CALIFORNIA

Mortgage

AND

Deed of Trust

Practice

SECOND EDITION

CALIFORNIA

Mortgage
AND
Deed of Trust
Practice

SECOND EDITION

ROGER BERNHARDT

Edited by Craig H. Scott
CEB Attorney

CONTINUING EDUCATION OF THE BAR ▪ CALIFORNIA

Berkeley, California
For supplement information, call (415) 642-6810

Library of Congress Catalog Card No. 89–83396
© 1990 by The Regents of the University of California
Printed in the United States of America
ISBN 0–88124–177–6

RE–31340

CONTINUING EDUCATION OF THE BAR ▪ CALIFORNIA

By agreement between the Board of Governors of the State Bar of California and The Regents of the University of California, California Continuing Education of the Bar offers an educational program for the benefit of practicing lawyers. The program is administered by a Governing Committee through the University of California in cooperation with local bar associations and the Joint Advisory Committee made up of the State Bar Committee on Continuing Education of the Bar and the Deans of accredited law schools.

Practice books are published as part of the educational program. Authors are given full opportunity to express their individual legal interpretations and opinions, and these obviously are not intended to reflect any position of the State Bar of California or of the University of California. Chapters written by employees of state or federal agencies are not to be considered statements of governmental policies.

California Continuing Education of the Bar publications and oral programs are intended to provide current and accurate information about the subject matter covered and are designed to help attorneys maintain their professional competence. Publications are distributed and oral programs presented with the understanding that CEB does not render any legal, accounting, or other professional service. Attorneys using CEB publications or orally conveyed information in dealing with a specific client's or their own legal matters should also research original sources of authority.

CEB considers that the publication of any CEB practice book is the beginning of a dialogue with our readers. The periodic supplements to this book will give us the opportunity to make corrections or additions you suggest. If you know something we did not include, or if we erred, please share your knowledge with other California lawyers. Send your comments to:

Supplement Editor
California Continuing Education of the Bar
2300 Shattuck Avenue
Berkeley, California 94704

EDUCATION OF THE BAR

Richard Pearl, San Francisco
Bruce E. Ramsey, Modesto
James J. Scherer, Oakland
Richard L. Schwartzberg, Santa Ana
Anthony F. Sgherzi, Los Angeles
Suzelle M. Smith, Los Angeles
Richard Neil Snyder, San Francisco
Gary L. Waldron, Fresno
David M. Zeligs, Fair Oaks

Law School Dean Members
Dean Florian Bartosic, University of California (Davis)
Dean Scott H. Bice, University of Southern California Law Center
Dean Paul A. Brest, Stanford University
Dean Benjamin Bycel, Ventura/Santa Barbara Colleges of Law
Dean Jesse H. Choper, University of California (Berkeley)
Dean Charles E. D'Arcy, Lincoln Law School of Sacramento
Dean Michael H. Dessent, California Western School of Law
Dean Barbara S. Evans, Monterey College of Law
Dean John A. FitzRandolph, Whittier College School of Law
Dean H. Jay Folberg, University of San Francisco School of Law
Dean Arthur N. Frakt, Loyola Law School
Dean Nels B. Fransen, Humphreys College of Law
Dean Seymour Greitzer, Glendale University College of Law
Dean Kenneth Held, University of LaVerne/University of LaVerne at
San Fernando Valley Colleges of Law
Dean Chris Kanios, New College of California School of Law
Acting Dean George Kraft, Western State University College of Law of
San Diego
Dean Jeffrey Kupers, John F. Kennedy University School of Law
Dean Robert Leahy, Empire College School of Law
Dean Mark Owens, Jr., San Francisco Law School
Dean Anthony J. Pagano, Golden Gate University School of Law
Dean Janice L. Pearson, San Joaquin College of Law
Dean Ronald F. Phillips, Pepperdine University School of Law
Dean Perry Polski, University of West Los Angeles School of Law
Dean Susan Westerberg Prager, University of California (Los Angeles)
Dean Franklin Thompson Read, Hastings College of Law
Dean Gordon D. Schaber, McGeorge School of Law,
University of the Pacific
Dean Wade V. Shang, Northrop University Law Center
Dean Kristine Strachan, University of San Diego School of Law
Dean Leigh H. Taylor, Southwestern University School of Law
Dean William H. J. Tiernan, National University School of Law
Dean Gerald F. Uelmen, University of Santa Clara School of Law
Dean Marcia B. Wilbur, Western State University College of Law of
Orange County

Table of Contents

Preface

The original edition of this book provided a much-needed practice-oriented guide for attorneys representing any of the parties to real property secured transactions, combining legal forms, checklists, and other practice aids with extensive substantive discussion. Since the first edition was published, CEB has undertaken publication of its three-volume practice series on real property financing (see 1, 2 California Real Property Financing (Cal CEB 1988, 1989)). Although that series covers many aspects of real property financing, the bar still needs a practical guide to the enforcement of real property security devices. In addition, many changes have taken place in the law governing real property security since publication of the first edition. Accordingly, this second edition has been reorganized to emphasize remedies aspects of real property secured transactions, while bringing practitioners up to date on legal developments during the past decade and covering all the substantive material in the previous edition.

Professor Roger Bernhardt has extensively reviewed, reorganized, and rewritten the original material. His discussion of tax considerations of real property secured transactions is based in part on chap 8 of the first edition, written by Robert C. Livsey of Brobeck, Phleger & Harrison, San Francisco. Professor Bernhardt's discussion of bankruptcy aspects of real property foreclosures is based in part on material written for the supplement to the first edition by Edward A. Weiner of Pillsbury, Madison & Sutro, San Francisco. Each chapter was reviewed by consultants from throughout the state, who provided valuable insight into all aspects of real property security practice. The consultants are listed on the acknowledgments pages that follow this preface.

Legal editing of this book was performed by CEB attorney Craig H. Scott. CEB senior editor Maryann Aberg handled copyediting and production, assisted in the final production process by CEB editor Sharon Welch. Principal research assistants and citation checkers were David Fuller, Paula Hyman, April Nelson, Lane Parker, Mary Bruce Reid, Mindy Spatt, and Janette Tom. Ted Francis prepared the index.

Ann Becker, Jean Hohenthal, Kathryn Murphy, Sue Weaver, and Myra Wysinger were the compositors of the book, which was illustrated by David Gentry.

Legal editing of this book was completed at the end of September 1989. Statute and case citations were checked through October 1, 1989. CEB intends to supplement the book on a regular basis.

William A. Carroll
Director

About the Author

Roger Bernhardt, who received his B.A., M.A., and J.D. degrees from the University of Chicago, is Professor of Law at Golden Gate University, San Francisco. He is also the editor of CEB's California Real Property Law Reporter and the author of Real Property in a Nutshell (West Publishing, 1981), Black Letter Law of Real Property (West Publishing, 1983), and California Real Estate Finance (Carolina Academic Press, 1988). Admitted to practice law in California and New York, Professor Bernhardt is a member of the American Law Institute and the American College of Real Estate Lawyers.

Acknowledgments

CEB is grateful to each of the following attorneys, who served as consultants on the book by reviewing and commenting on one or more chapter manuscripts. Their valuable insights and suggestions made the book more accurate, more practical, and more reflective of California practice.

Alice L. Akawie
Wilson, Sher, Marshal & Peterson, Oakland

William R. Biel
Rutan & Tucker, Costa Mesa

Professor Gail B. Bird
Hastings College of Law, San Francisco

Michael S. Cucchissi
Pettis, Tester, Kruse & Krinsky, Irvine

Alan Dempster
San Francisco

Stephen W. Dyer
Horan, Lloyd, Karachale & Dyer, Monterey

Stephen B. Fainsbert
Fainsbert, Mase & Snyder, Los Angeles

Gordon L. Graham
CEB Attorney, Berkeley

Frederick D. Holden, Jr.
Brobeck, Phleger & Harrison, San Francisco

Kathleen A. Knox
Home Savings of America, Pasadena

Jeffrey C. Krause
Stutman, Treister & Glatt, Los Angeles

John F. Lehr, Jr.
Drummy, Garrett, King & Harrison, Costa Mesa

David A. Leipziger
Cox, Castle & Nicholson, Los Angeles

Robert C. Livsey
Brobeck, Phleger & Harrison, San Francisco

Hal M. Marzell
Home Savings of America, Pasadena

John A. Mase
Fainsbert, Mase & Snyder, Los Angeles

Professor Cynthia A. Mertens
University of Santa Clara School of Law, Santa Clara

James Murad
Cooper, White & Cooper, San Francisco

Rose Pothier
Pothier & Hinrichs, Santa Ana

Professor Edward H. Rabin
University of California School of Law, Davis

C. Darrell Sooy
Tobin & Tobin, San Francisco

Bruce C. Stuart
Stradling, Yocca, Carlson & Rauth, Newport Beach

Anthony Theophilos
McCutchen, Doyle, Brown & Enersen, San Francisco

W. Stephen Wilson
Wilson, Sher, Marshall & Peterson, Oakland

Gary York
Dewey, Ballantine, Bushby, Palmer & Wood, Los Angeles

Author's Foreword and Acknowledgments

CEB was kind enough to permit me to revise this book entirely, rather than merely updating it for a second edition. I have reorganized and rewritten most of the text to take advantage of the fact that, in the interim, CEB had published the first two volumes of California Real Property Financing. The existence of that work permitted me to rewrite this one as a remedy-oriented book. Attorneys are thus able to turn to California Real Property Financing when they need information on negotiating, documenting, and closing loans, and to use this book for help on collecting, attacking, or defending those loans. Material on documentation has been retained to give this book a slightly broader base and to make it, to some degree, a primer on all of mortgage law. The book's primary thrust, however, is on handling a mortgage loan already in existence, rather than drafting one from scratch.

To a large degree, creation of a loan is easy because the debtor so often simply signs what the creditor's lawyers have drafted. But a key party—the judiciary—is absent from that process. It is what the judges later say about the documents, not what the parties originally said, that matters the most. The easier part for the creditor is getting the debtor to sign the new clause its attorneys have drafted; the harder part is getting the clause upheld in court. That is the subject of this book.

This edition also incorporates into the text two topics previously treated independently. In the first edition, tax consequences constituted a separate chapter, and readers were forced to go to one chapter for discussion of the legal aspects of a transaction and to another chapter for discussion of the tax aspects. Now, tax consequences are integrated with the underlying issues. Much of my learning on this issue came from Robert Livsey, who authored the excellent tax chapter in the first edition. The rest came from my former student and brilliant tax attorney (and CPA), Alan Dempster.

The other newly integrated material is the discussion of bankruptcy. At the time the first edition was written, that topic did not have the significance it subsequently acquired, and so was not covered at all there. Ed Weiner was kind enough to write an appendix on bankruptcy law for the supplement while the rest of us started to catch up. As with taxation, bankruptcy is too important to be confined to isolated treatment, so I have taken Ed's material and dispersed it to appropriate places in the book.

I do wish to apologize for the title of the book. "California Mortgage and Deed of Trust Practice" is dull and cumbersome. It is accurate, however, because California attorneys use deeds of trust while generally referring to them as mortgages. (But who can blame us for not wanting to be referred to as "deed of trust lawyers"?)

Roger Bernhardt
San Francisco

Chapter 1: **Basics of Real Property Secured Transactions**

1

Basics of Real Property Secured Transactions

§1.1   I. SCOPE OF BOOK

A person may purchase or improve real property by paying the entire price in cash. One can also borrow the money needed to purchase or improve real property on an unsecured basis, *i.e.*, without putting up the real property as security for the obligation to repay the loan. See §1.2. Such activities do not constitute real property financing transactions as the term is generally understood, nor are they the subject of this book.

This book is about borrowing money and using real property as security for the loan. For discussion of the basics of real property transactions, including their financing aspects, see §§1.2–1.8. The purpose of the loan may be to acquire the very property that is given as security for the loan (a purchase-money loan), to construct improvements on the land (a construction loan), or to enhance the existing improvements (a home improvement or improvement loan). Even if the purpose of the loan is unrelated to real property (*e.g.*, for a vacation), the loan is still characterized as a real property loan if real property is given as security for the loan. The basic characteristic of a real property loan is that a mortgage or deed of trust on the borrower's title to real property secures the borrower's promissory note. Basics of the promissory note are discussed in §§1.9–1.20; mortgages and deeds of trust are discussed in §§1.21–1.34. The installment land sale contract, another real property financing device, is covered only briefly in this book, in §1.35.

§1.2   A. Secured Versus Unsecured Loans

In the simplest kind of credit transaction, the unsecured loan, the lender merely takes back a promissory note from the borrower. The note itself is unnecessary as long as the loan is outside the requirements of the statute of frauds. CC §1624. The drawback of such an unsecured loan is that, if the debtor defaults and the creditor is forced to sue, the creditor's only remedy is to obtain a judgment that is not self-executing, *i.e.*, that does not automatically recover money or other assets from the debtor. Whether the judgment can be converted into money depends on the effectiveness of execution and other postjudgment remedies. Collection on a judgment is fruitful only if the judgment debtor has assets and only if those assets have not already been taken by other creditors.

To avoid these drawbacks, a lender often insists on security for its loan. When security is given, certain assets of the borrower are set aside ("hypothecated") so that the creditor may reach and sell them if the debtor defaults. Taking security gives the lender two significant advantages:

■ The debtor is no longer able to convey these assets free from the creditor's claims on them, which eliminates the risk that there will be no assets on which to levy (CC §2923); and

■ Once the creditor's security interest is perfected, all later creditors acquire inferior interests in the same property, which eliminates the risk that other claims will take priority (CC §2897).

A security agreement (or instrument) is a promise by the debtor that a certain asset may be reached by the creditor if the obligation is not paid. The security agreement does not create the obligation to pay, which is usually evidenced by a promissory note (see §1.10). The agreement is a second document, usually accompanying the note, that gives the creditor rights to an asset if the obligation is not performed. See §§1.21–1.34. In lay terms, the note says "I promise to pay," and the security instrument says "If I fail to pay, you can have this property."

This book is concerned primarily with real property security, *i.e.*, security in the form of an interest in land that is available to the creditor on default. Personal property security is governed by Division 9 of the Commercial Code (Com C §§9101–9508) (see CC §§2914, 2944) and is outside the scope of this book, except when it constitutes a fixture (see §1.34) or is given in conjunction with real property as security for a loan (see §8.7). See Secured Transactions in California Commercial Law Practice (Cal CEB 1986) for a thorough discussion of Division 9.

§1.3   B. Terminology in Real Property Finance Transactions

A typical real property loan involves two parties and two documents. One party to the loan is the *borrower, debtor,* or *obligor.* Because a note is usually executed, that person may also be known as a *maker.* The other party is the *lender, creditor,* or *obligee,* who may be the *payee* or *holder* of the note. Sometimes the terms "bank," "savings and loan association," or "lending institution" are used to describe the lender.

The promissory note is often secured by a *security instrument,* which entitles the lender to reach some asset of the debtor if the note is not paid. In California, the security instrument is most commonly a *deed of trust* (with the debtor and creditor known as *trustor* and *beneficiary* and a neutral third party known as *trustee*). The security instrument may also be a *mortgage* (with *mortgagor* and *mortgagee,* as participants). In either case, the creditor is said to have a *lien* on the property given as security, which is also referred to as *collateral.* The terms "deed of trust," "trustor," and "beneficiary" are used interchangeably in this book with "mortgage," "mortgagor," and "mortgagee," respectively, unless the context indicates otherwise. Deed of trust terminology has generally been used in preference to mortgage terminology because of the prevalent use of the deed of trust in California.

If the financing is incidental to a sale of land, the *seller* or *vendor* may be the creditor, and the *buyer* or *purchaser* may be the debtor. If the purchaser is borrowing money from both a bank and the seller, there will be two loans and two deeds of trust. Inevitably, the bank will hold the *senior* or *first* deed of trust, and the seller will be a *second* or *junior* beneficiary. In this book, the senior beneficiary is usually treated as a lending institution and referred to as "it." For installment land sale contract terminology, see § 1.35.

Just as the terms "deed of trust," "mortgage," and "security instrument" are used somewhat interchangeably (because for most purposes their differences are not significant), the similarity among the terms "obligation," "debt," "note," and "purchase price" is sufficient to permit frequent substitution of these words. See Hetland, *Deficiency Judg-*

ment Limitations in California—A New Judicial Approach, 51 Calif L
Rev 1 (1963). Nevertheless, there are times when the distinctions matter. (Code of Civil Procedure §580a refers to "obligation"; §580b, to
"purchase price"; §580d, to "note"; and §726, to "debt.") "Obligation"
is the broadest term because it is not limited to payment of money and
therefore is the only correct term to use when the deed of trust secures
a contractual obligation other than payment. See §1.9. "Debt" refers to
an obligation to pay money and is broader than "price" because a construction or improvement loan on real property is a debt even though
it forms no part of the property's purchase price. A "note" is merely evidence of the debt, not the debt itself, which is what is secured. *Matthews v Hinton* (1965) 234 CA2d 736, 44 CR 692.

§1.4   II. OVERVIEW OF REAL PROPERTY SALES
AND FINANCING TRANSACTION

The purchase and financing of real property involve a number of
steps and participants. A brief overview follows for the attorney who
has no experience in handling a real property sales transaction:

■ *Listing.* The first step normally occurs when the owner of property signs a listing agreement with a real estate broker, authorizing the
broker to seek a buyer for the property and agreeing to pay the broker
a commission if a sale is made. There are various types of listing agreements, with differing legal consequences. See California Real Property Sales Transactions §§2.45–2.85 (Cal CEB 1981).

■ *Purchase and sale agreement.* The broker will locate a person interested in purchasing the property and arrange for the prospective
buyer to make an offer to purchase it. This offer is often labeled a
"deposit receipt," but it is much more than merely a receipt for the
deposit. If the seller accepts the offer contained in the deposit receipt,
a binding purchase and sale agreement is created between the parties.
See Real Property Sales §§3.39–3.40.

■ *Escrow.* The purchase and sale agreement is usually performed
through an escrow. An escrow agent, who is a neutral party and usually licensed, holds the buyer's money and the seller's deed and, when
all conditions have been met, transfers each to the other party. The
escrow agent acts only according to written instructions signed by each
party. See Real Property Sales, chap 11.

■ *Title insurance.* In California, the buyer almost always obtains a title insurance policy insuring that the deed received conveys marketable title to the property (subject only to exceptions disclosed in the policy and acceptable to the buyer). The policy also insures the lender's lien. A preliminary title report is usually issued earlier in the transaction to enable the parties to cure any title defects before escrow closes. See Real Property Sales §§3.79, 3.98. For discussion of title insurance, see California Title Insurance Practice (Cal CEB 1980).

■ *Financing.* Financial institutions provide most of the funds used for the acquisition of real property in California. See Real Property Sales, chap 6; 1, 2 California Real Property Financing (Cal CEB 1988, 1989). These "third party" lenders deposit their loan funds into escrow with instructions that the funds not be disbursed until the buyer has executed satisfactory loan documents (including a note and deed of trust). At the close of escrow, the loan proceeds will go to the seller (to pay the purchase price) and the buyer's loan documents will go to the lender. The lender's deed of trust, which is insured by a title policy, is recorded immediately after the deed is recorded.

When the seller finances part of the price, the escrow instructions will indicate that the seller will receive a note and deed of trust from the buyer for the amount financed. See Real Property Sales, chap 5.

A. Representing Seller

§1.5   1. Attorney's Role as Advisor

An owner who sells real property is either "cashed out," by receiving the entire price (or the owner's entire equity) in cash, or else accepts all or part of the purchase price on a deferred basis. In a simple seller-financed situation, the seller accepts a note and deed of trust from the buyer for all or part of the purchase price, and no third party loan funds are involved. The seller's attorney must explain to the seller the consequences of being a secured lender. A seller who provides all or a portion of the financing on a one-to-four-unit family residence is characterized as an "arranger of credit" subject to significant disclosure requirements. CC §§2956–2957; see Fishkin, *Disclosures in Creative Financing,* 6 CEB Real Prop L Rep 133 (Oct. 1983). For a form disclosure statement, see California Real Property Practice Forms Manual §2.5 (Cal CEB 1988).

More common than sole vendor financing is the case in which the buyer borrows part of the purchase price from an institutional lender and also defers payment on part of the balance of the price to the seller. For example, in the sale of a $100,000 house, the buyer may make a downpayment of $15,000, borrow $80,000 from a bank, and give the seller a note and deed of trust for the remaining $5000. In this case the seller must be told not only what it means to be a beneficiary of a deed of trust, but also what it means to be a junior beneficiary, because the bank will undoubtedly hold the senior position.

The seller's attorney must also keep in mind the tax consequences of the transaction. The amount realized by the seller in excess of his or her basis in the property constitutes taxable gain. The amount realized includes cash, promissory notes, and the unpaid balance on any existing mortgages on the property that are not paid off in connection with the sale. See §2.30. A tax-deferred exchange under IRC §1031 may enable the seller to avoid recognition of such gain. For further discussion, see Real Property Exchanges (Cal CEB 1982).

Beneficiaries' foreclosure rights are covered in chaps 2–3, which also discuss the problems of a junior beneficiary when a senior beneficiary forecloses. Chapter 5 covers the rights of both senior and junior beneficiaries to recover the rents and profits from the property ancillary to foreclosing on it. The restrictions on a beneficiary's right to obtain a money judgment against the trustor, including the rights of the sold-out junior after a senior foreclosure sale, are discussed in chap 4. The tax consequences of foreclosure are discussed as they arise throughout the book.

§1.6   2. Checklist for Seller's Attorney

The seller's attorney should review (and in some cases draft) the documents necessary for the transaction. These include:

_____ *Listing agreement.* Seller's attorney sometimes negotiates terms in advance with broker. See California Real Property Sales Transactions, chap 2 (Cal CEB 1981).

_____ *Purchase and sale agreement.* Often prepared by broker or salesperson; sometimes negotiated and drafted by attorney for buyer or seller. See Real Property Sales, chap 3.

_____ *Seller's escrow instructions.* Should be prepared by seller's attorney; often based on information supplied by escrow holder. See Real Property Sales, chap 11.

_____ *Various disclosures:*

a. Real estate agency relationship disclosure form (CC §2375) (see California Real Property Practice Forms Manual §2.1 (Cal CEB 1988));

b. Confirmation of agency relationship (CC §2375.5) (see Real Property Forms §2.2);

c. Equity seller's right of cancellation (agreements for purchase of seller's equity in owner-occupied, one-to-four-unit residence in foreclosure (CC §§1695–1695.14) (see Real Property Forms §2.3));

d. Seller financing disclosure statement (CC §§2956–2957; see §1.5) (see Real Property Forms §2.5); and

e. Real estate transfer disclosure statement (CC §§1102–1102.14) (see California Real Property Sales Transactions Supp §1.69A (Cal CEB); California Real Property Practice Forms Manual Supp §2.6 (Cal CEB)).

_____ *Preliminary title report.* Should be requested and reviewed by seller's attorney at earliest possible date, preferably before purchase contract is executed, unless attorney is familiar with state of seller's title. See California Title Insurance Practice §§3.18–3.19 (Cal CEB 1980); Real Property Sales §3.98.

_____ *Seller's existing loan documents.* Should be checked for prepayment rights; if seller is to pay off existing loan, make certain seller is not "locked in." See §7.20.

_____ *Buyer's promissory note to seller.* Must contain provisions for:

a. Acceleration on default (see §§7.2–7.6);

b. Attorneys' fees (see §§7.29–7.33); and

c. Prepayment rights, if any (see §§7.19–7.25).

Also consider provisions for late charges (see §§7.7–7.9) and due-on-sale clause (see §§7.10–7.18).

_____ *Buyer's deed of trust to seller.* When drafting:

a. Consider provision for acceleration of balance due on note for buyer's default, and provision for foreclosure if default not cured (see §7.42);

b. Include provision giving lender a right (1) to pay, *e.g.,* senior liens, taxes, and insurance; (2) to add amounts paid to indebtedness secured by deed of trust; and (3) to require immediate reimbursement from borrower (CC §2924c; see §§7.34–7.36);

c. Consider whether to include due-on-sale clause (see §7.10);

d. Consider provision requiring borrower to pay one twelfth of the estimated annual costs monthly into an impound account for taxes and insurance premiums (see §7.34); and

e. If deed of trust contains future-advance clause (most title company forms do; see §8.34), be certain it is not excessively broad (see §8.42).

_____ *Note and deed of trust given by purchaser to senior lender.* Determine whether there are any obligatory future advances. See §8.44.

_____ *Notice to senior lender.* Give notice of junior lien to senior lender. Obtain estoppel certificate or statement of condition from any existing senior lienholders. See §8.44.

_____ *Notice under CC §2924b.* Record request for notice under CC §2924b (senior liens). See §2.15.

_____ *Title insurance policy.* Insure seller's deed of trust (usually a California Land Title Association joint protection policy issued at no additional cost).

_____ *Fire insurance policy.* Should include lender's loss payable endorsement. Require that first year's premium be paid through escrow. See §§7.26–7.28.

_____ *Truth-in-lending or RESPA documents.* Review any required truth-in-lending or Real Estate Settlement Procedures Act of 1974 (RESPA) (12 USC §§2601–2617) documents. See Real Property Sales §§1.50, 6.58, 11.85–11.89.

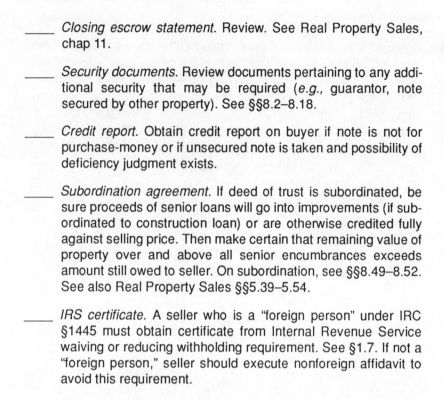

_____ *Closing escrow statement.* Review. See Real Property Sales, chap 11.

_____ *Security documents.* Review documents pertaining to any additional security that may be required (*e.g.,* guarantor, note secured by other property). See §§8.2–8.18.

_____ *Credit report.* Obtain credit report on buyer if note is not for purchase-money or if unsecured note is taken and possibility of deficiency judgment exists.

_____ *Subordination agreement.* If deed of trust is subordinated, be sure proceeds of senior loans will go into improvements (if subordinated to construction loan) or are otherwise credited fully against selling price. Then make certain that remaining value of property over and above all senior encumbrances exceeds amount still owed to seller. On subordination, see §§8.49–8.52. See also Real Property Sales §§5.39–5.54.

_____ *IRS certificate.* A seller who is a "foreign person" under IRC §1445 must obtain certificate from Internal Revenue Service waiving or reducing withholding requirement. See §1.7. If not a "foreign person," seller should execute nonforeign affidavit to avoid this requirement.

B. Representing Buyer
§1.7   1. Attorney's Role as Advisor

Except for the rare all-cash buyer, a person acquiring real property usually borrows a considerable amount of money to complete the sale. Thus, the usual buyer acquires title to real property and becomes a debtor at the same time. The buyer's liability is usually secured by the real property he or she has just purchased. The buyer's attorney must explain the consequences of these facts to the client. In rare cases, the buyer may constitute an "arranger of credit" who must make significant disclosures to the seller under CC §§2956–2957. See §1.5.

If the seller is a "foreign person" under IRC §1445, the buyer may be required to withhold 10 percent of the purchase price unless the seller provides a certificate from the Internal Revenue Service waiving or reducing the withholding requirement. IRC §1445(a); see Offer,

Federal Tax Withholding Obligations Become Effective on January 1, 1985, for Purchasers of Real Property Interests From Foreign Persons, 8 CEB Real Prop L Rep 29 (Mar. 1985). Failure to comply with the withholding requirements of IRC §1445 may subject the buyer to liability for payment of the seller's tax together with penalties and interest. IRC §1461.

The deed of trust that the buyer signs gives the lender (or seller) a lien on the property. If the buyer fails to pay the note as it falls due, a lien creditor may institute proceedings to enforce the lien by foreclosure and sale of the property. See chaps 2–3. Before foreclosing, the creditor may also seek to have a receiver appointed to take possession of the property and to sequester the rents and profits from it for satisfaction of the debt. See chap 5. Under certain circumstances, the creditor may also obtain a deficiency judgment against the buyer if the foreclosure sale does not produce enough funds to cover its claim. See chap 4. On the other hand, the buyer has certain statutory rights to cure defaults (see §§2.22, 3.51) and may be immune from liability for a deficiency (see chap 4), depending on the nature of the sales transaction and the foreclosure proceedings.

The buyer's attorney must also consider the tax consequences of the transaction. The amount paid by the buyer usually determines his or her basis in the property for federal income tax purposes. IRC §1012. The amount paid includes any mortgages created, assumed, or taken "subject to" by the buyer as part of the purchase price, as well as transactional costs of acquiring the property. See generally Taxation of Real Property Transfers, chap 2 (Cal CEB 1981). When the seller supplies mortgage financing, however, the buyer's ability to claim deductions against basis (as qualified nonrecourse financing) is subject to the at-risk rules. IRC §465; see Taxation RP Transfers §1.6. When property is acquired as part of a tax-deferred exchange under IRC §1031, the buyer's basis consists of the property's acquisition price reduced by the amount of gain deferred. IRC §1031(b); see Real Property Exchanges §3.10 (Cal CEB 1982).

§1.8   2. Checklist for Buyer's Attorney

The buyer's attorney should review (and in some cases prepare) the necessary documents in the transaction. These include:

_____ *Offer to purchase ("deposit receipt").* Usually prepared by broker or salesperson; sometimes negotiated and drafted by attorney for buyer or seller. See California Real Property Sales Transactions §§3.39–3.40 (Cal CEB 1981).

_____ *Buyer's escrow instructions.* Should be drafted by buyer's attorney; often based on information supplied by escrow holder. See Real Property Sales §§11.42–11.65.

_____ *Preliminary title report.* See Real Property Sales §3.98.

_____ *Loan application.* See 1 California Real Property Financing, chap 1 (Cal CEB 1988).

_____ *Promissory note to lender.* See chaps 7–8, App A.

_____ *Promissory note to seller.* Consider use of nonnegotiable note or, if purchase-money note, nonrecourse provision in note. See §§1.18–1.19. If note is given to noninstitutional lender (*e.g.,* seller), consider requiring that it be deposited with bank or savings and loan association as collecting agent who is to endorse on note the fact of payment as each installment is paid.

_____ *Deed of trust to third party lender.* See chaps 7–8, App B.

_____ *Deed of trust to seller.* See chaps 7–8, App B.

_____ *Truth-in-lending statement.* See Real Property Sales §1.50.

_____ *Various disclosure statements,* if required. See §1.5.

_____ *Real Estate Settlement Procedures Act of 1974 (RESPA) (12 USC §§2601–2617) settlement statement.* See Real Property Sales §§11.85–11.89.

_____ *Reports and clearances* on structural pests or any other conditions called for in purchase agreement. See Real Property Sales §§3.116–3.130.

_____ *Fire insurance policy.* See Real Property Sales, chap 10.

_____ *Closing escrow statement.* See Real Property Sales, chap 11.

_____ *Title insurance policy.* Be certain escrow instructions provide that title is to be subject only to specified exceptions to which buyer has agreed.

_____ *IRS certificate.* Buyer must withhold 10 percent of purchase price (and remit it to Internal Revenue Service) if seller is a "foreign person" under IRC §1445 (see §1.7), unless seller produces certificate waiving the requirement. If buyer is purchasing property for use as a residence and amount realized is less than $300,000, withholding is not required. IRC §1445.

§1.9   III. OBLIGATION

Most secured obligations take the form of written promises to pay money. For most purposes, the words "debt" and "note" are used interchangeably with "obligation" in this book (but see §1.3). The secured obligation need not, however, be a note or even a debt. The statutory definition of liens and mortgages as security for "performance of an act" (CC §§2872, 2920) is not limited to payment of money. See *Stub v Belmont* (1942) 20 C2d 208, 124 P2d 826 (crop servicing contract); *Congregational Church Bldg. Soc'y v Osborn* (1908) 153 C 197, 94 P 881 (promise to use property for church purposes); *Valley Vista Land Co. v Nipomo Water & Sewer Co.* (1968) 266 CA2d 331, 72 CR 181 (promise to furnish water and sewer facilities). See also *Willys of Marin Co. v Pierce* (1956) 140 CA2d 826, 296 P2d 25. In nonmoney situations, the promisee can count on a meaningful foreclosure action only if there is some provision for liquidating damages in the contract. See *Feraud v Anaheim Inv. Co.* (1934) 138 CA 227, 31 P2d 1092 (lump-sum damages provided for breach of lifetime annuity contract). Because California prohibits strict foreclosure (see §3.1), there must be a sale when the security interest is foreclosed, and the promisee is entitled only to as much of the sale proceeds as are necessary to cover the loss. Foreclosure becomes almost impossible if the obligation lacks liquidity. See Nelson & Whitman, Real Estate Finance Law §2.2 (2d ed 1985).

The statute of frauds (CC §1624) may require that the obligation be in writing, but otherwise there is no independent mortgage law requirement of a writing. An enforceable oral promise is a sufficient obligation to support the mortgage or deed of trust. *Todd v Todd* (1912) 164 C 255, 128 P 413; *Hickox v Lowe* (1858) 10 C 197; *Dool v First Nat'l Bank* (1930) 107 CA 585, 290 P 478. There is no requirement that the obligation be unconditional. *Congregational Church Bldg. Soc'y v Osborn, supra*; *Purser v Eagle Lake Land & Irrig. Co.* (1896) 111 C 139, 43 P 523. For discussion of considerations in drafting the note, see §1.20 and 1 California Real Property Financing, chap 3 (Cal CEB 1988).

In future-advance (see §§8.34–8.48) and line of credit (see §8.45) arrangements, if there is no present loan the obligation to pay arises only if and when an advance is made. *Moss v Odell* (1901) 134 C 464, 66 P 581; *Langerman v Puritan Dining Room Co.* (1913) 21 CA 637, 132 P 617. See also *Frank H. Buck Co. v Buck* (1912) 162 C 300, 122 P 466. Similarly, in contracts of indemnity and guaranty, the obligation to perform arises only after loss or nonperformance by another. *Fernandez v Tormey* (1898) 121 C 515, 53 P 1119 (indemnity); *Indusco Management Corp. v Robertson* (1974) 40 CA3d 456, 114 CR 47 (guaranty); *Kelley v Goldschmidt* (1920) 47 CA 38, 190 P 55 (guaranty).

§1.10   A. Relationship of Obligation to Security

In many respects, the obligation is more important than the security. An obligation can exist with or without security; if there is no security, the obligation is unsecured but still valid. On the other hand, a security interest cannot exist without an underlying obligation. See *Henley v Hotaling* (1871) 41 C 22; *Turner v Gosden* (1932) 121 CA 20, 8 P2d 505. See also *Lee v Joseph* (1968) 267 CA2d 30, 72 CR 471.

The term "security" includes the concept that something (*i.e.,* the obligation) is secured. It is impossible to define security apart from its relationship to the promise or obligation that it secures. See CC §§2872, 2909, 2920. Furthermore, the primacy of the obligation is such that, if there are inconsistencies between the language of the note (evidence of the obligation) and the deed of trust (evidence of the security), the terms of the note will control. *Pacific Fruit Exch. v Duke* (1930) 103 CA 340, 284 P 729.

§1.11   1. Consideration

An illustration of the failure to observe the differences between the obligation and the security (see §1.10) is found in the maxim that one cannot make a gift of a mortgage. The maxim is correct, but there are right and wrong reasons for it. That a mortgage needs consideration is incorrect, even though several early California Supreme Court decisions have held that it does. See, *e.g., McDonald v Randall* (1903) 139 C 246, 72 P 997; *Chaffee v Browne* (1895) 109 C 211, 41 P 1028. That a valid mortgage needs a valid underlying obligation and that a valid obligation needs consideration are correct. A note is valid only when it is supported by consideration, because otherwise it is merely a promise to pay in the future. Com C §3408; *Shipley Co. v Rosemead Co.* (1929) 100 CA 706, 280 P 1017; *Allen's Collection Agency v Lee* (1925) 73 CA 68, 238 P 169. Thus, a gift of a note and a mortgage will fail not because the mortgage is without consideration, but because the note is without consideration; when the note fails as an obligation, the mortgage fails along with it. *Coon v Shry* (1930) 209 C 612, 289 P 815. See also *Lee v Joseph* (1968) 267 CA2d 30, 72 CR 471; Nelson & Whitman, Real Estate Finance Law §2.3 (2d ed 1985).

Mortgages, and particularly deeds of trust, are more like conveyances than contracts and should not need independent consideration any more than gift deeds do. See CC §1040. In fact, many mortgages and deeds of trust are upheld when there is no real consideration (except under a strained construction), as when one person gives a mortgage to secure the debt of another (see *Garretson Inv. Co. v Arndt* (1904) 144 C 64, 77 P 770; *Carson v Reid* (1902) 137 C 253, 70 P 89) or when a debtor gives a mortgage to secure an existing debt (see *Ekmann v Plumas County Bank* (1932) 215 C 671, 12 P2d 433; *Smitton v McCullough* (1920) 182 C 530, 189 P 686; *Frey v Clifford* (1872) 44 C 335).

Although a deed of trust can secure an existing debt without new consideration (*Ekmann v Plumas County Bank, supra*), when the security interest is given by one who is insolvent, the conveyance may be deemed fraudulent under the Uniform Fraudulent Transfer Act (UFTA) (CC §§3439–3439.12). *Kirkland v Risso* (1979) 98 CA3d 971, 976, 159 CR 798, 801. A deed of trust may be voided in connection with a bankruptcy case (a) as a preference if the deed of trust was given to secure a preexisting debt within three months before the case was begun (11 USC §547) and (b) if the deed was given within one year before the case was begun for less than reasonably equivalent value (11 USC §548). See §6.51.

§1.12   2. Destruction

Because the obligation is primary (see §1.10), destruction of the security does not affect the obligation, other than to convert it from a secured to an unsecured debt. *Frost v Witter* (1901) 132 C 421, 64 P 705. It is therefore possible for an unpaid beneficiary to reconvey its deed of trust to the trustor without automatically sacrificing its claim for payment. See *Sherwood v Dunbar* (1856) 6 C 53. Any such relinquishment of the security must be mutual because the beneficiary cannot unilaterally waive its security to proceed against its trustor as an unsecured creditor (CCP §726; *Barbieri v Ramelli* (1890) 84 C 154, 23 P 1086; *Hartman v Smith* (1963) 219 CA2d 415, 33 CR 147), nor can the debtor unilaterally reconvey the security back to himself or herself (*Duley v Westinghouse Elec. Corp.* (1979) 97 CA3d 430, 158 CR 668). On the other hand, destruction of the obligation seriously affects survival of the security. If, for any reason, the debt is extinguished, the security becomes meaningless. See *Trowbridge v Love* (1943) 58 CA2d 746, 137 P2d 890 (forgiveness of debt); *Burd v Downing* (1923) 60 CA 493, 213 P 287 (mutual rescission of lease).

Destruction, as used in this context, does not mean mere physical loss of the security instrument. If the loan documents are lost, the beneficiary remains secured (although the trustee may require posting of a lost instrument indemnity bond as a condition to reconveyance or foreclosure). *Huckell v Matranga* (1979) 99 CA3d 471, 160 CR 177. See also §7.41.

§1.13   3. Purchase-Money Notes

The character of the obligation may have an important impact on the character of the security, particularly when the obligation is a purchase-money debt. Two consequences spring from the determination that a deed of trust secures a purchase-money obligation: first, and most important, that the creditor has no right to recover a deficiency judgment after foreclosure (CCP §580b), subject to certain exceptions (see §§4.23–4.30); and, second, that security for purchase-money has priority over other liens on the property, subject to the recording laws (CC §2898).

Priority under CC §2898 means that a purchase-money lien is a senior lien on the property, even when there are outstanding judgment liens against the purchaser that immediately attach to any asset the purchaser acquires. *Majewski v Empire Constr. Co.* (1970) 2 C3d 478, 85 CR 819; *Mercantile Collection Bureau v Roach* (1961) 195 CA2d 355, 15 CR 710; *Ludy v Zumwalt* (1927) 85 CA 119, 259 P 52. It does not mean that the purchase-money deed of trust has priority over a previously recorded mechanics' lien or mortgage. *Avery v Clark* (1891)

87 C 619, 25 P 919; see *Walley v P.M.C. Inv. Co.* (1968) 262 CA2d 218, 68 CR 711.

The priority accorded to purchase-money liens is not limited to liens of vendors who finance all or part of the sale. Third party money is purchase-money if it was given to enable the purchaser to acquire the property. See *Van Loben Sels v Bunnell* (1898) 120 C 680, 53 P 266.

The descriptions of purchase-money in CCP §580b and CC §2898 are not identical. Thus, a deed of trust may be called a purchase-money deed of trust for priority purposes (under CC §2898) but not for anti-deficiency purposes (under CCP §580b). Section 580b excludes third party financing of dwellings for more than four families that are not owner occupied, but §2898 does not. See *Kistler v Vasi* (1969) 71 C2d 261, 78 CR 170. Consequently, any analogy between the two sections is of dubious validity.

In addition, the mere fact that an obligation is a purchase-money debt creates certain security rights in the vendor. Civil Code §3046 gives the vendor a lien "for so much of the price as remains unpaid and unsecured otherwise than by the personal obligation of the buyer." See, *e.g., McGreevy v Constitution Life Ins. Co.* (1965) 238 CA2d 364, 47 CR 711.

For federal income tax purposes, indebtedness incurred to acquire real property is included in the buyer's basis in the property, whether or not the loan is secured. IRC §1012. Funds borrowed to improve the property may also be added to the basis. Reg §§1.263(a)–1(a), 1.1016–2(a). (The cost of repairs, however, is deducted rather than capitalized and therefore is not added to the basis. IRC §§162, 212.) For discussion, see Taxation of Real Property Transfers §§2.56–2.60 (Cal CEB 1981).

B. Provisions for Payment

§1.14   ## 1. Principal and Interest

Although promissory notes contain numerous varieties of payment schemes, residential mortgage notes usually call for equal (level) payments of principal and interest on a periodic basis (monthly or sometimes quarterly) for 15, 20, or 30 years until the loan is entirely repaid. Because interest is always calculated on the outstanding unpaid balance, the interest component in the early years of the loan may constitute 90 percent or more of the payments, declining over the life of the loan to a relatively insignificant share at the end. See 1 California Real Property Financing §§1.19–1.20 (Cal CEB 1988). The rate may either be fixed over the life of the loan or be tied to some index and recalculated periodically (adjustable and variable rate loans). See 1 Real Property Financing §§1.21–1.22; California Real Property Sales Transactions §§6.47–6.52 (Cal CEB 1981). When the rate is adjustable, changes in the index lead either to altered periodic payments or to an altered duration for the loan. Lenders employing such devices must be careful to comply with state usury laws. See 1 Real Property Financing §§3.27, 5.45–5.50.

Second mortgages on residential property are often written for shorter periods of time (*e.g.,* three, five, or seven years) and without full amortization. The monthly payment may be only 1 percent of the principal balance, which means that a large balloon payment is required at the end of the term (and expected to be paid by refinancing at that time). Under CC §§2924i and 2966, balloon notes must contain a legend advising the borrower of the right to notice of the balloon payment 90 to 150 days before its due date, whenever the final payment is more than twice the regular monthly payment and the security for the note consists of residential real property.

Installment notes commonly contain a provision accelerating the unpaid balance on default by the borrower. For discussion of acceleration clauses, see §§7.2–7.6. An installment note may also contain a due-on-sale clause that provides for acceleration if the borrower transfers or encumbers the property. For discussion, see §§7.10–7.18.

To assist first-time home buyers, lending institutions sometimes employ "graduated payment" notes that provide for smaller than average payments in the early years of the loan, compensated for by increasingly larger payments as the years pass (and the borrowers' income presumably grows). The payments at the beginning of the loan term may actually be less than the interest that accrues during that period, leading to "negative amortization," *i.e.,* the enlargement rather than the reduction of the loan principal with each periodic payment. See 1 Real Property Financing §1.18.

To accommodate senior citizens, who have little current income because of retirement but who have accumulated wealth in the form of a paid-up home, some lenders offer "reverse annuity" mortgages. The lender lends the homeowner a monthly amount, and repayment is not required until the borrower sells the property or dies.

Lenders may offer commercial borrowers a lower basic interest rate in return for receipt of a "contingent interest," *i.e.,* a share of the profits of the borrower's venture or a share in the capital appreciation of the security over all or part of the life of the loan. Shared appreciation mortgages are regulated by CC §§1917–1917.005. Arguments that such arrangements might be held to constitute joint ventures rather than loans, or be held to violate usury laws, are eliminated by CC §§1917.001 and 1917.005.

§1.15   2. Tax Consequences of Interest Payments on Note

■ *Mortgagee.* Interest payments received by the mortgagee constitute ordinary income. IRC §1001; see generally Taxation of Real Property Transfers §§3.1–3.9 (Cal CEB 1981). This is true whether the payments are collected regularly during the term of the loan or received at the foreclosure sale (from third party bidding or from the credit-bidding of accrued interest as well as unpaid principal). See §2.30. When the loan is paid prematurely and the mortgagee thus forgoes receipt of anticipated interest, only an accrual-basis taxpayer (or cash-basis taxpayer subject to original-issue discount treatment; see below) who has already included the anticipated interest payment in income may deduct unreceived anticipated interest. Reg §1.166–1(e), 1.166–6(a)(2); see *Fitzhugh L. Odom,* TC Memo 1979–53.

■ *Mortgagor.* Treatment of interest paid by the mortgagor depends on the character of the debt, which in turn may depend on the nature of the asset being financed. If the security consists of business property, the interest paid may be deducted as a business expense under IRC §163(a). If the property is held for investment, interest is deductible to the extent of net investment income. IRC §163(d). If the property is subject to passive activity treatment, interest is deductible in accordance with IRC §469. Home mortgage acquisition interest is deductible up to $1 million of acquisition debt (plus $100,000 of debt in a nonacquisition case as home equity interest, *i.e.,* a home equity credit line). IRC §163(h). The California rule differs, however, with respect to home mortgage interest. See Rev & T C §17024.5. Personal interest that does not qualify under any of the foregoing provisions is nondeductible. IRC §163(h). For discussion, see Taxation of Real Property Transfers Supp §2.4A (Cal CEB). Points paid at the inception of the loan are deductible ratably over the life of the loan except when the loan was taken to purchase or improve (but not refinance) the taxpayer's principal residence (and are then deductible in the year paid). IRC §461(g); *James Richard Huntsman* (1988) 91 TC 917.

Whenever interest is set at below-market rates, deferred, or made subject to balloon treatment, the transaction may be subject to treatment by the Internal Revenue Service under the original-issue discount (or imputed interest) rules. IRC §§483, 1271–1274. For discussion, see Taxation RP Transfers Supp §2.45A. When the amount of nonrecourse debt greatly exceeds the property's value, interest deductions may be denied, either for the excess debt (see *Pleasant Summit Land Corp. v Commissioner* (3d Cir 1988) 863 F2d 263, cert denied (Oct. 10, 1989) ___ US ___, 110 S Ct 260, ___ L Ed 2d ___) or for the entire debt in an abusive situation (see *Estate of Isaacson v Commissioner* (2d Cir 1988) 860 F2d 55).

§1.16   C. Obligor

A security instrument needs an obligation to be enforceable, but it does not need an obligor, *i.e.,* one personally responsible for performing. See CC §2890; *Shelley v Byers* (1925) 73 CA 44, 238 P 177. The purchase-money situation is the most common example of this rule; the effect of CCP §580b is that no individual is personally liable for the debt. Although there is still an obligation to pay, because nonpayment will lead to foreclosure, only the property is liable for payment. See §4.23. It is also possible to draft a nonpurchase-money note as a "nonrecourse" note to insulate its maker from personal responsibility for payment. See App A.

The debtor need not be the trustor. If *A* gives a deed of trust to a lender to secure *B*'s promissory note, *A* is a trustor but *B* is the debtor. If the note is not paid, *A* may lose her property by foreclosure, but she has no obligation to pay the note if the foreclosure proceeds do not discharge the entire debt. See *Garretson Inv. Co. v Arndt* (1904) 144 C 64, 77 P 770. See also *Carson v Reid* (1902) 137 C 253, 70 P 89. *A* is personally liable on the note only if she cosigns, endorses, or guarantees it. *Lange v Aver* (1966) 241 CA2d 793, 50 CR 847; *Stephenson v Lawn* (1957) 155 CA2d 669, 318 P2d 132. But see *Lopez v Puzina* (1966) 239 CA2d 708, 49 CR 122. If *A* assumes personal liability and also gives a deed of trust, the deed of trust may stand either as security for her own guaranty of payment or as additional security for *B*'s promise to pay the note. *Commercial Bank v Kershner* (1898) 120 C 495, 52 P 848; *Kelley v Goldschmidt* (1920) 47 CA 38, 190 P 55.

A subsequent grantee of encumbered property is not always personally liable for the debt. Assume that *A* borrows $100,000, giving a note and deed of trust on her property. She then conveys the property to *B,* and nothing is said about the loan. In this case, the creditor may foreclose on the property now held by *B,* and may possibly obtain a deficiency judgment against *A,* but cannot have a deficiency judgment against *B* because *B* never promised to pay the note. *B* is a nonassuming grantee and, as such, is not personally liable, although he takes the property subject to the lien of the deed of trust. *Braun v Crew* (1920) 183 C 728, 192 P 531; *Hibernia Sav. & Loan Soc'y v Dickinson* (1914) 167 C 616, 140 P 265; *Wolfert v Guadagno* (1933) 130 CA 661, 20 P2d 360. Moreover, once a nonassuming grantee enters the picture, subsequent grantees share that immunity, even when they personally attempt to assume the loan. See *Dail v Campbell* (1961) 191 CA2d 416, 12 CR 739, and cases cited therein. Whenever the grantor has no personal liability, subsequent grantees will not be liable whether or not they are assuming grantees, because there is nothing to assume. See *Weaver v Bay* (1963) 216 CA2d 559, 31 CR 211; §8.22.

§1.17   D. Transfers

Transfers of mortgage paper are common among institutional lenders, and there is an active secondary market, assisted by the federal government, for the exchange of secured notes. When the payee anticipates the prospect of later transferring the note, the note should be made negotiable (see §§1.18–1.19) and should be drafted to comply with the requirements of the secondary market agencies. See 1 California Real Property Financing §§1.40–1.43, 3.1 (Cal CEB 1988).

Because the obligation and the security are different, they commonly appear as separate documents (promissory note and deed of trust). The creditor holding both a note and a deed of trust may transfer one and retain the other. If it transfers the note but not the deed of trust, the transferee still gets a secured note; the security follows the note, legally if not physically. CC §2936; *Seidell v Tuxedo Land Co.* (1932) 216 C 165, 13 P2d 686. The transferee of the note may utilize the security even if it was not transferred along with the note. *Lewis v Booth* (1935) 3 C2d 345, 44 P2d 560; *Burnett v Lyford* (1892) 93 C 114, 28 P 855.

On the other hand, if the deed of trust is given to the transferee without the note accompanying it, the transferee has nothing except the possibility of an action against the transferor to compel it to transfer the note as well as the deed, if that was part of the agreement. *Kelley v Upshaw* (1952) 39 C2d 179, 246 P2d 23; *Polhemus v Trainer* (1866) 30 C 685. Consequently, when one transferee takes the note and another takes the deed of trust, the one holding the note prevails, regardless of who took first (*Adler v Sargent* (1895) 109 C 42, 41 P 799), unless the transferee of the note is subject to estoppel by virtue of having permitted the transferor to continue to appear as owner (*Domarad v Fisher & Burke, Inc.* (1969) 270 CA2d 543, 76 CR 529). See §8.28 on multiple notes.

Transfers of mortgage paper may be made outright (sale) or by pledge (as security for a loan to the transferor). In either case, the note should be delivered physically to the transferee to perfect the transfer. Without a physical transfer, a sale could be invalidated as a fraudulent conveyance under CC §3440, and a transfer in pledge could be invalidated as unperfected under Com C §9301(1)(b). See *In re Executive Growth Invs.* (Rechnitzer v Boyd) (Bankr CD Cal 1984) 40 BR 417. Sales and investments in speculative notes have often led to heavy losses for innocent investors who received impressive-looking "certificates" from their investment advisors rather than the actual notes required to protect themselves when the schemes went into bankruptcy. See *In re Staff Mortgage & Inv. Corp.* (Greiner v Wilke) (9th Cir 1980) 625 F2d 281; *In re Bruce Farley Corp.* (Starr v Bruce Farley Corp.) (9th Cir 1980) 612 F2d 1197. But see *In re Golden Plan* (Bear v Coben) (9th Cir 1987) 829 F2d 705.

E. Negotiability

§1.18   1. Negotiable Secured Paper

The promissory note may be written to be negotiable or nonnegotiable. See 1 California Real Property Financing §§3.3, 3.6, 3.8 (Cal CEB 1988). Negotiability is important not to the immediate payee, but to the transferee who thus qualifies for holder-in-due-course status and thereby takes free of many defenses to the note. See Com C §§3302, 3305.

To be negotiable, an instrument must contain an unconditional promise to pay. Com C §3104. California courts initially took the position that a secured note was not negotiable, on the ground that the one-action rule (CCP §726; see §§4.3–4.11) converted the unconditional obligation to one conditioned on the absence of a prior deficiency judgment. *National Hardware Co. v Sherwood* (1913) 165 C 1, 130 P 881; *Kelly v Universal Oil Supply Co.* (1924) 65 CA 493, 224 P 261; *Helmer v Parsons* (1912) 18 CA 450, 123 P 356. This case-law rule was abrogated by the legislature when it enacted former CC §3265, which explicitly eliminated security as an impediment to negotiability. Stats 1923, ch 98. Although former CC §3265 was repealed in 1963 when the Commercial Code was enacted, it appears that Com C §3104 continues to permit making a secured note negotiable.

Commercial Code §3105 provides that a promise otherwise unconditional is not made conditional by a statement in it that it is secured. Thus, if an otherwise-negotiable promissory note contains merely an additional sentence stating that it is secured by a mortgage or deed of trust, its negotiability is not thereby impaired. See Com C §3105(2)(a). See also Official Comment No. 8 to UCC §3–105. Incorporation of too many of the provisions of the security instrument into the text of the note could, however, impair negotiability. See *Siebenhauer v Bank of Cal. Nat'l Ass'n* (1930) 211 C 239, 294 P 1062; *People's Bank v Porter* (1922) 58 CA 41, 208 P 200; *Holly Hill Acres, Ltd. v Charter Bank* (D Fla 1975) 314 S2d 209 (incorporation of mortgage instrument by reference).

Even though the note recites that it is secured, the transferee could still be a holder in due course (see §1.19), subject of course to the one-action rule of CCP §726. It is unknown whether the transferee would take subject to CCP §580b (see §4.23) if the note recites that it is secured but does not indicate whether it is a purchase-money instrument.

If, on the other hand, the note makes no reference to the security, a different set of problems arises. The mortgagor runs the risk that a holder in due course may claim ignorance of the security and seek to recover on the note as if it were unsecured. Under these circumstances, the mortgagor may lose the protection of the one-action and antideficiency rules. See *Kish v Bay Counties Title Guar. Co.* (1967) 254 CA2d 725, 62 CR 494; *Van Vleck Realty v Gaunt* (1967) 250 CA2d 81, 58 CR 246. The fact that the mortgage was recorded may not help the mortgagor, because the principles of constructive notice generated by the recording laws (see CC §2934) are generally inapplicable to holders in due course, on the sensible ground that the free transferability of commercial paper would be impaired if each taker had to examine the records before purchasing negotiable paper. Com C §3304(5). See also *Haulman v Crumal* (1936) 13 CA2d 612, 57 P2d 179; *Ross v Title Guar. & Trust Co.* (1934) 136 CA 393, 29 P2d 236.

When a secured note has been properly made negotiable, negotiability is also imparted to the security instrument. *Hayward Lumber & Inv. Co. v Naslund* (1932) 125 CA 34, 13 P2d 775. Thus, a holder in due course takes both the note and the mortgage free of hidden defenses.

Negotiation of the note may be accomplished by making an endorsement directly on it or by attaching a second sheet (an allonge) to the note. Com C §3202(2).

§1.19   2. Holder in Due Course

For a transferee of the note to gain holder-in-due-course status, it is not enough that the note itself be negotiable. The transferee must also act in good faith, give value, and not have actual notice of any defense or claim on the part of the obligor. Com C §3302. As discussed in §1.18, principles of constructive notice under the recording laws are not applied to holders in due course. Thus, for example, the notice given by a lis pendens does not affect a holder in due course. *Ross v Title Guar. & Trust Co.* (1934) 136 CA 393, 29 P2d 236. The basic principle is that demands and considerations of negotiability are sufficiently important to override inconsistent principles appropriate to real property and the real property recording system. See Com C §3304(5).

Federal Trade Commission regulations have restricted the scope of the holder-in-due-course doctrine in the consumer credit field by permitting debtors to raise against transferees the same defenses they could have raised against sellers. See 16 CFR §433.2. California courts have also limited application of the doctrine in consumer credit cases. See *Vasquez v Superior Court* (1971) 4 C3d 800, 94 CR 796; *Morgan v Reasor Corp.* (1968) 69 C2d 881, 73 CR 398; *Commercial Credit Corp. v Orange County Mach. Works* (1950) 34 C2d 766, 214 P2d 819. See §1.17 on transfers of notes.

§1.20   F. Drafting Checklist

A transaction of any consequence should include a note tailored to the circumstances. The following questions may be used as a checklist for drafting notes. For discussion and form provisions for the promissory note, see 1 California Real Property Financing, chap 3 (Cal CEB 1988).

Financial data. What information does the client have regarding the background, assets, and financial responsibility of each of the proposed obligors?

_____ What information can the proposed payee supply?

_____ What are the assets of each obligor?

_____ Is it advisable to ask for a statement of such information?

_____ Is it advisable to obtain a credit report?

_____ If a proposed obligor is a business organization, will it furnish a balance sheet and profit-and-loss statements for preceding years?

Security. What security is available?

_____ Should the note given to the seller be secured by the real property sold? See §§1.21–1.34.

_____ Should the note be secured by other real property owned by the purchaser? See §§8.2–8.6.

_____ Should the note be secured by an assignment of rents and profits of the real property? See chap 5.

_____ Should an unsecured note be given (do the disadvantages of being a secured creditor outweigh the advantages)?

_____ Should a guarantor be required? See §§8.10–8.18.

_____ Should personal property be taken as part of the security? If so, what is required to perfect a security interest in the personal property? For discussion of multiple- and mixed-security issues, see §§8.2–8.8.

_____ What is the value of the security? How will the security's value be determined? Should there be an appraisal of the property?

Negotiability

_____ Does the note contain words of negotiability? See §§1.18–1.19.

_____ If it is intended that the note be sold on the secondary mortgage market, does it comply with the requirements of agencies that purchase loans on that market? See 1 Real Property Financing §§1.40–1.43, 3.1.

Payment

_____ Does the note designate a place of payment that will give the holder a convenient forum in which to file a legal action in case of default? See §3.9.

_____ Is it intended that the maker will have the right to prepay the note? See §§7.19–7.25.

_____ Will an unrestricted right of prepayment restrict marketability of the note in the hands of the payee?

_____ Will a prepayment penalty enhance the marketability of the note?

Interest

_____ Will a provision for late-charges payment induce the maker to pay promptly? See §§7.7–7.9.

_____ Has provision been made for interest on delinquent interest?

_____ Have usury restrictions been considered, and does the note guard against the possibility of usury? See 1 Real Property Financing §§3.47, 5.45–5.50.

_____ Is stated interest rate sufficient to avoid application of original-issue discount rules? See §1.15.

Related agreements

_____ If the note is the product of an underlying contract (*e.g.,* real property purchase and sale agreement), is the note consistent with that contract? See California Real Property Sales Transactions, chap 3 (Cal CEB 1981).

_____ Has care been taken to provide for all terms of the note in the underlying contract, or has a copy of the proposed note been made a part of the underlying contract?

_____ Is provision made in the underlying contract for title insurance and recording and filing?

_____ Will the inclusion of various securing clauses impress on the maker the formality and strictness of the transaction?

Acceleration. Should the holder be given the right to accelerate maturity of the note for reasons other than nonpayment of an installment? See §§7.2–7.6, 7.10–7.18.

_____ What will happen if the maker dies or becomes incapacitated, sells the business, withdraws from active participation in the business, suffers a casualty loss in or out of the business, or obtains a divorce?

_____ What will happen if the maker sells real or personal property on which a deed of trust or chattel mortgage has been given as security for the note? See §§7.10–7.18.

_____ Does a prepayment penalty apply when the debt is accelerated? CC §2954.10 (see §§7.22, 7.25).

Costs and attorneys' fees

_____ Have costs and attorneys' fees in event of default been fully provided for to enforce the security as well as the note? See §§7.29–7.33.

_____ Have all obligors (*i.e.,* guarantors and endorsers as well as makers) been made liable for attorneys' fees? See §§8.9–8.27.

Liability. Has the liability of guarantors, accommodation endorsers, and other endorsers been made as unconditional and extensive as they will permit? See §§8.9–8.27. See also 1 Real Property Financing, chap 7.

_____ Has each waived due presentment and notice of dishonor?

_____ Has each waived discharge for impairment of recourse or collateral?

_____ Has each consented to extensions or renewals of the note?

Choice of law. Has the law governing the note been established? See §§4.44–4.46.

Obligations of signers. Are the capacities in which obligors will be liable clear? See §§8.9–8.27; 1 Real Property Financing, chap 7.

_____ Are guarantors clearly distinguished from makers?

_____ Is it clear that guarantors are guarantors of payment and not merely of collection?

_____ If the note is being executed by partners, is it clear that the note will be executed on behalf of the partnership?

_____ Have all obligors been made jointly and severally liable?

Obligor's capacities to execute note

_____ Have partnership agreements and corporation bylaws been examined to ascertain the extent of the authority to execute notes and by whom that authority may be exercised?

_____ Are such partnerships and corporations prohibited from acting as guarantors or sureties?

_____ Does a duly executed corporate resolution specifically authorize execution of the note in the form in which it is proposed to be executed?

_____ If an obligor is married, must the note be executed by the spouse? See Real Property Sales §3.15.

Execution. Will the note be duly executed in all respects? Will each party sign in the intended capacity? See Real Property Sales §§3.9–3.31.

_____ If the note will be executed by a corporation, does it satisfy formal requirements for corporate execution? Will it be executed by authorized officers? Has a certified copy of the resolution authorizing the note been obtained? See Real Property Sales §3.26.

_____ If the note will be executed by a person acting in a representative capacity, does he or she have authority to do so? Has, *e.g.,* a duly executed power of attorney or court order been obtained? See Real Property Sales §§3.18–3.21.

_____ Are signature lines constructed and labeled to make eminently clear the capacity in which each party will sign? Be specific by expressly labeling the party, *e.g.,* "Principal," "Agent," "Individually and as Comaker" (when party will also sign in representative capacity), or "Guarantor of Payment."

§1.21   IV. SECURITY INSTRUMENT

The peculiar nature of real property has always required that its use as security be treated differently from the use of chattels for this purpose. One cannot carry real property to the nearest pawn shop or bank and leave it there until the debt is paid. This unique character of real property led to development of a system of documentation that gave creditors a measure of security equal to what they would have had by retaining possession of a chattel. The documents evidencing the transaction replace manual delivery of the security and must conform to the law of real property conveyancing in effect at the time they are executed. Thus, the earliest mortgages could not read "I will convey my land to you if I fail to pay my debt," because that would have violated the common law prohibition against springing interests (repealed in California by CC §767). Instead, early mortgages stated, "I convey my property to you now, but if I pay my debt on time, then title will revert to me." This estate in fee simple subject to condition subsequent conformed to feudal rules for conveyancing and thus became the first generally used mortgage device in England. See Nelson & Whitman, Real Estate Finance Law §§1.2–1.3 (2d ed 1985).

Under the common law system of estates, the debtor's failure to pay the debt by its due date ("law day") meant that the condition subsequent had failed to occur, the debtor's power of termination had ended, and the creditor's fee simple subject to condition subsequent was enlarged into a fee simple absolute. The debtor had no right to pay late and recover the land. This result was countenanced by the English common law courts, but courts of equity looked behind the form of the transaction and recognized that although the transaction appeared to be a conveyance, it was in fact a loan; the deed had been given not to convey land but as security for the debt. Therefore, if the grantee under the deed was treated as a lender rather than as a purchaser, late payment of the debt would not prejudice it (as long as interest was added for the delay). Thus, a debtor who failed to pay the debt on time could proceed to a court of equity and, on showing that the deed was really security for a loan, obtain the right to pay the debt late and thus "redeem" the property. This "equity of redemption" came to be part of every real property loan, leading to the further development that on default the creditor was compelled to go to court to "foreclose" this equity of redemption before claiming title to the mortgaged property. See *McMillan v Richards* (1858) 9 C 365. The common law equity of redemption is codified in CC §§2903–2905 (see §§2.22, 3.51).

The important principle to note in this development is that redemption rights were given to the debtor not by the language of the mortgage, but rather by the courts, usually in contradiction of the wording of the mortgage. The judiciary recognized that debtors were too necessitous to bargain for any rights and would have to be protected by the courts. These "superior equities" created by the courts came to be read into all mortgage loans, and the courts held that they were not waivable by any language or artifice in the mortgage papers.

§1.22   A. Mortgage

The mortgage was originally written as a common law fee simple subject to condition subsequent (see §1.21), but ultimately came to be simply a document by which the debtor-borrower "mortgaged" the real property to the creditor as "security" for a debt. This basic mortgage format is embodied in CC §2948 as a statutory form.

Unlike the common law fee simple subject to condition subsequent, the California mortgage does not give the mortgagee title to the property. It is not a deed; the mortgagee receives a lien on the property, *i.e.,* the right to have the property sold to satisfy the indebtedness. This is the "lien theory" of mortgages, followed in California and numerous other states. CC §§2888, 2926; *Harp v Calahan* (1873) 46 C 222, 233; *Mack v Wetzlar* (1870) 39 C 247, 254; *Goodenow v Ewer* (1860) 16 C 461, 467; *Nagle v Macy* (1858) 9 C 426.

§1.23   B. Deed of Trust

In California, the deed of trust has completely eclipsed the mortgage as the lending industry's preferred security instrument. The reasons for its rise in popularity illustrate a peculiar aspect of California mortgage law.

The general tendency of English courts of equity and American courts is to treat as a mortgage any instrument that secures a debt with real property. The instrument is thus subject to all the rules governing mortgages. If changes in form could insulate a mortgage instrument from the rules protecting debtors, creditors would automatically compel their debtors to execute such variant instruments. Thus, the threshold question for a court examining a real property instrument is whether the document serves a mortgage function. If it does, it will be treated as a mortgage, regardless of its form. This rule has been followed in California with regard to many forms of disguised security. See §4.35.

Historically, however, the California Supreme Court declined to follow this approach with respect to deeds of trust, holding that, if a deed of trust did not look like a mortgage, it was not a mortgage. *Koch v Briggs* (1859) 14 C 256. The strictly formal differences between the two instruments were held in *Koch* to make them different in effect. (A mortgage declares that the debtor "mortgages" the property; a deed of trust recites that the trustor "grants, transfers, and assigns [the property] to trustee in trust" as security for the loan.) The court went on to hold that, because the instrument was not a mortgage, it was not subject to the debtor-protection rules that govern mortgages. Given this advantage, the deed of trust rapidly became the dominant real property security instrument in California.

It was not until 1933 that the supreme court recognized its error and brought the deed of trust back within the coverage of California's mortgage policy. In *Bank of Italy Nat' l Trust & Sav. Ass'n v Bentley* (1933) 217 C 644, 20 P2d 940, the court held that, if a deed of trust served the same economic function as a mortgage, it should be treated as a mortgage and thus be subject to the same set of rules that govern mortgages. The one-action rule of CCP §726 (see §§4.3–4.10) was thus held to apply to a note secured by a deed of trust as well as to a mortgage.

The *Bank of Italy* decision did not precipitate a return by lenders to the mortgage as the preferred security instrument. Although the decision deprived the deed of trust of its perceived advantages over the mortgage, 70 years of judicial analysis of use of the deed of trust as a security instrument were invaluable to an industry interested in certainties. Thus, the deed of trust continued to be the standard security document.

Subsequent decisions have continued the merger of mortgage and deed of trust law; it is difficult to find meaningful legal differences between them any longer. Although the deed of trust was originally held to be a "title" rather than a "lien" document, the functional aspects of that distinction have vanished, and both mortgages and deeds of trust now have the same effect, or lack of it, on title. Compare, *e.g., People ex rel Dep't of Pub. Works v Nogarr* (1958) 164 CA2d 591, 330 P2d

858, with *Hamel v Gootkin* (1962) 202 CA2d 27, 20 CR 372. There remains today only the early holding that the power of sale in a deed of trust is not outlawed by time, although the same power in a mortgage is subject to the statute of limitations. *Travelli v Bowman* (1907) 150 C 587, 89 P 347; *Sipe v McKenna* (1948) 88 CA2d 1001, 200 P2d 61. This distinction was narrowed by the legislature in the Marketable Record Title Act (CC §§880.020–887.090), which imposed finite time limits on the enforceability of all real property security instruments (CC §882.020). Distinctions remain between mortgages and deeds of trust, however, in terms of time limitations. See §§3.11, 6.17. If the courts ultimately eliminate even this distinction as unreasonable and unnecessary, it will then be accurate to say that there is no functional distinction between a mortgage and deed of trust in California. The sole remaining advantage of the deed of trust for private lenders will then be the presence of an independent trustee able to handle a sale or foreclosure when necessary. See 1 Real Property Financing §4.1 (Cal CEB 1988).

§1.24   1. Forms of Deeds of Trust

Although there is a suggested statutory model for mortgages in CC §2948, there is no statutory form for a deed of trust. Most noninstitutional lenders use the printed forms supplied by title companies. An annotated title company form appears in App B. Various title company forms are substantially identical. Both long-form and short-form printed deeds of trust are available from title companies. The form in App B is a short form. The substantive provisions of the long form and the short form are identical, but in the short form many of the provisions are incorporated by reference to a recorded fictitious deed of trust, so that the reverse side, on which the provisions are reprinted in full, need not be recorded. In the long form, the provisions are restated in the body of the form and must be recorded. Although title companies usually supply the short form unless the long form is specifically requested, the parties should seriously consider using the long form because its provisions may more easily be modified. There is also more space on the long form for adding additional provisions. The fact that the provisions are contained in the body of the long form above the signature line, rather than appearing in small print on the back of the form, also makes it more difficult for a party later to claim ignorance of the provisions. Finally, use of the long form eliminates the risk of defective incorporation by reference.

An attorney advising a party who is using a title company form should remember that the deed of trust can be modified even though it is on a printed form. Many of the provisions (*e.g.*, right to insurance or condemnation proceeds, interest on sums advanced by beneficiary to protect the security) affect only the trustor and the beneficiary and are of no concern to the trustee (usually a title company). Provisions in title company forms often attempt to strike a balance between the perceived interests of the lender and the borrower, but the parties' attorneys may wish to modify or add certain provisions. Attorneys who frequently represent trustors or beneficiaries may wish to add a predrafted rider to the printed form to serve as a starting point for negotiations.

Institutional lenders, *e.g.*, banks and savings and loan associations, usually use their own forms or uniform instruments approved by the Federal National Mortgage Association ("Fannie Mae") and the Federal Home Loan Mortgage Corporation ("Freddie Mac"). For discussion of the requirements of the various agencies in the secondary mortgage market, see 1 California Real Property Financing §§1.40–1.43 (Cal CEB 1988). Institutional deeds of trust also contain special provisions for loans insured by the Federal Housing Administration or guaranteed by the Veterans Administration. The discussion in this book is generally confined to the common title company form deeds of trust.

§1.25   2. Requirements for Validity

Mortgages and deeds of trust must each comply with the formalities necessary for grants of real property. The mortgage is specifically required to do so by statute. CC §2922. The deed of trust is technically a grant of real property. See *Hahn v Hahn* (1954) 123 CA2d 97, 266 P2d 519. Thus, the instrument must be in the form of a writing that adequately identifies the parties and the property (CC §1091; *Dool v First Nat'l Bank* (1929) 207 C 347, 278 P 233; *Watkins v Bryant* (1891) 91 C 492, 504, 27 P 775, 777) and must be properly signed and delivered (CC §1091; *Le Mesnager v Hamilton* (1894) 101 C 532, 35 P 1054). Acknowledgment is not required, but without it the instrument cannot be recorded. CC §2952; *Bank of Ukiah v Petaluma Sav. Bank* (1893) 100 C 590, 35 P 170; *Williams v Nieto* (1929) 98 CA 615, 277 P 513. Requirements for establishing the identity of the parties whose signatures are acknowledged in the instrument are set out in CC §1185(c). The mortgage or deed of trust must secure an obligation in order for a lien to attach to the property. See §1.10. The lien may, however, secure a promise to pay future debts as they arise. *Moss v Odell* (1901) 134 C 464, 66 P 581; see §8.34.

If the trustor fails to execute and deliver the deed of trust as the parties have agreed, the would-be beneficiary may have an equitable lien on the property. See *In re Destro* (Pellerin v Stuhley) (9th Cir 1982) 675 F2d 1037.

§1.26   C. Convertible Mortgage

A convertible mortgage gives the lender (in addition to the note and deed of trust) an option to buy the encumbered property at some time in the future. When the option is exercised, the note is canceled and the deed of trust is reconveyed as part of the purchase price. The convertible mortgage permits the borrower to keep the property for the short term, and thus to retain the early tax and ownership benefits and risks, and enables the lender to buy a valuable mature property in an increasingly competitive market. See *Financing Real Estate During the Inflationary 80s,* ABA Sec Real Prop, Prob & Trust L (Strum, ed., 1981).

Concerns that such arrangements might constitute an impermissible "clogging" of the equity of redemption were eliminated by enactment of CC §2906, which provides that an option granted to a mortgagee or a beneficiary under a deed of trust to acquire encumbered (nonresidential) real property is valid as long as its exercise does not depend on a default by the borrower. See Nellis, *Convertible Mortgages: A Brief Review of the Legal and Drafting Issues,* 8 CEB Real Prop L Rep 1 (Jan. 1985).

D. Parties
§1.27   1. Trustor

A deed of trust must identify the trustor, whose signature is necessary to the instrument's effectiveness. *Le Mesnager v Hamilton* (1894) 101 C 532, 35 P 1054; *Welch v Security-First Nat'l Bank* (1943) 61 CA2d 632, 143 P2d 770. Because the instrument transfers an interest in real property, the trustor must own all or some part of that interest. This doctrine is qualified, however, by application of the doctrine of after-acquired title. See CC §2930. See also 2 Bowman, Ogden's Revised California Real Property Law §17.13 (TI Corp-CEB 1975). Note, however, that a deed of trust that was recorded before the trustor acquired record title is outside the chain of title and thus does not acquire priority over a subsequently recorded deed of trust. *Far W. Sav. & Loan Ass'n v McLaughlin* (1988) 201 CA3d 67, 246 CR 872.

The trustor need not be sole owner of the property as long as his or her signature alone can convey some fractional interest in it. See §1.31. When the property is held as community property, both spouses must be named and both must execute the deed of trust. CC §§5125, 5127; *O'Banion v Paradiso* (1964) 61 C2d 559, 39 CR 370; *Jack v Wong Shee* (1939) 33 CA2d 402, 415, 92 P2d 449, 455; *Italian Am. Bank v Canepa* (1921) 52 CA 619, 199 P 55. When property is presumed to be community property under CC §4800.1, but appears of record to be held in joint tenancy or tenancy in common, however, the signature of one spouse may be effective to encumber his or her half of the property. *Kane v Huntley Fin.* (1983) 146 CA3d 1092, 194 CR 880; *Mitchell v American Reserve Ins. Co.* (1980) 110 CA3d 220, 167 CR 760. See also *In re Nelson* (Security Pac. Fin. Corp. v Nelson) (9th Cir 1985) 761 F2d 1320 (wife bound by husband's forgery of her signature when he believed he had her consent and she accepted benefits of transaction). See also §1.31. Third party creditors of the married couple do not, however, have standing to challenge the validity of a note and deed of trust executed by only one of the spouses. *Clar v Cacciola* (1987) 193 CA3d 1032, 238 CR 726 (holder of third deed of trust sought unsuccessfully to challenge validity of second deed of trust signed only by husband).

The trustor need not be the debtor for the deed of trust to be valid. One can give a mortgage or deed of trust to secure the debt of another. *Everly Enters. v Altman* (1960) 54 C2d 761, 8 CR 455; *Garretson Inv. Co. v Arndt* (1904) 144 C 64, 77 P 770; *Exchequer Acceptance Corp. v Alexander* (1969) 271 CA2d 1, 76 CR 328; see §1.16. One can also give a deed of trust to secure a strictly contingent obligation, such as a guaranty. See §1.9.

§1.28   2. Trustee

The trustee under a deed of trust is not a true trustee and is not subject to the general rules governing trusts. *Lupertino v Carbahal* (1973)

35 CA3d 742, 747, 111 CR 112, 115. The function of the trustee is to conduct a sale of the property on default or to reconvey the property to the trustor according to the beneficiary's instructions on the trustor's performance of the obligation. The trustee has no other duties. The trustee has been referred to as a common agent rather than as a true trustee, but even this label is misleading because the trustee is not required to obtain the trustor's consent as a precondition to selling the trustor's interest on foreclosure. *Jones v Sierra Verdugo Water Co.* (1923) 63 CA 254, 218 P 454.

Because the trustee has no real function other than to foreclose on demand, title companies will often serve as trustees in accordance with their printed forms even though they have not specifically consented to the appointment or been given notice of it. See *Huntoon v Southern Trust & Commerce Bank* (1930) 107 CA 121, 290 P 86. They undertake their task only when requested to do so by the beneficiary.

The beneficiary may choose to substitute its own attorney or other nominee as trustee if he or she does not want to pay the charges that title companies exact for foreclosure, or if the trustee refuses to foreclose when requested to do so. See §2.7. Procedures for substitution are set forth in CC §2934a. Apparently the provisions of §2934a need not be followed if the beneficiary complies with alternative procedures set forth in the deed of trust. See *U.S. Hertz, Inc. v Niobrara Farms* (1974) 41 CA3d 68, 116 CR 44. Unless the attorney is familiar with foreclosure procedures, it may be preferable to permit an experienced title company to handle the mechanics of the trustee's foreclosure sale. See §2.2.

§1.29   3. Beneficiary

The beneficiary must be an obligee of the secured obligation (usually payee of a note), because otherwise the deed of trust in its favor is meaningless. *Watkins v Bryant* (1891) 91 C 492, 27 P 775; *Nagle v Macy* (1858) 9 C 426. See §1.10 on the need for an obligation. The deed of trust is only an incident of the obligation and has no existence apart from it. *Goodfellow v Goodfellow* (1933) 219 C 548, 27 P2d 898; *Adler v Sargent* (1895) 109 C 42, 41 P 799; *Turner v Gosden* (1932) 121 CA 20, 8 P2d 505. When the beneficiary and trustee are too closely connected, a court might hold that the deed of trust is not supported by an actual obligation, or that the deed of trust merges into the underlying fee interest. See *In re Universal Farming Indus.* (Spacek v Thomen) (9th Cir 1989) 873 F2d 1334. The holder of the note can enforce the deed of trust whether or not he or she is named as beneficiary or mortgagee. CC §2936; see §1.17.

The beneficiary may also serve as trustee under the deed of trust. *More v Calkins* (1892) 95 C 435, 30 P 583. This arrangement has drawbacks, however. See the discussion of trustees in the Comment to App B. The beneficiary cannot also serve as trustor, because that arrangement would effect a merger of the two interests and thus destroy the deed of trust as an effective instrument. *Wilson v McLaughlin* (1937) 20 CA2d 608, 67 P2d 710. But see *Anglo-Californian Bank v Field* (1908) 154 C 513, 98 P 267. The beneficiary may serve as beneficiary of other deeds of trust on the same real property, but there are risks of merger if liens in favor of the beneficiary are not separated by intervening liens of third parties. See *Anglo-Californian Bank v Field, supra*; *Union Bank v Wendland* (1976) 54 CA3d 393, 126 CR 549; *Investcal Realty Corp. v Edgar H. Mueller Constr. Co.* (1966) 247 CA2d 190, 55 CR 475.

§1.30   E. Property Given as Security

The deed of trust should contain a legal description of the property or adequate reference to a prior recorded instrument containing such a description. *Wemple v Yosemite Gold Mining Co.* (1906) 4 CA 78, 87 P 280. An inadequate description of the property will invalidate the instrument. *Sepulveda v Apablasa* (1938) 25 CA2d 381, 77 P2d 526; *Staterstrom v Glick Bros. Sash, Door & Mill Co.* (1931) 118 CA 379, 5 P2d 21.

Civil Code §2947 provides that any interest in real property capable of being transferred may be mortgaged. Thus, it is possible to mortgage less than the full fee. Some of the more common lesser interests given as security are discussed in §§1.31–1.32. When the security consists of a nonfee interest, the deed of trust should describe the interest as well as the property.

§1.31   1. Fractional Interests

A fractional interest in property may be mortgaged. CC §2947. One tenant in common may subject his or her individual interest to a deed of trust, leaving the interest of the other tenant in common unencumbered. *Haster v Blair* (1940) 41 CA2d 896, 107 P2d 933. If a deed of trust is signed by only one of the co-owners, only that owner's interest is encumbered unless the signing owner is authorized to act on behalf of the others. When all co-owners execute the deed of trust, it constitutes an encumbrance on the entire fee. *Caito v United Cal. Bank* (1978) 20 C3d 694, 144 CR 751.

The rules are similar for joint tenancies. One joint tenant may encumber his or her fractional interest without the consent or signature of the others. *Schoenfeld v Norberg* (1970) 11 CA3d 755, 90 CR 47; *Clark v Carter* (1968) 265 CA2d 291, 70 CR 923; see §1.27. Although execution of a mortgage by one joint tenant severs the joint tenancy in some states, California courts have not followed this rule. *Clark v Carter, supra; People ex rel Dep't of Pub. Works v Nogarr* (1958) 164 CA2d 591, 330 P2d 858. Civil Code §683.2(a)(1) now provides that the joint tenancy is severed whenever a joint tenant executes and delivers a deed conveying legal title to another, "whether or not pursuant to an agreement that requires the third person to reconvey legal title to the joint tenant," but it is unlikely that the legislature intended to alter the existing rule in enacting this section. Under existing case law, the mortgagee takes a lien on the joint-tenancy interest. A foreclosure sale will effect a severance, however, and the purchaser at the sale becomes a tenant in common with the remaining joint tenant. If either joint tenant dies before foreclosure, however, the consequences are different. Because the joint tenancy remains in effect despite the mortgage, the principles of survivorship regulate the consequences of a death. Thus, if the nonmortgaging joint tenant dies first, the other joint tenant succeeds to the entire estate and the mortgage previously executed expands to cover the entire estate. See CC §2930; *Sherman v McCarthy* (1881) 57 C 507; *Parry v Kelley* (1877) 52 C 334. If the mortgaging joint tenant dies first, the mortgage is lost along with the estate and the surviving joint tenant takes the property free of the mortgage. See *Schoenfeld v Norberg, supra; Clark v Carter, supra; Hamel v Gootkin* (1962) 202 CA2d 27, 20 CR 372; *People ex rel Dep't of Pub. Works v Nogarr, supra.* For discussion of property held by spouses in joint tenancy, see §1.27.

When a junior lien exists on a fractional interest in property and the entire fee is sold to satisfy a senior lien, any surplus is divided between the junior and the holders of the other fractional interest. *Caito v United Cal. Bank, supra.*

Only under very unusual circumstances will a lender consider accepting a fractional interest as security because of the problem of selling the partial estate. A partition action may be necessary if cooperation cannot be obtained from the other co-tenants. On partition, see California Real Property Remedies Practice, chap 8 (Cal CEB 1982).

§1.32   2. Estates Smaller Than a Fee Simple

A life estate or term of years may be mortgaged. *McLeod v Barnum* (1901) 131 C 605, 63 P 924; *Commercial Bank v Pritchard* (1899) 126 C 600, 59 P 130; *San Francisco Breweries v Schurtz* (1894) 104 C 420, 38 P 92. Leasehold mortgages are common financing arrangements in modern commercial transactions. If the tenant defaults, the leasehold interest is sold at a foreclosure sale and the foreclosure purchaser becomes the new tenant. The landlord's reversionary interest is unaffected by the sale. Sometimes a landlord will subordinate the reversion to the mortgage instrument, in which case the foreclosure will result in sale of the entire fee rather than just the leasehold. *Matthews v Hinton* (1965) 234 CA2d 736, 44 CR 692.

One appellate court has held that a leasehold mortgage constitutes a personal property, rather than a real property, security interest. *Taylor v Bouissiere* (1987) 195 CA3d 1197, 241 CR 253. If followed, this surprising decision could cause serious complications for leasehold financing arrangements, because the Uniform Commercial Code expressly excludes leaseholds from its coverage, leaving leasehold security interests unregulated by any existing legal regimen. The historical fact that the leasehold was once regarded as a "chattel real," rather than as true real property, is a doubtful basis for excluding such interests from the operation of traditional real property rules. See Munoz, *Taylor v Bouissiere: Confusion for Leasehold Mortgage Holders,* 11 CEB Real Prop L Rep 61 (Apr. 1988).

It is also possible for a landlord to mortgage only the reversionary interest in the property. This occurs whenever a mortgage is executed after the property is already subject to a lease, unless the tenant has agreed to subordinate the leasehold to the mortgage. *Enos v Cook* (1884) 65 C 175, 3 P 632. When only the reversion is mortgaged, a foreclosure sale merely conveys the reversion and the purchaser becomes the new landlord. If the leasehold has been subordinated to the mortgage, the foreclosure sale terminates the leasehold and disposes of it along with the reversion, thus giving the foreclosure sale purchaser the entire fee. *McDermott v Burke* (1860) 16 C 580. When the leasehold and the reversion are subsequently acquired by the same party, the existence of a leasehold mortgage will prevent a merger of the two estates. *6424 Corp. v Commercial Exch. Prop.* (1985) 171 CA3d 1221, 217 CR 803.

It is possible for the vendor and purchaser under an installment land sale contract (see §1.35) to mortgage their respective interests separately. Each fits within the statutory requirement for transferability. CC §2947; see *Tripler v MacDonald Lumber Co.* (1916) 173 C 144, 159 P 591. The rights under an option to purchase real property and the right to redeem from a tax sale may also be mortgaged. When an installment land contract has been completely performed, or an option exercised, the doctrine of after-acquired title enlarges the mortgage to include the newly acquired interest. CC §2930. In case of foreclosure on one of these lesser interests, the purchaser at the foreclosure sale acquires no greater rights than the trustor had, but the purchased rights are also no smaller, and thus the purchaser may complete performance under the land sale contract, exercise the option (*Chapman v Great W. Gypsum Co.* (1932) 216 C 420, 14 P2d 758), or redeem the property from the tax sale.

§1.33   3. Encumbered Property

Property subject to a mortgage or deed of trust remains fully alienable and thus can be subjected to further encumbrances. Accordingly, a deed of trust may be executed on property that is already subject to an existing deed of trust. The beneficiary of the later instrument merely acquires a junior rather than a senior lien on the property. There is no legal limit to the number of mortgages or deeds of trust that may be imposed on property, although the latest creditor will want to ascertain that the property has sufficient value to satisfy all the prior liens plus this one. The interest acquired following a sale on foreclosure of a junior lien is subject to all prior liens. *Streiff v Darlington* (1937) 9 C2d 42, 68 P2d 728; *Wardlow v Middleton* (1909) 156 C 585, 105 P 738; see §2.27. For discussion of the beneficiary's right to accelerate the debt on further encumbrance of the property under a due-on-sale clause, see §7.10.

Prior easements, convenants, and equitable servitudes are encumbrances on property that do not impair its alienability or, therefore, its mortgageability. If property subject to an easement or similar burden is foreclosed, the purchaser at the sale will obtain the encumbered title (*Kreichbaum v Melton* (1874) 49 C 50; *Cook v De La Guerra* (1864) 24 C 237), unless the mortgage or deed of trust has priority over the encumbrance (*Sain v Silvestre* (1978) 78 CA3d 461, 144 CR 478).

§1.34   4. Personal Property and Improvements

A real property mortgage or deed of trust does not encumber personal property that is not affixed to the land. *McLeod v Barnum* (1901) 131 C 605, 63 P 924. A beneficiary who seizes or sells such personalty may be liable for conversion. *Strutt v Ontario Sav. & Loan Ass'n* (1972) 28 CA3d 866, 105 CR 395. The creditor who wants a security interest in personalty as well as realty should execute a separate security instrument for it and file that instrument in accordance with the Commercial Code. Com C §§9201, 9203; *Freedland v Greco* (1955) 45 C2d 462, 289 P2d 463. For discussion of issues that arise when the collateral consists of both real and personal property ("mixed collateral"), see §8.7.

Once personal property is affixed to the land, it becomes part of the real property under the doctrine of fixtures. CC §§658, 660. As such, it is subject to any subsequently executed real property mortgage or deed of trust. It also becomes subject to previously executed mortgages or deeds of trust under the doctrine of after-acquired title. CC §2930; *Commercial Bank v Pritchard* (1899) 126 C 600, 59 P 130; *Hill v Gwin* (1875) 51 C 47. Thus, a typical residential mortgage covers not only the land but also the house. For discussion, see 2 Bowman, Ogden's Revised California Real Property Law §17.14 (TI Corp-CEB 1975).

Third parties with chattel liens, who compete with real property creditors because the goods have become fixtures, have priority under Com C §9313 when:

■ The chattel security interest was a purchase-money security interest that attached before the goods became fixtures, and the claimant made a "fixture filing" (*i.e.,* recorded a document at the county recorder's office, rather than with the Secretary of State as is customary for most Commercial Code filings) within ten days after the goods became fixtures (Com C §9313(4)(a));

■ The chattel security interest was not a purchase-money security interest, but the fixture filing occurred before the deed of trust was recorded (Com C §9313(4)(b));

■ The fixtures are readily removable factory or office machines or readily removable replacements of domestic consumer appliances (Com C §9313(4)(c));

■ The lien on the real property was obtained by legal or equitable proceedings after the security interest in the fixtures was perfected (Com C §9313(4)(d)); or

■ The holder of the real property interest has consented (Com C §9313(5)(a)).

In all other cases, the real property interest is paramount. Special rules apply when the property is subject to a construction loan mortgage and the goods were affixed to the property during construction (Com C §9313(6)), and when the debtor has removal rights (Com C §9313(5)(b)), *e.g.,* when a tenant has the right to remove trade fixtures (see *Goldie v Bauchet Props.* (1975) 15 C3d 307, 124 CR 161).

Under Com C §§9402–9403, a deed of trust may be effective as a financing statement filed as a fixture filing. See Secured Transactions in California Commercial Law Practice §§3.72, 3.77 (Cal CEB 1986).

§1.35   F. Installment Land Sale Contract

An alternative to the deed of trust in California is the installment land sale contract. As a device that was once perceived as circumventing the consequences of a due-on-sale clause in a deed of trust (see §7.12), it acquired considerable popularity during the early 1970s. The installment land contract was also widely employed in the early 1960s and before, as an inexpensive and expedient financing vehicle, until a series of California court decisions eliminated any legal or financial advantage it offered sellers over a promissory note secured by a deed of trust.

This section gives only a brief summary of installment land contracts so that the attorney who has never encountered one will be familiar with its legal effect. For a more extensive discussion of installment land contracts, see California Real Property Sales Transactions §§1.65, 5.4–5.7, 12.2 (Cal CEB 1981); Graham, *The Installment Land Contract in*

California: Is It Really a Mortgage?, 4 Real Prop L Rep 117 (Oct. 1981).

In a land contract transaction, a single document is used in place of the separate note and security instrument used in a conventional financing arrangement. The land contract is executed by both parties rather than just the debtor; the seller agrees to convey title to the buyer when paid in full, and the buyer agrees to pay the price to the seller in installments. Because the seller retains title until the contract price is paid in full, the seller does not need to receive a security interest in the property (the title retained functions as security) and thus no deed of trust or mortgage is used. Because the contract embodies the buyer's promise to pay the purchase price, there is no need for the buyer to execute a note to the seller agreeing to pay. Instead of interest, the seller pays a time-price differential. See *Boerner v Colwell Co.* (1978) 21 C3d 37, 145 CR 380. The installment land contract thus operates like a conditional sales contract.

Early cases gave the California seller a package of remedies on the buyer's breach that was in many ways superior to the remedies available under a mortgage or deed of trust. See, *e.g., Longmaid v Coulter* (1898) 123 C 208, 55 P 791; *Glock v Howard & Wilson Colony Co.* (1898) 123 C 1, 55 P 713. These remedies included benefit-of-the-bargain damages, the right to forfeiture of the buyer's past payments, specific performance, rescission, quiet title, and liquidated damages.

In the past few decades, however, the courts have significantly eroded the seller's formerly favored position. The reference to contracts in CCP §580b was held to include land contracts within the section's bar against deficiency judgments (see §4.23), thus prohibiting a seller from recovering unpaid back installments owed by the buyer. *Venable v Harmon* (1965) 233 CA2d 297, 43 CR 490. This logic, of course, also bars an action to recover future installments (*i.e.,* to recover the price), although such actions had previously been authorized in *Longmaid v Coulter, supra.* Compare the mortgagee's right to monetary relief under CCP §726. See §4.4. As of 1986, the power-of-sale procedures of CC §§2924–2924h apply to an installment land sale contract that contains a power of sale. CC §2920(b).

In *Barkis v Scott* (1949) 34 C2d 116, 208 P2d 367, the supreme court permitted defaulting buyers to resist the seller's attempt to quiet title and allowed them to reinstate their breached contract even though it provided that time was of the essence. Compare the statutory right to reinstate mortgages and deeds of trust under CC §2924c. See §2.22. The court in *Barkis* limited its decision to nonwillfully defaulting purchasers, but this limitation was later dropped in *MacFadden v Walker* (1971) 5 C3d 809, 97 CR 537, in which the court permitted a willfully defaulting purchaser to reinstate her installment land contract. In *McFadden,* the court held that awarding reinstatement as a remedy was discretionary with the trial court, but that discretion was eliminated in *Petersen v Hartell* (1985) 40 C3d 102, 219 CR 170, in which the court held that a willfully defaulting buyer has an absolute right to redeem the property (*i.e.,* to pay the full balance of the purchase price) whenever the buyer has paid a substantial portion of the purchase price before the default.

The defaulting buyer is not limited to a right to reinstate the contract. After breach, the buyer is still entitled to recover, as restitution, any amounts paid to the seller in excess of the seller's actual damages. *Freedman v The Rector* (1951) 37 C2d 16, 230 P2d 629. By contrast, a mortgagee or beneficiary is not required to return any funds to the debtor, unless there is a surplus after a foreclosure sale. *Smith v Allen* (1968) 68 C2d 93, 65 CR 153. The seller's actual damages are held to be nonexistent if the seller subsequently resells the property for a higher price. On the other hand, a resale at a loss does not fix the seller's damages at that amount, because the statutory measure is the difference between the contract price and the market value on the date of the breach (which may be different from the difference between the contract price and the resale price on the resale date). *Royer v Carter* (1951) 37 C2d 544, 233 P2d 539. The seller may, however, choose to rescind and recover rental-value rather than difference-value damages, and the buyer cannot complain of that election. See *Honey v Henry's Franchise Leasing Corp.* (1966) 64 C2d 801, 52 CR 18. See also *Kudokas v Balkus* (1972) 26 CA3d 744, 103 CR 318. This rule applies, however, only within the context of determining the amount of restitution to be paid to the buyer; it is difficult for the seller to recover a money judgment against the buyer under CCP §580b. *Venable v Harmon, supra.* Amendments to CC §3307 in 1983 added consequential damages and interest to the benefit-of-the-bargain damages that the seller may recover.

In *Freedman v The Rector, supra,* the court also held that a provision liquidating the seller's damages at the amount actually paid by the buyer was invalid. See also *Caplan v Schroeder* (1961) 56 C2d 515, 15

CR 145. In 1977, California's liquidated damages rules were extensively revised, and new provisions were written to cover purchases of residential real property (see CC §§1675–1680). Installment land contracts were specifically excluded from the special real property provisions (see CC §1681) and are presumably subject to the more relaxed general standard of presumptive validity set forth in CC §1671 (rather than the former standard of presumptive invalidity, now confined to residential leases and retail installment contracts). See Real Property Sales §3.179; Guggenhime, *California's New Liquidated Damages Law,* 1 CEB Real Prop L Rep 17 (Feb. 1978). By comparison, the beneficiary under a deed of trust is absolutely entitled to retain what it has received from the trustor, but it does not also obtain the trustor's title, except by purchase at a foreclosure sale. See §§3.61–3.62.

Finally, the seller may not bring an unlawful detainer action against a defaulting purchaser who refuses to leave, because the unlawful detainer statute does not cover this situation. CCP §1161. The vendor must sue in ejectment instead. *Francis v West Va. Oil Co.* (1917) 174 C 168, 162 P 394. A mortgagee is not so limited. CCP §1161a.

Judicial and statutory protections for buyers under installment land contracts are primarily of benefit to defaulting buyers. For the non-defaulting buyer, there remains the risk that the seller (who still has title) may default. The seller may jeopardize the purchaser's expectant title by failing to protect it against liens or by failing to keep it or even to acquire it. See, *e.g., Luette v Bank of Italy Nat'l Trust & Sav. Ass'n* (9th Cir 1930) 42 F2d 9. The buyer may be unable to seek any relief until the final payment is due, because the installment land contract may have been drafted so that the seller has no obligation to obtain good title until the price has been fully paid. *Lloyd v Locke-Paddon Land Co.* (1935) 5 CA2d 211, 42 P2d 367. But see *Prentice v Erskine* (1913) 164 C 446, 129 P 585. See generally Graham, 4 RPLR at 117. A trustor or mortgagor holds title to the property and therefore has no comparable fears concerning the seller's performance. See §§1.22–1.23. Buyers are afforded some protection by CC §§2985–2985.6, which impose certain obligations on sellers under installment land contracts.

The buyer's measure of damages against a defaulting seller is the price paid, the expenses of examining title and preparing documentation, the difference between the agreed price and the value at the time of breach, expenses of preparing to enter on the land, consequential damages, and interest. CC §3306. See generally California Real Property Remedies Practice §§4.11–4.16 (Cal CEB 1982). The buyer also has a "purchaser's lien" on the property for sums paid to the seller. CC §3050.

Formal distinctions between an installment land sale contract and a purchase-money mortgage or deed of trust usually do not affect the tax treatment of the parties to the sale; recognition of gain or loss is the same under either arrangement. *Harold R. Smith* (1939) 39 BTA 892.

Chapter 2: **Trustees' Sales**

2

Trustees' Sales

§2.1   I. INTRODUCTION

When the beneficiary under a deed of trust (or a mortgagee) wishes to foreclose the lien, an alternative to judicial foreclosure (described in chap 3) is to conduct a private sale of the property under the procedures set forth in CC §§2924–2924h. The remedy of a private foreclosure sale is available only if the deed of trust (or mortgage) contains a power-of-sale clause (see §2.5). This private-sale alternative is variously referred to as a trustee's sale or as a power-of-sale, private sale, extrajudicial, or nonjudicial foreclosure. These terms are used interchangeably in this chapter.

§2.2   A. Attorney's Role

An attorney's involvement in a private foreclosure sale often comes about when the holder of a secured note reports that the loan is delinquent and seeks advice on how to proceed. After investigating the common informal collection methods (*e.g.,* telephone calls, letters), the attorney must explain a foreclosure sale and its attendant consequences to the client and, perhaps, assist the client in carrying out the sale.

The attorney may also be contacted by a mortgagor or trustor who is claimed to be in default. The attorney must advise the debtor concerning conduct of the sale and possible avenues for protecting the debtor's interests. The attorney may eventually be retained to seek various remedies on the debtor's behalf, such as filing a legal action attacking the sale or pursuing various bankruptcy strategies. For discussion of debtor's strategies, see chap 6. An attorney for a debtor threatened with foreclosure should be aware of CC §§1695–1695.14, regulating home equity sales contracts. This statute applies to the sale of any one-to-four-unit owner-occupied residence that is sold by the trustor ("equity seller") within one year after a notice of default (see §2.12) has been recorded. Under CC §1695.13, it is unlawful for anyone to take unconscionable advantage of an owner whose residential property is in foreclosure, *e.g.,* by purchasing it for little or no money with the promise to reconvey later if paid. The debtor is entitled to rescind a home equity sales contract within two years of the date of recordation of the notice of default. CC §1695.14. The debtor's attorney should also be aware of CC §§2945–2945.8, regulating mortgage foreclosure consultants.

If a secured creditor client chooses to proceed with a private sale, the client must decide whether to have the matter handled by the trustee named in the deed of trust, to substitute another person or entity as trustee (see §2.7), or to conduct the proceeding itself. The attorney will usually advise that the creditor select a corporate trustee experienced in such matters (*e.g.,* a title company) to handle the sale, either the trustee originally named in the deed of trust or a substitute trustee. The attorney's role will then be to assist the client by (1) explaining the proceedings to the client, (2) monitoring those proceedings on the client's behalf, (3) providing advice in making strategic decisions when necessary, and (4) helping the client furnish the necessary information and documents to the trustee.

The attorney should be familiar with all the steps in the trustee's sale procedure to ensure that they are carried out correctly so that the title conveyed to the purchaser will be marketable. A trustee's sale guaranty is often obtained from a title company at the inception of trustee's sale proceedings, although its cost may make it advisable to record the notice of default first, in the hope that the notice will encourage payment of the delinquent amount. For discussion of the trustee's sale guaranty, see California Title Insurance Practice §§3.24, 4.13 (Cal CEB 1980). For a form guaranty, see Title Ins, App G. Failure to obtain this guaranty may leave the trustee unaware that the trustor has filed a bankruptcy petition, and thus make recording of the notice of default a violation of the automatic stay. See §6.49. If the notice of default is recorded through a title company, however, the title company should ascertain whether a bankruptcy petition has been filed and should refrain from recording the notice of default.

Attorneys are seldom involved in the details of conducting the trustee's sale, because it is usually more efficient to let the trustee handle those details. Accordingly, this chapter does not instruct the attorney on how to conduct a trustee's sale. The chapter is intended to impart sufficient information to enable the attorney to work with the trustee and instruct the client on the procedures of the foreclosure sale. Beginning with §2.11, the chapter leads the reader, step by step, through the trustee's sale procedures.

§2.3 B. Choosing Between Private Sale and Judicial Foreclosure

There are many reasons for preferring a private sale to judicial foreclosure (see chap 3). A private sale bypasses the courts altogether, which means that the matter can usually be handled with less time and expense than judicial foreclosure. Trustees' fees are often less than attorneys' fees would be, and the entire process can be completed within about four months from the recording of the notice of default, assuming that the trustor does not pursue any of the methods discussed in chap 6 for forestalling the sale. A trustee's sale is not subject to postsale redemption rights (CCP §§729.010–729.090; see §§3.73–3.80) and will therefore often command a higher price from a third party, so that the creditor has a better chance of being paid in full or (when the creditor is the purchaser) of obtaining title free from redemption rights. For discussion of combining either remedy with an action for appointment of a receiver to collect rents from the property, see §5.14.

A further advantage, in the case of multiple deeds of trust or mortgages securing a single note, is that (if the deed of trust so provides; see §2.23) extrajudicial foreclosures may be conducted in separate, piecemeal fashion, with the order of sales at the creditor's discretion, while judicial foreclosure requires consolidation of all the security into a single action. CCP §726; *Hatch v Security-First Nat'l Bank* (1942) 19 C2d 254, 120 P2d 869; see §8.4. For discussion of the order of sale after judgment when multiple parcels are involved, see §3.55. Finally, in the case of deeds of trust, foreclosure under a power of sale is not subject to the statute of limitations. *Flack v Boland* (1938) 11 C2d 103,

77 P2d 1090; see *Faxon v All Persons* (1913) 166 C 707, 137 P 919. (Under the Marketable Record Title Act, however, the life of a lien is subject to a finite ceiling. CC §882.020. For discussion, see §1.23.)

The major disadvantage of nonjudicial foreclosure is that the creditor is not entitled to a deficiency judgment after the sale. CCP §580d. Thus, when nonpurchase-money security is involved, the bar to a deficiency judgment may be a significant disincentive. See §4.14. The client should be advised, however, that a deficiency judgment can probably be discharged in bankruptcy.

In certain situations, the creditor may be forced into a judicial foreclosure even though a trustee's sale would otherwise be preferable, *e.g.*, when the security instrument lacks a power of sale or when a hidden security device has been used. See §2.5. In addition, if some issues remain unsettled between the creditor and the debtor, or among the creditors, judicial resolution of these matters may be necessary, and it may be safer to have the foreclosure sale conducted under judicial supervision at the same time as the collateral disputes are being resolved. See *Scott v Security Title Ins. & Guar. Co.* (1937) 9 C2d 606, 72 P2d 143; *Hamilton v Carpenter* (1942) 52 CA2d 447, 126 P2d 395.

§2.4   C. Election of Remedies

The creditor is not bound by an initial decision to begin proceedings under a power of sale and may drop the process at any time for any reason. *Flack v Boland* (1938) 11 C2d 103, 77 P2d 1090; *Commercial Centre Realty Co. v Superior Court* (1936) 7 C2d 121, 59 P2d 978. The decision either to proceed with or to abandon the extrajudicial sale is strictly within the creditor's discretion, and the creditor is not considered to have made an irrevocable election of remedy until the trustee's sale is conducted. *Carpenter v Title Ins. & Trust Co.* (1945) 71 CA2d 593, 163 P2d 73.

Conversely, the fact that a judicial foreclosure action has previously been filed does not bar the creditor from electing to abandon the action in favor of nonjudicial proceedings (or constitute its one action under CCP §726) as long as a judgment has not been obtained. *McDonald v Smoke Creek Live Stock Co.* (1930) 209 C 231, 286 P 693. Creditors sometimes initiate both types of foreclosure simultaneously, to obtain appointment of a receiver immediately in the judicial foreclosure action (see §5.13) and then to obtain the benefits of a nonredeemable sale in a nonjudicial foreclosure sale. See *Turner v Superior Court* (1977) 72 CA3d 804, 140 CR 475.

§2.5   D. Power-of-Sale Clause a Prerequisite

No security instrument can be foreclosed extrajudicially unless it contains language authorizing such a procedure, *i.e.*, a power-of-sale clause. *Huene v Cribb* (1908) 9 CA 141, 98 P 78. A mortgage or deed of trust without such a clause is still a valid security instrument, but it must be foreclosed judicially. *Fogarty v Sawyer* (1861) 17 C 589; *Huene v Cribb, supra.* A power-of-sale clause creates an independent right, given to the creditor by the debtor, to dispose of the security on default. *McDonald v Smoke Creek Live Stock Co.* (1930) 209 C 231, 286 P 693; *Fogarty v Sawyer, supra.*

No particular form is required for a power-of-sale clause. The conventional deed of trust merely states in the granting clause that the trustor grants the property to the trustee "with power of sale" (see App B). Courts interpret such language liberally to be sufficient to constitute a power-of-sale clause. *Fogarty v Sawyer, supra.* The detailed provisions in a standard title company deed of trust dealing with the mechanics of sale do little more than recapitulate many of the provisions already contained in CC §§2924–2924h, which are automatically part of the power of sale (*Curti v Pacific Mortgage Guar. Co.* (9th Cir 1936) 87 F2d 42) and which probably cannot be altered, at least to the debtor's detriment, by contrary language in the security instrument (CC §2953). See §7.42. The deed of trust may contain notice provisions more favorable to the debtor, and the creditor is bound by such provisions. *Fogarty v Sawyer, supra.* More liberal notice provisions may be required, for example, if the instruments are to be sold on the federal secondary mortgage market. See 1 California Real Property Financing §4.65 (Cal CEB 1988).

Any security instrument may include a power-of-sale clause. Civil Code §2932 specifically authorizes inclusion of power-of-sale clauses in mortgages, but the parties to real property transactions included them in mortgages long before the statute was enacted. *Fogarty v Sawyer, supra.* Deeds of trust have customarily contained power-of-sale clauses, although there has never been any statutory authorization for them. *Koch v Briggs* (1859) 14 C 256. The power of sale is transferred automatically along with an assignment of the deed of trust. *Strike v*

Trans-West Discount Corp. (1979) 92 CA3d 735, 155 CR 132. Deeds absolute may also contain such clauses (*Felton v Le Breton* (1891) 92 C 457, 28 P 490), although the presence of such language in a hidden security instrument would usually be inconsistent with the desire to mask the fact that the instrument is intended to create a security interest.

Civil Code §2920(b) expressly authorizes inclusion of a power-of-sale clause in installment land sale contracts (see §1.35). This statute, which provides that the provisions of CC §§2924–2924h apply to installment land contracts with a power of sale, should remove any doubt that may exist concerning the enforceability of power-of-sale clauses in installment land contracts and should overcome any reluctance by title companies to insure the title that results from enforcement of a power-of-sale clause in an installment land contract.

Finally, a power of sale may exist in its own right, embodied in an independent document. In that case, the mere creation of the remedy by the parties implies that a security interest was intended, making the document into a mortgage. *Pfeiffer v Hesse* (1930) 107 CA 616, 290 P 501.

As long as the security instrument does not make sale under the power of sale the creditor's exclusive remedy, a power-of-sale clause merely adds a cumulative remedy to the existing remedy of judicial foreclosure. CCP §725a; *Fighiera v Radis* (1919) 180 C 660, 182 P 418; *Godfrey v Monroe* (1894) 101 C 224, 35 P 761; *Cormerais v Genella* (1863) 22 C 116. A creditor may ignore the power and judicially foreclose the lien created by the security instrument instead. *Commercial Centre Realty Co. v Superior Court* (1936) 7 C2d 121, 59 P2d 978; *Loretz v Cal-Coast Dev. Corp.* (1967) 249 CA2d 176, 57 CR 188.

§2.6   E. Constitutionality of Private Sales

The California Supreme Court has upheld the constitutionality of trustees' sales conducted under CC §§2924–2924h. *Garfinkle v Superior Court* (1978) 21 C3d 268, 146 CR 208. The court ruled that a private foreclosure sale does not constitute state action and is therefore not subject to the due process clauses of the federal and state constitutions (US Const amend XIV; Cal Const art I, §7(a)). The *Garfinkle* court reasoned that:

■ The power of sale arises from contract (the mortgage or deed of trust provisions) rather than from statute;

■ Although there is extensive statutory regulation of private sales, the statutes are designed to restrict creditor behavior and do not constitute governmental encouragement of the procedure;

■ The ministerial role of the county recorder does not mean that government officials are significantly involved in the process; and

■ There is no delegation of judicial power to private parties.

See also *U.S. Hertz, Inc. v Niobrara Farms* (1974) 41 CA3d 68, 116 CR 44; *Strutt v Ontario Sav. & Loan Ass'n* (1972) 28 CA3d 866, 105 CR 395.

The *Garfinkle* court reached its conclusion with respect to application of both the federal and state constitutions. Because it can speak authoritatively only on state law, the somewhat remote possibility remains that the federal courts will reach a different conclusion on the fifth and fourteenth amendment issues. The California trustee's sale has been held not to constitute state action for federal constitutional purposes by the federal district court for the Northern District of California (*Lawson v Smith* (ND Cal 1975) 402 F Supp 851), and several federal courts of appeals have reached the same conclusion concerning similar private sales in other states (see *Charmicor, Inc. v Deaner* (9th Cir 1978) 572 F2d 694 (Nevada power of sale not state action even though created by statute, not contract); *Northrip v Federal Nat'l Mortgage Ass'n* (6th Cir 1975) 527 F2d 23 (Michigan power-of-sale statute); *Bryant v Jefferson Fed. Sav. & Loan Ass'n* (DC Cir 1974) 509 F2d 511 (Washington D.C. statute)).

Early decisions of the United States Supreme Court upheld power-of-sale foreclosures (see *Scott v Paisley* (1926) 271 US 632; *Bell Silver & Copper Mining Co. v First Nat'l Bank* (1895) 156 US 470). In more recent cases, however, the Supreme Court has invoked the due process clause of the United States Constitution to invalidate state procedures that sanction the seizure or sale of a debtor's property without a prior hearing. See *Sniadach v Family Fin. Corp.* (1969) 395 US 337 (prejudgment wage garnishment); *North Georgia Finishing, Inc. v Di-Chem, Inc.* (1975) 419 US 601 (garnishment of bank account). See also *Fuentes v Shevin* (1972) 407 US 67 (summary seizure of debtor's property under replevin statute). But see *Mitchell v W.T. Grant Co.* (1974) 416 US 600, in which the court upheld a statute that did not require preseizure notice or a hearing. The *Sniadach* line of decisions should not constitute a basis for invalidating the California trustee's sale if the high court agrees that no state action is involved.

After the decision in *Garfinkle v Superior Court, supra,* the California Supreme Court held that a trustee has no duty to provide the trustor with actual notice as long it complies with the notice formalities of CC §2924b. *I. E. Assoc. v Safeco Title Ins. Co.* (1985) 39 C3d 281, 216 CR 438. In *Garfinkle,* the court specifically refrained from expressing an opinion on the validity of the provision in CC §2924 that recitals in a trustee's deed that proper notice was given are conclusive in favor of a bona fide purchaser for value. *Garfinkle v Superior Court* (1978) 21 C3d 268, 279 n16, 146 CR 208, 215 n16. See §6.39 for discussion of deed recitals. Because trustees' sales have largely been construed as constituting private action rather than state action, judicial review of such sales must proceed along common law and statutory, rather than constitutional, grounds. For discussion of challenges to trustees' sales, see chap 6.

II. PRELIMINARY CONSIDERATIONS; SPECIAL PROBLEMS

§2.7   A. Substitution of Trustee

The beneficiary's attorney should examine the deed of trust to determine who is named as trustee. When the attorney is representing a private party, the deed of trust will often be a title company printed form, with the name of the title company that supplied the form printed on the form as trustee. Attorney and beneficiary must decide whether to ask the named title company to act as trustee to handle the foreclosure proceedings or to substitute another title company or other entity as trustee. Under certain circumstances, such as when the default is of a nonpecuniary nature (*e.g.,* failure to maintain the premises), the named title company may be unwilling to act as trustee in the foreclosure proceedings.

Deeds of trust almost invariably contain a provision for substituting the trustee. Typically, the provision vests the power to appoint a new trustee in the beneficiary alone. See clause B9 in App B. Occasionally, however, the deed of trust will require that the new trustee be substituted, jointly, by the trustor and the beneficiary. In very rare instances, the deed of trust will require that, in addition to the consent of the beneficiary (and, sometimes, the trustor), the original trustee must convey title to the substituted trustee.

Civil Code §2934a provides a procedure for substitution of trustees. Although CC §2934a(a)(1) provides that the statutory procedure controls despite any contrary provision in a deed of trust executed on or after January 1, 1968, the procedures apparently need not be followed if the deed of trust contains alternative provisions and they are complied with (see, *e.g., U.S. Hertz, Inc. v Niobrara Farms* (1974) 41 CA3d 68, 116 CR 44). In any case, CC §2934a applies only when the deed of trust confers "no other duties" on the trustee than those incidental to exercise of the power of sale. If more duties are conferred, the instrument may control. Under CC §2934a(a)(1), a substitution of trustees may be effected by recording in the county in which the property is located a substitution executed and acknowledged by all the beneficiaries under the deed of trust or their successors in interest. The substitution must contain (1) the date on which the deed of trust was recorded, (2) the name of the trustor, (3) the book and page where the deed of trust is recorded, and (4) the name of the new trustee. CC §2934a(a)(2). Further provisions for substituting trustees under multiple deeds of trust recorded in the same county are contained in CC §2934a(a)(2)–(3). Provisions requiring the substituted trustee to give notice of default and sale are contained in CC §2934a(b)–(c).

§2.8   B. Federally Insured or Guaranteed Loans

If the loan has been insured by the Federal Housing Administration (FHA) or guaranteed by the Veterans Administration (VA), the beneficiary is required to notify the appropriate agency before initiating foreclosure proceedings. See, *e.g.,* 38 USC §1816(a)(1) (VA). Each agency also has certain procedures that must be followed with respect to the sale and subsequent events in order for the secured creditor to be able to recover from the agency on the insured loan or the guaranty if the property does not sell for enough on foreclosure to satisfy the debt. See 12 USC §§1707—1715z–20 (FHA); 38 USC §§1801–1827 (VA). The beneficiary should contact the agency involved before initiating foreclosure proceedings to determine the required procedures, and should ensure that they are followed. Attorneys should advise clients with VA-guaranteed loans that the VA will probably seek to recover a deficiency from a defaulting buyer, notwithstanding provisions of state law barring a deficiency, if the VA acquires the property from the lender after the foreclosure sale and suffers a loss on resale. See §4.46; 2 California Real Property Financing §§3.23, 3.36 (Cal CEB 1989).

§2.9   C. Soldiers' and Sailors' Civil Relief Act

The Soldiers' and Sailors' Civil Relief Act of 1940 (50 USC App §§501–591) provides that foreclosure of a lien on real property for non-payment of any amount due and secured by a mortgage or deed of trust is invalid if made while the debtor is in military service, or within three months thereafter, except on court order. 50 USC App §532. This provision applies only if the obligation was incurred before the debtor entered military service. 50 USC App §532(1).

When the Act applies, it effectively precludes foreclosure by private sale without court intervention. Consequently, before conducting the foreclosure sale, trustees customarily require assurance that the trustor is not a member of the armed forces. The beneficiary usually provides this assurance by executing an affidavit on a form supplied by the trustee. If the beneficiary has no direct knowledge of the trustor's military status, it may be necessary to obtain certificates from the personnel branches of each of the armed forces stating that the trustor is not in the military service.

§2.10   D. Federal Tax Liens; Senior Citizen's Property Tax Postponement

Federal tax liens filed more than 30 days before the date of the trustee's sale are not extinguished by the sale, unless the Internal Revenue Service was given appropriate notice at least 25 days before the date of the sale. IRC §7425. If notice is given and the lien extinguished, the United States has a 120-day period following the trustee's sale within which to redeem the property. IRC §7425; see *Little v U.S.* (9th Cir 1986) 794 F2d 484. The IRS currently redeems properties on a fairly regular basis, although it rarely did so in years past. In any case, existence of the IRS lien effectively keeps the foreclosure-sale purchaser from reselling the property during the 120-day redemption period. A title company will usually except the IRS lien from coverage, in which case title is not marketable. If the title company issues a policy dating back only to the date of the foreclosure sale (*i.e.,* missing the

IRS lien), the title company may be liable under the policy. Litigation often arises when a title insurer is forced to pay under its policy after having failed to find an IRS lien because it was recorded under a different name than that appearing on other documents regarding the property. See, *e.g., First Am. Title Ins. Co. v U.S.* (9th Cir 1988) 848 F2d 969; *U.S. v Polk* (9th Cir 1987) 822 F2d 871. See also *Olympic Fed. Sav. & Loan Ass'n v Regan* (9th Cir 1981) 648 F2d 1218.

To comply with these requirements, after expiration of the notice of default, trustees customarily set the sale date at least 31 days in advance (rather than the minimum 20 days required by CC §2924f) and order from the title company a "date down" of the trustee's sale guaranty. The timing must be such that the record is searched as of 31 days before the sale date, thus revealing whether any federal tax liens were filed more than 30 days before the sale date.

If any IRS liens appear of record, the trustee must notify the IRS of the sale at least 25 days before the sale date. Operation of these two requirements tends to narrow the time within which the title company can report to the trustee and, if necessary, the trustee can notify the IRS. Because of these time constraints, it is almost impossible to complete foreclosure from the date of recording the notice of default to the date of the trustee's sale in the minimum period of three months plus 20 days. At least 121 days, and often longer, are required to ensure compliance with the federal tax lien law.

If the State of California has a lien on the property for postponed property taxes under the Senior Citizens and Disabled Citizens Property Tax Postponement Law of 1977 (Rev & T C §§20581–20586), in the event of a trustee's sale the State Controller must be given notice, as provided in CC §2924b, of any lien having priority over the state's lien. Govt C §16187. If the notice of lien for postponed property taxes is recorded after the notice of default was recorded, but at least 30 days before the date of the sale, the Controller must be given notice of the sale not less than 25 days before the sale. Govt C §16187.

III. NOTICE OF DEFAULT

§2.11   A. First Steps

The Civil Code prescribes certain procedures for giving the notices required before a sale may be conducted. CC §§2924, 2924c (notice of default), 2924f (notice of sale). The deed of trust may contain provisions adding additional notice requirements. The uniform deed of trust form approved for use in California by the Federal National Mortgage Association and the Federal Home Loan Mortgage Corporation imposes such further duties on the beneficiary and should be read carefully to ensure that these additional requirements are met. See 1 California Real Property Financing §4.66 (Cal CEB 1988).

The notice of default prescribed in CC §§2924 and 2924c is usually prepared by the trustee at the beneficiary's request. See *Jones v Sierra Verdugo Water Co.* (1923) 63 CA 254, 218 P 454. If the trustee fails to record the notice, the beneficiary or person holding the note may do so. CC §2924; *Birkhofer v Krumm* (1938) 27 CA2d 513, 81 P2d 609. When the trustee disagrees with the beneficiary about the propriety of the sale, either the trustee should resign or the beneficiary should substitute a more compliant trustee (see §2.7).

The trustee may be faced with problems when there are multiple beneficiaries, but the trustee probably should act on the instructions of any one beneficiary unless the others give contrary orders. *Bliss v Security-First Nat' l Bank* (1947) 81 CA2d 50, 183 P2d 312. The right to protect the common estate from injury enables any co-beneficiary of a deed of trust to elect independently to initiate a trustee's sale when the trustor is in default. *Perkins v Chad Dev. Corp.* (1979) 95 CA3d 645, 157 CR 201. On multiple notes, see §§8.28–8.30.

Trustees frequently require manual delivery of the note and deed of trust when asked to foreclose, although they are not legally required to do so. *California Trust Co. v Smead Inv. Co.* (1935) 6 CA2d 432, 44 P2d 624. Deed of trust provisions usually require that the beneficiary deliver those documents for the trustee's protection. The trustee will usually insist that the beneficiary furnish a lost instrument indemnity bond if the original papers cannot be located. See *Huckell v Matranga* (1979) 99 CA3d 471, 160 CR 177. The promissory note is a negotiable instrument (Com C §§3104, 3302, 3305; see §1.18) and, if the beneficiary cannot produce it, the trustee has no assurance that it has not been transferred.

Attorneys should be aware that additional notice requirements are imposed when the foreclosure involves a mortgage or deed of trust containing a power of sale that is secured by real property containing a single-family, owner-occupied residence and that secures an obligation contained in a contract for goods or services under the Unruh Retail Installment Sales Act (CC §§1801–1812.20). CC §2924f(c). If the default of an obligation secured by such a security instrument has not been cured within 30 days after recordation of the notice of default, the trustee must mail an additional notice to the trustor or mortgagor at his or her last-known address. For a copy of the required notice, see §2.13.

From July 1, 1985, until January 1, 1991, the beneficiary or mortgagee of a senior lien on real property either containing one-to-four residential units or given to secure an original obligation not exceeding $300,000 must, on written request accompanied by $40, inform a junior beneficiary or mortgagee of delinquencies of four months or more on the senior obligation by the trustor or mortgagor. CC §2924e. The junior's request for notice of delinquency expires after five years but may be renewed within six months before its expiration date on payment of the $15 renewal fee. The rights and obligations of the various parties under CC §2924e inure to the benefit of those parties' successors and assigns. CC §2924e.

§2.12   B. Form: Notice of Default

NOTICE OF DEFAULT AND ELECTION TO SELL UNDER DEED OF TRUST

IMPORTANT NOTICE
[14-point boldface type if printed or in capital letters if typed]

IF YOUR PROPERTY IS IN FORECLOSURE BECAUSE YOU ARE BEHIND IN YOUR PAYMENTS, IT MAY BE SOLD WITHOUT ANY COURT ACTION [14-point boldface type if printed or in capital letters if typed], and you may have the legal right to bring your account in good standing by paying all of your past due payments plus permitted costs and expenses within the time permitted by law for reinstatement of your account, which is normally five business days prior to the date set for the sale of your property. No sale date may be set until three months from the date this notice of default may be recorded (which date of recordation appears on this notice). This amount is _____ as of ____(Date)____, and will increase until your account becomes current. You may not have to pay the entire unpaid portion of your account, even though full payment was demanded, but you must pay the amount stated above. However, you and your beneficiary or mortgagee may mutually agree in writing prior to the time the

notice of sale is posted (which may not be earlier than the end of the three-month period stated above) to, among other things, (1) provide additional time in which to cure the default by transfer of the property or otherwise; or (2) establish a schedule of payments in order to cure your default; or both (1) and (2).

Following the expiration of the time period referred to in the first paragraph of this notice, unless the obligation being fore-closed upon or a separate written agreement between you and your creditor permits a longer period, you have only the legal right to stop the sale of your property by paying the entire amount demanded by your creditor.

To find out the amount you must pay, or to arrange for payment to stop the foreclosure, or if your property is in foreclosure for any other reason, contact:

> _____
> (Name of Beneficiary or
> Mortgagee)
>
> _____
> (Mailing Address)
>
> _____
> (Telephone)

If you have any questions, you should contact a lawyer or the government agency which may have insured your loan.

Notwithstanding the fact that your property is in foreclosure, you may offer your property for sale, provided the sale is con-cluded prior to the conclusion of the foreclosure.

Remember, YOU MAY LOSE LEGAL RIGHTS IF YOU DO NOT TAKE PROMPT ACTION. [14-point boldface type if printed or in capital letters if typed]

NOTICE IS HEREBY GIVEN THAT _ _[name]_ _, as _ _[trustee/ beneficiary]_ _, under the deed of trust executed by _ _[name]_ _, as trustor, to _ _[name]_ _, as trustee, and _ _[name]_ _, as beneficiary, dated _ _ _ _ _ _, and recorded on _ _[date]_ _, in Book No. _ _ at page _ _ of the Official Records of _ _ _ _ _ _ _ _ County, California, hereby declares that a breach of the obligation secured by the deed of trust has occurred, that the nature of the breach is the failure to _ _[number and specify omissions constitut-

ing breach]_ _, **and that the beneficiary (1) declares that all sums secured by the deed of trust are immediately due and payable and (2) elects to sell or cause to be sold the trust property to satisfy the obligation.**

Dated: _ _ _ _ _ _

> ___[Signature of_ _[trustee/
> beneficiary]_ _]___
> _ _[Typed name]_ _

Comment: The language of the headings and of the first six paragraphs of the notice is required by CC §2924c. If the notice is printed, the entire notice must appear in at least 12-point boldface type. The notice of default must be in Spanish if the agreement is one covered by CC §1632 and the trustor requested a Spanish translation of the agreement. CC §2924c(b)(1).

Under CC §2924, the notice of default must name the trustor, give either the book and page number in which the instrument is recorded or a description of the mortgaged property, state that a breach of the obligation has occurred, specify the nature of the breach, and state the beneficiary's election to sell the property to satisfy the obligation. The notice need not include the names of parties other than the original trustor or mortgagor. *Rogers v Evans* (1934) 137 CA 538, 31 P2d 233.

No special language is required to describe the breach; a general description (*e.g.,* "failure to pay January installment") is adequate. See *Engelbertson v Loan & Bldg. Ass'n* (1936) 6 C2d 477, 58 P2d 647; *Middlebrook-Anderson Co. v Southwest Sav. & Loan Ass'n* (1971) 18 CA3d 1023, 96 CR 338. But see *System Inv. Corp. v Union Bank* (1971) 21 CA3d 137, 98 CR 735. Too much specificity may be dangerous because, even if it is inaccurate, the beneficiary is bound by it and may not reject a tender that complies with the precise wording or amount stated in the demand. *Tomczak v Ortega* (1966) 240 CA2d 902, 50 CR 20; *Hayward Lumber & Inv. Co. v Corbett* (1934) 138 CA 644, 33 P2d 41. Similarly, for installment obligations, general language may be sufficient to indicate an intent to accelerate. *Engelbertson v Loan & Bldg. Ass'n, supra.* The beneficiary should try to make the statement of the outstanding default broad but not uncertain. If the statement is too specific, later independent defaults by the trustor (*e.g.,* the beneficiary needing to advance additional sums to keep senior liens current) will usually not be regarded as falling within the specification of default and will thus require preparation of an additional notice of default. See *Little v Harbor Pac. Mortgage Invs., No. 79B* (1985) 175 CA3d 717, 221 CR 59. The statement should also include all known defaults. For example, if only defaults in payment are listed, the beneficiary cannot refuse reinstatement even though the trustor is also in default for having failed to pay taxes on the property. Unknown defaults should not, however, be included; a notice of default that includes other breaches "if any" is improper and may nullify the sale (*Anderson v Heart Fed. Sav.* (1989) 208 CA3d 202, 256 CR 180). See Stillman, *Using "If Any" Clauses To Describe Postnotice Breaches in a Notice of Default: Is It Still a Viable Practice?*, 12 CEB Real Prop L Rep 145 (July 1989).

§2.13   C. Form: Special Notice for Unruh Act Deeds of Trust

Copies: One copy for trustor or mortgagor; copies for other parties; office copies.

YOU ARE IN DEFAULT UNDER A _ _*[DEED OF TRUST/ MORT-GAGE]*_ _, DATED _ _ _ _ _ _ . UNLESS YOU TAKE ACTION TO PROTECT YOUR PROPERTY, IT MAY BE SOLD AT A PUBLIC SALE. IF YOU NEED AN EXPLANATION OF THE NATURE OF THE PROCEEDING AGAINST YOU, YOU SHOULD CONTACT A LAWYER.

Comment: This notice is required by CC §2924f(c)(3) whenever the security instrument being foreclosed is secured by real property containing a single-family, owner-occupied residence and secures an obligation contained in a contract for goods or services under the Unruh Retail Installment Sales Act (CC §§1801–1812.20). For discussion of the Unruh Act, see 1 California Debt Collection Practice §§2.59–2.67 (Cal CEB 1987). Apparently, CC §2924f(c)(3) does not require that this notice be recorded. The trustee or beneficiary sending the Unruh Act notice should be sure to send it by registered or certified mail to be able at a later time to prove that the notice was given. For discussion of sale requirements peculiar to Unruh Act contracts, see §2.25.

§2.14   D. Recording, Mailing, and Publishing Notice

The trustee or beneficiary must comply with several statutory requirements concerning the notice of default. Under CC §2924, the notice must be recorded but need not be acknowledged. *U.S. Hertz, Inc. v Niobrara Farms* (1974) 41 CA3d 68, 116 CR 44. The form for the notice is specified in CC §2924c(b), which also requires that it be in Spanish in specified instances (see Comment to form in §2.12).

The mailing, publication, and delivery requirements of CC §2924b must also be met. This section requires that a copy of the notice, including the recording date, be sent by registered or certified mail within ten days of the actual recordation to any persons who have recorded a request for notice and to the trustor or mortgagor at his or her last-known address. CC §2924b(b)(1). The buyer under an installment land sale contract is also a party entitled to notice. *Perry v O'Donnell* (9th Cir 1984) 749 F2d 1346. A copy of the notice must also be mailed, within one month, to any person holding an interest of record in the property who would be affected by the foreclosure, including successor owners, contract purchasers, junior lienors, and their various assignees. CC §2924b(c). In addition, the trustee or beneficiary must mail the notice by first-class mail to the trustor or mortgagor, all persons who have recorded requests for notice, and all persons enumerated in CC §2924b(c), at the same address to which the notice was sent by certified or registered mail, and execute and retain an affidavit of the mailing. CC §2924b(e). A second notice by mail must be given one month later for mortgages securing an obligation under the Unruh Retail Installment Sales Act (CC §§1801–1812.20). CC §2924f(c)(3); see §§2.13, 2.25.

There are some gaps in the statutory notice requirements. For example, notice apparently need not be mailed to guarantors, endorsers, or former owners of the property (other than the original trustor) who may have assumed the obligation, all of whom might be liable for a deficiency judgment, despite the effect of CCP §580d. See §8.13. Thus, these parties should record a request for notice to protect their interests. Furthermore, any party, including the trustor, who is entitled to receive notice, but whose address has changed, should inform the secured creditor by recording a new request for notice of default. Junior lienholders should always be advised to record a request for notice when their liens first attach to the property. Even parties assured of receiving notice under CC §2924b(b) or §2924b(c) can accelerate receipt of the notice by 20 days by recording a request for notice.

Government Code §27321.5 requires that, to be recordable, a deed of trust must contain a trustor's request for notice of default. Under CC §2924b(d), if a deed of trust or mortgage does not contain a request for notice, or the request does not contain an address, and no subsequent request has been recorded, a copy of the notice must be published for at least four weeks in a newspaper of general circulation. This requirement is somewhat superfluous in light of the mandatory mailing requirements discussed above, but nevertheless it should not be overlooked.

The trustor should record a request for notice under CC §2924b(a) (see §2.15), setting forth his or her address if it is other than the property in question, to impose on the trustee a duty to deliver notice to the correct address. Under CC §2924b(b)(3), the trustor's "last-known address" is an address *actually* known by the trustee, beneficiary, or other person authorized to record the notice of default. The beneficiary must inform the trustee if the beneficiary actually knows the trustor's last address, but the trustee has no duty to locate a trustor who has changed address without informing the trustee. *Lupertino v Carbahal* (1973) 35 CA3d 742, 111 CR 112; *McClatchey v Rudd* (1966) 239 CA2d 605, 48 CR 783. If the trustee or beneficiary has communicated with the trustor at the new address, however, the trustee will be assumed to be aware of it. *Lupertino v Carbahal, supra.* Although in *Garfinkle v Superior Court* (1978) 21 C3d 268, 279 n16, 146 CR 208, 215 n16, the supreme court hinted at a duty to locate the trustor, it subsequently held that the trustee need merely comply with the statutory requirements and has no additional duty to attempt to give the trustor actual notice (*I. E. Assoc. v Safeco Title Ins. Co.* (1985) 39 C3d 281, 216 CR 438). Institutional lenders often find it difficult to coordinate the "last-known address" requirement with their normal operations. The trustor may communicate by any of various means with any number of the lender's employees, and the lender may be held to a duty to provide this information to the trustee, sometimes years after the loan was funded.

To ensure that notice is given to all parties entitled to it, most trustees regularly obtain a trustee's sale guaranty from a title company, which gives them a listing of all parties entitled to receive the notice of default. See §2.2; California Title Insurance Practice §§3.24, 4.13 (Cal CEB 1980).

§2.15   E. Form: Request for Notice

**REQUEST FOR COPY OF NOTICE OF DEFAULT
AND NOTICE OF SALE UNDER DEED OF
TRUST OR MORTGAGE**

In accordance with Civil Code section 2924b, I hereby request that a copy of any notice of default or notice of sale under the _ _[deed of trust/mortgage] _ _ **recorded   on** _ _[date] _ _, _ _[in Book No. _ _ at page _ _ of the Official Records/filed for record with recorder's serial number _ _] _ _ of _ _ _ _ _ _ _ _ **County, California, be mailed to me,** _ _[name] _ _, **at** _ _[state address] _ _. **The** _ _[deed of trust/mortgage] _ _ **was executed by** _ _[name] _ _ **with** _ _[name of beneficiary/mortgagee] _ _, **as** _ _[beneficiary/mortgagee] _ _, **and** _ _[name] _ _, **as trustee.**

NOTICE: A copy of any notice of default and of any notice of sale will be sent only to the address contained in this recorded request. If your address changes, a new request must be recorded.

Dated: _ _ _ _ _ _

___[Signature] ___
_ _[Typed name] _ _

[Acknowledgment]

Comment: The request need not be signed by the party to whom the notice is requested to be sent. It may be signed by a third party, *e.g.*, the attorney for the party who is to receive the notice. The request for notice must be acknowledged (CC §2924b(a)), although the actual notice need not be. The notice is prescribed by statute and must be in substantially the form set forth in CC §2924b(a). There is no requirement that a copy of the request for notice be mailed to the beneficiary from whom notice is requested. Accordingly, CC §2924b(f) provides that recording the request is not deemed to be notice to the beneficiary that the requestor has or claims any interest in the property. If the requestor wishes to notify the beneficiary of such a claim, the facts should be stated in a separate certified or registered letter to the beneficiary. To be protected against optional future advances, a junior creditor must give such independent notice to a senior creditor whose securing instrument contains a future-advance or dragnet clause. See §§8.44, 8.48.

§2.16   F. Failure To Send Notice

The trustee's failure to notify a party who requested notice, or a party who is otherwise entitled to notice under CC §2924b, may void the sale. Recitals of regularity (see §§2.26, 6.34) in the trustee's deed may overcome this defect, however, when the buyer at the trustee's sale is a bona fide purchaser. See *Little v CFS Serv. Corp.* (1987) 188 CA3d 1354, 233 CR 923. Lack of formal notice may not invalidate the sale if the requesting party nevertheless receives actual notice. *Crummer v Whitehead* (1964) 230 CA2d 264, 40 CR 826. When no notice of default is given to a party who is entitled to it and who holds a significant interest in the property, the omission may be analogous to a failure to effect service of process on an equivalent party in a judicial foreclosure proceeding. See *Garfinkle v Superior Court* (1978) 21 C3d 268, 146 CR 208; §2.6. This probably means that failure to give notice to a trustor voids the sale entirely (*Goodenow v Ewer* (1860) 16 C 461), but failure to notify a requesting junior might result in a sale that does not extinguish the junior interest (*Carpentier v Brenham* (1870) 40 C 221).

Civil Code §2924b(b)(1) requires that the trustee provide the trustor with notice at the trustor's last-known address if different from the address specified in the deed of trust. "Last-known address" is defined as an address actually known to the trustee (see §2.14). CC §2924b(b)(3). The trustee incurs no liability for failing to send a notice of default or sale to the trustor's latest address unless the trustee has actual knowledge of the address. CC §2924b(b)(3).

§2.17   G. Reinstatement Rights

The trustor, the trustor's successor in interest, and junior lienors are entitled to reinstate the obligation by paying the amount stated in the notice of default plus reasonable costs and expenses of enforcement and trustees' or attorneys' fees. CC §2924c(a). The reinstatement period extends until five business days before the date of sale set forth in

the notice of sale. CC §2924c(e). If the sale is later postponed or renoticed, the reinstatement period is automatically extended to five business days before the new date of sale. There is no right to reinstatement
during the final five days before the sale. CC §2924c(e). Precise calculation of the expiration of the reinstatement period has yet to be determined by case law and can cause dilemmas for trustees, *e.g.,* when
reinstatement is offered on the fifth business day before the sale.

The reinstatement period is not merely a moratorium that gives the
trustor an additional period of possession. It is also a grace period
during which the trustor (and others) may reinstate any obligation accelerated by the beneficiary because of the default. *Magnus v Morrison*
(1949) 93 CA2d 1, 208 P2d 407. Because most secured real property
loans are repayable on an installment basis, and almost all such installment notes contain an acceleration clause providing that the entire unpaid balance of the loan may be called due whenever one installment
is missed (see §7.2), the right of reinstatement becomes an essential
shield against the sword of acceleration. Under CC §2924c, if the trustor misses a monthly installment and the beneficiary then records a
notice of default demanding payment of the entire balance, the trustor
(or junior lienors) may ignore the demand and reinstate the loan within
the reinstatement period merely by making up the missed installments
(plus specified costs and fees). Reinstatement is thus different from
redemption in that it does not require that the entire loan be paid off,
but restores the loan to its original installment basis by paying off only
the past defaulted installments. An important protective device, reinstatement is a remedy available to the debtor, the debtor's successors,
and anyone with a subordinate lien or encumbrance of record on the
property (CC §2924c(a)). *Magnus v Morrison, supra.*

Reinstatement is effected by tendering to the beneficiary the amount
set forth in the notice of default, plus reasonable costs and expenses,
as determined under CC §2924c(c), and trustees' or attorneys' fees, as
determined under CC §2924c(d). CC §2924c(a). The trustee is entitled
to charge the beneficiary the costs of recording, mailing, publishing,
and posting notices required by CC §§2924–2924i, the costs of postponement on the request of the trustor under CC §2924g (not to exceed
$50 per postponement), and a fee for a trustee's sale guaranty or, in the
event of a judicial foreclosure, a litigation guaranty. CC §2924c(c). In
addition, trustees' or attorneys' fees may be charged in the amount of
$200 ($300 after the mailing of the notice of sale) on the first $50,000

or less of the unpaid principal sum, plus 0.5 percent (1 percent after the mailing of the notice of sale) of the unpaid principal sum between $50,000 and $150,000, plus 0.25 percent (0.5 percent after the mailing of the notice of sale) of any portion of the unpaid principal sum secured between $150,000 and $500,000, plus 0.125 percent (0.25 percent after the mailing of the notice of sale) for any amounts over $500,000. CC §§2924c(d), 2924d. See also *Sweatt v Foreclosure Co.* (1985) 166 CA3d 273, 212 CR 350. The statutory limitations on trustees' and attorneys' fees may not apply to attorneys' fees that the beneficiary may be entitled to recover under specific provisions of the deed of trust. *Buck v Barb* (1983) 147 CA3d 920, 195 CR 461; see §§3.51, 7.30. For example, the beneficiary may incur attorneys' fees to obtain relief from a bankruptcy automatic stay (see §6.49).

The amount then due under the obligation for purposes of reinstatement is the amount specified in the notice of default (CC §2924c(b)) together with any subsequent arrearages. See *Anderson v Heart Fed. Sav.* (1989) 208 CA3d 202, 256 CR 180. If the proper amount is tendered, it is improper for the trustee or beneficiary to reject it and proceed with the foreclosure sale. *Munger v Moore* (1970) 11 CA3d 1, 89 CR 323. The trustor must, however, unambiguously tender the entire amount due; the beneficiary is not obligated to go through its receipts and total up various partial payments to determine whether the proper amount has been tendered. *Gaffney v Downey Sav. & Loan Ass'n* (1988) 200 CA3d 1154, 246 CR 421. Rejection of a proper tender does not cancel the debt, but it does destroy the right to foreclose based on the asserted default. *Magnus v Morrison, supra.* The trustor must pay only those amounts correctly specified in the notice of default (plus periodically accruing arrearages, usually monthly payments) even if other, independent defaults have since occurred. *Anderson v Heart Fed. Sav., supra.* But see *Little v Harbor Pac. Mortgage Invs., No. 79B* (1985) 175 CA3d 717, 221 CR 59 (beneficiary under second deed of trust not entitled to demand payments made to cure default under first deed of trust but not claimed in notice of default). See also *Napue v Gor-Mey W., Inc.* (1985) 175 CA3d 608, 220 CR 799.

When the beneficiary exercises its rights under a rents-and-profits clause in the deed of trust by taking over collection of the rents during the default period, the rents collected may be sufficient to effect an inadvertent reinstatement of the loan, perhaps entitling the trustor to have the receivership terminated. See §§5.18, 5.21. Many institutional deeds of trust, however, provide that collection of rents does not cure the default. Whether such a provision is valid is an open question.

Partial payments made during the reinstatement period do not effect a reinstatement or extend the reinstatement period. Thus, a trustor who owes $200 every month and who misses January's payment must tender the full $400 in February (plus costs and trustees' or attorneys' fees), or $600 in March or $800 in April, to effect reinstatement. A tender of $100 in February or $700 in April will do nothing toward postponing or defeating a foreclosure sale. *Sellman v Crosby* (1937) 20 CA2d 562, 67 P2d 706. See also *Gaffney v Downey Sav. & Loan Ass'n, supra*. Attorneys representing creditors usually advise their clients, however, not to accept partial payments unless the debtor is clearly advised by letter that partial payments do not waive the default. Otherwise, acceptance of a partial payment leaves a creditor open to claims of waiver or estoppel based on the trustor's contention that he or she would not have paid but for the beneficiary's agreement to delay or stop the sale. Courts tend to view with suspicion a beneficiary who accepts the trustor's partial payments and continues with the foreclosure sale. See *Altman v McCollum* (1951) 107 CA2d Supp 847, 236 P2d 914.

The right of reinstatement extends until five business days before the specified date of sale. CC §2924c(e). Courts are likely to extend the period well past the sale date, however, when the trustor has filed an action challenging the validity of the foreclosure sale. In *Bisno v Sax* (1959) 175 CA2d 714, 346 P2d 814, the trustors filed an action to enjoin the sale after the three-month period (the former reinstatement period before 1985 amendments to CC §2924c that extended the period to five days before the date of sale) had ended and cured their existing defaults while the injunction was in effect and the case was awaiting trial (seven months later). This late reinstatement was held to be sufficient reason to set aside the sale as improper. In *Hunt v Smyth* (1972) 25 CA3d 807, 101 CR 4, the trustors sought an injunction on the seventy-seventh day of the notice period, but it was not until more than two years later that an appellate court ruled against them and then gave them their remaining 13 days to reinstate. On the other hand, trustors who have too precipitately enjoined foreclosure sales have rendered themselves liable for extensive damages. See *Surety Sav. & Loan Ass'n v National Auto. & Cas. Ins. Co.* (1970) 8 CA3d 752, 87 CR 572.

For discussion of trustors' actions challenging foreclosure sales, see chap 6; on damages for improper actions by the trustor, see §6.37. See also *Baypoint Mortgage Corp. v Crest Premium Real Estate Inv. Retirement Trust* (1985) 168 CA3d 818, 214 CR 531. For discussion of the *Baypoint* decision, see 8 CEB Real Prop L Rep 129 (Aug. 1985).

§2.18   IV. NOTICE OF SALE

After expiration of three months from the date on which the notice of default (see §2.12) was recorded, if the trustor (or a junior lienor) has not exercised the right to reinstate the obligation, the trustee next gives notice of sale. CC §2924. (Note, however, that the trustor has until five business days before the sale date to reinstate the obligation; see §2.17.) The contents of the notice are prescribed by CC §2924f(b). For a form notice of sale, see §2.19. For the notice issued by a levying officer in connection with an execution sale or judicial foreclosure under CCP §701.540, see §3.58.

The notice must be given at least 20 days before the date set for sale of the property. CC §2924f(b). Thus, a trustee's sale requires a total time period of three months (after recording the notice of default; see §2.14) and 20 days (given by the notice of sale), assuming there are no delays. In actual practice, the minimum time will probably be slightly longer to comply with federal tax lien notice requirements. See §2.10.

Any time a new trustee is substituted on the deed of trust, a new notice of sale must be given, containing the name, street address, and telephone number of the substituted trustee; otherwise, the sale is void. CC §2934a(c). Consequently, any substitution of trustees (see §2.7) is best made before the foreclosure process has been started.

§2.19   A. Form: Notice of Sale

NOTICE OF TRUSTEE'S SALE

YOU ARE IN DEFAULT UNDER A _ _[*DEED OF TRUST/ MORTGAGE*]_ _, DATED _ _ _ _ _ _. UNLESS YOU TAKE ACTION TO PROTECT YOUR PROPERTY, IT MAY BE SOLD AT A PUBLIC SALE. IF YOU NEED AN EXPLANATION OF THE NATURE OF THE PROCEEDING AGAINST YOU, YOU SHOULD CONTACT A LAWYER.

NOTICE IS HEREBY GIVEN that the real property situated in _ _ _ _ _ _ _ _ County, California, known as _ _[state street address or other designation]_ _, and described as:

[Legal description]

will be sold at public auction _ _[e.g., on the steps of the County Courthouse]_ _ on _ _[date]_ _, at _ _ _ _.m., to the highest bidder for cash, cashier's check drawn on a state or national bank, check drawn on a state or federal savings and loan association, savings association, or savings bank specified in Financial Code section 5102 and authorized to do business in California, or _ _[other designated cash equivalent]_ _.

The sale will be made without covenant or warranty regarding title, possession, or encumbrances, to satisfy the obligation secured by the deed of trust executed by _ _[name]_ _, as trustor, to _ _[name]_ _, as trustee, for the benefit and security of _ _[name]_ _, as beneficiary, dated _ _ _ _ _ _, and recorded in Book No. _ _ at page _ _ of the Official Records of _ _ _ _ _ _ _ _, County, California, in the amount of $_ _ _ _ _ _, including the total amount of the unpaid balance and reasonably estimated costs, expenses, and advances at the time of initial publication of this notice.

[Add, if appropriate]

The beneficial interest under the deed of trust and the obligations secured by it were assigned to _ _[name]_ _ by an assignment dated _ _ _ _ _ _, and recorded on _ _[date]_ _, in Book No. _ _ at page _ _ of the Official Records of the County.

[Add, if appropriate]

The undersigned trustee was appointed and substituted as trustee under the deed of trust by an instrument dated _ _ _ _ _ _, and recorded on _ _[date]_ _, in Book No. _ _ at page _ _ of the Official Records of _ _ _ _ _ _ _ _ County, California, and executed by _ _[name]_ _ under the provisions of the deed of trust.

[Add, if appropriate]

This notice is republished by the undersigned trustee under Civil Code section 2924h(d) because of cancellation by the previous last and highest bidder of an instrument submitted to the trustee as a cash equivalent.

[Add, if property has no street address or other common designation]

This sale is conducted at the request of _ _[name] _ _, as beneficiary, whose address is _ _[state address] _ _. Directions to the property may be obtained by submitting a written request to the beneficiary within ten days of the first publication of this notice.

[Continue]

Notice of default and election to sell the described real property under the deed of trust was recorded in Book No. _ _ at page _ _ of the Official Records of the County.

Dated: _ _ _ _ _ _

                                    ___[Signature]___
                                    _ _[Typed name] _ _
                                    Trustee

_ _[Trustee's name] _ _

_ _[Street address] _ _

_ _[Telephone number] _ _

Comment: Civil Code §2924f(b) requires that the notice of sale (1) give the time and place of the sale, (2) describe the property to be sold, and (3) be given at least 20 days before the date of the sale. In addition to a description of the property, the notice must give the street address or other common designation, if any. If the property has no street address or other common designation, the notice must state the name and address of the beneficiary and that directions for locating the property may be obtained from the beneficiary by requesting them in writing within ten days of the first publication of the notice. An error or omission in the street address or common designation, or in the directions, does not affect the validity of the notice if it includes the legal description. CC §2924f(b). Most title companies have printed notice-of-sale forms generally available.

All notices of sale must contain the notice that is required to be given 30 days after recordation of the notice of default by CC §2924f(c)(3) for Unruh Retail Installment Sales Act mortgages (see §§2.13–2.14). CC §2924f(b). The required additional notice appears in capitals at the beginning of the above form. The notice must include the street address of the sale and the specific location at the address where the sale will be held. CC §2924f(b). In addition, the notice must contain a statement of the total amount of the unpaid balance, the reasonable estimated costs, expenses, and advances since initial publication of the notice, and the name, address, and telephone number of the trustee or person conducting the sale. The notice must include the name of the original trustor and state whether the notice is a republication following cancellation by the last and highest bidder of an instrument given to the trustee as a cash equivalent under CC §2924h(d). CC §2924f(b). On the bidder's failure to pay the bid price, see §2.23.

§2.20   B. Recording, Publishing, and Mailing Notice of Sale

The requirements for distributing the notice of sale differ from those for the notice of default (see §2.14):

■ The notice of sale must be given at least 20 days before the sale date (see §2.21) and must be recorded at least 14 days before the sale date. CC §2924f(b). The notice of default must be recorded as the first step in the trustee's sale process. CC §2924b(b)(1).

■ The notice of sale must be published in addition to being mailed as required by CC §2924b(b). CC §2924f(b). Publication of the notice of default is required only when the trustor has not requested notice of default. CC §2924b(d).

■ The notice of sale must be posted both in a public place and on the property. CC §2924f(b). If the property is a single-family residence, the notice of sale must be posted on a door of the residence, if possible, and, if this is not possible, in a conspicuous place on the property. CC §2924f(b). Posting is not required for the notice of default (see §2.14).

The notice of sale must be mailed by registered or certified mail to all persons who are entitled to receive a notice of default. CC §2924b(b)(2)–(3). The notice must also be mailed to the trustor or mortgagor by first-class mail in addition to the notice by registered or certified mail required by CC §2924b(b)(2), and the trustee or beneficiary must execute and retain an affidavit of the mailing. CC §2924b(e); see §2.14.

The trustee should conduct a record search just before recording the notice of default to determine those persons who are entitled to receive notice, but need not search a second time for persons who acquired interests after the notice of default was recorded. Accordingly, a party who acquires an interest in the property after a notice of default has been recorded cannot expect to receive further notice of the proceeding by then recording an instrument or a request for notice; such a purchaser should contact the trustee or beneficiary directly to obtain information regarding the foreclosure. Otherwise, a purchaser must rely on the posted or published notices of sale.

Under CC §2924f(b), the notice of sale must also be published once a week over a period of at least 20 days in a newspaper of general circulation in the city, judicial district, or county where all or part of the property is situated. The inexact divisibility of 20 days to a weekly publication requirement has been noted and held to mean that the notice must appear three times during the period, even though that may amount to a spread of only 14 days between the first and last notice. *Hotchkiss v Darling* (1933) 130 CA 625, 20 P2d 343; *McCabe v Willard* (1931) 119 CA 122, 6 P2d 258. The requirements that copies of the notice be posted both on the property in a conspicuous place and in a public place in the appropriate city, judicial district, or county of sale, and be published in a newspaper of general circulation (CC §2924f(b)), presumably afford wide dissemination of the notice. Difficulties obviously arise in meeting the posting requirements when the property consists of multiple lots, but the trustee is not required to post each lot separately. *Py v Pleitner* (1945) 70 CA2d 576, 161 P2d 393; *Peterson v Corporation of America* (1937) 21 CA2d 527, 69 P2d 904; *Security-First Nat' l Bank v De La Cuesta* (1936) 15 CA2d 302, 59 P2d 542. Separate postings are usually made only when the lots are noncontiguous. The courthouse or city hall is the usual locale for the public posting. See *McCabe v Willard, supra.* The requirement is that the notice be posted, not that it be kept posted; testimony of an initial posting is sufficient. *Hotchkiss v Darling, supra.*

The procedures for demanding and giving notice are not cumbersome and coordinate well with an institutional beneficiary's normal operations. Before a creditor takes a security interest, it should search the records to see whether there are any liens that take priority over its interest. If the beneficiary discovers a prior lien that is not in default, it need merely record a request for notice of default. If, on the other hand, the creditor learns of a lien already in default, it should contact the creditor involved before deciding whether to take a security interest in the property at all.

§2.21   C. When Notice of Sale May Be Given

Civil Code §2924 requires that at least three months elapse after the notice of default is recorded before the notice of sale may be given, and CC §2924f(b) requires that the notice of sale be given at least 20 days before the sale. Trustees frequently allow more than the minimum required time when giving the notice of sale. A defaulting trustor will usually benefit if the foreclosure process advances more slowly than required; it will be difficult to attack the sale if the beneficiary or trustee has given generous time allowances. *Arata v Downer* (1937) 21 CA2d 406, 69 P2d 213. See also §2.11.

Notice that does not allow the required times may postpone or invalidate the sale. Not only is it improper to conduct the sale on less than 20 days' notice, but the notice of sale cannot be given until at least three months after the notice of default was recorded. CC §2924. See also *The Work of the 1939 Legislature,* 13 S Cal L Rev 1, 47 (1939). If the notice of sale sets a date that is too early, the appropriate cure is to postpone the sale (*Mack v Golino* (1950) 95 CA2d 731, 213 P2d 760 (two months' postponement at trustor's request)) or, more safely, to cancel that sale and republish the notice with a proper sale date. The sale may be canceled or postponed without risk because the trustor is not entitled to demand that the property be taken by foreclosure at a particular time. *Scott v Security Title Ins. & Guar. Co.* (1937) 9 C2d 606, 72 P2d 143.

As with the notice of default, a properly noticed sale is valid whether or not the trustor has actual knowledge of it. *Sargent v Shumaker* (1924) 193 C 122, 223 P 464; see §§2.14, 2.16. Strict compliance with the statutory requirements is all that is required. *Lopez v Bell* (1962) 207 CA2d 394, 24 CR 626. The notice must comply with the statute in effect at the time of the sale, not the one in force at the time the deed of trust was executed, even though the deed of trust incorporates the earlier statutory requirements. *United Bank & Trust Co. v Brown* (1928)

203 C 359, 264 P 482. A sale that does not comply with the notice requirements is probably void (*United Bank & Trust Co. v Brown, supra*), although the trustor's attendance (and bidding) probably cures any defects in the notice (see *Stevens v Plumas Eureka Annex Mining Co.* (1935) 2 C2d 493, 41 P2d 927).

Although failure to comply with service and time requirements for the notice of sale may render the sale defective, especially if the failures prejudice the trustor's rights, minor defects in the wording of the notice will usually not render the notice invalid. See *Williams v Koenig* (1934) 219 C 656, 28 P2d 351; *Savings & Loan Soc'y v Burnett* (1895) 106 C 514, 39 P 922.

§2.22 D. Reinstatement and Redemption After Notice Has Been Given

The statutory right to reinstate the obligation under CC §2924c extends until five business days before the date of the foreclosure sale. CC §2924c(e). Under former CC §2924c, the trustor's reinstatement rights extended only for three months from the date on which the notice of default was recorded, which is also the point at which a notice of sale may first be given (CC §2924; see §2.21), so that service of the notice of sale usually coincided with expiration of the reinstatement period. Under 1985 amendments to CC §2924c, expiration of the three-month period no longer terminates the right to reinstate, which now runs until five business days before the sale date specified in the notice of sale and is automatically extended if the sale is postponed. To reinstate under CC §2924c, the trustor must pay the amount then in default plus costs and expenses as specified in CC §2924c(c) and trustees' or attorneys' fees as specified in CC §2924c(d). CC §2924c(a). For discussion of reinstatement rights, see §2.17. If the deed of trust gives the trustor more generous reinstatement rights, those provisions will control. More liberal provisions are often required in the case of loans that are to be sold on the federal secondary mortgage market. For discussion of the requirements of the Federal National Mortgage Association's and Federal Home Loan Mortgage Corporation's uniform deed of trust, see 1 California Real Property Financing §§4.60–4.70 (Cal CEB 1988).

Reinstatement is possible even within five days before the sale if the beneficiary is willing, because the notice of sale may be vacated by the parties' agreement at any time. If the beneficiary does not agree, the debtor's sole right after expiration of the reinstatement period is to redeem the property under CC §§2903 and 2905 by paying off the entire debt plus costs, not just the past arrearages. *Wadleigh v Phelps* (1906) 149 C 627, 87 P 93; *Randall v Duff* (1894) 101 C 82, 35 P 440; see §2.17.

Even redemption rights end once bidding at the foreclosure sale starts, and the auctioneer must sell to the highest bidder. CC §2924g. Therefore, trustors or junior lienors who have raised sufficient funds to pay off the defaulted loan must make their tenders to invoke redemption rights under CC §§2903–2905 before the sale commences or take their chances on the public bidding. *Sullivan v Superior Court* (1921) 185 C 133, 195 P 1061. They may redeem until the sale under CC §§2903–2905, and a timely tender of the appropriate sum must lead to cancellation of the sale. *Kleckner v Bank of Am. Nat'l Trust & Sav. Ass'n* (1950) 97 CA2d 30, 217 P2d 28; *Lichty v Whitney* (1947) 80 CA2d 696, 182 P2d 582. As with other inadequate tenders, however, the trustee need not cancel or even postpone the sale unless the full amount properly due is proffered. *Karlsen v American Sav. & Loan Ass'n* (1971) 15 CA3d 112, 92 CR 851.

§2.23   V. THE SALE

Under CC §2924g(a), a trustee's sale must be conducted by public auction in the county where all or part of the property is situated, between 9 a.m. and 5 p.m. on any business day. When the property consists of multiple lots, they must be sold separately, and the trustor may direct the order in which the lots are sold, unless the deed of trust provides otherwise. CC §2924g(b); *Humboldt Sav. Bank v McCleverty* (1911) 161 C 285, 119 P 82. Most deeds of trust permit the trustee to sell the property in a block or in an order determined by the trustee. See §7.42. Usually the parcels are sold separately, unless there is an overriding lump-sum bid for all the parcels that is greater than the total of the individual bids. The trustor is entitled to direct the order of sale (CC §2924g(b)), unless the deed of trust provides otherwise (which it inevitably does; see §7.42). The trustee's refusal to honor the trustor's requests concerning the order of sale may jeopardize the validity of the sale if it can be shown that a better price would have resulted from following the trustor's proposal. See *Pacific States Sav. & Loan Co. v O'Neil* (1936) 7 C2d 596, 61 P2d 1160.

When the debtor has equity in more than one property subject to sale by the trustee, but transferred the property to third parties before the sale, CC §2899 (on marshaling of assets) requires that the assets be sold in the reverse order of alienation by the debtor. That is, the first property to be sold is the last alienated by the debtor (if the purchasers of that property had notice that the debtor's prior conveyance was subject to the abstracts of judgment), then the second to last property, and so on. *Commonwealth Land Title Co. v Kornbluth* (1985) 175 CA3d 518, 220 CR 774. On the right of junior lienholders to require marshaling of assets under CC §2899, see §8.52.

The sale commences when the auctioneer announces that the property is for sale and that bids are invited. The trustee usually acts as auctioneer, but anyone appointed by the trustee may serve. *Central Sav. Bank v Lake* (1927) 201 C 438, 257 P 521. The trustee's attorney may conduct the sale. CC §2924a. Terms of sale are announced, and the trustee usually declares that the sale is without warranties of title. See *Brown v Busch* (1957) 152 CA2d 200, 313 P2d 19. The trustee has a duty to make reasonable efforts to make the sale fair and equitable, even to the extent of interrupting the sale to explain the bidding procedures to potential bidders. *Bank of Seoul & Trust Co. v Marcione* (1988) 198 CA3d 113, 244 CR 1.

Bidding at the sale is regulated by CC §2924h, which provides that each bid constitutes an irrevocable offer that is automatically canceled by any higher bid (CC §2924h(a)) or by postponement or cancellation of the sale (CC §2924h(e)). With the exception of bids by the foreclosing beneficiary, all bids must be in cash or otherwise acceptable to the trustee, and the trustee may reject any bid not backed by cash or cash equivalent. CC §2924h(b); *Hill v Gibraltar Sav. & Loan Ass'n* (1967) 254 CA2d 241, 62 CR 188; *Kleckner v Bank of Am. Nat'l Trust & Sav. Ass'n* (1950) 97 CA2d 30, 217 P2d 28. In addition to cash, acceptable bids may be in the form of a cashier's check drawn on a state or national bank, a check drawn on a state or federal credit union, or a check drawn on a state or federal savings and loan association, savings association, or savings bank specified in Fin C §5102 and authorized to do business in California, or other cash equivalent previously designated in the notice of sale. CC §2924h(b). In *Baron v Colonial Mortgage Serv. Co.* (1980) 111 CA3d 316, 168 CR 450, the court held that the trustee should have accepted a high bid in the form of a cashier's check made out to the bidder but endorsed to the trustee. Note, however, that this case was decided under a 1979 amendment to CC §2924h(b) (subsequently re-amended) that provided that payment must be in a form "reasonably satisfactory" to the trustee; the court held that this standard was also applicable to pre-1979 sales. The current version of CC §2924h(b) provides that a cash equivalent must be "designated in the notice of sale as acceptable to the trustee."

Even a junior lienor who stands to receive all the surplus after the senior lien is paid must bid all cash or cash equivalent and cannot use any part of the junior lien for a credit-bid. *Nomellini Constr. Co. v Modesto Sav. & Loan Ass'n* (1969) 275 CA2d 114, 79 CR 717. The foreclosing beneficiary is allowed to credit-bid because its sale has been properly noticed and the trustor has had adequate time to challenge the amount demanded. *Witter v Bank of Milpitas* (1928) 204 C 570, 269 P 614.

For a number of reasons, the foreclosing beneficiary may wish to bid less than the amount of its debt. See §2.29; Johnson & Smith, *The Case Against the Full Value Bid*, 12 CEB Real Prop L Rep 141 (July 1989). For example, a beneficiary will often underbid to obtain rents that may be held in a receivership. See §5.21. Underbidding may also be appropriate if the obligation is secured by other collateral or guaranties. See §§4.14–4.16. Another reason to underbid is that a full credit-bid may waive the beneficiary's right to recover insurance proceeds on the property. See §§7.21, 8.8. A bid that does not include unpaid interest may reduce the amount realized by the beneficiary for income tax purposes. See §2.30. If the property is in need of repairs, and the beneficiary does not want to incur the expense of rehabilitating it, the beneficiary may underbid in an attempt to encourage others to acquire the property. See Crocker, *Beneficiary's Underbid—A Neglected Tool*, 44 LA B Bull 295 (1969). On the other hand, underbidding increases the risk of having the sale set aside as a fraudulent conveyance if the trustor subsequently files a petition in bankruptcy. See §6.51.

Because the demands of other parties have not been similarly established, their bids are no different from bids by strangers and must be in cash or cash equivalent. *Py v Pleitner* (1945) 70 CA2d 576, 161 P2d 393. A junior creditor interested in seeing that the property is not undersold, but who is unable to bid the necessary cash to cover the senior lien, should reinstate the senior lien before the sale (under CC §2924c;

see §§2.17, 2.22) and then foreclose the junior lien and credit-bid at the junior sale. See *United Sav. & Loan Ass'n v Hoffman* (1973) 30 CA3d 306, 106 CR 275.

No party is barred from bidding, although a bid by the trustee on its own behalf is always suspect. *Copsey v Sacramento Bank* (1901) 133 C 659, 66 P 7. It is proper for the beneficiary to bid, because a contrary rule would deprive the sale of probably its best customer and therefore lower the selling price. *Bank of Am. Nat'l Trust & Sav. Ass'n v Century Land & Water Co.* (1937) 19 CA2d 194, 65 P2d 109. Junior lienholders may also bid, and successful junior bids do not jeopardize any other rights the lienholders may have under their security instruments. *Investcal Realty Corp. v Edgar H. Mueller Constr. Co.* (1966) 247 CA2d 190, 55 CR 475. See also *Pacific Loan Management Corp. v Superior Court* (1987) 196 CA3d 1485, 242 CR 547 (Small Business Administration, as junior lienholder, entitled to surplus sale proceeds over those owed senior lienholder, even though SBA purchased property at trustee's sale for less than property's value). It is unlawful to offer or to accept consideration not to bid, to fix bidding, or to restrain bidding. If an interested party is defrauded as a result of any of these activities, the wrongdoer can be fined, imprisoned, or both. CC §2924h(g). See also 11 USC §363(n). Conspiracies between bidders to chill the bidding are improper, of course, but only the trustor can complain of such behavior, because other parties can protect themselves by competitive bidding of their own. *Bertschman v Covell* (1928) 205 C 707, 272 P 571.

The sale should be made to the highest bidder and will usually be upheld even if the winning bid is far below the property's value. *Crofoot v Tarman* (1957) 147 CA2d 443, 305 P2d 56. An inadequate sale price is more likely, however, to be subjected to judicial scrutiny. Although court approval of the sale is not required (*California Trust Co. v Smead Inv. Co.* (1935) 6 CA2d 432, 44 P2d 624), evidence of gross inadequacy of the sale price will lead to invalidation of the sale if there is also evidence of irregularity in the sale procedures. See *In re Worcester* (Rosner v Worcester) (9th Cir 1987) 811 F2d 1224. For discussion of actions to set aside the sale, see chap 6. On acceptance of the high bid, the purchaser must deposit the full amount of the bid with the trustee. Failure to do so may render the high bidder liable for damages and may also be punishable as a misdemeanor if the failure is willful. CC §2924h(d). If the funds tendered at a trustee's sale are not made available to the payee or endorsee because of a failure of consideration, then the sale is subject to automatic rescission. CC §2924h(c). In the event of a rescission, a notice of rescission must be sent by the trustee to the last and highest bidder if the bidder's address is known to the trustee, and the interest of any lienholder will be reinstated to the same priority as if the sale had not occurred. If the last and highest bidder cancels an instrument submitted to the trustee as a cash equivalent, the trustee may recover from the bidder the cost of a new notice of sale. CC §2924h(d).

Although the sale is final when the trustee accepts the last and highest bid (CC §2924h(c)), the trustee is not required to deliver a deed to the bidder immediately but may arrange to do so later. *Kleckner v Bank of Am. Nat' l Trust & Sav. Ass' n, supra.* When the trustee believes that no bid is adequate, all bids may be rejected. *Pacific Ready-Cut Homes, Inc. v Title Guar. & Trust Co.* (1929) 103 CA 1, 283 P 963.

§2.24   A. Postponements

Civil Code §2924g(a) requires that any postponement of a sale be announced at the time and location specified in the notice of sale. The trustee may postpone the sale at the trustee's discretion on instructions from the beneficiary or on written request of the trustor to obtain sufficient cash to pay the debt or to bid at the sale. The trustor is entitled to make one such request, and any postponement in response to such a request is limited to one business day. CC §2924g(c)(1). The trustor's request must be in writing and must be accompanied by a statement identifying the source from which the funds to satisfy the obligation will be obtained. *Whitman v Transtate Title Co.* (1985) 165 CA3d 312, 211 CR 582.

After three postponements, a new notice of sale must be given. CC §2924g(c)(1). The following types of postponements, however, do not count against the total of three: postponements at the trustor's request (CC §2924g(c)(1)); postponements by court order, as in the case of an automatic stay under the Bankruptcy Code (11 USC §362(a)); postponements by mutual agreement of trustor and beneficiary; or postponements resulting from the prohibition on sale within seven days of the expiration of an injunction, restraining order, or stay (CC §2924g(c)(2)). In *California Livestock Prod. Credit Ass' n v Sutfin* (1985) 165 CA3d 136, 211 CR 152, the court held that three postponements of a trustee's sale did not require renoticing the sale when the postponements were required to comply with the automatic stay in a bankruptcy proceeding.

At the time and location specified in the notice of sale, the trustee must publicly announce the postponement, the reason for the postponement, and the subsequent date, time, and place of sale. If the sale is postponed by injunction, restraining order, or otherwise stayed by operation of law, it must be held no sooner than seven days after the earlier of (1) dismissal of the action, or (2) the expiration or termination of the injunction, order, or stay, unless a court having jurisdiction over the matter orders otherwise. CC §2924g(d). When the sale is postponed, the time within which the trustor may reinstate the obligation is automatically extended until five business days before the new sale date. CC §2924c(e).

To extinguish a tax lien junior to the interest being foreclosed, the trustee must give the district director of the Internal Revenue Service or State Controller notice of the trustee's sale if notice of the tax lien was filed more than 30 days before the date set for sale. See §2.10. An oral announcement of a postponement that complies with state law provides notice of the postponement to the district director and State Controller. Reg §301.7425–3(a)(2); CC §2924g(d). If notice of sale was originally not required because the tax lien was not filed more than 30 days before the date originally set for sale, a postponement may make it necessary to give notice of the sale to the appropriate taxing authority. When the postponement delays the sale until more than 30 days after the filing of the tax lien, notice to the district director or State Controller is required. Reg §301.7425–3(a)(2); Govt C §16187. See §2.10 on the time requirements for the notice.

A common reason for exercise of the trustee's discretion in delaying the sale is to give the bidders time to obtain the cash necessary to cover their bids. See *Security-First Nat' l Bank v Cryer* (1940) 39 CA2d 757, 104 P2d 66. The trustee may, however, reject the request for a delay and proceed with the sale. *Hill v Gibraltar Sav. & Loan Ass' n* (1967) 254 CA2d 241, 62 CR 188; *Kleckner v Bank of Am. Nat' l Trust & Sav. Ass' n* (1950) 97 CA2d 30, 217 P2d 28. As noted above, the trustor is entitled to one delay to raise sufficient cash (CC §2924g(c)(1)), and the trustee almost certainly has discretion to grant the trustor a further delay to raise the necessary funds. See *Foge v Schmidt* (1951) 101 CA2d 681, 226 P2d 73. Requests by junior lienors present a similar problem, but the decision not to postpone the sale will be upheld if it constitutes a reasonable exercise of the trustee's discretion. *Hill v Gibraltar Sav. & Loan Ass'n, supra.*

Trustors commonly contend that they had received oral assurances from the beneficiary that the sale would be postponed. Such oral, gratuitous promises are not enforceable, and the trustee may proceed with the sale as it was noticed. *Raedeke v Gibraltar Sav. & Loan Ass'n* (1974) 10 C3d 665, 111 CR 693; *Karlsen v American Sav. & Loan Ass'n* (1971) 15 CA3d 112, 92 CR 851. Note that under CC §2924g(c)(1) the trustor's request for a postponement must be in writing to be enforceable. A postponement agreement between trustor and beneficiary that is supported by consideration is enforceable, but the beneficiary should exercise caution concerning the amount charged for a delay, because consideration may constitute a "loan or forbearance" of money and therefore be subject to usury rules. See *Buck v Dahlgren* (1972) 23 CA3d 779, 100 CR 462. Although it may be proper for the beneficiary to insist on a partial payment of the loan as a condition for the delay, any demand for a sum of money not to be applied to the loan should be calculated carefully.

§2.25   B. Unruh Act Mortgages and Deeds of Trust

Civil Code §2924f(c) contains special requirements for mortgages or deeds of trust that contain a power of sale, that are secured by real property containing a single-family owner-occupied residence, and that secure an obligation contained in a contract for goods or services subject to the Unruh Retail Installment Sales Act (Unruh Act) (CC §§1801–1812.20). An attorney representing a client involved in an Unruh Act mortgage or deed of trust foreclosure should carefully examine CC §2924f(c), which applies to real property on which a notice of default was filed after July 10, 1980. The statute's most important requirements are:

■ If the mortgagor or trustor has failed to cure the default within 30 days after the notice of default was recorded, the statement set forth in §2.13 must be mailed to the trustor or mortgagor at his or her last-known address. CC §2924f(c)(3).

■ The procedure for notice of sale for properties on which notices of default were filed after July 10, 1980, is the same as for other sales of properties when the mortgage or deed of trust contains a power of sale (see §§2.18–2.20). CC §2924f(c)(2).

■ Sales of residential real property subject to Unruh Act mortgages or deeds of trust must be held in the county in which the residence is located. CC §2924f(c)(4).

■ All sales must be made to the person making the highest offer. The trustee may receive offers to purchase for ten days before the time of sale, and the noticed sale must be postponed to a specific date if any such offer is accepted in writing before the sale date by both the trustor and the beneficiary. The trustor may convey the property to the offeror before the date set for the postponed sale. The conveyance will terminate any further proceeding under the notice of sale, and the notice will be considered revoked. CC §2924f(c)(4).

■ In addition to the trustee's fee provided by CC §2924c, the trustee or mortgagee acting under CC §2924f(c) is entitled to charge an additional $50 fee. CC §2924f(c)(5).

§2.26   C. Form: Trustee's Deed

TRUSTEE'S DEED

_ _[Name]_ _, _ _[state capacity, e.g., a California corporation]_ _, **as trustee under the deed of trust described below, hereby grants without warranty to _ _[name]_ _ all the real property situated in _ _ _ _ _ _ _ _ County, California, known as _ _[state street address** or other designation]_ _, **and described as:**

[Legal description]

This conveyance is made under the powers conferred on the grantor by the deed of trust executed by _ _[name]_ _, as trustor, and naming _ _[name]_ _, as trustee, and _ _[name]_ _, as beneficiary, dated _ _ _ _ _ _, and recorded on _ _[date]_ _, in Book No. _ _ at page _ _ of the Official Records of _ _ _ _ _ _ _ _ County, California;

[Add, if appropriate]

and assigned to _ _[name]_ _ by an assignment dated _ _ _ _ _ _, in Book No. _ _ at page _ _ of the Official Records of _ _ _ _ _ _ _ _ County;

[Add, if appropriate]

and by the appointment and substitution of the trustee under the deed of trust by an instrument dated _ _ _ _ _ _, and recorded on _ _[date]_ _, in Book No. _ _ at page _ _ of the Official Records of _ _ _ _ _ _ _ _ County, and executed by _ _[name]_ _;

[Continue]

and after fulfilling the conditions specified in the deed of trust authorizing the conveyance as follows:

1. The trustor defaulted on the obligations for which the transfer in trust was made as security, and notice of default was recorded in the office of the County Recorder of _ _ _ _ _ _ _ _ County, the nature of the default being the failure to _ _[specify]_ _. This default still existed at the time of sale.

2. Not less than three months elapsed between the recording of the notice of default and the posting and first publication of the notice of sale of the property.

3. The beneficiary made due and proper demand on the trustee to sell the property under the terms of the deed of trust.

4. The trustee gave notice of the time and place of the sale of the property in accordance with the laws of California and the terms of the deed of trust.

5. The trustee complied with all requirements of law concerning the mailing of copies of notices _ _[and the _ _[publication/personal delivery]_ _ of the notice of default/_ _[and the]_ _ _ _[posting/publication]_ _ of the notice of sale]_ _.

6. The property was sold by the grantor at public auction on _ _[date]_ _, in _ _ _ _ _ _ _ _ County, California, in which the property _ _[or part of it]_ _ is situated, in full accordance with the laws of the State of California and the terms of the deed of trust.

The grantee, as the highest bidder at the sale, became the purchaser of the property and paid the trustee $_ _ _ _ _ _, the amount bid, in lawful money of the United States.

Dated: _ _ _ _ _ _

> _ _ _[Signature]_ _ _
> _ _[Typed name]_ _
> **Trustee**

[*Acknowledgment*]

Comment: The recitals in the trustee's deed concerning compliance with the notice-of-default and notice-of-sale requirements are important in protecting third party purchasers from subsequent attacks. CC §2924. See §6.39 on the effect of the recitals when the trustor seeks to attack a trustee's sale.

§2.27 D. Title Conveyed by Trustee's Deed

Title conveyed by a trustee's deed relates back in time to the date on which the deed of trust was executed. The trustee's deed therefore passes the title held by the trustor as of that earlier time plus any after-acquired title, rather than passing the title that the trustor held on the date of the foreclosure sale. *Hohn v Riverside County Flood Control & Water Conserv. Dist.* (1964) 228 CA2d 605, 39 CR 647; *Bracey v Gray* (1942) 49 CA2d 274, 121 P2d 770. Thus, liens that attached to the property after execution of the foreclosed deed of trust are eliminated, and the purchaser at the trustee's sale takes title to the property free of those junior liens. *Carpenter v Smallpage* (1934) 220 C 129, 29 P2d 841; *Dugand v Magnus* (1930) 107 CA 243, 290 P 309. Certain governmental liens, *e.g.,* for real property taxes and assessments (Rev & T C §2192.1), are superior despite having been recorded later than the deed of trust and are therefore not subject to elimination. See §2.10. Mechanics' liens are eliminated only if the date on which the work commenced (rather than the date of recording) was subsequent to the date on which the foreclosed deed of trust was recorded. CC §3134.

The trustee's deed also conveys title free and clear of the lien of the deed of trust or mortgage under which the foreclosure sale was conducted. Because the sale proceeds are to be used to satisfy that lien, it no longer exists as an encumbrance on the property, even if the sale proceeds do not satisfy the claim. CC §2910; CCP §726; see, *e.g., Ralph C. Sutro Co. v Paramount Plastering, Inc.* (1963) 216 CA2d 433, 31 CR 174.

The trustee's deed conveys the property subject to all senior liens on it. *Streiff v Darlington* (1937) 9 C2d 42, 68 P2d 728. A junior foreclosure has no effect on senior liens, with the possible exception that a senior lienor may have the right to accelerate based on language in the senior instrument. See §§7.10–7.18. The title conveyed at the junior sale relates back only to the date on which the junior deed of trust was executed, and title is therefore subject to the senior lien. The foreclosure purchaser at the junior sale receives only the interest held by the trustor on the day on which the junior lien was given. *Hohn v Riverside County Flood Control & Water Conserv. Dist., supra; Bracey v Gray, supra.*

The title covenants in CC §1113 are probably not implied, despite the use of the word "grant" in the trustee's deed. *National Pac. Oil Co. v Watson* (1920) 184 C 216, 193 P 133; *Mitchell v California-Pacific Title Ins. Co.* (1926) 79 CA 45, 248 P 1035, discussed in Comment, *Grantor and Grantee: Recovery by the Grantee of Money Paid under Mistake as to Vendor's Title*, 15 Calif L Rev 53 (1926). Civil Code §1113 does not apply when "restrained by express terms contained in such conveyance" (*Babb v Weemer* (1964) 225 CA2d 546, 37 CR 533; see also *Lippman v Sears, Roebuck & Co.* (1955) 44 C2d 136, 280 P2d 775; *Cousins Inv. Co. v Hastings Clothing Co.* (1941) 45 CA2d 141, 113 P2d 878), and trustees' deeds are always expressly made without warranties. For discussion of covenants of title, see California Real Property Sales Transactions, chap 9 (Cal CEB 1981).

Note that a foreclosure sale is not subject to CC §§1102–1102.14, which impose certain disclosure requirements on transfers of specified residential property. CC §1102.1(b).

§2.28   E. Possession Following Sale

The purchaser at a trustee's sale is entitled to immediate possession of the property. *Farris v Pacific States Auxiliary Corp.* (1935) 4 C2d 103, 48 P2d 11. The purchaser may bring an unlawful detainer action against a trustor, or anyone holding under the trustor, who refuses to relinquish possession after the sale. CCP §1161a; *MCA, Inc. v Universal Diversified Enters. Corp.* (1972) 27 CA3d 170, 103 CR 522. Although the trustor may challenge the purchaser's title by asserting that the sale did not meet statutory requirements, no triable issue of fact is presented unless the trustor first offered to pay the full amount of the debt. 27 CA3d at 176, 103 CR at 525; *Crummer v Whitehead* (1964) 230 CA2d 264, 40 CR 826; *Py v Pleitner* (1945) 70 CA2d 576, 582, 161 P2d 393, 396.

Tenants of the former trustor may also be evicted by the purchaser if their leases are junior to the foreclosed deed of trust. *Dugand v Mag-*

nus (1930) 107 CA 243, 290 P 309. The right to evict may, however, be subject to local rent control restrictions. See *Gross v Superior Court* (1985) 171 CA3d 265, 217 CR 284. A lease junior to the deed of trust gives the tenant merely a leasehold interest in mortgaged premises, and foreclosure constitutes eviction by paramount title (*Sullivan v Superior Court* (1921) 185 C 133, 195 P 1061). Although a senior foreclosure and sale is a breach of the trustor-landlord's covenant of quiet enjoyment and may result in liability to the tenant, the tenant is not insulated from the foreclosure purchaser's superior right to possession (*Sullivan v Superior Court, supra*) in the absence of a local rent or eviction control ordinance (*Gross v Superior Court, supra*). Although the trustor is entitled to just three days' written notice before commencement of unlawful detainer proceedings (CCP §1161a(b)), a tenant of the trustor is entitled to written notice to quit "at least as long as the term of the hiring itself but not exceeding 30 days" (CCP §1161a(c)). The tenant, as well as the trustor, may defend an unlawful detainer action under CCP §1161a by challenging the purchaser's title, *i.e.*, by attacking the validity of the trustee's sale (although not the validity of the underlying mortgage). *Cheney v Trauzettel* (1937) 9 C2d 158, 69 P2d 832. For further discussion, see California Residential Landlord-Tenant Practice §6.48 (Cal CEB 1986).

The fact that foreclosure terminates junior leases may adversely affect the purchaser if the leases are favorable to the landlord. In this situation, the tenants will claim that the foreclosure sale terminates the tenancy. *Dugand v Magnus, supra*. Abandonment by the tenants may possibly be avoided in a judicial foreclosure if they are not named as defendants in the action, at least when they occupy under a recorded lease. See CCP §726; *Carpenter v Hamilton* (1944) 24 C2d 95, 147 P2d 563. There is no precise equivalent of this device in a trustee's sale. The same end may possibly be achieved by including in the notice of sale the reversion and right to rents but not the leasehold estate, because the estates are legally separable. *Commonwealth Memorial, Inc. v Telophase Soc'y of Am., Inc.* (1976) 63 CA3d 867, 134 CR 58. This strategy is analogous to foreclosing and selling only one of two lots included as security in the deed of trust. The trustor has no valid objection to this device, because the trustor can have no liability for a deficiency under CCP §580d (although the existence of other security could give rise to a deficiency; see §8.6), and the possibility of a surplus is increased by omitting a favorable leasehold from the sale. The tenants cannot complain either, because their right to quiet enjoyment is preserved. This device is consistent with the doctrine of marshaling assets in inverse order of alienation. CC §2899. See §§8.2–8.8 on multiple security. The purchaser should also examine the tenants' leases because many commercial leases require the tenants to attorn to any purchaser at a sale.

A lease that was executed before the deed of trust was executed is superior to the deed of trust. The beneficiary takes a deed of trust on leased property and acquires merely a lien on the reversion. *Fahrenbaker v E. Clemens Horst Co.* (1930) 209 C 7, 284 P 905. Foreclosure of the interest conveys to the purchaser only the same reversion. The purchaser may not, therefore, evict the tenant, nor may the tenant terminate its obligations under the lease. The purchaser becomes the new landlord and is entitled to the rents as they become due. *Fahrenbaker v E. Clemens Horst Co., supra.* If the tenant under a prior lease is not visibly in possession of the property, and the lease was not recorded, the purchaser at the foreclosure sale should be able to take the property free of the lease as a bona fide purchaser.

§2.29 F. Disposition of the Proceeds

The trustee should disburse the proceeds of sale in the following order:

■ Reimbursement of its own costs and the expenses of the sale (CC §§2924c(c)–(d), 2924d);

■ Satisfaction of the beneficiary's debt;

■ Payment to junior lienors in order of priority (*Dockrey v Gray* (1959) 172 CA2d 388, 341 P2d 746; *Sohn v California Pac. Title Ins. Co.* (1954) 124 CA2d 757, 269 P2d 223); and

■ Payment of any surplus to the trustor (*Atkinson v Foote* (1919) 44 CA 149, 186 P 831).

If there is a dispute about how much should be paid, or to whom, the trustee should interplead the proceeds into court for a judicial determination. An erroneous payment may subject the trustee to liability to a party injured by the error. *Atkinson v Foote, supra.*

Items that are not paid out of the sale proceeds include prior liens, expenditures made by the purchaser after the sale, and usurious interest. *Arneill Ranch v Petit* (1976) 64 CA3d 277, 134 CR 456. Trustees may encounter pitfalls in attempting to disburse the proceeds properly. For example, a junior lienholder is entitled to make an advance to keep the senior from foreclosing, as a way of protecting the junior security. *Windt v Covert* (1907) 152 C 350, 93 P 67; *United Sav. & Loan Ass'n v Hoffman* (1973) 30 CA3d 306, 106 CR 275. A junior who makes such an advance may include the advance as part of the junior debt and recover out of the sale proceeds. If the junior does not cure the senior arrearages until after acquiring the property at a junior foreclosure sale, however, then the junior cannot claim these advances as part of the debt. *Streiff v Darlington* (1937) 9 C2d 42, 68 P2d 728. This should also be true for insurance and tax payments made by the creditor. Thus, the right to recover such expenditures from the sale proceeds may depend on when they were made. See *United Sav. & Loan Ass'n v Hoffman, supra.*

The trustee must also exercise caution when the beneficiary has had a receiver appointed to collect rents from the property during the foreclosure period. *United Sav. & Loan Ass'n v Hoffman, supra.* The rents are available as additional security and may be reached by the beneficiary only if the foreclosure sale fails to satisfy the entire debt. The debt is satisfied whenever there is a bid equal to it. *Cornelison v Kornbluth* (1975) 15 C3d 590, 125 CR 557. A full bid therefore deprives the beneficiary of access to the rents held by the receiver, which will then go either to junior lienors (*United Sav. & Loan Ass'n v Hoffman, supra*) or to the trustor (*Eastland Sav. & Loan Ass'n v Thornhill & Bruce, Inc.* (1968) 260 CA2d 259, 66 CR 901). To avoid this result, a beneficiary should reduce its bid by the amount of the rents held by the receiver. See §5.21. The same principles apply to fire insurance proceeds. See §§7.26–7.28.

Any surplus that must be paid to juniors or to the trustor includes only the amount received at the foreclosure sale in excess of the amount owed the foreclosing party and costs of sale. A profitable resale after the foreclosure sale does not create a surplus for the benefit of the juniors or the trustor. *Strutt v Ontario Sav. & Loan Ass'n* (1972) 28 CA3d 866, 105 CR 395.

The purchaser at the foreclosure sale need not be concerned with disposition of any surplus. Although misallocation of the sale proceeds may lead to litigation among the various claimants, it has no effect on the purchaser's title. *Hohn v Riverside County Flood Control & Water Conserv. Dist.* (1964) 228 CA2d 605, 39 CR 647.

VI. TAX CONSEQUENCES OF FORECLOSURE

§2.30   A. For Mortgagor

The gain or loss to the mortgagor on foreclosure is the difference between the mortgagor's adjusted basis in the property and the amount realized from the foreclosure. *Helvering v Hammel* (1941) 311 US 504. In effect, the foreclosure sale is treated as if the mortgagor had sold the property to the highest bidder; when the proceeds of the foreclosure sale do not exceed the mortgage debt, the amount realized is the face amount of the obligation, even if the property is worth less than the outstanding obligation and the mortgagor remains liable for a deficiency. See *Mendham Corp.* (1947) 9 TC 320.

The amount realized by the mortgagor includes any surplus foreclosure sale proceeds received by the mortgagor. Reg §1.1001–2(c), Example (2). It also includes the unpaid balance of any nonrecourse mortgage loan (*i.e.,* a loan for which a deficiency judgment is prohibited by law or language in the note) as the discharge of an indebtedness, even when the debt exceeds the value of the security. Reg §1.1001–2; *Commissioner v Tufts* (1983) 461 US 300; see *Allan v Commissioner* (8th Cir 1988) 856 F2d 1169; Taxation of Real Property Transfers §3.6 (Cal CEB 1981). When a deficiency judgment is possible, the amount realized is the lesser of the amount bid at the foreclosure sale or the unpaid balance of the mortgage debt. Reg §1.1001–2. If a deficiency judgment is obtained and is later forgiven, additional income is realized from discharge of that debt. Reg §1.1001–2(c), Example (8).

Interest arrearages included in the discharged debt are also part of the amount realized by the mortgagor, but if payment of that interest would have generated a deduction for the mortgagor, then an offsetting deduction is allowed on foreclosure. IRC §108(e)(2). If the mortgagor was insolvent at the time of foreclosure, income realized from discharge of the debt may not be recognized; instead, that income may reduce net operating loss or other tax attributes if there are any. IRC §108(b).

The character of the mortgagor's gain or loss on foreclosure usually depends on the use of the asset constituting the security. If the asset is a capital asset, the mortgagor's gain or loss is capital. IRC §1221. If the asset is property used for a trade or business, the amount realized may be treated as capital gain or ordinary loss, subject to the netting rules of IRC §1231. If the asset was property held for personal use, any gain is capital and no loss deduction is allowed. IRC §262. If the mortgagor has a statutory right to postsale redemption, gain or loss is recognized when the redemption right expires rather than when the sale occurs. *Derby Realty Corp.* (1937) 35 BTA 335, acq 1938–1 Cum Bull 9. The mortgagor may, however, accelerate recognition by quitclaiming the right of redemption and thus obtain a loss deduction in the year in which the foreclosure occurs. *Commissioner v Hill* (6th Cir 1941) 119 F2d 421.

B. For Mortgagee

§2.31   **1. When Third Party Acquires Property at Foreclosure Sale**

When a foreclosure sale of the mortgaged property occurs, either by trustee's sale or judicial foreclosure, the amount of the mortgagee's gain or loss is measured by the difference between the amount received by the mortgagee and the mortgagee's basis in the mortgage. Reg §1.166–6. Any loss sustained is treated as a bad-debt loss. Reg §1.166–6(a). Any gain recognized by the mortgagee is usually ordinary gain. IRC §1222; see Taxation of Real Property Transfers §3.35 (Cal CEB 1981). In the case of a nonrecourse mortgage, the mortgagee will collect only the net proceeds of the foreclosure sale, because no deficiency will survive the sale. When the mortgagor is personally liable on the mortgage obligation, the amount received by the mortgagee will include any additional amount that the mortgagee collects after foreclosure. The amount realized probably does not include the amount of a deficiency judgment that the mortgagee manages to obtain, unless the judgment is actually collected.

The mortgagee's basis in the mortgage note is usually the amount loaned, plus any loan expenses (plus accrued interest if the mortgagee is an accrual-basis taxpayer), and less any payments of principal received. For discussion of determining basis, see Taxation RP Transfers §§2.1–2.76. If the mortgagee purchased an existing note, the price paid for it establishes the basis. IRC §§1011–1012. A mortgagee's basis in a purchase-money note is the face value of the note. If the mortgagee has reported gain on the sale under the installment method, the basis in the note is the excess of its face value over the gain that would be recognized if the note were paid. IRC §453.

Any amount received on foreclosure by the mortgagee, in excess of basis, is treated as income. See generally Taxation RP Transfers §§3.1–3.9. If the amount received is interest income, it is treated as discussed in §1.15. If it is other income (because the mortgagor's basis in the note was different from the balance due on the note), then it is capital gain or ordinary income depending on the character of the asset. See §2.30. There is a loss if the amount received is less than the mortgagee's basis in the note (typically when the amount bid at the sale is less than the unpaid principal balance of the note). The loss is an ordinary loss if the mortgagee was a professional lender (IRC §166); otherwise, it is a capital loss (IRC §§165, 1221).

Gain or loss occurs in the year of the foreclosure sale if the obligation is nonrecourse or the mortgagee does not obtain a deficiency judgment. Reg §1.166–6(a). If the mortgagee obtains a deficiency judgment, which then proves uncollectible, the mortgagee is entitled to a bad-debt deduction in the year in which the deficiency judgment becomes worthless. Reg §1.166–3(b), 1.166–6(a). The existence of a postsale right of redemption in the mortgagor does not change the timing of the mortgagee's gain or loss. The amount of a deficiency judgment that is later collected should be added to the amount realized. *Security Mortgage Co.* (1972) 58 TC 667.

§2.32   2. When Mortgagee Acquires Property at Foreclosure Sale

■ *Seller.* A seller-mortgagee's reacquisition of the property at the foreclosure sale is viewed as an exchange of the debt for the property and is subject to IRC §1038. Gain is thus realized to the extent that the property's value exceeds the seller's basis in the debt. Recognition of this gain is limited, however, to the extent by which the amounts previously received by the seller exceed previously reported gain. IRC §1038. Any earlier-recognized loss is deducted from the seller's new basis in the property. IRC §1038(d).

Nonrecognition is greater if the seller is over age 55 and qualifies under IRC §121 for a one-time gain exclusion of $125,000 (or the earlier sale to the buyer qualified under §121 and is now being undone by the foreclosure). The sale may also qualify under IRC §1034 for rollover of gain on a principal residence if the seller-mortgagee purchases another residence within two years and disposes of the repossessed residence within one year of repossession. In these cases, there is no recognition of any part of the gain or loss. IRC §1038(e); Reg §1.1038–2.

■ *Third party lender.* When a mortgagee who is a third party lender purchases at the sale, IRC §1038 does not apply. A bad-debt loss is recognized to the extent that the amount bid is less than the mortgagee's basis in the debt, and there is gain or loss to the extent that the amount bid differs from the fair market value of the property acquired. *Community Bank v Commissioner* (9th Cir 1987) 819 F2d 940. If the property is worth less than the debt, an underbid will usually generate an ordinary loss if the mortgagee is a professional lender and a capital loss otherwise. See IRC §§165(a), 166. Conversely, a credit-bid that includes interest arrearages produces ordinary income for the interest thus considered to have been collected, even if the property's fair market value is less than the unpaid loan balance. *Helvering v Midland Mut. Life Ins. Co.* (1936) 300 US 216; *National Life Ins. Co. v U.S.* (Ct Cl 1933) 4 F Supp 1000; *Prudential Ins. Co.* (1935) 33 BTA 332. As purchaser, the mortgagee has a basis in the property that is usually the amount bid. Reg §1.166–6(b)(2).

Chapter 3: **Judicial Foreclosure**

VI. SALE
  A. Intermediate Steps Between Judgment and Sale §3.55
  B. Judicial Council Form: Writ of Sale §3.56
  C. Judicial Council Form: Notice of Levy §3.57
  D. Form: Notice of Sale §3.58
  E. Eligible Bidders §3.59
  F. Method of Bidding §3.60
  G. Steps Following Sale §3.61
  H. When Sale Is Subject to Redemption Rights
    1. Certificate of Sale §3.62
    2. Form: Certificate of Sale §3.63
    3. Form: Notice of Right of Redemption §3.64
  I. Form: Receiver's Report and Account of Sale §3.65
  J. Form: Deed of Sale §3.66

VII. DEFICIENCY JUDGMENT §3.67
  A. Form: Notice of Motion for Deficiency Judgment §3.68
  B. Hearing §3.69
  C. Form: Application for and Order Appointing Probate Referee §3.70
  D. Deficiency Judgment §3.71
  E. Form: Deficiency Judgment §3.72

VIII. POSTSALE REDEMPTION §3.73
  A. Who May Redeem §3.74
  B. Order of Redemption §3.75
  C. Time in Which To Redeem §3.76
  D. Effect of Redemption §3.77
  E. Amount Necessary To Redeem §3.78
  F. Possession, Rents, and Profits During Redemption Period §3.79
  G. After Expiration of Redemption Period §3.80

3

Judicial Foreclosure

I. INTRODUCTION

§3.1   **A. Judicial Foreclosure Defined**

Judicial foreclosure is a procedure by which the beneficiary of a deed of trust (or mortgagee) may enforce its lien on the property: The beneficiary obtains a judgment ordering the sale of the property, the sale is conducted by a levying officer, and the proceeds are then applied toward reduction of the debt. A deficiency judgment may then be obtainable if the sale proceeds are insufficient to cover the indebtedness. The effect of the foreclosure sale is to terminate the trustor's equity of redemption, *i.e.,* the trustor's right to clear its title of the encumbrance by paying the debt, even after the stated due date. CC §§2903, 2931; see *Hibernia Sav. & Loan Soc'y v Lauffer* (1940) 41 CA2d 725, 107 P2d 494. The common law device of strict foreclosure, under which the property was turned over to the mortgagee directly, without a sale, in satisfaction of the debt, is not permitted in California. CC §2889; CCP §744. For a technical exception to this rule, see §3.24. For discussion of the common law method of foreclosure, see Nelson & Whitman, Real Estate Finance Law §§7.1–7.32 (2d ed 1985).

Because the entire procedure is conducted under court supervision, judicial foreclosure is distinct from a trustee's sale conducted under CC §§2924–2924i, which bypasses the judiciary entirely (and is appropriately referred to as nonjudicial or extrajudicial foreclosure). Nonjudicial foreclosure is discussed in chap 2. For discussion of considerations in choosing between judicial and nonjudicial foreclosure, see §§2.3–2.4, 3.2–3.6.

For discussion of the tax consequences of foreclosure, whether by trustee's sale or judicial foreclosure, see §2.30.

B. Considerations in Choosing Judicial Foreclosure

1. Advantages

§3.2   **a. Availability of Deficiency Judgment**

The reason a secured creditor elects to foreclose judicially is usually that it wants to obtain a deficiency judgment. A creditor who uses judicial foreclosure may be able to obtain a deficiency judgment if the amount realized on sale of the property is insufficient to satisfy the debt (CCP §726); a deficiency judgment is never permitted after nonjudicial foreclosure (CCP §580d). Even when judicial foreclosure is used, a deficiency judgment is allowable only in cases involving nonpurchase-money secured debts and certain exempt third party purchase-money secured debts and is therefore not available to a creditor holding a purchase-money mortgage or deed of trust. See §4.23.

§3.3   **b. Lack of Power-of-Sale Clause**

Only security instruments that contain appropriate language (*i.e.*, power-of-sale clauses) can be foreclosed extrajudicially. See §2.5. Irregular mortgage substitutes or hidden security instruments (*e.g.*, a covenant not to convey, a deed absolute intended as a mortgage; see §4.35) usually lack a power of sale and must therefore be foreclosed judicially.

§3.4   **c. Other Reasons**

Judicial foreclosure may also be preferable when disagreements exist between the foreclosing creditor and the debtor (*e.g.*, about the amount of the debt or the right to foreclose) or between the foreclosing creditor and other creditors about priorities. The disagreements can often be better resolved as part of a foreclosure action, rather than by a private foreclosure followed by a lawsuit to determine the effect of the foreclosure. See *Dobbins v Economic Gas Co.* (1920) 182 C 616,

189 P 1073; *Mercantile Trust Co. v Sunset Road Oil Co.* (1920) 50 CA 485, 195 P 466. But see *Rowley v Davis* (1915) 169 C 678, 147 P 958.

Before 1960, a nonjudicial sale did not eliminate junior federal tax liens. Because that rule was changed (see *U.S. v Brosnan* (1960) 363 US 237), the existence of federal tax liens is no longer a reason to select judicial foreclosure. See §2.10 for discussion of federal tax liens and nonjudicial foreclosure.

§3.5   2. Disadvantages

The major drawback of judicial foreclosure has historically been the prospect of statutory redemption following the judicial sale. See §§3.73–3.80. The existence of postsale redemption rights has meant that a judicial sale does not give a purchaser the same nonredeemable title as a trustee's sale. This right of redemption carries with it the trustor's right to possession of the property for the redemption period. See §3.79. The existence of the trustor's rights to redemption and possession generally caused bidding at such sales to be lower than at nonjudicial foreclosure sales. See *U.S. v Stadium Apartments* (9th Cir 1970) 425 F2d 358, 365. The beneficiary can now avoid postsale redemption by waiving its right to a deficiency judgment (CCP §§726(e), 729.010), and can thus obtain the benefits of a judicial resolution of its disagreements with the trustor, without losing the benefits of a nonredeemable sale. See §3.71. Redemption is therefore confined to its original role of offsetting inflated deficiency judgments.

Judicial foreclosure proceedings frequently take longer and are more expensive to conduct than out-of-court private trustees' sales (although, if the debt is large enough, trustees' fees may exceed the costs of judicial foreclosure).

A judicial foreclosure action may be completely prohibited by the statute of limitations. See §3.11. A nonjudicial sale is not affected by limitation periods if a deed of trust rather than a mortgage is involved. *Flack v Boland* (1938) 11 C2d 103, 77 P2d 1090; *Sipe v McKenna* (1948) 88 CA2d 1001, 200 P2d 61; see §§6.17–6.19.

§3.6   3. When To Decide

The beneficiary under a deed of trust need not determine at the outset which type of foreclosure to use, because neither filing a complaint for judicial foreclosure nor recording a notice of default constitutes an election of remedies. See §2.4. The beneficiary may discontinue a judicial foreclosure action at any time in order to conduct a trustee's sale unless the trustor can show that some special harm will result from this decision. *Flack v Boland* (1938) 11 C2d 103, 77 P2d 1090; *Commercial Centre Realty Co. v Superior Court* (1936) 7 C2d 121, 59 P2d 978; *Mayhall v Eppinger* (1902) 137 C 5, 69 P 489; *Carpenter v Title Ins. & Trust Co.* (1945) 71 CA2d 593, 163 P2d 73. The beneficiary may file a judicial foreclosure action primarily to obtain appointment of a receiver, without intending to proceed to a foreclosure judgment. See §5.13. Such an action is often filed simultaneously with commencement of proceedings for nonjudicial foreclosure. *Baumann v Harrison* (1941) 46 CA2d 84, 115 P2d 530.

II. PREPARING THE ACTION

§3.7   A. Nature of Action

In California there is only one form of judicial action to recover a debt or enforce a right secured by a mortgage or deed of trust on real property. CCP §726. This action, known as a foreclosure action (or judicial foreclosure action), is basically an action to enforce a lien for payment of a debt. It results in the sale of the property in satisfaction of the obligation and the issuance of a sheriff's or receiver's deed. Foreclosure is complete when the trustor's equity of redemption is completely extinguished. CC §§2903, 2931; see *Duff v Randall* (1897) 116 C 226, 48 P 66; *Hibernia Sav. & Loan Soc'y v Lauffer* (1940) 41 CA2d 725, 107 P2d 494. Because the action is equitable in nature, equitable principles apply. *Kirkpatrick v Stelling* (1940) 36 CA2d 658, 98 P2d 566; *Brichetto v Raney* (1926) 76 CA 232, 245 P 235. There is no right to a jury trial even if a personal judgment for a deficiency is sought. *Downing v Le Du* (1890) 82 C 471, 23 P 202; *Van Valkenburgh v Oldham* (1910) 12 CA 572, 108 P 42.

The customary steps in a foreclosure action are:

■ Filing complaint (see §§3.29–3.44);

■ Recording lis pendens (notice of pendency of action; CCP §409) (see §§3.45–3.46);

■ Serving summons and complaint on the defendants (see §3.10);

■ Filing of responsive pleadings by the defendants (see §§3.47–3.51);

■ Trial of the action (see §3.52);

■ Entry of judgment of foreclosure and order of sale (see §§3.53–3.55);

■ Obtaining writ of sale (see §3.56);

■ Giving notice of levy and notice of sale (see §§3.57–3.58);

■ Conducting the sale (see §§3.59–3.60);

■ Issuance of certificate of sale (if postsale redemption rights exist) or deed of sale (see §§3.62–3.64);

■ Filing of levying officer's accounting (see §3.65); and

■ Issuance of deed of sale if the property is not redeemed (see §3.66).

§3.8   B. Jurisdiction

California courts have jurisdiction only over California real property and may not foreclose liens on property outside the state. *Title Ins. & Trust Co. v California Dev. Co.* (1915) 171 C 173, 152 P 542; *Lilly-Brackett Co. v Sonnemann* (1910) 157 C 192, 106 P 715; *Felton v West* (1894) 102 C 266, 36 P 676; *Allen v Allen* (1892) 95 C 184, 30 P 213. Conversely, the courts of sister states have no power to foreclose mortgages secured by California real property. *Lilly-Brackett Co. v Sonnemann, supra.* If the security instrument covers real property situated in more than one state, a California court may foreclose the lien on the part of the property that is located in California. *Hartwick v Superior Court* (1959) 174 CA2d 809, 345 P2d 304.

An action to foreclose a lien on real property is an equitable action that is subject to the subject-matter jurisdiction of the superior court. Cal Const art VI, §10; CCP §86; see *Curtin v Salmon River Hydraulic Gold Mining & Ditch Co.* (1903) 141 C 308, 74 P 851; *Downing v Le Du* (1890) 82 C 471, 23 P 202; *La Societe Francaise D'Eparngnes et de Prevoyance Mutuelle v Selheimer* (1881) 57 C 623. On the proper superior court in which to file the action, see §3.9.

The action may be brought in federal court if the United States is a defendant (28 USC §2410) or if the requirements for federal diversity jurisdiction are met (28 USC §1332). If an action naming the United

States as a defendant is brought in state court, the United States may have it removed to federal court. 28 USC §1444.

§3.9   C. Venue

In an action to foreclose a lien on real property, the proper venue is the county in which the property or some part of it is located (CCP §392(1)), even if a deficiency judgment is sought or if an additional cause of action seeking a personal judgment is joined. *Appel v Hubbard* (1957) 155 CA2d 639, 318 P2d 164; *Case v Kirkwood* (1931) 119 CA 207, 6 P2d 110. If there is a single mortgage or deed of trust covering real property in more than one county, venue is proper in either county. CCP §726; *Kent v Williams* (1905) 146 C 3, 79 P 527; *Murphy v Superior Court* (1902) 138 C 69, 70 P 1070. When multiple deeds of trust secure a single debt, they should be foreclosed in one action even though the property is located in more than one county; otherwise, the omitted security may be lost under CCP §726 (see §§4.3–4.4). *Stockton Sav. & Loan Soc'y v Harrold* (1900) 127 C 612, 60 P 165; *Appel v Hubbard, supra.* Under CCP §392(1), venue is proper in any county in which the property securing the obligation, or some part of it, is located. But see contrary dictum in *Merced Sec. Sav. Bank v Casaccia* (1894) 103 C 641, 37 P 648.

§3.10   D. Service of Process

Only the interests of parties who are subject to the court's jurisdiction will be properly terminated by the judgment and the succeeding foreclosure sale. *Morrissey v Gray* (1911) 160 C 390, 117 P 438; *Johnston v San Francisco Sav. Union* (1883) 63 C 554; *Montgomery v Tutt* (1858) 11 C 307; *Hurt v Pico Inv. Co.* (1932) 127 CA 106, 15 P2d 203. To acquire jurisdiction over a party, the plaintiff in a foreclosure action must cause that party to be properly served with the summons and complaint. CCP §415.10. Substituted service on a party under CCP §415.20(b) is sufficient to confer jurisdiction over that party, including jurisdiction to enter a deficiency judgment. *Korea Exch. Bank v Yang* (1988) 200 CA3d 1471, 246 CR 619. A party's general appearance in the action confers the court's jurisdiction over that party as if personal service had been effected. CCP §1014.

Service of the summons and complaint in foreclosure actions is effected in the same manner as in civil actions generally. See CCP §§410.10–418.11. For discussion of jurisdiction and service of process, see 1 California Civil Procedure Before Trial, chaps 2, 8 (Cal CEB 1977).

§3.11 E. Statute of Limitations

There is no statute of limitations specifically governing actions to foreclose liens (although the Marketable Record Title Act (CC §§880.020–887.090), discussed below, imposes a ceiling on the life of a lien). The lien is incidental to the principal obligation and is extinguished when the statute runs on the principal obligation. CC §2911. Although no statute of limitations bars the power of sale under deeds of trust (see §3.5), judicial foreclosure of both deeds of trust and mortgages is subject to the statute of limitations. *Flack v Boland* (1938) 11 C2d 103, 77 P2d 1090.

Judicial foreclosure actions are subject to the four-year limitation period of CCP §337, which applies generally to actions on written contracts. *Flack v Boland, supra.* The action must be filed within four years after the maturity date of the obligation (*Flack v Boland, supra*) and within four years after the maturity date of any installment payment that is to be enforced by the action (*Trigg v Arnott* (1937) 22 CA2d 455, 71 P2d 330). Partial payments made within the statutory limitation period start the running of a new period but are not effective to revive a cause of action once it is completely time-barred. CCP §360.

When the statute of limitations has run on a note secured by a mortgage (as opposed to a note secured by a deed of trust), the owner of the mortgaged property may be able to bring a quiet title action to clear the records of the stale claim. Although this remedy is denied to the original mortgagor who executed the note, on the ground that one who seeks equity must do equity (see *Aguilar v Bocci* (1974) 39 CA3d 475, 114 CR 91), a successor-owner to the mortgagor is entitled to such relief (*Faxon v All Persons* (1913) 166 C 707, 137 P 919) even when the successor purchases the property with knowledge of the old mortgage (*Mix v Sodd* (1981) 126 CA3d 386, 178 CR 736).

Civil Code §882.020 provides that the lien of a mortgage or deed of trust expires ten years after the maturity date of the obligation, if that date can be determined from the recorded document, or 60 years after the date of recordation, if no maturity date can be ascertained. This expiration date can be extended for ten years by recording a "notice of intent to preserve interest" under CC §880.340. CC §882.020(a)(3).

§3.12   F. Title Company Services

Before filing an action to foreclose a mortgage or deed of trust, an attorney should obtain a litigation or foreclosure guaranty from the title company. The foreclosure guaranty shows the present condition of the record as to ownership, encumbrances, taxes, and parties who should be joined in the action. It also includes other information that may be helpful in preparing the complaint. For further discussion of litigation guaranties, see California Title Insurance Practice §3.23 (Cal CEB 1980). The guaranty may not, however, cover certain items, such as a notice of default under a deed of trust. See *Glavinich v Commonwealth Land Title Ins. Co.* (1984) 163 CA3d 263, 209 CR 266. See also §2.2 for discussion of title company services regarding trustees' sales.

§3.13   G. Federally Insured or Guaranteed Loans

If the loan has been insured or guaranteed by the Federal Housing Administration (FHA) or the Veterans Administration (VA), the foreclosing creditor's attorney should contact the applicable agency before filing a foreclosure action to determine what procedures must be followed. Formal notice to the agency of the default and pending foreclosure may be required. See, *e.g.,* 38 USC §1816(a)(1) (VA). Each agency also has procedures that must be followed concerning the sale for the creditor to be able to recover from the agency on the insured loan or the guaranty for any shortfall from the sale. See 12 USC §§1707—1715z–20 (FHA); 38 USC §§1801–1827 (VA).

These federal agencies are not obliged to act when a deed of trust is in default and, instead of exercising their rights of repurchase, may permit the beneficiary to complete its foreclosure. *Rank v Nimmo* (9th Cir 1982) 677 F2d 692 (VA).

H. Parties

§3.14   1. Plaintiffs

A foreclosure action may be brought by the mortgagee under a mortgage, by either the beneficiary or the trustee under a deed of trust, or by their successors in interest. CCP §725a. If there are two or more holders of the secured obligation, all should join as plaintiffs, and any holder who refuses to join or cannot join should be joined as a defendant. Lack of consent from the other beneficiaries does not prohibit one of the beneficiaries from foreclosing to protect the common estate. *Perkins v Chad Dev. Corp.* (1979) 95 CA3d 645, 157 CR 201; see §2.11. For discussion of joinder of parties, see 1 California Civil Procedure Before Trial §§7.12–7.15 (Cal CEB 1977).

2. Defendants

§3.15   a. Owners: Past, Present, and Future

The present owner of the mortgaged property must be named as a defendant in the foreclosure action. Even though the present owner may not have been the original mortgagor or debtor or ever have assumed the obligation, the property cannot be sold in a foreclosure sale unless the current owner has had an opportunity to be heard in the foreclosure action. *Burton v Lies* (1862) 21 C 87; *City & County of San Francisco v Lawton* (1861) 18 C 465; *Boggs v Fowler & Hargrave* (1860) 16 C 559. For discussion of compulsory and permissive joinder, see 1 California Civil Procedure Before Trial §§7.12–7.15 (Cal CEB 1977).

If the property is owned in fractional interests, omission of any owner insulates that fractional interest from the foreclosure sale, although the sale is valid as to the interests of owners who are named in the action. See §8.3. When the foreclosure sale is invalid because an indispensable owner has been omitted, CCP §701.680(c) provides that the debtor (1) may have the sale set aside if the beneficiary is the purchaser and (2) may recover damages for the impropriety. Early case law, however, held the sale absolutely invalid as to the omitted interest, and the debtor can still probably have the sale set aside regardless of the purchaser's identity. *Goodenow v Ewer* (1860) 16 C 461, 469. The predecessor code section to CCP §701.680 (former CCP §708) also provided that the frustrated bidder at such a sale could recover the purchase price from the foreclosing creditor, and this remedy is probably still available when the sale is set aside because an essential party was not before the court. The purchaser, having acquired some interest in the property because other trustor-owners were included in the action, may alternatively bring a second foreclosure action against the omitted trustor because the lien of the mortgage was not extinguished as to that trustor. *Burns v Hiatt* (1906) 149 C 617, 87 P 196; *Hagan v Gardner* (9th Cir 1960) 283 F2d 643; *Tutt v Van Voast* (1939) 36 CA2d 282, 97 P2d 869.

There is no reason to name as a defendant any mortgagor or trustor who no longer owns the property, unless a deficiency judgment is being sought against him or her. *Hutchison v Barr* (1920) 183 C 182, 190 P 799; *San Diego Realty Co. v Hill* (1914) 168 C 637, 143 P 1021. Intermediate owners who did not assume the debt and do not currently own an interest in the real property need not be named as defendants because they are not personally liable. See *Johnson v Home Owners' Loan Corp.* (1941) 46 CA2d 546, 116 P2d 167 (present grantee who takes subject to mortgage is necessary party; grantee who has transferred his or her interest is proper, but not necessary, party). Former owners who have signed the note or assumed the debt can be held liable for a deficiency, and they should therefore be included as defendants if the action seeks a deficiency judgment. *Braun v Crew* (1920) 183 C 728, 192 P 531; *Robson v O'Toole* (1923) 60 CA 710, 214 P 278; *Robson v O'Toole* (1919) 45 CA 63, 187 P 110.

b. Holders of Other Interests in Property

§3.16   (1) Tenants

Tenants whose leases are *prior* to the deed of trust need not be included as parties in a foreclosure action, because their leaseholds are not affected by elimination of the mortgagor's reversionary interest. See §5.38; California Residential Landlord-Tenant Practice §6.48 (Cal CEB 1986). For discussion of compulsory and permissive joinder rules, see 1 California Civil Procedure Before Trial §§7.12–7.15 (Cal CEB 1977). Tenants whose leases are subordinate to the deed of trust are probably proper defendants (CCP §379) in a judicial foreclosure action and should be named as defendants if the foreclosing creditor wishes to terminate their leases.

It is not clear whether tenants whose interests are subordinate to the deed of trust are subject to compulsory joinder requirements under CCP §389. Because they hold real property interests that will be extinguished by foreclosure, most states hold them to be necessary parties. See Nelson & Whitman, Real Estate Finance Law §7.12 (2d ed 1985). See also *Sullivan v Superior Court* (1921) 185 C 133, 195 P 1061 (dictum that tenant entitled to surplus from foreclosure sale and to statutory redemption). In CC §2924b, the legislature has required that copies of the notice of sale and notice of default be mailed to such tenants, seemingly regarding them as parties who must be joined. In *McDermott v Burke* (1860) 16 C 580, the court appears to have held to the contrary, but the opinion probably refers only to tenants who acquire an interest in the mortgaged property after a foreclosure action has been filed. On tenants' rights following foreclosure, see §§5.34–5.41.

§3.17 (2) Purchasers Under Installment Land Sale Contracts

Persons who have recorded installment land sale contracts (see §1.35) (and purchasers under unrecorded contracts who are known to the beneficiary) should be named as defendants in the foreclosure action to eliminate their equitable ownership interests in the property. See *Perry v O'Donnell* (9th Cir 1984) 749 F2d 1346; *Wienke v Smith* (1918) 179 C 220, 176 P 42; *Fish v Fowlie* (1881) 58 C 373. See §3.19 on unrecorded interests.

§3.18 (3) Persons Acquiring Interests After Complaint Filed

Persons who acquire an interest in the property after commencement of a judicial foreclosure action need not be joined as defendants as long as the plaintiff records and serves a lis pendens immediately on filing the complaint. The lis pendens binds such persons as effectively as if they had been joined in the action. CCP §§409, 1908(a)(2); see §§3.45–3.46; California Lis Pendens Practice §1.3 (Cal CEB 1983).

§3.19 (4) Unrecorded Interests

Persons with unrecorded interests in the property need not be named as defendants and are nevertheless bound by the judgment as if they had been included. CCP §726. Courts have read CCP §726 so literally as to excuse the omission even of successors to the original owners whose unrecorded interests were known to the foreclosing mortgagee. *Redondo Improvement Co. v O' Shaughnessy* (1914) 168 C 323, 143 P 538; *Hager v Astorg* (1904) 145 C 548, 79 P 68; *Hibernia Sav. & Loan Soc'y v Cochran* (1904) 141 C 653, 75 P 315; *Johnson v Home Owners' Loan Corp.* (1941) 46 CA2d 546, 116 P2d 167. Despite the rule in CCP §726, it is better practice to name all persons known to have interests in the property to be sure that their interests are eliminated. In light of cases such as *Sniadach v Family Fin. Corp.* (1969) 395 US 337 and *Randone v Appellate Dep't* (1971) 5 C3d 536, 96 CR 709, the continued vitality of a rule that an interest in property may be foreclosed without notice to its holder may be open to question.

§3.20   (5) Adverse Owners

Persons who own interests in the property that are not subject to the mortgage or deed of trust should not be included in the foreclosure action. *Cody v Bean* (1892) 93 C 578, 29 P 223; *Ord v Bartlett* (1890) 83 C 428, 23 P 705. If two or more persons own individual interests in the property and fewer than all the co-owners executed the mortgage or deed of trust, the nonsigning co-owners need not be named in the complaint because the decree and sale will not affect their interests. *Hoppe v Hoppe* (1894) 104 C 94, 37 P 894. If the security consists of a leasehold interest in the property, the lessor need not be included in the action unless the lessor's reversionary interest has been subordinated to the mortgage or deed of trust. See *Matthews v Hinton* (1965) 234 CA2d 736, 44 CR 692. Although a foreclosure action is generally not an appropriate action in which to try title, if an adverse claimant who has been named as a defendant elects to have the issue determined, the court may resolve the conflicting claims in the foreclosure action. *Beronio v Ventura County Lumber Co.* (1900) 129 C 232, 61 P 958; see *Cady v Purser* (1901) 131 C 552, 63 P 844. See also *Williams v Cooper* (1899) 124 C 666, 57 P 577.

(6) Other Lienors
§3.21   (a) Senior Lienors

A foreclosure action has no effect on liens that are senior to the lien being foreclosed. Therefore, senior lienors need not be joined as defendants in the foreclosure action. A senior lienor is a proper party, however, if named as a defendant, and may cross-complain to foreclose the superior lien if it is otherwise due or in default. *Van Loben Sels v Bunnell* (1901) 131 C 489, 63 P 773. If the senior lien is due, and the senior lienor cross-complains, the judgment may then provide that the sale should be conducted to satisfy both liens. When there is disagreement about the priority of the liens involved, the foreclosure action is an appropriate vehicle to resolve it. See §3.4. Joining a senior lienor may also be appropriate to resolve conflicting claims of priority over rents and profits from the property. On rents and profits, see chap 5.

§3.22   (b) United States or State of California as Lien Claimant

The United States should be made a defendant in the foreclosure action when the federal government claims a mortgage or other lien on the property junior to the lien being foreclosed. In such a case, the complaint must specify the details regarding the liens to be affected by the foreclosure. 28 USC §2410.

The State of California should be joined as a defendant if it holds a junior lien on the property. CC §2931a; see *Wayland v State Dep't of Employment* (1958) 161 CA2d 679, 326 P2d 954.

§3.23   (c) Junior Lienors

Junior lienors of record should be named as defendants in a foreclosure action in order to cut off their liens and terminate their rights to reinstate the loan and to redeem the property from the senior lien under CC §§2903–2905 and 2924c. Under former CCP §701, junior lienors also had the right to redeem the property after a judicial foreclosure sale, and, under former CCP §703, junior liens reattached to the property on postsale redemption by the debtor. Under CCP §§701.630 and 729.080(e), however, junior liens are extinguished by a senior foreclosure sale, do not have postsale redemption rights, and do not reattach on redemption by the debtor. For further discussion, see Dyer, *Judicial Foreclosure After the Revised Enforcement of Judgments Act,* 6 CEB Real Prop L Rep 53, 56 (Apr. 1983).

§3.24   (d) Effect of Omitting Junior Lienor

When a junior lienholder has been omitted from the senior foreclosure action and sale, the property remains subject to the junior lien and the termination of rights discussed in §3.23 does not occur. *Fox v California Title Ins. Co.* (1932) 120 CA 264, 7 P2d 722; *Carpentier v Brenham* (1870) 40 C 221. The foreclosure and sale are not void but are invalid as far as the junior lien is concerned. *Carpentier v Brenham, supra.* The purchaser at such a defective foreclosure sale has two choices: to acknowledge the defect and pay off the junior lien or to act as if he or she has purchased the senior lien (rather than the property) at the sale. As assignee of the senior lien, the purchaser may bring a separate foreclosure action against the junior and insist that the junior either pay off the senior lien or lose the right to redeem the property under CC §§2903–2905 and 2924c. This second foreclosure action against the junior will not include the original mortgagor (whose interest in the property was terminated by the first foreclosure and sale) and will be a "strict" foreclosure because there is nothing left to sell. *Goodenow v Ewer* (1860) 16 C 461.

The omitted junior should be placed as nearly as possible in the same position (*i.e.,* with the same remedies) as if the senior had not foreclosed. The junior retains redemption rights under CC §§2903–2905 and 2924c. The junior may also elect to foreclose the junior lien, but must do so as a junior lienholder; omitting the junior from the foreclosure action does not alter the parties' respective priorities.

Either the foreclosure sale purchaser or the omitted junior may elect to act first. If the omitted junior believes that the property is worth more than the senior debt, the junior should offer to pay off the senior debt and then foreclose. If the property is worth less than the senior debt, there is no reason for the junior to take any action; the junior has not been prejudiced by the omission from the senior's foreclosure action. The junior may, however, be compelled to bring a foreclosure action to obtain a deficiency judgment because the lien has not been eliminated and the junior cannot sue for a deficiency as a "sold-out" junior (see §4.31).

The foreclosure sale purchaser must take some action to eliminate the omitted junior lien. If the property is worth less than the combined amounts of the junior and senior liens, the purchaser should foreclose against the junior in a separate action. Only if the purchaser believes the property to be worth more than both debts should he or she offer to pay off the junior debt instead and keep the property.

§3.25   c. Persons Liable for Deficiency Judgment

All persons who may be liable for a deficiency judgment should be named as defendants to avoid defenses based on their exclusion. *Hubbard v University Bank* (1899) 125 C 684, 58 P 297; *Craiglow v Williams* (1920) 45 CA 514, 188 P 76. See also *White v Schader* (1921) 185 C 606, 198 P 19. Guarantors (see §§8.9–8.18), endorsers (see §8.19), and former property owners who either originally executed the note or subsequently assumed it should be named as defendants if a deficiency is to be sought against them.

§3.26   d. Trustee as Defendant

The trustee may bring the foreclosure action as plaintiff. If the beneficiary brings the action, the trustee may either be named as a defendant or be omitted entirely. *Field v Acres* (1937) 9 C2d 110, 69 P2d 422. Although joinder of the trustee is not compulsory (CCP §389), the trustee may be joined as a defendant. *Carpenter v Title Ins. & Trust Co.* (1945) 71 CA2d 593, 163 P2d 73. See also *Churchill v Woodworth* (1906) 148 C 669, 84 P 155. On rules for compulsory and permissive joinder of defendants, see 1 California Civil Procedure Before Trial §§7.12–7.15 (Cal CEB 1977). If some affirmative relief is sought against the trustee, it should definitely be named.

If the trustee is named only as a nominal defendant, the trustee should be served and the plaintiff's attorney should prepare a notice of appearance to be signed by the trustee, stating that the trustee's default may be taken subject to the condition that no monetary or other relief will be sought against the trustee.

3. Death or Incompetency of Beneficiary or Trustor

§3.27   a. Beneficiary

If the beneficiary is deceased, the representative of the estate chooses and pursues the remedy on default in the name of the representative alone. *Fox v Tay* (1890) 89 C 339, 24 P 855. In the case of an incompetent, the foreclosure action is brought in the name of the ward by his or her conservator. *Dixon v Cardozo* (1895) 106 C 506, 39 P 857. For discussion of the powers of representatives and conservators in dealing with the parties' interests under mortgages and deeds of trust, see 1 California Decedent Estate Practice, chap 10 (Cal CEB 1986); 3 California Decedent Estate Practice, chaps 23, 33 (Cal CEB 1987); 2 Bowman, Ogden's Revised California Real Property Law, chap 29 (TI Corp-CEB 1975).

§3.28 b. Trustor

When a judicial foreclosure action is commenced after the death of the trustor, a representative must be appointed for the estate and made a defendant. Prob C §573. Minor and incompetent defendants not having a general guardian or conservator must be represented by a guardian ad litem. CCP §372; see generally 2 Bowman, Ogden's Revised California Real Property Law, chap 29 (TI Corp-CEB 1975).

III. COMPLAINT FOR FORECLOSURE
§3.29 A. Necessary Allegations

A complaint for judicial foreclosure must contain the following allegations:

■ That the promissory note or other obligation was executed and delivered and, if applicable, assumed. See §§3.31, 3.35.

■ That the mortgage or deed of trust securing the original obligation was executed and delivered. The date of recordation should be alleged to establish priority over subsequent liens. See §3.32.

■ The plaintiff's status as payee, mortgagee, beneficiary, or assignee. If the plaintiff is an assignee, the facts of the assignment should be alleged. See §3.34.

■ The event entitling the plaintiff to bring the action. Most notes contain an acceleration clause that permits the mortgagee or beneficiary to declare the entire principal sum due in the event of default, which should be pleaded along with the fact that the plaintiff elected to accelerate. See §§3.37–3.40.

■ The interests of other defendants. See §3.36.

■ That the plaintiff is entitled to a lien for attorneys' fees and other expenses, if provided for in the mortgage or deed of trust. See §3.42.

For further discussion of the elements of an action for judicial foreclosure, see 5 Witkin, California Procedure, *Pleading* §§627–630 (3d ed 1985). For discussion of the formal aspects of drafting a complaint, see 1 California Civil Procedure Before Trial §§7.16–7.41 (Cal CEB 1977).

B. Form: Complaint for Foreclosure
§3.30   1. Introductory Allegations

Copies: Original (filed with court clerk with proof of service); copies for service (one for each attorney of record and unrepresented party); office copies.

_ _[*Name, address, telephone*]_ _
Attorney for plaintiff(s)

[*Title of court*]

[*Title of case*]   **No.** _ _ _ _ _ _

**COMPLAINT FOR
FORECLOSURE OF
DEED OF TRUST**

Plaintiff alleges:

1. _ _[*State capacity, corporate or otherwise, of plaintiff(s)*]_ _.

2. _ _[*State identity and capacity of named defendant(s)*]_ _.

3. **Plaintiff does not know the true names of defendants sued as Doe 1 through Doe _ _[*number of fictitiously named defendants*]_ _. Each of the defendants sued as Doe 1 through Doe _ _ has, or claims to have, some interest in the property subject to the deed of trust described in paragraph _ _, which is subsequent to and subject to the lien of the deed of trust.**

[Continue as follows, if appropriate]

[4.] Defendant, _ _[name]_ _, is the trustee named in the deed of trust described in paragraph _ _ and is made a party for the purpose of having all interested parties appear before the Court.

Comment: Either the beneficiary or the trustee may bring the action to foreclose. CCP §725a. See §3.28 on naming the trustee as a plaintiff or defendant.

The complaint must state a cause of action against each fictitiously named defendant. This may be done either in the fictitious-name paragraph or in the paragraph containing the particular charging allegation. For example, in the case of unknown guarantors or assuming grantees who might be liable for a deficiency judgment, the Doe defendants could be designated as such in the paragraph alleging liability of a guarantor or assuming grantee. See §3.28. For discussion of fictitious defendants, see 1 California Civil Procedure Before Trial §§7.19–7.20 (Cal CEB 1977).

§3.31   2. Execution of Note

[5.] On _ _[date]_ _, for valuable consideration, defendant, _ _[name]_ _, made, executed, and delivered to plaintiff, _ _[name]_ _, _ _[his/her]_ _ written promissory note in the amount of $ _ _ _ _ _ _. A copy of the note is attached as Exhibit _ _ and incorporated in this complaint.

Comment: This allegation assumes that the deed of trust being foreclosed secures a promissory note. Technically, only an obligation is necessary (see §1.10), and the obligation need not be evidenced by a writing except as required by the statute of frauds (CC §1624(f)). The writing evidencing the obligation may be in a form other than a note. See §2.1. When a deed absolute has been used as a hidden mortgage, the defendant (grantee) may maintain that there is no obligation and that the cash given by the plaintiff was payment of the purchase price rather than a loan of funds (see §4.35).

§3.32   3. Execution of Deed of Trust

[6.] To secure payment of the principal sum and interest as provided in the promissory note, and as part of the same transac-

tion, defendant, _ _[name] _ _, made, executed, and delivered to plaintiff, as beneficiary, a deed of trust dated _ _ _ _ _ _, by the terms of which defendant, _ _[name] _ _, as trustor, conveyed to _ _[name] _ _, as trustee, real property in _ _ _ _ _ _ _ _ County, California.

The deed of trust was acknowledged on _ _[date] _ _, and recorded on _ _[date] _ _, in Book No. _ _ at page _ _ of the Official Records of _ _ _ _ _ _ _ _ County, California.

A copy of the deed of trust, marked Exhibit _ _, is attached and incorporated in this complaint.

Comment: If the security instrument is a mortgage instead of a deed of trust, the drafter of the complaint should make appropriate changes in terminology. The wording of the instrument need not be included verbatim. Both mortgages and deeds of trust are proper subjects for judicial foreclosure. CCP §725a; *Talcott v Meakin* (1915) 26 CA 293, 146 P 897. The date of recordation is included to establish priority. If a copy of the security instrument is attached as an exhibit and incorporated by appropriate language, reference to it in the complaint also constitutes a sufficient description of the property. *Johnston v McDuffee* (1890) 83 C 30, 23 P 214.

§3.33   4. Alternate Language if Hidden Security Device Used

[6.] As security for the payment of the _ _[note/debt] _ _, defendant, _ _[name] _ _, made, executed, and delivered to plaintiff an instrument captioned _ _ _ _ _ _ _, a copy of which, marked Exhibit _ _, is attached and incorporated in this complaint. This instrument was agreed to by plaintiff and defendant and was intended to operate as a mortgage on real property in _ _ _ _ _ _ _ _ County, California, described as:

[Legal description]

Comment: Foreclosure is the appropriate remedy for hidden security instruments, *i.e.*, documents that do not appear on their faces to be mortgages but serve the same economic function. See §4.35. If an instrument is determined to have been intended to function as a mortgage, it is treated as a mortgage, and the one-action rule (CCP §726; see §4.3) mandates foreclosure. *Kaiser Indus. Corp. v Taylor* (1971) 17 CA3d 346, 94 CR 773. Because such instruments almost by necessity omit a power-of-sale clause, judicial foreclosure is necessary unless the underlying security is worthless. *Kaiser Indus. Corp. v Taylor, supra*; see §4.6. The appropriate procedure is for the creditor to bring an action to have the instrument declared to be a mortgage and simultaneously foreclosed as such. The most common kinds of hidden mortgages are deeds absolute and covenants not to convey. *Coast Bank v Minderhout* (1964) 61 C2d 311, 38 CR 505, disapproved on other grounds in 21 C3d 953; *Keese v Beardsley* (1923) 190 C 465, 213 P 500; *Vance v Gilbert* (1918) 178 C 574, 174 P 42; *Russell v Zink* (1939) 32 CA2d 566, 90 P2d 360. But see *Tahoe Nat' l Bank v Phillips* (1971) 4 C3d 11, 92 CR 704; *Orange County Teachers Credit Union v Peppard* (1971) 21 CA3d 448, 98 CR 533.

§3.34   5. Plaintiff's Ownership of Note and Beneficial Interest

[*Choose appropriate paragraph*]

[*Either*]

[7.] Plaintiff is now, and at all times material to this action was, the lawful owner and holder of the promissory note and beneficial interest under the deed of trust.

[*Or*]

[7.] On _ _[*date*]_ _, the note and beneficial interest in the deed of trust were assigned _ _[*and endorsed over*]_ _ to plaintiff. A copy of the assignment, marked Exhibit _ _, is attached and incorporated in this complaint. Plaintiff is now and at all times since _ _[*date of assignment*]_ _, has been the lawful owner and holder of the promissory note and beneficial interest in the deed of trust.

§3.35   6. Interest of Guarantors, Endorsers, or Assuming Grantees

[8.] On _ _[*date*]_ _, defendant, _ _[*name*]_ _, _ _[*guaranteed/endorsed/assumed*]_ _ the promissory note. A copy of the _ _[*guaranty/endorsement/assumption agreement*]_ _, marked Exhibit _ _, is attached and incorporated in this complaint.

Comment: If a deficiency judgment is sought against a guarantor, endorser, or assuming grantee, the complaint must contain an allegation justifying naming that person as defendant. An assumption agreement must be in writing. CC §1624(f). In the paragraph demanding a deficiency, the prayer should also include any defendant sued as guarantor, endorser, or assuming grantee. For discussion of guarantors, endorsers, and assuming grantees, see §§8.9–8.27.

§3.36   7. Interest of Other Defendants

[9.] Defendant, _ _[*name*]_ _, has, or claims to have, some interest in the real property or some part of it. Among defendant _ _[*name*]_ _'s claims are those asserted by reason of _ _[*list claims in detail*]_ _, which are subsequent to and subject to the lien of plaintiff's deed of trust.

Comment: Holders of recorded subordinate interests in the property must be named as defendants to terminate their presale reinstatement and redemption rights. See §3.23. Included in this category are holders of junior judgment liens, purchasers under recorded contracts of sale, and tenants under recorded leases. See §§3.16–3.24. If there are multiple claimants to the property with different types of claims, separate paragraphs should be used for each type of claim.

§3.37   8. Right of Acceleration on Default

[10.] The promissory note (Exhibit _ _) provides that, if the payor defaults in payment of any installment when due, or in the performance of any agreement in the deed of trust securing payment of the note, the entire principal and interest will become immediately payable and due at the option of the noteholder.

The deed of trust provides that, if the trustor defaults in the payment of any indebtedness secured by the deed of trust, or in the performance of any agreement in the note or deed of trust, the entire principal and interest secured by the deed of trust will, at the option of the beneficiary, become immediately due and payable.

Comment: If neither the note nor the deed of trust contains a clause accelerating an installment obligation on default, the beneficiary must rely on CCP §728, which provides that, if property cannot be sold in portions, without injury to the parties, then all of it may be ordered sold and the entire debt paid off in a foreclosure action. *Yoakam v White* (1893) 97 C 286, 32 P 238. If the property is severable, the foreclosure sale must cease as soon as there is a bid sufficient to cover the installments unpaid as of the date of the foreclosure decree. *Bank of Napa v Godfrey* (1888) 77 C 612, 20 P 142; *Hunt v Dohrs* (1870) 39 C 304. After that sale, the beneficiary may conduct further foreclosure sales to cover later unpaid installments, either by making supplementary motions in the same action (*Byrne v Hoag* (1899) 126 C 283, 58 P 688), as provided in the original decree (*Bank of Napa v Godfrey, supra*), or by filing periodic, successive foreclosure actions (*Higgins v San Diego Sav. Bank* (1900) 129 C 184, 61 P 943; *McDougal v Downey* (1872) 45 C 165; *Zingheim v Marshall* (1967) 249 CA2d 736, 57 CR 809). See also *Furesz v Garcia* (1981) 120 CA3d 793, 174 CR 803 (beneficiary may elect not to enforce acceleration clause and conduct piecemeal foreclosure (dictum)). See §§7.2–7.6 for discussion of acceleration clauses.

§3.38   9. Default in Loan Payments

[11.] **By the terms of the promissory note (Exhibit _ _), defendant, _ _[name] _ _, promised and agreed to pay to plaintiff monthly installment payments of $_ _ _ _ _ _, principal and interest, on the _ _ _ day of each month beginning _ _[date] _ _. Defendant has wholly failed, neglected, and refused to make payment of $_ _ _ _ _ _, principal and interest, due on _ _[date] _ _, and subsequent months, up to and including _ _[date] _ _. The total of the monthly payments in default is $_ _ _ _ _ _. For such failure and default, plaintiff has exercised _ _[his/her/its] _ _ option and elected to declare the entire sum of principal and interest immediately due and payable. The total amount due consists of the principal sum of $_ _ _ _ _ _, plus annual interest from _ _[date] _ _, to _ _[date] _ _, at _ _ percent. Interest on $_ _ _ _ _ _ amounts to $_ _ _ _ _ _ per day for each additional day from _ _[date] _ _, to the date of entry of judgment in this action.**

Comment: This paragraph assumes that the action is based on an installment note containing an acceleration clause. If a single payment note, or a note on which the obligation has matured, is involved, the references to acceleration can be omitted. If the note is an installment note without an acceleration clause, but the property cannot be sold in portions, allegations conforming to CCP §728 should be used to overcome the omission of a contract right to accelerate. See §3.37.

§3.39   10. Default in Payment of Taxes

[12.] By the terms of the deed of trust (Exhibit _ _), defendant, _ _[name]_ _, promised and agreed to pay, at least _ _ _ days before delinquency, all general and special city and county taxes affecting the real property described in the deed of trust. Defendant, _ _[name]_ _, has failed and refused to pay _ _[describe unpaid taxes]_ _, and because of this default the real property was sold on _ _[date]_ _, to the State of California. The total amount now in default and delinquent, including the redemption fee and penalties, is $_ _ _ _ _ _, which is the total amount necessary to redeem as of the date on which this complaint is filed.

Comment: For discussion of the trustor's obligation to pay taxes on the property, see §7.35.

§3.40   11. Default in Payment of Insurance

[13.] By the terms of the deed of trust (Exhibit _ _), defendant, _ _[name]_ _, promised and agreed to provide and to maintain in force at all times fire, earthquake, and other insurance, each in an amount satisfactory to and with loss payable to _ _[name]_ _. Since _ _[date]_ _, defendant has failed and refused to renew and to maintain in force fire, earthquake, and other insurance. Because of defendant's failure and refusal to pay the premium on the insurance policies at the time of renewal, plaintiff has been required to pay, and has paid, the premiums on the insurance policies to keep the real property described in the deed of trust and the building on it insured at all times. The payments were made on the following dates and in the following amounts:

[*State dates of payments, amounts paid, and
periods covered*]

By the terms of the deed of trust, when plaintiff is required to make such payments because of the failure and refusal of defendant to pay the premiums on the insurance policies, the amounts paid by plaintiff will be charged to the principal due on the note secured by the deed of trust. The sum of $_ _ _ _ _ _, representing plaintiff's payments on the insurance policies, is not included in, but is in addition to, the principal sum due on the note (see paragraph _ _).

Comment: For discussion of the trustor's obligation under the deed of trust to pay insurance premiums, see §§7.26–7.27.

§3.41　　12. Future Sums To Protect Security

[14.] Plaintiff may hereafter be required to expend additional sums to protect _ _[his/her/its]_ _ security in the property described in the deed of trust. In the deed of trust (Exhibit _ _), defendant(s), _ _[names of any defendants personally liable]_ _, agreed to pay any such sums expended by plaintiff. Plaintiff will amend this complaint to allege the nature and amounts of such sums if plaintiff is required to make such additional expenditures.

Comment: For discussion of the beneficiary's right to reimbursement for sums expended to protect the security, see §7.37.

§3.42　　13. Payment of Attorneys' Fees

[15.] By the provisions of the promissory note (Exhibit _ _) and the deed of trust (Exhibit _ _), defendant, _ _[name]_ _, agreed that, if any action were instituted on the note or deed of trust, defendant would pay the sum fixed by the Court as plaintiff's attorneys' fees, and that these charges would also become a lien on the real property. Because of defendant's defaults, it has become necessary for plaintiff to employ an attorney to commence and prosecute this foreclosure action. The reasonable value of services of counsel in this action _ _[is $_ _ _ _ _ _ /should be determined by the Court at the time of trial]_ _ .

Comment: For discussion of the beneficiary's right to attorneys' fees, see §§7.29–7.33.

§3.43 14. Demand for Judgment (Prayer)

WHEREFORE, plaintiff demands judgment as follows:

1. That the Court order judgment against defendant, _ _[name] _ _, for:

a. The sum of $_ _ _ _ _ _ principal, together with interest from _ _[date] _ _, to _ _[date] _ _, at the annual rate of _ _ percent as provided in the note, amounting to $_ _ _ _ _ _, making a combined total, principal and interest, of $_ _ _ _ _ _, together with interest at the rate of $_ _ _ _ _ _ per day from _ _[date] _ _, to the date of entry of judgment;

b. _ _[Specify any amounts expended, plus interest, and desired relief for any other default alleged in the complaint] _ _;

c. Costs of this action and attorneys' fees that the Court considers reasonable; and

d. Additional sums, if any, that plaintiff hereafter expends to protect its security interest in the property described in the deed of trust, together with interest at the annual rate of _ _ percent, according to proof.

2. That the Court enter its judgment determining that the rights, claims, ownership, liens, titles, and demands of defendant(s) _ _[name(s)] _ _ are subject, subsequent, and subordinate to plaintiff's deed of trust.

3. That the Court order that the deed of trust (Exhibit _ _) be foreclosed and that judgment be entered for sale of the premises, according to law, by the Sheriff of _ _ _ _ _ _ _ _ County or a receiver to be appointed by the Court; that the proceeds of the sale be applied in payment of the amounts due to plaintiff; and that defendant, _ _[name] _ _, and all persons claiming under _ _[him/her/it] _ _ subsequent to the execution of plaintiff's deed of trust, as lien claimants, judgment creditors, claimants under a junior deed of trust, purchasers, encumbrancers, or otherwise, be barred and foreclosed from all rights, claims, interests, or equity of redemption in the premises when time for redemption has elapsed.

4. That the Court award plaintiff judgment and execution a-gainst defendant, _ _[name]_ _, for any deficiency that may remain after applying all the proceeds of the sale of premises properly applicable to the satisfaction of the amounts found due by the Court under paragraph 1 of this demand for judgment.

5. That the Court permit plaintiff or any other party to this action to become a purchaser at the foreclosure sale, that _ _[when *the time for redemption has elapsed*]_ _ **the Sheriff or receiver execute a deed to the purchaser of the property at the sale, and that the purchaser be let into possession of the property on production of the Sheriff's or receiver's deed.**

6. That the Court award all other appropriate relief.

Dated: _ _ _ _ _ _

> ___[*Signature of attorney*]___
> _ _[*Typed name*]_ _
> **Attorney for** _ _[*name*]_ _

Comment: The demand for monetary relief in the judgment should be for the entire unpaid principal plus accrued interest. Attorneys' fees and costs are customarily set by the court at or after entry of judgment. See *Monroe v Fohl* (1887) 72 C 568, 14 P 514. See generally 2 California Civil Procedure During Trial, chap 22 (Cal CEB 1984); California Attorney's Fees Award Practice, chaps 5–6 (Cal CEB 1982). Attorneys' fees are authorized by CCP §730.

To terminate the interests of additional defendants, the request for a sale foreclosing the trustor's interest (see ¶3) should be expanded. See §§3.17–3.24.

The request for a deficiency judgment (see ¶4) should also be expanded, if appropriate, to include other defendants who may be liable for a deficiency. See §3.25. If no deficiency judgment is sought, the attorney should consider attempting to eliminate the redemption period by inserting a statement in the prayer that a deficiency judgment is waived. There is no need, however, to waive the right to a deficiency judgment at the time the complaint is filed. The plaintiff can also attempt to waive a deficiency judgment by making a full credit-bid at the sale. CCP §§726(e), 716.020, 729.010–729.090. For discussion of waiver of the redemption period, see §3.73; Dyer, *Judicial Foreclosure After the Revised Enforcement of Judgments Act,* 6 CEB Real Prop L Rep 53, 56 (Apr. 1983).

§3.44   C. Receivers

Foreclosure complaints often contain additional causes of action for specific performance of a rents-and-profits clause and for appointment of a receiver to collect the rents and profits. See §§5.12–5.18.

§3.45   D. Lis Pendens

Immediately on filing the complaint, the plaintiff should record a notice of action pending (lis pendens) in the same county. On lis pendens generally, see California Lis Pendens Practice (Cal CEB 1983). A lis pendens, once recorded and served, imparts constructive notice of the legal action underlying it and thus binds subsequent purchasers or encumbrancers to any judgment eventually entered in the action. CCP §409; see *Albertson v Raboff* (1956) 46 C2d 375, 295 P2d 405. If the lis pendens names all the parties to the foreclosure action and has been properly recorded, subsequent owners and junior lienors will be bound by the judgment and their interests will be terminated by the foreclosure sale. *Dobbins v Economic Gas Co.* (1920) 182 C 616, 189 P 1073; *Hibernia Sav. & Loan Soc'y v Cochran* (1904) 141 C 653, 75 P 315; *Johnson v Friant* (1903) 140 C 260, 73 P 993; *McNamara v Oakland Bldg. & Loan Ass'n* (1901) 132 C 247, 64 P 277. If no lis pendens has been recorded, these persons still take subject to the mortgage or deed of trust if it was recorded, but they are not affected by the foreclosure action. A new foreclosure action must be brought against them. See *Carpenter v Lewis* (1897) 119 C 18, 50 P 925.

A trustor who merely answers the judicial foreclosure complaint is not entitled to record a lis pendens, even when appealing from a foreclosure judgment, because the trustor retains no interest that could be the subject of a lis pendens. Under CCP §409, a party must have filed a complaint or cross-complaint to be entitled to record a lis pendens. *Arrow Sand & Gravel, Inc. v Superior Court* (1985) 38 C3d 884, 215 CR 288.

§3.46   E. Form: Lis Pendens

Copies: Original (filed with county recorder); duplicate originals to record if property is situated in more than one county; copies for service (one for each attorney of record and unrepresented party); office copies.

Recording Requested By	)
	)
	)
	)
After Recording Return To	)
	)
	)
	) (Space above this line for recorder's use)

[*Title of court*]

[*Title of case*]   **No.** _ _ _ _ _ _

NOTICE OF ACTION PENDING
_ _[*(CCP §409)/(OTHER STATUTE(S) AS APPROPRIATE)*] _ _

PLEASE TAKE NOTICE that this action was commenced on _ _[*date*]_ _, **by** _ _[*specify all plaintiffs*] _ _, **plaintiff(s), against** _ _[*specify all defendants*] _ _, **defendant(s), and is now pending in the above-entitled Court.**

Plaintiff(s) seek(s) relief in this action affecting _ _[*title to/the right to possession of*] _ _ **real property located in** _ _ _ _ _ _ _ _ **County, California, known as** _ _[*state street address or other designation*] _ _, **and described as follows:**

[*Legal description*]

The object of the _ _[*action/cross-action*] _ _ **is** _ _[*briefly describe nature of causes of action concerning real property in complaint or cross-complaint*] _ _.

Dated: _ _ _ _ _ _

> ___*[Signature of attorney]*___
> _ _*[Typed name]*_ _
> **Attorney for** _ _*[name]*_ _

[Acknowledgment, if required by local recorder]

Comment: The rules governing preparation, recording, and service of a notice of action pending (lis pendens) are contained in CCP §§409–409.7. For extensive discussion of lis pendens requirements, see California Lis Pendens Practice (Cal CEB 1983). The caption of the lis pendens must include the full names of all defendants; merely listing the first defendant, followed by "et al.," is not sufficient. The lis pendens gives notice of the pendency of the action only against parties designated by their real names. CCP §409; see Lis Pendens §2.13. The lis pendens should be recorded on the same day the complaint is filed and must be served on the defendants to be effective. CCP §409(c). Code of Civil Procedure §409 does not require that the notice of lis pendens be acknowledged, but some local recorders impose this requirement. See Lis Pendens §2.22. Under 1984 amendments to CCP §409, a litigant filing an action in propria persona must have the lis pendens issued by the court or obtain a certificate from the court that the action concerns real property. These additional requirements need not be met if the lis pendens is issued by an attorney of record in the action. CCP §409(b).

IV. DEFENDANTS' RESPONSIVE PLEADINGS

§3.47   A. By Trustor

Any defenses the trustor has to an action on the note (*e.g.*, lack of consideration, illegality) are equally good against an action to foreclose the instrument securing the note. On defenses against enforcement of the note, see §§6.14–6.19. If the note was negotiable, however, defenses against the original creditor may not be effective against a foreclosing creditor who is a holder in due course. See Com C §§3104, 3302, 3305; §§1.18–1.19. Judicial foreclosure actions are governed by a four-year statute of limitations when a written obligation is in default. CC

§2911; CCP §337(1); see §3.11. The statute of limitations may be raised by general demurrer if the defect appears on the face of the complaint (CCP §430.10(e)), or in the answer whether or not the defect appears on the face of the complaint. See *California Safe Deposit & Trust Co. v Sierra Valleys Ry.* (1910) 158 C 690, 698, 112 P 274, 278. The trustor may also have defenses relating solely to the security, *e.g.,* a denial of the allegation that the obligation is secured. Such a defense may be available when the beneficiary contends that some special instrument (*e.g.,* a covenant not to convey) is a mortgage and the debtor denies it, or when, under a dragnet clause in a deed of trust (see §8.34), the beneficiary contends that the obligation in question is secured and the trustor disagrees.

§3.48   B. By Junior Lienors

Junior creditors may attack the validity of the senior obligations on the same grounds as are available to the trustor (see §3.47), because an improper senior obligation detrimentally affects the juniors' priority. See *Caito v United Cal. Bank* (1978) 20 C3d 694, 702, 144 CR 751, 755; *Valley Title Co. v Parish Egg Basket, Inc.* (1973) 31 CA3d 776, 107 CR 717; *Hayward Lumber & Inv. Co. v Naslund* (1932) 125 CA 34, 13 P2d 775.

Junior lienholders are automatically entitled to the surplus after a foreclosure sale and need do nothing to preserve that right. See CCP §§701.810, 727; *Livingston v Rice* (1955) 131 CA2d 1, 280 P2d 52. It is also appropriate, however, for a junior either to demand the surplus in his or her answer or to cross-complain for foreclosure of the junior debt along with the senior. *Camp v Land* (1898) 122 C 167, 54 P 839. A cross-complaint for foreclosure does not enlarge the junior's rights to the surplus; formerly, a junior's cross-complaint had the effect of cutting off the junior's statutory postsale redemption rights (*San Jose Water Co. v Lyndon* (1899) 124 C 518, 57 P 481), but a junior lienor no longer has such rights (CCP §729.020; see §3.74).

§3.49   C. By Trustee

If the complaint seeks affirmative relief against the trustee, the trustee should file an answer and defend the action. If, as is usually the case, the trustee is named only as a nominal defendant, the trustee should be willing to agree to a formal notice of appearance stating that the trustee's default may be taken on the condition that no relief will be sought against the trustee. See §3.26. The trustee cannot recover costs or attorneys' fees for an unnecessary appearance in the action. *Field v Acres* (1937) 9 C2d 110, 69 P2d 422; see *Carpenter v Title Ins. & Trust Co.* (1945) 71 CA2d 593, 163 P2d 73.

§3.50 D. Defenses to Claims for Deficiency

If the note constituting the basis for the action was executed for a purchase-money loan, a deficiency judgment is not available even if the deed of trust is foreclosed judicially. CCP §580b; see §4.23. Application of CCP §580b should be raised as an affirmative defense; if §580b is not raised, it may be held to have been waived. See *United Cal. Bank v Tijerina* (1972) 25 CA3d 963, 102 CR 234.

When a deficiency judgment is appropriate in the action generally, but has been improperly asserted against a particular defendant, this defect must be raised as an affirmative defense. *Treat v Craig* (1901) 135 C 91, 67 P 7. Defendants who may assert such a defense include a nonassuming grantee (or even an assuming grantee of a nonassuming grantee) (see §§8.21–8.27) and any party initially liable but whose liability has been eliminated by subsequent acts of the parties, *e.g.,* a guarantor or original debtor who has not consented to some alteration of the basic obligation. See *Sumitomo Bank v Iwasaki* (1968) 70 C2d 81, 73 CR 564.

§3.51 E. Reinstatement and Presale Redemption Rights

In addition to the statutory right to redeem following the sale under CCP §§729.010–729.090 (see §§3.73–3.80), the trustor or mortgagor and certain other persons having an interest in the property (1) have a statutory right to reinstate the loan (*i.e.,* to pay the unaccelerated balance due) at any time before the judgment of foreclosure is entered (CC §2924c) and (2) have a codified common law right to redeem the property from the mortgage or deed of trust by paying the full amount due to the foreclosing creditor at any time before the foreclosure sale (CC §§2903–2905).

Under CC §2924c, the trustor or mortgagor (or their successors in interest), a beneficiary under a subordinate deed of trust, or any other person having a subordinate lien or encumbrance of record may cure the default and reinstate the mortgage or deed of trust at any time before entry of the judgment of foreclosure by paying the mortgagee or beneficiary the entire amount that would then be due had there been no default, plus trustees' or attorneys' fees actually incurred, not exceeding $200, plus a decreasing percentage of any unpaid principal sum greater than $50,000. Amendments to CC §2924c(a) (Stats 1981, ch 427) eliminated language requiring that, to be recoverable, the attorneys' fees be "actually incurred." Under *Buck v Barb* (1983) 147 CA3d 920, 195 CR 461, the beneficiary may be able to claim attorneys' fees over the statutory limits. In *Buck,* the court held that the limitation on attorneys' fees in CC §2924c does not apply to fees that a beneficiary claims for "protecting the security," provided the deed of trust contains language authorizing payment of such fees and the notice of default includes a claim for the fees. 147 CA3d at 925, 195 CR at 463. Note, however, that in *Bruntz v Alfaro* (1989) 212 CA3d 411, 260 CR 488, the court held that the trustor's tender to reinstate the debt must include only the attorneys' fees enumerated in CC §2924c(d), even when the beneficiary forecloses judicially and may have already incurred far greater attorneys' fees than the statutory limits.

The common law equity of redemption (*i.e.,* the right to redeem the property from the lien by paying the debt) is codified in CC §§2903–2905. This right, which is terminated by the foreclosure sale, may be exercised by any person having an interest in property subject to the deed of trust. CC §2903. Redemption is made by paying the full amount of the debt plus any damages to which the lienholder is entitled because of the delay. CC §2905.

Federal agencies that have made loans secured by deeds of trust may be subject to state law governing reinstatement and redemption. *U.S. v Ellis* (9th Cir 1983) 714 F2d 953; see §4.46.

V. OBTAINING JUDGMENT
§3.52   A. Trial

It is not uncommon for all the defendants in a judicial foreclosure action to fail to answer. In such a case, their defaults may be entered by the court clerk on the plaintiff's request (CCP §585(b)), and the court then enters a judgment of foreclosure and order of sale (see §3.54). If any of the defendants were served by publication, the clerk cannot enter a default, and an plaintiff must apply to the court in writing for entry of judgment. CCP §585(c). The attorney must, of course, present proof of service on the defendants and an affidavit, as required by the Soldiers' and Sailors' Civil Relief Act of 1940 (50 USC App §§501–585), that the defendants are not serving in the armed services.

If any of the defendants file answers, the court sets the case for trial. On trial-setting generally, see 1 California Civil Procedure Before Trial, chap 3 (Cal CEB 1982). Despite the possibility of a deficiency judgment, the parties are not entitled to a jury trial. *Downing v Le Du* (1890) 82 C 471, 23 P 202; *Van Valkenburgh v Oldham* (1910) 12 CA 572, 108 P 42.

The plaintiff must present the following evidence:

■ The original note;

■ The original mortgage or deed of trust or a certified copy of the recorded mortgage or deed of trust;

■ If the plaintiff is an assignee, the original or a certified copy of the assignment;

■ The written assumption agreement if the defendant is an assuming grantee of the original trustor (CCP §1624(f));

■ A statement of the account, including the date of the original default, the date to which interest is credited, and the unpaid balance of the obligation;

■ Proof of advancements for taxes, insurance, or other expenditures secured by the deed of trust (if applicable); and

■ Proof of the recording date of the deed of trust to prove priority.

If the default consists of a violation of a general covenant in the mortgage or deed of trust (*e.g.*, failure to keep the property in good repair or to cultivate farmland; see §4.40), the plaintiff must present evidence of the breach from witnesses qualified in that field.

If the court finds in favor of the plaintiff on all elements of the case, it enters a judgment of foreclosure and an order of sale, directing either the sheriff or a receiver appointed by the court to sell the real property or as much of it as may be required to satisfy the debt. See §3.54.

As in other contested cases, a statement of decision (see CCP §632) may be requested by any party and will usually be prepared, at the court's direction, by the prevailing party. A statement of decision is not required unless requested by one of the parties within ten days after the court announces a tentative decision. If the trial is concluded within one calendar day or less than eight hours over two days, however, the request must be made before the case is submitted for decision. CCP §632; Cal Rules of Ct 232(b). For discussion, see 2 California Civil Procedure During Trial §§20.16–20.24 (Cal CEB 1984).

§3.53   B. Judgment

The following requirements for a judgment of foreclosure (also referred to, apparently interchangeably, as a "decree" of foreclosure) are set forth in CCP §726:

■ The judgment must direct the sale of all or part of the property and order the sale proceeds applied first to court costs and the expenses of the levy and sale and then to the amount due the plaintiff, including reasonable attorneys' fees if the security instrument provides for them. CCP §726(a).

■ The judgment must appoint either the sheriff or a receiver to sell the property in the manner provided for execution of judgments in CCP §716.020 (deficiency waived or prohibited) or §§729.010–729.090 (deficiency permitted). CCP §726(e); see §§3.55–3.60.

■ The judgment must declare the amount of the indebtedness and either determine the personal liability of any defendant who may be subject to a deficiency judgment or declare that a deficiency judgment is waived or prohibited. CCP §726(b). For discussion of procedures for obtaining a deficiency judgment after the sale, see §§3.67–3.72.

When a deficiency judgment is available and the proceeds of the sale are insufficient to satisfy the indebtedness, on the plaintiff's application made within three months after the sale the court must take evidence and enter a deficiency judgment against the defendants for the amount by which the indebtedness plus interest and costs of sale exceeds the fair value of the property on the date of sale. CCP §726(b). The amount of the deficiency judgment may not exceed the difference between the indebtedness and the sale price. CCP §726(b); see §3.67.

§3.54 C. Form: Judgment of Foreclosure and Order of Sale

Copies: Original (filed with court clerk when signed by judge); copies for service (one for each attorney of record and unrepresented party); office copies.

[*Title of court*]

[*Title of case*]   **No.** _ _ _ _ _ _

**JUDGMENT OF
FORECLOSURE AND
ORDER OF SALE**

The above-entitled case came on regularly for _ _[*trial/default hearing*]_ _**on**_ _[*date*]_ _**. Plaintiff,**_ _[*name*]_ _**, appeared by**_ _[*his/her/ its*]_ _**attorney,**_ _[*name*]_ _**, and defendant,**_ _[*name*]_ _**, appeared by**_ _[_ _[*his/her/its*]_ _*attorney,*_ _[*name*]_ _*,/default*]_ _**. The Court, having heard the testimony and considered the evidence,**_ _[*and having already filed its statement of decision on*_ _[*date*]_ _*,/ makes the following statement of decision:*_ _[*State factual and legal basis for decision; see CCP §632*]_ _*and/and a statement of decision not having been requested,*]_ _**enters its judgment as follows:**

1. Plaintiff is entitled to entry of judgment against defendant on the terms set forth in the following paragraphs.

2. Defendant is indebted to plaintiff in the following sums:

    a. Principal and interest in the amount of $_ _ _ _ _ _**;**

    b. Attorneys' fees in the amount of $_ _ _ _ _ _**;**

    c. Money expended for _ _[*e.g., taxes, insurance*]_ _ **under the terms of the deed of trust, as alleged in the complaint, in the amount of $**_ _ _ _ _ _**; and**

    d. Actual costs of foreclosure and sale.

These amounts are secured by the deed of trust set forth in the complaint.

[Choose appropriate paragraph]

[Either]

3. The real property described in paragraph 9, or as much of it as may be necessary, will be sold in the manner prescribed by law, and the writ of sale will issue to the Sheriff of _ _ _ _ _ _ _ _ County, ordering and directing _ _*[him/her]*_ _ to conduct such sale. Any party to this action may purchase at the sale.

[Or]

3. _ _*[Name]*_ _ is appointed as receiver by this Court to sell the real property described in paragraph 9, or as much of it as may be necessary, in the manner prescribed by law._ _*[He/She]*_ _will swear to perform _ _*[his/her]*_ _ duties according to law and will execute an undertaking in the amount of $_ _ _ _ _ _, with sufficient sureties.

[Continue]

4. From the proceeds of the sale, the _ _*[Sheriff/receiver]*_ _will pay to plaintiff, after deducting costs of Court and the expenses of the levy and sale, the sums adjudged due, together with interest at the annual rate of _ _ percent from the date of this judgment.

5. If any surplus remains after the payments specified in paragraph 2 are made, the surplus will be paid to _ _*[name(s) of person(s) entitled to share in surplus in order of priority]*_ _.

[Choose appropriate paragraph]

[Alternative 1]

6. Defendant, _ _*[name]*_ _, is personally liable for payment of the sums secured by the deed of trust and is a defendant against whom a deficiency judgment may be ordered. The Court retains jurisdiction to determine the amount of the deficiency, if any.

[Alternative 2]

6. Defendant, _ _*[name]*_ _, is not a person against whom a deficiency judgment may be ordered and is not personally liable for payment of the sums secured by the deed of trust.

[Alternative 3]

6. Plaintiff has waived judgment for any deficiency and therefore defendant, _ _[name]_ _, is not personally liable for payment of the sums secured by the deed of trust.

[After Alternative 1, add]

7. After the time allowed by law for redemption has expired, defendant, _ _[name]_ _, will be forever barred from any right of redemption. At that time, the _ _[Sheriff/receiver]_ _ will execute a deed of sale to the purchasers, who may then take possession of the property, if necessary with the assistance of the Sheriff of _ _ _ _ _ _ _ _ County.

[After Alternative 2 or 3, add]

7. On completion of the sale, the _ _[Sheriff/receiver]_ _ will execute a deed of sale to the purchasers, who may then take possession of the property, if necessary with the assistance of the Sheriff of _ _ _ _ _ _ _ _ County.

[Continue]

8. Defendant, _ _[name]_ _, all persons claiming from or under _ _[him/her]_ _, all persons and their personal representatives having liens subsequent to the deed of trust by judgment or decree on the described real property, all persons and their heirs or personal representatives having any lien or claim by or under such subsequent judgment or decree, all persons claiming under them, and all persons claiming to have acquired any estate or interest in the premises after the recording of notice of the pendency of this action with the County Recorder are forever barred and foreclosed from all equity of redemption in and claim to the premises, from and after delivery of the deed by the _ _[Sheriff/receiver]_ _.

9. The property that is the subject of this judgment and order is described as:

[Legal description]

Dated: _ _ _ _ _ _

_____
Judge of the Superior Court

**Entered on _ _[date] _ _, in the Judgment Book, Volume No. _ _
at page _ _.**

_____
**Clerk
By _ _ _ _ _ _ _ _, Deputy**

Comment: The judgment in a foreclosure action must indicate clearly
that foreclosure of the plaintiff's lien has been ordered, set forth the
amounts found to be due the plaintiff, and order the property sold to
satisfy the amount due the plaintiff. *Laubisch v Roberdo* (1954) 43 C2d
702, 277 P2d 9; *Sichler v Look* (1892) 93 C 600, 29 P 220.

Paragraph 6 of the form presents options for the attorney drafting
the judgment for the foreclosing creditor. The creditor must decide
whether it is willing to risk redemption and a redemption period, which
are the costs of seeking a deficiency judgment. There is a redemption
period (of either three months or one year; see §3.76), regardless of the
amount realized at the foreclosure sale, whenever a deficiency is not
waived or prohibited.

Paragraph 7 (first alternative) refers to the right of statutory postsale
redemption (CCP §§729.010–729.090), *i.e.*, the right to redeem the
property after the foreclosure sale by paying the purchase price. The
defendant has no right to reinstate the obligation (*i.e.*, to pay the amount
in default) once judgment has been entered. CC §2924c; see §3.51. The
common law equity of redemption, *i.e.*, the right to pay off the entire
debt (referred to in ¶8), ends at the moment of sale. CC §§2903–2905;
see §3.51.

As an alternative to sale by the sheriff, the court may appoint a
receiver to conduct the sale. CCP §712.060. The court apparently must
require a bond of the receiver (CCP §566), whose powers and duties
are established by statutory provisions concerning receivers. See CCP
§§568, 568.5, 708.610–708.620. If the sheriff is ordered to conduct the
sale, no bond is required and the sheriff's fees are prescribed by law.
See Govt C §26730. The court must determine the appropriate award
of attorneys' fees regardless of any contrary provision in the security
instrument. CCP §730.

VI. SALE

§3.55   A. Intermediate Steps Between Judgment and Sale

The foreclosure sale is conducted in the manner provided in the Enforcement of Judgments Law (CCP §§680.010–724.260). If a deficiency judgment is waived or prohibited, the property is sold as provided in CCP §716.020. If a deficiency is not waived or prohibited, the property is sold subject to the debtor's right of redemption as provided in CCP §§729.010–729.090. CCP §726(e).

Whether a deficiency judgment is available (and thus whether the mortgagor has a right of redemption) also determines the amount of notice that must be given before the property can be sold by the levying officer. If a deficiency judgment has been waived or is prohibited, the debtor must first be given a notice of levy requiring 120 days' notice (CCP §§700.015, 701.545) and then, after the 120-day period has run, a notice of sale giving 20 days' notice (CCP §701.540). Thus, when the debtor has no postsale redemption rights (see §§3.73–3.80), he or she is entitled to 140 days' notice before the foreclosure sale. (During this period, the debtor retains his or her right to redeem the property from the lien under CC §2903. See §3.51.)

If a deficiency judgment is available, the levying officer need not give the debtor 120 days' notice before serving a notice of sale (CCP §729.010(b)(2)), although a notice of levy must still be recorded and served (CCP §§700.015, 729.010(b)(2)). A 20-day notice of sale must also be recorded and served (CCP §701.540), but it may be given immediately on entry of the judgment (CCP §729.010(b)(2)). The provisions of CCP §701.540(h), requiring that the creditor instruct the levying officer, no earlier than 30 days after the notice of levy, to mail notice of sale to lienholders of record, do not apply when the property is being sold subject to a deficiency judgment. CCP §729.010(b)(3). When the deficiency is not waived or prohibited, the debtor has a period within which to redeem the property of either three months (if the proceeds of the sale are sufficient to satisfy the indebtedness; CCP §729.030(a)) or one year (if the proceeds are not sufficient to satisfy the indebtedness; CCP §729.030(b)).

For a useful explanation of the application of the Enforcement of Judgments Law to judicial foreclosure, see Dyer, *Judicial Foreclosure*

After the Revised Enforcement of Judgments Act, 6 CEB Real Prop L Rep 53, 56 (Apr. 1983). For a notice of levy form, see §3.57; for a notice of sale form, see §3.58; for discussion of presale common law redemption rights, see §3.51; for discussion of postsale redemption rights, see §§3.73–3.80.

The plaintiff's first step after judgment is to obtain a writ of sale from the court clerk. CCP §§716.010–716.020, 712.010–712.060. Before enactment of the Enforcement of Judgments Law, the plaintiff apparently had to obtain only a copy of the order directing either the sheriff or the commissioner to conduct the sale. See *Granger v Sheriff* (1903) 140 C 190, 73 P 816.

The levying officer (*i.e.,* the sheriff or receiver appointed by the court) must record the writ of sale and notice of levy and serve the notice on the judgment debtor and any occupant of the property. Requirements for service are specified in CCP §700.015. Time requirements between the notice of levy and notice of sale are discussed above. The levying officer must also give 20 days' notice of the sale. Requirements for serving the notice of sale are set forth in CCP §701.540. In addition to serving the debtor and any occupants of the property (CCP §701.540(c), (e)), the levying officer must post the notice in a public place and on the property (CCP §701.540(d)) and publish the notice in a newspaper of general circulation in accordance with Govt C §6063. CCP §701.540(g). The levying officer must also mail the notice of sale to any person who has filed a request for notice with the clerk of the court that entered the judgment. CCP §701.550.

The sale must be held in the county in which some of the property is located and must be conducted between 9 a.m. and 5 p.m. CCP §701.570(a). Although the deed of trust usually recites that the beneficiary may direct the order of sale if multiple properties are involved, the statute provides that the judgment debtor may request that the sale be conducted in a particular order, and the levying officer may honor this request if, in his or her opinion, the requested manner of sale is likely to yield an amount at least equal to any other manner of sale or the amount required to satisfy the judgment. CCP §701.570(d). The order of sale is, however, subject to the "marshaling of assets" rules of CC §2899. See *Commonwealth Land Title Co. v Kornbluth* (1985) 175 CA3d 518, 220 CR 774. For further discussion of marshaling assets, see §8.52. The parties may agree to postpone the sale, in which case the only notice necessary is a public announcement by the levying officer at the time and place set for the original sale. CCP §701.580.

§3.56   B. Judicial Council Form: Writ of Sale

ATTORNEY OR PARTY WITHOUT ATTORNEY *(Name and Address)*:   TELEPHONE NO.:   *FOR RECORDER'S USE ONLY*

☐ Recording requested by and return to:

☐ ATTORNEY FOR   ☐ JUDGMENT CREDITOR   ☐ ASSIGNEE OF RECORD

NAME OF COURT:
STREET ADDRESS:
MAILING ADDRESS:
CITY AND ZIP CODE:
BRANCH NAME:
PLAINTIFF:
DEFENDANT:

WRIT OF   ☐ **EXECUTION (Money Judgment)**
       ☐ **POSSESSION OF**   ☐ **Personal Property**
                       ☐ **Real Property**
       ☐ **SALE**

CASE NUMBER:

FOR COURT USE ONLY

1. **To the Sheriff or any Marshal or Constable of the County of:**

   You are directed to enforce the judgment described below with daily interest and your costs as provided by law.

2. **To any registered process server:** You are authorized to serve this writ only in accord with CCP 699.080 or CCP 715.040.

3. *(Name):*
   is the ☐ judgment creditor ☐ assignee of record whose address is shown on this form above the court's name.

4. **Judgment debtor** *(name and last known address):*

   ☐ additional judgment debtors on reverse

5. **Judgment entered** on *(date):*
6. ☐ **Judgment renewed** on *(dates):*

7. **Notice of sale** under this writ
   a. ☐ has not been requested.
   b. ☐ has been requested *(see reverse).*
8. ☐ Joint debtor information on reverse.

[SEAL]

9. ☐ See reverse for information on real or personal property to be delivered under a writ of possession or sold under a writ of sale.
10. ☐ This writ is issued on a sister-state judgment.

11. Total judgment . . . . $
12. Costs after judgment (per filed order or memo CCP 685.090) . $
13. Subtotal *(add 11 and 12)* . . . . . $
14. Credits . . . . $
15. Subtotal *(subtract 14 from 13)* . $
16. Interest after judgment (per filed affidavit CCP 685.050) . . . . . . $
17. Fee for issuance of writ . . . . . . $
18. **Total** *(add 15, 16, and 17)* . . . . $
19. Levying officer: Add daily interest from date of writ *(at the legal rate on 15)* of . . . . $

20. ☐ The amounts called for in items 11–19 are different for each debtor. These amounts are stated for each debtor on Attachment 20.

Issued on *(date):*

Clerk, by _____ , Deputy

— NOTICE TO PERSON SERVED: SEE REVERSE FOR IMPORTANT INFORMATION —

(Continued on reverse)

Form Approved by the
Judicial Council of California
EJ-130 [Rev. January 1, 1989]   **WRIT OF EXECUTION**   CCP 699.520, 712.010, 715.010

SHORT TITLE:	CASE NUMBER:

Items continued from the first page:

4. ☐ **Additional judgment debtor** *(name and last known address)*:

7. ☐ **Notice of sale** has been requested by *(name and address)*:

8. ☐ **Joint debtor** was declared bound by the judgment (CCP 989–994)
   a. on *(date)*:   a. on *(date)*:
   b. name and address of joint debtor: b. name and address of joint debtor:

   c. ☐ additional costs against certain joint debtors *(itemize)*:

9. ☐ *(Writ of Possession or Writ of Sale)* **Judgment** was entered for the following:
   a. ☐ Possession of real property. The complaint was filed on *(date)*:
      (1) The court will hear objections to enforcement of the judgment under CCP 1174.3 on the following dates *(specify)*:
      (2) The daily rental value on the date the complaint was filed is *(specify)*: $
   b. ☐ Possession of personal property
      ☐ If delivery cannot be had, then for the value *(itemize in 9e)* specified in the judgment or supplemental order.
   c. ☐ Sale of personal property
   d. ☐ Sale of real property
   e. Description of property:

— NOTICE TO PERSON SERVED —

Writ of execution or sale. Your rights and duties are indicated on the accompanying Notice of Levy.

Writ of possession of personal property. If the levying officer is not able to take custody of the property, the levying officer will make a demand upon you for the property. If custody is not obtained following demand, the judgment may be enforced as a money judgment for the value of the property specified in the judgment or in a supplemental order.

Writ of possession of real property. If the premises are not vacated within five days after the date of service on the occupant or, if service is by posting, within five days after service on you, the levying officer will remove the occupants from the real property and place the judgment creditor in possession of the property. Personal property remaining on the premises will be sold or otherwise disposed of in accordance with CCP 1174 unless you or the owner of the property pays the judgment creditor the reasonable cost of storage and takes possession of the personal property not later than 15 days after the time the judgment creditor takes possession of the premises.
A Claim of Right to Possession form accompanies this writ.

Comment: After entry of judgment in a foreclosure action, the plaintiff should obtain a writ of sale from the court clerk and deliver it to the sheriff or receiver for execution of the judgment. CCP §§716.010–716.020, 712.010–712.060. Contents of the writ are specified in CCP §699.520, and the Judicial Council form reproduced in this section covers these requirements. Procedures for return of the writ by the levying officer are set forth in CCP §699.560. Note that a description of the property must be filled in at 9e on the reverse side of the form.

§3.57   C. Judicial Council Form: Notice of Levy

ATTORNEY OR PARTY WITHOUT ATTORNEY *(Name and Address)*: TELEPHONE NO.:	FOR RECORDER'S USE ONLY
☐ Recording requested by and return to:	
ATTORNEY FOR *(Name)*:	
NAME OF COURT:	
STREET ADDRESS:	
MAILING ADDRESS:	
CITY AND ZIP CODE:	
BRANCH NAME:	
PLAINTIFF:	
DEFENDANT:	LEVYING OFFICER *(Name and Address)*:
NOTICE OF LEVY under Writ of ☐ Execution (Money Judgment) ☐ Sale	
TO THE PERSON NOTIFIED *(name)*:	LEVYING OFFICER FILE NO.: COURT CASE NO.:

1. The judgment creditor seeks to levy upon property in which the judgment debtor has an interest and apply it to the satisfaction of a judgment as follows:
   a. judgment debtor *(name)*:
   b. the property to be levied upon is described
   ☐ in the accompanying writ of possession or writ of sale.
   ☐ as follows:

2. The amount necessary to satisfy the judgment creditor's judgment is *(specify total amount due under the writ less partial satisfactions plus daily interest from the date of the writ until the date of levy)*:
   $

3. You are notified as
   a. ☐ a judgment debtor.
   b. ☐ a person other than the judgment debtor *(state capacity in which person is notified)*:

   (Read Information for Judgment Debtor or Information for Person Other Than Judgment Debtor on reverse.)

Notice of Levy was
☐ mailed on *(date)*:
☐ delivered on *(date)*:
☐ posted on *(date)*:
☐ filed on *(date)*:
☐ recorded on *(date)*:

Signed by:

_____

☐ Levying officer   ☐ Registered process server
(Continued on reverse)

Form Approved by the
Judicial Council of California
EJ-150 (Rev. January 1, 1985)

NOTICE OF LEVY
(Enforcement of Judgment)

CCP 699.540

SHORT TITLE:	LEVYING OFFICER FILE NO.:	COURT CASE NO.:

— INFORMATION FOR JUDGMENT DEBTOR —

1. The levying officer is required to take custody of the property described in item 1 in your possession or under your control.

2. You may claim any available exemption for your property. A list of exemptions is attached. **If you wish to claim an exemption for personal property, you must do so within 10 days after this notice was delivered to you or 15 days after this notice was mailed to you** by filing a claim of exemption and one copy with the levying officer as provided in section 703.520 of the Code of Civil Procedure. **If you do not claim an exemption, you may lose it and the property is subject to enforcement of a money judgment. If you wish to seek the advice of an attorney, you should do so immediately so that a claim of exemption can be filed on time.**

3. You are not entitled to claim an exemption for property that is levied upon under a judgment for sale of property. This property is described in the accompanying writ of sale. You may, however, claim available exemptions for property levied upon to satisfy damages or costs awarded in such a judgment.

4. You may obtain the release of your property by paying the amount of a money judgment with interest and costs remaining unpaid.

5. If your property is levied upon under a writ of execution or to satisfy damages and costs under a writ of possession or sale, the property may be sold at an execution sale, perhaps at a price substantially below its value. Notice of sale will be given to you. Notice of sale of real property (other than a leasehold estate with an unexpired term of less than two years) may not be given until at least 120 days after this notice is served on you. This grace period is intended to give you an opportunity to settle with the judgment creditor, to obtain a satisfactory buyer for the property, or to encourage other potential buyers to attend the execution sale.

6. All sales at an execution sale are final; there is no right of redemption.

— INFORMATION FOR PERSON OTHER THAN JUDGMENT DEBTOR —

1. If the property levied upon is in your possession or under your control and you do not claim the right to possession or a security interest, you must deliver the property to the levying officer. If you do not deny an obligation levied upon or do not claim a priority over the judgment creditor's lien, you must pay to the levying officer the amount that is due and payable and that becomes due and payable during the period of the execution lien which lasts two years from the date of issuance of the writ of execution. You must execute and deliver any documents needed to transfer the property.

2. You must complete the accompanying Memorandum of Garnishee.

3. If you claim ownership or the right to possession of real or personal property levied upon or if you claim a security interest in or lien on personal property levied upon, you may make a third-party claim and obtain the release of the property pursuant to sections 720.010–720.800 of the Code of Civil Procedure.

4. **Make checks payable to the levying officer.**

Comment: The notice of levy is issued by the sheriff or court-appointed receiver to carry out the terms of the writ of sale (see §3.56). CCP §§700.015, 699.540–699.545, 716.010–716.020. When the debtor has postsale redemption rights (*i.e.,* when a deficiency judgment is not waived or prohibited), the notice of levy must be served on the defendants (CCP §700.015), and a 20-day notice of sale may be given at the same time (CCP §729.010(b)(2)). When a deficiency judgment has been waived or is prohibited, the notice of levy must be given at least 120 days before notice of sale may be given. CCP §§700.015, 701.545; see §3.55. The contents of the notice of levy are specified in CCP §699.540. Use of the Judicial Council form should suffice to comply with these requirements.

§3.58   D. Form: Notice of Sale

Copies: Original (issued by levying officer and served on judgment debtor); one copy for court file; one copy for sheriff's file; copies for each other defendant; office copies.

[*Title of court*]

[*Title of case*]   No. _ _ _ _ _ _

NOTICE OF SALE

PLEASE TAKE NOTICE that the above-entitled Court has ordered me, as levying officer, to sell the real property located in _ _ _ _ _ _ _ _ County, California, known as _ _[*state street address or other designation*]_ _, and described as:

[*Legal description*]

[*Add, if property has no street address or other common designation*]

Directions to the location of the real property to be sold may be obtained from the undersigned on request.

[*Continue*]

The judgment of foreclosure of the deed of trust on the property

and the order of sale were entered on _ _[date]_ _, in the Judgment Book, Volume No. _ _ at page _ _ and recorded on _ _[date]_ _.

The sale will begin at _ _ _ _.m. on _ _[date]_ _, at _ _[state address]_ _, City of _ _ _ _ _ _ _,_ _ _ _ _ _ _ _ County, California. The property will be sold to the highest bidder for cash or certified or cashier's check, except that, if the highest bid exceeds $5000, the highest bidder may elect to deposit either $5000 or 10 percent of the amount bid, whichever is greater, and within ten days after the date of the sale must pay the balance due plus costs and interest accruing from the date of sale to the date of payment. As much of the property as is necessary will be sold to pay the expenses of sale and to satisfy the judgment of $_ _ _ _ _ _, plus costs and interest.

Prospective bidders should refer to sections 701.510 to 701.680, inclusive, of the Code of Civil Procedure for provisions governing the terms, conditions, and effect of the sale and the liability of defaulting bidders.

[Add, if deficiency judgment is not waived or prohibited]

The property will be sold subject to the right of redemption under Code of Civil Procedure sections 729.010–729.090.

[Continue]

Dated: _ _ _ _ _ _

> ___[Signature]___
> _ _[Typed name]_ _
> _ _[Sheriff/Court-Appointed
> Receiver]_ _

Comment: The notice of sale must comply with the requirements of CCP §701.540. In addition to the legal description of the property, the notice must give its street address or other common designation. If the property has no street address or other common designation, the notice must indicate that directions to the property's location may be obtained from the levying officer by an oral or written request. CCP §701.540(a). The language in the next-to-last paragraph of the notice is required by CCP §701.547. For discussion of the manner of bidding, see §3.60. Requirements for posting, publication, and mailing of the notice of sale are set forth in CCP §701.540 (see §3.55).

The notice of sale must always be preceded by, or served simultaneously with, a notice of levy (see §3.57), but the time within which the notice of sale may be served after service of the notice of levy varies depending on the nature of the judgment. If a deficiency judgment has been waived or is prohibited, the debtor has no postsale redemption rights, but the notice of sale cannot be served until 120 days after service of the notice of levy. CCP §701.545. During this 140-day period preceding the sale, the debtor retains the common law right to redeem the property from the lien (see CC §2903). When the debtor has statutory postsale redemption rights (*i.e.*, when a deficiency judgment is neither waived nor prohibited), the notice of sale may be served immediately on entry of the foreclosure judgment. CCP §729.010(b)(2). In that case, however, the notice of sale must state that the property is sold subject to the statutory right of redemption (CCP §729.010(b)(1)), and the debtor has either three months or one year to redeem the property from the foreclosure sale (CCP §729.030) (see §3.76).

§3.59 E. Eligible Bidders

Any party may bid at the foreclosure sale (CCP §701.570) except for the levying officer, whose participation in the sale is expressly forbidden (CCP §701.610). The foreclosing creditor may bid, and a purchase in satisfaction of the judgment makes the creditor a bona fide purchaser within the meaning of the recording statutes. *Foorman v Wallace* (1888) 75 C 552, 17 P 680. Note, however, that if the creditor purchases the property at the sale, the debtor may commence an action within six months to have the sale set aside for irregularities in the proceedings. CCP §701.680(c); see §3.15. The trustor is also an eligible bidder, although the levying officer should scrutinize the trustor's bid carefully to ensure that it is backed by cash. *Security-First Nat'l Bank v Cryer* (1940) 39 CA2d 757, 104 P2d 66.

Any junior liens are extinguished by the sale. CCP §§701.630, 729.080(e). These sections abrogate the earlier rule under which junior liens would reattach to the property if the trustor were the successful bidder at the foreclosure sale or subsequently redeemed the property (see *Call v Thunderbird Mortgage Co.* (1962) 58 C2d 542, 25 CR 265). Junior lienors may, of course, bid at the sale, and this practice is likely to become more frequent as a means of protecting junior lien rights in light of CCP §§701.630 and 729.080(e). See Dyer, *Judicial Foreclosure After the Revised Enforcement of Judgments Act,* 6 CEB Real Prop L Rep 53, 56 (Apr. 1983).

§3.60   F. Method of Bidding

The judgment creditor may bid by giving the levying officer a written receipt crediting all or part of the amount required to satisfy the judgment, except that certain claims, such as the levying officer's costs, preferred labor claims, exempt proceeds, and any other claim required by statute to be satisfied, must be paid in cash. CCP §701.590(b). By virtue of the credit-bid, however, the foreclosing creditor need not pay cash up to the amount of the judgment, although any bid in excess of the judgment must be made in cash. *Central Sav. Bank v Lake* (1927) 201 C 438, 257 P 521.

Before July 1, 1983, the effective date of the Enforcement of Judgments Law, all other bidders were required to support their bids with cash. Under CCP §701.590(c), if the bid price exceeds $5000, the successful bidder has the additional option of depositing the greater of $5000 or 10 percent of the amount bid and paying the balance within ten days of the sale. A bidder electing this option must also pay additional costs and interest that accrue between the sale and the date of payment.

If the bidder fails to pay the balance due within ten days, the levying officer conducts a new sale. CCP §701.600(a). The defaulting bidder is liable for costs of the original sale and resale, interest, attorneys' fees, and the amount of the original bid less the amount bid for the property in the second sale. CCP §701.600(b)–(c).

Because any deficiency judgment will be limited to the difference between the fair value of the property and the amount of the debt (CCP §726; see §4.17), the foreclosing creditor must make certain that the bid price equals the fair value. If the property is sold for less than its fair value, the trustor will have a transferable right to purchase the property by redeeming at the sale price, but the creditor's deficiency judgment will be limited by the fair value. See §§4.18–4.22 for discussion of fair-value limitations. Consequently, it is usually advisable for the foreclosing creditor to credit-bid the amount of the debt, at least up to the property's fair value. For discussion of underbidding, see §§2.23,

8.8. The foreclosing creditor should have the property appraised before the sale in order to determine its fair value.

§3.61 G. Steps Following Sale

Once the sale is completed, the sheriff or court-appointed receiver must dispose of the proceeds in accordance with the judgment. The costs of sale and sums owed to the creditor must be paid, and any surplus goes to the debtor unless there are junior creditors to be paid out of the surplus. CCP §§701.810–701.830. If the property is not sold subject to a deficiency, the levying officer must give the purchaser a deed of sale. CCP §701.660; see §3.66. If a deficiency judgment is not waived or prohibited, however, the debtor has postsale redemption rights and the levying officer must give the purchaser a certificate of sale. CCP §729.040; see §§3.62–3.63. If the property is not redeemed within the redemption period, the levying officer must give the purchaser a deed of sale. CCP §729.080(a). When the property is sold subject to redemption rights, the levying officer must give the debtor notice of the right of redemption "promptly after the sale." CCP §729.050; see §3.64.

A creditor who seeks a deficiency judgment must make an application for it within three months after the foreclosure sale. CCP §726(b); see §§3.67–3.72.

H. When Sale Is Subject to Redemption Rights

§3.62 1. Certificate of Sale

When a deficiency judgment is not available (and the debtor therefore has no postsale redemption rights), the levying officer must execute and deliver a deed of sale (see §3.66) when the foreclosure sale purchaser pays the amount due. CCP §701.660. When a deficiency judgment is not waived or prohibited, however, the levying officer must execute and deliver a certificate of sale to the purchaser on receipt of the purchase price. CCP §729.040. The certificate of sale procedure is used because the property is still subject to redemption rights under CCP §§729.010–729.090. If the property is not redeemed within the applicable redemption period (see §3.76), the levying officer must execute a deed of sale and deliver it to the foreclosure sale purchaser. CCP §729.080(b). The certificate of sale must state that the property is sold subject to the right of redemption. CCP §729.040(b)(3). A certificate of sale may be sold or otherwise transferred. See *Foorman v Wallace* (1888) 75 C 552, 17 P 680. The levying officer must serve the judgment debtor with a notice of the debtor's redemption rights. CCP §729.050; see §3.64.

Under former CCP §§700–700a, and cases interpreting these sections, the certificate of sale passed title to the purchaser equal to the title held by the trustor as of the date of execution and recordation of the deed of trust (and subject to statutory redemption rights). The title conveyed was subject to all senior liens but free and clear of all junior liens. *Dickey v Gibson* (1898) 121 C 276, 53 P 704; see *Freelon v Adrian* (1911) 161 C 13, 118 P 220; *Johnson v Friant* (1903) 140 C 260, 73 P 993. This is undoubtedly still the rule, although no statute expressly so provides.

§3.63   2. Form: Certificate of Sale

Copies: Original (filed with county recorder); duplicate originals to record if property is situated in more than one county; copies for service (one for each attorney of record and unrepresented party); office copies.

Recording Requested By)
)
)
)
After Recording Return To)
)
)
) **(Space above this line for recorder's use)**

[*Title of court*]

[*Title of case*]   **No. _ _ _ _ _ _**

CERTIFICATE OF SALE

I, _ _[*name of sheriff/or court-appointed receiver*]_ _, **certify that I was appointed levying officer by the above-entitled Court to sell**

the real property known as _ _[*state street address or other designation*]_ _ **and described as:**

[*Legal description*]

and to apply the proceeds to the necessary expenses of sale, and to the judgment of $_ _ _ _ _ _, plus interest and costs. The judgment of foreclosure of the deed of trust on the property and the order of sale were entered in favor of _ _[*creditor*]_ _, **of** _ _[*state address*]_ _, **and against** _ _[*debtor*]_ _, **whose last-known address is** _ _[*state address*]_ _, **on** _ _[*date*]_ _, **and entered on** _ _[*date*]_ _ **in the Judgment Book, Volume No. _ _ at page _ _.**

The sale was advertised and conducted according to the provisions of the Code of Civil Procedure. The sale took place on _ _[*date*]_ _. **The real property consisted of** _ _[*e.g., one lot/three parcels*]_ _, **and the successful bid for** _ _[*the/each*]_ _ _ _[*lot/parcel*]_ _ **was** _ _[*enumerate lot(s) or parcel(s) and successful bid(s)*]_ _, **made by, and sold at auction to,** _ _[*name(s) of successful bidder(s)*]_ _. **The total price paid was $_ _ _ _ _ _.**

The real property was sold subject to the right of redemption under Code of Civil Procedure sections 729.010–729.090 and may be redeemed within _ _[*three months/one year*]_ _ after the date of sale.

Dated: _ _ _ _ _ _

> ___[*Signature*]___
> _ _[*Typed name*]_ _
> _ _[*Sheriff/Court-Appointed
> Receiver*]_ _

[*Acknowledgment*]

Comment: Whenever real property is sold at a judicial sale subject to postsale redemption rights under CCP §§729.010–729.090, the levying officer must give the purchaser a certificate of sale. CCP §729.040. For all other foreclosure sales (*i.e.*, those in which deficiency judgment is waived or prohibited so that the debtor has no postsale redemption rights), the levying officer gives the purchaser a deed of sale. CCP

§701.660. For discussion, see §3.62. The required contents of a certificate of sale are prescribed in CCP §§701.670 and 729.040. Specifically, the certificate of sale must contain the following information:

■ The name of the court in which the judgment was entered and the
name and number of the case (CCP §701.670(a));

■ The date of entry of judgment and any subsequent renewals, and
notation of where the judgment was entered in the court's records (CCP
§701.670(b));

■ The name and address of the judgment creditor and the name and
last-known address of the judgment debtor (CCP §701.670(c));

■ A description of the property (CCP §701.670(d));

■ The date of sale (CCP §701.670(e));

■ The price paid for each distinct lot or parcel sold subject to the
right of redemption (CCP §729.040(b)(1));

■ The total price paid (CCP §729.040(b)(2)); and

■ A statement that the property is sold subject to the right of redemption, indicating the applicable redemption period (CCP §729.040(b)(3)).

Because a duplicate of the certificate must be recorded with the
county recorder as well as executed and delivered to the purchaser
(CCP §729.040(a)), the certificate should comply with requirements
for recordation.

§3.64   3. Form: Notice of Right of Redemption

Copies: Original for service on judgment debtor; one copy for each
other party; one copy for sheriff's file; office copies.

[*Title of court*]

[*Title of case*]   No. _ _ _ _ _ _

                                               NOTICE OF RIGHT OF
                                               REDEMPTION

To: _ _[*Name of judgment debtor*]_ _

**PLEASE TAKE NOTICE that you have the right to redeem the
real property described below from the foreclosure sale con-**

ducted by the undersigned under a writ of sale issued by the above-entitled Court on the judgment of foreclosure entered in this action. The real property is described as follows:

[Legal description]

The real property was sold by the undersigned levying officer in accordance with the provisions of the Code of Civil Procedure to __[name of purchaser]__ for the sum of $_____ on __[date]__.

The real property may be redeemed any time within __[three months/one year]__ after the date of sale.

Dated: _____

___[Signature]___
__[Typed name]__
__[Sheriff/Court-Appointed Receiver]__

Comment: This notice must be given by the levying officer "promptly after the sale." CCP §729.050. Service may be made personally or by mail. The notice must state the applicable redemption period. If the proceeds of the foreclosure sale are sufficient to satisfy the secured indebtedness with interest and the costs of the action and the sale, the redemption period is three months from the date of sale. CCP §729.030(a). If the proceeds are not sufficient to satisfy the indebtedness plus interest and costs, the redemption period is one year. CCP §729.030(b); see §3.76.

§3.65 I. Form: Receiver's Report and Account of Sale

Copies: Original (filed with court clerk with proof of service); copies for service (one for each attorney of record and unrepresented party); office copies.

[Title of court]

[Title of case] **No. _____**

RECEIVER'S REPORT AND ACCOUNT OF SALE

I, _ _[name] _ _, am the receiver appointed by this Court to conduct a sale of the real property known as _ _[state street address or other designation]_ _ and described as:

[Legal description]

and to distribute the proceeds according to the Court's judgment entered in this action. This is my report and account of the sale.

1. The judgment of foreclosure of the deed of trust on the described property and the order of sale were entered on _ _[date]_ _, in the Judgment Book, Volume No. _ _ at page _ _.

2. I swore an oath to perform my duties according to law and _ _[executed an undertaking/obtained a bond]_ _ in the amount of $_ _ _ _ _ _, as set and approved by the Court, _ _[and supported by sufficient sureties]_ _.

3. The sale was advertised and conducted in accordance with the provisions of the Code of Civil Procedure. Written notice describing the property to be auctioned and the place of auction was posted on the property and in a public place on _ _[date]_ _. The notice was published weekly in a newspaper of general circulation in the _ _[city/judicial district]_ _ in which _ _[all/part of]_ _ the property is located. Posting and publication preceded the sale by at least 20 days. Affidavits of posting and publication in the described manner are attached as Exhibits _ _ and _ _.

4. The property was offered for sale at auction at the advertised time and place. The real property consisted of _ _[e.g., one lot, three parcels]_ _ and the highest bid for _ _[the/each]_ _ _ _[lot/parcel]_ _ was _ _[enumerate lot(s) or parcel(s) and successful bid(s)]_ _, made by _ _[name(s)]_ _.

[Choose appropriate paragraph]

[Either]

5. I gave _ _[the/each]_ _ purchaser a deed of sale and recorded a duplicate of _ _[the/each]_ _ deed in the office of the recorder of _ _ _ _ _ _ _ _ County.

[Or]

5. I gave _ _[the/each]_ _ purchaser a certificate of sale and recorded a duplicate of _ _[the/each]_ _ certificate in the office of the recorder of _ _ _ _ _ _ _ County. The certificate of sale contained the following information:

   a. The name of the Court in which judgment was entered and the name and number of the case;

   b. The date of entry of judgment and any subsequent renewals, and notation of where judgment was entered in the Court's records;

   c. The name and address of the judgment creditor and the name and last-known address of the judgment debtor;

   d. A description of the property;

   e. The date of sale;

   f. The price paid for each lot or parcel sold subject to the right of redemption;

   g. The total price paid; and

   h. A statement that the property is sold subject to the right of redemption, indicating the applicable redemption period.

[Continue]

6. The expenses of the sale totaled $_ _ _ _ _ _ and consisted of the following items:

[Itemize expenses]

This amount was deducted from $_ _ _ _ _ _, the proceeds of the sale, leaving a balance of $_ _ _ _ _ _.

7. In accordance with the judgment and order of sale, I disbursed $_ _ _ _ _ _ to _ _[name of plaintiff]_ _. A receipt for this amount is attached as Exhibit _ _.

[*Add, if there were surplus funds*]

8. After satisfying the judgment, as indicated in paragraph 7, a surplus of $_ _ _ _ _ _ remained, which I_ _[*paid to defendant, _ _[name]_ _,/deposited with the court clerk*]_ _, in accordance with the judgment. A receipt for the surplus is attached as Exhibit _ _.

ACCOUNT

[9.] _ _[*Itemize receiver's accounting of details of sale and disbursal of funds*]_ _.

I declare under penalty of perjury under the laws of the State of California that the foregoing is true and correct.

Dated: _ _ _ _ _ _

___[*Signature*]___
_ _[*Typed name*]_ _
Court-Appointed Receiver

Comment: The levying officer should file a report with the court describing the sale and itemizing the financial details of the sale and the disbursal of funds. See CCP §§712.050, 699.560. If the sale is conducted by the sheriff, the sheriff's return will be made in the same manner as for execution sales. The property should be identified both by its street address and its legal description. The buyer's name and address and the price paid for the property should be included. The accounting should recount the expenses in detail, *e.g.,* cost of publishing notice of sale, costs of service. A deficiency or surplus in the sum realized should be noted.

§3.66   J. Form: Deed of Sale

Copies: Original (filed with county recorder); duplicate originals to record if property is situated in more than one county; copies for service (one for each attorney of record and unrepresented party); office copies.

Recording Requested By)
)
)
)
After Recording Return To)
)
)
) **(Space above this line for recorder's use)**

[*Title of court*]

[*Title of case*]   **No. _ _ _ _ _ _**

DEED OF SALE

I, _ _[*name*]_ _, **having been appointed levying officer in this matter by the above-entitled Court, grant to and confirm in** _ _[*name and capacity of purchaser(s)*]_ _ **the real property situated in _ _ _ _ _ _ _ _ County, California, known as** _ _[*state street address or other designation*]_ _, **and described as:**

[*Legal description*]

This deed is given under the powers granted to me by the Court in its judgment of foreclosure of the _ _[*deed of trust/mortgage*]_ _ **on the described property, which was entered in favor of** _ _[*judgment creditor*]_ _, **of** _ _[*state address of judgment creditor*]_ _ **and against** _ _[*judgment debtor*]_ _, **of** _ _[*state last-known address of judgment debtor*]_ _, **on** _ _[*date*]_ _, **and entered on** _ _[*date*]_ _ **in the Judgment Book, Volume No. _ _ at page _ _.**

The sale was conducted according to the provisions of the Code of Civil Procedure. The property was sold, _ _[*subject to redemption*]_ _, **at public auction on** _ _[*date*]_ _, **in _ _ _ _ _ _ _ _ County, California. The above-named grantee(s)** _ _[*was/were*]_ _ **the highest bidder(s) for the** _ _[*lot/parcel*]_ _ **and paid the successful bid in lawful currency of the United States.**

[*Add, if sale was subject to redemption rights*]

I issued a certificate of sale to the purchaser(s) and recorded a duplicate certificate on _ _[*date*]_ _, **in Book No. _ _ at page _ _ of the Official Records of _ _ _ _ _ _ _ _ County, California.**

The time for redemption under the Code of Civil Procedure has now elapsed, and all rights of redemption have expired.

Dated: _ _ _ _ _ _

> ___[*Signature*]___
> _ _[*Typed name*]_ _
> _ _[*Sheriff/Court-Appointed
> Receiver*]_ _

[*Acknowledgment*]

Comment: If the property is not subject to redemption after the foreclosure sale, the levying officer must execute and deliver a deed of sale to the purchaser. CCP §701.660. If the property is sold subject to redemption rights (*i.e.,* if a deficiency judgment is not waived or prohibited), the levying officer must first deliver to the purchaser a certificate of sale. CCP §729.040; see §3.63. After the time for redemption has expired (see §3.76), if the property has not been redeemed, the levying officer must execute and deliver a deed of sale to the purchaser. CCP §729.080(a). The deed of sale must contain the following provisions (CCP §701.670(a)–(e)):

■ The title of the court in which the judgment was entered and the name and number of the foreclosure action;

■ The date of entry of judgment and the date on which the judgment was entered in the court records;

■ The name and address of the judgment creditor and the name and last-known address of the judgment debtor;

■ A description of the property; and

■ The date of sale.

§3.67   VII. DEFICIENCY JUDGMENT

Procedures for obtaining a deficiency judgment are discussed in §§3.68–3.72. For substantive discussion of the right to a deficiency judgment, and antideficiency protections, see chap 4.

The procedure for obtaining a deficiency judgment is set forth in CCP §726(b). The foreclosing creditor must file an application for a deficiency judgment within three months after the date of the foreclosure sale. Application is customarily accomplished by noticed motion under CCP §1010, although it may also be done by filing a document labeled "Application for Deficiency," together with an order to show cause.

To qualify for a deficiency judgment, the secured creditor must:

■ Hold a nonpurchase-money deed of trust (CCP §580b) (see §4.23);

■ Not have extrajudicially foreclosed on any part of the security (see §4.14);

■ Have drafted the original foreclosure judgment to provide for a deficiency against named defendants (see §3.53);

■ Have received less than the full amount of the judgment indebtedness from the sale proceeds;

■ Apply to the court for a deficiency judgment within three months following the foreclosure sale (CCP §726(b)) (see §3.68); and

■ Establish that the fair value of the property is less than the debt (see §3.69).

A sold-out junior creditor need not comply with the requirement in CCP §726(b) that an application for a deficiency judgment be made within three months after the foreclosure sale. A sold-out junior may bring an independent action on the promissory note for any balance still owed after having received the surplus, if any, from the foreclosure sale. *Roseleaf Corp. v Chierighino* (1963) 59 C2d 35, 27 CR 873. The suit must be commenced before the expiration of the statute of limitations applicable to the junior note. See §§4.31–4.33.

§3.68   A. Form: Notice of Motion for Deficiency Judgment

Copies: Original (filed with court clerk with proof of service); copies for service (one for each attorney of record and unrepresented party); office copies.

[*Title of court*]

[*Title of case*]   **No.** _ _ _ _ _ _

                                           **NOTICE OF MOTION FOR
                                           DEFICIENCY JUDGMENT**

                                           Hearing: _ _[*date and time*]_ _
                                           Department: _ _ _ _

To each party and attorney of record:

PLEASE TAKE NOTICE that on _ _[*date*]_ _, **at** _ _ _ _.**m., or as
soon thereafter as the matter can be heard, in Department No.** _ _ **of
the above-entitled Court, plaintiff,** _ _[*name*]_ _, **will move the Court
for a deficiency judgment.**

**This motion will be made on the ground that neither the pro-
ceeds from the foreclosure sale nor the fair value of the property
is equal to the amount of the indebtedness with interest and costs.
This motion is based on this notice, all the pleadings, records,
and files in this action, the attached memorandum of points and
authorities, and oral and documentary evidence to be presented
at the hearing of the motion.**

Dated: _ _ _ _ _ _

                                    _ _ _[*Signature of attorney*]_ _ _
                                    _ _[*Typed name*]_ _
                                    Attorney for _ _[*name*]_ _

Comment: The notice must be served on all persons against whom a
deficiency judgment is sought at least 15 days before the hearing. CCP
§726(b). Any additional facts needed to support the motion that are not
contained in documents in the court file may be supplied by attaching
a separate declaration or affidavit by the plaintiff or the plaintiff's attorney or may be presented at the hearing on the motion. The most important fact, obviously, is the price for which the property was sold at
the foreclosure sale. The sale price should be obtainable from the levying officer's certificate of sale (see §3.63), notice of right to redeem
(see §3.64), or report and account of sale (see §3.65). The creditor's
attorney should check local procedure to determine whether the judge
who presided at the trial will preside at the deficiency hearing.

§3.69   B. Hearing

The court must hold a hearing on the application for the deficiency judgment and take evidence of the fair value of the property. CCP §726(b). On the application of any party made at least ten days before the hearing, or on the court's own motion, the court may appoint a probate referee to appraise the property. CCP §726(b). The report may be put into evidence or the referee may be examined as a witness. See §3.70 for a form for the application. Other witnesses may also be called for their opinions on value. The owner is competent to testify concerning the property's value; other witnesses must be qualified as experts. Evid C §813; see *Everts v Matteson* (1942) 21 C2d 437, 132 P2d 476.

The hearing is limited to determining the amount by which the indebtedness, plus interest and costs of levy and sale, exceeds the fair value of the property on the date of sale. CCP §726(b). Defenses to the plaintiff's right to a deficiency judgment, as opposed to the amount of the deficiency, must be raised before the initial foreclosure judgment and may not be raised at the deficiency hearing. See *United Cal. Bank v Tijerina* (1972) 25 CA3d 963, 102 CR 234.

§3.70   C. Form: Application for and Order
              Appointing Probate Referee

Copies: Original (filed with court clerk with proof of service); copies for service (one for each attorney of record and unrepresented party); office copies.

[*Title of court*]

[*Title of case*]   No. _ _ _ _ _ _

                                     APPLICATION FOR AND
                                     ORDER APPOINTING
                                     PROBATE REFEREE

I, _ _[*name of moving party*]_ _, **declare:**

1. The above-entitled Court entered its judgment of foreclosure of the deed of trust in this matter on _ _[*date*]_ _, determining the amount of the indebtedness to plaintiff to be $_ _ _ _ _ _, together with interest and costs, and directed that

the real property be sold by auction according to law. The Court retained jurisdiction to enter a deficiency judgment.

2. The property was sold on _ _[date] _, and the proceeds of the sale amounted to $_ _ _ _ _ _. After deducting expenses, the net proceeds amounted to $_ _ _ _ _ _.

3. The plaintiff in this matter applied to the Court for a deficiency judgment on _ _[date] _. The application is set for hearing on _ _[date] _.

I declare under penalty of perjury under the laws of the State of California that the foregoing is true and correct. I hereby apply for an order appointing a probate referee to appraise the property at the time of sale, _ _[date] _ _, and to file _ _[his/her] _ appraisal with the court clerk, under the provisions of Code of Civil Procedure section 726(b).

Dated: _ _ _ _ _ _

                        ___[Signature]___
                        _ _[Typed name] _ _

ORDER

Good cause appearing from _ _[name of party] _ _'s application for an order appointing a probate referee,

IT IS ORDERED that _ _[name] _ _ is appointed to appraise the real property described as:

[Legal description]

as of _ _[date] _ _, the date of sale. The referee will be paid $_ _ _ _ _ _, plus costs and expenses, and is directed to file _ _[his/her] _ _ appraisal, under oath, with the court clerk on or before _ _[date] _ _.

Dated: _ _ _ _ _ _

                        _____
                        Judge of the Superior Court

Comment: Code of Civil Procedure §726 provides that any party may apply to the court at least ten days before the date set for the deficiency hearing for appointment of a probate referee to appraise the property. The court may also appoint a referee on its own motion. As a practical matter, because of fair-value limitations, the foreclosing creditor will need an appraisal even before the sale takes place. See §3.60.

§3.71 D. Deficiency Judgment

Following the hearing and the determination of the fair value of the property on the date of sale, the court must enter its judgment. If a deficiency is found to exist, the court enters a money judgment in favor of the plaintiff in an amount equal to the difference between the indebtedness, plus interest and costs of levy and sale, and the property's fair value. In any event, the amount of the deficiency judgment, exclusive of interest and costs, may not exceed the difference between the entire amount of the secured indebtedness and the sale price. CCP §726(b). If the court finds no deficiency by applying these measures, then it should enter judgment in favor of the defendant on this issue.

§3.72 E. Form: Deficiency Judgment

Copies: Original (filed with court clerk when signed by judge); copies for service (one for each attorney of record and unrepresented party); office copies.

[*Title of court*]

[*Title of case*] No. _ _ _ _ _ _

DEFICIENCY JUDGMENT

The plaintiff's _ _[*motion/application*]_ _ for a money judgment for a deficiency after sale of real property in this action for foreclosure of a deed of trust came on regularly for hearing on _ _[*date*]_ _. Plaintiff appeared by attorney _ _[*name*]_ _; defendant, _ _[*name*]_ _, appeared by attorney _ _[*name*]_ _. The Court, having heard the testimony and considered the evidence, _ _[*makes the following statement of decision: _ _[State factual and legal basis for decision; see CCP §632*]_ _and/and a *statement of decision not having been requested,*]_ _ **enters its judgment as follows:**

Plaintiff, _ _[*name*]_ _, recover from defendant, _ _[*name*]_ _, the sum of $_ _ _ _ _ _, with interest at the annual rate of _ _ percent from _ _[*date*]_ _, together with the sum of $_ _ _ _ _ _ as costs.

Dated: _ _ _ _ _ _

_____
Judge of the Superior Court

Entered on _ _[*date*]_ _, in the Judgment Book, Volume No. _ _ at page _ _.

_____
Clerk
By _ _ _ _ _ _ _ _, Deputy

Comment: This is a conventional money judgment, enforceable by all traditional means. It may, among other things, be recorded and become a lien on all property owned and later acquired by the judgment debtor. See 4 Miller & Starr, Current Law of California Real Estate §9.171 (2d ed 1989). Before enactment of the Enforcement of Judgments Law (CCP §§680.010–724.260) and CCP §§729.010–729.090, a deficiency judgment would have become a lien on the originally mortgaged property if the property were ever reacquired by the debtor. *Simpson v Castle* (1878) 52 C 644. Under CCP §729.080(e), however, the lien of a deficiency judgment does not reattach to the property if the debtor redeems it after the sale. See §3.77; Dyer, *Judicial Foreclosure After the Revised Enforcement of Judgments Act,* 6 CEB Real Prop L Rep 53, 57 (Apr. 1983).

§3.73   VIII. POSTSALE REDEMPTION

Although the foreclosure judgment cuts off the right of reinstatement (CC §2924c) and the foreclosure sale terminates the traditional equity of redemption (CC §§2903–2905; see §3.51), the sale creates in the judgment debtor and his or her successor in interest a new right of redemption (commonly referred to as statutory redemption) whenever the right to a deficiency judgment is not waived or prohibited. CCP §§726(e), 729.010–729.090. Unlike the equitable right of redemption before sale, the statutory right of redemption is asserted not against the secured creditor but against the purchaser at the foreclosure sale. Furthermore, the amount necessary to redeem depends on the foreclosure sale price, not on the amount of the secured debt. See §3.78. For example, if the amount of the indebtedness before foreclosure was $100,000 and the purchaser at the foreclosure sale paid $150,000 for the property, the trustor must pay $150,000, not $100,000, to redeem, and the money is paid to the purchaser, not to the beneficiary. Conversely, if the property was sold for less than the indebtedness, the debtor can redeem by paying the purchaser only the amount bid. The mechanics of redemption are covered in considerable detail in CCP §§729.010–729.090. The logic of subjecting foreclosure sales to a postsale right of redemption is dubious in light of the presale rights of redemption already afforded the mortgagor and the generally acknowledged fact that the prospect of redemption lowers the bids made at a sale (see *Rainer Mortgage v Silverwood, Ldt.* (1985) 163 CA3d 359, 209 CR 294; *U.S. v Stadium Apartments* (9th Cir 1970) 425 F2d 358).

The right to postsale redemption exists only when a deficiency judgment is not waived or prohibited. CCP §§726(e), 729.010. This is a significant departure from the pre-1983 rule (which permitted postsale redemption after any judicial foreclosure sale). The new rule permits beneficiaries who are required to foreclose judicially for reasons other than to obtain a deficiency judgment (*e.g.,* to resolve other disputes between the parties) to obtain the benefits of a nonredeemable sale by waiving any possibility of a deficiency judgment. On the other hand, the debtor is given a longer period within which to exercise *presale* redemption rights when a deficiency judgment has been waived (because an additional 120 days must elapse before the notice of sale can be served). See §3.55. A waiver must be made no later than entry of the judgment of foreclosure if it is to cut off redemption rights, because CCP §726 requires that the judgment specify whether a deficiency judgment may be ordered against the defendant. For discussion of whether a proper waiver has been made, and whether the beneficiary can unilaterally waive a deficiency judgment, see Dyer, *Judicial Foreclosure After the Revised Enforcement of Judgments Act,* 6 CEB Real Prop L Rep 53, 56 (Apr. 1983). The mere fact that no deficiency judgment is awarded (because the entire debt was matched by the bid or because a fair-value hearing determined that the value equaled the debt) does not eliminate the redemption period; it merely shortens the period from one year to three months. CCP §729.030; see Dyer, 6 CEB RPLR at 56.

For federal income tax purposes, the existence of the statutory right of postsale redemption does not delay recognition of gain or loss by the creditor, although it may do so for the debtor. See §2.30.

§3.74   A. Who May Redeem

Only the judgment debtor and the judgment debtor's successor in interest are permitted to redeem the property after a foreclosure sale. CCP §729.020. This rule departs from the law as it existed before 1983, when the Enforcement of Judgments Law (CCP §§680.010–724.260) and CCP §§729.010–729.090 became effective. Under former CCP §701(2), creditors with junior liens on the property (referred to as "redemptioners") were also permitted to redeem. See *Salsbery v Ritter* (1957) 48 C2d 1, 306 P2d 897; *Clark v Cuin* (1956) 46 C2d 386, 295 P2d 401; *Eldridge v Wright* (1880) 55 C 531; *Simpson v Castle* (1878) 52 C 644. Under CCP §§729.010–729.090, postsale redemption rights are not extended to juniors. A junior who fears underbidding at an impending senior sale must either be prepared to enter the bidding at the senior sale and bid up the property sufficiently to cover the junior debt (assuming that the property is of adequate value for this purpose) or else avoid the sale by reinstating the senior loan. Reinstatement is usually cheaper than bidding at the senior sale, at which the junior will need cash to cover his or her bid (CCP §701.590(c); see §3.60).

A junior was formerly entitled to conduct a separate foreclosure sale after the senior sale and acquire the property at it, thus becoming the trustor's successor in interest and, as such, entitled to redeem the property from the senior sale. See *Fry v Bihr* (1970) 6 CA3d 248, 85 CR 742. It is doubtful, however, that this procedure is currently permitted by CCP §§729.010–729.090, which no longer characterize the purchaser at a foreclosure sale as a "successor in interest" of the judgment debtor (CCP §729.020). Case law pre-dating CCP §§729.010–729.090 treated purchasers at preceding or subsequent foreclosure sales as successors and permitted them to exercise redemption rights. See *Call v Thunderbird Mortgage Co.* (1962) 58 C2d 542, 25 CR 265. It is unclear whether that doctrine has been altered by the new code provision. See *Pollard v Harlow* (1903) 138 C 390, 71 P 454; *Bateman v Kellogg* (1922) 59 CA 464, 211 P 46. For further discussion of this issue, see Dyer, *Judicial Foreclosure After the Revised Enforcement of Judgments Act,* 6 CEB Real Prop L Rep 53, 56 (Apr. 1983).

§3.75 B. Order of Redemption

Under former CCP §701, junior lienholders were permitted to redeem the property but no particular order for redemption was specified. This rule resulted in "scramble redemption" in which the property could be re-redeemed by other persons with redemption rights. As a result of changes enacted in the law regarding redemption rights with passage of the Enforcement of Judgments Law (CCP §§680.010–724.260) and CCP §§729.010–729.090, there is no significant scrambling in the redemption process. Redemption rights are limited by CCP §729.020 to the judgment debtor and the judgment debtor's successor in interest. See §3.74.

"Scramble" issues conceivably could still arise when redemption is first made by the judgment debtor's successor, who acquired title at what was itself a redeemable sale, and the original debtor then seeks to redeem from the successor. See *Bateman v Kellogg* (1922) 59 CA 464, 211 P 46.

§3.76 C. Time in Which To Redeem

The period during which property may be redeemed from a foreclosure sale is three months from the date of sale if the proceeds of the sale are sufficient to satisfy the secured indebtedness plus interest and costs. CCP §729.030(a). If the sale proceeds are not sufficient to satisfy the indebtedness together with interest and costs, the redemption period is one year from the date of sale. CCP §729.030(b).

Changes brought about by enactment of the Enforcement of Judgments Law (CCP §§680.010–724.260) and CCP §§729.010–729.090 on redemption simplified the law concerning the time in which to redeem. Redemption is now permitted only if a deficiency judgment is not waived or prohibited (CCP §726(e)), and the time periods specified by CCP §729.030 apply only when a deficiency judgment is available. Under former CCP §§702 and 725a, redemption periods of three or 12 months existed whenever there was a foreclosure sale, even if a deficiency judgment was waived or prohibited. Also, under former CCP

§703, there were 60-day re-redemption periods after redemptions by junior lienors. Under CCP §729.020, however, redemption by junior lienors is no longer permitted (see §3.75), and therefore there is no possibility of re-redemption.

Although courts are divided on the issue, the weight of authority holds that an automatic bankruptcy stay under 11 USC §362 does not toll the three-month and one-year redemption periods, but rather that 11 USC §108(b) extends the period to a date 60 days after the bankruptcy case was filed if expiration would otherwise have occurred during the 60-day period. See, *e.g., In re Eagles* (California Thrift & Loan Ass'n v Downey Sav. & Loan Ass'n) (Bankr 9th Cir 1984) 36 BR 97. See also *Napue v Gor-Mey W., Inc.* (1985) 175 CA3d 608, 220 CR 799. For further discussion, see §6.50.

§3.77   D. Effect of Redemption

Redemption has the effect of terminating the foreclosure sale and restoring the redeeming party to the estate that had been sold. CCP §729.080(d). This rule contrasts with former CCP §703, under which the sale was terminated only on redemption by the debtor but not by redemption by a junior lienholder. See *Kaiser v Mansfield* (1958) 160 CA2d 620, 628, 325 P2d 865, 870. Redemption by junior lienors was eliminated when former CCP §701 was repealed by enactment of the Enforcement of Judgments Law (CCP §§680.010–724.260). See §3.75.

A further change is contained in CCP §729.080(e), which provides that liens extinguished by the sale do not reattach to the property after redemption and that the property that was subject to the extinguished lien may not be applied to the satisfaction of the claim or judgment under which the lien was created. Under former CCP §703, liens that had been cut off by the foreclosure sale were automatically reinstated on redemption by the debtor or the debtor's successor in interest.

Junior liens are thus destroyed by the sale. These liens were always eliminated by a senior sale, but formerly juniors were entitled to redeem and also to have their liens reattach if the judgment debtor redeemed. See *Lindsey v Meyer* (1981) 125 CA3d 536, 178 CR 1, in which the court held that under former CCP §703 redemption by the debtor causes the lien for any unsatisfied portion of the debt to reattach even though a deficiency judgment following the sale would have been barred by CCP §580b. A sold-out junior is relegated by CCP §729.080(e) to the position of an unsecured creditor and must sue on the underlying debt, if possible. See §4.31. For discussion of the rationale for the new rule, see Dyer, *Judicial Foreclosure After the Revised Enforcement of Judgments Act,* 6 CEB Real Prop L Rep 53, 56 (Apr. 1983).

A junior lienor who bids at the senior sale need not bid up to the combined total of junior and senior liens to protect the junior lien from redemption by the trustor. Under CCP §729.060(b)(5), a redeeming debtor must pay off any liens held by the purchaser that are subordinate to the foreclosing lien. This protection exists only when the junior is the purchaser; if a third party purchases, redemption does not entail payment of the junior lien. Thus, the junior has an incentive to outbid third parties until the junior lien is covered (assuming that the value of the security warrants it). See Dyer, 6 CEB RPLR at 57.

The effect of CCP §729.080(e) on deficiency judgments is unclear. Its purpose seems to be to prohibit selling the property a second time to satisfy the same debt. Thus, a lien for the unsatisfied portion of the lien that was the subject of the foreclosure action seemingly will not reattach even if the debtor reacquires the property, as it would have under former law (see *Lindsey v Meyer, supra*). It is not clear, however, whether a recorded deficiency judgment would become a lien on all property owned or later acquired by the debtor, including the redeemed property. When a successor of the debtor redeems, instead of the debtor, the lien of the deficiency judgment does not bind the successor. To avoid the possibility that CCP §729.080(e) might be interpreted so that a lien for a deficiency would attach, the debtor apparently can still convey his or her interest to a third party to redeem. See *Fry v Bihr* (1970) 6 CA3d 248, 85 CR 742 (judgment lien reattached following redemption after execution sale).

It is also unclear what effect CCP §729.080(e) has when a sold-out junior later obtains a money judgment on the junior debt and records an abstract of judgment. Arguably, §729.080(e) would bar that judgment from becoming a lien if the property is redeemed or required by the debtor. For additional analysis of §729.080(e), see Dyer, 6 CEB RPLR at 57.

§3.78   E. Amount Necessary To Redeem

To redeem the property, the debtor or the debtor's successor in interest must deposit the redemption price with the levying officer during the redemption period. A successor in interest who seeks to redeem must also file with the levying officer proof of the right to redeem in the form of a conveyance, an assignment, or other evidence of an interest. CCP §729.060(a). When the redeeming party deposits the redemption price, the levying officer must tender it to the foreclosure sale purchaser. If the purchaser accepts the tender, the levying officer must execute a certificate of redemption, deliver it to the redeeming party, and record it. CCP §729.080(b).

The redemption price consists of the total of the following amounts:

■ The purchase price at the foreclosure sale (as opposed to the fair value of the property; see *Lindsey v Meyer* (1981) 125 CA3d 536, 178 CR 1). CCP §729.060(b)(1).

■ Any assessments or taxes and reasonable amounts for fire insurance, maintenance, upkeep, and repair of improvements on the property. CCP §729.060(b)(2).

■ Amounts paid by the purchaser on a prior obligation secured by the property to the extent payment was necessary to protect the purchaser's interest. CCP §729.060(b)(3).

■ Interest on the above amounts, at the rate of interest on money judgments, from the time such amounts were paid until the date on which the redemption price is deposited with the levying officer. CCP §729.060(b)(4).

■ The amount of any liens the foreclosure sale purchaser has on the property that are subordinate to the lien under which the property was sold, plus interest. CCP §729.060(b)(5). Under former CCP §702, this principle was applied when a creditor held both first and second mortgages (or other liens) on the property but foreclosed only the first lien and purchased the property at that lien sale. A redeeming party was required to pay the purchaser the amount bid at the sale plus the amount of the second lien. *Salsbery v Ritter* (1957) 48 C2d 1, 306 P2d 897. If the creditor foreclosed the second mortgage instead, the property was sold subject to the first mortgage, which would not be a lien to be considered in the redemption price. A deficiency judgment held by the foreclosing creditor was also held not to be a lien on the property that must be paid by a party seeking to redeem. *Simpson v Castle* (1878) 52 C 644.

Any rents and profits from the property that were paid to the purchaser, or the value of the purchaser's use and occupation of the property, may be offset against the amounts that comprise the redemption price under CCP §729.060(b). CCP §729.060(c).

If the purchaser and the redeeming party disagree on the amount of the redemption price or on whether the party seeking redemption is entitled to redeem, or if the purchaser refuses a tender of the purchase price, the party seeking redemption may file a petition with the court for an order determining the redemption price or determining whether the party seeking redemption is entitled to redeem. When the petition is filed, the petitioner must deposit the undisputed amount of the redemption price with the levying officer and give the levying officer written notice that the petition has been filed. CCP §729.070(a).

The petition must be written and must include the following statements (CCP §729.070(b)):

■ The amounts demanded to which the petitioner objects and the reasons for the objections.

■ Any amounts offset to which the purchaser objects and the justification for the offset.

■ The petitioner's status (*i.e.,* judgment debtor or successor in interest (CCP §729.020; see §3.74) that qualifies the petitioner to redeem. A copy of a recorded conveyance, an assignment, or other evidence of interest must be filed with the petition (see CCP §729.060(a)).

The court must hold a hearing on the petition within 20 days after its filing unless the hearing is continued for good cause. CCP §729.070(c). The purchaser must be served with a copy of the petition and notice of the time and place of the hearing at least ten days before the hearing. CCP §729.070(d). The person seeking to redeem the property has the burden of proof at the hearing. CCP §729.070(e). On affidavit or other evidence, the court must determine by order the amount required to redeem. CCP §729.070(f). If an amount in addition to that already deposited is required to redeem, the redeeming party has ten days after issuance of the order to pay the additional amount to the levying officer. CCP §729.070(g).

Tender of the redemption price determined by the court, or agreed on by the purchaser and redeeming party, is equivalent to payment (requiring the levying officer to deliver and record a certificate of redemption under CCP §729.080(b)) and, if the tender is refused, the levying officer must deposit the amount tendered with the county treasurer. If the purchaser does not claim the deposit within five years, it is paid into the county general fund. CCP §729.080(c).

§3.79 F. Possession, Rents, and Profits During Redemption Period

The debtor retains the right to possession of the property during the redemption period. CCP §729.090; see *Carpenter v Hamilton* (1944) 24 C2d 95, 147 P2d 563; *Munzinger v Caffrey* (1942) 49 CA2d 180, 121 P2d 13. The foreclosure purchaser is entitled to receive from the person in possession the rents and profits from the property or the value of the use and occupation of the property. CCP §729.090(a); see *Shintaffer v Bank of Italy Nat' l Trust & Sav. Ass'n* (1932) 216 C 243, 13 P2d 668; *House v Lala* (1963) 214 CA2d 238, 29 CR 450. The purchaser is liable, however, to a person who redeems the property, for any rents and profits the purchaser has received (CCP §729.090(b)) and, as discussed in §3.78, the amount of the rents and profits or the value of use and occupation may be offset against the redemption price (CCP §729.060(c)).

The purchaser is entitled to enter the property during the redemption period to repair and to maintain the premises and is entitled to an order from the court restraining waste on the premises. CCP §729.090(c). The court may grant an order restraining waste without notice. CCP §729.090(c). For further provisions concerning protection against waste, see CCP §§86, 564, 568.5, and 746.

§3.80 G. After Expiration of Redemption Period

If the redemption price is not deposited with the levying officer within the redemption period, or if any additional deposit required by the court under CCP §729.070(g) is not deposited within ten days after issuance of the order, the levying officer must promptly execute, deliver, and record a deed of sale that complies with CCP §701.670 (see §3.66) in favor of the execution sale purchaser. If a tender of the redemption price is accepted by the purchaser, or if the redeeming party tenders the redemption price determined by the court under CCP §729.070 (see §3.78) or a redemption price agreed on by the purchaser, the levying officers must execute, deliver, and record a certificate of redemption in favor of the party seeking to redeem. CCP §729.080(b)–(c). On redemption, the effect of the foreclosure sale is terminated (see §3.77), and the party who redeemed the property is restored to the estate that was sold by foreclosure. CCP §729.080(d).

Various remedies may be invoked to recover possession of the property after expiration of the redemption period, depending on which party has obtained title and which party is then in possession of the property. If the property has not been redeemed, then the purchaser at the foreclosure sale will usually be seeking to obtain possession from the debtor who is entitled to possession during the redemption period. CCP §729.090(a); see §3.79. The purchaser is entitled to bring an unlawful detainer action against the debtor under CCP §1161a(b)(2). See, e.g., *Moss v Williams* (1948) 84 CA2d 830, 191 P2d 804. The purchaser is also entitled to the less-expeditious remedy of ejectment. See *Dickey v Gibson* (1898) 121 C 276, 53 P 704. For discussion of ejectment, see California Real Property Remedies Practice, chap 10 (Cal CEB 1982). In cases under earlier judicial foreclosure statutes, the courts speak of the purchaser's right to obtain a "writ of assistance" from the court that issued the foreclosure judgment as a means of obtaining possession. See *Sullivan v Superior Court* (1921) 185 C 133, 195 P 1061; *Rafftery v Kirkpatrick* (1938) 29 CA2d 503, 85 P2d 147. It is unclear whether a writ of assistance is available under the Enforcement of Judgments Law (CCP §§680.010–724.260), which makes no mention of it. In any case, unlawful detainer under CCP §1161a is a relatively speedy summary remedy, although its use would require filing a separate action.

The foreclosure sale purchaser may be subject to the restrictions of a local rent control ordinance when attempting to evict a tenant of the trustor. See *Gross v Superior Court* (1985) 171 CA3d 265, 217 CR 284. For discussion of the situation that arises when the property is occupied by a tenant of the debtor, see California Residential Landlord-Tenant Practice §6.48 (Cal CEB 1986).

In some cases, the redeeming party may need to recover possession of the property. A redeeming party who is the debtor in the foreclosure action will often already be in possession because that right exists under CCP §729.090(a). If the foreclosure sale purchaser or some other party has actually taken possession during the redemption period, the redeeming party's remedies will depend on the facts. No unlawful detainer remedy has been expressly given to the debtor as redeeming party under CCP §1161a. Ejectment would almost certainly be available, however, as a remedy. See Real Property Remedies, chap 10.

If the redeeming party is a successor in interest to the debtor, the successor may need to recover possession of the property if the debtor has remained in possession. In that case, the successor would seem to be entitled under CCP §1161a(b)(4) to unlawful detainer as a remedy as the purchaser of the debtor's interest in the property. The successor would also probably be entitled to use ejectment as a remedy. See Real Property Remedies, chap 10.

Chapter 4: **One-Action and Antideficiency Rules**

4

One-Action and Antideficiency Rules

I. INTRODUCTION

§4.1   **A. History of Antideficiency Legislation**

California has a distinctive body of law regulating the right of a mortgagee or beneficiary to obtain a personal judgment against the mortgagor or trustor in addition to the amount realized from a sale of the security. See Poteat, *State Legislative Relief for the Mortgage Debtor During the Depression,* 5 Law & Contemp Probs 517 (1938). Before the 1930s, the common law mortgagee had the basic options of foreclosing on the security, bringing an action on the underlying note, or both. See Nelson & Whitman, Real Estate Finance Law §§8.1, 8.3 (2d ed 1985). The lender is not given this choice under California law. Recognizing debtors' inability to bargain effectively for their rights in a loan transaction and the need to halt the wholesale destruction of the small landowner class during the depression of the 1930s, the legislature enacted antideficiency rules (CCP §§580a, 580b, and 580d) to regulate the mortgagee's remedies. Because these remedial statutes are not part of any comprehensive plan, the courts have been compelled to fill in the legislative gaps with judicial lawmaking. As a result, confusion is high and predictability is low in this area.

See chap 8 on the application of these rules in multiple-security and multiple-party situations. For another extensive discussion of California antideficiency rules, see 2 California Real Property Financing, chap 3 (Cal CEB 1989).

§4.2   B. Application of Rules to Both Mortgages and Deeds of Trust

The fair-value provisions (CCP §§580a and 726), the one-action rule (CCP §726), and the antideficiency protections (CCP §§580b and 580d) all apply equally to both mortgages and deeds of trust. Sections 580a–580b and 580d specifically refer to both. Although §726 refers only to mortgages, CCP §725a makes the provisions of §726 applicable to deeds of trust.

Historically, the prevalent use of deeds of trust in California probably results from the fact that until 1933 the lending industry did not regard them as subject to the one-action rule. See §1.23. This belief was based on CCP §726's reference to mortgages, which are defined in CC §2924 to exclude transfers in trust. See *Koch v Briggs* (1859) 14 C 256; *Pierce v Robinson* (1859) 13 C 116. See also *Commercial Nat'l Bank v Catron* (10th Cir 1931) 50 F2d 1023 (one-action rule not applicable to deeds of trust); *Herbert Kraft Co. v Bryan* (1903) 140 C 73, 80, 73 P 745, 747; *Bateman v Burr* (1881) 57 C 480. In 1933, however, the California Supreme Court held that, because a deed of trust serves precisely the same economic function as a mortgage, it was to be treated as a mortgage and was therefore subject to all the rules restricting mortgage enforcement. *Bank of Italy Nat'l Trust & Sav. Ass'n v Bentley* (1933) 217 C 644, 20 P2d 940. Thus, the creditor who attempted to sue on its note, without first foreclosing or alleging that the security was worthless, was denied this remedy. Intimations in the opinion that the deed of trust might be rewritten to permit a waiver of CCP §726 were subsequently rejected in *Winklemen v Sides* (1939) 31 CA2d 387, 402, 88 P2d 147, 155.

§4.3   II. ONE-ACTION RULE

The one-action rule (CCP §726) begins: "There can be but one form of action for the recovery of any debt or the enforcement of any right secured by mortgage upon real property . . . ." This provision was first enacted in 1851 (as Practice Act §246) to provide for "one action," was reenacted in 1872 as CCP §726, and was amended in 1933 to refer to "one form of action." The 1933 change has never been treated as significant (see Comment, *Mortgages and Trust Deeds: Foreclosure Sale of a Portion of the Mortgaged Premises: Remedies Open to the Mortgagee When the Security Is Valueless: Pleading the Existence of Security,* 25 Calif L Rev 469 (1937)), and the rule is often still referred to as the one-action rule.

The general effect of the provision is to make foreclosure the sole remedy available to an unpaid mortgagee or beneficiary in California and thus deny it the possibility of an action solely on the note. A secured creditor cannot treat its debt as an ordinary debt and base an independent cause of action on it; the existence of real property security denies the creditor remedies open to unsecured creditors. See *Taylor v Bouissiere* (1987) 195 CA3d 1197, 241 CR 253 (one-action rule does not apply when leasehold is considered to constitute personal rather than real property; see §1.32). For further discussion of the one-action rule, see 2 California Real Property Financing §§3.37–3.53 (Cal CEB 1989).

§4.4   A. Purpose and Effects

The commonly stated purpose of CCP §726 is to eliminate the possibility that a multiplicity of actions will be brought against the defaulting debtor. See *Bank of Italy Nat' l Trust & Sav. Ass' n v Bentley* (1933) 217 C 644, 20 P2d 940; *Felton v West* (1894) 102 C 266, 36 P 676; *Ould v Stoddard* (1880) 54 C 613. The section was originally derived from §905 of New York's proposed Code of Civil Procedure, which was never adopted. Proposed §905 provided that, when a debt was secured by a mortgage, (1) separate actions on the debt and the security were not allowed, and (2) all the creditor's claims were required to be included in one action. The New York one-action principle would have limited the mortgagee to one remedy while permitting it to choose which one. California, however, limits the choice as well as the remedy. Because CCP §726 bars an independent action on the note, the only method by which a beneficiary may recover from the trustor's personal estate is by a deficiency judgment after a foreclosure sale has failed to produce enough to satisfy the debt. Thus, CCP §726 is a security-first rule as well as a one-action rule. A beneficiary seeking relief must pursue the security before looking to the trustor for satisfaction of the debt. *Porter v Muller* (1884) 65 C 512, 4 P 531; *Winklemen v Sides* (1939) 31 CA2d 387, 88 P2d 147.

This security-first principle has the further effect of converting the debtor's promise to pay from an absolute to a conditional obligation. A California trustor who signs a note does not promise unconditionally to pay the note, but rather promises to pay any deficiency that remains if a sale of the encumbered property does not satisfy the note. *Otto v Long* (1900) 127 C 471, 477, 59 P 895, 896; *Commercial Bank v Kershner* (1898) 120 C 495, 52 P 848. It is, of course, difficult to justify the security-first principle on antimultiplicity grounds because multiplicity is avoided equally well by a simple election-of-remedies doctrine, such as the one New York first considered. See Comment, *Mortgages & Trust Deeds: Enforcement of a Secured Debt in California*, 31 Calif L Rev 429 (1943). The courts have suggested no other reason for the existence of the one-action rule. See *Bank of Italy Nat'l Trust & Sav. Ass'n v Bentley, supra.*

A second major aspect of CCP §726 is that, although it confines the beneficiary to one remedy, it expands the scope of that remedy to provide the beneficiary with more comprehensive relief than was previously available. A common law mortgagee who foreclosed had to file a separate action to seek a deficiency judgment, and a mortgagee who sued on the note alone could not foreclose except by independent action. See *Felton v West, supra.* Under CCP §726, the California mortgagee or beneficiary may have both a foreclosure and a deficiency judgment in the same judicial action. *Felton v West, supra; Ould v Stoddard, supra.*

A previous drawback of the one-action rule (from the creditor's point of view) was that it delayed the creditor's opportunity to reach any other assets of the debtor until after a deficiency judgment had been obtained. Although unsecured creditors of the same debtor could attach other assets of the debtor when filing their action on the debt, the secured creditor was not allowed a prejudgment attachment. See §4.7. Under a 1977 amendment to CCP §483.010, however, a secured creditor may obtain a prejudgment attachment of the debtor's assets if the value of the security has decreased to less than the amount of the claim. On prejudgment attachment, see 1 Debt Collection Practice in California, chap 4 (Cal CEB 1987).

A more significant impact of CCP §726 on the mortgagee results from California's restrictions on deficiency judgments. See Leipziger, *Deficiency Judgments in California: The Supreme Court Tries Again,* 22 UCLA L Rev 753 (1975). Without the restrictions of CCP §726, a secured creditor could avoid most of the limitations on deficiency judgments by ignoring the security and obtaining a judgment on the note (and then perhaps executing on the same property). This approach is barred by §726. See *James v P.C.S. Ginning Co.* (1969) 276 CA2d 19, 80 CR 457. The rules governing deficiency judgments become even more important when any personal recovery against the debtor is confined to such judgments. In cases in which the antideficiency rules completely prohibit deficiency judgments, the effect of §726 is to limit the beneficiary to the real property security and nothing else; in those situations it becomes a security-only rule as well as a security-first and one-action rule. See §4.23.

§4.5   B. What Is an Action?

Creditors may discover to their chagrin that a step taken as part of the process of collecting a debt may constitute their one action under CCP §726. See generally 2 California Real Property Financing §3.38 (Cal CEB 1989). When mutual obligations exist between the parties, the one-action rule may deny the secured creditor the ability to assert its claim by cross-complaint against the debtor. *Pitzel v Maier Brewing Co.* (1912) 20 CA 737, 130 P 705. The deficiency may be used as an offsetting claim only after the security has first been exhausted. *Nelson v Bank of Am. Nat' l Trust & Sav. Ass' n* (1946) 76 CA2d 501, 173 P2d 322. But see *Bidart Bros. v Elmo Farming Co.* (1973) 35 CA3d 248, 110 CR 819.

The one-action rule has been held to prohibit banks from asserting "bankers' lien" rights against their customers (*McKean v German-American Sav. Bank* (1897) 118 C 334, 50 P 656; *Woodruff v California Republic Bank* (1977) 75 CA3d 108, 141 CR 915) and also from asserting the right of set-off, *i.e.,* reaching into accounts maintained by the debtor when the secured loan is in default (*Bank of America v Daily* (1984) 152 CA3d 767, 199 CR 557). See Rowan & Mertens, *Bank of America v Daily: Setoff versus the Right to Foreclose,* 8 CEB Real Prop L Rep 73 (June 1985). The status of sanctions for violation of the one-action rule in this manner is presently before the California Supreme Court in *Security Pac. Nat' l Bank v Wozab* (rev granted Aug. 24, 1989, S010502; superseded opinion at 210 CA3d 1119 (advance reports), 258 CR 850). See Munoz & Rabin, *The Sequel to Bank of America v Daily: Security Pac. Nat' l Bank v Wozab,* 12 CEB Real Prop L Rep 193 (Oct. 1989).

Bankers' offsets involve no judicial assistance and, in the author's view, cannot truly be characterized as CCP §726 actions, although the courts treat the appropriation (by judicial action or otherwise) of any of the debtor's unpledged assets before foreclosure as a violation of the security-first aspect of §726. See *In re Kristal* (Carnation Co. v Lampi) (9th Cir 1985) 758 F2d 454. Following the analogy of the multiply-secured creditor who omits some or all of the security from the collection process (see §§8.2–8.8), the courts have held that the appropriate sanction is loss of the security and consequent loss of the right to recover on the debt itself (because the security was never exhausted and could not be, in light of the sanction). The consequences of a misstep can be exceedingly costly for the creditor, as in *Security Pac. Nat' l Bank v Wozab, supra,* in which premature assertion of a banker's lien on a $2800 account cost the creditor its right to recover on its $976,000 note, guaranty, and deed of trust. Other courts are likely to find a more appropriate sanction than loss of the entire amount of a legitimate claim when an unpaid creditor has inadvertently taken an asset out of order.

§4.6   C. Worthless Security Exception

The one-action rule does not apply when the creditor's security is legally worthless, *e.g.,* when the real property is nonexistent (see *Dyer Law & Collection Co. v Abbott* (1921) 52 CA 545, 199 P 340), non-mortgageable (see *Republic Truck Sales Corp. v Peak* (1924) 194 C 492, 515, 229 P 331, 340), not owned by the mortgagor or trustor (see *Otto v Long* (1900) 127 C 471, 59 P 895), or not subject to being encumbered by the debtor (see *Curtin v Salmon River Hydraulic Gold Mining & Ditch Co.* (1903) 141 C 308, 74 P 851; *Powell v Patison* (1893) 100 C 236, 34 P 677). See also *McPhee v Townsend* (1903) 139 C 638, 73 P 584. See generally 2 California Real Property Financing §3.44 (Cal CEB 1989). In such situations, foreclosure would be meaningless, and the courts permit the creditor to proceed directly on its note without first having to obtain a deficiency judgment for the entire debt. *Otto v Long, supra.* A bankruptcy court's decision, holding that a motion for relief from the bankruptcy automatic stay (see §6.50) constitutes the creditor's one action (see *In re Rivers* (McReynolds v Rivers) (Bankr CD Cal 1984) 39 BR 608) cast terror in the lending industry until it was reversed on appeal (see *In re Rivers* (McReynolds v Rivers) (CD Cal 1984) 55 BR 699).

The exception does not apply when the security is valueless for economic rather than legal reasons. *Barbieri v Ramelli* (1890) 84 C 154, 23 P 1086; *Giandeini v Ramirez* (1936) 11 CA2d 469, 54 P2d 91. The beneficiary cannot justify avoiding foreclosure because it erred in its valuation of the security at the time the security was taken. A beneficiary who contends that its security has no value can best resolve the question through a foreclosure sale (where the market will demonstrate value) and may not compel a court to substitute its opinion of value for that of the marketplace. *Security-First Nat' l Bank v Chapman* (1939) 31 CA2d 182, 87 P2d 724; *Giandeini v Ramirez, supra.* See also *Bartlett v Cottle* (1883) 63 C 366.

§4.7 D. Subsequently Worthless Security Exception

When the security is destroyed after execution of the deed of trust, the beneficiary may sue immediately on its note and need not foreclose first. See *Cohen v Marshall* (1925) 197 C 117, 122, 239 P 1050, 1052 (mortgaged crops destroyed by rain and insects); *Toby v Oregon Pac. R.R.* (1893) 98 C 490, 33 P 550 (dictum concerning mortgaged ship lost at sea). The source of this exception is a section of California's attachment law, which originally provided that attachment would issue either on a suit on a note that was not secured or on a note for which the security had "without any act of the plaintiff . . . become valueless." Former CCP §537 (earlier wording), now CCP §483.010(b). See Comment, *Mortgages and Trust Deeds: Foreclosure Sale of a Portion of the Mortgaged Premises: Remedies Open to the Mortgagee When the Security Is Valueless: Pleading the Existence of Security,* 25 Calif L Rev 469 (1937). These provisions from the attachment statute have been read into CCP §726, so that a beneficiary whose security has become valueless is permitted not only to attach (CCP §483.010 (former CCP §537)) but also to sue on the note without foreclosing as would otherwise be required by §726. Because the attachment provision refers only to security that has *become* valueless, relief from the sanctions of §726 has been denied when the security was worthless when the lien was created. *Barbieri v Ramelli* (1890) 84 C 154, 23 P 1086.

The exception for subsequently worthless security does not include cases in which the creditor itself makes the security worthless. See CCP §483.010(b). Although security is usually regarded as something a creditor takes strictly for its own benefit (and which, therefore, the creditor can ignore when the security becomes inconvenient), the one-action rule condemns a creditor to its security and does not permit a unilateral divestment of it. *Western Fuel Co. v Sanford G. Lewald Co.* (1922) 190 C 25, 210 P 419; *Commercial Bank v Kershner* (1898) 120 C 495, 52 P 848. Only if the debtor consents may a creditor dispense with its security and proceed directly on the note. See CC §3513; *Martin v Becker* (1915) 169 C 301, 146 P 665; *Hibernia Sav. & Loan Soc'y v Thornton* (1895) 109 C 427, 42 P 447. See also *Salter v Ulrich* (1943) 22 C2d 263, 138 P2d 7. Thus, a creditor who loses its security through a culpable act does not come within the exception to the one-action rule. See *Hibernia Sav. & Loan Soc'y v Thornton, supra* (security discharged by improper probate proceedings by mortgagee); *Page v Latham* (1883) 63 C 75 (statute of limitations barred relief on security); *Pacific Valley Bank v Schwenke* (1987) 189 CA3d 134, 234 CR 298 (release of security to one debtor gives co-debtor a CCP §726 defense, even though second debtor was not trustor under deed of trust); *Cooper v Burch* (1906) 3 CA 470, 86 P 719 (mortgagee released security of record).

The worthless security exception does not apply to security that declines in value in a falling market to a point at which the creditor believes it to be valueless. See §4.6. When an opinion of worth is required, the creditor must foreclose to let the market determine that fact. *Bartlett v Cottle* (1883) 63 C 366; *Security-First Nat'l Bank v Chapman* (1939) 31 CA2d 182, 87 P2d 724; *Giandeini v Ramirez* (1936) 11 CA2d 469, 54 P2d 91. See §§4.40–4.42 on security impaired by waste.

The exception for subsequently worthless security includes a junior lienholder whose security is rendered valueless by a senior foreclosure sale. Thus, a "sold-out junior" is permitted to sue directly on the note despite CCP §726. *Roseleaf Corp. v Chierighino* (1963) 59 C2d 35, 27 CR 873; see §4.8.

The doctrine of worthless security has caused courts to create numerous and dubious distinctions between "legally worthless" and "economically worthless" security and between "originally worthless" and "subsequently worthless" security. Nothing in CCP §726 indicates that foreclosure may be avoided because of inadequacy of the security;

nothing in CCP §483.010 indicates that foreclosure (which is not mentioned in that section) is affected by the existence of worthless security. The natural reading of the two statutes would be to require foreclosure in all cases but to permit attachment to issue in foreclosure proceedings in which the security had become worthless. There is nothing inherently incompatible between foreclosure and attachment. In all cases in which the creditor originally held real property security, an action to foreclose on it would then be required. If the creditor believes the security to be worthless (or to have become worth less than the debt; see CCP §483.010(b)), it should also apply promptly for a writ of attachment. If the mortgagor disputes the allegation that the security is worthless, the question before the court would be whether to issue attachment, not whether to foreclose on the security. Foreclosure would always be required and the integrity of the one-action rule preserved. See Leipziger, *Deficiency Judgments in California: The Supreme Court Tries Again*, 22 UCLA L Rev 753, 790 n105 (1975).

§4.8 E. Sold-Out Junior Mortgagee or Beneficiary

Changes in market conditions and property values affect the holder of a junior deed of trust far more than the senior. When the senior's lien is large in relation to the total value of the property, a slight decline in property value may render the junior's security partially or even totally worthless. Thus, on a $200,000 house, when the first deed of trust secures a loan of $160,000 and the second deed of trust secures a $20,000 loan, the junior's security is affected by any decline in market value of more than 10 percent. Such a decline in value does not by itself, however, permit the junior to ignore the security and proceed against the trustor directly. *Barbieri v Ramelli* (1890) 84 C 154, 23 P 1086; *Giandeini v Ramirez* (1936) 11 CA2d 469, 54 P2d 91. A junior who believes that the security has no value because of the amount of the senior liens may not use that as an excuse to bypass the one-action rule; the junior must first foreclose judicially and sell the property subject to the paramount liens. If the junior is correct about the property's value, the sale will not produce enough to cover what is owed on the junior obligation, and the junior may obtain a deficiency judgment for the entire amount of the debt.

The situation changes, however, if the senior lienholder forecloses its lien. A senior foreclosure sale conveys the property free of all junior liens (see §§2.27, 3.23). Thus, the junior no longer has a lien on the property, and the security has been entirely destroyed. A sold-out junior thus holds security that has "become valueless" and is permitted to sue directly on the note. *Roseleaf Corp. v Chierighino* (1963) 59 C2d 35, 27 CR 873; *Savings Bank v Central Mkt. Co.* (1898) 122 C 28, 54 P 273; see *Greenebaum v Davis* (1900) 131 C 146, 63 P 165.

For federal income tax purposes, a junior mortgagee may claim a bad-debt loss after being sold out by a senior foreclosure if it can be shown that the junior debt has actually become worthless. The mere fact that the senior foreclosed, however, may not be sufficient. *Arthur Berenson* (1939) 39 BTA 77. The loss is either ordinary or capital, depending on whether the junior is a professional lender. IRC §§166, 1221.

§4.9   1. Sold-Out Junior's Complaint

Because the courts permit a junior to sue directly on the note when the senior has foreclosed (see §4.8), the complaint may take the form of a simple action for collection of an unsecured note. To eliminate the prospect of CCP §726's being raised as a defense, however, the complaint should also include an allegation that the security is worthless (see §4.10).

§4.10   2. Form: Allegation of Worthless Security

The note was originally secured by a deed of trust executed by defendant and delivered to plaintiff. The security interest created by the deed of trust has become valueless without any act of plaintiff, because the property encumbered by the deed of trust has been foreclosed on and sold under a deed of trust senior and paramount to the deed of trust given to plaintiff. _ _[No portion of the proceeds from the senior sale was available for the satisfaction of plaintiff's note./$_ _ _ _ _ _ was received from the sale, providing only partial satisfaction of plaintiff's note, leaving a balance of $_ _ _ _ _ _ due and unpaid.]_ _

Comment: This allegation should be used in the complaint when a sold-out junior lienor sues directly on the note. See §4.9.

§4.11 3. Problems Created by Sold-Out Junior Exception

The sold-out junior lienor is a common phenomenon. A defaulting trustor is likely to default on both the senior and junior notes, and a foreclosing senior beneficiary is likely to bid no more than the amount owed on the first deed of trust. In such a case, the trustor may be subject to two separate proceedings: a foreclosure by the senior and a subsequent action by the sold-out junior on the second note. The one-action rule thus does not protect the trustor from a multiplicity of actions when the property is subject to two deeds of trust. The junior may sue on its note even when the senior forecloses judicially, so that the trustor will be sued twice. More important, because an action on the note also bypasses many of California's antideficiency rules, the sold-out junior exception also strips the trustor of many antideficiency protections. See §§4.4, 4.31–4.35.

The sold-out junior exception came into existence because in early cases the courts held (without seriously considering the matter) that the junior lienholder was not required to foreclose along with the senior lienholder. See, *e.g., Savings Bank v Central Mkt. Co.* (1898) 122 C 28, 54 P 273. In a judicial foreclosure action brought by the first lienholder, the second lienholder will inevitably be named as a defendant to validate and perfect the foreclosure sale. See §3.23. Under the general rules of pleading, a cross-complaint by the junior for foreclosure of its lien would be proper. See *Hibernia Sav. & Loan Soc'y v London & Lancashire Fire Ins. Co.* (1903) 138 C 257, 71 P 334 (judgment lienor); *Stockton Sav. & Loan Soc'y v Harrold* (1900) 127 C 612, 60 P 165. Adherence to the policy of avoiding multiplicity of actions should have dictated that the junior join in any senior foreclosure action, foreclose its own deed of trust along with the senior's, and claim all surplus proceeds from the sale. This policy would also mean that a junior who failed to do this, having been served as a defendant, should be treated as having made the security worthless by its own inaction and thus rendered itself ineligible for relief. *Hibernia Sav. & Loan Soc'y v Thornton* (1895) 109 C 427, 42 P 447, discussed in §4.7. The law, however, developed contrary to this policy. If the junior cross-complained to foreclose its own deed of trust, it lost its right to redeem from the senior sale. *San Jose Water Co. v Lyndon* (1899) 124 C 518, 57 P 481. On postsale redemption, see §3.73. Thus, juniors usually concluded that it was wiser not to cross-complain for foreclosure of their liens as part of senior foreclosures.

§4.12   III. DEFICIENCY JUDGMENTS

California law presents a series of obstacles, known collectively as the antideficiency rules, to a mortgagee or beneficiary seeking a deficiency judgment. Substantive aspects of these rules are discussed in §§4.13–4.30; procedures for obtaining a deficiency judgment are discussed in §§3.67–3.72. There are three major pieces of antideficiency legislation in California: the private-sale bar (see §§4.14–4.16), the fair-value limitation (see §§4.17–4.22), and the purchase-money prohibition (see §§4.23–4.30).

§4.13   A. Deficiency Judgment Defined

Technically, a deficiency judgment is a judgment against the trustor for the difference between the unpaid balance of the secured debt (plus expenses) and the amount produced by the sale. Thus, for example, if at the time of foreclosure $35,000 is owed to the beneficiary and the high bid at the foreclosure sale is $28,000, the deficiency is $7000, and the beneficiary may obtain a personal judgment for this amount if a deficiency judgment is permitted. *Toby v Oregon Pac. R.R.* (1893) 98 C 490, 33 P 550; see §3.67.

The California courts have expanded the definition of deficiency judgment to include actions brought by sold-out juniors (see *Brown v Jensen* (1953) 41 C2d 193, 259 P2d 425 (junior's suit on note barred by CCP §580b)) and actions to recover damages for waste (see *Cornelison v Kornbluth* (1975) 15 C3d 590, 125 CR 557 (waste damages barred by CCP §§580b and 580d, except for bad-faith waste (dictum))). On the other hand, fraud actions have been exempted from the antideficiency provisions. See Fin C §§779, 7459–7460; CCP §726(f)–(h) (not applicable to loans of $150,000 or less (adjusted for inflation) on single-family residential property); *Lassar & Gross Int'l v Dunham* (1987) 196 CA3d 496, 241 CR 854; *Guild Mortgage Co. v Heller* (1987) 193 CA3d 1505, 239 CR 59; *Manson v Reed* (1986) 186 CA3d 1493, 231 CR 446; *Glendale Fed. Sav. & Loan Ass'n v Marina View Heights Dev. Co.* (1977) 66 CA3d 101, 138, 135 CR 802, 824. Financial Code §§779, 7459–7460 and CCP §726(f)–(h) were enacted to modify the decision in *First Fed. Sav. & Loan Ass'n v Lehman* (1984) 159 CA3d 537, 205 CR 600, in which the court subjected fraud actions to antideficiency rules unless the complaint alleged misrepresentations concerning the value of the security.

Damages may also be recovered for other types of fraudulent behavior as an exception to the antideficiency rules. *Bell v Roy* (1986) 187 CA3d 694, 232 CR 83 (trustor falsely released vendor's deed of trust); *Sawyer v First City Fin. Corp.* (1981) 124 CA3d 390, 177 CR 398 (conspiracy between trustor and senior to eliminate junior lien); see §4.43. See also *Passanisi v Merit-McBride Realtors* (1987) 190 CA3d 1496, 1509, 236 CR 59, 66 (attorneys' fees not barred by CCP §580d when beneficiary successfully resists trustor's action to enjoin foreclosure sale); *Kass v Weber* (1968) 261 CA2d 417, 67 CR 876 (rescission by defrauded beneficiary). An action for rent-skimming under CC §§890–894 is not subject to the one-action and antideficiency rules. CC §891(g). (Rent-skimming is defined as the practice of using revenue received from the rental of residential real property, during the first year after acquiring the property, without first applying the revenue to payments due on all mortgages and deeds of trust encumbering the property. CC §890(a).)

§4.14   B. Private-Sale Prohibition (CCP §580d)

Code of Civil Procedure §580d provides:

No judgment shall be rendered for any deficiency upon a note secured by a deed of trust or mortgage upon real property hereafter executed in any case in which the real property has been sold by the mortgagee or trustee under power of sale contained in such mortgage or deed of trust.

The provisions of this section shall not apply to any deed of trust, mortgage or other lien given to secure the payment of bonds or other evidences of indebtedness authorized or permitted to be issued by the Commissioner of Corporations, or which is made by a public utility subject to the provisions of the Public Utilities Act.

The section became effective in 1941 as the last of California's depression-era mortgagor-protection legislation. It imposes a complete bar against any deficiency judgment when the mortgagee or beneficiary has elected to foreclose by power of sale rather than judicially. Regardless of the inadequacy of the foreclosure sale proceeds, there is no further recovery. For discussion of the private-sale prohibition, see 2 California Real Property Financing §§3.28–3.36 (Cal CEB 1989).

§4.15   1. Section 580d and Redemption

Code of Civil Procedure §580d imposes no limitations on deficiency judgments following judicial foreclosures as opposed to power-of-sale foreclosures. Judicial sales, however, are subject to redemption by the trustor following the sale in cases in which a deficiency judgment is permitted. See §3.73. Thus, the purpose ascribed to §580d is to equalize judicial and nonjudicial foreclosure sales by burdening them, respectively, with the risk of redemption and a deficiency bar. The beneficiary who seeks a deficiency judgment must conduct a sale that is subject to redemption; the beneficiary who wants to make a nonredeemable sale must give up the right to a deficiency judgment. *Roseleaf Corp. v Chierighino* (1963) 59 C2d 35, 27 CR 873.

Although both forms of sale have drawbacks, the deterrents are clearly different, and the beneficiary chooses which device to employ. Consequently, the impact of the limitations is considerably lessened. When the property is worth at least enough to cover the debt still due, the creditor will usually choose a private sale, which will pay off the entire debt and also cut off the debtor's right of redemption. When the property is not valuable enough to cover the debt, the creditor may seek a judicial sale and deficiency judgment. A debtor may be subject to a deficiency judgment or to a nonredeemable sale, at the creditor's election. Section 580d provides only that the creditor cannot have both remedies against the debtor.

§4.16   2. Section 580d as Deterrent to Underbidding

The purpose of the deficiency bar in trustees' sales and the right of redemption in judicial sales is to deter underbidding at the sale. *Roseleaf Corp. v Chierighino* (1963) 59 C2d 35, 27 CR 873. Both accomplish this purpose, but in different ways, and neither eliminates underbidding in all cases.

Postsale redemption deters underbidding by making underbids subject to nullification through later redemption. For discussion of redemption rights, see §3.73. If the market value of the property is $400,000, the beneficiary is owed $400,000, and the beneficiary bids $400,000 at the sale, the trustor is unlikely to redeem the property. If the beneficiary bids only $300,000 for the property, however, the trustor may be motivated to redeem in order to acquire a $400,000 property for only $300,000. See §3.73. Redemption for $300,000 leaves the beneficiary without the property and still owed $100,000. Thus, one effect of the underbid is that the proceeds from the property do not satisfy the full debt, although the property was worth enough to do so. To avoid this risk, a beneficiary will often bid the value of the property at least up to the extent of debt (although there may be an incentive to underbid in some cases; see §8.8).

In nonjudicial foreclosure sales, redemption does not deter underbidding, because such sales are absolute. Neither the trustor nor junior lienholders have redemption rights once the sale is concluded. See §2.3. Although eliminating redemption should encourage greater competitive bidding, it is not always enough and, during the 1930s, nonredeemable sales combined with deficiency judgments based on underbidding were common. Code of Civil Procedure §580d was enacted to eliminate this situation. See also the discussion of CCP §580a in §§4.17–4.22.

Section 580d does not so much discourage underbidding as make underbidding irrelevant. The total deficiency bar nullifies the prospective profit from an underbid. A beneficiary conducting a trustee's sale of the property is treated as having bid the full amount of its debt, and no actual bid for a lesser sum will make any difference as far as deficiency judgments are concerned. There may be other reasons for underbidding at a private sale, but a deficiency judgment is not one of them. See Johnson & Smith, *The Case Against the Full Value Bid,* 12 CEB Real Prop L Rep 141 (July 1989); Crocker, *Beneficiary's Underbid— A Neglected Tool,* 44 LA B Bull 295 (1969). Underbidding may be appropriate, for example, if the beneficiary intends to seek recovery on other claims such as waste, when a full credit-bid would bar the claim. See *Sumitomo Bank v Taurus Developers* (1986) 185 CA3d 211, 229 CR 719. On underbidding in connection with seeking insurance proceeds as additional security, see §8.8.

Both the redemption statute and CCP §580d operate effectively only when the market value of the property is less than the debt. When the value of the property exceeds the debt, neither provision fully protects the debtor against underbidding. For example, assume that the property is worth $500,000, with a debt of $400,000. If the sale is private, the beneficiary has no inducement to bid over $400,000 unless there are other bidders. Section 580d eliminates the possibility of a profit from bidding less than $400,000, because no deficiency judgment will ensue, but the statute creates no incentive to bid over $400,000; it regulates deficiencies, not surpluses. A similar situation occurs in the judicial sale. The beneficiary is discouraged from bidding less than $400,000 but is not encouraged to bid more than $400,000. Although property worth $500,000 is more likely to be redeemed if it sold for $400,000 than if it sold for $500,000, this provides no motivation for the beneficiary to bid more than $400,000. Every cent bid by the beneficiary over what it is owed must be in the form of cash and will be turned over to the trustor or to junior creditors; a more expensive redemption thus returns to the beneficiary only what it has previously paid out. If the beneficiary prefers to have cash rather than to hold land, it will bid only $400,000, hoping that this low figure will encourage someone else to redeem.

Because neither system protects the trustor from underbidding when the property is worth more than the debt, the combined effect leads a beneficiary into making a choice, usually to the debtor's detriment:

■ If the property is worth more than the debt, the beneficiary should foreclose by power of sale; the bid will be less than the market value of the property, the sale will be nonredeemable, and there will be no surplus for the debtor or junior lienholders.

■ If the property is worth less than the debt, the beneficiary should foreclose judicially and make a credit-bid at close to market value; the trustor's right of redemption will be of little value, and the beneficiary will seek a deficiency judgment.

For discussion of bankruptcy courts' treatment of foreclosure sales as fraudulent transfers in underbidding cases, see §6.56.

§4.17   C. Fair-Value Limitation (CCP §§726, 580a)

Code of Civil Procedure §726(b) provides that a deficiency judgment is limited to

the amount by which the amount of the indebtedness . . . exceeds the fair value of the property . . . as of the date of sale [provided, however, that in] no event shall the amount of the judgment . . . exceed the difference between the amount for which the property was sold and the entire amount of the indebtedness . . . .

(References to interest and costs are omitted.) Section 726(b) also provides that (1) within three months after the judicial foreclosure sale the plaintiff may apply to the court for a deficiency judgment, (2) the court must take evidence of fair value before rendering judgment, and (3) the amount of the judgment is limited as provided.

Code of Civil Procedure §580a, which applies to nonjudicial foreclosure sales, requires the creditor to file a complaint for the deficiency within three months after the sale and imposes a fair-value hearing and judgment limitation similar to that of CCP §726(b). See §4.21. The three-month limitation period also applies to an action on the note brought by a sold-out junior following a trustee's sale at which the junior was the successful bidder. *Bank of Hemet v U.S.* (9th Cir 1981) 643 F2d 661.

These two sections limit the size of the deficiency judgment to either (1) the difference between the unpaid debt and the fair value of the security or (2) the difference between the debt and the sale price of the security, whichever is smaller. Thus, if the foreclosing beneficiary is owed $500,000 at the time of sale and the high bid is $400,000, the beneficiary will be able to obtain a deficiency judgment for $100,000 if the court finds that the fair value of the property is $400,000 or less, *i.e.,* the fair value is less than the amount bid. If the court finds that the fair value at the time of sale was $420,000, the beneficiary is restricted to an $80,000 deficiency judgment (the difference between the debt and the fair value, which in this case is smaller than the difference between the debt and the selling price). Because of redemption rights, a creditor should bid the value of the property at least up to the amount of the debt. If the fair value is found to be only $350,000, the deficiency will be $100,000, not $150,000, because the amount bid ($400,000), not the fair value ($350,000), governs when the amount bid is larger.

On procedures for determining fair value, see §§3.68–3.69. On the effectiveness of fair-value rules on bidding behavior, see §4.20. For extensive discussion of the fair-value provisions, see 2 California Real Property Financing §§3.24–3.27 (Cal CEB 1989).

Fair-value limitations do not apply to a sale of real property made "free and clear of all liens" under bankruptcy law (11 USC §363(f)) rather than by foreclosure. *Coppola v Superior Court* (1989) 211 CA3d 848, 259 CR 811.

§4.18 1. Definition of Fair Value

Code of Civil Procedure §726 uses the term "fair value"; CCP §580a uses "fair market value" instead. In *Roseleaf Corp. v Chierighino*

(1963) 59 C2d 35, 27 CR 873, the court used the terms interchangeably, but this indifference was characterized by the court in *Rainer Mortgage v Silverwood, Ltd.* (1985) 163 CA3d 359, 366 n5, 209 CR 294, 298 n5, as improvident dicta. Section 726 originally used the term "fair market value," but the statute was amended in 1937 to refer only to "fair value." A proposal at that time to use the term "intrinsic value" was dropped, but the court in *Rainer* nevertheless held that intrinsic (or underlying) value was the concept intended by the legislature; market value is only one factor to consider in calculating this amount.

How the court is to appraise the property's intrinsic value is not entirely clear. In *Rainer,* the court held that the appraisal should not take into account the price-reducing fact that the judicial foreclosure sale was subject to redemption, because redemption was only a temporary possibility. In *Nelson v Orosco* (1981) 117 CA3d 73, 172 CR 457, however, the court held that the fact that the property was subject to a lis pendens at the time of sale would be considered in determining its fair value.

For discussion of procedures for the fair-value hearing, see §3.69.

§4.19   2. Rationale

The fair-value provisions of CCP §§726 and 580a were enacted in 1933 when it became apparent that the traditional debtor-protection mechanisms were no longer working. It had previously been assumed that a defaulting trustor could expect that the property would be sold for a reasonable price because (a) the foreclosure sale would be by public auction, and (b) there was a right of redemption following the sale and the trustor or junior creditors would repurchase the property if it had been underbid. The depression so depleted cash and credit, however, that only the beneficiary ever bid at its foreclosure sale and neither the junior creditor nor the trustor had the means to redeem, even when redemption was a bargain. (The beneficiary could afford to bid at the sale because it was allowed to credit-bid the debt owed to it and thus did not need cash.) On redemption, see §§3.73–3.80.

§4.20   3. Effectiveness

The fair-value provisions limit only deficiency judgments; when no deficiency judgment is sought, there is no fair-value hearing. This means that a trustor is protected against bids that are both below the value of the property and below the amount owed on the debt, but is not protected against any bid that equals or exceeds the debt even though it is below the value of the property. The fair-value provisions thus operate much the same as CCP §580d. See §4.16. If the property has a market value of $500,000 and the balance unpaid on the note is $400,000, nothing in the fair-value sections prevents the beneficiary from bidding only $400,000, and nothing in them encourages the beneficiary to bid more than $400,000. Because most beneficiaries make loans for less than the current market value of the security, the value of the foreclosed property often exceeds the debt at the time of sale. In such instances, the fair-value provisions do nothing to ensure a fair bid. See also §4.33. For further discussion, see 2 California Real Property Financing §3.25 (Cal CEB 1989).

§4.21 4. Fair Value Following Exercise of Power of Sale

For eight years, between 1933 (when CCP §580a was enacted) and 1941 (when CCP §580d became effective), §580a limited the size of money judgments following nonjudicial foreclosure sales. Enactment of §580d, however, created a complete bar to a deficiency judgment after a private sale, preempting §580a in most situations.

Nevertheless, the legislature has never repealed CCP §580a, and its continued existence requires that it be given some role in the fore-closure system. It is applied to a sold-out junior who was the success-ful bidder at the senior lienor's sale. See §4.33. It may eventually be held to be similarly applicable to guarantors and in multiple-security cases. See §§4.33, 8.5, 8.13. Section 580a refers to "the balance due upon an obligation"; CCP §580d mentions only a "note." Possibly §580a would be called into play in private foreclosure sales of nonnote obligations to which §580d might not apply. See *Willys of Marin Co. v Pierce* (1956) 140 CA2d 826, 296 P2d 25.

§4.22 5. Fair Value and One-Action Rule

Without the limitations of the one-action rule, a secured creditor could easily avoid the restrictions of the fair-value provisions: The creditor could merely file an action on the note, obtain a personal judgment, and levy on the same property. See *Salter v Ulrich* (1943) 22 C2d 263, 138 P2d 7; *James v P.C.S. Ginning Co.* (1969) 276 CA2d 19, 80 CR 457. The creditor could then bid less than the amount owed on the judgment, leaving the judgment partially unsatisfied. There is no provision for a fair-value hearing at an execution sale. CCP §701.570; see *Rauer v Hertweck* (1917) 175 C 278, 165 P 946; *Winbigler v Sherman* (1917) 175 C 270, 165 P 943; *Central Pac. R.R. v Creed* (1886) 70 C 497, 11 P 772; *Smith v Randall* (1856) 6 C 47. Because the one-action rule forces secured creditors to foreclose, however, the rule also forces them into a fair-value hearing whenever they seek more than the value of their security.

§4.23   D. Purchase-Money Prohibition (CCP §580b)

In its present form, CCP §580b provides:

No deficiency judgment shall lie in any event after any sale of real property for failure of the purchaser to complete his contract of sale, or under a deed of trust, or mortgage, given to the vendor to secure payment of the balance of the purchase price of real property, or under a deed of trust, or mortgage, on a dwelling for not more than four families given to a lender to secure repayment of a loan which was in fact used to pay all or part of the purchase price of such dwelling occupied, entirely or in part, by the purchaser.

Where both a chattel mortgage and a deed of trust or mortgage have been given to secure payment of the balance of the combined purchase price of both real and personal property, no deficiency judgment shall lie at any time under any one thereof if no deficiency judgment would lie under the deed of trust or mortgage on real property.

The statute was first enacted in 1933, although some provisions were added later. The reference to contracts of sale in the first paragraph was added in 1935; the entire second paragraph, dealing with combined real and personal property security, was added in 1949; and the distinction between vendor and third party financing was added in 1963.

The basic rule of CCP §580b may be simply stated: Deficiency judgments are prohibited after the foreclosure sale of real property that secures a purchase-money loan. Purchase-money, as presently included within §580b, means either money loaned by the seller to the purchaser or, if loaned by a third party, money used to pay all or part of the purchase price of a dwelling of not more than four units occupied entirely or in part by the purchaser. See §4.25 for discussion of the "standard transaction" falling within the scope of §580b. See generally 2 California Real Property Financing §§3.3–3.23 (Cal CEB 1989).

The basic rule has not been simple to apply, however, and has caused attorneys considerable uncertainty when advising clients on whether a particular transaction falls within the purchase-money prohibition.

§4.24   1. Section 580b Contrasted With Other Antideficiency Rules

Code of Civil Procedure §580b operates within a different frame of reference than do the one-action, extrajudicial sale, and fair-value provisions of the code. The other rules all relate to the process of foreclosure and do not apply to preforeclosure events. Section 580b has nothing to do with foreclosure but denies deficiency judgments to certain creditors regardless of what happens at the foreclosure. Whether obligations come under §580b depends on the nature of the secured transaction when it first occurs, *i.e.,* whether the loan was originally made for the purpose of purchasing the real property security. Subsequent events do not alter the effect of §580b. *Brown v Jensen* (1953) 41 C2d 193, 259 P2d 425. See discussion in §4.26. Thus, in contrast to the other antideficiency rules, application of §580b depends on the circumstances involved in making the loan rather than on what happens when the loan is in default. *Paramount Sav. & Loan Ass'n v Barber* (1968) 263 CA2d 166, 69 CR 390. Similar purchase-money antideficiency rules apply to mobilehomes (CC §2983.8; see *Bank of Sonoma County v Dorries* (1986) 185 CA3d 1291, 230 CR 459) and floating homes (Health & S C §18038.7; see *Security Pac. Nat'l Bank v Cassavant* (1988) 205 CA3d 127, 252 CR 175).

§4.25   2. Scope of §580b: Standard Transactions

The California Supreme Court has held that CCP §580b covers only "standard" purchase-money transactions and certain variations that come within the purposes of §580b. *Spangler v Memel* (1972) 7 C3d 603, 102 CR 807; *Roseleaf Corp. v Chierighino* (1963) 59 C2d 35, 27 CR 873. The standard two-party transaction is one in which the seller takes back a deed of trust (or mortgage) on the property that secures a note from the buyer for all or part of the price. If the seller's deed of trust (or mortgage) is a first deed of trust, the transaction clearly comes under §580b. If the deed of trust is a second deed of trust, it still fits within the notion of a "standard" purchase-money transaction, at least when the senior deed of trust secures a conventional first loan on the property. *Brown v Jensen* (1953) 41 C2d 193, 259 P2d 425. On application of §580b when the property is subsequently conveyed to new owners, see §§8.23–8.26.

Since 1963, the scope of CCP §580b has included a loan from a third party given to enable the buyer to purchase a one-to-four-unit dwelling that the buyer will personally occupy, in whole or in part. *Prunty v Bank of America* (1974) 37 CA3d 430, 112 CR 370; see §4.29.

In all the transactions described above, CCP §580b is applied automatically to prohibit any deficiency judgment against the purchaser. Presumably no arguments by the creditor based on equity or policy will change the result. In all transactions that differ from the standard, however, the supreme court has stated that application of §580b depends on whether its purposes will be met by giving or refusing deficiency protection to the purchaser. *Spangler v Memel* (1972) 7 C3d 603, 613, 102 CR 807, 814; *Roseleaf Corp. v Chierighino* (1963) 59 C2d 35, 41, 27 CR 873, 876. Thus, a natural first line of attack for any beneficiary seeking a deficiency judgment is to contend that the particular transaction before the court is a variation that does not fall within the purposes of §580b (see §§4.26–4.28). See *Clayton Dev. Co. v Falvey* (1988) 206 CA3d 438, 253 CR 609 (defective mortgage valid as equitable mortgage but still subject to §580b); *Allstate Sav. & Loan Ass'n v Murphy* (1979) 98 CA3d 761, 159 CR 663 (loan to finance construction of swimming pool not subject to §580b). For further discussion of the *Clayton* decision and its ramifications, see Little & Anscher, *Avoiding the Equitable Mortgage Trap,* 12 CEB Real Prop L Rep 193 (Oct. 1989).

§4.26   3. Section 580b: Purposes

There is no significant legislative history concerning the enactment of CCP §580b. There is much judicial explanation of its purposes, but many of the court's arguments are circular or contradictory. The opinion in *Brown v Jensen* (1953) 41 C2d 193, 259 P2d 425, was the first to ascribe purposes to §580b. In *Brown,* the supreme court stated that the section was intended to ensure that the beneficiary can look only to the security for recovery of a purchase-money debt, because the seller who takes back a deed of trust knows the value of the security and therefore assumes the risk that it will become inadequate. Ten years later, however, the court effectively rejected this position, stating that (a) it is doubtful that the legislature intended to base the protection on the relative astuteness of buyer and seller, and (b) the statement in *Brown* that a beneficiary must look only to the security states a conclusion without an explanation. *Roseleaf Corp. v Chierighino* (1963) 59 C2d 35, 27 CR 873. The *Roseleaf* court declared instead (59 C2d at 42, 27 CR at 877) that, by placing the risk of inadequate security on the vendor, a

vendor is thus discouraged from overvaluing the security. Precarious land promotion schemes are discouraged, for the security value of the land gives purchasers a clue as to its true market value [and that if] inadequacy of the security results, not from overvaluing, but from a decline in property values during a general or local depression, section 580b prevents the aggravation of the downturn that would result if defaulting purchasers were burdened with large personal liability. Section 580b thus serves as a stabilizing factor in land sales.

These two purposes of CCP §580b, that of preventing overvaluation and of stabilizing property values (referred to as overvaluation and stabilization), are analyzed at length in §§4.27–4.28. Because the courts subject all but standard transactions to an analysis of whether the purposes of §580b will be met by granting a deficiency judgment (see §4.25), a full understanding of both concepts is necessary.

§4.27 a. Overvaluation

Although the courts have stated that CCP §580b was intended to prevent overvaluation of real property (see *Roseleaf Corp. v Chierighino* (1963) 59 C2d 35, 27 CR 873; see §4.26), the statute generally produces the opposite result. A purchaser who knows that he or she will be immune from personal liability for any default on the purchase price is likely to offer more rather than less for the property. If the market rises, there is a profit but if the market falls, the loss is cushioned or completely avoided by CCP §580b. Section 580b may have been expected to discourage the seller from asking too high a price for property, but nothing in its operation encourages the seller to take a lower price: If the note is paid, the seller is better off; if the note is not paid, its large size permits a greater credit-bid at the foreclosure sale. The note cannot be collected beyond the property's worth, but a larger uncollectible note is no worse than a smaller uncollectible one. Thus, instead of discouraging sellers from taking second deeds of trust, §580b has often led sellers to raise prices to compensate for the risk of the worthlessness of their second deeds of trust, and buyers have just as often been willing to pay these higher asking prices instead of making substantial downpayments because of §580b antideficiency protection.

The courts have analyzed overvaluation in the construction field differently from overvaluation in real property sales. One court of appeal held that CCP §580b should be applied to a lender supplying funds for construction of the borrower's personal residence on the ground that this would "discourage construction borrowing which is 'unsound' because the financed construction is overvalued." *Prunty v Bank of America* (1974) 37 CA3d 430, 441, 112 CR 370, 377. In *Spangler v Memel* (1972) 7 C3d 603, 102 CR 807, however, the court held that a purchaser of raw land who gives a first deed of trust to the construction lender and a second subordinated deed of trust to the seller of the land is not protected against a personal judgment in favor of the seller following a senior foreclosure sale, on the opposite ground that denial of protection to the purchaser is the best deterrent to overvaluation in that context. The decisions in *Prunty* and *Spangler* make it apparent that a court can allocate the risk as it pleases, justifying either result on the ground of overvaluation. This judicial inconsistency, of course, makes prediction of future results difficult. See also *Boyle v Sweeney* (1989) 207 CA3d 998, 255 CR 153.

A construction loan on commercial property is not subject to CCP §580b, because the funds come from a third party and do not involve a personal dwelling. Dictum in *Spangler v Memel* (1972) 7 C3d 603, 614 n9, 102 CR 807, 814 n9, that a seller of vacant land who subordinates to a construction loan for the buyer's personal residence might be treated differently from a seller who subordinates to a construction loan for a commercial building, suggests that the commercial-residential distinction could someday be applied to sellers as well as to third party lenders. But see *Ziegler v Barnes* (1988) 200 CA3d 224, 246 CR 69, discussed in §4.35. When subordination is agreed on but does not occur, there is no reason to give the vendor the benefit of the *Spangler* exemption for CCP §580b. See *Budget Realty v Hunter* (1984) 157 CA3d 511, 204 CR 48.

§4.28 b. Stabilization

Overvaluation (see §4.27) and stabilization are supposed to operate in complementary situations. The overvaluation mechanism is intended to function when the initial selling price is so unrealistically high as to guarantee that a deficiency judgment will follow any foreclosure sale, because the value of the property is not equal to the amount of the debt. The stabilization mechanism, on the other hand, is intended to apply when the parties initially set a proper selling price, but the market then declines and the security can no longer cover the debt. *Roseleaf Corp. v Chierighino* (1963) 59 C2d 35, 27 CR 873.

The stabilization policy set forth in *Roseleaf* is not directed at the immediate parties but is aimed at slowing down an overall economic depression. The assumption appears to be that a trustor who loses the security is more likely to default on his or her other obligations if also faced with a deficiency judgment. This may lead the unpaid creditors into financial difficulties, thus aggravating a downturn in the economy.

The stabilization policy has been as difficult to justify as the overvaluation policy. Depressions can be more effectively impeded by giving all debtors, not just purchase-money trustors, antideficiency protection. Furthermore, denial of a deficiency judgment in an otherwise proper case (*i.e.,* when the property is truly not worth the debt) does not eliminate a loss but merely shifts it from trustor to beneficiary. The beneficiary then becomes the one likely to default on debts, thus aggravating an economic downturn. Finally, the 1963 amendment to CCP §580b, which partially exempts third party lenders from the statute, tends to discredit the notion that the purpose of the statute is to make creditors a buffer against depressions.

In the construction field, one court of appeal has stated that the stabilization policy covers natural disasters (*e.g.,* landslides) as well as economic ones. In *Prunty v Bank of America* (1974) 37 CA3d 430, 442, 112 CR 370, 377, the court stated that the construction lender is able to bear such risks because it controls the entire construction process and can purchase insurance against physical risks. *Prunty v Bank of America, supra.* (If this line of reasoning is followed, the unavailability of depression insurance should result in protection for lenders during economic downturns.)

§4.29   4. Third Party Loans; History and Rationale of §580b

Until 1963, CCP §580b did not specify the categories of lenders covered by its "purchase-money" prohibition. Early commentators, interpreting decisions in other states, took the prohibition to refer only to seller financing. See Currie & Lieberman, *Purchase-Money Mortgages and State Lines: A Study in Conflict-of-Laws Method,* 1960 Duke LJ 1; Nelson & Whitman, Real Estate Finance Law §5.35 (2d ed 1985). Although some early supreme court dicta indicated that third party lenders would be considered purchase-money creditors (see *Stockton Sav. & Loan Bank v Massanet* (1941) 18 C2d 200, 114 P2d 592), one court of appeal held that they were not (*Peterson v Wilson* (1948) 88 CA2d 617, 199 P2d 757).

In *Roseleaf Corp. v Chierighino* (1963) 59 C2d 35, 27 CR 873, the court clearly implied inclusion of third party lenders because the policies of overvaluation and stabilization work best (if at all) when so applied. Three weeks after *Roseleaf* was decided, the supreme court ruled that a third party (the seller's broker) who advanced credit to enable the buyer to conclude the sale came within CCP §580b and was therefore barred from obtaining a deficiency judgment. *Bargioni v Hill* (1963) 59 C2d 121, 28 CR 321 (disapproving *Peterson v Wilson, supra*).

In response, the legislature amended CCP §580b (in 1963) to cover third party lenders. This amendment makes buyer protection dependent on the nature of the property purchased. Residential property of one to four units, on which the buyer will reside, has §580b protection. Residential property of over four units, commercial property, or raw land has no deficiency protection. This distinction is relevant only to third party loans, not to vendor financing. The vendor cannot have a deficiency judgment regardless of the kind of property involved. See §4.23.

The legislative standards for third party lenders make rational application of the judicial policies of overvaluation and stabilization all the more difficult. A policy against overvaluation can be effective in the third party loan context, because a third party lender does not set the selling price or profit from it and will therefore lend only as much as the property is worth if antideficiency rules prohibit recourse beyond the security. (Even without CCP §580b, institutional lenders may be restricted by loan-to-value ratio requirements from lending more than a stated percentage of the property's appraised value. See, *e.g.,* Fin C §§1227 (state banks), 7509 (state savings and loan associations); 12 CFR §545.32(d) (federal savings and loan associations).) The amount that a third party is willing to lend furnishes the parties a clue to the value of the property and could lead to a realistic selling price. *Spangler v Memel* (1972) 7 C3d 603, 102 CR 807; see Rintala, *California's Anti-Deficiency Legislation and Suretyship Law: The Transversion of Protective Statutory Schemes,* 17 UCLA L Rev 245 (1969). When commercial property is involved, however, the California lender is not affected by CCP §580b and can look to the buyer-borrower for a deficiency. Consequently, the lender is not dependent on a proper valuation of the property, but the seller, who sets the price, is bound by §580b. A serious overvaluation approach would reverse this arrangement, subject the lender to §580b, and not bar the seller by it.

The stabilization policy justifies a complete lender exemption from CCP §580b, even on loans for small residential properties, because a third party lender who is denied an otherwise proper deficiency judgment (*i.e.,* when the property is worth less than the debt) suffers a real loss (because actual dollars were loaned and not recovered), which could cause the lender to default on its own obligations elsewhere and thereby fuel a depression. Thus, neither policy seems consistent with the actual provisions of §580b concerning third party lenders.

§4.30   5. Structuring Transactions To Avoid §580b

Because CCP §580b gives protection in some cases and denies it in others (see §4.23), it is not surprising that parties structure transactions to try to avoid the statute's debtor protections. The courts have been erratic in deciding which arrangements permissibly avoid §580b and which do not. The basic principle, of course, should be that courts will look beyond form and into the substance of transactions. See *Bank of Italy Nat'l Trust & Sav. Ass'n v Bentley* (1933) 217 C 644, 20 P2d 940.

Shortly after determining the policies underlying CCP §580b (see *Roseleaf Corp. v Chierighino* (1963) 59 C2d 35, 27 CR 873; §§4.25–4.29), however, the California Supreme Court permitted a transparent avoidance device to succeed. In *Kistler v Vasi* (1969) 71 C2d 261, 78

CR 170, a purchaser of raw land paid part of the price in the form of a note and deed of trust to the seller's broker. Although the transaction was an exchange, the broker took the note in satisfaction of its commission; *i.e.,* essentially the buyer gave a note to the seller for part of the purchase price, and the seller turned it over to the broker to satisfy the seller's liability to the broker for the commission. Accordingly, recovery of a deficiency on the note should have been barred by §580b because the note was, in effect, assigned to the broker. The court permitted recovery, however, on the rationale that the parties were free to structure the transaction either to give or to withhold deficiency protection to the buyer. Moreover, the buyer presumably paid a lower price in return for executing an unprotected note (which is hardly consistent with the notion that §580b is intended to prevent overvaluation, if a protected purchase-money note would have generated a higher price).

Conversely, in *Ziegler v Barnes* (1988) 200 CA3d 224, 246 CR 69, the court held that a similar arrangement did not escape CCP §580b protection in a case in which the true seller had the buyer execute a note to a third party as part of the ostensible acquisition of a different parcel (which was then traded to the true seller as part of a tax-deferred exchange). Without reference to *Kistler v Vasi, supra,* the court refused to allow the form of the transaction to override its substance, *i.e.,* that the buyer gave a note to the true seller for the property ultimately acquired by the buyer.

Giving priority to substance over form does not, however, necessarily guarantee predictability. In *BMP Prop. Dev. v Melvin* (1988) 198 CA3d 526, 243 CR 715, the seller exchanged its property with the buyers and also loaned them $80,000 to cover cash-flow shortages and for other nonpurchase-money purposes. Although most observers would have predicted that it would not be treated as protected by CCP §580b, the court held that it was a purchase-money loan that was necessary to the sale because the buyers could not have afforded the transaction otherwise. Because the loan was not in the form of a purchase-money loan (it was made through a separate escrow after the sale was completed), this outcome rests solely on the substance of the transaction. The outcome does not aid predictability of results in other cases, however; practitioners can only guess whether a court will decide that a related transaction is necessary to the sale.

As discussed more thoroughly elsewhere, a lender who wishes to avoid CCP §580b protection may also consider using one of the following devices:

■ Securing the note with property other than that being purchased with the loan proceeds (see §8.6);

■ Securing the note with multiple security (see §§8.2–8.8);

■ Splitting the debt into several notes, each separately secured (see §§8.28–8.30);

■ Representing some part of the debt by an unsecured note (see §4.38); and

■ Requiring that the note be guaranteed (see §§8.10–8.18).

§4.31   IV. SOLD-OUT JUNIOR AND ANTIDEFICIENCY RULES

A nonselling junior creditor whose security is destroyed when the senior forecloses is permitted to bring an action on the note directly against the trustor, because the security-first aspect of the one-action rule does not apply in this situation. See §4.8. When the sold-out junior brings an action on the trustor's note, a series of special problems arise concerning application of the antideficiency rules. These problems are discussed in §§4.32–4.35.

§4.32   A. Nonjudicial Sales

The California Supreme Court has held that a nonselling junior creditor is not barred from bringing an action directly on the note merely because the senior foreclosure was conducted under the senior power of sale rather than by court action. *Roseleaf Corp. v Chierighino* (1963) 59 C2d 35, 27 CR 873. The selling senior is barred from obtaining a deficiency judgment by CCP §580d, but the nonselling junior is not. See §4.14 on CCP §580d. The rationale stated in *Roseleaf* is that the junior should not be penalized for a choice (concerning the method of foreclosure) that the junior did not make. A junior's action on the note is not barred by CCP §580d, even when the junior is the successful bidder at the senior sale and thus obtains the benefit of the nonredeemable title such a sale provides (although CCP §580a does apply in determining the amount of the deficiency; see §4.33). *Walter E. Heller W., Inc. v Bloxham* (1985) 176 CA3d 266, 221 CR 425. A junior's action on the note is barred, however, if the junior previously conducted its own sale and purchased the property at that sale. *Ballengee v Sadlier* (1986) 179 CA3d 1, 224 CR 301.

This rule helps the junior at the expense of the trustor, who thus faces the prospect of both losing the property in a nonredeemable sale (through the senior foreclosure) and remaining subject to personal liability on the junior note. The basic policy of CCP §580d (*i.e.,* that a trustor should be subject to deficiency liability only when there is a right to redeem; see *Union Bank v Gradsky* (1968) 265 CA2d 40, 71 CR 64, and *Roseleaf v Chierighino, supra*) is thereby thwarted. The senior lienor commonly bids no more than what it is owed on its senior lien, leaving no surplus for the junior. The junior is then entitled to obtain a personal judgment against the trustor, even if the property was worth enough to pay off both liens. See §§4.8, 4.33.

§4.33   B. Fair-Value Rules

The California Supreme Court has held that a nonselling junior creditor is not bound by the fair-value provisions of CCP §§580a and 726 (see §§4.17–4.22). *Roseleaf Corp. v Chierighino* (1963) 59 C2d 35, 27 CR 873. The court's treatment of the fair-value provisions is thus analogous to its treatment of CCP §580d, *i.e.,* that neither restriction applies to junior deeds of trust following senior foreclosures. See §4.32. The court's rationale is that the fair-value provisions are intended to influence only the selling creditor who is able to credit-bid the amount of its debt (although the statute contains no language to this effect). To hold the junior responsible for a fair selling price at a senior sale would compel the junior to bid cash, which (according to the supreme court) the trustor can do equally well. Thus, a junior who brings an action on the note is not required to prove the fairness of the price bid at the senior sale, and the trustor is not permitted the defense that the property was undersold at the senior sale. *Roseleaf Corp. v Chierighino, supra*. As noted in §4.32, fairness to the junior comes at the expense of the trustor. If the security was worth $500,000 and the first and second loans were for $400,000 and $40,000, respectively, the trustor has an equity of $60,000. If the senior bids only $400,000 (or less) at its trustee's sale, however, and the junior is then permitted to obtain a $40,000 money judgment against the trustor, the $60,000 asset is converted into a $40,000 liability by application of the fair-value rules.

The fair-value rules apply when the junior is the high bidder at the senior sale. A money judgment for the balance due on the junior note is then limited to the difference between the fair value of the property (or its selling price, if greater) and the combined total of the junior and senior debts. *Walter E. Heller W., Inc. v Bloxham* (1985) 176 CA3d 266, 221 CR 425; *Bank of Hemet v U.S.* (9th Cir 1981) 643 F2d 661. Otherwise, the junior would gain the double advantage of a successful underbid and the equivalent of a deficiency judgment based on the underbid. (This is the one situation in which CCP §580a is clearly held to apply. See §4.20.) The court in *Bank of Hemet v U.S., supra,* also held that in such a situation the junior would be subject to the three-month period for seeking a deficiency judgment (see §3.67), although a nonbidding, sold-out junior is not so limited (*Roseleaf Corp. v Chierighino, supra*).

C. Purchase-Money Restrictions

§4.34   1. Other Security

Except for special cases, the sold-out junior creditor is barred from bringing a personal action against the trustor when the junior lien secures a purchase-money loan. Thus, unlike the other antideficiency doctrines (see §§4.32–4.33), CCP §580b applies to a sold-out junior. See *Brown v Jensen* (1953) 41 C2d 193, 259 P2d 425. See also *Mortgage Guar. Co. v Sampsell* (1942) 51 CA2d 180, 124 P2d 353. Only a junior creditor who holds a nonpurchase-money note is permitted to sue on it following a senior foreclosure sale. The formal basis of the holding in *Brown* was the assertion that a sold-out junior suing on the note is seeking a deficiency judgment. Technically, the action is not for a deficiency, because the junior has not held a previous foreclosure sale. In *Brown,* however, the supreme court held that a foreclosure sale is a precondition only when it would not be an idle act; when there is no security left to foreclose, a judgment on the note is the functional equivalent of a deficiency judgment and is therefore subject to CCP §580b.

In *Roseleaf Corp. v Chierighino* (1963) 59 C2d 35, 27 CR 873, this logic was limited to the "standard purchase-money mortgage transaction" and, accordingly, CCP §580b was held not to apply when the seller of property took back notes secured by second deeds of trust on other properties owned by the buyer. The supreme court held that, when a note is secured by other property, the overvaluation and stabilization principles (see §§4.27–4.28) do not apply. Thus, a seller who declines to accept a junior deed of trust on the property being sold, but instead accepts a junior deed of trust on other property owned by the buyer, may later sue on the note if that other property is foreclosed by its senior lienor. Despite apparent inconsistencies between *Roseleaf* and *Brown,* the courts steadfastly maintain that *Brown* remains good law. See *Spangler v Memel* (1972) 7 C3d 603, 609, 102 CR 807, 810; *Barash v Wood* (1969) 3 CA3d 248, 83 CR 153.

The seller's lien on the other security in *Roseleaf* was a junior lien, but the opinion does not treat that fact as significant for CCP §580b purposes. Conceivably, even if the seller had held a first lien on the other security, it could have recovered a deficiency judgment under appropriate circumstances. An action directly on the note and an action for a deficiency judgment following a trustee's sale by the seller are probably both barred, because the other security exception seems to apply only to §580b and not also to CCP §726 or §580d.

§4.35   2. Nonstandard Transactions

The California Supreme Court has held that a seller who takes back a second deed of trust on the property is not engaging in a "standard" transaction (see §4.34) when the second lien is subordinated to a senior deed of trust securing a construction loan rather than a purchase-money loan, and the seller is therefore not barred by CCP §580b from recovering a deficiency. *Spangler v Memel* (1972) 7 C3d 603, 102 CR 807. In *Spangler,* the court held that overvaluation in a construction context is best prevented by imposing the risk of failure on the buyer rather than on the seller, and that stabilization is not furthered by making the seller rather than the buyer bear the loss after the senior foreclosure has eliminated both interests. See *Roffinella v Sherinian* (1986) 179 CA3d 230, 224 CR 502; §§4.27–4.28.

The reasoning in *Spangler v Memel, supra,* casts considerable doubt on the logic of the rule in *Roseleaf Corp. v Chierighino* (1963) 59 C2d 35, 27 CR 873 (see §4.34), in standard transactions, because it applies with equal force to standard as well as nonstandard situations. Because the overvaluation policy relates to the purchase price of the property as set by the buyer and the seller, not the lender, the effect of shifting the risk of an inflated price from seller to buyer is the same whether the first loan is for construction or purchase, at least when the property is commercial. The effect of a senior sale on a junior deed of trust (*i.e.,* leaving the junior without security or payment) is also independent of the nature of the senior deed of trust.

This difficulty in applying the *Spangler* logic has continued to plague the courts. In *Nickerman v Ryan* (1979) 93 CA3d 564, 155 CR 830, after a judgment of dissolution converted community property to a tenancy in common, the former wife transferred her interest in their motel and apartment building to her former husband, taking a note secured by a deed of trust on the motel as partial payment. Despite its clear purchase-money nature, the note was held by the court not to be subject to CCP §580b, because the wife had entered into the transaction to be "free of the vicissitudes of the commercial enterprises" (93 CA3d at 574, 155 CR at 836), a statement that describes most vendors. In *Long v Superior Court* (1985) 170 CA3d 499, 216 CR 337, the vendor sold a $150,000 parcel for $250,000 (its speculative value) and then was permitted to recover on his subordinated $118,000 purchase-money note after being sold out by foreclosure of the senior subordinating construction loan. Despite the admitted overvaluation and the vendor's receipt of a downpayment nearly equal to the real value of the property, the court declined to impose the restrictions of CCP §580b against the vendor, holding that he had merely "prudently attempted to realize maximum value" from the property. Statements such as these make it difficult to predict what a court will hold to constitute purchase-money in a given case.

The opinion in *Spangler v Memel* (1972) 7 C3d 603, 614 n9, 102 CR 807, 814 n9, suggests that CCP §580b might be held to apply if the property were to be used as the buyer's personal residence, rather than for commercial purposes, thus possibly introducing into vendor financing the same commercial-residential distinction that the legislature has inserted into third party financing. See §4.29. This suggestion was ignored in *Ziegler v Barnes* (1988) 200 CA3d 224, 246 CR 69, however, in which the court held that a subordinated seller is entitled to seek a deficiency under the *Spangler* rule even though the building constructed was a single-family residence. The commercial-residential distinction was given yet another application in *Boyle v Sweeney* (1989) 207 CA3d 998, 255 CR 153, in which a single-family residence was replaced with three condominiums, and the court held that this change in intensity of use was equivalent to the change from residential to commercial use that justified the deficiency judgment in *Spangler*. See also *Wright v Johnston* (1988) 206 CA3d 333, 253 CR 418, in which the seller subordinated to subsequent refinancing of the senior loans and was permitted to recover a deficiency judgment because he was left with no equity cushion. The *Spangler* rule was held inapplicable in *Budget Realty v Hunter* (1984) 157 CA3d 511, 204 CR 48, a case in which subordination was intended but never occurred.

V. APPLICATION OF ONE-ACTION AND ANTIDEFICIENCY RULES TO OTHER INSTRUMENTS

§4.36 A. Installment Land Sale Contracts

The normal remedies available to a seller for the buyer's breach of an installment land sale contract (see §1.35) are quiet title, ejectment, damages, and rescission. *Honey v Henry's Franchise Leasing Corp.* (1966) 64 C2d 801, 52 CR 18; *Longmaid v Coulter* (1898) 123 C 208, 55 P 791; see 2 California Real Property Financing §3.10 (Cal CEB 1989); California Real Property Sales Transactions §§5.4–5.7 (Cal CEB 1981); California Real Property Remedies Practice §§4.45–4.50 (Cal CEB 1982); Graham, *The Installment Land Contract in California: Is It Really a Mortgage?*, 4 CEB Real Prop L Rep 117 (Oct. 1981).

The purchase-money antideficiency provisions of CCP §580b apply to installment land contracts. A provision to this effect was added by the legislature in 1935, two years after the section was first enacted, to avoid widespread circumvention of the purchase-money policy through use of land sale contracts instead of deeds of trust. See Currie & Lieberman, *Purchase-Money Mortgages and State Lines: A Study in Conflict-of-Laws Method*, 1960 Duke LJ 1. Thus, a purchaser who buys property under an installment land contract receives antideficiency protection functionally equivalent to that given a buyer who gives back a deed of trust or mortgage for the unpaid portion of the purchase price. The seller can neither sue to collect unpaid back installments (*Venable v Harmon* (1965) 233 CA2d 297, 43 CR 490) nor accelerate and sue for the unpaid balance of the price (*Powell v Alber* (1967) 250 CA2d 485, 58 CR 657). See Real Property Remedies §4.47.

Despite the legislature's failure to limit the language of CCP §580b to long-term contracts that are intended as mortgage substitutes, the courts nevertheless do not generally apply §580b to installment land contracts that are actually real property purchase and sale agreements (also known as "marketing contracts" or "deposit receipts"; see Real Property Sales, chap 3). *Freedman v The Rector* (1951) 37 C2d 16, 230 P2d 629; *Venable v Harmon, supra.* Code of Civil Procedure §580b is not treated as a complete bar to specific enforcement of a purchase and sale agreement by the seller. See *Landis v Blomquist* (1967) 257 CA2d 533, 64 CR 865; *Laske v Lampasona* (1948) 89 CA2d 284, 200 P2d 871. If the purchaser fails to comply with a judgment for specific performance, however, the seller is forced to initiate a judicial sale as the next step. See *Ward v Union Bond & Trust Co.* (9th Cir 1957) 243 F2d 476. Then, the language of §580b, if taken literally, would bar the seller's right to a money judgment against the buyer following the sale. See *Longmaid v Coulter, supra*; Graham, 4 CEB RPLR at 117.

§4.37   B. Mortgage Substitutes

Once a court determines that an instrument is a security device, all the antideficiency rules come into operation. Holding agreements found to be disguised mortgages have been so treated. *Lucky Invs.v Adams* (1960) 183 CA2d 462, 7 CR 57 (CCP §580b); *Jensen v Friedman* (1947) 79 CA2d 494, 179 P2d 855 (CCP §580d). Covenants not to convey, once found to be mortgages, have been held to come under the one-action rule and would therefore probably also fall under the antideficiency rules. *Kaiser Indus. Corp. v Taylor* (1971) 17 CA3d 346, 94 CR 773. The same is true of deeds absolute that are shown to be mortgages. *Wilson v Anderson* (1930) 109 CA 467, 293 P 627. It may be expected that agreements held to constitute disguised security devices (*e.g.,* sale-leasebacks, ground leases) will also be subject to the antideficiency and one-action rules. See, *e.g., Golden State Lanes v Fox* (1965) 232 CA2d 135, 42 CR 568; *Orlando v Berns* (1957) 154 CA2d 753, 316 P2d 705.

§4.38   C. Unsecured and Partially Secured Notes

An unsecured note does not come under the one-action or antideficiency rules. *Childs v Hunt* (1970) 9 CA3d 276, 88 CR 34. Even if the note is given as part of the purchase price for real property, it does not come under CCP §580b. *Jonathan Manor, Inc. v Artisan, Inc.* (1967) 247 CA2d 651, 56 CR 14. Courts have held that the policy against overvaluation is not served by extending the restrictions of §580b to unsecured notes (see *Van Vleck Realty v Gaunt* (1967) 250 CA2d 81, 58 CR 246), although overvaluation seems all the more probable when the seller looks to the buyer rather than to the property for full payment. Nevertheless, nothing in the antideficiency statutes applies to unsecured notes.

Some creditors seek the best of both worlds by separating the purchase price or obligation into secured and unsecured components, each represented by separate notes. In this case, the debt must be fractionalized so that the sum of all notes does not exceed the total indebtedness. *Freedland v Greco* (1955) 45 C2d 462, 289 P2d 463. Section 580b has no effect on the unsecured notes (*Nevin v Salk* (1975) 45 CA3d 331, 342, 119 CR 370, 376; *Christopherson v Allen* (1961) 190 CA2d 848, 12 CR 658), nor do the other antideficiency rules apply to them. This makes it possible for the seller to retain a forecloseable lien on the property and also to recover a personal judgment against the buyer, even if the redeemed note is foreclosed extrajudicially. The drawback is that each remedy is exclusive to that note, and the seller (1) is without a remedy against a wealthy buyer on the secured note if the security is wiped out by a senior sale and (2) has no recourse to the property for the unsecured note (except by execution) if the buyer becomes insolvent, even if the property soars in value. Some sellers attempt to write notes that appear secured and unsecured simultaneously (see, *e.g.*, *Freedland v Greco, supra*; *Loretz v Cal-Coast Dev. Corp.* (1967) 249 CA2d 176, 57 CR 188), but such devices inevitably fail.

§4.39   D. Environmental Indemnity Agreements

Lenders have recently become concerned about the potential effects of various environmental clean-up statutes on real property held as security for their loans. Federal and state statutes require responsible parties to pay the costs of cleaning up sites contaminated with hazardous substances. See, *e.g.*, the Comprehensive Environmental Response, Compensation, and Liability Act of 1980 (CERCLA or Superfund; 42 USC §§9601–9675); Health & S C §§25300–25395 (State Superfund). For a summary of statutory requirements, see Thornton, *Developing a*

Hazardous Substance Policy for Lenders Secured by Real Property, 12 CEB Real Prop L Rep 85 (Apr. 1989); Finkelstein, Hansen, & Steel, *Buying Contaminated Property: How to Avoid a Toxic Surprise,* 6 Cal Real Prop J 1 (Spring 1988).

As possessor of the property, the trustor can be held responsible for clean-up costs (regardless of his or her personal lack of fault concerning the contamination) and is therefore likely to default on the mortgage loan if the loan balance plus the potential clean-up costs make retaining the property no longer profitable. Although clean-up liens do not take priority over preexisting mortgage liens, the fact that the purchaser at a foreclosure sale may be required to pay the response costs of subsequently decontaminating the property will naturally enter into its bidding calculations, thus giving the future clean-up costs de facto priority over the mortgage. Of even greater concern to the lender is the risk that it, too, may be held responsible for clean-up costs (which may easily exceed the loan balance). See Thornton, 12 CEB RPLR at 94; Burhenn & Howard, *Lender Liability,* 6 Cal Real Prop J 17 (Spring 1988).

CERCLA exempts from clean-up liability a lender who "without participating in the management . . . holds indicia of ownership primarily to protect his security interest." 42 USC §9601(20)(A). This exception does not, however, protect a lender who actively supervises the borrower's workout or who takes title to the property at the foreclosure sale. *U.S. v Mirabile* (ED Pa 1985) 15 Envtl L Rep 20994; *U.S. v Maryland Bank & Trust Co.* (D Md 1986) 632 F Supp 573. These decisions have generated substantial concern within the lending industry over how best to protect against the risk that contaminated property is held as loan security. See Thornton, 12 CEB RPLR at 87.

A much-discussed measure for lenders' protection is to obtain an environmental indemnity agreement from the borrower when the loan is made. See Cooper, *Unsecured Environmental Indemnity Agreements,* 12 CEB Real Prop L Rep 95 (Apr. 1989). Besides warranting to the lender that there are no hazardous substances on the site, and covenanting not to deploy any, the borrower also agrees to indemnify the lender for any environmental problems concerning the security. It is unknown how enforceable such indemnities are under California's antideficiency rules. See Roberts, *California Antideficiency Laws and Environmental Indemnities,* 7 Cal Real Prop J, no. 3, p 1 (1989).

To secure an environmental indemnity agreement by the same property given as security for the loan accomplishes nothing: If the presence of contaminants on the property reduces its value below the loan balance, the property is of no use as security for the indemnity agreement. Except for purchase-money loans, the lender can obtain the same relief by foreclosing judicially and obtaining a deficiency judgment (probably equal to the entire debt, because there will be no purchasers when the response costs exceed the property's value). The problem can also be avoided by securing the indemnity with other collateral, but additional security is often not available.

A suggested alternative to this dilemma is the use of an unsecured indemnity agreement. See Cooper, 12 CEB RPLR at 98. The label is somewhat misleading, because such an agreement often merely repeats identical indemnity language contained in the security instrument, giving the lender duplicate secured and unsecured indemnity agreements. Such an arrangement raises the risk that the unsecured indemnity agreement will be held to have merged into the secured agreement, just as an unsecured note duplicating a secured note for the same obligation has no independent effect. See *Freedland v Greco* (1955) 45 C2d 462, 289 P2d 463. The identity between the secured and unsecured indemnities cannot entirely be avoided by providing that the secured indemnity terminates on foreclosure and the unsecured indemnity survives foreclosure. An attempt to invoke the indemnity after foreclosure, for a liability known to the lender before foreclosure, would be barred by CCP §580d (for a trustee's sale) and by CCP §726. If the unsecured postforeclosure indemnity were restricted, however, to environmental problems discovered only after foreclosure (*i.e.*, after the lender acquires title), the courts might regard it as sufficiently unrelated to the secured obligation to fall outside the antideficiency rules. See *Nevin v Salk* (1975) 45 CA3d 331, 119 CR 370, and *Christopherson v Allen* (1961) 190 CA2d 848, 12 CR 658, in which the courts held that unsecured purchase-money notes are not subject to CCP §580b restrictions when they represent debts that are separate from secured notes also given by the purchaser. See §4.38. To the extent that such an arrangement is upheld as constituting unrelated secured and unsecured obligations, it may also survive a full credit-bid by the lender. See *Cornelison v Kornbluth* (1975) 15 C3d 590, 125 CR 557. For discussion, see Cooper, 12 CEB RPLR at 100.

An arrangement of separate unsecured and secured notes depends for its validity on being viewed as creating an indemnity agreement analogous to one executed by the seller in favor of a buyer of real property, which is clearly valid. The difference is that the loan indemnity is executed *not* when title passes from the borrower to the lender (*i.e.,* at the foreclosure sale) but when the loan was made and in conjunction with the making of that loan. In this respect, the arrangement appears to be similar to a deed in lieu of foreclosure (see §6.2), which is entirely valid if given to a preexisiting lender for an immediate (not time-based) consideration (see *De Martin v Phelan* (1897) 115 C 538, 47 P 356), valid only after very close scrutiny otherwise (see *Bradbury v Davenport* (1896) 114 C 593, 46 P 1062) and never valid when given by the borrower when the loan is made (*Hamud v Hawthorne* (1959) 52 C2d 78, 338 P2d 387). See §§6.4–6.7.

To the extent that unsecured postforeclosure indemnity agreements are viewed as advance waivers of antideficiency protections, they are likely to be held invalid; to the extent that they are treated as independent and truly unsecured obligations, they may be upheld. The view to be taken by the judiciary is as yet unknown.

VI. WASTE AND OTHER ACTIONS

§4.40   A. Waste

Civil Code §2929 imposes on the trustor a duty not to commit waste. The standard title company form deed of trust (see App B) amplifies this requirement as follows:

To protect the security of this Deed of Trust, Trustor agrees:

1. To keep said property in good condition and repair; not to remove or demolish any building thereon; to complete or restore promptly and in good and workmanlike manner any building which may be constructed, damaged, or destroyed thereon and to pay when due all claims for labor performed and materials furnished therefor; to comply with all laws affecting said property or requiring any alterations or improvements to be made thereon; not to commit or permit waste thereof; not to commit, suffer, or permit any act upon said property in violation of law; to cultivate, irrigate, fertilize, fumigate, prune, and do all other acts which from the character or use of said property may be reasonably necessary, the specific enumerations herein not excluding the general.

In many respects, CC §2929 provides a beneficiary better protection than the clause does, because the courts have held that the clause does not run with the land and bind nonassuming successor owners, while the statutory duties imposed by §2929 apply to nonassuming grantees. *Cornelison v Kornbluth* (1975) 15 C3d 590, 125 CR 557.

A trustor's failure to maintain the premises is commonly referred to as "waste," but technically the clause gives the beneficiary the right not to have its security impaired rather than the right not to have waste committed. *Cornelison v Kornbluth, supra*; see *Easton v Ash* (1941) 18 C2d 530, 116 P2d 433; *Southern Pac. Land Co. v Kiggins* (1930) 110 CA 56, 293 P 708. The security interest held by a beneficiary is different from the future interest held by, *e.g.,* a landlord. Thus, cases dealing with a landlord's remedies for waste may be inapplicable. See *People ex rel Dep't of Transp. v Redwood Baseline, Ltd.* (1978) 84 CA3d 662, 149 CR 11. As yet, however, the courts have not made such a distinction. See generally 2 California Real Property Financing §3.20 (Cal CEB 1989).

Code of Civil Procedure §§580b and 580d both apply to protect a trustor from liability for all except bad-faith waste. *Cornelison v Kornbluth, supra*. Thus, in the case of a purchase-money obligation, the beneficiary cannot recover for waste unless bad faith can be shown under CCP §580b. If the obligation is not a purchase-money obligation, there can be a recovery for non-bad-faith waste only if the beneficiary forecloses judicially and the sale results in a deficiency; if the foreclosure is by trustee's sale, §580d bars relief for any waste except bad-faith waste. Even if the property is sold at a judicial foreclosure sale, and even if the waste was committed in bad faith, the beneficiary cannot recover if the bidding at the foreclosure sale produces an amount large enough to satisfy the entire obligation. *Cornelison v Kornbluth, supra*. See also *Sumitomo Bank v Taurus Developers* (1986) 185 CA3d 211, 229 CR 719. For discussion of what constitutes bad-faith waste, see *Osuna v Albertson* (1982) 134 CA3d 71, 184 CR 338; *Hickman v Mulder* (1976) 58 CA3d 900, 130 CR 304; *In re Mills* (Mills v Sdrawde Titleholders, Inc.) (9th Cir 1988) 841 F2d 902.

The federal courts have rejected application of the *Cornelison* rule to loans insured by the Federal Housing Administration (FHA), characterizing the rule as one that encourages the spread of blight. Recovery is permitted for waste on property securing FHA-insured loans despite CCP §580b and without the requirement that the waste have been committed in bad faith. *U.S. v Haddon Haciendas Co.* (9th Cir 1976) 541 F2d 777. But see *In re Mills, supra* (state law on waste applied in bankruptcy proceeding). See §4.46 for discussion of federal law and antideficiency rules.

§4.41   1. Waste and One-Action Rule

A question not directly resolved by the court in *Cornelison v Kornbluth* (1975) 15 C3d 590, 125 CR 557 (see §4.40), is whether CCP §726 applies to actions for waste brought against the trustor and requires that the beneficiary first foreclose on the security. An 1889 supreme court decision indicated, in dictum, that the mortgagee could sue the mortgagor for damages for removal of fixtures without first foreclosing. See *Lavenson v Standard Soap Co.* (1889) 80 C 245, 22 P 184. In 1968, however, the supreme court indicated that the beneficiary's right to sue separately for waste was an open question (*American Sav. & Loan Ass'n v Leeds* (1968) 68 C2d 611, 68 CR 453), and the logic of *Cornelison* seems to require a prior sale to determine the remaining value of the security and thus measure the extent of the waste. See *United States Fin. v Sullivan* (1974) 37 CA3d 5, 112 CR 18. Dictum in *Osuna v Albertson* (1982) 134 CA3d 71, 184 CR 338, however, appears to imply that an action for waste might have been permissible even though no foreclosure sale had taken place. See also *Krone v Goff* (1975) 53 CA3d 191, 127 CR 390.

If CCP §726 applies, then the beneficiary must be permitted to foreclose solely because waste has been committed. Civil Code §2929 does not provide for foreclosure for waste, however; the appropriate relief is damages or an injunction. See *Easton v Ash* (1941) 18 C2d 530, 116 P2d 433; *Conde v Sweeney* (1911) 16 CA 157, 116 P 319. Under CCP §564(2), the beneficiary may have a receiver appointed to prevent waste, but only as an incident to a foreclosure sale, the propriety of which has not yet been established. What is necessary to insulate the trustor from independent actions for waste, and simultaneously to give the beneficiary some immediate cause of action when waste is being committed, is a rule that foreclosure is an appropriate remedy for breach of the mortgage covenant against waste, even when the basic obligation (the note) is not in default. If the trustor disputes the claim of waste, this contention could be tested judicially either as a defense to a judicial foreclosure action or in an action to enjoin a trustee's sale. Even though the covenant against waste does not subject subsequent owners to personal liability for its breach unless they specifically assume the obligations under the deed of trust, all successors nevertheless take subject to the covenant (along with all other provisions of the deed of trust) so that breach of it should be grounds for foreclosure against them as well. *Braun v Crew* (1920) 183 C 728, 192 P 531; see §7.43.

§4.42   2. Third Party Waste

When waste is committed by a third party, neither the clause in the deed of trust (see §4.40) nor CC §2929 applies, and the beneficiary's rights against the third party come under general tort principles. *United States Fin. v Sullivan* (1974) 37 CA3d 5, 112 CR 18. Because the defendant is not the debtor in such cases, the protections of CCP §§726, 580b, and 580d do not apply, and the beneficiary may sue for impairment of the security without first foreclosing. When the waste is the result of joint actions of the trustor and a third party, as in *Lavenson v Standard Soap Co.* (1889) 80 C 245, 22 P 184, certain procedural problems arise for which no simple solution is available.

Waste by a third party may often be actionable by the trustor as well as the beneficiary. *American Sav. & Loan Ass'n v Leeds* (1968) 68 C2d 611, 68 CR 453; *Duarte v Lake Gregory Land & Water Co.* (1974) 39 CA3d 101, 113 CR 893. Nothing in clause A1 of the standard title company form deed of trust (see §4.40, App B) prohibits the trustor from suing third parties for damage to the real property nor gives the beneficiary a right to demand all or part of the award.

§4.43   B. Fraud

Institutional lenders and loan brokers are permitted to sue borrowers for damages for fraudulently inducing them to make loans, despite the one-action and antideficiency rules. See *Guild Mortgage Co. v Heller* (1987) 193 CA3d 1505, 239 CR 59 (lender may recover for fraud despite CCP §§726, 580b, and 580d); *Manson v Reed* (1986) 186 CA3d 1493, 231 CR 446. See also *Bell v Roy* (1986) 187 CA3d 694, 232 CR 83. There are statutes to the same effect (see CCP §726(f), (h); Fin C §§779, 7459–7460), but they do not apply to loans of $150,000 or less (adjusted for inflation) secured by owner-occupied, single-family residential property. CCP §726(g). For further discussion, see 2 California Real Property Financing §3.21 (Cal CEB 1989). Another exception to the one-action rule is an action for "rent skimming" under CC §§890–894 (see §4.13).

§4.44 VII. CHOICE OF LAW

The one-action and antideficiency rules clearly apply when both the real property and the debtor are located in California. On jurisdiction and venue in such cases, see §§3.8–3.9. Choice-of-law problems arise when either the mortgaged property or the mortgagor is located out of state. These issues are discussed in §4.45. Similar problems arise when all interests are local, but the mortgage is federal or federally insured. See §4.46.

§4.45 A. California Versus Foreign Law

Code of Civil Procedure §726 applies only when the real property serving as security is located in California. *First-Trust Joint Stock Land Bank v Meredith* (1936) 5 C2d 214, 53 P2d 958; *Felton v West* (1894) 102 C 266, 36 P 676. Thus, a creditor holding non-California real property as security may sue on its note in California without first having to foreclose, assuming that the state in which the property is located does not have a one-action rule (if it does, California would probably enforce the sister-state rule; see 2 California Real Property Financing §3.53 (Cal CEB 1989)). Restatement (Second) of Conflict of Laws §229 (1971) suggests, however, that the security-first aspect of CCP §726 should still apply (even though the one-action aspect would not) under the principle that local law applies to foreclosure issues. The restatement rule would permit the creditor to bring a separate action for a deficiency judgment, but only after first having foreclosed. See *Younker v Reseda Manor* (1967) 255 CA2d 431, 63 CR 197.

Even when the security is located out of state, a California debtor is protected by CCP §§580b (*Kish v Bay Counties Title Guar. Co.* (1967) 254 CA2d 725, 62 CR 494; *Hersch & Co. v C & W Manhattan Assoc.* (9th Cir 1982) 700 F2d 476) and 580d (*Consolidated Capital Income Trust v Khaloghli* (1986) 183 CA3d 107, 227 CR 879) if the note specifies that California law applies or the transaction has sufficient contacts with California (see 2 Real Property Financing §3.22). Thus, a

California purchaser of out-of-state real property will seldom be subject to a deficiency judgment in a California court. Conversely, a foreign deficiency judgment may be entitled to full faith and credit (unless the foreign judgment conflicts with a California judgment) even though a California court would not have entered such a judgment itself. See *Stuart v Lilves* (1989) 210 CA3d 1215, 258 CR 780.

When the security for the debt is California real property but the debtor resides elsewhere, the antideficiency rules do not always apply. If the out-of-state debtor is sued personally in another state, a money judgment entered in that state may release the California security under CCP §726. *Ould v Stoddard* (1880) 54 C 613. The foreign judgment would presumably be valid in California. If a foreclosure action were attempted instead, it would have to be commenced in California for the court to have jurisdiction over the security (see §3.8), and California antideficiency protections might then apply. If the note provided that it was governed by foreign law, however, and the applicable foreign law did not prohibit deficiency judgments, a foreign deficiency judgment would be valid in California. See *Kerivan v Title Ins. & Trust Co.* (1983) 147 CA3d 225, 195 CR 53; *United Bank v K & W Trucking Co.* (1983) 147 CA3d 217, 195 CR 49.

For discussion of issues concerning conflict of laws and California antideficiency rules, see Comment, *Application of California's Antideficiency Statutes in Conflict of Laws Contexts,* 73 Calif L Rev 1332 (1985); 2 Real Property Financing §§3.22, 3.35, 3.53.

§4.46   B. State Versus Federal Law

Federal law permits the United States government to recover from borrowers on Federal Housing Administration (FHA) insured or Veterans Administration (VA) guaranteed loans. See, *e.g.,* 38 CFR §36.4323(e). These provisions override the protections of CCP §580b. *Herlong-Sierra Homes, Inc. v U.S.* (9th Cir 1966) 358 F2d 300; *U.S. v Rossi* (9th Cir 1965) 342 F2d 505. See also *U.S. v Allgeyer* (9th Cir 1972) 466 F2d 1195. (Note, however, that the *Rossi* decision involved an action by the VA to recover amounts it paid under the loan guaranty, rather than an action for a deficiency judgment under California law.)

The Ninth Circuit Court of Appeals has also held that federal policy considerations override CCP §580d in an action by the VA for a deficiency judgment after a trustee's sale. *Branden v Driver* (9th Cir 1971) 441 F2d 1171. See generally 2 California Real Property Financing §§3.23, 3.36 (Cal CEB 1989). The United States government can, however, waive its rights. In *U.S. v Stewart* (9th Cir 1975) 523 F2d 1070, the parties had deleted the standard clause in a deed of trust on a VA direct loan, a clause providing that federal laws govern the rights and liabilities of the parties. As a result, the government was held to be bound by state antideficiency law.

The fair-value provisions of Nevada law and redemption rights existing under Arizona law have been held to apply to Small Business Administration loans which, unlike FHA loans, are negotiated individually. *U.S. v MacKenzie* (9th Cir 1975) 510 F2d 39. See also *U.S. v Yazell* (1966) 382 US 341.

The Ninth Circuit has rejected CCP §§580b and 580d defenses to an action by the United States government for damages for waste against a borrower on a loan insured under the National Housing Act (12 USC §§1701–1750g). *U.S. v Haddon Haciendas Co.* (9th Cir 1976) 541 F2d 777. (In contrast, the California Supreme Court permits the borrower to raise CCP §§580b and 580d defenses to an action for waste, other than "bad-faith" waste. *Cornelison v Kornbluth* (1975) 15 C3d 590, 125 CR 557. See §§4.40–4.42 regarding waste.) See also *U.S. v Stadium Apartments* (9th Cir 1970) 425 F2d 358 (rejecting application of state postsale redemption provisions to FHA-insured loan).

In general, loans made by federal agencies are held to be subject to (or free from) state law regarding mortgage remedies, such as redemption rights and antideficiency rules, depending on whether the state law hinders or encourages the policy behind the federal loan program in question, in addition to the language of the loan documents and provisions of federal statutes or regulation, as discussed above. See *U.S. v Ellis* (9th Cir 1983) 714 F2d 953.

§4.47 VIII. WAIVER

Civil Code §2953 provides that CCP §§726 and 580a protections cannot be waived by the borrower when making or renewing a secured loan. Although §2953 does not refer to CCP §580b or §580d, the courts have usually prohibited waivers of all the antideficiency rules. The relevant considerations are when the waiver is made, who made it, and (in some cases) either how it is made or which antideficiency protec-

tion is being waived. These considerations are discussed in §§4.48–
4.51.

§4.48   A. Advance Waivers

California courts have consistently refused to permit waivers of antideficiency protections that are made contemporaneously with the
making of the loan. The courts take the view that, to obtain a loan, a
necessitous borrower will always waive all of his or her rights at the
creditor's insistence. See *Salter v Ulrich* (1943) 22 C2d 263, 138 P2d
7; *Winklemen v Sides* (1939) 31 CA2d 387, 88 P2d 147. Thus, a contemporaneous waiver of CCP §726 is invalid, as are waivers of the fair-
value provisions of CCP §§726 and 580a (*Winklemen v Sides, supra*)
and waivers of the three-month limitation period set forth in those sections (*California Bank v Stimson* (1949) 89 CA2d 552, 201 P2d 39).
Code of Civil Procedure §§580d and 580b cannot be waived in advance. See *Freedland v Greco* (1955) 45 C2d 462, 289 P2d 463 (CCP
§580d); *Powell v Alber* (1967) 250 CA2d 485, 58 CR 657 (CCP §580b).

The proscription against waivers and attempted waivers of the antideficiency protections is not limited to explicit waivers in the note or
security instrument. The courts will invalidate a transaction when they
perceive that it has been structured with the underlying purpose of
depriving the debtor of antideficiency or one-action protections. Thus,
a deed in lieu of foreclosure given to the creditor contemporaneously
with the mortgage or deed of trust will be held invalid as an attempt to
make the debtor waive the right to have the property sold at a public
sale after default. *Hamud v Hawthorne* (1959) 52 C2d 78, 338 P2d 387;
see §6.5. A debtor's agreement to indemnify a mortgage guaranty insurer cannot be used to waive the debtor's protection under CCP §580d.
Commonwealth Mortgage Assur. Co. v Superior Court (1989) 211
CA3d 508, 259 CR 425. A deed absolute that is found to have been intended as a mortgage is subject to all the foreclosure rules. See *Byrne
v Hudson* (1899) 127 C 254, 59 P 597. An agreement in which the
guarantor is actually the debtor is also invalid for the same reasons.
Valinda Builders v Bissner (1964) 230 CA2d 106, 40 CR 735. See also
§8.18.

For many years, use of a deed of trust deprived the debtor of the
protection of rules that applied to mortgages, but the supreme court's
decision in *Bank of Italy Nat' l Trust & Sav. Ass' n v Bentley* (1933) 217

C 644, 20 P2d 940, eliminated the distinction and subjected deeds of trust to the one-action rule. See §1.23.

Various other mortgage substitutes, such as covenants against encumbrances, at one time enabled creditors to escape antideficiency protections, but when courts see through the form to characterize such instruments as security devices, all the antideficiency rules apply. See §4.35.

§4.49 B. Subsequent Waivers

In contrast to the rule invalidating contemporaneous waivers (see §4.48), the courts have often upheld "subsequent" waivers made by the mortgagor after the mortgage was executed. See, *e.g., Salter v Ulrich* (1943) 22 C2d 263, 138 P2d 7. Presumably, the duress that might compel the waiver vanishes once the loan has been made, although a debtor in distress with regard to the existing loan may be in even more desperate straits than one who has not yet borrowed at all. See *Palm v Schilling* (1988) 199 CA3d 63, 244 CR 600. Civil Code §2953 (see §4.47) applies to waivers made in conjunction with the renewal of loans, but the courts have held that §2953 does not prevent a trustor from waiving mortgage protections in return for an extension of the loan. *Morello v Metzenbaum* (1944) 25 C2d 494, 154 P2d 670.

In *Russell v Roberts* (1974) 39 CA3d 390, 114 CR 305, the court held that the debtor had waived the CCP §580b defense as consideration for various concessions by the purchase-money mortgagee. In *Goodyear v Mack* (1984) 159 CA3d 654, 205 CR 702, the court upheld a subsequent waiver that was made as part of a resale and refinancing of the debt. See also *Wright v Johnston* (1988) 206 CA3d 333, 253 CR 418, discussed in §8.25; *Shepherd v Robinson* (1981) 128 CA3d 615, 180 CR 342. One California court refused to follow the logic of *Russell v Roberts, supra,* holding that public policy prohibits a debtor from waiving CCP §580b protection. *Palm v Schilling, supra.* This holding tempts the purchase-money creditor to foreclose when the debtor defaults, rather than to refinance the debt with a bargained-for waiver, an outcome that does not necessarily leave the debtor in a better position. For discussion of deeds in lieu of foreclosure given after execution of the mortgage, see §6.6.

What the courts will characterize as a subsequent waiver may not always be clear. Is it a subsequent or contemporaneous waiver when an existing mortgage is assumed by a purchaser who also executes a waiver of some of the antideficiency protections? It is subsequent to execution from the mortgagee's point of view, but contemporaneous from the purchaser's perspective. Because the purchaser executes the instrument, it is likely to be treated as an advance waiver (and therefore held invalid; see §4.48).

§4.50   C. Only Debtor Can Waive

A valid waiver requires an act of the debtor; the creditor alone cannot waive the debtor protection rules. Although creditors holding worthless security are exempt from several of the debtor protection rules (see §§4.6–4.7), these exemptions do not apply when the creditor is personally responsible for loss of the security. See *Hibernia Sav. & Loan Soc'y v Thornton* (1895) 109 C 427, 42 P 447. Thus, a mortgagee may not cancel its security to sue on its note as an unsecured creditor. *Merced Sec. Sav. Bank v Casaccia* (1894) 103 C 641, 37 P 648; *Barbieri v Ramelli* (1890) 84 C 154, 23 P 1086. The mortgagee may release the security, but the mortgagor must join in the release for it to have the effect of waiving the one-action and antideficiency rules. A unilateral release does not exempt the transaction from debtors' antideficiency protections. See *Crisman v Lanterman* (1906) 149 C 647, 87 P 89. In one case, the court suggested that a mortgagee who releases part of its security may still obtain a deficiency judgment by first crediting the mortgagor with the full value of the released portion (see *Woodward v Brown* (1897) 119 C 283, 51 P 2), but there is a greater likelihood that the release of even part of the security without the mortgagor's consent may totally bar a deficiency judgment if the mortgagor makes a timely objection to the release. See §8.3.

Code of Civil Procedure §726 may be waived by the mortgagor's agreement either that the mortgagee may release the security if it so desires or that the mortgagor will not plead the section in an action brought on the promissory note. *Russell v Roberts* (1974) 39 CA3d 390, 114 CR 305. For discussion of the effect of the mortgagor's failure to plead CCP §726 as a defense, see §4.51. Both agreements have the effect of permitting the mortgagee to ignore its security and violate the one-action rule by bringing an action on its note as an unsecured creditor. The agreement to allow the mortgagee to release the security may also have the effect of waiving the other antideficiency rules.

The purchase-money antideficiency protection (CCP §580b) is usually waived by an agreement that the mortgagor will not raise §580b as a defense in any proceeding instituted by the mortgagee to obtain a deficiency judgment following a judicial foreclosure sale. For discussion of other devices for waiving §580b, see *Russell v Roberts, supra.* If the mortgagee intends to seek a deficiency judgment after a nonjudicial sale, then it must also obtain a waiver of CCP §580d. The fair-value provisions of CCP §580a must also be waived if the mortgagee intends to have the deficiency judgment measured solely by the sale price rather than by the fair market value of the property. For what might have worked as a limited waiver of §580d had it not been made in advance, see *Loretz v Cal-Coast Dev. Corp.* (1967) 249 CA2d 176, 57 CR 188, in which the parties stipulated that the value of the security was only a part of the debt.

For discussion of use of a deed in lieu of foreclosure as a waiver of the requirement that the mortgagee foreclose the lien and sell the property, see §6.2.

§4.51   D. Mortgagor's Failure To Plead CCP §726 as Defense

When a beneficiary brings an action on the note, the trustor may plead CCP §726 as an affirmative defense, contending that the beneficiary must foreclose on the security instead (see §4.4). See *Western Fuel Co. v Sanford G. Lewald Co.* (1922) 190 C 25, 210 P 419; *Barbieri v Ramelli* (1890) 84 C 154, 23 P 1086. If the trustor fails to plead §726 defensively, the action will proceed and the beneficiary may obtain a money judgment on the note. See *Salter v Ulrich* (1943) 22 C2d 263, 138 P2d 7. It is the trustor's obligation to raise the defense; if the defense is not raised, it is waived. See *Spector v National Pictures Corp.* (1962) 201 CA2d 217, 20 CR 307.

Although it is generally the debtor's loss when CCP §726 is not pleaded, other undesired consequences may be imposed on the beneficiary. As well as being an affirmative defense, §726 has a "sanction" aspect. See *Walker v Community Bank* (1974) 10 C3d 729, 111 CR 897. If the beneficiary ignores its security and proceeds to obtain a judgment solely on the note, it loses any advantage the security would have given it. The beneficiary then may look to the property only as an execution creditor and loses any priority over other creditors that its former lien might have afforded. *James v P.C.S. Ginning Co.* (1969) 276 CA2d 19, 80 CR 457. See also *Salter v Ulrich, supra.*

In multiple-security cases, the beneficiary's omission of part of the security leads to loss of the lien on the omitted part but apparently does not prohibit the beneficiary from obtaining a deficiency judgment following sale of the security that was included. *Walker v Community Bank, supra*; see §8.3. If the trustor prefers that all the security be included (to reduce the size of any deficiency), this point must be raised defensively at the appropriate time in the proceedings and before the foreclosure sale. *United Cal. Bank v Tijerina* (1972) 25 CA3d 963, 102 CR 234; §8.3.

A trustor's failure to plead CCP §726 in a personal action brought against that trustor alone does not seem to create a §726 defense in favor of the other trustors when the beneficiary later proceeds against their interests in the security. *Williams v Reed* (1957) 48 C2d 57, 307 P2d 353; see §8.4.

Chapter 5: **Rents and Profits**

5

Rents and Profits

§5.1   I. CREDITOR'S RIGHT TO POSSESSION AND RENTS; IN GENERAL

A mortgage or deed of trust gives the creditor a lien against the debtor's title which can be satisfied by judicial foreclosure or a trustee's sale of that title. The security instrument in and of itself does not give the creditor any independent right, however, either to possession of the real property (*People's Sav. Bank v Jones* (1896) 114 C 422, 46 P 278) or to the rents derived from the property (*Lee v Ski Run Apartments Assoc.* (1967) 249 CA2d 293, 57 CR 496). CC §2927. In this chapter, possession and rents are treated as separate interests in encumbered property, distinct both from each other and from the title given as security.

Most current deed of trust forms contain some type of rents-and-profits clause that gives the beneficiary rights to possession and rents immediately on the trustor's default. Enforcing such a clause is discussed in §§5.10–5.18. For discussion of assignments of rents, see 1 California Real Property Financing, chap 6 (Cal CEB 1988). Most hidden security instruments (which fall within the statutory definition of "mortgage"; CC §2924) lack such language because a provision giving one party the right to take possession or rents on the other's nonperformance might unmask the instrument and reveal its true mortgage character. For discussion of hidden mortgages, see §§4.36–4.37. Thus, deeds absolute, or deeds and options intended as mortgages, rarely include rents-and-profits clauses. The "agreement not to encumber," employed in *Coast Bank v Minderhout* (1964) 61 C2d 311, 38 CR 505, disapproved on other grounds in 21 C3d 953, which the supreme court held to be an equitable mortgage, apparently did not contain such language. If any of these instruments is determined to be a mortgage, it is treated as a mortgage without a provision giving the beneficiary the right to possession and rents, and the creditor is limited to the remedies described in §§5.7–5.9.

If there is no special enabling language in the security instrument, then the creditor is not entitled to possession of the property or to any rents generated by it before foreclosure. When the property is sold at a foreclosure sale, the purchaser becomes entitled to both possession and rents as a result of the transfer of title, but the transfer does not create any corresponding presale rights in the mortgagee. On the rights of purchasers after the sale, see §§5.33–5.41.

After the trustor's default, the presence or absence of a rents-and-profits clause will have a significant effect on the remedies available to the beneficiary. The property may deteriorate markedly while the foreclosure proceeds, because a debtor in default is unlikely to be ready or willing to spend much money on maintenance of property that is about to be lost. In addition, delinquent debtors often maximize their efforts to collect rents and other profits during this period while allowing the loan to remain in default. Rents-and-profits clauses are designed to prevent "waste" and "skimming" that confront a creditor during the foreclosure period and that may jeopardize the creditor's ability to recover on the obligation. See *U.S. v Haddon Haciendas Co.* (9th Cir 1976) 541 F2d 777. See also *Cornelison v Kornbluth* (1975) 15 C3d 590, 125 CR 557. For recent legislation regulating rent-skimming, see CC §§890–895. For discussion of waste, see §§4.40–4.42.

II. POSSESSION AND RENTS BEFORE FORECLOSURE SALE

§5.2　　　A. Mortgagee in Possession

A creditor can protect against waste and reach the property's rents and profits by becoming a mortgagee in possession. "Mortgagee in possession" is a specialized legal concept that carries more consequences then those created under a normal deed of trust or mortgage. A creditor usually becomes a mortgagee in possession by entering into possession of the property with the trustor's consent. See §5.5. A creditor who becomes a mortgagee in possession acquires both advantages and liabilities. In the cases cited in §5.3, the creditor claimed to be a mortgagee in possession in order to take advantage of that status. In the cases cited in §5.4, the debtor claimed that the creditor was a mortgagee in possession in order to penalize the creditor.

§5.3   1. Rights of Mortgagee in Possession

A creditor who becomes a true mortgagee in possession may retain possession of the property until the debt is paid. *Snyder v Western Loan & Bldg. Co.* (1934) 1 C2d 697, 37 P2d 86. Even when an action to collect on the promissory note would be outlawed by the statute of limitations, the mortgagee in possession may remain in possession as long as the obligation is unsatisfied. *Spect v Spect* (1891) 88 C 437, 26 P 203. This is of little importance to the beneficiary under a deed of trust because the power-of-sale remedy is not subject to time limitations (see §2.3), but possession can be important to the creditor because mortgages and most hidden security instruments are subject to statutes of limitation. See *Aguilar v Bocci* (1974) 39 CA3d 475, 114 CR 91.

Possession of the property carries with it the right to rents and profits. A mortgagee in possession may apply the profits from the property toward payment of the debt even if there is no rents-and-profits clause in the security instrument. *Nelson v Bowen* (1932) 124 CA 662, 12 P2d 1083; see *Johns v Moore* (1959) 168 CA2d 709, 336 P2d 579. The courts treat the debtor's delivery of possession to the creditor as conferring the right to rents and profits, which are dependent on the possessory right.

§5.4   2. Liabilities of Mortgagee in Possession

A mortgagee in possession must account to the trustor for management of the property and is liable for failing to act in a businesslike way. *Davis v Stewart* (1944) 67 CA2d 415, 154 P2d 447. The mortgagee in possession is not responsible for ensuring the profitability of the premises but is responsible for any losses caused by his or her negligence. *Murdock v Clarke* (1891) 90 C 427, 438, 27 P 275, 278. This liability extends to junior creditors as well as to the trustor. See *Anglo-Californian Bank v Field* (1908) 154 C 513, 98 P 267. The risk of accountability for improvident behavior should encourage the creditor to include a rents-and-profits clause in the security instrument to facilitate appointment of a receiver to take possession of the property (which does not lead to mortgagee in possession status) in the event of a default. See §§5.10–5.18.

§5.5   3. Becoming Mortgagee in Possession

The debtor may agree to let the creditor take possession of the property, either at the inception of the loan or at a later time. CC §2927. No additional consideration is required. *Nelson v Bowen* (1932) 124 CA 662, 12 P2d 1083.

The most common way for a creditor to become a mortgagee in possession is to enter onto the property with the trustor's consent. A formal agreement between the two parties is not necessary; consent to the entry is readily implied in favor of the beneficiary, especially when it has entered after a default and without objection by the trustor. *Hooper v Young* (1903) 140 C 274, 74 P 140 (deed absolute); *Spect v Spect* (1891) 88 C 437, 26 P 203 (mortgage). Some courts have even indicated that a peaceable entry may be all that is required for a creditor to become protected as a mortgagee in possession. *Snyder v Western Loan & Bldg. Co.* (1934) 1 C2d 697, 37 P2d 86; *Nelson v Bowen, supra.* But see *Freeman v Campbell* (1895) 109 C 360, 42 P 35. A forcible entry, however, will not produce mortgagee in possession status but will subject the intruding beneficiary to liability for forcible entry and trespass. *McGuire v Lynch* (1899) 126 C 576, 59 P 27 (trespass); *Calidino Hotel Co. v Bank of Am. Nat' l Trust & Sav. Ass' n* (1939) 31 CA2d 295, 306, 87 P2d 923, 929 (forcible entry). The courts have not fashioned a consistent rule to cover entry after an invalid foreclosure sale. The supreme court has held that a purchaser who took possession was a mortgagee in possession when the judicial sale was void for lack of an indispensable party (*Burns v Hiatt* (1906) 149 C 617, 87 P 196), but the court has held to the contrary when a private sale under a power of sale in a mortgage (as distinct from a deed of trust) was barred by the statute of limitations (*Faxon v All Persons* (1913) 166 C 707, 137 P 919).

When a creditor takes possession under circumstances that do not entitle it to claim mortgagee in possession status, it loses all the advantages accompanying that status. The creditor cannot retain possession until paid (*Faxon v All Persons, supra*) and cannot apply the rents and profits toward reduction of its debt (*Freeman v Campbell, supra*).

Any money collected must be turned over to the mortgagor even though the mortgage debt remains unpaid. *Belcher v Aaron* (1937) 8 C2d 180, 64 P2d 402. Thus, the creditor must return to the debtor rents that it may never be able to recover under California antideficiency laws. See chap 4.

§5.6   4. Avoiding Mortgagee in Possession Status

A mortgage in and of itself does not give the mortgagee a right to possession of the real property. CC §2927; *Snyder v Western Loan & Bldg. Co.* (1934) 1 C2d 697, 37 P2d 86. The same is true for a deed of trust. *Bank of Am. Nat' l Trust & Sav. Ass' n v Bank of Amador County* (1933) 135 CA 714, 28 P2d 86. A deed absolute intended as a mortgage likewise does not authorize the creditor to take possession of the property unless the deed expressly so provides. *McGuire v Lynch* (1899) 126 C 576, 59 P 27.

Inclusion of a rents-and-profits clause in a deed of trust does not convert the beneficiary into a mortgagee in possession. *Freeman v Campbell* (1895) 109 C 360, 42 P 35; *Bank of Am. Nat' l Trust & Sav. Ass' n v Bank of Amador County, supra.* Even if the beneficiary personally collects rents from the tenants under such a clause, it does not thereby become a mortgagee in possession. *Strutt v Ontario Sav. & Loan Ass' n* (1972) 28 CA3d 866, 879, 105 CR 395, 404. Additional possessory acts of property management beyond rent collection are required before a creditor becomes a mortgagee in possession. *Bank of Am. Nat' l Trust & Sav. Ass' n v Bank of Amador County, supra.* Entering the premises to make repairs to preserve the security is similarly not considered a possessory act, and the repairing creditor does not become a mortgagee in possession. *Gudel v Ellis* (1962) 200 CA2d 849, 858, 19 CR 751, 757. Obtaining appointment of a receiver to manage the property does not impose mortgagee in possession status on the creditor. *Tourny v Bryan* (1924) 66 CA 426, 226 P 21. See also *Murdock v Clarke* (1891) 90 C 427, 27 P 275. Persuading the debtor after default to allow the creditor to collect the rents without assuming responsibility for property management should also not have this effect. In all these situations, the creditor must account for rents actually collected but is not subject to the prudent business standard that courts apply to a true mortgagee in possession. See §5.4.

B. Remedies in Absence of Rents-and-Profits Clause

§5.7   **1. Damages**

Civil Code §2929 imposes a duty on the owner of encumbered property not to impair the security, and impliedly gives the secured party a right to sue for damages if the duty is breached. The beneficiary has a limited ability to sue third parties (*e.g.*, developers, contractors) for impairment of the security. *United States Fin. v Sullivan* (1974) 37 CA3d 5, 12, 112 CR 18, 22. See also *Cornelison v Kornbluth* (1975) 15 C3d 590, 598 n3, 125 CR 557, 563 n3.

Any recovery of damages for waste against the trustor or the trustor's successor is barred, however, if CCP §580b or §580d applies, unless the beneficiary can show that the waste was committed in "bad faith." *Cornelison v Kornbluth, supra*; see *Osuna v Albertson* (1982) 134 CA3d 71, 184 CR 338. Thus, if the security was given for purchase-money, or if foreclosure occurs by trustee's sale, the beneficiary may recover damages from the trustor only if the beneficiary can show that the trustor committed the acts of waste in bad faith. As a result, when the trustor's lack of care causes the value of the property to fall, the beneficiary generally will be unable to recover because bad faith usually requires affirmative acts ("active" waste rather than mere "passive" or "permissive" waste). *Hickman v Mulder* (1976) 58 CA3d 900, 130 CR 304; *Krone v Goff* (1975) 53 CA3d 191, 127 CR 390. Furthermore, in order to recover for waste, the beneficiary must first foreclose and sell the property. See *Cornelison v Kornbluth, supra*.

See §§4.40–4.42 for discussion of a beneficiary's rights concerning waste under deed of trust provisions.

§5.8   **2. Injunctive Relief**

Under CCP §745(a), a beneficiary may bring an action to enjoin acts of waste during the foreclosure period. Although an injunction is rarely effective to compel a defaulting trustor to take care of the property, it may be valuable when the trustor threatens to dismantle or remove some of the property (see *Robinson v Russell* (1864) 24 C 467). A temporary restraining order is sometimes helpful as a provisional remedy to preserve the status quo while the creditor seeks to have a receiver appointed. See §§5.11–5.22. The temporary restraining order can further direct the debtor to keep and account for all rents collected until the receiver is appointed.

§5.9 3. Receiver

A common method for protecting the property and collecting the rents for the beneficiary after the trustor's default is the appointment of a receiver, *i.e.,* a person who, under court appointment and supervision, takes possession of the property and collects the rents and profits from it. CCP §564; *Neider v Dardi* (1955) 130 CA2d 646, 279 P2d 598. The beneficiary is not held responsible for the receiver's behavior or misbehavior and is not charged with mortgagee in possession status by virtue of the receivership. *Tourny v Bryan* (1924) 66 CA 426, 226 P 21; see §5.6. For discussion of receivers, see 2 California Real Property Financing, chap 1 (Cal CEB 1989).

When the deed of trust contains a rents-and-profits clause, the beneficiary may have a receiver appointed under CCP §564(8) (see §§5.10–5.18). Even when the security instrument lacks a rents-and-profits clause, the beneficiary can seek to have a receiver appointed in order to protect the property as part of a judicial foreclosure proceeding. In such a case, the receiver must be appointed under CCP §564(2), which is somewhat more restrictive and requires a stronger showing than CCP §564(8). See §5.13. If there is a basis for foreclosure, the court may, as ancillary relief, put a receiver in possession of the property pending the foreclosure sale. The trustor's neglect of the property does not appear to constitute a ground for foreclosure, even if the security instrument contains a covenant against waste, unless the mortgage or deed of trust specifies foreclosure or acceleration if waste occurs. The standard title company form deed of trust contains such a provision. See §7.42, App B. Nothing in CC §2929 or CCP §745 (see §5.7) authorizes a foreclosure on the basis of waste alone. See Leipziger, *The Mortgagee's Remedies for Waste,* 64 Calif L Rev 1086 (1976).

Without a rents-and-profits clause in the security instrument, an unpaid beneficiary must make a showing of the following facts to obtain appointment of a receiver under CCP §564(2): (1) that the property is in danger of being lost, removed, or materially injured; or (2) that a condition of the mortgage or deed of trust has not been performed, and that the property is probably insufficient to satisfy the debt. Thus, it is not enough for the beneficiary to show nonpayment of the debt and a decline in the value of the security; the value of the property must have fallen below the unpaid balance. *Hibernia Sav. & Loan Soc'y v Ellis Estate Co.* (1933) 132 CA 408, 22 P2d 806. Because the appointment of a receiver is viewed, in this situation at least, as a harsh and drastic remedy, a clear showing of need is required.

A further difficulty confronting the creditor whose instrument lacks a rents-and-profits clause is that a receiver appointed under CCP §564(2) may be limited to preserving the property from waste and may not be entitled to claim rents except as needed to avoid waste. Rent and title are different interests, and one may have title to property without also having the right to receive rents from it. *Walmsley v Holcomb* (1943) 61 CA2d 578, 143 P2d 398. Thus, mortgaging the title does not itself convey any present right to the rents from the property, which belong to the titleholder rather than to one with merely a lien against title. *Locke v Klunker* (1898) 123 C 231, 55 P 99; *Turner v Superior Court* (1977) 72 CA3d 804, 140 CR 475. Even if the rents are treated as directly connected to the title, title technically remains in the trustor until the foreclosure sale is completed. Thus, without a rents-and-profits clause, the rents from the property are treated as a separate and unencumbered asset. See *Snyder v Western Loan & Bldg. Co.* (1934) 1 C2d 697, 37 P2d 86. Appointment of a receiver does not enlarge the scope of the mortgage lien; if the deed of trust does not include rents, the receivership might not either. Even though CCP §568 empowers a court to authorize a receiver to collect rents, that power may be limited to situations in which there is an independent ground for placing the rents under the court's control, *i.e.,* when the mortgage has a rents-and-profits clause or when the rents must be used to preserve the property. *Gudel v Ellis* (1962) 200 CA2d 849, 19 CR 751.

Early creditors sought to avoid these difficulties by including a stipulation in the mortgage instrument that a receiver would be appointed whenever the debtor defaulted. Such a stipulation is of little help without a rents-and-profits clause, however, because the courts have held that jurisdiction to appoint a receiver cannot be conferred by consent. *Baker v Varney* (1900) 129 C 564, 62 P 100. See also *Barclays Bank v Superior Court* (1977) 69 CA3d 593, 137 CR 743. Even when there is a stipulation in the instrument for appointment of a receiver, the beneficiary still must prove probable insufficiency of the security to obtain an appointment under CCP §564(2). *Bank of Woodland v Stephens* (1904) 144 C 659, 79 P 379.

C. Rents-and-Profits Clause

§5.10   1. Absolute Assignment of Rents; Absolute Assignment Conditional on Default

When a loan is made, the creditor may take an absolute assignment of the rents or an absolute assignment conditional on default. Under an absolute assignment, the creditor rather than the trustor or mortgagor is entitled to collect the rents. An absolute assignment is rarely given at the time the loan is made. Usually the creditor has no desire to collect rents directly as long as the loan remains out of default. The creditor must also take care not to become a mortgagee in possession with its attendant obligations. See *Johns v Moore* (1959) 168 CA2d 709, 336 P2d 579, and discussion in §5.4. Likewise, the borrower is reluctant to permit the creditor to receive rents directly as long as there is no default.

A creditor who wishes access to the rents only on default may obtain either an absolute assignment conditional on default or an assignment as additional security (at the time the loan is made). By taking an absolute assignment conditional on default, the creditor hopes to obtain the rents and profits in preference to junior lienholders and trustees in bankruptcy and without the necessity of perfecting the lien through possession or appointment of a receiver. The typical assignment of rents as additional security creates only an inchoate lien and requires that the creditor take some sort of action to perfect its lien on the rents. See §5.11.

No California court has ever interpreted or upheld a clause as absolutely assigning the rents on default; the beneficiary has always been required to take possession or to have a receiver appointed (see, *e.g., Malsman v Brandler* (1964) 230 CA2d 922, 41 CR 438). The supreme court has said in dictum that a clause absolutely assigning the rents to the beneficiary on the occurrence of a condition (*e.g.,* default) transfers to the beneficiary the trustor's right to the rents on the occurrence of the specified condition. *Kinnison v Guaranty Liquidating Corp.* (1941) 18 C2d 256, 115 P2d 450. The Ninth Circuit Court of Appeals has similarly interpreted California law to validate such absolute-assignment-on-default clauses. *In re Ventura-Louise Prop.* (Great W. Life Assur. Co. v Rothman) (9th Cir 1974) 490 F2d 1141. See also *In re Charles C. Stapp, Inc.* (Equitable Mortgage Co. v Fishman) (9th Cir 1981) 641 F2d 737. In other states, however, such clauses have not been upheld. See Kratovil & Werner, Modern Mortgage Law & Practice §§20.07–20.07(a) (2d ed 1981). Whether an assignment that is absolute in form, but that is in fact a component of a security arrangement, will be permitted to operate according to its terms is doubtful. See CCP §744; CC §2924.

For discussion of the relationship between the rents-and-profits clause and bankruptcy, see Comment, *Assignment of Rents Clauses under California Law and in Bankruptcy: Strategy for the Secured Creditor,* 31 Hastings LJ 1433 (1980).

§5.11   2. Assignment of Rents as Additional Security (Rents-and-Profits Clause)

The deed of trust forms supplied by most title companies pledge the title "together with the rents, issues, and profits thereof" as security for the loan. See App B. The reverse side of the instrument usually contains a provision such as the following (see clause B5 in App B):

As additional security, Trustor hereby gives to and confers upon Beneficiary the right, power, and authority, during the continuance of these Trusts, to collect the rents, issues, and profits of said property, reserving unto Trustor the right, prior to any default by Trustor in payment of any indebtedness secured hereby or in performance of any agreement hereunder, to collect and retain such rents, issues, and profits as they become due and payable. Upon any such default, Beneficiary may at any time without notice, either in person, by agent, or by a receiver to be appointed by a court, and without regard to the adequacy of any security for the indebtedness hereby secured, enter upon and take possession of said property or any part thereof, in his own name sue for or otherwise collect such rents, issues, and profits, including those past due and unpaid, and apply the same, less costs and expenses of operation and collection, including reasonable attorneys' fees, upon any indebtedness secured hereby, and in such order as Beneficiary may determine. The entering upon and taking possession of said property, the collection of such rents, issues, and profits, and the application thereof as aforesaid, shall not cure or waive any default or notice of default hereunder or invalidate any act done pursuant to such notice.

This language gives the beneficiary a lien on the rents and profits of the property in addition to the claim against the title. *Childs Real Estate Co. v Shelburne Realty Co.* (1943) 23 C2d 263, 143 P2d 697. If the trustor defaults, the beneficiary may apply any rents it collects after the default, as well as the proceeds of a later foreclosure sale, to the satisfaction of its debt. Thus, the rents collected are a form of additional security for repayment of the debt. *Mortgage Guar. Co. v Sampsell* (1942) 51 CA2d 180, 186, 124 P2d 353, 356.

Because the rents and the title are treated as distinct interests in the property, the debtor can pledge one or the other, or both, to the creditor. *Title Guar. & Trust Co. v Monson* (1938) 11 C2d 621, 626, 81 P2d 944, 946. A mortgage or deed of trust, without more, hypothecates the title but not the rents (see §5.1); an assignment of rents, without more, pledges the rents but not the title. A deed of trust with a rents-and-profits clause creates a lien on both interests in the property, but, unless it is an absolute assignment, creates only an inchoate lien on the rents, which must be perfected. See §5.12.

In practice, lenders often obtain a pledge of the rents in a separate document labeled an "assignment of rents." See *Johns v Moore* (1959) 168 CA2d 709, 336 P2d 579. Separate documentation emphasizes the distinct nature of the rents from the title. See §5.1. Problems of priority can arise if this second document is not recorded or if it is recorded later than the deed of trust. Including a conventional rents-and-profits clause in the deed of trust should eliminate this risk. *Snyder v Western Loan & Bldg. Co.* (1934) 1 C2d 697, 37 P2d 86; see *Pacific Fruit Exch. v Schropfer* (1929) 99 CA 692, 279 P 170. In general, the effect is the same whether the clause is in the deed of trust or a separate document. *In re Ventura-Louise Prop.* (Great W. Life Assur. Co. v Rothman) (9th Cir 1974) 490 F2d 1141.

§5.12   a. Perfecting the Lien

The lien given to the beneficiary by a provision that assigns rents as additional security (see §5.11) is inchoate; it must be perfected before it actually enables the beneficiary to prevail against a trustor or junior creditor. *Carlon v Superior Court* (1934) 2 C2d 17, 38 P2d 149; *Lee v Ski Run Apartments Assoc.* (1967) 249 CA2d 293, 57 CR 496.

The beneficiary can often perfect the lien by making a demand on the tenants to pay future rents to the beneficiary. See *Johns v Moore*

(1959) 168 CA2d 709, 336 P2d 579. The demand will be successful if the debtor-landlord agrees that the beneficiary is entitled to direct payment of the rents. Even if the debtor disputes the claim to the rents, the demand may still succeed if it is coupled with an agreement that the beneficiary will indemnify the tenants against any loss. Another informal and effective method may be to appoint the defaulting trustor as agent to collect the rents for the beneficiary's account. *Snyder v Western Loan & Bldg. Co.* (1934) 1 C2d 697, 37 P2d 86.

A mere demand on the trustor to turn over the rents, or on the tenants to pay rent to the beneficiary, does not perfect the lien if the trustor or tenants fail to cooperate. *Childs Real Estate Co. v Shelburne Realty Co.* (1943) 23 C2d 263, 143 P2d 697; *Lee v Ski Run Apartments Assoc., supra; Malsman v Brandler* (1964) 230 CA2d 922, 41 CR 438. In bankruptcy cases, however, the federal courts may follow a different rule, as discussed below. See *In re Ventura-Louise Prop.* (Great W. Life Assur. Co. v Rothman) (9th Cir 1974) 490 F2d 1141 n1 (mere demand on tenants would perfect lien).

If neither the trustor nor the tenants respond to the beneficiary's demand, the beneficiary can perfect the lien of the rents-and-profits clause by seeking court appointment of a receiver to collect the rents. See §5.13. Even if the trustor and the tenants are cooperative, the beneficiary may still wish to seek appointment of a receiver, rather than to collect the rents directly, if the property involves management responsibilities that could make the beneficiary a mortgagee in possession. See §5.2.

If the trustor refuses the beneficiary's demand for rents, it is dangerous for the beneficiary to take additional action without court authorization. An entry without the trustor's consent might entail liability for forcible entry. *Calidino Hotel Co. v Bank of Am. Nat'l Trust & Sav. Ass'n* (1939) 31 CA2d 295, 87 P2d 923. In such a case, the rents-and-profits clause would not be a defense to the breach of the peace involved. See *Jordan v Talbot* (1961) 55 C2d 597, 12 CR 488 (forcible entry by landlord after tenant's default).

Because state law governs the scope of security interests in bankruptcy proceedings, a security interest in rents and profits perfected under state law before the commencement of bankruptcy proceedings extends to rents and profits that accrue afterwards. *Butner v U.S.* (1979) 440 US 48; *In re Ventura-Louise Prop., supra.* Despite prior perfection by the beneficiary, however, the rents and profits are the property of the bankruptcy estate and must be turned over to the trustee or debtor under 11 USC §§542–543. Such property is "cash collateral" that may be used by the trustee or debtor in possession only with the secured creditor's consent or with court authorization, after notice and hearing, and subject to the provision of adequate protection of the secured creditor's interest. 11 USC §363; see Comment, *Assignment of Rents Clauses under California Law and in Bankruptcy: Strategy for the Secured Creditor,* 31 Hastings LJ 1433 (1980); §6.54.

§5.13 b. Specific Performance of Rents-and-Profits Clause

The usual method for obtaining appointment of a receiver in case of default is for the beneficiary to seek specific performance of the trustor's promise to transfer the rents and profits to it immediately on default as embodied in the rents-and-profit clause (see §5.11). See *Mines v Superior Court* (1932) 216 C 776, 16 P2d 732. Rather than asking for a receiver as part of a judicial foreclosure proceeding (under CCP §564(2)), the beneficiary has the receiver appointed as part of the specific performance action, which is a proceeding in equity and therefore may include appointment of a receiver under CCP §564(8). By this device, the difficulties encountered in obtaining a receiver under CCP §564(2) are avoided. The beneficiary need not prove that the value of the property is declining or is probably insufficient to discharge the debt (see §5.9), and judicial concerns about the harshness of receivership do not appear to interfere with appointments made under CCP §564(8) rather than CCP §564(2) (see §5.9).

Receivership may be granted under CCP §564(8) at the request of the secured creditor, as long as the security instrument contains a proper rents-and-profits clause and the complaint pleads a proper cause of action for specific performance. See *Mines v Superior Court, supra; Turner v Superior Court* (1977) 72 CA3d 804, 140 CR 475. In an action brought under CCP §564(8), the creditor is not required to show that the property is insufficient to discharge the debt. Even when the deed of trust contains a rents-and-profits clause, however, appointment of a receiver under CCP §564(8) is discretionary, not automatic. The recital in the deed of trust that the beneficiary is entitled to appointment of a receiver on default is not binding on the courts. *Barclays Bank v Superior Court* (1977) 69 CA3d 593, 137 CR 743.

§5.14   c. Procedures for Appointing Receiver

The beneficiary must file an action (or a motion in a pending action, usually for judicial foreclosure) in order to have the court appoint a receiver to take over management and control of the mortgaged property. The complaint should plead a cause of action for specific performance of the rents-and-profits clause, with a prayer for appointment of a receiver to collect the rents as pendente lite relief. See *Mercantile Mortgage Co. v Chin Ah Len* (1935) 3 CA2d 504, 39 P2d 817; §5.15. The beneficiary's attorney should be careful not to proceed to a final judgment in the receivership action, which could create a one-action bar to either judicial or nonjudicial foreclosure (see §§4.3–4.10).

The beneficiary may also add a cause of action for judicial foreclosure of the deed of trust (see §§3.29–3.43) to the action for a receiver, although this is unnecessary because the real purpose of the action is usually to have the receiver in control from the time of default until the trustee's sale. Normally, the beneficiary will commence a trustee's sale by recording a notice of default (see chap 2) at the same time that it files its action to enforce the rents-and-profits clause. The receiver will continue in possession until the trustee's sale is conducted, and then turn over the rents collected to the beneficiary if they are needed to cover a shortfall in the bidding. See §5.21.

The beneficiary may be able to obtain ex parte appointment of a receiver under Cal Rules of Ct 349 and 351 and local court rules. The nature of the emergency and the basis for a claim of irreparable injury must be shown by verified complaint or affidavit. Cal Rules of Ct 349(a)(1). Other facts that must be shown are set forth in Cal Rules of Ct 349(a)(2)–(4), (b). When a receiver is appointed ex parte, the matter must be made returnable by an order to show cause and a hearing must be held confirming appointment of the receiver. Cal Rules of Ct 351. For discussion of procedures for ex parte appointments, see 2 California Real Property Financing, chap 1 (Cal CEB 1989); 1 California Civil Procedure Before Trial §§18.22–18.27 (Cal CEB 1977). See also Comment to form in §5.17.

Selection of a qualified receiver is of obvious importance to the court and the parties because the receiver must have the experience to manage the property competently. See CCP §566 on receivers' qualifications and CCP §567 on the receiver's bond and oath. In most jurisdictions, a small number of persons (who are also frequently trustees in bankruptcy) receive most of the appointments as receivers.

§5.15 d. Form: Complaint for Specific Performance of Rents-and-Profits Clause

Copies: Original (filed with court clerk); copies for service (one for each defendant to be served); office copies.

_ _[Name, address, telephone]_ _
Attorney for plaintiff

[*Title of court*]

[*Title of case*]   **No.** _ _ _ _ _ _

COMPLAINT FOR SPECIFIC PERFORMANCE OF RENTS-AND-PROFITS CLAUSE

Plaintiff alleges:

1. _ _[*See §3.30 for introductory allegations*]_ _.

2. _ _[*Allegation concerning execution of note; see §3.31*]_ _.

3. _ _[*Allegation concerning execution of deed of trust; see §3.32*]_ _.

4. _ _[*Allegation concerning plaintiff's ownership of note and beneficial interest under deed of trust; see §3.34*]_ _.

5. _ _[*Allegation concerning nature of default; see §3.38. Plaintiff need not allege an election to accelerate balance due but should allege that demand was made to cure default*]_ _.

6. The deed of trust provides _ _[*quote provisions pledging the rent*]_ _.

7. In addition to the foregoing provision and the other provisions, paragraph _ _ **of the deed of trust provides** _ _[*quote provisions pertaining to enforcement of the rents-and-profits clause*]_ _.

8. Plaintiff has no adequate remedy at law to enforce the provisions of the deed of trust set forth in paragraphs 6–7.

WHEREFORE, plaintiff demands judgment as follows:

1. That the Court enter its order appointing a receiver, pendente lite, to take possession of the real property and to conserve and manage it, and to collect any and all rents and profits from it;

2. That the Court enter its judgment directing defendant and anyone holding title to the real property under defendant to deliver possession of the property and the rents and profits from it to plaintiff; and

3. That the Court award plaintiff costs and all other appropriate relief.

> ___*[Signature of attorney]*___
> _ _*[Typed name]*_ _
> **Attorney for Plaintiff**

[Verification, if desired]

Comment: For a second cause of action for foreclosure, see §§3.29–3.43. On procedures for the action, see §5.14 and Comment to form in §5.17.

§5.16   e. Form: Notice of Motion for Appointment of Receiver

Copies: Original (filed with court clerk); copies for service (one for each defendant to be served); office copies.

[Title of court]

[Title of case]   **No. _ _ _ _ _ _**

> **NOTICE OF MOTION FOR APPOINTMENT OF RECEIVER; MEMORANDUM OF POINTS AND AUTHORITIES; SUPPORTING DECLARATIONS**
>
> **Hearing:** _ _*[date and time]*_ _
> **Department:** _ _ _ _
> **Trial Date:** _ _*[if set]*_ _

To defendants and their attorneys:

PLEASE TAKE NOTICE that on _ _[date and time]_ _, or as soon thereafter as counsel can be heard, in _ _[e.g., Department No. _ _]_ _ of the above-entitled Court, located at _ _[state address]_ _, California, plaintiff, _ _[name]_ _, will move the Court for an order appointing a receiver to take possession, conserve, manage, and collect any and all rents and profits from the real property located in the County of _ _ _ _ _ _ _ _, California, known as _ _[state street address or other designation]_ _, and described as:

[Legal description]

This motion will be made on the grounds that defendant has defaulted in _ _[his/her/its]_ _ obligations under the deed of trust as alleged in the verified complaint on file in this action and that appointment of a receiver is necessary for the collection of rents and profits from the property as provided in the deed of trust.

The motion will be based on the allegations of the _ _[complaint/verified complaint]_ _ on file in this action and of plaintiff's _ _[supporting affidavits/declarations]_ _, _ _[and]_ _ on plaintiff's memorandum of points and authorities _ _[, and on oral and documentary evidence to be presented at the hearing on the motion]_ _.

Dated: _ _ _ _ _ _

_ _ _[Signature of attorney]_ _ _
_ _[Typed name]_ _
Attorney for plaintiff

Comment: The notice of motion must be accompanied by a memorandum of points and authorities (Cal Rules of Ct 313) and supporting declarations (Cal Rules of Ct 349, 351). In courts with more than one department, the proper department in which to move for appointment of a receiver is determined by local court rules. For the date on which the hearing should be set, see CCP §1005. The beneficiary may proceed by order to show cause instead of following the motion procedure. Using an order to show cause may be advantageous when time is important, because the order can be issued before the defendant appears in the action; a motion can be used only after the defendant has made an appearance. In an emergency, the beneficiary can make an ex parte application for appointment of a receiver, followed by a hearing to confirm the appointment on an order to show cause. Cal Rules of Ct 349, 351; see Comment to form in §5.17.

§5.17   f. Form: Declaration for Appointment of Receiver

Copies: Original (filed with court clerk); copies for service (one for each defendant to be served); office copies.

[*Title of court*]

[*Title of case*]   No. _ _ _ _ _ _

                                          DECLARATION OF _ _*[NAME OF DECLARANT]*_ _

                                          Hearing: _ _*[date and time]*_ _
                                          Department: _ _ _ _
                                          Trial Date: _ _*[if set]*_ _

I declare that:

1. I am _ _*[the plaintiff/insert other description of declarant]*_ _ **in the above-entitled action to obtain specific performance of the provisions of the deed of trust alleged in the complaint in this action that authorize plaintiff to take possession of the real property described in the deed of trust and to collect the rents and profits from the real property on default of defendant,** _ _*[name]*_ _.

2. The following defaults have been committed by defendant under the note and the deed of trust securing it:

[*List defaults*]

3. The real property consists of _ _*[e.g., a four-unit apartment building]*_ _ **that produces an income of $**_ _ _ _ _ _ **per month, which defendant is presently receiving and withholding from plaintiff.**

4. _ _*[Name of proposed receiver]*_ _, **whose address is** _ _ _ _ _ _ _ _, **is a disinterested and qualified person to be**

apointed receiver (a) on filing an undertaking, in a sum to be approved by the Court, to the effect that _ _[he/she]_ _ will faithfully discharge _ _[his/her]_ _ duties as receiver in this action and obey the orders of the Court; and (b) on taking an oath to perform the duties of receiver faithfully.

I declare under penalty of perjury under the laws of the State of California that the foregoing is true and correct.

Dated: _ _ _ _ _ _

                    ___[Signature of declarant]___
                    _ _[Typed name]_ _

Comment: There are three methods for seeking appointment of a receiver once the action has been filed:

■ *By ex parte application* (Cal Rules of Ct 349). This method may be used immediately after the complaint is filed, but requires an additional showing as discussed below. When appointment is sought ex parte, the court must also issue an order to show cause setting a date and time for a hearing to confirm appointment of the receiver. Cal Rules of Ct 351. If a receiver is appointed ex parte, the plaintiff must post an undertaking in addition to that required of the receiver. CCP §566(b); see generally 1 California Civil Procedure Before Trial §§18.22–18.27 (Cal CEB 1977).

■ *By order to show cause* (see *Nichols v Superior Court* (1934) 1 C2d 589, 36 P2d 380; see also *Olsan v Comora* (1977) 73 CA3d 642, 140 CR 835). When this method is used, the court sets the hearing date and directs the defendant to show cause on that date why a receiver should not be appointed. This method may also be used as soon as the complaint is filed and before the defendant has entered an appearance in the action. See 1 Civ Proc Before Trial §15.39.

■ *By noticed motion* (Cal Rules of Ct 353(a)). When this method is used, the plaintiff must wait to file the notice of motion until the defendant has entered an appearance. CCP §1014; see 1 Civ Proc Before Trial §15.41.

When the beneficiary seeks ex parte appointment of a receiver, an additional showing of necessity must be made either in declarations or in a verified complaint. Cal Rules of Ct 349. Among other matters, the beneficiary must show the existence of an emergency sufficient to cause the beneficiary irreparable injury during the time necessary for a noticed hearing (Cal Rules of Ct 349(a)(1)) and that the receivership will not seriously interfere with the trustor's business operations (Cal Rules of Ct 349(a)(4)). These and other matters required by Rule 349 must be incorporated into the declaration for appointment of a receiver when the application is made ex parte. When the appointment is made ex parte, an order to show cause must also be issued, setting a hearing to confirm the appointment within ten days. Cal Rules of Ct 351(a). The beneficiary must post an undertaking when the receiver is appointed ex parte. CCP §566(b). The receiver must post an undertaking before acting in that capacity, whether appointed on noticed motion or ex parte. CCP §567(b).

For discussion of receiverships in general, including procedures and forms, see 2 California Real Property Financing, chap 1 (Cal CEB 1989); 1 Civ Proc Before Trial, chap 18. See also Leipziger, *The Mortgagee's Remedies for Waste,* 64 Calif L Rev 1086 (1976).

§5.18　　　g. Order Appointing Receiver

A well-drafted order is essential in a receivership proceeding. Permissible powers and duties of receivers are specified in CCP §568. The lender's attorney should give considerable thought to the contents of the order when drafting it. The order should provide for:

■ Authorization for the receiver to manage, repair, and lease the property and to collect rents and profits;

■ Payment by the receiver of real property taxes, insurance premiums, assessments, and senior liens, and the order in which they must be paid;

■ A method for determining the receiver's compensation (*e.g.,* an hourly rate based on declarations by the receiver to the court);

■ Authorization for the receiver to retain counsel and pay counsel fees out of the rents collected;

■ Periodic accountings to be rendered by the receiver to the court; and

■ Payments by the receiver to the beneficiary on the debt secured by the deed of trust.

Orders commonly provide that all rents collected by the receiver must be applied first to the expenses of administering the receivership, second to the payment of all expenses incurred by the receiver in managing the property, third to the payment of taxes and secured debts having priority, and fourth to retention by the receiver of a working capital fund, with the balance of the rents to be paid periodically to the secured creditor who obtained appointment of the receiver. Periodic payments to the secured creditor may inadvertently reinstate the debt (thus justifying termination of the receivership; see §5.21), but most creditors prefer to have the money as soon as possible, even if this cures the default and the trustor is therefore entitled to have the receivership terminated.

For a form order appointing a receiver on notice, see 1 California Civil Procedure Before Trial §18.33 (Cal CEB 1977). For a form ex parte order appointing a receiver and order to show cause why the appointment should not be confirmed, see 1 Civ Proc Before Trial §18.35.

D. Receiver and Rents

§5.19   1. Previously Collected Rents

The receiver has the power, subject to continuing control and instruction from the court, to take and keep possession of the property and to receive the rents from it. CCP §568. Under this rule, it appears that the receiver is entitled to all rents uncollected on the date on which the receiver takes possession, even if the rents have already accrued. *Childs Real Estate Co. v Shelburne Realty Co.* (1943) 23 C2d 263, 143 P2d 697; *Title Guar. & Trust Co. v Monson* (1938) 11 C2d 621, 81 P2d 944; *Mortgage Guar. Co. v Sampsell* (1942) 51 CA2d 180, 124 P2d 353. For discussion of these cases and the receiver's right to accrued but uncollected rents, see Comment, *Assignment of Rents Clauses Under California Law and in Bankruptcy: Strategy for the Secured Creditor,* 31 Hastings LJ 1433, 1442 (1980). Apparently, the trustor may retain any previously collected rents even though they were obtained after the default on the loan and even after the beneficiary's demand for possession. See *Childs Real Estate Co. v Shelburne Realty Co., supra*; 31 Hastings LJ at 1443. Without an absolute assignment (or an absolute assignment conditional on default), it appears that the lien on rents and profits is perfected only by the beneficiary's actual entry on the property, or by appointment of a receiver (see §5.12), and, until then, the trustor may properly collect and retain the rents. The conventional rents-and-profits clause assigning the rents only as additional security is not construed as including a promise by the trustor to turn over all rents to the beneficiary as of the moment of default. Instead, the courts have held that such a clause merely permits perfection of the inchoate lien by appropriate proceedings. See *Childs Real Estate Co. v Shelburne Realty Co., supra.* See also *Carlon v Superior Court* (1934) 2 C2d 17, 38 P2d 149; *Lee v Ski Run Apartments Assoc.* (1967) 249 CA2d 293, 57 CR 496. See discussion in §5.12.

§5.20   2. Control of Receiver

The receiver's obligation is to collect the rents and hold or dispose of them under the court's order. The receiver is an agent of the court, and not of the beneficiary, and as such is bound to do what the court instructs rather than to do what either the trustor or the beneficiary desires. *Belcher v Aaron* (1937) 8 C2d 180, 64 P2d 402. The receiver's powers are limited to preserving and protecting the property, not to upgrading or enhancing its value. See CCP §568. To justify sale of the property, a receiver (a) must show that an imminent financial crisis will occur if the sale is not made (*Cal-American Income Prop. Fund VII v Brown Dev. Corp.* (1982) 138 CA3d 268, 187 CR 703) and (b) must obtain the court's approval (CCP §568.5).

Appointment of a receiver does not make the beneficiary a mortgagee in possession. *Bank of Am. Nat'l Trust & Sav. Ass'n v Bank of Amador County* (1933) 135 CA 714, 28 P2d 86; see §§5.2–5.6. Conversely, the beneficiary is not liable for any misconduct by the receiver. *Tourny v Bryan* (1924) 66 CA 426, 226 P 21. On the powers of receivers generally, see CCP §§568–570.

§5.21   3. Disposition of Rents

The receiver must retain possession of rents collected until ordered by the court to pay them out. *Garretson Inv. Co. v Arndt* (1904) 144 C 64, 77 P 770. When a receiver is appointed at the behest of a junior creditor, the court's order may authorize the receiver to make regular payments on the senior mortgage to keep it out of foreclosure. *Lovett v Point Loma Dev. Corp.* (1968) 266 CA2d 70, 71 CR 709; *Johns v Moore* (1959) 168 CA2d 709, 336 P2d 579. Turning over to the beneficiary any rents collected may have the effect of reinstating the debt and thus nullifying both the receivership and the foreclosure proceedings. Reinstatement may also be held to occur even when the receiver does not turn over the rents, if the amount held by the receiver is sufficient to cure the arrearages; however, compensation for the receiver must first be deducted from the amount held. See *Maggiora v Palo Alto Inn, Inc.* (1967) 249 CA2d 706, 57 CR 787. The receiver should not turn over any part of the funds to anyone, including the beneficiary, without prior court authorization. *Miller v Fidelity & Deposit Co.* (1935) 3 CA2d 580, 40 P2d 951. It may be appropriate to draft the order to provide for periodic payments to the beneficiary or to senior creditors.

The customary method of dealing with the rents held by the receiver is for the beneficiary first to conduct and complete a trustee's sale and then for the receiver to make an accounting to the court (see Cal Rules of Ct 353). Before the sale, the beneficiary should obtain an estimate from the receiver of the funds left in the receivership for distribution to the beneficiary at the time of the receiver's final accounting. The beneficiary will then usually underbid at the sale by an amount at least equal to the available rents held by the receiver. This "deficiency" is then satisfied by application of the rents (as "additional security"; see §§5.22, 8.8) when the receiver files the accounting. Because the trustee's sale is extrajudicial, it does not constitute an action barring the subsequent award of rents to the beneficiary. If a final judicial disposition of the rents were to occur first, that judgment could bar further relief under the one-action rule. CCP §726; see *Walker v Community Bank* (1974) 10 C3d 729, 111 CR 897; §5.22. For discussion of the one-action rule, see §§4.3–4.10. The beneficiary must not only conduct the nonjudicial foreclosure sale first but must also bid less than the amount owed to it if it wants to recover the rents. A full bid would constitute complete satisfaction of its debt and preclude it from making any claim to the rents held by the receiver. *Eastland Sav. & Loan Ass'n v Thornhill & Bruce, Inc.* (1968) 260 CA2d 259, 66 CR 901.

§5.22 4. Application of One-Action and Antideficiency Rules

A rents-and-profits clause allows the beneficiary to treat the rents as additional security as far as the one-action and antideficiency rules are concerned. As long as only one judicial action is undertaken, the one-action mandate of CCP §726 is met. See §8.3. A judicial foreclosure judgment that did not include rents already sequestered would lead to loss of the security interest in them (see *Walker v Community Bank* (1974) 10 C3d 729, 111 CR 897), but a completed trustee's sale (which is not an "action") does not stop the beneficiary from then claiming rents held by the receiver to cover an insufficient sale price. See §5.21. To avoid loss of the real property security as a sanction under the one-action rule, a final judgment should not be taken in the receivership proceedings until after the trustee's sale of the real property on foreclosure. See §8.3. Appointment of a receiver and initiation of trustee's sale proceedings may be undertaken simultaneously because no election of remedies is involved. *Mortgage Guar. Co. v Sampsell* (1942) 51 CA2d 180, 186, 124 P2d 353, 356.

Judicial characterization of the rents as additional security has eliminated most antideficiency defenses raised by debtors. For discussion of antideficiency rules, see §§4.12–4.34. Code of Civil Procedure §580d does not prohibit the beneficiary from recovering rents even when the foreclosure sale is nonjudicial, because realizing on further security is not treated as equal to collecting a deficiency. See *Freedland v Greco* (1955) 45 C2d 462, 289 P2d 463. For the same reasons, the beneficiary may obtain the rents even though it holds a purchase-money deed of trust, because CCP §580b has been held not to prohibit taking (and collecting) additional security. *Mortgage Guar. Co. v Sampsell, supra*; see §8.6. Finally, the courts have held that the fair-value provisions of CCP §§726 and 580a (see §§4.17–4.22) do not apply to rents, and the beneficiary is therefore not required to demonstrate fair bidding at the trustee's sale as a precondition to taking the rents. *Hatch v Security-First Nat'l Bank* (1942) 19 C2d 254, 120 P2d 869; *Mortgage Guar. Co. v Sampsell, supra*. As a result of this last rule, it is not uncommon for the beneficiary to calculate its bid by subtracting the rents thus far collected from the balance owing on the debt and then to bid that amount (or less) (see §5.21). Although this method of determining a bid should be considered conduct that the fair-value provisions of CCP §§726 and 580a were intended to prevent (see §4.19), the courts will probably continue to approve such conduct as long as the rents are treated as further security and the seizure of further security is not recognized as a deficiency device.

§5.23   E. Conflicting Creditors' Claims; Priorities

If both senior and junior deeds of trust contain rents-and-profits clauses and both creditors perfect their liens, the senior is entitled to collect the rents first. *Baumann v Bedford* (1941) 18 C2d 366, 115 P2d 437. None of the rents will be applied toward satisfaction of the junior deed of trust until after the senior debt has been fully satisfied. Thus, if, at the senior trustee's sale, the senior underbids by an amount equal to or greater than the rents held by the receiver (see §5.22), all rents will go to satisfy the senior "deficiency." Only if the bidding at the senior sale is adequate to retire the senior debt will the rents held by the receiver become surplus and available to the junior. Thus, it is often the junior who must bid at the senior sale to enforce the intent of the fair-value provisions of the antideficiency rules. See §4.17. For discussion of the procedure a junior should follow to obtain surplus rents after a senior sale, see *United Sav. & Loan Ass'n v Hoffman* (1973) 30 CA3d 306, 106 CR 275.

The senior deed of trust has priority to claim the rents only when the senior's lien on the rents and profits has been perfected. As long as the senior lien on rents and profits remains unperfected (see §5.24), the junior lienholder may be able to reach the rents under its own rents-and-profits clause. This result can occur whenever the senior either fails to act or is rendered unable to act by the junior lienholder's reinstatement and cure of the default on the senior lien. *Carlon v Superior Court* (1934) 2 C2d 17, 38 P2d 149; see §5.25. Then, it is the junior who has the receiver appointed and the rents applied to the junior "deficiency." *Mortgage Guar. Co. v Sampsell* (1942) 51 CA2d 180, 124 P2d 353.

§5.24   1. When Senior Fails To Perfect Senior Lien

Priority of mortgage gives the senior lienholder priority to claim the rents only from the time the senior perfects its lien on the rents and profits. If the trustor defaults on both deeds of trust and the junior beneficiary perfects the junior lien on the rents and profits but the senior does not, the junior has the right to collect the rents. If the junior is the only party seeking to have a receiver appointed, then the receiver will collect the rents strictly on the junior's behalf, even though the senior lien is also in default. *Childs Real Estate Co. v Shelburne Realty Co.* (1943) 23 C2d 263, 143 P2d 697; *Carlon v Superior Court* (1934) 2 C2d 17, 38 P2d 149. The senior may file its own action to have a receiver appointed or it may intervene in the junior receivership proceedings, but until it does so, the rents collected by the receiver are solely for the junior's benefit. Once the senior has a receiver appointed, rents thereafter collected are held for its account (*Baumann v Bedford* (1941) 18 C2d 366, 115 P2d 437), but the senior action has no retroactive effect, and rents previously collected may be retained by or for the junior (*Carlon v Superior Court, supra*).

There may be no need for the senior beneficiary to act if the order appointing a receiver for the junior provides for protection of senior rights. See *Lovett v Point Loma Dev. Corp.* (1968) 266 CA2d 70, 71 CR 709. Of course, the senior should intervene to protect its priority when the junior receivership does not recognize its rights.

When the rents have been assigned absolutely to the senior beneficiary, not as security, but as a means of satisfying the debt (see §5.10), the senior need not perfect its claim; the junior receivership has no effect at all on the senior's right to rents. *Kinnison v Guaranty Liquidating Corp.* (1941) 18 C2d 256, 115 P2d 450; *Malsman v Brandler* (1964) 230 CA2d 922, 41 CR 438. Although it is uncertain whether a senior beneficiary may rely on a provision that assigns the rents to it absolutely contingent on the trustor's default, as a means of gaining priority over a junior who already has a receiver appointed, there is no doubt that such a clause will give the senior priority over a trustee in bankruptcy. *In re Ventura-Louise Prop.* (Great W. Life Assur. Co. v Rothman) (9th Cir 1974) 490 F2d 1141; see §5.10. If the junior has an absolute assignment of rents, and the senior's rents-and-profits clause is merely a security assignment, the senior should nevertheless prevail when there is a default and the senior perfects its own lien. *Childs Real Estate Co. v Shelburne Realty Co., supra; Lovett v Point Loma Dev. Corp., supra.* If the absolute assignment to the senior is unrecorded, the junior may be able to obtain permanent priority for its claim to the rents. *Pacific Fruit Exch. v Schropfer* (1929) 99 CA 692, 279 P 170. But see *Snyder v Western Loan & Bldg. Co.* (1934) 1 C2d 697, 37 P2d 86.

§5.25   2. When Junior Reinstates Senior Lien

A junior beneficiary may effectively disable the senior from sequestering the rents by ensuring that the senior mortgage is kept current or by curing any defaults under it. If the trustor has failed to pay the senior, the junior may pay the amounts due; by reinstating the senior, the junior can prevent appointment of a receiver on the senior loan. Invariably, the junior deed of trust provides that a default on the senior obligation is also a breach of the junior obligation, thus permitting the junior to seek a receivership whenever there is a default on the senior loan under the rents-and-profits clause in the junior deed of trust. The junior deed of trust typically provides that the junior may advance the funds necessary to protect the security (*i.e.*, cure the senior default) and demand reimbursement from the trustor. See §7.37. Thus, the trustor's failure to pay the junior for curing a senior default constitutes an additional ground of default and occasion for appointment of a receiver under the junior rents-and-profits clause. When the senior deed of trust is allowed to become delinquent, usually the junior deed of trust has also not been paid, providing yet another basis for a junior foreclosure and appointment of a receiver.

Once a junior beneficiary cures the senior default and then has a receiver appointed, the junior may arrange to have the receiver keep the senior mortgage current through application of the rents collected. *Lovett v Point Loma Dev. Corp.* (1968) 266 CA2d 70, 71 CR 709. Meanwhile, the junior may proceed with foreclosure of the junior lien. The junior may add the amounts advanced to cure the senior default to the total amount owed the junior and may reach any remaining rents held by the receiver as additional security in the event that the foreclosure sale fails to satisfy the entire junior claim. *United Sav. & Loan Ass'n v Hoffman* (1973) 30 CA3d 306, 106 CR 275.

F. Receivership and Existing Leases

§5.26 1. When Lease Is Prior to Deed of Trust

If a lease was executed by the trustor before the deed of trust was executed, and the beneficiary takes title to the property with notice of the lease (*e.g.*, if the tenant is in possession of the property), the beneficiary is bound by the lease's terms. See *Bories v Union Bldg. & Loan Ass'n* (1903) 141 C 74, 74 P 552. See also *Scheerer v Cuddy* (1890) 85 C 270, 24 P 713; *Rosenkranz v Pellin* (1950) 99 CA2d 650, 222 P2d 249. The receiver may collect the rents owed by the tenants but cannot evict the tenants or terminate their leases unless they are in default. When a deed of trust is subordinate to a lease, it is merely a lien on the lessor's reversion and does not constitute an encumbrance on a possessory tenant's leasehold estate. See Nelson & Whitman, Real Estate

Finance Law §§4.20–4.21 (2d ed 1985). If the deed of trust is fore-closed and the property sold, the purchaser obtains only the benefi-ciary's reversionary interest, *i.e.,* an interest subject to the lease. See *Calidino Hotel Co. v Bank of Am. Nat'l Trust & Sav. Ass'n* (1939) 31 CA2d 295, 87 P2d 923. The receiver has no greater rights or lien than the beneficiary, *i.e.,* no rights superior to a prior leasehold estate. This same relationship exists when the deed of trust preceded the lease but the beneficiary has agreed to subordinate to the lease or to leave the tenant's interest undisturbed. See *Bank of Am. Nat'l Trust & Sav. Ass'n v Hirsch Mercantile Co.* (1944) 64 CA2d 175, 148 P2d 110. See also *Security-First Nat'l Bank v Marxen* (1938) 28 CA2d 446, 82 P2d 727.

§5.27   2. When Deed of Trust Is Prior to Lease

The beneficiary's interest under the deed of trust is usually superior to all tenants' interests under their leases because the leases were ex-ecuted after the deed of trust was recorded or the existing leases all have clauses subordinating the leaseholds to subsequently executed deeds of trust.

The deed of trust is also superior to an unrecorded prior lease if the beneficiary qualifies as a bona fide encumbrancer without notice under the recording acts (*Tropical Inv. Co. v Brown* (1919) 45 CA 205, 187 P 133), as might be the case, for example, if the tenant is not visibly in possession of the property. The rights of a receiver in such cases are covered in §§5.28–5.31.

§5.28   a. When Deed of Trust Lacks Rents-and-Profits Clause

If the deed of trust does not contain a rents-and-profits clause, then a receiver appointed under CCP §564(2) (see §5.9) has authority only to maintain and conserve the property and has no power to terminate existing leases, even those executed subsequent to the mortgage. Leases inferior to the mortgage will be terminated by a foreclosure sale but remain in full force and effect before such a sale and are unaffected by the receivership. *McDermott v Burke* (1860) 16 C 580; see Kratovil & Werner, Modern Mortgage Law & Practice §§20.03–20.04(d) (2d ed 1981). The rents paid by the tenants may also be beyond the receiver's reach because of the lack of a rents-and-profits clause. See §5.9.

§5.29   b. When Deed of Trust Includes Rents-and-Profits Clause

When a deed of trust with priority under the recording acts contains a rents-and-profits clause, and a receiver is appointed to enforce it, two separate questions are raised:

■ May the tenants terminate their leases before the foreclosure sale when a receiver has been appointed? See §5.30.

■ May the receiver terminate the tenants' leases before the trustee's sale? See §5.31.

§5.30   (1) Termination by Tenants

Although no reported California decision has ruled on the issue, it seems unlikely that the courts would permit tenants to terminate their leases merely because a receiver had been appointed to collect the rents on the beneficiary's behalf. Nothing in the appointment of the receiver dispossesses the tenants or constitutes a breach of their leases. *Wright v Standard Eng'g Corp.* (1972) 28 CA3d 244, 104 CR 539. Appointment of a receiver in such circumstances is like a sale of the reversion by the landlord; the tenants are merely required to pay their rents to a new landlord. CC §§821, 1111; see *Tourny v Bryan* (1924) 66 CA 426, 226 P 21.

§5.31   (2) Termination by Receiver

A more difficult question than the tenants' right to terminate (see §5.30) is the right of the receiver or beneficiary to reject undesirable leases and either terminate the tenancies or compel the tenants to pay a reasonable rent ("occupational value") rather than the rents reserved in their leases. Inferior leases are terminated by a properly conducted trustee's sale (*McDermott v Burke* (1860) 16 C 580; *Tropical Inv. Co. v Brown* (1919) 45 CA 205, 187 P 133), but no reported California decision deals with the powers of a receiver concerning the existing tenancies before the foreclosure sale.

A lease that is subject to the deed of trust is also subject to the rents-and-profits clause in the deed of trust. Is the beneficiary therefore entitled to direct the receiver, before foreclosure, to override the right of possession given to the tenants in their leases? It has been argued that the receiver should be able to disaffirm leases whenever doing so is necessary to maintain the beneficiary's margin of security, and that tenants who sign leases on encumbered property take their leasehold interests subject to this risk. See Nelson & Whitman, Real Estate Finance Law §§4.37–4.38 (2d ed 1985). On the other hand, the New York court of appeals has held that a receiver cannot terminate inferior existing leases or charge the tenants a higher rent even though the mortgage contains a rents-and-profits clause. *Prudence Co. v 160 W. Seventy-Third St. Corp.* (1932) 257 NYS 691, 183 NE 365, 86 ALR 361.

There are arguments both ways. Tenants whose leases are subject to a deed of trust are already in jeopardy of having their leases terminated prematurely if the deed of trust is foreclosed; termination of leases on appointment of a receiver three or four months before a foreclosure only mildly accelerates the event. Moreover, the chance of collecting greater rent from new tenants will benefit the trustor as well as the beneficiary. Not all defaulted deeds of trust, however, are ultimately foreclosed by sale. The trustor will be subject to serious long-term consequences if a lease can be terminated before the potential sale, or if the present tenants can quit the premises rather than pay a higher rent. Subsequent reinstatement of the deed of trust will not enable the trustor to retain tenants whose leaseholds have already been terminated. The receiver could possibly be held liable if termination of the leases constituted bad judgment, but a more workable rule might be to allow the leases to survive until the trustor's default becomes irreversible and leads to the transfer of title to a foreclosure purchaser. Although the latter rule may lead to some loss of income by the beneficiary (who is thus limited to the actual rent provided in the leases during that period), this loss is a direct result of the California policy of requiring a four-month period between default and sale under a power of sale. See §2.21. This statutory procedure is based on the assumption that the beneficiary will require a sufficient margin of security to protect against loss from the delay. A rule postponing termination of leases until foreclosure is complete would also eliminate the risk of sham defaults designed only for early termination of unfavorable leases.

The same principles probably apply to tenants who have in good faith prepaid all or part of their rents to the trustor before the default. They should be permitted to remain on the premises according to their leases until foreclosure is completed. When prepayment was merely part of a scheme to deprive the beneficiary of rents during the default period, however, the receiver may be able to overcome the scheme and charge an appropriate rent. *Prudence Co. v 160 W. Seventy-Third St. Corp., supra.* The deed of trust may prevent this problem by prohibiting prepayment of rents. See *Kirkeby Corp. v Cross Bridge Towers, Inc.* (NJ Super 1966) 219 A2d 343.

If tenants have prepaid rent for a period beyond the date of a private foreclosure sale or beyond the redemption period following a judicial foreclosure, such prepayment should not entitle them to possession, against the foreclosure purchaser, for that period (see §§2.28, 3.79). Any claim by the tenants for reimbursement of the prepaid rent would have to be asserted against the trustor who received it rather than against the foreclosure purchaser.

§5.32   G. Charging the Trustor Rent

An unresolved issue in California is whether the trustor in possession may be charged rent when he or she remains in possession of the property after default but before the foreclosure sale. For discussion of liability for rent after the sale, see §5.37. The New York rule is that a mortgagor in possession is not liable for rent for the period during which the property was occupied before the foreclosure sale. In *Holmes v Gravenhorst* (1933) 263 NY 148, 188 NE 285, 91 ALR 1230, the court held that under a conventional rents-and-profits clause the mortgagor's basic right to possession of the premises until the foreclosure sale exempts him or her from liability for rent before the sale.

At least one authority has argued that when the margin of security is inadequate, the beneficiary should be entitled to charge the trustor rent, which would then be applied to the debt and reduce the trustor's liability for a deficiency, if any. See Nelson & Whitman, Real Estate Finance Law §4.40 (2d ed 1985). This rationale for imposing liability for rent on the trustor as an offset to a potential deficiency would make little sense under California antideficiency statutes. The California legislature has allocated the risk of impaired security to the secured creditor in most cases (see, *e.g., Roseleaf Corp. v Chierighino* (1963) 59 C2d 35, 27 CR 873), and this risk generally may not be shifted back to the debtor. See §§4.23–4.30.

Most California deeds of trust do not provide expressly that the trustor will be liable for rent as of the moment of default, and such a clause is not likely to be enforceable in California. If the clause imposed a liability for rent on the trustor, in addition to the existing obligation to pay the debt, it would be no more than a penalty provision requiring the debtor to pay an additional amount because of the default. See *Garrett v Coast & S. Fed. Sav. & Loan Ass'n* (1973) 9 C3d 731, 108 CR 845. A host of other problems would follow from the effect of such a clause on, *e.g.,* the right of reinstatement, the lender's right to recover the unpaid "rent" from any surplus after the sale, and the possibility of a personal judgment for unpaid rent despite CCP §§580b and 580d.

§5.33   III. RENTS AND POSSESSION AFTER FORECLOSURE SALE

The previous sections of this chapter discuss the parties' rights before a foreclosure sale. The foreclosure sale completely changes their respective rights to rents and profits. The beneficiary's right to satisfy its obligation from the property ends with the sale. A deficiency judgment may then be available, but it usually will not be collectible out of the property. See chap 4. Rights to possession and rents are transferred by the sale to the foreclosure purchaser, who often replaces the beneficiary as the trustor's adversary. The most important distinction to be made with regard to postsale problems is whether the foreclosure sale is judicial or extrajudicial. Consequences of a judicial foreclosure sale are covered in §§5.34–5.39; consequences of an extrajudicial sale are covered in §5.41.

A. Consequences of Judicial Foreclosure Sale

§5.34   1. Possession

Despite the absence of express statutory language requiring such a conclusion, California courts have long held that the trustor and those claiming under the trustor are entitled to retain possession of the previously encumbered property during the redemption period that follows sale of the property after a judicial foreclosure action. See, *e.g., Shintaffer v Bank of Italy Nat'l Trust & Sav. Ass'n* (1932) 216 C 243, 13 P2d 668. On the debtor's redemption rights, see §§3.73–3.80. The combined drawbacks of redemption and possession for up to a year after the sale no doubt account for the lending industry's general avoidance of judicial foreclosure, even at the expense of forgoing deficiency judgments (see §3.5).

§5.35 2. Duration of Trustor's Right to Possession

The purchaser at a judicial foreclosure sale is denied possession of the property, and the trustor retains the right to possession until the end of the statutory redemption period. See §§3.79, 5.34. Following a judicial foreclosure sale, redemption is permitted if the beneficiary has a right to a deficiency judgment (see CCP §726(e)). CCP §729.010. On when the right to a deficiency judgment exists, see §3.67. If the proceeds of the foreclosure sale are sufficient to satisfy the secured indebtedness plus interest and costs, the redemption period is three months. CCP §729.030(a). If the sale proceeds were insufficient to satisfy the indebtedness, the redemption period is one year. CCP §729.030(b); see §3.76. During the redemption period, the purchaser may restrain waste (CCP §729.090(c)) and may have a receiver appointed, but the receiver is authorized only to collect rents, not to take possession (CCP §§564(4), 729.090(a)).

§5.36 3. Rents During Redemption Period

Although the trustor is given possession during the redemption period (see §5.34), the purchaser at the foreclosure sale is entitled to recover the rents and profits from the property. CCP §729.090(a). Rents so collected must be applied as a credit on the amount needed to redeem. CCP §729.090(b); *First Nat'l Trust & Sav. Bank v Staley* (1933) 219 C 225, 25 P2d 982; *Clarke v Cobb* (1898) 121 C 595, 54 P 74.

Many problems arise from the fact that the redemption statutes separate the right to possession from the right to rents. See CCP §729.090. The trustor is entitled to possession but does not control the rents; the purchaser is entitled to the rents but lacks the right to possession. A basic question that has not been resolved is who can seek what sort of relief when a third party tenant in possession does not pay the rent. Because common law jurisprudence usually assumes a connection between the right to possession and the right to rents, few analogies are available from other fields of real property law.

§5.37 4. Trustor in Possession

The trustor has no right to rent-free possession during the redemption period that follows the judicial foreclosure sale. The trustor may retain possession for the redemption period, but the purchaser can charge rent for this occupancy. CCP §729.090(a); *Carpenter v Hamil-*

ton (1944) 24 C2d 95, 147 P2d 563; see §3.79. The amount owed will be the value of the use and occupation of the premises. CCP §729.090(a); *Walls v Walker* (1869) 37 C 424; *McDevitt v Sullivan* (1857) 8 C 592. The trustor's monthly rent is often computed by applying one twelfth of the legal rate to the redemption price (see CCP §729.060(b)) because the redemption price increases by that amount each month (CCP §729.060(b)(4)), and the rent is applied as a credit on the amount necessary to redeem (CCP §729.090(b)). Thus, if the trustor pays the rent, the redemption price remains constant. *Murdock v Clarke* (1891) 88 C 384, 26 P 601.

If the trustor fails to pay the rent, the foreclosure sale purchaser probably cannot bring either an unlawful detainer action or an ejectment action because the trustor is entitled to possession during the redemption period. CCP §729.090(a); *Petersen v Jurras* (1935) 2 C2d 253, 40 P2d 257; *First Nat' l Trust & Sav. Bank v Staley* (1933) 219 C 225, 25 P2d 982. The purchaser can have a receiver appointed, but the receiver would have no greater power to evict a nonpaying trustor than did the purchaser. *Stevens v De Cardona* (1879) 53 C 487. The purchaser cannot insist on payment of back rent as a condition for statutory redemption, but such payment is virtually mandated anyway because the redemption price increases by one twelfth of the legal rate each month unless rent is paid to offset it. CCP §729.060(b)(4).

If the trustor does not redeem the property, the purchaser should be able to obtain a money judgment for the rental value during the period that the trustor was in possession. CCP §729.090(a); *First Nat' l Trust & Sav. Bank v Staley, supra; Reynolds v Lathrop* (1857) 7 C 43. This remedy should not be considered to be a deficiency judgment, because it is based on conduct by the trustor that is completely different from and subsequent to the trustor's breach under the deed of trust. *Honey v Henry's Franchise Leasing Corp.* (1966) 64 C2d 801, 52 CR 18.

§5.38   5. Rights and Duties of Trustor's Tenants

Although the courts in some early cases held that the purchaser had no right to recover rents directly from the trustor's tenants (see *First Nat' l Trust & Sav. Bank v Staley* (1933) 219 C 225, 25 P2d 982), that rule has apparently been changed by amendment of the receivership statute to permit the purchaser to have a receiver collect the rents. CCP

§564(4). Only if the tenants are unaware of the purchaser's existence will subsequent rent payments to the trustor be protected. *Title Ins. & Trust Co. v Pfenninghausen* (1922) 57 CA 655, 207 P 927. On receiving notice of the foreclosure sale, the tenants must pay their rent to the purchaser, or to a receiver appointed at the purchaser's behest, and not to the trustor. CCP §729.090(a); *Munkelt v Kumberg* (1937) 22 CA2d 369, 70 P2d 997. The tenants' security deposits usually cannot be retained by the foreclosing beneficiary or receiver. See CC §§1950.5(g), 1950.7(d). For discussion of security deposits generally, see California Residential Landlord-Tenant Practice §§6.140–6.149 (Cal CEB 1986).

The tenants probably have the trustor's superior right of possession against the purchaser for the redemption period. See §5.34. Thus, the purchaser appears to lack the power to evict the tenants, probably even when they fail to pay rent. *Carpenter v Hamilton* (1944) 24 C2d 95, 147 P2d 563. For the same reason, nothing in the foreclosure sale relieves the tenants of their liability for rent during the redemption period. Their right to possession is undisturbed by the sale and they are not, therefore, entitled to abandon their leases. See §2.28. During the redemption period, they remain tenants of the trustor. *Metropolitan Life Ins. Co. v Childs Co.* (1921) 230 NY 285, 130 NE 295, 14 ALR 658.

If the rents reserved in existing leases are low, it is unclear whether the purchaser may raise them to a reasonable level. Code of Civil Procedure §729.090(a) provides that the purchaser is entitled to receive the rents or the value of the use and occupation of the property, but the statute does not specify which measure should be applied when the rent and the occupational value differ. Occupational value probably applies only when there is no stated rent (*Webster v Cook* (1869) 38 C 423; *Munkelt v Kumberg, supra*) or when the trustor remains in possession and does not pay rent (see §5.37). There is no apparent mechanism for the purchaser to raise the rents owed by the trustor's tenants during the redemption period, or to evict them if they fail to pay.

When the leases have priority over the deed of trust, the measure of the tenants' liability is the rents reserved in their leases. In such cases, the foreclosure sale passes only the trustor's reversionary interest to the purchaser. See generally Nelson & Whitman, Real Estate Finance Law §§4.20–4.21, 4.23 (2d ed 1985). Even when the leases were executed after the deed of trust was recorded, however, the tenants are still probably liable only for the rent specified in their leases during the redemption period. If the trustor agreed to a rent lower than the value of the use and occupation of the property, the tenants should be entitled to the benefit of their bargain for as long as the trustor's possessory right exists, *i.e.*, until the end of the redemption period. If the purchaser is able to demand a higher rent, the tenants should have the option of quitting the premises rather than paying more than their leases provide. The tenants' departure in response to the purchaser's demand for more money would have undesirable long-term effects if the trustor were later to redeem, because the trustor would not be able to retrieve the departed tenants. See §5.31. Because the tenants are entitled to undisturbed possession until the redemption period expires, the trustor is not in default with respect to the trustor's obligations under the leases until expiration of the redemption period. See *Lloyd v Locke-Paddon Land Co.* (1935) 5 CA2d 211, 42 P2d 367; *Luette v Bank of Italy Nat'l Trust & Sav. Ass'n* (9th Cir 1930) 42 F2d 9. The purchaser's superior title should not jeopardize the tenant's contractual arrangements until that time.

Tenants who have prepaid all or part of their rents before the redemption period should likewise be entitled to enjoy their prepaid possession even though it occurs during the statutory redemption period. Only when the prepayment is made by tenants with actual knowledge of the fact that foreclosure is already underway (see *Harris v Foster* (1893) 97 C 292, 32 P 246; *Fowler v Lane Mortgage Co.* (1922) 58 CA 66, 207 P 919), or by tenants who are otherwise in collusion with the trustor-landlord, should the prepayment be ignored. Whenever rent has been prepaid in good faith, the purchaser may be able to hold the trustor accountable for the loss but should not be able to make the tenants pay twice. If the tenants have prepaid rent for a period beyond the redemption period, such prepayment will not entitle them to possession against the foreclosure purchaser. See §5.39.

When the rent is postpaid, and part of it is for possession before the foreclosure sale, the rent should be apportioned so that the increment that relates to the period before foreclosure is returned to the trustor (unless the beneficiary has perfected its claim to back rents under the rents-and-profits clause). See *Clarke v Cobb* (1898) 121 C 595, 54 P 74. See also *Eastland Sav. & Loan Ass'n v Thornhill & Bruce, Inc.* (1968) 260 CA2d 259, 66 CR 901.

§5.39 6. Effect of Expiration of Redemption Period on Inferior Leases

The purchaser's subordination to existing junior leases (see §5.38) ends once the redemption period is completed; thereafter, the purchaser is entitled to recover possession from the junior tenants. Anyone who remains in possession, either a tenant of the trustor or the trustor personally, is immediately subject to an unlawful detainer action. CCP §1161a. If the tenants are permitted to remain, the purchaser is entitled to set the terms and the rent. *McDermott v Burke* (1860) 16 C 580; see Nelson & Whitman, Real Estate Finance Law §§4.20–4.21 (2d ed 1985). If the tenants' leases purport to run for longer periods, their remedy is against the trustor for breach of the covenant of quiet enjoyment under CC §1927.

The converse of the foregoing is that the purchaser cannot compel the trustor's tenants to remain under the terms of their former leases. On expiration of the redemption period, the tenants' leasehold estates terminate; they are free to quit the premises and to be released from the obligations of their leases. See Nelson & Whitman, Finance Law §4.21.

The purchaser remains subject to leases that were executed before the deed of trust if the purchaser had notice of the leases and they were not subordinated to the deed of trust. Retaining their rights until the leases expire, the tenants under these leases are as unaffected by the end of the redemption period as they were by the foreclosure. *Tropical Inv. Co. v Brown* (1919) 45 CA 205, 187 P 133; see Nelson & Whitman, Finance Law §4.21. These prior tenants must recognize the purchaser as their new landlord (CC §1111) and must honor all the covenants in their leases that benefit the purchaser and run with the land; in all other respects, however, their leasehold estates remain unchanged.

§5.40 7. Holding Tenants to Preexisting Lease

In California, the beneficiary under a deed of trust may hold junior tenants to their leases by omitting them from the judicial foreclosure action. *Sullivan v Superior Court* (1921) 185 C 133, 195 P 1061; *Goodenow v Ewer* (1860) 16 C 461. But see *McDermott v Burke* (1860) 16 C 580 (tenants held not proper parties in foreclosure action). By this device, the tenants' leasehold estates in the property are not foreclosed, and the judgment and sale terminate only the trustor's reversion in the property. See §§2.28, 3.16. Some other states follow this rule. See, *e.g.*, *Metropolitan Life Ins. Co. v Childs Co.* (1921) 230 NY 285, 130 NE 295, 14 ALR 658. When tenants are not included in the judicial foreclosure action, their leaseholds should not be considered terminated; the tenants should retain their rights and obligations under their leases for the duration of their leaseholds. Of course, the courts will not tolerate bad-faith arrangements; whenever it appears that the trustor and beneficiary are using a default to terminate uneconomic leases, the scheme should be disallowed.

Tenants in possession under unrecorded leases apparently need not be named as defendants in a foreclosure action in order for their leases to be terminated by the foreclosure sale. See CCP §726(c); §3.19.

§5.41   B. Effect of Trustee's Sale

Because there is no right of redemption after a trustee's sale, the trustor has no right of possession after the sale. *Farris v Pacific States Auxiliary Corp.* (1935) 4 C2d 103, 48 P2d 11. A trustor who remains in possession after a trustee's sale is subject to an immediate unlawful detainer action. CCP §1161a. The same is true for the trustor's tenants, unless their leases were superior to the mortgage. See §5.26. In this respect, completion of a trustee's sale is similar to expiration of the period of redemption for judicial foreclosure sales. See §5.30. If existing tenants wish to remain tenants, they must agree on new lease terms with the purchaser.

It is unclear whether any mechanism exists by which junior tenants can be held to their leases following a trustee's sale when the purchaser or lender desires such an outcome. The method for holding junior tenants to their leases following a judicial foreclosure (*i.e.*, omission of the tenants as parties to the action; see §5.40) cannot be applied following a trustee's sale because there is no action from which the tenants can be omitted as parties. The beneficiary may be able to tailor the sale so that it results in a sale only of the reversion and does not include the leasehold estate, by analogy to the way in which only part of a multiple security is offered for sale. See §2.28. A sale of the reversion alone would leave the tenants' leases unaffected. The tenants come into privity of estate with the foreclosure purchaser and are bound and benefited by all covenants that run with the land. CC §§818–834.

Chapter 6: **Debtor Strategies**

6

Debtor Strategies

§6.1   I. INTRODUCTION

This chapter discusses various strategies the trustor's attorney may pursue when the trustor is faced with foreclosure. A trustor who views the situation as hopeless may attempt to convey the property to the beneficiary rather than suffer the inevitable and embarrassing trustee's sale (see chap 2) or judicial foreclosure (see chap 3). Deeds in lieu of foreclosure as a debtor strategy are discussed in §§6.2–6.11. When the foreclosure sale appears to be improper, the trustor may challenge it, either beforehand by an action to enjoin the sale (see §§6.13–6.37) or afterwards by an action to set aside the sale (see §§6.38–6.47). Finally, the trustor may take advantage of various debtor protections offered under the federal Bankruptcy Code (see 11 USC §§101–1301; §§6.48–6.56) or may file an action for damages against the lender (see §6.57).

§6.2   II. DEEDS IN LIEU OF FORECLOSURE

A deed executed by the trustor to the beneficiary to avoid having the beneficiary foreclose on its deed of trust is referred to as a "deed in lieu of foreclosure," a "deed in lieu," or merely a "lieu deed." Such a transaction may be advantageous to both parties, but there are serious risks involved, especially for the beneficiary.

A beneficiary who accepts a lieu deed avoids the delays and costs of foreclosure. Instead of paying trustees' or attorneys' fees and waiting approximately four months for the sale, the beneficiary receives title to the property immediately with negligible transaction costs. If the property's value exceeds the amount of the debt, the beneficiary obtains more than it could expect from a public sale with competitive bidding. When the trustor is irretrievably in default and has no appreciable equity in the property, use of a lieu deed prevents the embarrassment and impaired credit rating of a public foreclosure sale and also gives the trustor immunity from a possible deficiency judgment.

The beneficiary runs certain risks in accepting a lieu deed. The grantor-trustor may later regret the action and sue to set aside the deed. See §6.4. Junior lienors may claim that the deed was not effective to extinguish or impair their claims. See §6.9. In addition, the broader coverage of the standard CLTA owner's policy is not as effective in protecting the beneficiary if it acquires title by deed in lieu rather than by purchase at a foreclosure sale. There is also the risk that the lieu deed may be treated as a fraudulent conveyance or preference in bankruptcy. See §§6.51, 6.56.

Lieu deeds are exempted from the constraints placed on home equity sales contracts by CC §§1695–1695.14. CC §1695.1(a)(2). For discussion of CC §§1695–1695.14, see §2.2.

From the trustor's federal income tax perspective, a deed in lieu of foreclosure is equivalent to a foreclosure sale at which the beneficiary bids the unpaid balance of the note. See §2.30. For the beneficiary, it is equivalent to collecting the debt to the extent of the fair market value of the property (which may be different from acquisition at a foreclosure sale for the amount bid). *Commissioner v Spreckels* (9th Cir 1941) 120 F2d 517. If the property is worth less than the principal loan balance, no interest income results to the beneficiary from receipt of the lieu deed. See *Helvering v Missouri State Life Ins. Co.* (8th Cir 1934) 78 F2d 778; *Manhattan Mut. Life Ins. Co.* (1938) 37 BTA 1041.

§6.3   A. Form and Contents

A deed in lieu of foreclosure need not necessarily differ in form from any other deed passing a fee title. It may take the form of a quitclaim deed (*Hamud v Hawthorne* (1959) 52 C2d 78, 338 P2d 387; *Smith v Sharp* (1924) 70 CA 336, 233 P 374), a grant deed, or any other valid deed (*Beeler v American Trust Co.* (1944) 24 C2d 1, 147 P2d 583; *Bastajian v Brown* (1943) 57 CA2d 910, 135 P2d 374; *Corcoran v Hinkel* (1893) 4 CU 360, 34 P 1031).

Title insurers customarily require either special recitals in the lieu deed or an estoppel affidavit from the trustor before they will insure a lieu deed. The recital should state that the conveyance was freely and fairly made. If the trustor was personally liable on the debt, the recital should add that the conveyance was made in full satisfaction of the debt. If the trustor was not personally liable for the debt, title insurers may require a recital that consideration equal to the fair value of the trustor's equity was paid. For form recitals, see 2 Bowman, Ogden's Revised California Real Property Law §§17.48–17.49 (TI Corp-CEB 1975). For a form estoppel affidavit, see 2 Ogden's Real Property §17.50. The affidavit is admissible but is not conclusive evidence of its contents. *Beeler v American Trust Co., supra.* The same is probably true for the recitals.

The beneficiary should also execute a reconveyance of the deed of trust (*Miller v Taber* (1957) 149 CA2d 792, 309 P2d 110) and should cancel the trustor's note. See *Holmes v Warren* (1904) 145 C 457, 78 P 954; *Chapman v Hicks* (1919) 41 CA 158, 182 P 336. Although cancellation of the note and deed of trust is technically unnecessary, failure to cancel them may furnish support to the trustor's later contention that the deed in lieu is invalid because a debtor-creditor relationship still exists (see §6.4). Sometimes the note is converted to nonrecourse status rather than canceled. *Shusett, Inc. v Home Sav. & Loan Ass'n* (1964) 231 CA2d 146, 41 CR 622. Reconveyance of the deed of trust is evidence that the lien has been extinguished. *Miller v Taber, supra.*

§6.4 B. Challenges by Trustor

Two contrary principles govern the validity of deeds in lieu of foreclosure. Supporting the validity of lieu deeds is the principle that a trustor's title to encumbered property is freely alienable. See CC §711. The trustor may convey his or her interest to any person, including the beneficiary under the deed of trust. *Phelan v De Martin* (1890) 85 C 365, 24 P 725; *Gronenschild v Ritzenthaler* (1947) 81 CA2d 138, 183 P2d 720. The deed can be set aside or reformed only when grounds exist that would support its cancellation or reformation. *Phelan v De Martin, supra.* On cancellation of instruments, see California Real Property Remedies Practice, chap 6 (Cal CEB 1982); on reformation, see Real Property Remedies, chap 2.

Undercutting the validity of lieu deeds is CC §2889, which voids contracts that (1) forfeit property that is subject to a lien or (2) restrain the right of redemption. The trustor has an equity of redemption in the encumbered property, *i.e.,* the right to pay the debt late and to receive any surplus from a foreclosure sale. CC §§2903–2905, 2924c; see §§2.17, 3.51. A lieu deed given by the trustor terminates both these rights. *Bradbury v Davenport* (1896) 114 C 593, 46 P 1062; *Winklemen v Sides* (1939) 31 CA2d 387, 88 P2d 147. Because deeds in lieu of foreclosure appear to fall squarely within the statutory prohibition, they are sometimes declared invalid even when their execution is absolutely free from fraud or any other defect. *Hamud v Hawthorne* (1959) 52 C2d 78, 338 P2d 387; see Nelson & Whitman, Real Estate Finance Law §6.19 (2d ed 1985).

California courts have not applied a consistent rationale in ruling on the validity of lieu deeds. Most reported decisions have upheld lieu deeds, following the principle that the trustor's interest is freely alienable. See, *e.g., Rogers v Mulkey* (1944) 63 CA2d 567, 147 P2d 62; *Borden v Boyvin* (1942) 55 CA2d 432, 130 P2d 718; *Davis v Stewart* (1939) 31 CA2d 574, 88 P2d 734. Some courts, however, have held lieu deeds invalid as violating the principles underlying CC §2889. See, *e.g., Hamud v Hawthorne, supra.* See also *First Fed. Trust Co. v Sanders* (1923) 192 C 194, 219 P 440.

A lieu deed may be intended to function either as a deed or as a mortgage. When a lieu deed is intended as a deed, it should be held valid except when it is tainted by fraud or some similar defect. *Gronenschild v Ritzenthaler, supra.* When the lieu deed is intended as a mortgage, however, it should be held invalid because the trustor has already given the beneficiary a deed of trust on the property and retains only the equity of redemption, which cannot be waived. CC §2889. (The trustor may give the beneficiary a second deed of trust on the property, but this still leaves the trustor with the right either to pay late or to receive the surplus from a sale, *i.e.,* the equity of redemption. *Union Bank v Wendland* (1976) 54 CA3d 393, 126 CR 549. A lieu deed is thus quite different from a second mortgage.)

The test of whether a deed in lieu is intended as a deed or as a mortgage is not very different from the traditional test used to determine whether a deed absolute is intended as a deed or as a mortgage (see §§4.36–4.37). The issue is whether the parties view the trustor as still owning the property, with the right to cure any default and to receive any surplus above the obligation in case of a foreclosure sale. If the trustor is viewed as still owning the property, the deed in lieu of foreclosure should be treated as a mortgage and not as a deed. If, on the other hand, the trustor has exchanged his or her equity for some consideration and has thus become merely a former owner of the property, with no further claim on or interest in the title, then the deed is a true deed and should be valid. The test turns on the intent of both parties in light of the circumstances. *Greene v Colburn* (1958) 160 CA2d 355, 325 P2d 148; *Mealy v Sunland Ref. Corp.* (1950) 96 CA2d 700, 216 P2d 59; *Jensen v Friedman* (1947) 79 CA2d 494, 179 P2d 855.

The distinction can be most clearly seen when comparing a prospective lieu deed with one that is to take effect immediately. When a trustor in default gives the beneficiary a deed to take effect in six months if the default has not been cured by then, the deed is actually a mortgage. *McGuigan v Millar* (1931) 117 CA 739, 4 P2d 607. When the trustor delivers an immediately effective deed and receives, in exchange, immediate debt forgiveness and cash consideration equal to the value of his or her equity in the property (if any), the transaction is a true conveyance and the deed is not a mortgage. Most lieu-deed transactions are variations of one of these two situations. See §§6.5–6.7.

§6.5   1. Lieu Deed Executed Contemporaneously With Loan

Civil Code §2889 is applied automatically to invalidate (a) a lieu deed made at the time of executing the original loan or (b) a provision for a lieu deed in the loan documents. *Bradbury v Davenport* (1896) 114 C 593, 46 P 1062. See also *Adams v Hopkins* (1904) 144 C 19, 77 P 712. A beneficiary is categorically prohibited from taking both a deed of trust and a deed absolute to take effect at some future date if the note is not paid. *Hamud v Hawthorne* (1959) 52 C2d 78, 338 P2d 387. The equity of redemption is granted to trustors by law, not by agreement, and provisions that seek to waive or restrict it are invalid. *Green v Butler* (1864) 26 C 595; *McMillan v Richards* (1858) 9 C 365. In such a case, the lieu deed is nothing but an attempted waiver of the right of redemption, because it operates only in a prospective fashion (*i.e.,* as a security instrument).

Invalidity of such a lieu deed is automatic. The beneficiary cannot defend the lieu deed by claiming that the loan was made on more generous terms because of it. *Beeler v American Trust Co.* (1944) 24 C2d 1, 147 P2d 583. The prohibition of CC §2889 undoubtedly also covers any disguised form of lieu-deed provision in the original loan documents. Any provision in the loan documents, however worded, that enables the beneficiary to obtain title on the trustor's default without a foreclosure and sale will fail.

§6.6   2. Subsequent Lieu Deeds

A lieu deed executed after the original loan was made is not automatically invalid. *Bradbury v Davenport* (1896) 114 C 593, 46 P 1062. Although a trustor is not permitted to waive the right of redemption in advance, California law permits waiver at any time after the trustor has received the loan proceeds. Deeds in lieu of foreclosure that are executed after the loan was made are upheld as long as they are fair, regardless of when they were given. *Bradbury v Davenport* (1898) 120 C 152, 52 P 301; *Watson v Edwards* (1894) 105 C 70, 38 P 527. Thus, courts have upheld lieu deeds given when the trustor was already in default (see *Watson v Edwards, supra*) and those given after the beneficiary had obtained a judgment of foreclosure and was awaiting the sale (see *Hines v Ward* (1898) 121 C 115, 53 P 427).

The distinction between a lieu deed given simultaneously with the mortgage and one that is given at a later time is that a contemporaneous lieu deed is always intended to function prospectively and can never be anything but a security device, while a later deed could be intended to function as a deed rather than as another mortgage (*i.e,* to transfer title absolutely, rather than as security, to the beneficiary; see §6.7). Nevertheless, it is surprising that a prospectively operative lieu deed, even when given after the deed of trust was executed, is not subjected to the same kind of critical judicial scrutiny and treatment as any other mortgage substitute. See §§4.37, 6.4.

§6.7   3. Conditional Lieu Deeds

For a deed in lieu of foreclosure to be effective, it must be treated by the parties as a final and complete passage of title from trustor to beneficiary and as a cancellation of all related financial obligations between them. *Beeler v American Trust Co.* (1944) 24 C2d 1, 147 P2d 583. Any arrangement that permits the trustor's continued connection with the property may lead a court to find that the deed is actually a mortgage. Thus, in *Beeler,* even though the deed was accompanied by a trustor's affidavit that the deed was only a deed, the California Supreme Court held it to be a mortgage because the beneficiary-grantee immediately leased the property back to the trustor with an option to repurchase and failed to cancel the trustor's earlier promissory note. See also *Strike v Trans-West Discount Corp.* (1979) 92 CA3d 735, 155 CR 132 (deed absolute, given after deed of trust, held to be security instrument when given as part of agreement under which (a) trustor was to remain in possession and pay taxes and assessments and (b) grantee-lender was to reconvey when trustor brought loan current). In other cases involving leasebacks and options, lieu deeds have been upheld, but probably only because this issue was not raised. See, *e.g., In re San Francisco Indus. Park, Inc.* (ND Cal 1969) 307 F Supp 271; *Shusett, Inc. v Home Sav. & Loan Ass'n* (1964) 231 CA2d 146, 41 CR 622; *Jensen v Burton* (1931) 117 CA 66, 3 P2d 324.

§6.8 C. Lieu Deeds and Third Parties

A deed that is acquired by the beneficiary from a third person is always treated as a valid deed rather than as a mortgage substitute. *Lineker v McColgan* (1921) 54 CA 771, 202 P 936.

A deed from the trustor to the original beneficiary, who had meanwhile transferred the note and deed of trust to another person, does not effect a merger of title and beneficial interest, because it is not a conveyance to the lienholder. Instead, the former beneficiary becomes the present titleholder subject to the lien of a deed of trust held by the transferee of that interest. *Rodgers v Peckham* (1898) 120 C 238, 52 P 483.

When the beneficiary conveys to a bona fide purchaser after having received a lieu deed, the trustor may not be able to attack the lieu deed by showing that it was not intended to be a true deed. CC §2925. The trustor's only remedy is against the beneficiary for wrongfully depriving the trustor of the equity of redemption. See *Munger v Moore* (1970) 11 CA3d 1, 89 CR 323.

§6.9 D. Lieu Deeds and Junior Creditors

Any conveyance by a trustor passes the trustor's title to the transferee subject to all existing liens. *Streiff v Darlington* (1937) 9 C2d 42, 68 P2d 728. Thus, if the title is encumbered by two deeds of trust, the grantee takes subject to both of them. If the grantee is the beneficiary under the first deed of trust, its lien would normally merge into its title and be destroyed. However, this would have the effect of giving the beneficiary title subject to another creditor's junior deed of trust, a result that is clearly contrary to the intent of the beneficiary when it took the lieu deed. See *Sheldon v La Brea Materials Co.* (1932) 216 C 686, 15 P2d 1098.

To avoid this result when there are junior lienors of record, courts have held that a beneficiary's lien and title do not merge when a lieu deed is given. *Anglo-Californian Bank v Field* (1905) 146 C 644, 80 P 1080. But see *Jensen v Burton* (1931) 117 CA 66, 3 P2d 324. Even when the deed was intended as a true deed and consideration was paid for it, or the beneficiary went into possession, or both, a merger will still be averted if it would harm the beneficiary. *Anglo-Californian Bank v Field, supra.* The junior lienor should be treated as a junior who has been omitted from a judicial foreclosure sale: The junior's rights are unimpaired, but the sale is otherwise valid. See *Carpentier v Brenham* (1870) 40 C 221. The junior should be allowed to redeem from the senior lien (under CC §§2903–2905), and the senior should be allowed to bring a foreclosure action against the junior. Alternatively, the senior should be able to act as trustor-owner and redeem from the junior lien. See §3.24 on the effect of omitting a junior from a judicial foreclosure action. Mishandled lieu-deed cases are always troublesome and generally lead to litigation. The beneficiary should not accept a deed in lieu of foreclosure unless it is absolutely certain that there are no junior liens of record or that the junior lienors have consented to the arrangement.

§6.10   E. Consequences of Lieu Deed Being Declared Mortgage

The issue of whether the lieu deed is a deed or a mortgage (see §6.4) is generally raised when the trustor sues to have the lieu deed declared a mortgage or to have it canceled altogether. If the trustor prevails, the court grants the appropriate relief, but the trustor remains liable for the debt (which the complaint must allege still to be in existence) and title remains encumbered. *Beeler v American Trust Co.* (1944) 24 C2d 1, 147 P2d 583. The trustor's liability remains even if the previous mortgage or deed of trust has been released or reconveyed. *Beeler v American Trust Co., supra.* The court may set a time within which the trustor may redeem the property (see §6.4), or it may merely declare that the instrument is a mortgage and leave the beneficiary to enforce its claim. See, *e.g., Hodgkins v Wright* (1900) 127 C 688, 60 P 431. The trustor may also contend, as a defense to an eviction action brought under the deed, that the lieu deed is actually a security instrument and compel the grantee-mortgagee to foreclose instead. See *Strike v Trans-West Discount Corp.* (1979) 92 CA3d 735, 155 CR 132.

A further possible consequence of executing what is apparently a lieu deed, but is in fact a mortgage, is that the court may impose a constructive trust in favor of the grantor. *Woodard v Hennegan* (1900) 128 C 293, 60 P 769; *Vance v Lincoln* (1869) 38 C 586. See also *Windt v Covert* (1907) 152 C 350, 93 P 67.

§6.11   F. Additional Consideration; Partial Lieu Deeds

Sometimes a deed in lieu will be desirable from a business point of view only if it is accompanied by additional consideration; *i.e.,* the lender will agree to accept the deed in lieu and cancel the debt only if the borrower also agrees to pay additional consideration to mitigate the lender's loss. This additional consideration may take the form of cash, secured or unsecured notes, or additional property. Additional consideration may also be required when the lender accepts a deed in lieu as satisfaction for only part of the debt (usually referred to as a partial deed in lieu), with the balance of the debt being restructured, usually as part of a workout. On workouts, see 2 California Real Property Financing, chap 1 (Cal CEB 1989).

A requirement for additional consideration raises the question of whether the deed in lieu constitutes an impermissible waiver of the protection of CCP §726, because the beneficiary obtains the equivalent of a deficiency judgment without judicial scrutiny or fair-value limitations. On waiver of antideficiency protections, see §§4.47–4.51. The borrower is losing the property and paying additional money to the lender. Even though the lieu deed is consensual and subsequent to the original security instrument (see §6.6), it still may violate CC §2953, which prohibits waiver of the protection of CCP §726 when making or renewing a loan. "Renewal" seems to describe a situation in which the initial obligation is replaced with a new obligation of essentially the same kind or nature. *Morello v Metzenbaum* (1944) 25 C2d 494, 154 P2d 670; *Russell v Roberts* (1974) 39 CA3d 390, 114 CR 305 (criticized on other grounds in *Palm v Schilling* (1988) 199 CA3d 63, 244 CR 600;

see §4.49). A partial deed in lieu does not appear to constitute a renewal, because the remaining obligation is usually significantly different from the original obligation. Prudent counsel should (1) state that the additional consideration does not constitute a renewal and (2) carefully highlight the differences between the original obligation and the new one. See *Russell v Roberts, supra.*

§6.12   III. ATTACKING TRUSTEE'S SALE

There is no automatic judicial review or supervision of a trustee's sale, although a sale may be subject to judicial review if the purchaser at the sale seeks judicial intervention to obtain possession of the property. Usually, however, judicial review of the trustee's sale occurs because the trustor or another interested party files an action attacking the sale. See *Smith v Allen* (1968) 68 C2d 93, 65 CR 153; *Meadows v Bakersfield Sav. & Loan Ass'n* (1967) 250 CA2d 749, 59 CR 34; *Py v Pleitner* (1945) 70 CA2d 576, 161 P2d 393.

The relief available to a person aggrieved by a trustee's sale depends first on whether the action is filed before or after the sale. A plaintiff who sues before the sale may seek to enjoin it until the court can decide the underlying issues, *e.g.*, whether a default occurred, whether the amount claimed to be owed is correct, whether a lien exists at all, or whether proper presale notice procedures have been followed. See §§6.13–6.37. The relief ultimately depends on what is proved at trial. An injunction is not available if the sale has been concluded. A completed sale may be set aside by the court unless it was made to a bona fide purchaser (see §§6.38–6.39), in which case the plaintiff may be limited to money damages. See §§6.38–6.47.

A party in possession of the property who seeks to invalidate the sale may refuse to leave the premises and then challenge the sale by defending an unlawful detainer or ejectment action brought by the purchaser. CCP §1161a; *Crummer v Whitehead* (1964) 230 CA2d 264, 40 CR 826. See also *MCA, Inc. v Universal Diversified Enters. Corp.* (1972) 27 CA3d 170, 103 CR 522. For discussion of defenses to an unlawful detainer action brought under CCP §1161a, see California Residential Landlord-Tenant Practice §6.48 (Cal CEB 1986). On ejectment, see California Real Property Remedies Practice, chap 10 (Cal CEB 1982).

§6.13 A. Injunctive Relief

The statutory requirement of a three-month period between the notice of default and the notice of sale, followed by an additional 20-day period between the notice of sale and the actual sale (CC §§2924, 2924(f); see §§2.11, 2.18), gives the trustor ample time to file an action to enjoin the sale. For discussion of requirements and procedures for obtaining injunctive relief, see 1 California Civil Procedure Before Trial, chap 15 (Cal CEB 1977).

§6.14 1. Grounds

Grounds for enjoining trustees' sales fall into two general categories. Under the first category, the trustor challenges the trustee's right to foreclose because, *e.g.*, (a) there was no default on the obligation (see, *e.g., Salot v Wershow* (1958) 157 CA2d 352, 320 P2d 926; *Rice v Union Trust Co.* (1920) 50 CA 643, 195 P 720), (b) the beneficiary does not have a valid lien against the property, or (c) there was fraud in the original transaction (*U.S. Hertz, Inc. v Niobrara Farms* (1974) 41 CA3d 68, 116 CR 44; *Stockton v Newman* (1957) 148 CA2d 558, 307 P2d 56; *Daniels v Williams* (1954) 125 CA2d 310, 270 P2d 556). See §§6.15–6.19. Included in this category are cases in which the trustor concedes the default but disputes the amount. See §6.20.

Under the second category, the trustor concedes the right to foreclose but contends that the sale violates the procedural requirements of CC §§2924–2924i because of defects in the notice of default, notice of sale, or proposed conduct of the sale. See *Crummer v Whitehead* (1964) 230 CA2d 264, 40 CR 826; §6.21.

§6.15 a. General Challenges to Right To Foreclose

The trustor may be able to contest foreclosure on one or more grounds that are potentially available as defenses against enforcement of an unsecured obligation. In litigation involving a secured transaction, the creditor is put to the same proof regarding the existence and validity of the debt as would be required of the creditor for an unsecured debt. The trustor may challenge not only the obligation but also the existence and validity of the security. The creditor loses the right both to sue on the obligation and to foreclose on the security if the obligation is unenforceable. *Savings Bank v Asbury* (1897) 117 C 96, 48 P 1081 (failure to lend full amount destroys right to accelerate); *Benson v Andrews* (1955) 138 CA2d 123, 292 P2d 39 (failure of consideration); *Trowbridge v Love* (1943) 58 CA2d 746, 137 P2d 890 (forgiveness of debt); *Burd v Downing* (1923) 60 CA 493, 213 P 287 (release of obligation). See generally Nelson & Whitman, Real Estate Finance Law §5.17 (2d ed 1985).

§6.16   (1) Payment

Payment in full completely discharges both the obligation and the security. A mortgage is extinguished by payment because it is merely a lien that depends for its existence on the continuance of an underlying obligation. See CC §2909; *McMillan v Richards* (1858) 9 C 365. A deed of trust, although theoretically a title transaction rather than a lien, exists only as long as there is a valid trust purpose. See Prob C §§15407, 15409. See also *MacLeod v Moran* (1908) 153 C 97, 94 P 604. If an obligation has been entirely performed but the record title has not been cleared, the landowner may bring an appropriate action to compel reconveyance of the deed of trust. See CC §2941. Wrongful refusal to clear the title can result in civil or criminal penalties. CC §§2941–2941.5.

§6.17   (2) Passage of Time

The only substantive difference between a mortgage with a power of sale and a deed of trust lies in application of the statute of limitations. Each secures an obligation that, if not performed, generates a cause of action for four years following the breach of a written obligation (CCP §337) or for two years following the breach of an oral obligation (CCP §339). *San Jose Safe Deposit Bank of Sav. v Bank of Madera* (1904) 144 C 574, 78 P 5. The lapse of four years does not have the same effect on a deed of trust, however, as it does on a mortgage. See §§6.18–6.19.

§6.18   (a) Mortgages

A mortgage is a lien on the mortgagor's real property under which the mortgagor retains title to the mortgaged premises. CC §2920; *Adler v Sargent* (1895) 109 C 42, 41 P 799. Civil Code §2911 provides that a lien is extinguished by the lapse of time during which an action could have been brought on the underlying obligation, which means that the mortgage is extinguished four years after the mortgagor defaults on the obligation if the mortgagee takes no action. *Wells v Harter* (1880) 56 C 342. Because a power of sale in a mortgage is merely an incident of the mortgage lien, it too is lost four years after nonpayment. *Faxon v All Persons* (1913) 166 C 707, 137 P 919. The right to foreclose or to sell is not extended by giving the mortgagee possession of the premises, although a "mortgagee in possession" may retain possession until the mortgage balance is paid. *Spect v Spect* (1891) 88 C 437, 26 P 203; see §5.3.

A creditor holding a mortgage must pay close attention to the time periods involved. The mortgagee cannot compel the debtor to execute an indefinite waiver of the statute of limitations, because CCP §360.5 limits the validity of such waivers to four-year periods. The creditor can obtain from the mortgagor an agreement to extend or renew the mortgage. Subsequent grantees of the mortgagor may validly consent to such extensions. *Curtis v Holee* (1921) 184 C 726, 195 P 395; *Cotcher v Barton* (1920) 49 CA 251, 193 P 169. If the renewal agreement is made after the limitation period has already run, all formalities for creating a mortgage in the first instance must be met. CC §2922; *Wells v Harter, supra*; see *Easton v Ash* (1941) 18 C2d 530, 116 P2d 433, for an example of an acceptable renewal form.

Although the mortgagee may be able to compel the mortgagor to agree to an extension of the mortgage, difficulties may be encountered with junior lienors. Unless the junior lienors also consent, they are not affected by an extension agreement between the first mortgagee and the mortgagor, and they may plead the statute of limitations as a bar to any foreclosure action or sale undertaken by the first mortgagee. *Ekmann v Plumas County Bank* (1932) 215 C 671, 12 P2d 433. A junior's right to strict compliance with the statute of limitations is entirely independent of the mortgagor's right and, even if the senior's statutory period is suspended by some disability, the junior may still successfully object to late foreclosure. See *Wood v Goodfellow* (1872) 43 C 185.

If the time to enforce the mortgage lien has passed, there is little that the mortgagee can do. It has lost both the right to foreclose and the right to sue for collection of the debt. All the mortgagee has in its favor is the recorded lien on the land, which cannot be removed by the mortgagor without payment. See *Chapman v Hicks* (1919) 41 CA 158, 182

P 336. Even the recorded lien has limited value, however, because the mortgagor may convey the property to another person after the statutory period expires, and the grantee may then quiet title and thus terminate the cloud on title created by the mortgage, as long as the grantee paid consideration for the property and the lien has expired. *Faxon v All Persons, supra.* In the rare cases in which the mortgagee has been given possession, the mortgagee is immune from ejectment until it has been paid, either by the mortgagor or from the profits of the land, even though its possession does not extend the time to foreclose. *Spect v Spect, supra;* see §5.3.

§6.19   (b) Deeds of Trust

The picture is brighter for the beneficiary of a deed of trust than for a mortgagee (see §6.18). Unlike a mortgage, a deed of trust gives the beneficiary (actually the trustee) title to the land rather than merely a lien on it. See *Koch v Briggs* (1859) 14 C 256. This trust title, together with the power of sale, had been held to endure for as long as the underlying trust purpose survives. *Hohn v Riverside County Flood Control & Water Conserv. Dist.* (1964) 228 CA2d 605, 39 CR 647. Under 1982 marketable title legislation (Stats 1982, ch 1268), however, a deed of trust is no longer the perpetual security that it once was. The lien of a mortgage or deed of trust now expires ten years after the due date of the obligation, if that date can be determined from the recorded document, or 60 years after the date of recordation of the instrument, if no due date can be determined (which will be the case for most recorded deeds of trust). CC §882.020. The expiration date can be extended for ten years by recording a "notice of intent to preserve interest" under CC §880.340. CC §882.020(a)(3).

Thus, apart from the Marketable Title Act provisions, the trustee under a deed of trust may exercise the power of sale despite any statute of limitations bar on the underlying obligation. *Welch v Security-First Nat'l Bank* (1943) 61 CA2d 632, 143 P2d 770; see §1.23. Junior lienors cannot complain of later foreclosure, because they are presumed to have known that the senior had no obligation to hasten collection of its debt. *Summers v Hallam Cooley Enters.* (1942) 56 CA2d 112, 132 P2d 60. The only effect of the statute of limitations in such a situation is that there can be no deficiency judgment, both because the obligation itself is immune after four years (CCP §337) and because the remedy of judicial foreclosure is lost at the same time (*Flack v Boland* (1938) 11 C2d 103, 77 P2d 1090), leaving exercise of the power of sale (which precludes any deficiency judgment under CCP §580d; see §4.14) as the only method of foreclosure.

§6.20 b. Disputed Obligations

Misunderstandings among the parties are common in complicated loan transactions, and the trustor's failure to make a payment demanded by the beneficiary may or may not be a breach of the trustor's obligations, depending on the circumstances. See, *e.g.*, *Hauger v Gates* (1954) 42 C2d 752, 269 P2d 609 (trustor's offset against beneficiary excused default); *Strike v Trans-West Discount Corp.* (1979) 92 CA3d 735, 155 CR 132 (notice of default based on usurious claim vacated); *Hunt v Smyth* (1972) 25 CA3d 807, 101 CR 4 (beneficiary's previous acceptance of partial payments might have waived other deficiencies); *System Inv. Corp. v Union Bank* (1971) 21 CA3d 137, 98 CR 735 (beneficiary should use funds in building loan account to satisfy payment due); *Ripley Improvement Co. v Hellman Commercial Trust & Sav. Bank* (1928) 90 CA 83, 265 P 835 (creditor held sufficient funds of debtor to pay obligation). See also *Gaffney v Downey Sav. & Loan Ass'n* (1988) 200 CA3d 1154, 246 CR 421 (foreclosure upheld despite beneficiary's receipt of separate, partial checks equaling amount due). In cases involving a bona fide dispute, the court may enjoin the pending sale while it decides what amount is properly due. See *More v Calkins* (1890) 85 C 177, 24 P 729; *Baypoint Mortgage Corp. v Crest Premium Real Estate Inv. Retirement Trust* (1985) 168 CA3d 818, 214 CR 531. But see *Hazen v Nicholls* (1899) 126 C 327, 58 P 816; *Ravano v Sayre* (1933) 135 CA 60, 26 P2d 515. If the trustor admits liability and disputes only the amount, the court may limit the trustor to temporary injunctive relief (see *Producers Holding Co. v Hill* (1927) 201 C 204, 256 P 207), or it may enjoin the particular sale without prejudice to future foreclosures based on different defaults (see *Lockwood v Sheedy* (1958) 157 CA2d 741, 321 P2d 862).

It is common in such cases for the plaintiff to combine the cause of action for injunctive relief with one for declaratory relief. Both causes of action are included in the form complaint in §6.34.

A temporary restraining order or preliminary injunction is commonly sought in such cases. See *Producers Holding Co. v Hill, supra; More v Calkins, supra; Strike v Trans-West Discount Corp., supra; Lenard v Edmonds* (1957) 151 CA2d 764, 312 P2d 308; *Stockton v Newman* (1957) 148 CA2d 558, 307 P2d 56. The injunction is usually requested to preserve the status quo until the court can resolve the underlying issues in dispute. The permanent relief sought will vary depending on the grounds alleged. The plaintiff will usually seek an accounting to determine the amount still owed or the correct amount necessary to reinstate the loan. Pending the result of the accounting, the plaintiff may seek to reinstate the loan or to redeem the property from the lien on payment of the full amount found to be due. If the plaintiff contends that nothing is owed, either because full payment has already been made or set-offs equal the balance due, or that the lien is otherwise invalid because of, *e.g.,* fraud or the trustor's lack of capacity to hypothecate the property, then the plaintiff will pray that the deed of trust be canceled and that title to the property be quieted free of the lien as part of the permanent relief.

A trustor who contends that the proposed trustee's sale is improper because the loan is not in default will seek to have the court reinstate the loan by ordering the trustee to record a rescission of the notice of default and enjoining the trustee from proceeding with the sale. This relief should not bar the beneficiary from later foreclosing based on new or different defaults. See *Lockwood v Sheedy, supra.*

§6.21   c. Improper Procedures

The trustee's failure to comply with statutory requirements regulating private sales is an additional ground for granting injunctive relief. For example, the sale may be enjoined if the trustee failed to give proper notice of default. *System Inv. Corp. v Union Bank* (1971) 21 CA3d 137, 98 CR 735; *Lockwood v Sheedy* (1958) 157 CA2d 741, 321 P2d 862.

Attacks based on improper procedures are usually made by a plaintiff who seeks to set aside a completed sale rather than to enjoin a pending sale. If the only basis for the plaintiff's attack is an improper procedure, the remedy is limited to ordering that the sale not proceed until proper procedures have been followed. The plaintiff may gain some advantage by the delay, however, *e.g.,* by obtaining additional time either to refinance the property and pay off the loan or to cure the default and reinstate the existing loan.

§6.22 d. Statutory Basis for Injunctive Relief

Under CCP §526, a court may issue provisional injunctive relief (*i.e.*, a temporary restraining order or preliminary injunction) against acts that:

■ Threaten waste or great or irreparable injury. In a foreclosure context, irreparable injury is usually alleged by contending that the property is unique. See CC §3387; *Wheat v Thomas* (1930) 209 C 306, 287 P 102; *Wright v Rodgers* (1926) 198 C 137, 243 P 866. See also *United Sav. & Loan Ass' n v Reeder Dev. Corp.* (1976) 57 CA3d 282, 129 CR 113. This allegation may not suffice if the real property was held only for investment. See *Jessen v Keystone Sav. & Loan Ass' n* (1983) 142 CA3d 454, 191 CR 104 (condominium units are like any other commodity; damages are readily ascertainable). The presumption of uniqueness under CC §3387 is conclusive for single-family residences; for all other real property, the burden of proof is on the party contending that pecuniary compensation is adequate. For further discussion, see Bird, *Toward Understanding California's Rebuttable Presumption That Land is Unique,* 1 Cal Real Prop J 21 (Summer 1983).

■ Violate another party's rights in the subject of the action and tend to render final judgment ineffectual.

■ Produce injury for which money damages are inadequate or extremely difficult to ascertain.

■ Threaten to cause a multiplicity of judicial proceedings.

■ Violate a trust obligation.

In addition, CCP §526 authorizes injunctive relief to restrain commission or continuance of an act if the complaint alleges "that the plaintiff is entitled to the relief demanded," and the relief sought consists of restraining the commission or continuance of the act, either for a limited time or perpetually. See *Stockton v Newman* (1957) 148 CA2d 558, 307 P2d 56.

Civil Code §3422 authorizes permanent injunctive relief to prevent the breach of an obligation existing in favor of the plaintiff when (1) pecuniary compensation would not afford adequate relief, (2) money damages are inadequate or difficult to ascertain, (3) the relief will prevent a multiplicity of judicial proceedings, or (4) the obligation arises from a trust.

Civil Code §3368 also authorizes injunctive relief whenever necessary to prevent a party "from doing that which ought not to be done." See *City of Pasadena v Superior Court* (1910) 157 C 781, 109 P 620 (CC §3368 conforms with general grant of equity jurisdiction in California Constitution).

§6.23   e. Tender Required for Provisional Relief

The court will usually condition a temporary restraining order or preliminary injunction on a requirement that the trustor pay, or tender payment, of any amounts admittedly owed the beneficiary (*Bisno v Sax* (1959) 175 CA2d 714, 346 P2d 814; *Young v Burchill* (1929) 96 CA 341, 274 P 379); the court may dissolve the injunction if such payments are not made (*Meetz v Mohr* (1904) 141 C 667, 75 P 298). This requirement may be excused, however, if bad-faith acts by the beneficiary lulled the trustor into not paying. *McCue v Bradbury* (1906) 149 C 108, 84 P 993. Tender may also be excused when payment might be construed as waiver of the right to rescind. See *Stockton v Newman* (1957) 148 CA2d 558, 307 P2d 56.

Courts usually deny an injunction sought solely to gain the trustor time to accumulate enough money to cure the default. *Gordon v Mc-Gaslin* (1943) 61 CA2d 540, 143 P2d 359. A court may stay the effect of its denial of a preliminary injunction, however, if it believes the trustor should have more time to raise the funds necessary for a tender (*Lupertino v Carbahal* (1973) 35 CA3d 742, 746, 111 CR 112, 114), or it may continue an order postponing the sale (*In re Reader* (1939) 32 CA2d 309, 89 P2d 654).

No tender is required when nothing is due, *e.g.*, when the trustor's set-off claims exceed the amount owed the beneficiary. *Hauger v Gates* (1954) 42 C2d 752, 269 P2d 609. When the hearing on a preliminary injunction is the debtor's only presale means of obtaining a judicial determination of the amount due or whether any amount is due, a tender is unnecessary. See *More v Calkins* (1890) 85 C 177, 24 P 729. See also *Stockton v Newman, supra*.

2. Parties

§6.24   a. Plaintiffs

Parties entitled to seek to enjoin a trustee's sale should include any party with the right to cure defaults under the deed of trust (see CC

§2924c), to redeem the property from the lien of the deed of trust (CC §§2903–2904), or to receive notice of default under CC §2924b(b)–(c) without recording a request for special notice. See §2.14.

The trustor is usually the plaintiff in an action to enjoin a trustee's sale, but other parties may seek an injunction even when the trustor does not challenge the sale. See *Hall v Citizens Nat'l Trust & Sav. Bank* (1942) 53 CA2d 625, 128 P2d 545 (constructive trustee); *Vaughan v People's Mortgage Co.* (1933) 130 CA 632, 20 P2d 335 (trustor's brother).

A junior creditor may sue to enjoin a sale that is improper and that will impair the junior's rights. See *Landsdown v Smith & Sons Reserve Corp.* (1934) 1 CA2d 618, 37 P2d 127. Guarantors probably have similar standing. See CC §§2810, 2819; *Union Bank v Gradsky* (1968) 265 CA2d 40, 71 CR 64. A senior lienor lacks standing to enjoin a junior sale, however, because the senior cannot redeem or challenge the junior lien. CCP §527. Similarly, former owners of the property have no interest in the trustee's sale, because its nonjudicial nature immunizes them from liability for a deficiency, which is their only possible concern. CCP §580d. A former owner who has taken back a second deed of trust or has a vendor's lien would have standing to sue as a junior creditor.

The trustor's tenants, whose leases may be terminated by a completed foreclosure sale, should have standing to enjoin the sale. See CC §§2924b(c)(1), 2924b(c)(2)(D)–(E), and 2924b(c)(3), which respectively require that notice of default and notice of sale be mailed to holders of leaseholds "acquired by an instrument sufficient to impart constructive notice" and to subsequent takers and encumbrancers.

§6.25 b. Defendants

The defendant in an action to enjoin the sale is usually the trustee responsible under the deed of trust for giving the notices and conducting the sale. CC §2924. On the trustee's duty to the trustor, see *Block v Tobin* (1975) 45 CA3d 214, 119 CR 288; *Pierson v Fischer* (1955) 131 CA2d 208, 280 P2d 491. See also *Garfinkle v Superior Court* (1978) 21 C3d 268, 146 CR 208. The term "trustee" includes any agent of the trustee authorized to conduct the sale. See *Orloff v Pece* (1933) 134 CA 434, 25 P2d 484. The beneficiary under the deed of trust should also be named as a defendant, because the foreclosure is based on the beneficiary's allegation of default. If not included, the beneficiary may be free to substitute a new trustee and continue the sale through the substitute. See §2.7. In addition, the trustor will often want to seek additional relief against the beneficiary, *e.g.*, damages for fraud. Service of process on the trustee neither constitutes service on the beneficiary nor requires the trustee to notify the beneficiary of the action. CC §2937.7.

National banks were formerly regarded as immune from state court injunctions against foreclosure sales. See, *e.g., Kemple v Security-First Nat' l Bank* (1967) 249 CA2d 719, 57 CR 838; *First Nat' l Bank v Superior Court* (1966) 240 CA2d 109, 49 CR 358. In *Third Nat' l Bank v Impac, Ltd.* (1977) 432 US 312, however, the United States Supreme Court held that 12 USC §91 does not bar an injunction to restrain the bank's foreclosure sale pending a hearing on the trustor's claim.

§6.26   3. Jurisdiction and Venue

Jurisdiction to issue injunctive relief rests initially in the trial courts; appellate courts do not have original jurisdiction over actions seeking injunctive relief. See Cal Const art VI, §10; *Walsh v Railroad Comm' n* (1940) 16 C2d 691, 107 P2d 611.

An action to enjoin a trustee's sale will usually be filed in the superior court of the county in which all or some of the real property is located. Superior courts have original jurisdiction in all civil cases, except when jurisdiction is conferred by statute on other courts. Cal Const art VI, §10. A superior court may issue provisional or final injunctive relief even though the complaint demands additional relief below the court's jurisdictional threshold. See *St. James Church v Superior Court* (1955) 135 CA2d 352, 287 P2d 387 (superior court has jurisdiction in action demanding permanent injunction and $240 in damages). Municipal and justice courts may, in cases otherwise within their subject-matter jurisdiction, issue temporary restraining orders and preliminary injunctions but not permanent injunctions. CCP §86(a)(8); see *St. James Church v Superior Court, supra*. Court commissioners do not have jurisdiction to issue injunctive relief. CCP §259. See also 2 Witkin, California Procedure, *Courts* §§274–275 (3d ed 1985).

The county in which the real property or some part of it is located is the proper county for trial of actions for the "determination in any form" of a right or interest in real property, subject to the court's power to transfer actions. CCP §392(1)(a). An action to enjoin a trustee's sale and to reform the power-of-sale clause in the deed of trust is local rather than transitory, even when incidental relief (*e.g.,* damages) is also sought. Thus, the action is properly filed in the county where the real property is located and may not be transferred to the county in which the beneficiary resides. *Massae v Superior Court* (1981) 118 CA3d 527, 173 CR 527.

4. Procedures for Obtaining Temporary Restraining Orders and Preliminary Injunctions

§6.27   a. Distinctions Among Types of Injunctive Relief

A temporary restraining order (TRO) is an interim order issued to preserve the status quo pending the hearing on an application for a preliminary injunction. See CCP §527; *Biasca v Superior Court* (1924) 194 C 366, 228 P 861. Although a TRO is not technically an injunction (because it may be issued ex parte without a requirement for a bond or undertaking), it has the same force and effect. See CCP §527. A TRO expires automatically 15 days after issuance or, on a showing of good cause, 20 days after issuance. CCP §527; see *Sharpe v Brotzman* (1956) 145 CA2d 354, 302 P2d 668 (interpreting earlier ten-day provision). The restraining order terminates if a preliminary injunction is denied or is superseded by issuance of a preliminary injunction. See *Houser v Superior Court* (1932) 121 CA 31, 8 P2d 483.

A preliminary injunction is an order issued to preserve the status quo pending final determination of an action on the merits. CCP §527; see *Continental Baking Co. v Katz* (1968) 68 C2d 512, 528, 67 CR 761, 771; *State Bd. of Barber Examiners v Star* (1970) 8 CA3d 736, 87 CR 450. The court usually conditions a preliminary injunction on the posting of a bond to protect the enjoined party. CCP §529; see §6.33. After the case has been heard on its merits, the preliminary injunction is either merged into a permanent injunction or dissolved if a permanent injunction is denied. See *Shahen v Superior Court* (1941) 46 CA2d 187, 115 P2d 516.

The court's decision to issue or deny a preliminary injunction is not an adjudication of the ultimate issues in the action (*People v Black's*

Food Store (1940) 16 C2d 59, 105 P2d 361), although it may indicate what the final judgment will be. Indeed, a court will ordinarily not issue a preliminary injunction unless there is a reasonable likelihood that the plaintiff will prevail at trial. See *Continental Baking Co. v Katz, supra.*

The court issues a permanent injunction after trial or other resolution of the case on its merits. Because a permanent injunction is not a provisional remedy, it need not have the same scope and effect as a preliminary injunction previously issued by the court. *San Diego Water Co. v Pacific Coast S.S. Co.* (1894) 101 C 216, 35 P 651. Because it represents final resolution of the action, issuance of a permanent injunction is not conditioned on a bond or undertaking. *Shahen v Superior Court, supra.*

§6.28   b. Procedures for Moving Party

The attorney for the party seeking to enjoin the trustee's sale must decide whether first to request a temporary restraining order (TRO) and order to show cause (see §§6.29–6.30) or simply to seek a preliminary injunction on notice (see §§6.31–6.32). A TRO should be sought immediately if the proposed trustee's sale is to take place in less than the 15 days required for noticing a motion for a preliminary injunction. See CCP §1005. Although the trustor has at least 110 days (after the notice of default is recorded; see §2.18) in which to seek to enjoin the sale, much of this time may already have passed before the attorney is contacted.

(1) When Temporary Restraining Order Is Sought

§6.29   (a) Checklist

To obtain a temporary restraining order (TRO) and order to show cause, the plaintiff's attorney must:

Prepare and file

_____ Complaint or cross-complaint (and have summons issued).

_____ Affidavits or declarations in support of TRO (and preliminary injunction).

_____ Memorandum of points and authorities.

_____ TRO and order to show cause.

_____ Bond or undertaking, if required by court (counsel should be prepared in advance with adequate sureties; see §6.33).

Record

_____ Lis pendens. See §6.35.

Notify

_____ Attorney for responding party or, if unknown, responding party of hearing on TRO. Under CCP §527, plaintiff's attorney must, except in certain situations, certify under oath that (1) he or she informed the opposing party or opposing party's attorney of time and place of hearing; (2) he or she attempted to give such notice, specifying efforts made; or (3) he or she should not be required to give such notice, for the reasons specified. See 1 California Civil Procedure Before Trial §15.38 (Cal CEB 1977).

Serve on responding party

_____ Copies of complaint or cross-complaint, summons, affidavits or declarations, points and authorities, and TRO and order to show cause, within time ordered by court and at least two days before show-cause hearing.

§6.30 (b) Form: Order To Show Cause and Temporary Restraining Order

Copies: Original (presented to judge for signature and filed with court clerk); copies for service and notice; office copies.

[*Title of court*]

[*Title of case*] **No. _ _ _ _ _ _**

ORDER TO SHOW CAUSE AND TEMPORARY RESTRAINING ORDER

Good cause appearing in the complaint, supporting declarations, and memorandum of points and authorities on file in this

action, and it appearing that this is a proper case for issuance of an order to show cause and a temporary restraining order, and that unless a temporary restraining order issues plaintiff will suffer irreparable injury before the matter can be heard on notice,

IT IS ORDERED that defendant, _ _[name] _ _, appear on _ _[date] _ _, at _ _ _ _.m., in Department No. _ _ of the above-entitled Court at _ _[state address] _ _, to show cause why a preliminary injunction should not be issued enjoining defendant from selling or attempting to sell, or causing to be sold, the trust property described in the complaint on file in this action either under the power of sale in the deed of trust or by foreclosure action.

IT IS FURTHER ORDERED that, pending the hearing on the order to show cause, defendant, _ _[name] _ _, defendant's agents, officers, employees, and representatives, and all persons acting in concert or participating with them, are hereby restrained and enjoined from selling, attempting to sell, or causing to be sold the trust property described in the complaint on file in this action either under the power of sale in the deed of trust or by foreclosure action.

IT IS FURTHER ORDERED that a copy of the complaint, supporting declarations, and memorandum of points and authorities, together with a copy of this order to show cause and temporary restraining order, be served on defendant no later than _ _[date set by Court; at least two days before hearing] _ _.

[Add, if appropriate; see §6.33]

BOND _ _[or undertaking] _ _ on this temporary restraining order is hereby fixed at _ _[amount to be inserted by Court] _ _.

Dated: _ _ _ _ _ _

_____
Judge of the Superior Court

(2) When Preliminary Injunction Is Sought by Noticed Motion

§6.31   (a) Checklist

To obtain a hearing on the application for a preliminary injunction when no temporary restraining order is sought, the plaintiff's attorney must:

Prepare and file

____ Complaint or cross-complaint (and have summons issued).

____ Affidavits or declarations in support of preliminary injunction.

____ Memorandum of points and authorities.

____ Notice of motion, or order to show cause, with proof of service of moving papers, within time specified by local rule.

____ Bond or undertaking, if required by court (counsel should be prepared in advance with adequate sureties; see §6.33).

Record

____ Lis pendens, if real property is involved. See §6.35.

Serve on responding party

____ Notice of motion or order to show cause, memorandum of points and authorities, affidavits or declarations, summons, and complaint or cross-complaint. For notice of motion, service must be made at least 15 days before hearing (unless time has been shortened; time is extended an additional five days if service is made by mail to California defendant). CCP §1005. Responding party's papers opposing motion must be filed and served at least five days before hearing. CCP §1005. Plaintiff's attorney may also proceed by obtaining from trial court an order to show cause why preliminary injunction should not issue, in which case service must be made within time ordered by court, but no later than two days before hearing.

§6.32   (b) Form: Notice of Motion for Preliminary Injunction

Copies: Original (filed with court clerk with proof of service); copies for service (one for each attorney of record and unrepresented party); office copies.

[*Title of court*]

[*Title of case*]   **No. _ _ _ _ _ _**

**NOTICE OF MOTION FOR
PRELIMINARY INJUNCTION;
MEMORANDUM OF POINTS
AND AUTHORITIES;
SUPPORTING DECLARATIONS**

Hearing: _ _[*date and time*]_ _
Department: _ _ _ _
Trial Date: _ _[*if set*]_ _

To defendant and defendant's attorney:

PLEASE TAKE NOTICE that on _ _[*date*]_ _, at _ _ _ _.m., or as soon thereafter as counsel can be heard, in Department No. _ _ of the above-entitled Court at _ _[*state address*]_ _, plaintiff will move the Court for a preliminary injunction as prayed for in the complaint on file in this action, enjoining defendant, and defendant's agents, officers, employees, and representatives, from selling, attempting to sell, or causing to be sold the trust property described in the complaint on file in this action, either under the power of sale in the deed of trust or by foreclosure action. This motion will be made on the grounds stated in the complaint on file in this action and in plaintiff's _ _[*supporting affidavits/declarations*]_ _ and memorandum of points and authorities, which are attached to this notice of motion and filed with it.

Plaintiff's motion for preliminary injunction will be based on all pleadings, papers, and records on file in this action and on evidence that may be presented at the hearing on this motion.

Dated: _ _ _ _ _ _

_____[*Signature of attorney*]_____
_ _[*Typed name*]_ _
Attorney for _ _[*name*]_ _

Comment: The notice of motion must be accompanied by a memorandum of points and authorities (Cal Rules of Ct 313) and supporting declarations (CCP §527). In courts with more than one department, the proper department in which to move for a preliminary injunction is determined by local court rules. The hearing on the preliminary injunction must be set at least 15 days after the notice of motion is filed (20 days if service is made by mail and the place of mailing and address are within California). CCP §1005.

The first page of each paper filed must show the date, time, and location (if known) of the hearing immediately below the case number. Cal Rules of Ct 311(b). The trial date must also be shown if one has been set. Rule 311(b) also requires that the first page of the notice show the nature or title of attached documents other than exhibits. Documents bound together must be consecutively paginated. Cal Rules of Ct 311(b). The first paragraph of a notice of motion must state both the nature of the order being sought and the grounds for issuing the order. Cal Rules of Ct 311(a).

§6.33   c. Bond or Undertaking

The trial court has discretion to require a bond or undertaking when issuing a temporary restraining order (TRO), and courts usually exercise this discretion by imposing a bonding requirement. See *Biasca v Superior Court* (1924) 194 C 366, 228 P 861. If a bond or undertaking is required, the TRO does not become effective until the bond or undertaking is deposited with the court. *Armstrong v Superior Court* (1916) 173 C 341, 159 P 1176; *Heyman & Co. v Landers* (1859) 12 C 107.

When a court issues a preliminary injunction, it must require that the moving party give a written undertaking with sufficient sureties (CCP §529), unless the enjoined party waives the requirement (see *City of Los Angeles v Superior Court* (1940) 15 C2d 16, 98 P2d 207) or the court, in its discretion, waives the requirement for an indigent (*Conover v Hall* (1974) 11 C3d 842, 114 CR 642).

The undertaking provides security for damages suffered by the responding party as a result of the preliminary injunction if the court subsequently decides that the injunction was wrongly granted. See §6.37. Because the deed of trust protects the beneficiary against defaults by the trustor, the undertaking is needed only to give the beneficiary further protection against any delays in realizing on its deed of trust. Requiring an undertaking for exactly the same amount as the obligation is therefore probably improper because there is no reason to duplicate the deed of trust. Setting a bond that is excessively large or unrelated to any damage that an injunctive delay could possibly cause may constitute a denial of due process to the trustor. *Lindsey v Normet* (1972) 405 US 56.

The undertaking requirement on preliminary injunctions, when applicable, is jurisdictional; if the court does not require an undertaking, or if the undertaking is not given, the injunction is inoperative (*Federal Automotive Servs. v Lane Buick Co.* (1962) 204 CA2d 689, 22 CR 603) and may be dissolved by the enjoined party (*Neumann v Moretti* (1905) 146 C 31, 79 P 512). An undertaking given on a TRO expires with the order and a new undertaking must be given for a preliminary injunction. *Maier v Luce* (1923) 61 CA 552, 215 P 399.

The sureties on an undertaking may be either individual or corporate. CCP §995.310. Challenges to the sufficiency of the undertaking are made by noticed motion under CCP §§995.910–995.960 and must be filed within five days after the date on which the undertaking is filed. CCP §529. The quality and not the mere number of sureties determines their sufficiency under CCP §529. *River Trails Ranch Co. v Superior Court* (1980) 111 CA3d 562, 168 CR 747.

Because it is not a provisional remedy (see §6.27), a permanent injunction issued after trial is not conditioned on a bond or undertaking. *Shahen v Superior Court* (1941) 46 CA2d 187, 115 P2d 516.

§6.34   d. Form: Complaint To Enjoin Trustee's Sale

Copies: Original (filed with court clerk); copies for service (one for each defendant to be served); office copies.

_ _[Name, address, telephone]_ _
Attorney for plaintiff

[Title of court]

[Title of case]   **No. _ _ _ _ _ _**

**COMPLAINT FOR
DECLARATORY AND
INJUNCTIVE RELIEF**

Plaintiff alleges:

FIRST CAUSE OF ACTION

**1. Plaintiff, _ _[name]_ _, is now, and at all times mentioned in
this complaint was, _ _[indicate plaintiff's ownership interest in real
property]_ _ of real property known as _ _[state street address or
other designation]_ _ and described as:**

[Legal description]

**2. Defendant, _ _[name of trustee]_ _, is a _ _[e.g., California
corporation, national banking association]_ _ authorized to engage in, and at all times mentioned in this complaint engaged
in, _ _[e.g., title insurance, banking and trust]_ _ business as a
_ _[e.g., title insurance company, California state bank]_ _.**

**3. Defendant, _ _[name]_ _, is now and at all times relevant to
this complaint was, _ _[beneficiary under the deed of trust alleged in
paragraph 6 and is a resident of _ _ _ _ _ _ _ _ _ County, California/al-
lege other capacity and residence]_ _.**

**4. Plaintiff does not know the true names of defendants
sued as Doe 1 through Doe _ _[number of fictitiously named defendants]_ _.**

**5. On _ _[date]_ _, _ _[plaintiff/plaintiff's predecessor in inter-
est]_ _, for a valuable consideration, made, executed, and delivered to defendant, _ _[name of beneficiary]_ _, a written
promissory note. A copy of the promissory note is attached as
Exhibit _ _ and incorporated by reference.**

6. **To secure payment of the principal sum and interest as provided in the note and as part of the same transaction,** _ _[plaintiff/plaintiff's predecessor in interest]_ _ **executed and delivered to defendant,** _ _[name]_ _, **a deed of trust dated** _ _ _ _ _ _, **by the terms of which plaintiff, as trustor, conveyed to defendant,** _ _[name]_ _, **as trustee, the real property described in paragraph 1. On** _ _[date]_ _, **the deed of trust was recorded in Book No.** _ _ **at page** _ _ **of the Official Records of** _ _ _ _ _ _ _ _ **County, California. A copy of the deed of trust is attached as Exhibit** _ _ **and incorporated by reference.**

7. **On** _ _[date]_ _, **defendant,** _ _[name]_ _, **caused to be recorded a notice of default and of election to sell in Book No.** _ _ **at page** _ _ **of the Official Records of** _ _ _ _ _ _ _ _ **County, California, alleging (a) that a breach of the obligation secured by the deed of trust had occurred, consisting of plaintiff's alleged failure to** _ _[summarize default, e.g., pay certain monthly installments of principal and interest]_ _, **and (b) that defendant, as beneficiary, elects to sell, or cause to be sold, the trust property to satisfy that obligation. A copy of the notice of default and election to sell is attached as Exhibit** _ _ **and incorporated by reference.**

[Choose appropriate paragraph]

[Either 1: If alleged that trustee lacks right to conduct sale]

8. **A breach of the obligation for which the deed of trust is security** _ _[has not occurred/is excusable because, e.g., defendant, _ _[name]_ _, refused plaintiff's tender of arrearages]_ _. **An actual controversy exists between plaintiff and defendant concerning their respective rights and duties in the trust property in the described transactions in that (a) plaintiff contends that** _ _[state legal consequences resulting from facts alleged in preceding paragraphs]_ _, **and (b) defendant disputes this contention and contends that** _ _[state contentions]_ _.

[Or 2: If improper sale procedures alleged]

8. **Defendant,** _ _[name]_ _, _ _[state improprieties, e.g., has failed to comply with the publishing and posting requirements of Civil Code section 2924f in that_ _[state facts constituting noncompliance or establishing fraudulent or collusive arrangements]_ _]_ _. **An actual controversy exists between plaintiff and defendant concern-**

ing their respective rights and duties in the trust property in the described transactions in that (a) plaintiff contends that _ _[*state legal consequences resulting from facts alleged in preceding paragraphs*]_ _, and (b) defendant disputes this contention and contends that _ _[*state contentions*]_ _.

[*Continue*]

9. **Plaintiff desires a judicial determination and declaration of plaintiff's and defendants' respective rights and duties; specifically,** _ _[*state declaration requested, e.g., that plaintiff did not breach his or her obligations, or that trustee failed to comply with statutory requirements for conducting the sale*]_ _. **Such a declaration is appropriate at this time so that plaintiff may determine** _ _[*his/her/its*]_ _ **rights and duties before the real property that is the subject of this dispute is sold at a foreclosure sale.**

SECOND CAUSE OF ACTION

10. **Plaintiff realleges and incorporates by reference the allegations in paragraphs 1 through 8 of the First Cause of Action.**

11. **Defendant,** _ _[*as trustee*]_ _, **intends to sell, and unless restrained will sell or cause to be sold, the trust property, to plaintiff's great and irreparable injury in that** _ _[*specify, e.g., defendant has given notice that the sale of the property will take place on* _ _[*date*]_ _, *at* _ _ _ _.m., *at* _ _[*state address*]_ _, _ _ _ _ _ _ _ _ *County, California, and, if the sale takes place as scheduled, plaintiff, having no right to redeem* _ _[*his/her/its*]_ _ *property from the sale, will forfeit it*]_ _.

12. **The scheduled sale is wrongful and should be enjoined in that** _ _[*specify grounds for this contention, e.g., there was no breach, trustee did not follow statutory sale procedures*]_ _. **Plaintiff has no other plain, speedy, or adequate remedy, and the injunctive relief prayed for below is necessary and appropriate at this time to prevent irreparable loss to plaintiff's interests.**

THIRD CAUSE OF ACTION

13. **Plaintiff realleges and incorporates by reference the allegations in paragraphs 1 through 8 of the First Cause of Action.**

14. The amount of money due and owing from plaintiff to defendant, _ _[name of beneficiary] _ _, is unknown to plaintiff and cannot be determined without an accounting.

WHEREFORE, plaintiff demands judgment as follows:

1. That the Court issue a declaration of the rights and duties of the parties; specifically, _ _[specify declaration desired, e.g., (a) *that trustee has no right to conduct the sale because, e.g., no breach occurred or there is no valid lien, or (b) that trustee has not followed required sale procedures*] _ _.

2. That the Court issue a _ _[temporary restraining order] _ _, preliminary injunction, and permanent injunction restraining defendant, _ _[name of trustee] _ _, defendant's agents, attorneys, and representatives, and all persons acting in concert or participating with them, from selling, attempting to sell, or causing to be sold the trust property either under the power of sale in the deed of trust or by foreclosure action.

3. That the Court render an accounting between plaintiff, _ _[name] _ _, and defendant, _ _[name of beneficiary] _ _, determining the amount, if any, actually due and owing from plaintiff to defendant, _ _ [beneficiary] _ _.

4. That plaintiff recover _ _[his/her/its] _ _ attorneys' fees and costs incurred in this action, and that the Court award all other appropriate relief.

Dated: _ _ _ _ _ _

> ___[Signature of attorney]___
> _ _[Typed name] _ _
> **Attorney for _ _[name] _ _**

Comment: This form is illustrative of a complaint seeking declaratory and injunctive relief concerning a scheduled foreclosure sale; obviously, the allegations of the complaint must be tailored to fit the facts and legal contentions of a particular trustee's sale. In an appropriate case, the plaintiff might add a cause of action for an accounting (see Third Cause of Action and ¶3 of the prayer) to determine the amounts actually owed by the plaintiff. On formal aspects of drafting the complaint, see 1 California Civil Procedure Before Trial §§7.16–7.41 (Cal CEB 1977); on declaratory relief, see 2 California Civil Procedure Before Trial, chap 24 (Cal CEB 1978); on injunctive relief, see 1 Civ Proc Before Trial, chap 15. A debtor who is successful in enjoining a sale may be entitled to recover attorneys' fees under CC §1717 if the promissory note or deed of trust provides for attorneys' fees. *Valley Bible Center v Western Title Ins. Co.* (1983) 138 CA3d 931, 188 CR 335; see §§7.29–7.33.

§6.35   e. Lis Pendens

A notice of action pending (lis pendens) should be recorded immediately after the complaint seeking to enjoin the sale is filed. The purpose of the lis pendens is to put all subsequent purchasers of the property on notice of the plaintiff's claim. *Putnam Sand & Gravel Co. v Albers* (1971) 14 CA3d 722, 92 CR 636. Consequently, even if a preliminary injunction is denied and the trustee's sale takes place, the fact that a lis pendens has been recorded will cause the purchaser to take subject to the plaintiff's claims. The purchaser will not qualify as a bona fide purchaser able to take advantage of the presumptions of regularity in the recitals of the trustee's deed. See CC §2924.

The lis pendens form in §3.46 may be used by a plaintiff seeking to enjoin a sale. For extensive discussion of use of a lis pendens, see California Lis Pendens Practice (Cal CEB 1983).

§6.36   5. Appeals

A direct appeal may be taken from an order issuing or dissolving, or refusing to issue or dissolve, a temporary restraining order (TRO) or preliminary injunction. CCP §§904.1(f) (superior court), 904.2(g) (municipal or justice court). Direct appeals of interim injunctive orders are not particularly effective, however, because the case may proceed to trial and judgment before the appeal can be heard. Accordingly, extraordinary writs are often used to challenge interim orders. See 1 California Civil Procedure Before Trial §§15.81–15.82 (Cal CEB 1977); California Civil Writ Practice (2d ed Cal CEB 1987).

A final judgment either issuing or denying a permanent injunction is also appealable. CCP §§904.1(a), 904.2(a); *U.S. Hertz, Inc. v Niobrara Farms* (1974) 41 CA3d 68, 116 CR 44.

When an injunction has been denied, the trial court, to preserve the status quo pending appeal, has authority either to issue a TRO or to continue a preliminary injunction previously issued. *City of Pasadena v Superior Court* (1910) 157 C 781, 109 P 620. The trial court has this power even after a notice of appeal has been filed. *General Elec. Co. v Federal Employees' Distrib. Co.* (1955) 132 CA2d 649, 282 P2d 941. If the trial court has dissolved a previously issued injunction or has otherwise refused to enjoin a trustee's sale pending appeal, the appellant may petition the appellate court for a stay or writ of supersedeas to preserve the status quo pending appeal. CCP §923; Cal Rules of Ct 49; see *People ex rel San Francisco Bay Conserv. & Dev. Comm'n v Town of Emeryville* (1968) 69 C2d 533, 72 CR 790. See generally California Civil Appellate Practice, chap 6 (2d ed Cal CEB 1985).

Under the decision in *Hunt v Smyth* (1972) 25 CA3d 807, 101 CR 4, it appears that a trustor who obtains a preliminary injunction before expiration of the reinstatement period, but who ultimately loses on the merits after an appeal, may be allowed the unexpired portion of the reinstatement period that remained when the action for an injunction was filed. In *Hunt*, the notice of default was recorded on April 11, 1969; the trustors sued for an injunction on July 3, 1969, 13 days before the (then) three-month reinstatement period would have ended. On May 22, 1972, almost three years later, the court of appeal ruled against the trustors but ordered that on remand they be allowed the remaining 13 days to reinstate their loan. See §2.17.

§6.37 6. Consequences of Improper Attempts To Enjoin

If, after having granted a temporary restraining order or preliminary injunction, the court determines on the merits that the plaintiff was not entitled to injunctive relief, the plaintiff is liable for any decline in the value of the security that occurs during the period in which the sale was postponed. *Surety Sav. & Loan Ass'n v National Auto. & Cas. Ins. Co.* (1970) 8 CA3d 752, 87 CR 572. Thus, if property originally worth $100,000 has declined in value to $95,000 during the pendency of an interim injunctive order, a beneficiary owed $100,000 or more may recover $5000 in damages for the delay. If the beneficiary is owed $95,000 or less, however, sale of the reduced security will still satisfy the debt, and no damages are allowed under these circumstances. In addition, the beneficiary may recover special items of damages such as attorneys' fees for defending the action for an injunction, interest, loss of rental income, and costs of protecting the property. *Surety Sav. & Loan Ass'n v National Auto. & Cas. Ins. Co., supra.*

The debtor's attorney may also be liable for engaging in dilatory tactics in enjoining a foreclosure. *Kapelus v Newport Equity Funds, Inc.* (1983) 147 CA3d 1, 194 CR 893 (sanctions of $5000 imposed against debtor and his attorney). On the other hand, a debtor who is successful in enjoining a sale should recover attorneys' fees under CC §1717. *Valley Bible Center v Western Title Ins. Co.* (1983) 138 CA3d 931, 188 CR 335.

Code of Civil Procedure §529 requires that the plaintiff post a bond or undertaking as a prerequisite to obtaining a preliminary injunction. See §6.33. The statutory language limiting the defendant's damages to those "not exceeding an amount to be specified" (CCP §529) may, however, restrict the damages recoverable for an improper injunction to the amount of the bond. See *Surety Sav. & Loan v National Auto. & Cas. Ins. Co., supra.* Further damages may then be recovered only by a separate action for abuse of process or malicious prosecution. See *Dickey v Rosso* (1972) 23 CA3d 493, 100 CR 358.

Whether the antideficiency rules protect a trustor from liability for improperly delaying a sale has never been decided by an appellate court, but such an argument is unlikely to succeed. A beneficiary always runs the risk that the security will decline in value in purchase-money situations and when it elects to foreclose by trustee's sale, but the delay and decline in value resulting from an injunction are not part of its bargain. This loss is analogous to that caused by the trustor's bad-faith waste (see §4.40). Both are affirmative acts not related to financial inability to care for the property and should not, therefore, be protected by the antideficiency laws. See *Cornelison v Kornbluth* (1975) 15 C3d 590, 125 CR 557.

§6.38   B. Setting Aside Sale

After a trustee's sale has taken place, the trustor or other party (*e.g.,* junior lienor) may bring an action to have the sale set aside or to quiet title against the purchaser at the sale. See *Crummer v Whitehead* (1964) 230 CA2d 264, 40 CR 826; *Taliaferro v Crola* (1957) 152 CA2d 448, 313 P2d 136; *Brown v Busch* (1957) 152 CA2d 200, 313 P2d 19; *Standley v Knapp* (1931) 113 CA 91, 298 P 109; *Henderson v Fisher*

(1918) 38 CA 270, 176 P 63. The plaintiff is not required to have first tried to enjoin the sale and is not estopped from raising issues that could have been argued before the sale. See *Hauger v Gates* (1954) 42 C2d 752, 269 P2d 609. It is more difficult to set aside a sale to a bona fide purchaser, however, than it would have been to have enjoined the sale beforehand. See *Weingard v Atlantic Sav. & Loan Ass'n* (1970) 1 C3d 806, 819, 83 CR 650, 656; §6.39. A plaintiff challenging the sale has the burden of proof on all issues and must show that he or she was injured by the alleged irregularity. See *California Trust Co. v Smead Inv. Co.* (1935) 6 CA2d 432, 44 P2d 624; *American Trust Co. v deAlbergaria* (1932) 123 CA 76, 10 P2d 1016.

The action to set the sale aside is often accompanied by separate causes of action:

■ To quiet title (CCP §§760.010–764.070; see California Real Property Remedies Practice, chap 7 (Cal CEB 1982));

■ To cancel the trustee's deed (CC §3412; see Real Property Remedies, chap 6);

■ For an accounting; and

■ For recovery of possession through ejectment (see Real Property Remedies, chap 10) or for recovery of damages for withholding possession (CCP §740).

On nonmonetary causes of action, see §6.41; on relief in the form of damages, see §6.42.

An action brought solely to set aside the sale is equitable and therefore does not entitle the parties to a jury trial. When a claim for damages is joined with the action, the court may hear the equitable cause of action first. *Raedeke v Gibraltar Sav. & Loan Ass'n* (1974) 10 C3d 665, 111 CR 693; *Rablin v Greiner* (1935) 4 C2d 255, 48 P2d 696. The trustor is not required to seek damages for wrongful sale of the property if he or she seeks to have title restored. See *Marlenee v Brown* (1943) 21 C2d 668, 134 P2d 770; *Strutt v Ontario Sav. & Loan Ass'n* (1970) 11 CA3d 547, 90 CR 69; *Standley v Knapp, supra.*

A junior lienor will have more difficulty than the trustor in setting aside the sale, because damages are usually an adequate remedy. See *U.S. Cold Storage v Great W. Sav. & Loan Ass'n* (1985) 165 CA3d 1214, 212 CR 232. The court in *Arnolds Management Corp. v Eischen* (1984) 158 CA3d 575, 205 CR 15, stated that a junior lienor may have the sale set aside only after having tendered the entire balance due on the senior obligation (a requirement disapproved by the court in *U.S. Cold Storage*). See also *FPCI RE-HAB 01 v E&G Invs.* (1989) 207 CA3d 1018, 255 CR 157, in which the court held that a sold-out junior lienor failed to show that it was damaged when the beneficiary under a wraparound deed of trust claimed the entire amount due on the wraparound and the underlying deed of trust in the notice of sale. For discussion of these cases, see the commentary in 12 CEB Real Prop L Rep 135 (May 1989).

§6.39 1. Disadvantages of Action To Set Aside; Conclusiveness of Trustee's Deed Recitals

The client's rights can best be preserved if the trustor's attorney seeks to enjoin the foreclosure sale beforehand, rather than waiting and filing an action to set aside the sale afterwards. In terms of the issues that may be raised, however, the plaintiff is usually permitted to assert the same grounds that could have been raised to enjoin the sale. Whether the facts in a case justify setting aside a trustee's sale is largely a matter for the trial court's discretion. *Crummer v Whitehead* (1964) 230 CA2d 264, 40 CR 826; *Brown v Busch* (1957) 152 CA2d 200, 313 P2d 19. In the absence of evidence to the contrary, the sale is presumed to have been conducted regularly and fairly. *Hohn v Riverside County Flood Control & Water Conserv. Dist.* (1964) 228 CA2d 605, 39 CR 647; *Brown v Busch, supra.*

A major disadvantage of an action to set aside the sale is that the sale stands if the trustor loses on the merits, and the trustor has no further opportunity to reinstate the loan. In contrast, if the trustor loses an action to enjoin the sale, the court often grants additional time to reinstate. See *Hunt v Smyth* (1972) 25 CA3d 807, 101 CR 4; §6.37.

A second disadvantage is that, by waiting until after the foreclosure sale, the trustor risks losing the right to set aside the sale against a bona fide purchaser for value who purchased either at the foreclosure sale or subsequently from the beneficiary who has credit-bid at the sale. See *Weingard v Atlantic Sav. & Loan Ass'n* (1970) 1 C3d 806, 819, 83 CR 650, 656; *Strutt v Ontario Sav. & Loan Ass'n* (1970) 11 CA3d 547, 90 CR 69. A beneficiary who purchases at its own sale by a credit-bid does not qualify as a bona fide purchaser. *20th Century Plumbing Co. v*

Sfregola (1981) 126 CA3d 851, 179 CR 144; *Tomczak v Ortega* (1966) 240 CA2d 902, 50 CR 20. It is unclear whether the beneficiary can elevate itself to bona fide purchaser status by adding some cash to its credit-bid. A third party who purchases at the trustee's sale without notice of any claim of invalidity qualifies as a bona fide purchaser. *Sorenson v Hall* (1934) 219 C 680, 28 P2d 667. A third party who later purchases for value, and without notice, from a beneficiary who purchased at its own sale may be similarly protected. But see *Di Nola v Allison* (1904) 143 C 106, 76 P 976 (sale after judicial foreclosure action). The plaintiff in an action to set aside the sale should therefore record a lis pendens as soon as the complaint is filed to prevent subsequent takers from qualifying as bona fide purchasers. See *System Inv. Corp. v Union Bank* (1971) 21 CA3d 137, 98 CR 735; §6.35. If the property is acquired by a bona fide purchaser, the plaintiff's recovery may be limited to damages against the beneficiary or trustee.

If the trustee's deed recites that the trustee has complied with all requirements concerning the mailing, posting, publication, or personal delivery of the notice of default and the notice of sale, the recitals are conclusive in favor of bona fide purchasers and encumbrancers for value and without notice. CC §2924; see *Garfinkle v Superior Court* (1978) 21 C3d 268, 279 n16, 146 CR 208, 215 n16. In the absence of a bona fide purchaser, the recitals are only prima facie evidence of the facts that they allege to be true. CC §2924; *Wolfe v Lipsy* (1985) 163 CA3d 633, 209 CR 801; *Beck v Reinholtz* (1956) 138 CA2d 719, 292 P2d 906; *Seidell v Tuxedo Land Co.* (1934) 1 CA2d 406, 36 P2d 1102.

In addition to the conclusive presumption created by CC §2924, and despite the language of the statute, deeds of trust commonly recite that all the recitals in the trustee's deed are conclusive in all cases. See §7.42. Thus, the trustor may be bound by the recitals by virtue of having signed the deed of trust. See *Mersfelder v Spring* (1903) 139 C 593, 73 P 452; *Pierson v Fischer* (1955) 131 CA2d 208, 280 P2d 491. But see *Seccombe v Roe* (1913) 22 CA 139, 133 P 507. See also *Little v CFS Serv. Corp.* (1987) 188 CA3d 1354, 1359, 233 CR 923, 925 (dictum). How third parties (*e.g.*, junior creditors) who did not sign the deed of trust, but take subject to its provisions, are affected by these nonstatutory recitals is unknown.

Civil Code §2924 limits the presumption to presale posting and publishing requirements and is silent concerning the conduct of the sale itself. The courts treat the conduct of the sale differently depending on the remedy sought rather than on the type of irregularity claimed. When the trustor files an equitable action to set aside the sale and restore the equity of redemption, any irregularities in the sale itself or in presale procedures may be attacked, and the courts will scrutinize the sale carefully. *Mersfelder v Spring, supra*; *Py v Pleitner* (1945) 70 CA2d 576, 161 P2d 393; *Holland v Pendleton Mortgage Co.* (1943) 61 CA2d 570, 143 P2d 493. In a postsale unlawful detainer action brought by the purchaser to oust the trustor or the trustor's tenant, the purchaser's title may be challenged to the limited extent of claiming noncompliance with the statutory foreclosure requirements, but further inquiry into the validity of the purchaser's title is not permitted. *Cheney v Trauzettel* (1937) 9 C2d 158, 69 P2d 832; *Abrahamer v Parks* (1956) 141 CA2d 82, 296 P2d 341. See also *Vella v Hudgins* (1977) 20 C3d 251, 142 CR 414; *Evans v Superior Court* (1977) 67 CA3d 162, 136 CR 596.

§6.40   2. Grounds for Setting Aside Sale

Grounds for setting aside a trustee's sale include those that would have supported an action to enjoin the sale (see §6.14):

■ Assertions that there was no breach or that the trustee was not otherwise authorized to foreclose. *Hauger v Gates* (1954) 42 C2d 752, 269 P2d 609 (set-off equaled amount due); *System Inv. Corp. v Union Bank* (1971) 21 CA3d 137, 98 CR 735 (waiver of breach); *Saterstrom v Glick Bros. Sash, Door & Mill Co.* (1931) 118 CA 379, 5 P2d 21 (void deed of trust); *Van Noy v Goldberg* (1929) 98 CA 604, 277 P 538 (debt not matured).

■ Attacks on the presale foreclosure process. *Strutt v Ontario Sav. & Loan Ass'n* (1972) 28 CA3d 866, 105 CR 395; *Standley v Knapp* (1931) 113 CA 91, 298 P 109; *Seccombe v Roe* (1913) 22 CA 139, 133 P 507.

In addition, improper conduct by the trustee or beneficiary at the sale itself generates a further ground for attack. *Pierson v Fischer* (1955) 131 CA2d 208, 280 P2d 491. The plaintiff must, however, overcome a presumption that the trustee's sale has been conducted regularly and fairly. CC §2924 (see §6.39); *Hohn v Riverside County Flood Control & Water Conserv. Dist.* (1964) 228 CA2d 605, 39 CR 647;

Brown v Busch (1957) 152 CA2d 200, 313 P2d 19. The fact that the amount bid is less than the property's market value is not a sufficient ground to set aside the sale in the absence of fraud, unfairness, or oppression. *Central Nat'l Bank v Bell* (1936) 5 C2d 324, 54 P2d 1107; *Crummer v Whitehead* (1964) 230 CA2d 264, 40 CR 826; *Brown v Busch, supra.* A gross disparity between price and value empowers the court, however, to set aside the sale if there is any evidence of unfairness or irregularity. See *Stevens v Plumas Eureka Annex Mining Co.* (1935) 2 C2d 493, 41 P2d 927; *Sargent v Shumaker* (1924) 193 C 122, 223 P 464; *Lopez v Bell* (1962) 207 CA2d 394, 24 CR 626; *Foge v Schmidt* (1951) 101 CA2d 681, 226 P2d 73. Sale price/market value ratios found insufficiently disproportionate to justify invalidation of the sale are $480/$4800 (see *Baldwin v Brown* (1924) 193 C 345, 224 P 462), $20,000/$50,000 (see *Crofoot v Tarman* (1957) 147 CA2d 443, 305 P2d 56), and $500/$2500 (see *Eigenhuis v Morris* (1934) 136 CA 333, 28 P2d 928).

3. Relief Available

§6.41   a. Nonmonetary Relief

When attacking a completed foreclosure sale, the trustor usually seeks to have the sale set aside and the trustee's deed canceled. Additional relief depends on the grounds advanced in seeking to set aside the sale. If the plaintiff contends that no lien exists, the complaint should seek cancellation of both the deed of trust and the trustee's deed and should include a cause of action to quiet title. If the plaintiff acknowledges a valid lien but contends that there was no default, the complaint will seek reinstatement of the loan in addition to having the sale set aside. An accounting should also be sought if the purported default was monetary. If the plaintiff admits the default but disputes the amount, the action may seek either reinstatement or redemption after the sale is set aside. A cause of action for an accounting will also be necessary. If defective sale procedures are alleged (either noncompliance with notice requirements or misconduct at the sale), the plaintiff will seek either to have the loan reinstated or to obtain the right to redeem the property from the lien after the sale is set aside.

When redemption is granted, the trial court will set a price and time for redemption. On redemption generally, see §2.22. The price should include the correct balance of the debt together with any proper costs the beneficiary (or purchaser) incurred after the sale, but the trustor may be given credit for reasonable rental income after the sale. Trustees' fees for conducting the sale probably should not be allowed to the beneficiary if the sale has been declared improper. *System Inv. Corp. v Union Bank* (1971) 21 CA3d 137, 98 CR 735. On attorneys' fees, see §§7.29–7.33. Interest and incidental expenses may be awarded at the trial court's discretion. See *Lupertino v Carbahal* (1973) 35 CA3d 742, 111 CR 112; *System Inv. Corp. v Union Bank, supra.*

The complaint may allege wrongdoing by a third party purchaser and not by either the trustee or the beneficiary. In such a case, the appropriate relief may be judicial imposition of a constructive trust. See *Roberts v Salot* (1958) 166 CA2d 294, 333 P2d 232; *Lantz v Stribling* (1955) 130 CA2d 476, 279 P2d 112. Further relief may be a mandatory injunction ordering the defendant to convey the property to the plaintiff or ordering that the trustee's deed be delivered to the court and canceled (CC §3412). See *Rablin v Greiner* (1935) 4 C2d 255, 48 P2d 696; *Vaughan v Roberts* (1941) 45 CA2d 246, 113 P2d 884.

§6.42 b. Damages

When a sale is voidable, the plaintiff is entitled to have the sale set aside or to recover damages. *Standley v Knapp* (1931) 113 CA 91, 298 P 109. When an improper sale cannot be set aside (*e.g.,* because title has passed to a bona fide purchaser), damages comparable to those for conversion of personal property are the usual and appropriate remedy. See *Munger v Moore* (1970) 11 CA3d 1, 89 CR 323. See also CC §§1708, 3333; *Murphy v Wilson* (1957) 153 CA2d 132, 314 P2d 507. Because an action for damages is legal rather than equitable, the parties are entitled to a jury trial. *Raedeke v Gibraltar Sav. & Loan Ass'n* (1974) 10 C3d 665, 111 CR 693.

The grounds for relief in actions for damages should be the same as those warranting cancellation of the sale, but allegations and proof of monetary loss must also be included. The measure of general damages due the trustor is the value of his or her lost equity in the property, *i.e.,* the value of the property at the time of sale in excess of all existing liens. *Munger v Moore, supra.* The measure of damages in favor of an aggrieved junior lienholder is the same, except that the junior's claim cannot exceed the amount due on the junior lien. *Munger v Moore, supra.* For example, if there is a first lien of $30,000 and a second lien of $5000 on property with a market value of $50,000, the senior lienor who wrongfully sells the property is liable to the trustor for $15,000 (market value less all liens) and liable to the junior for $5000 (market value less senior liens, but restricted to the amount of the junior lien).

§6.43   4. Parties

Any party with the right to reinstate the loan after a default under the deed of trust (see CC §2924c), to redeem the property from the lien of the deed of trust (CC §§2903–2904; see §2.17), or to receive automatic notice of default (CC §2924b(c)(2); see §2.14) should have standing to set aside an improper trustee's sale. *Munger v Moore* (1970) 11 CA3d 1, 89 CR 323. But see *Bertschman v Covell* (1928) 205 C 707, 272 P 571.

The party attacking the sale must demonstrate injury from the alleged impropriety. See *Sargent v Shumaker* (1924) 193 C 122, 223 P 464; *Dawes v Tucker* (1918) 178 C 46, 171 P 1068; *California Trust Co. v Smead Inv. Co.* (1935) 6 CA2d 432, 44 P2d 624; *American Trust Co. v deAlbergaria* (1932) 123 CA 76, 10 P2d 1016. A junior creditor who attacks the sale is required to show actual harm from the faulty sale, *i.e.*, that the value of the security was high enough to create a surplus for the junior. See *Hill v Gibraltar Sav. & Loan Ass'n* (1967) 254 CA2d 241, 62 CR 188. Because a senior creditor is unaffected by a junior sale, there is no reason to permit it to sue to have the sale set aside. After the sale, the senior may be able to accelerate under its due-on-sale clause. See §§7.10–7.18.

A guarantor normally has no need to set aside the sale because the sale's invalidity should constitute a defense to an action on the guaranty. See CC §2845. See also *System Inv. Corp. v Union Bank* (1971) 21 CA3d 137, 98 CR 735; *Mortgage Fin. Corp. v Howard* (1962) 210 CA2d 569, 26 CR 917. Such a defense, however, may be of no avail against a transferee of the note who is a holder in due course (see *Szczotka v Idelson* (1964) 228 CA2d 399, 39 CR 466) or if the guaranty waives the provisions of CC §2845 (as most form guaranties do). On guarantors, see §§8.10–8.18.

When the action is to set aside the sale rather than to enjoin it, the purchaser must be named as a defendant because he or she now holds title. The trustee and beneficiary should also be named as defendants, especially if the complaint seeks monetary as well as equitable relief. See §6.42.

§6.44   5. Jurisdiction and Venue

The superior court has original jurisdiction in all civil cases unless a statute specifically confers jurisdiction on another court. Cal Const art VI, §10. If the plaintiff elects to seek only money damages, jurisdiction is in the applicable municipal or justice court if the amount in controversy does not exceed $25,000. CCP §86(a)(1). If either the amount in controversy or the value of the property exceeds $25,000, or if the action is equitable, jurisdiction is in the superior court. A complaint to set aside a trustee's sale invariably involves requests for equitable relief (*e.g.*, quiet title, declaratory relief, accounting), which require that the action be filed in the superior court.

If the plaintiff seeks to have the trustee's sale set aside, the proper venue is the county in which the real property or some part of it is located. CCP §392(1)(a). The venue rules that govern an action to enjoin a trustee's sale also apply to an action to set aside the sale. See §6.26.

If the plaintiff seeks only damages, the general rules for transitory actions apply (see 1 California Civil Procedure Before Trial §§3.8–3.16, 3.30–3.34 (Cal CEB 1977)), and venue is proper in the county of residence of any one of the defendants (CCP §395(a)). In contract actions, venue is proper in the county in which the contract was entered into or was to be performed. CCP §395(a). If the plaintiff seeks both damages and to have the sale set aside, the court may treat the complaint as stating primarily a transitory cause of action (the damage claim) and will, therefore, treat the action as transitory for venue purposes. *Vaughan v Roberts* (1941) 45 CA2d 246, 113 P2d 884.

§6.45   6. Form: Complaint To Set Aside
     Trustee's Sale

Copies: Original (filed with court clerk); copies for service (one for each defendant to be served); office copies.

_ _[Name, address, telephone]_ _
Attorney for plaintiff

[Title of court]

[Title of case]   **No.** _ _ _ _ _ _

                               COMPLAINT TO SET ASIDE
                               TRUSTEE'S SALE

Plaintiff alleges:

FIRST CAUSE OF ACTION
[To set aside sale]

   1. Plaintiff, _ _[name]_ _, **is now, and at all times mentioned in this complaint was,** _ _[state plaintiff's interest in real property]_ _ **of real property known as** _ _[state street address or other designation]_ _ **and described as:**

[Legal description]

   2. Defendant, _ _[name]_ _, **claims to be the owner, by virtue of a trustee's deed from** _ _[name of trustee]_ _ **to the real property described in paragraph 1.**

[Add further defendant paragraphs as necessary]

   [3.] Defendant, _ _[name of trustee]_ _, **is a** _ _[e.g., California corporation, national banking association]_ _ **authorized to engage in, and at all times mentioned in this complaint engaged in,** _ _[e.g., title insurance, banking and trust]_ _ **business as a** _ _[e.g., title insurance company, California state bank]_ _.

   [4.] Defendant, _ _[name]_ _, **is now, and at all times relevant to this complaint was,** _ _[beneficiary under the deed of trust alleged in paragraph 1 and is a resident of _ _ _ _ _ _ _ _ _ County, California/ allege other capacity and residence]_ _.

   [5.] Plaintiff does not know the true names of defendants sued as Doe 1 through Doe _ _[number of fictitiously named defendants]_ _.

[*Continue*]

[6.] On _ _[*date*] _ _, plaintiff executed and delivered to defendant, _ _[*name*] _ _, a written promissory note in the amount of $_ _ _ _ _ _. A copy of the promissory note is attached as Exhibit _ _ and incorporated by reference.

[7.] To secure payment of the principal sum and interest as provided in the note and as part of the same transaction, plaintiff executed and delivered to defendant, _ _[*name*] _ _, as beneficiary, a deed of trust dated _ _ _ _ _ _, by the terms of which plaintiff, as trustor, conveyed to defendant, _ _[*name*] _ _, as trustee, real property described in paragraph 1. On _ _[*date*] _ _, the deed of trust was recorded in Book No. _ _ at page _ _ of the Official Records of _ _ _ _ _ _ _ _ County, California. A copy of the deed of trust is attached as Exhibit _ _ and incorporated by reference.

[8.] On _ _[*date*] _ _, defendant, _ _[*name*] _ _, caused to be recorded a notice of default and election to sell in Book No. _ _ at page _ _ of the Official Records of _ _ _ _ _ _ _ _ County, California, alleging that (a) a breach of the obligation secured by the deed of trust had occurred, consisting of plaintiff's alleged failure to _ _[*summarize default, e.g., pay certain monthly installments of principal and interest*] _ _, and (b) defendant beneficiary elected to sell, or cause to be sold, the trust property to satisfy that obligation. A copy of the notice of default and election to sell is attached as Exhibit _ _ and incorporated by reference.

[9.] Plaintiff alleges on information and belief that, on _ _[*date*] _ _, defendant beneficiary and defendant trustee published and posted, or caused to be published and posted, at various times and in various places certain notices of their intent to sell the trust property at public auction at _ _ _ _._m. on _ _[*date*] _ _, at _ _[*state address*] _ _, in the City of _ _ _ _ _ _, _ _ _ _ _ _ _ County, California, purportedly to satisfy the obligation secured by the deed of trust, on grounds of the alleged breach of the obligation, and under the power of sale in the deed of trust. Defendant trustee attempted and purported to sell the trust property as noticed, accepted valuable consideration from defendant, _ _[*name of purchaser*] _ _, and then executed and delivered or caused to be executed and delivered a trustee's deed to defendant, _ _[*name of purchaser*]_ _. **The deed was recorded in Book No.** _ _ **at page** _ _ **of the Official Records of** _ _ _ _ _ _ _ **County, California. A copy of the trustee's deed is attached as Exhibit** _ _ **and incorporated by reference.**

[10.] The sale was improperly held and the trustee's deed wrongfully executed, delivered, and recorded in that _ _[*state plaintiff's contentions, e.g., no breach of the obligation, absence of a valid lien, invalid presale procedures, improper sale procedures*]_ _ **in violation of the terms and conditions of the promissory note and deed of trust and in violation of the duties and obligations of defendant beneficiary and defendant trustee to plaintiff, all to plaintiff's loss and damage in that plaintiff has been wrongfully deprived of the beneficial use and enjoyment of the real property and has been deprived of legal title by forfeiture.**

[*Add, if plaintiff disputes amount owed but not fact of breach*]

[11.] Plaintiff _ _[*has tendered/offers to tender*]_ _ **to defendant beneficiary or defendant trustee all amounts due and owing so that the claimed default may be cured and plaintiff may be reinstated to all** _ _[*his/her/its*]_ _ **former rights and privileges under the promissory note and deed of trust. Plaintiff is ready, willing, and able to tender those sums, if any, that the Court finds due and owing on rendering the accounting requested in the Fourth Cause of Action of this complaint.**

[*Continue*]

SECOND CAUSE OF ACTION
[*To cancel trustee's deed*]

[12.] Plaintiff realleges and incorporates by reference the allegations in paragraphs 1 through 8.

[13.] Defendant, _ _[*name of purchaser*]_ _, **claims an estate or interest in the real property described in paragraph 1 adverse to that of plaintiff, but defendant's claims are without any right; defendant has no estate, right, title, or interest in the real property.**

[14.] The claims of defendant, _ _[*name of purchaser*]_ _, **are based on the trustee's deed (Exhibit** _ _), **described in paragraph**

[9], purporting to have been executed by defendant, _ _[name of trustee]_ _, and delivered to defendant, _ _[name of purchaser]_ _, on _ _[date]_ _, and purporting to convey the property to defendant, _ _[name of purchaser]_ _.

[15.] Although the trustee's deed (Exhibit _ _) appears valid on its face, it is invalid, _ _[void/voidable]_ _, and of no force or effect regarding plaintiff's interests in the real property described above, for the reasons set forth in paragraph [10].

[16.] The _ _[estate/interest]_ _ in the described real property claimed by defendant, _ _[name of purchaser]_ _, based on the trustee's deed, is a cloud on plaintiff's title in and to the real property, tends to depreciate its market value, restricts plaintiff's full use and enjoyment of the real property, and hinders plaintiff's right to unrestricted alienation of it. If the trustee's deed is not delivered and canceled, there is a reasonable fear that plaintiff will suffer serious injury.

THIRD CAUSE OF ACTION
[To quiet title]

[17.] Plaintiff realleges and incorporates by reference the allegations in paragraphs 1 through 8.

[18.] Plaintiff seeks to quiet title against the following claims of defendants: _ _[Describe claims held by each defendant, identifying, e.g., any supporting document, the nature of the interest the claim purports to create, recording information if any]_ _. Defendants' claims are without any right, and defendants have no right, title, estate, lien, or interest in the property described in paragraph 1.

[19.] Plaintiff names as defendants in this action all persons unknown, claiming (a) any legal or equitable right, title, estate, lien, or interest in the property described in the complaint adverse to plaintiff's title, or (b) any cloud on plaintiff's title to the property. The claims of each unknown defendant are without any right, and these defendants have no right, title, estate, lien, or interest in the property described in paragraph 1.

[20.] Plaintiff desires and is entitled to a judicial declaration quieting title in plaintiff as of _ _[date]_ _, _ _[and restoring possession to plaintiff]_ _.

FOURTH CAUSE OF ACTION
[*Accounting*]

[21.] Plaintiff realleges and incorporates by reference the allegations in paragraphs 1 through 8.

[22.] The amount of money still due and owing to defendant, _ _[*name of beneficiary*]_ _, is unknown to plaintiff and cannot be determined without an accounting.

WHEREFORE, plaintiff demands judgment as follows:

1. That the Court issue (a) a declaration that the sale of the trust property is null and void and of no force or effect, and (b) an order setting aside the trustee's sale of the real property.

2. That the Court (a) issue an order that defendant, _ _[*name of purchaser*]_ _, deliver the trustee's deed to the Court, and (b) cancel the trustee's deed.

3. That the Court order judgment quieting title in plaintiff as owner of the real property described in paragraph 1, declaring that defendant, _ _[*name of purchaser*]_ _, has no right, title, estate, lien, or interest in the property adverse to plaintiff _ _[*and ordering that plaintiff be restored to possession of the real property*]_ _.

4. That the Court render an accounting between plaintiff, _ _[*name*]_ _, and defendant, _ _[*name of beneficiary*]_ _, determining the amount, if any, actually due and owing from plaintiff to defendant, _ _[*name of beneficiary*]_ _.

5. That the Court award damages for the unlawful detention of the premises at the rate of $_ _ _ _ _ _ per month from _ _[*date*]_ _, until delivery of possession to plaintiff.

6. That plaintiff recover _ _[*his/her/its*]_ _ attorneys' fees and costs in this action, and that the Court award all other appropriate relief.

Dated: _ _ _ _ _ _

_ _ _[*Signature of attorney*]_ _ _
_ _[*Typed name*]_ _
Attorney for _ _[*name*]_ _

Comment: When the plaintiff seeks to set aside the sale, the complaint will always contain the first two causes of action: to set aside the trustee's sale and to cancel the trustee's deed. The other causes of action will depend on the basis for the plaintiff's claim. See §6.41 on non-monetary relief. A plaintiff who concedes that a sum is owed, but who disputes the existence of a default or contends that the default is excused, should ask the court to restore the plaintiff's estate, subject to the lien of the deed of trust, or to set a time and place for redemption (see ¶[8]). The plaintiff can probably recover possession of the property under the quiet-title cause of action. See California Real Property Remedies Practice §§7.9, 7.38 (Cal CEB 1982). An additional cause of action for ejectment may also be included to cover the possession issue. See Real Property Remedies §7.13, chap 10.

§6.46 7. Lis Pendens

A notice of action pending (lis pendens) should be recorded on the same day that the complaint is filed, if relief involving title is sought, to ensure that any subsequent purchaser or encumbrancer takes subject to the plaintiff's claims. See §6.35. For a form lis pendens, see §3.45.

§6.47 8. Improper Sale as Defense to Other Actions

A trustor who remains in possession of the property after a trustee's sale may be removed by an unlawful detainer action brought by the purchaser. CCP §1161a(b)(2); *MCA, Inc. v Universal Diversified Enters. Corp.* (1972) 27 CA3d 170, 103 CR 522. If the sale was improper, however, the unlawful detainer action may fail. *Crummer v Whitehead* (1964) 230 CA2d 264, 40 CR 826.

Because of the summary nature of unlawful detainer proceedings, a judgment for the purchaser is not necessarily res judicata and will probably not bar a subsequent suit by the trustor to set aside the sale or to recover damages. *Cheney v Trauzettel* (1937) 9 C2d 158, 69 P2d 832; *Byrne v Baker* (1963) 221 CA2d 1, 34 CR 178; *Patapoff v Reliable Escrow Serv. Corp.* (1962) 201 CA2d 484, 19 CR 886. An unlawful detainer judgment will have collateral estoppel or res judicata effect only on an issue that was actually raised, or could have been raised, in the unlawful detainer proceeding. *Vella v Hudgins* (1977) 20 C3d 251, 142 CR 414; *Gonzales v Gem Props.* (1974) 37 CA3d 1029, 112 CR 884.

A tenant on the property may raise an impropriety in the sale as a defense to an unlawful detainer action on the theory that the lease would otherwise still be in effect. See CC §1708; *Schubert v Lowe* (1924) 193 C 291, 223 P 550. See also *Pike v Hayden* (1950) 97 CA2d 606, 218 P2d 578; *Rishwain v Smith* (1947) 77 CA2d 524, 175 P2d 555.

Guarantors and other parties potentially liable for deficiency judgments after the sale should be able to use any impropriety in the sale as a defense to an action to recover a deficiency. See *System Inv. Corp. v Union Bank* (1971) 21 CA3d 137, 98 CR 735. See also *Block v Tobin* (1975) 45 CA3d 214, 119 CR 288; *Union Bank v Gradsky* (1968) 265 CA2d 40, 71 CR 64; §§8.15, 8.18.

§6.48   IV. BANKRUPTCY

One of the most effective ways for a debtor to halt a foreclosure, at least temporarily, is to file a petition in bankruptcy under the federal Bankruptcy Code (Title 11 of the United States Code). Under the Bankruptcy Code's automatic stay (see §6.49), filing the petition automatically stays most collection activities by any of the debtor's creditors, including secured real property creditors who are in the process of foreclosing. The automatic stay comes into effect when the debtor files a petition to initiate any of the most frequently utilized types of bankruptcy proceedings: Chapter 7 (liquidation), Chapter 11 (reorganization), Chapter 12 (adjustment of debts of a family farmer), or Chapter 13 (adjustment of debts of an individual with regular income). A trustee is appointed to take possession of the debtor's nonexempt property in Chapter 7 proceedings. 11 USC §701. In Chapter 11 proceedings, the debtor is usually left in possession of the property and has most of the powers of a bankruptcy trustee. 11 USC §1107. On Chapter 12 and Chapter 13 proceedings, see 11 USC §§1203, 1303.

Filing a bankruptcy petition creates a bankruptcy estate, which is comprised of all the debtor's legal and equitable interests in property, wherever located, as well as the proceeds, rents, and profits from that property. 11 USC §541(a). When the debtor holds bare legal title to real property, only that nominal interest passes to the bankruptcy estate. See *In re Torrez* (Torrez v Torrez) (9th Cir 1987) 827 F2d 1299. But see 11

USC §544(a)(3), which vests the trustee with bona fide purchaser status. The debtor is divested of ownership rights to real property that passes into the estate, and only the trustee (or debtor in possession exercising the rights and powers of a trustee (proceedings under Chapters 11–13; see above)) may create a security interest in such real property. 11 USC §§363–364; see *In re Crevier* (Crevier v Welfare & Pension Fund) (9th Cir 1987) 820 F2d 1553. The trustee represents the bankruptcy estate and has the power to begin actions and assert defenses on its behalf. 11 USC §323; Bankr R 6009; see *In re Kristal* (Carnation Co. v Lampi) (9th Cir 1985) 758 F2d 454 (see §4.5).

This book does not attempt to cover bankruptcy practice and procedure but provides an overview of issues concerning foreclosure of real property security. See §§6.49–6.56. For more extensive discussion of bankruptcy practice as it relates to real property security issues, see 2 California Real Property Financing, chap 2 (Cal CEB 1989). See also 2 Debt Collection Practice in California, chap 10 (Cal CEB 1987); King, Collier on Bankruptcy (15th ed 1979); King, Collier Bankruptcy Manual (3d ed 1979); Cherkis & King, Collier Real Estate Transactions and the Bankruptcy Code (1984); Cowans, Bankruptcy Law and Practice (1987).

§6.49   A. Automatic Stay

By filing a petition in bankruptcy under any chapter of the Bankruptcy Code (see §6.48), the trustor brings most creditors' collection efforts to a complete stop. The debtor's property is considered to have been transferred to a newly created bankruptcy estate (11 USC §541), controlled either by a trustee in bankruptcy (under Chapter 7) or by the debtor as debtor in possession (under Chapters 11–13). For extensive discussion of the automatic stay, see 2 California Real Property Financing §§2.3–2.42 (Cal CEB 1989). To protect this estate, filing the petition creates an automatic stay that prohibits virtually all attempts by creditors to collect debts or recover property in the debtor's possession until relief from the stay is obtained (see §6.50) or the stay terminates. 11 USC §362. Filing the petition stays the commencement or continuation of any proceeding to enforce a lien against the debtor's property or to recover any money claim against the debtor. 11 USC §362(a). The stay "stops all collection efforts, all harassment, and all foreclosure actions." *Barnett v Lewis* (1985) 170 CA3d 1079, 1088, 217 CR 80, 85.

A bankruptcy filing may also have the effect of staying foreclosure by a senior lien claimant against property in which the bankrupt estate has a junior lien or comparable interest. See *In re Bialic* (Harsh Inv. Corp. v Bialic) (9th Cir 1983) 712 F2d 426 (beneficiary stayed from foreclosing on other five sixths of the property when owner of the omitted one sixth had filed bankruptcy petition, because sale would depress value of one-sixth portion); 2 Real Property Financing §2.7. Juniors and other creditors, however, may lack standing to complain if the senior violates the automatic stay, because the purpose of the stay is to protect the debtor. See *In re Globe Inv. & Loan Co.* (Magnoni v Globe Inv. & Loan Co.) (9th Cir 1989) 867 F2d 556. But see *In re Mellor* (Pistole v Mellor) (9th Cir 1984) 734 F2d 1396 (reversing order lifting automatic stay to protect junior interests); Bankr R 4001(d) (requiring notice of agreements modifying stay).

The stay prohibits any act by a creditor to create, perfect, or enforce a lien against the debtor's property, including the use of any judicial or administrative proceeding. 11 USC §362. Because this language appears to preclude even the execution of a notice of default (see §2.12), it brings all judicial and nonjudicial foreclosure proceedings to a halt. A filing by one spouse, however, does not automatically stay creditors' acts affecting the other spouse's interest in the security. *In re Brooks* (James v Washington Mut. Sav. Bank) (9th Cir 1989) 871 F2d 89. A trustee's sale or similar activity may be set aside by the bankruptcy court. 11 USC §549(a). A willful violation may be punished by contempt proceedings, and the estate may recover both compensatory and punitive damages. 11 USC §362(h); see *In re Computer Communications, Inc.* (Computer Communications, Inc. v Codex Corp.) (9th Cir 1987) 824 F2d 725.

The stay, which is operative immediately, is effective whether or not the creditor has notice of it. 11 USC §362. Thus, a bankruptcy petition filed at 11:59 a.m. categorically prohibits a trustee's sale previously noticed for 12 noon on the same day, although an innocently conducted sale may lead to a subsequent bankruptcy order annulling the automatic stay (and thus validating the sale).

§6.50   B. Relief From Stay

Unless the automatic stay is modified by order of the bankruptcy court, it continues in effect until the case is closed or dismissed or a discharge is granted or denied to an individual bankrupt. 11 USC §362(c)(2). To the extent that the automatic stay prohibits actions against property of the estate, it terminates when the property is sold or abandoned. 11 USC §362(c)(1). Even when a stay against enforcement of a security interest on real property terminates because the property is abandoned from the estate to the debtor, enforcement of the secured claim is still barred by 11 USC §362(a)(5), which prohibits "any act to create, perfect, or enforce against property of the debtor any lien to the extent that such lien secures a claim that arose before the commencement of the [bankruptcy] case . . . ."

A motion for relief from the automatic stay must show either:

■ Cause for granting relief from the stay (11 USC §362(d)(1)); or

■ The debtor's lack of equity in the property when the property is not necessary to an effective reorganization (11 USC §362(d)(2)).

"Cause" for granting relief includes "lack of adequate protection" of the creditor's security interest. 11 USC §362(d)(1). Although the Bankruptcy Code does not define the term, it lists three forms of adequate protection to a secured creditor: periodic cash payments (11 USC §361(1)), an additional or replacement lien (11 USC §361(2)), and other relief that will give the creditor the "indubitable equivalent" of its original interest (11 USC §361(3)). An "equity cushion" in the property usually constitutes adequate protection for the beneficiary. See *In re Mellor* (Pistole v Mellor) (9th Cir 1984) 734 F2d 1396. See also *Stewart v Gurley* (9th Cir 1984) 745 F2d 1194. When the beneficiary is undersecured and the value of the security is declining, protection in the form of cash payments or additional security may be required. The undersecured beneficiary is not also entitled to postpetition interest, however, to compensate for the lost right of immediate foreclosure. *United Sav. Ass'n v Timbers of Inwood Forest Assoc.* (1988) 484 US 365.

Courts have held that "cause" for granting relief from the stay under 11 USC §362(d)(1) may include the debtor's bad faith. See *In re Yukon Enters.* (California Mortgage Serv. v Yukon Enters.) (Bankr CD Cal 1984) 39 BR 919. For discussion, see 2 California Real Property Financing §§2.16–2.20 (Cal CEB 1989). Bad faith is most commonly found when the original trustor conveys the property to a new entity, which immediately files bankruptcy (the "new debtor syndrome"), or when there are repeated filings intended to gain the benefit of successive automatic stays. See *In re Can-Alta Props.* (Can-Alta Props. v State Sav. Mortgage Co.) (Bankr 9th Cir 1988) 87 BR 89.

A creditor may request relief from the automatic stay to foreclose under a deed of trust on real property by filing a motion under 11 USC §362 and Bankr R 4001(a) and 9014. Notice and a hearing are required on a motion for relief from the stay unless the beneficiary can show that an ex parte proceeding is necessary to prevent irreparable damage to its security interest. 11 USC §362(f). Once a motion for relief from the stay has been filed, the stay terminates automatically 30 days later unless there is a preliminary hearing within 30 days and a final hearing within 30 days after that. 11 USC §362(e). All interested parties are entitled to participate in the hearing. Bankr R 7024. Making a motion for relief from the stay does not constitute an action within the meaning of the one-action rule of CCP §726. *In re Rivers* (McReynolds v Rivers) (CD Cal 1984) 55 BR 699.

The hearing on the stay may be an appropriate forum to resolve other questions requiring reference to state law. In *In re Kristal* (Carnation Co. v Lampi) (9th Cir 1985) 758 F2d 454, for example, the court refused to lift the automatic stay on the ground that the creditor had lost its security by behavior that violated the one-action rule (CCP §726). See §4.5.

If the stay is lifted, the beneficiary may continue with its foreclosure. *In re Suchy* (Community Thrift & Loan v Suchy) (9th Cir 1985) 786 F2d 900. According to the weight of authority, the automatic stay does not suspend either the reinstatement period under CC §2924c or the postsale redemption period under CCP §729.030. *In re Martinson* (Martinson v First Nat'l Bank) (8th Cir 1984) 731 F2d 543; *In re Eagles* (California Thrift & Loan Ass'n v Downey Sav. & Loan Ass'n) (Bankr 9th Cir 1984) 36 BR 97; *In re Pridham* (Steele v Pridham) (Bankr ED Cal 1983) 31 BR 497; *Triangle Management Servs. v Allstate Sav. & Loan Ass'n* (ND Cal 1982) 21 BR 699. See also *Napue v Gor-Mey W., Inc.* (1985) 175 CA3d 608, 220 CR 799. But see *In re Capital Mortgage & Loan, Inc.* (Bankr ED Cal 1983) 35 BR 967, in which the court held to the contrary.

Although the majority of decisions have held that 11 USC §362 does not toll such reinstatement or redemption periods, most courts have specified that, under 11 USC §108(b), such periods are extended in the debtor's favor to 60 days after commencement of the bankruptcy case if expiration would otherwise have occurred within that 60-day period.

Johnson v First Nat' l Bank (8th Cir 1983) 719 F2d 270; *In re Cucumber Creek Dev.* (Westergaard v Cucumber Creek Dev.) (D Colo 1983) 33 BR 820. In California, if the reinstatement period had not run when the stay went into effect, it would effectively be tolled under the new provision in CC §2924c that extends reinstatement until five business days before the sale, because the stay would delay the sale. For discussion, see 2 Real Property Financing §2.6.

Although CC §2924g(c)(1) provides that a trustee's sale that has been postponed three times must be renoticed (see §2.24), renoticing the sale is not required when the postponements are the result of a bankruptcy automatic stay. *California Livestock Prod. Credit Ass' n v Sutfin* (1985) 165 CA3d 136, 211 CR 152.

Sale of the property after the automatic stay has been lifted is insulated from attack (*In re Stivers* (Bryce v Stivers) (Bankr ND Cal 1983) 31 BR 735) unless the purchaser was the beneficiary or the trustor had obtained a stay pending appeal (*In re Onouli-Kona Land Co.* (Onouli-Kona Land Co. v Estate of Richards) (9th Cir 1988) 846 F2d 1170; *In re Sun Valley Ranches, Inc.* (Sun Valley Ranches, Inc. v Equitable Life Assur. Soc'y) (9th Cir 1987) 823 F2d 1373). If the bankruptcy court denies relief against the automatic stay, the beneficiary may appeal. *In re American Mariner Indus.* (Crocker Nat'l Bank v American Mariner Indus.) (9th Cir 1984) 734 F2d 426.

§6.51   C. Status of Claim

The fact that the creditor holds a mortgage on the debtor's property does not automatically guarantee that the bankruptcy court will recognize it as a secured claim.

Under 11 USC §548(a), a bankruptcy trustee has the power to set aside, as a fraudulent transfer, a lien created within one year before commencement of the bankruptcy case if the debtor voluntarily or involuntarily (1) made the transfer with actual intent to hinder, delay, or defraud creditors or (2) received less than "reasonably equivalent value" and (a) was insolvent or became insolvent as a result of the obligation, (b) was engaged in, or about to engage in, a business or transaction for which the debtor's capital was insufficient, or (c) intended or believed that the debtor would incur debt beyond the debtor's ability to pay as it became due. Note that these tests are virtually identical to those under California's version of the Uniform Fraudulent Transfer Act (UFTA) (CC §§3439–3439.12). CC

§3439.04. Trustees are also empowered to challenge transfers under the UFTA by 11 USC §544(a)(1)–(2) (as hypothetical lien creditors) and 11 USC §544(b) (as successors of actual creditors). Under 11 USC §548(a), the trustee is empowered to avoid liens created within one year before the bankruptcy filing; under the UFTA, liens may be set aside within four years after they were created (CC §3439.09). For further discussion, see 2 California Real Property Financing §2.57 (Cal CEB 1989).

If the lien was created to secure a preexisting debt within 90 days before commencement of the bankruptcy proceeding (one year in certain cases), the lien may be set aside as a preference. 11 USC §547. A mortgage or deed of trust that was not perfected by recordation before the bankruptcy filing may be set aside under the trustee's "strong-arm" powers as a hypothetical bona fide purchaser. 11 USC §544(a)(3); see *In re Marino* (Placer Sav. & Loan Ass'n v Walsh) (9th Cir 1987) 813 F2d 1562. The bankruptcy court may apply state law to resolve related or subsidiary questions. See *In re Destro* (Pellerin v Stuhley) (9th Cir 1982) 675 F2d 1037 (California doctrine of equitable mortgage protects creditor who received debtor's oral promise to give creditor a mortgage). See also *In re Mills* (Mills v Sdrawde Titleholders, Inc.) (9th Cir 1988) 841 F2d 902 (beneficiary's claim for waste barred because waste not shown to have been committed in bad faith as required by state law).

§6.52   D. Postpetition Interest and Charges

If the value of the security exceeds the value of the claim, the secured creditor is entitled to postpetition interest and reasonable fees, costs, and charges provided for in the note. 11 USC §506(b). Undersecured creditors have no claim to postpetition interest. See *United Sav. Ass'n v Timbers of Inwood Forest Assoc.* (1988) 484 US 365. For discussion, see 2 California Real Property Financing §2.14 (Cal CEB 1989). A provision in the note increasing the rate of interest on default appears to be enforceable in bankruptcy proceedings even though its status is uncertain under state law. *In re Southeast Co.* (Florida Partners Corp. v Southeast Co.) (9th Cir 1989) 868 F2d 335. See also *In re Skyler Ridge* (Bankr CD Cal 1987) 80 BR 500. Attorneys' fees, late charges, prepayment penalties, and other charges to reimburse an oversecured creditor for costs arising on default are recoverable under 11 USC §506(b) if provided for in the note. *In re 268 Ltd.* (Joseph F. Sanson Inv. Co. v 268 Ltd.) (9th Cir 1986) 789 F2d 674. These charges are subject to a judicial determination of reasonableness. See *In re Imperial Coronado Partners, Ltd.* (Imperial Coronado Partners, Ltd. v Home Fed. Sav. & Loan Ass'n) (Bankr 9th Cir 1989) 96 BR 997 (prepayment charge limited to difference between contract and market rates of interest).

Depending on the value of the security, a beneficiary is either over-secured or undersecured. If the debt exceeds the value of the security and is enforceable against the debtor, the beneficiary has (1) a secured claim equal to the value of the security and (2) an unsecured claim equal to the amount by which the claim exceeds the security. 11 USC §506.

In cases filed under Chapter 11, debtors may eliminate the default rate of interest or late charges by reinstating the obligation under a plan of reorganization. A secured creditor is not to be impaired if the plan cures any default, reinstates the claim for any damages caused by the default, and does not otherwise alter the legal, equitable, and contractual rights of the holder of the secured claim. 11 USC §1124(2); see *In re Southeast Co., supra.*

Thus, in Chapter 11 cases, the beneficiary may be entitled to an unsecured claim in addition to the security, even though a deficiency judgment against the debtor would have been barred by state law or because of a nonrecourse provision in the note. 11 USC §1111; *In re Woodridge N. Apartments* (Bankr ND Cal 1987) 71 BR 189. Alternatively, the beneficiary may elect to have the entire claim treated as secured despite the disparity between debt and value. 11 USC §1111(b); *In re Southern Mo. Towing Serv.* (Bankr WD Mo 1983) 35 BR 313.

§6.53   E. Use, Sale, or Lease of Security

The trustee in bankruptcy or debtor in possession is permitted to use, sell, or lease the security in the ordinary course of business as long as the creditor remains adequately protected (see §6.54). 11 USC §363. A hearing is required if the transaction is outside the ordinary course of business or on the creditor's request. 11 USC §363. The bankruptcy court may authorize the debtor or bankruptcy trustee to obtain new credit secured by a lien on the debtor's property, with priority senior to a preexisting security interest, if alternative financing is not available and the adequate protection requirement is met. 11 USC §364; see

In re Pine Mountain, Ltd. (Woods v Pine Mountain, Ltd.) (Bankr 9th Cir 1987) 80 BR 171; *In re Chevy Devco* (Bankr CD Cal 1987) 78 BR 585. Similarly, the security may be sold free of the lien if the standards of 11 USC §363(f), concerning substantive and procedural safeguards for the owner of the security, are met.

§6.54   F. Rents and Profits

Rents and profits from real property may be used by the debtor or the bankruptcy trustee, without a court order or the beneficiary's consent, if the beneficiary did not perfect its claim before the bankruptcy proceeding was initiated. If the claim was perfected, this "cash collateral" may be put to use only with the approval of the bankruptcy court or the creditor. 11 USC §363(c)(2); see *In re Center Wholesale, Inc.* (Owens-Corning Fiberglas Corp. v Center Wholesale, Inc.) (9th Cir 1985) 759 F2d 1440. Whether the right to the rents and profits was properly perfected is a question of state, rather than federal, law (*Butner v U.S.* (1979) 440 US 48; see §5.12); perfecting the claim is not accomplished merely by obtaining relief from the automatic stay (*In re Madera Farms Partnership* (John Hancock Mut. Life Ins. Co. v Madera Farms Partnership) (Bankr 9th Cir 1986) 66 BR 100). If the right to rents and profits was not perfected before the bankruptcy proceeding commenced, the creditor should give notice of perfection under 11 USC §546(b) and demand sequestration of the rents and an accounting. The creditor's receiver, if there is one, may be required to turn over any rents collected to the bankruptcy trustee or the debtor, unless grounds for retention can be shown. 11 USC §543. On receivers, see chap 5.

A request by the debtor or trustee for authority to use the rents is made by motion to the bankruptcy court. Bankr R 4001(b). On appropriate notice of motion (11 USC §102(1)(A)), the court must schedule a hearing and rule promptly (11 USC §363(c)(3)). Judicial approval of use of the rents cannot be given unless the beneficiary remains adequately protected. *In re Oak Glen R-Vee* (Santa Fe Fed. Sav. & Loan Ass'n v Oak Glen R-Vee) (Bankr CD Cal 1981) 8 BR 213.

§6.55   G. Reinstatement and Redemption Rights

A debtor under a Chapter 11 reorganization plan, without the consent or approval of the secured creditor, may:

■ Reinstate the maturity of a secured debt even though reinstatement would not be permitted under state law (11 USC §1124(2); on reinstatement in California, see §3.51); or

■ Pay off the secured claim in cash and redeem the security from the creditor's lien (11 USC §1124(3); see §3.51).

To reinstate, the debtor is required only to pay according to the original interest rate, despite provisions in the note increasing the rate on default. *In re Southeast Co.* (Florida Partners Corp. v Southeast Co.) (9th Cir 1989) 868 F2d 335; *In re Entz-White Lumber & Supply, Inc.* (Great W. Bank & Trust v Entz-White Lumber & Supply, Inc.) (1988) 850 F2d 1338.

A Chapter 13 plan may provide for reinstatement of a debt secured by a deed of trust or mortgage on the debtor's personal residence, even though reinstatement would not be permitted under applicable state law, as long as the foreclosure sale has not occurred. 11 USC §1322(b)(5). Reinstatement is permitted even when the Chapter 13 petition is filed immediately after a Chapter 7 discharge and the Chapter 13 plan does not provide for payments to unsecured creditors. *In re Metz* (Downey Sav. & Loan Ass'n v Metz) (9th Cir 1987) 820 F2d 1495.

A Chapter 11 debtor may also be able to obtain confirmation for a plan that (1) provides for the secured creditor to receive deferred payments on the secured claim and (2) is structured so that the present value of the payments equals or exceeds the value of the security. 11 USC §1129. Under this "cram-down" power of the bankruptcy court, the interest rate or payment schedule may be altered despite the secured creditor's opposition to the plan. See *In re Arnold* (Idaho v Arnold) (9th Cir 1986) 806 F2d 937; 2 California Real Property Financing §2.67 (Cal CEB 1989). The court's cram-down powers are more limited in Chapter 13 proceedings, especially when the loan is secured only by the debtor's residence. 11 USC §1322; see *In re Seidel* (Seidel v Larson) (9th Cir 1985) 752 F2d 1382 (debt may not be paid in installments when it has already come due before filing). See 2 Real Property Financing §2.71.

§6.56   H. Setting Aside Completed Foreclosure Sales

The bankruptcy court's power to set aside fraudulent transfers (see §6.51) includes the power to invalidate foreclosure sales conducted within one year after the bankruptcy filing if the court determines that the sale was made for less than reasonably equivalent value and the debtor was then insolvent. 11 USC §548. In *In re Madrid* (Madrid v Lawyers Title Ins. Corp.) (9th Cir 1984) 725 F2d 1197, the Ninth Circuit Court of Appeals held that the critical transfer occurs when the security interest is perfected, not at foreclosure, thus putting most foreclosure sales outside the one-year period for bankruptcy review of fraudulent transfers. The Ninth Circuit's interpretation of 11 USC §548 was rejected by some other circuits (see *In re Hulm* (First Fed. Sav. & Loan Ass'n v Hulm) (8th Cir 1984) 738 F2d 323; *Durrett v Washington Nat'l Ins. Co.* (5th Cir 1980) 621 F2d 201) and by Congress. In 1984 legislation, "transfer" was defined to include "foreclosure of the debtor's equity of redemption" (11 USC §101(50)), and 11 USC §548 was amended to include involuntary as well as voluntary transfers. See also the commentary in 8 CEB Real Prop L Rep 15 (Jan. 1985). The Ninth Circuit Bankruptcy Appellate Panel held, however, that the 1984 amendments did not overturn the holding in *In re Madrid, supra,* concerning the timing of fraudulent transfers (11 USC §548) or preferences (11 USC §547). *In re Ehring* (Ehring v Western Community Moneycenter) (Bankr 9th Cir 1988) 91 BR 897.

The extent of bankruptcy courts' power to scrutinize foreclosure sales has not been resolved by the amendments. The Bankruptcy Appellate Panel opinion in *In re Madrid* (Lawyers Title Ins. Corp. v Madrid) (Bankr 9th Cir 1982) 21 BR 424, held that a regularly conducted, noncollusive foreclosure sale was not a fraudulent conveyance even though the amount bid may have been only the amount owed to the foreclosing creditor. That decision was overruled by the Ninth Circuit, holding that the perfecting of the lien, not its foreclosure, constitutes a transfer under 11 USC §548 (*In re Madrid* (Madrid v Lawyers Title Ins. Corp.) (9th Cir 1984) 725 F2d 1197), but the 1984 Congressional inclusion of foreclosure sales within the definition of "transfers" did not resolve the substantive test for a fraudulent transfer proposed by the Bankruptcy Appellate Panel. See *In re Verna* (Verna v Dorman) (Bankr CD Cal 1986) 58 BR 246.

A bankruptcy court may also cancel a foreclosure on grounds that would have supported invalidation by a state court. *In re Worcester* (Rosner v Worcester) (9th Cir 1987) 811 F2d 1224 (irregularities at sale and gross inadequacy of price sufficient to set aside sale under state law).

§6.57   V. ACTIONS AGAINST LENDER

In recent years, aggrieved borrowers have gone beyond their traditional resistance to collection of their loans and foreclosure on real property security. With increasing frequency, borrowers have taken the initiative and sued their lenders for various actions not necessarily prohibited by the loan documents. The success of such actions has made lender liability a standard topic at meetings of lenders' counsel. Few of the reported decisions are California cases, and most theories of liability remain somewhat speculative.

Although lenders have always faced the risk of allegations of noncompliance with the loan agreement, causing borrowers to incur damages to be offset against the loan balance (see §§6.15–6.23), recent cases have raised the possibility of much more substantial liability (see *KMC Co. v Irving Trust Co.* (6th Cir 1985) 757 F2d 752 (judgment of $7.5 million against lender); *State Nat'l Bank v Farah Mfg. Co.* (Tex App 1984) 678 SW2d 661 (judgment of $18.6 million against lender)) and judicial recognition of many new duties (*e.g.*, a duty of good faith and fair dealing, a duty of commercial reasonableness, and a quasi-fiduciary duty). The cases have a common thread: To determine the legal duties of the lender, the court examines the entire relationship between lender and borrower and not just the provisions of the written documents. See, *e.g.*, *Barrett v Bank of America* (1986) 183 CA3d 1362, 229 CR 16; *State Nat'l Bank v Farah Mfg. Co., supra*; *Sahadi v Continental Illinois Nat'l Bank & Trust Co.* (7th Cir 1983) 706 F2d 193. For discussion of lender liability theories, see 2 California Real Property Financing §§4.10–4.14 (Cal CEB 1989).

Any aspect of a loan transaction, or even a prospective loan, contains the potential for lender liability. For example, delay in processing a loan application may be actionable when the final interest rate is higher than that originally offered, especially if the delay was intentional. See *Morosani v First Nat'l Bank* (11th Cir 1983) 703 F2d 1220 (lender liable under Racketeer Influenced and Corrupt Organizations Act (RICO) (18 USC §§1961–1968) for collecting loan fees based on fraudulent statements). See also Comment, *Lock-In Laws: Adding More Patches to the Mortgage Lending Quilt,* 37 Cath U L Rev 543 (1988). A lender that commits itself to fund a loan, and then improperly maneuvers to create a situation that would discharge its commitment, may be liable for any harm it causes the borrower. See *Penthouse Int'l v Dominion Fed. Sav. & Loan Ass'n* (2d Cir 1988) 855 F2d 963 ($128.7 million judgment for lost profits for breach of loan commitment); *Landes Constr. Co. v Royal Bank of Canada* (9th Cir 1987) 833 F2d 1365 ($18.5 million judgment plus forfeiture of $3 million already advanced for breach of oral loan commitment). See also Flick & Replansky, *Liability of Banks to Their Borrowers: Pitfalls & Protections*, 103 Banking LJ 220 (1986); Malloy, *Lender Liability for Negligent Real Estate Appraisals*, U Ill L Rev 53 (1984).

The single reported California decision on liability for preloan activities is less favorable to borrowers. In *Kruse v Bank of America* (1988) 202 CA3d 38, 248 CR 217, the court overturned a judgment of $20 million in compensatory damages and $27 million in punitive damages against a bank that had wrongly induced the borrower to believe that financing would be made available, holding that there is no tort liability for bad-faith denial of contract when there is no loan contract. This decision hardly guarantees, however, that creative borrowers' counsel will not be able to find more palatable theories of liability in the future. For discussion of lender liability during creation of the loan, see 2 Real Property Financing §§4.15–4.31.

During the life of the loan, the lender may be characterized as a fiduciary to the borrower, with attendant heightened obligations. In *KMC Co. v Irving Trust Co., supra*, the court upheld a $7.5 million judgment against a lender who refused to advance $800,000 under a discretionary $3.5 million line of credit. In *Barrett v Bank of America, supra*, the bank was held liable for failing to disclose that it did not intend to release guaranties it held as security. For discussion of lender liability for loan administration, see 2 Real Property Financing §§4.32–4.40.

Lenders have also been held liable for calling their loans in bad faith. See *Sahadi v Continental Illinois Nat'l Bank & Trust Co., supra; Brown v Avemco Inv. Corp.* (9th Cir 1979) 603 F2d 1367 (applying Texas law). In these decisions, the courts held lenders liable for invoking acceleration clauses in their notes, requiring good faith in the exercise of any "at-will" power analogous to the requirements of UCC §1–208. Two other courts have held, however, that good faith is not required when a lender calls a demand note. See *Flagship Nat'l Bank v Gray Distrib. Sys.* (Fla App 1986) 485 S2d 1336; *Centerre Bank v Distributors, Inc.* (Mo App 1985) 705 SW2d 42. No reported California case has yet considered this issue directly, but it could be raised in the future because

UCC §1–208 appears in California as Com C §1208. See *Gaffney v Downey Sav. & Loan Ass' n* (1988) 200 CA3d 1154, 246 CR 421 (judgment awarding punitive damages and damages for emotional distress for wrongful foreclosure reversed on ground that foreclosure was proper). For further discussion, see Secured Transactions in California Commercial Law Practice §§2.34–2.35, 5.7 (Cal CEB 1986).

Another troublesome issue in California is whether some recent creative financing arrangements have created joint ventures rather than mortgage loan financing between the parties. See, *e.g., Glendale Fed. Sav. & Loan Ass' n v Marina View Heights Dev.* (1977) 66 CA3d 101, 135 CR 802. If so, lenders recharacterized as joint venturers (with fiduciary obligations to their coventurers) may have considerably more trouble calling their loans or refusing to extend additional credit. For discussion of lender liability during the foreclosure process, see 2 Real Property Financing §§4.51–4.63.

California courts have also permitted third parties to recover from lenders despite lack of a lender-borrower relationship. See *Connor v Great W. Sav. & Loan Ass' n* (1968) 69 C2d 850, 73 CR 369, in which the court permitted buyers to sue the developer's construction lender for defective construction. The legislature promptly rejected the result in *Connor* by enacting CC §3434, but the broader questions of what obligations lenders owe, and to whom, remain open. See, *e.g.,* Note, *Lender Liability for Failure to Enforce Life-Threatening Housing Code Violations,* 8 Golden Gate L Rev 359 (1978).

Chapter 7: **Disputes Over Payment**

7

Disputes Over Payment

§7.1   I. TIME OF PAYMENT

This chapter discusses disagreements between the parties concerning whether an obligation is owed now or later, or how much is owed on the obligation at a given time. Demand notes are extremely rare, and most mortgage notes provide for some sort of periodic payment (either amortizing installments of principal and interest or calling for payments of interest alone). This installment feature of notes secured by real property inevitably generates concern about the consequences of a missed payment: Is the creditor limited to collection of only that installment or may the creditor consider the entire debt unsatisfied? To resolve this issue, mortgage notes usually contain an acceleration clause that permits the creditor to declare the entire obligation due when the debtor defaults on an installment. For discussion of acceleration clauses, see §§7.2–7.6. Acceleration of the note when there is a sale or encumbrance of the property rather than a default in payment depends on inclusion in the note of a due-on-sale clause that functions similarly to an acceleration clause. See §§7.10–7.18.

Another consequence of a missed installment payment on the note may be imposition on the borrower of a late charge, which requires inclusion of a late-charges clause in the note. See §§7.7–7.9. The mortgagee or beneficiary may also be entitled to impose a penalty if the debtor pays the debt prematurely (either voluntarily or involuntarily), under provisions in the note known as prepayment penalty (or prepayment privilege) provisions. See §§7.19–7.25.

Property insurance issues concerning the amount owed the beneficiary by the trustor are also discussed in this chapter, including demands by the beneficiary for (a) additional sums to cover insurance premiums that the trustor failed to pay and (b) using the proceeds of an insurance award to reduce the indebtedness rather than to restore the property. See §§7.26–7.28. The amount due may also be affected if the beneficiary makes tax payments when the trustor fails to do so. See §§7.34–7.37. Disagreements over the amount due or when it is due may eventually result in litigation and claims by either party for reimbursement of its attorneys' fees. See §§7.29–7.33. Other issues that may arise under the terms of the promissory note and relating to payment of the obligation are discussed in §§7.38–7.44.

§7.2   A. Form: Acceleration Clause

A note payable in installments should contain a clause permitting the creditor to accelerate the balance of the debt following a default in payment of an installment. A typical clause, such as that in the note in App A, should read:

If default occurs in the payment of any installment under this note when due, or in the performance of any of the agreements in the deed of trust securing this note, the entire principal sum and accrued interest will at once become due and payable, without notice, at the option of the holder of this note.

This clause fits most appropriately in the note, where all other provisions for payment are set out, but it may be included in the deed of trust as an additional remedy if the note contains no provisions antithetical to it. See Com C §§3105(1)(c), 3119; *Bryan v Swain* (1880) 56 C 616. See also *Pacific Fruit Exch. v Duke* (1930) 103 CA 340, 284 P 729.

An acceleration clause is commonly included in both the note and the deed of trust. Its presence in the note binds all parties who sign or guarantee the note (see *Burrill v Robert Marsh & Co.* (1934) 138 CA 101, 31 P2d 823), and it overrides any inconsistent provisions in the deed of trust (*Pacific Fruit Exch. v Duke, supra; San Gabriel Valley Bank v Lake View Town Co.* (1906) 4 CA 630, 89 P 360). The appearance of the acceleration clause in the recorded deed of trust gives constructive notice to all subsequent purchasers and lienors of the encumbered property. CC §1214.

For safety, the existence of an acceleration clause should be mentioned in the disclosure section of any credit agreement in order to comply with the Truth in Lending Act (15 USC §§1601–1681t). *Barrett v Vernie Jones Ford, Inc.* (ND Ga 1975) 395 F Supp 904; *Meyers v Clearview Dodge Sales* (ED La 1974) 384 F Supp 722; *Garza v Chicago Health Clubs* (ND Ill 1972) 347 F Supp 955; see Comment, *Acceleration Clause Disclosure Under the Truth in Lending Act,* 77 Colum L Rev 649 (1977). Concerning provisions for prepayment penalties on acceleration, see CC §2954.10, discussed in §7.25.

§7.3   1. Power-of-Sale Clause as Substitute

A power-of-sale clause in a mortgage or deed of trust may operate as an acceleration clause if it provides (a) for a sale on default and (b) that the sale proceeds will pay off the entire debt. *Phelps v Mayers* (1899) 126 C 549, 58 P 1048; *Kuster v Parlier* (1932) 122 CA 432, 10 P2d 124; see CC §2924. A power-of-sale clause is not always an adequate substitute, however, especially if the encumbered property is divisible and can be sold piecemeal. See *Yoakam v White* (1893) 97 C 286, 32 P 238; *Bank of San Luis Obispo v Johnson* (1878) 53 C 99; §8.14. See also *Hall v Jameson* (1907) 151 C 606, 91 P 518 (accelerated sale allowed, deficiency judgment postponed until end of entire installment period).

§7.4   2. Validity

The acceleration clause is a valid accessory to a secured note. See Com C §3109. Such a clause is not an illegal penalty, because it governs only the time of payment. See *Maddox v Wyman* (1892) 92 C 674, 28 P 838. It is viewed as giving the maker the limited privilege of delaying full repayment only as long as the installment payments are kept current. *Jump v Barr* (1920) 46 CA 338, 189 P 334. The courts have held that an acceleration clause does not work a forfeiture because it does not increase the size of the obligation. *Whitcher v Webb* (1872) 44 C 127. If acceleration would cause the trustor sufficient hardship, however, a court may invoke the doctrine of waiver to prohibit it. *Bisno v Sax* (1959) 175 CA2d 714, 346 P2d 814. Inclusion of an acceleration clause in the note may not compel the beneficiary to accelerate, if good reasons can be shown for seeking some other relief (*e.g.,* piecemeal foreclosure). See *Furesz v Garcia* (1981) 120 CA3d 793, 174 CR 803. For discussion of collection of prepayment penalties on acceleration, see §§7.22, 7.25.

§7.5   3. Income Tax Effects of Acceleration

For federal income tax purposes, if the seller provides all or some of the financing, reports the gain on the installment method under IRC §453, and then receives accelerated proceeds, the previously deferred gain is correspondingly accelerated. For discussion of installment sales, see Taxation of Real Property Transfers §§3.63–3.106 (Cal CEB 1981); California Real Property Sales Transactions §§5.10–5.15 (Cal CEB 1981).

§7.6   4. Effect of Absence of Acceleration Clause

When there is no clause accelerating an installment obligation on default, the beneficiary's next best hope is CCP §728, which provides that an indivisible piece of security may be sold in its entirety, and the entire debt paid off, in a foreclosure action. *Yoakam v White* (1893) 97 C 286, 32 P 238. If the property is severable, however, the foreclosure sale must cease as soon as a bid is sufficient to cover the installments unpaid as of the date of the foreclosure judgment. *Bank of Napa v Godfrey* (1888) 77 C 612, 20 P 142. After that sale, the beneficiary may hold further foreclosure sales to cover later unpaid installments, either after supplementary motions in the same action (*Byrne v Hoag* (1899) 126 C 283, 58 P 688) (for which the original decree should provide; see *Bank of Napa v Godfrey, supra*) or by the filing of periodic, successive foreclosure actions (CCP §1047; *Higgins v San Diego Sav. Bank* (1900) 129 C 184, 61 P 943; *McDougal v Downey* (1872) 45 C 165; *Zingheim v Marshall* (1967) 249 CA2d 736, 57 CR 809). See §3.37.

§7.7   B. Late Charges

Institutional notes commonly contain provisions imposing an additional charge on borrowers for failure to make timely payment of an installment. These clauses are designed to compensate lenders for administrative expense and loss of use of funds arising from delayed payment and also to pressure the borrower to pay on time. In the absence of a late-charges clause, the creditor cannot impose an additional fee on the borrower for making a late payment. *Roth v Department of Veterans Affairs* (1980) 110 CA3d 622, 167 CR 552. In such a case, the lender should be entitled only to additional interest for the delay under CC §3302. The validity of collecting such interest out of the next payment, reducing the amount of principal thus paid, has not been tested judicially.

In *Garrett v Coast & S. Fed. Sav. & Loan Ass'n* (1973) 9 C3d 731, 108 CR 845, the supreme court held that a late charge measured as a percentage of the unpaid principal balance of the loan was punitive and invalid. The note in *Garrett* provided that additional annual interest of 2 percent on the unpaid principal balance would be charged until the installment was paid. The court indicated that a late charge calculated in terms of the amount of the delinquent installment (rather than the entire unpaid principal) would be subject to different treatment.

Even a "reasonably calculated" late charge may possibly be judicially invalidated on the ground that late payment of a loan does not make actual damages difficult to calculate. See *Garrett v Coast & S. Fed. Sav. & Loan Ass'n* (1973) 9 C3d 731, 740, 108 CR 845, 851. Under CC §3302, interest is the measure of loss for the wrongful withholding of money, and interest is never difficult to ascertain. Judicial invalidation is unlikely, however, with liberalization of CC §1671's liquidated damages requirements, which place the burden of proving the provision's unreasonableness on the person attacking the provision. On the appropriateness of methods of calculation, see Comment, *Late-Payment Charges: Meeting the Requirements of Liquidated Damages*, 27 Stan L Rev 1133 (1975).

In other situations, late charges are treated as interest rather than as liquidated damages. See Anno, 63 ALR3d 50 (1975). As such, the charges may be subject to usury restrictions but are usually allowed on the ground that they come into play only at the debtor's election and are not conscious attempts by lenders to collect usurious interest. See, *e.g., Lew v Goodfellow Chrysler-Plymouth, Inc.* (Wash App 1971) 492 P2d 258; *Randall v Home Loan & Inv. Co.* (Wis 1944) 12 NW2d 915. In California, earlier decisions often referred to late charges as interest, especially in cases involving lenders who were exempt from usury restrictions. See *Clermont v Secured Inv. Corp.* (1972) 25 CA3d 766, 102 CR 340. The court in *Garrett v Coast & S. Fed. Sav. & Loan Ass'n, supra,* however, disapproved of that logic and declared that such clauses could not be treated as provisions for alternative performance, because the debtors had no real option to elect to pay late under the circumstances.

Late charges received by the mortgagee may be treated as additional interest for federal income tax purposes and therefore constitute ordinary income. See *Al S. Reinhardt* (1980) 75 TC 47; Rev Rul 74–187, 1974–1 Cum Bull 48. The mortgagor may treat such payments the same as other interest payments. See §1.15.

§7.8   1. Form: Late-Charges Clause

The maker(s) acknowledge(s) that late payment to payee will cause payee to incur costs not contemplated by this loan. Such costs include, without limitation, processing and accounting charges. Therefore, if any installment is not received by payee _ _[when due/within_ _ days of the due date]_ _, maker(s) will pay to payee an additional sum of _ _[e.g., 6 percent]_ _ of the overdue amount as a late charge. The parties agree that this late charge represents a reasonable sum considering all the circumstances existing on the date of this agreement and represents a fair and reasonable estimate of the costs that payee will incur by reason of late payment. The parties further agree that proof of actual damages would be costly or inconvenient. Acceptance of any late charge will not constitute a waiver of the default with respect to the overdue amount and will not prevent payee from exercising any of the other rights and remedies available to payee.

Comment: This clause has been drafted to satisfy the requirements of CC §1671(b) (liquidated damages), but its validity has not been tested in the courts. For other forms, see 1 California Real Property Financing §§3.13–3.14 (Cal CEB 1988). Note that nothing in the clause eliminates the need to send a notice of default before commencing trustee's sale proceedings. See §2.12.

§7.9   2. Restrictions on Late Charges

Civil Code §2954.4 permits late charges but limits the charge to 6 percent of the past-due installment or $5, whichever is greater. This statutory limitation applies only to loans made after 1976 on owner-occupied, single-family dwellings and not involving a credit union, industrial loan company, personal property loan broker, or real estate broker. Business and Professions Code §10242.5 limits late charges on loans negotiated through mortgage loan brokers to the greater of 10 percent of the installment or $5, but only if the loan is less than $20,000 (when secured by a first deed of trust) or $10,000 (when secured by a second deed of trust) (Bus & P C §10245). Loans insured by the Federal Housing Administration are limited to 2 percent of the installment after 15 days (24 CFR §241.105), and loans guaranteed by the Veterans Administration are limited to 4 percent after the same 15 days (38 CFR §36.4212(c)).

Civil Code §2954.5 requires that ten days' advance notice be given before a late charge may be assessed on a loan secured by real property. The lender can comply with this requirement either by (a) notifying the borrower in writing and giving the borrower ten days from the date of mailing to cure the delinquency or by (b) informing the borrower in the regular monthly billing of the date after which the late charge will be assessed. CC §2954.5(a). The Truth in Lending Act (15 USC §§1601–1681t) requires advance disclosure to the borrower of late-charges provisions. 12 CFR §226.4. There is a similar requirement in Uniform Consumer Credit Code §§2.203 and 3.203, as well as limitations on the amounts of such charges.

Misleading statements or representations about the note's late-charges provisions, in response to borrowers' inquiries, may violate a lender's or loan broker's duty of truthful disclosure and good-faith dealing, even though the loan documents themselves contain accurate information. *Wyatt v Union Mortgage Co.* (1979) 24 C3d 773, 782, 157 CR 392, 397.

§7.10 C. Form: Due-on-Sale Clause

Property subject to a mortgage or deed of trust is no less transferable than unencumbered property. CC §1044. The encumbrance is, of course, transferred with the property, so that the purchaser takes subject to the encumbrance whether or not the parties have so recited in their deed. Many security instruments contain due-on-sale clauses such as the following (abbreviated) form:

If the property, any part of it, or interest in it is sold _ _[or further encumbered]_ _, or if the trustor agrees to sell, convey, _ _[further encumber]_ _, or alienate the property, by operation of law or otherwise, all obligations secured by this instrument, regardless

of the maturity dates, at the option of the holder and without demand or notice will immediately become due and payable.

Such a clause usually appears in both the note and deed of trust. See, *e.g.,* the form note and deed of trust in 1 California Real Property Financing, chaps 3–4 (Cal CEB 1988). Its presence in the note does not impair negotiability (Com C §3105), and inclusion may be necessary to its validity under CC §2924.5, which requires that such a provision appear in both the note and deed of trust for any loan made after 1972 on a one-to-four-unit residence. The clause is also included in the deed of trust, in order to comply with CC §2924.5 and to give constructive notice to subsequent purchasers and encumbrancers. CC §1214. For another approach, see 1 Real Property Financing §3.19.

Due-on-sale clauses do not have the universal, constant wording found in acceleration clauses. The words "assigned, transferred, and/or disposed of" may replace or be added to "sold," "conveyed," or "alienated"; "voluntarily or involuntarily" may replace "by operation of law"; "if the trustor agrees to sell" may be omitted; and "further encumbered" may be added. For a combined form due-on-sale and due-on-encumbrance clause, see 1 Real Property Financing §4.45.

§7.11 1. Covenant Not To Convey as Due-on-Sale Clause

A document labeled as an agreement (or covenant) not to sell (or convey or encumber) may serve purposes similar to those of a due-on-sale clause. Such a document is usually used in lieu of a mortgage or deed of trust, but it is a poor substitute. When such a covenant is connected with an installment obligation, it permits the covenantee to accelerate the obligation, but does little else. Once accelerated, there is no follow-up right to sell the property, because such documents inevitably lack any power-of-sale clause. A power-of-sale clause cannot be included without defeating a major purpose of such an agreement, *i.e.,* to camouflage the fact that the holder of the note is taking security for it. To contain an effective power-of-sale clause, the agreement must describe itself as a deed of trust (or mortgage), which is what the lender is usually seeking to avoid. The lender may still be able to contend, as it did in *Coast Bank v Minderhout* (1964) 61 C2d 311, 38 CR 505, disapproved on other grounds in 21 C3d 953, that the agreement amounts to an equitable mortgage (lacking all the fine print), but that characterization will justify only judicial foreclosure. *Kaiser Indus. Corp. v Taylor* (1971) 17 CA3d 346, 94 CR 773. The debtor is more likely to succeed in arguing that a mortgage was not intended, in which case the lender becomes entirely unsecured. *Tahoe Nat' l Bank v Phillips* (1971) 4 C3d 11, 92 CR 704; *Orange County Teachers Credit Union v Peppard* (1971) 21 CA3d 448, 98 CR 533.

§7.12   2. Validity of Due-on-Sale Clauses

The due-on-sale clause has had a remarkable history in the courts and the United States Congress. Its first judicial recognition was as a separate document, *i.e.,* an agreement not to encumber or transfer property. In holding that such an instrument could be construed as an equitable mortgage, the California Supreme Court added that an a-greement providing for acceleration of an installment debt on the transfer of real property would not be an invalid restraint on alienation under CC §711. *Coast Bank v Minderhout* (1964) 61 C2d 311, 38 CR 505. The supreme court backed away from that position when it declared, in *Tahoe Nat' l Bank v Phillips* (1971) 4 C3d 11, 92 CR 704, that a functionally indistinguishable document was not a mortgage.

That same year, in *La Sala v American Sav. & Loan Ass' n* (1971) 5 C3d 864, 877, 97 CR 849, 857, the court, in construing a due-on-encumbrance clause in a deed of trust, ruled that the beneficiary could not automatically accelerate when the trustor imposed a second mortgage on the property. Automatic acceleration amounted to an unlawful restraint on alienation; acceleration could occur only when it was reasonably necessary to protect the lender's security. (The legislature later enacted CC §2949, which prohibits due-on-encumbrance clauses in loans secured by single-family, owner-occupied dwellings.)

Three years later, the supreme court ruled that a due-on-sale clause would not permit automatic acceleration when the trustor executed an installment land contract for sale of the property. *Tucker v Lassen Sav. & Loan Ass' n* (1974) 12 C3d 629, 116 CR 633. The court held that permissible acceleration depended on balancing the quantum of the restraint of alienation imposed on the trustor against the justification for the restraint on behalf of the lender. As applied to installment land contracts, the balance tipped against the lender. The quantum of restraint was heavy, because automatic acceleration prohibited such sales entirely. Conversely, the justification for the restraint was light: The lender was adequately protected against the risks of waste and default, and the lender's desire to use the sale as a device to correct interest rates in a rising market was not a legitimate justification.

Then, in 1978, the court ruled that automatic acceleration by an institutional lender was not allowed even when the borrower sold the property outright, *i.e.*, transferred legal title to the purchaser. *Wellenkamp v Bank of America* (1978) 21 C3d 943, 148 CR 379. Reconsidering and rejecting its earlier contrary dicta, the court held that alienation was restrained whenever the seller's lender threatened to call its loan or demanded an increased interest rate from the prospective buyer. The fact that acceleration merely compelled the buyer to borrow at current market rates did not lessen the restraint if a market rate loan was "economically unfeasible." The court found no counterbalancing justification for such restraint. In its previous decisions, the court had held the restraint unjustified because the seller's retention of an interest in the property constituted an incentive to keep the loan current. This incentive is obviously not present when the seller has been cashed out, but the court held that the downpayment would probably give the buyer enough of a stake in the property to deter a default. Thus, the court could find no justification for automatic acceleration, even in case of an outright sale. Again, the court rejected the lender's argument that acceleration was justified as a device to keep loans at current interest rates, admonishing the lending industry that the burden of bad economic projections should not fall on homeowners selling their properties.

In 1982, the supreme court held that automatic acceleration was prohibited, even for noninstitutional private lenders financing commercial real property. *Dawn Inv. Co. v Superior Court* (1982) 30 C3d 695, 180 CR 332. The same reason was given, *i.e.*, that the quantum of restraint outweighed its justification.

These decisions were unpopular in the lending industry and among many housing economists. Institutional lenders, who "lend short but borrow long," were trapped with portfolios of fixed-rate, low-interest loans against which they had to pay high interest rates to retain depositors. Home prices rose when sellers discovered that their ability to transfer low-interest loans to buyers added to the value of their properties. Many other state courts rejected the *Wellenkamp* logic, treating it either as bad economics or as inappropriate judicial intervention in the real estate market. More significantly, the Federal Home Loan Bank Board (FHLBB) authorized federally-chartered savings and loan associations to enforce due-on-sale clauses despite inconsistent state law (see 12 CFR §545.8–3(f)) and was upheld in doing so by the United States Supreme Court (see *Fidelity Fed. Sav. & Loan Ass'n v de la Cuesta* (1982) 458 US 141). California lenders began to convert to federal charters. The state's legislative response was to authorize various non-fixed-rate loans, such as the "adjustable-payment, adjustable-rate loan" (see CC §1916.7), the "renegotiable rate mortgage loan" (see CC §1916.8), and the "shared appreciation" mortgage (see CC §§1917.010–1917.075). See generally 1 California Real Property Financing §§1.19, 1.22 (Cal CEB 1988); California Real Property Sales Transactions §§6.47–6.52 (Cal CEB 1981).

The development of overriding importance was the enactment in 1982 of the Garn-St. Germain Depository Institutions Act of 1982 (12 USC §1701j–3), which validated all due-on-sale clauses notwithstanding contrary state law. (An initial "window period" during which state invalidation remained in effect expired in 1985.) The Garn Act's validation of due-on-sale clauses is now formalized in FHLBB regulations. Under 12 CFR §591.5(b)(1), due-on-sale clauses are valid according to their terms (*i.e.*, automatically) except that their exercise is prohibited for loans secured by an owner-occupied home in the following situations: creation of a subordinate lien, a transfer on the death of a joint tenant, the granting of a leasehold interest of not more than three years, transfers to certain named relatives, and a transfer into an inter vivos trust in which the borrower remains the occupant of the property. These restrictions do not apply to loans on commercial real property. Similar restrictions are embodied in state law in CC §2924.6.

It appears that due-on-encumbrance clauses on commercial real property are also made enforceable by the Garn Act. The Garn Act's definition of due-on-sale clauses is broad enough to include due-on-encumbrance clauses within its validating language. The original version of the Act excepted junior financing arrangements from its validating provisions, but 12 CFR §591.5(b)(1), discussed above, limits the exceptions to owner-occupied residential dwellings. Although there was some question whether the FHLBB regulations exceeded the Board's authority on this issue, the Garn Act itself was subsequently amended to incorporate the FHLBB's interpretation of the scope of the exception, thus implicitly validating due-onencumbrance clauses in the commercial context. See 12 USC §1701j–3(d). Civil Code §2924.6(a)(5) prohibits automatic acceleration of a loan secured by residential real property when the property is subjected to a junior encumbrance or lien. See 1 Real Property Financing §4.45.

§7.13   3. Enforcement

A due-on-sale clause does not provide that the trustor will not convey (or encumber) the property. Rather, it makes a conveyance (or subsequent encumbrance) an occasion for the lender to elect to accelerate the existing installment loan. The lender first declares an election to accelerate the loan; if the accelerated total is not paid, the lender records a notice of default and election to sell. See *Miller v Cote* (1982) 127 CA3d 888, 179 CR 753, in which the court held that a notice of default is defective if it states that the transfer is the specified default; the debtor's failure to pay the accelerated balance after the beneficiary accelerates is the default. See §§2.11–2.17.

Under existing case law, the lender cannot do anything other than accelerate when the specified event occurs, and nothing in the Garn-St. Germain Depository Institutions Act of 1982 (12 USC §1701j–3; see §7.12) suggests the existence of any additional remedies. Language in *Coast Bank v Minderhout* (1964) 61 C2d 311, 38 CR 505, disapproved on other grounds in 21 C3d 953, indicates that any more vigorous form of enforcement would probably constitute an unlawful restraint on alienation. As is true with the conceptually similar no-assignment clause in a lease, the provision does not entitle the beneficiary to void the objectionable transfer. *People v Klopstock* (1944) 24 C2d 897, 151 P2d 641; *Randol v Tatum* (1893) 98 C 390, 33 P 433; *Weisman v Clark* (1965) 232 CA2d 764, 43 CR 108. Similarly, the beneficiary cannot instruct the escrow agent to delay closing a sale until the beneficiary consents to the transfer. *Moss v Minor Props.* (1968) 262 CA2d 847, 69 CR 341. Thus, a due-on-sale clause cannot prevent a transaction covered by the clause; it permits no more than acceleration of the loan.

§7.14   4. Effect of Due-on-Sale Clause on Reinstatement Rights Under CC §2924c

A default declared because of a transfer, or because of failure to pay an accelerated debt following a transfer, is unlikely to be subject to reinstatement under CC §2924c. In this respect, the due-on-sale clause functions differently from the acceleration-for-default clause. See §§7.2–7.6. If the default is the transfer itself, it is a nonmoney default and therefore hardly qualifies for reinstatement by payment of arrearages under CC §2924c. See *Crowell v City of Riverside* (1938) 26 CA2d 566, 80 P2d 120. If the default is failure to pay the entire debt as accelerated (because of the transfer), then the default can be cured only by payment of the entire debt, and the right to reinstatement is meaningless. On the lender's right to impose a prepayment penalty following acceleration under a due-on-sale clause, see §7.25.

§7.15   5. Covered Transactions

Whenever the transaction is not covered by the language of the due-on-sale clause, or when there is no due-on-sale clause at all, the lender has no right to accelerate, because property subject to a mortgage is always fully alienable unless subject to a contrary agreement. CC §1044; see *Miller v Cote* (1982) 127 CA3d 888, 179 CR 753 (memorandum of intent is not a transfer, and therefore not covered by due-on-sale clause, even when accompanied by change of physical control of property).

Leases of the real property security are included within the class of transactions that may be covered by due-on-sale clauses under the Garn-St. Germain Depository Institutions Act of 1982 (12 USC §1701j–3; see §7.12). For discussion of considerations in negotiating a clause that includes leasing, see 1 California Real Property Financing §4.45 (Cal CEB 1988).

The parties must pay careful attention to drafting the due-on-sale clause to specify whether it will or will not apply to certain kinds of transfers such as sale of corporate assets, reorganizations, and shifts in partnership interests. The borrower will want to limit the definition of transfer as much as possible so that such activities are permitted; the lender, if wishing to limit such activities, should make the clause as specific as possible with respect to the activities that will qualify as a sale or transfer. Unless specifically described in the clause, such transfers may be held to be exempt from operation of a standard due-on-sale clause. See *Sexton v Nelson* (1964) 228 CA2d 248, 39 CR 407 (transfer from trustor to trustor's wholly owned corporation); *Ser-Bye Corp. v C.P. & G. Mkts.* (1947) 78 CA2d 915, 179 P2d 342 (sale of corporate stock). For further discussion and a sample clause, see 1 Real Property Financing §4.45.

Also exempt from automatic enforcement of a due-on-sale clause in connection with a mortgage or deed of trust on residential real property are the following (CC §2924.6(a)(2)–(5)):

■ A transfer by the obligor in which the spouse becomes a co-owner of the property;

■ A transfer resulting from a decree of dissolution of marriage or legal separation or a property settlement incidental to such a decree in which the obligor is required to continue loan payments by which a spouse who is an obligor becomes sole owner of the property;

■ A transfer by the obligor to an inter vivos trust of which the obligor is the beneficiary; and

■ The imposition of a junior lien or encumbrance on the property.

§7.16   6. Options

Due-on-sale clauses usually do not include granting an option to purchase the property among the trustor's actions that will lead to acceleration, and it is doubtful whether such clauses could do so, because an option gives the optionee only an inchoate interest in the property. *Pacific Southwest Dev. Corp. v Western Pac. R.R.* (1956) 47 C2d 62, 301 P2d 825; *Vierneisel v Rhode Island Ins. Co.* (1946) 77 CA2d 229, 175 P2d 63.

Once an option is exercised, however, the parties to the option become vendor and purchaser, and the principle of equitable conversion transfers equitable title to the purchaser. *Cates v McNeil* (1915) 169 C 697, 147 P 944. See also *Parr-Richmond Indus. Corp. v Boyd* (1954) 43 C2d 157, 272 P2d 16. Depending on the wording of the due-on-sale clause, the beneficiary may be entitled to accelerate either when the parties execute a purchase and sale agreement or when escrow closes.

§7.17   7. Waiver

A lender risks waiving its right to accelerate under a due-on-sale clause by knowingly accepting payments from the purchaser without exercising its right to accelerate. *Rubin v Los Angeles Fed. Sav. & Loan Ass' n* (1984) 159 CA3d 292, 205 CR 455. See also *Trubowitch v Riverbank Canning Co.* (1947) 30 C2d 335, 182 P2d 182 (lender accepted payments for a year with full knowledge of transfer). A lender may be able, however, to accept payments under a reservation of rights without waiving its right to exercise a due-on-sale clause. *Rubin v Los Angeles Fed. Sav. & Loan Ass' n, supra* (dictum).

The lender's lack of knowledge of the transfer is probably a defense to a waiver argument. *German-American Sav. Bank v Gollmer* (1909) 155 C 683, 102 P 932; *Weisman v Clark* (1965) 232 CA2d 764, 43 CR 108; *Weintraub v Weingart* (1929) 98 CA 690, 277 P 752; *Goodwin v Grosse* (1922) 56 CA 615, 206 P 138. See also *Mutual Fed. Sav. & Loan Ass' n v Wisconsin Wire Works* (Wis 1976) 239 NW2d 20.

No purchaser should acquire property, however, in the hope that the lender will be held to have waived its right to accelerate. An offer to purchase the property should be contingent on the seller's obtaining written consent from the beneficiary to transfer the loan whenever it includes a due-on-sale clause, although doing so may lead to an increase in interest. A solution will be much easier to find if the problem is confronted before escrow has closed (and the purchaser is still able to withdraw) than if it arises after title has passed and the lender has accelerated the loan.

§7.18   8. Form: Failure To Accelerate Does Not Waive Right To Accelerate for Later Breach

The beneficiary should add the following sentence to the due-on-sale clause:

Failure of the holder to exercise the option to accelerate the debt in the event of sale, assignment, or further encumbrance will not constitute waiver of the right to exercise this option in the event of subsequent sale, assignment, or further encumbrance.

By including this sentence, the beneficiary avoids any possibility that the "rule of *Dumpor*'s case" (see *Crowell v City of Riverside* (1938) 26

CA2d 566, 571, 80 P2d 120, 122) will be used against it. Consent to one assignment bars a landlord from objecting to a later assignment by that assignee. *Crowell v City of Riverside, supra*; *Kendis v Cohn* (1928) 90 CA 41, 265 P 844. If the sentence is omitted, the lender may still avoid this doctrine by giving only limited consent to the transfer and reserving the right to object to any further transfers. In *Rubin v Los Angeles Fed. Sav. & Loan Ass'n* (1984) 159 CA3d 292, 205 CR 455, the court implied in dictum that a reservation of rights could even overcome a waiver with respect to the present transfer, but that proposition remains untested.

§7.19   D. Prepayment Clause

The borrower's ability to repay the loan before its due date is governed by the note's prepayment provisions. The borrower has no right to prepay if the promissory note does not create one. The lender has the right to insist on being paid neither early nor late. *Smiddy v Grafton* (1912) 163 C 16, 124 P 433. But see *James Talcott, Inc. v Gee* (1968) 266 CA2d 384, 72 CR 168. A prepayment charge assessed under a clause in the note gives the lender the equivalent of unearned interest on foreclosure, a recovery that is not otherwise collectible. *Furesz v Garcia* (1981) 120 CA3d 793, 174 CR 803; see *Mann v Earls* (1964) 226 CA2d 155, 37 CR 877 (unsecured note). For discussion of prepayment clauses, see Stark, *Enforcing Prepayment Charges: Case Law and Drafting Suggestions,* 22 Real Prop, Prob & Trust J 549 (Fall 1987).

Lenders justify their resistance to prepayment on the grounds that prepayment increases their administrative costs, causes funds to sit idly in their coffers until they can be reloaned (perhaps at a lower rate) (see *Sacramento Sav. & Loan Ass'n v Superior Court* (1982) 137 CA3d 142, 186 CR 823), and allows borrowers to escape from old, high-interest loans in a declining market. See *Hellbaum v Lytton Sav. & Loan Ass'n* (1969) 274 CA2d 456, 79 CR 9, disapproved on other grounds in 21 C3d at 943. Courts have usually accepted these considerations, even when the loan being prepaid carries a below-market interest rate. See *Golden Forest Props. v Columbia Sav. & Loan Ass'n* (1988) 202 CA3d 193, 248 CR 316; *Trident Center v Connecticut Gen. Life Ins. Co.* (9th Cir 1988) 847 F2d 564; *Lazzareschi Inv. Co. v San Francisco Fed. Sav. & Loan Ass'n* (1971) 22 CA3d 303, 99 CR 417. But see *Williams v Fossler* (1980) 110 CA3d 7, 167 CR 545 (criticizing decisions in

Hellbaum v Lytton Sav. & Loan Ass' n, supra, and *Lazzareschi Inv. Co. v San Francisco Fed. Sav. & Loan Ass' n, supra*).

Sellers who carry all or part of the sale's financing often want to postpone prepayment in order to defer recognition of gain (this was particularly true under pre-1984 installment sale provisions of IRC §453). Under CC §2954.9(a)(3), the right to resist prepayment for installment sale reporting considerations is limited to the calendar year of sale. See *Donahue v LeVesque* (1985) 169 CA3d 620, 215 CR 388. For discussion of installment reporting, see Taxation of Real Property Transfers §§3.63–3.106 (Cal CEB 1981); California Real Property Sales Transactions §§5.10–5.15 (Cal CEB 1981). When a prepayment charge is received (by a seller or third party mortgagee), it is treated as additional interest income. *General Am. Life Ins. Co.* (1956) 25 TC 1265, acq 1956–2 Cum Bull 5. Conversely, the mortgagor may treat a prepayment charge as payment of additional interest expense. Rev Rul 57–198, 1957–1 Cum Bull 94; see §1.15.

A discount given to the mortgagor as an inducement to prepay a loan is treated as income from discharge of debt. IRC §108; *Sutphin v U.S.* (1988) 14 Cl Ct 545. When the discount comes from the seller as a price reduction, however, it is treated as a price adjustment rather than as income to the buyer. IRC §108(e)(5). The seller may correspondingly reduce the gain otherwise reported under IRC §453. See Rev Rul 72–570, 1972–2 Cum Bull 241.

§7.20   1. Sample Forms

The simplest prepayment clauses are the "or more" and the "on or before" clauses, which are simply added as phrases to installment notes. If the note recites that it is to be paid in "monthly installments of one thousand dollars or more," or is to be paid in "monthly installments on or before the first day of each month," the borrower thereby acquires the right to prepay the entire loan at any time without penalty. See *Fugate v Cook* (1965) 236 CA2d 700, 46 CR 291; *Born v Koop* (1962) 200 CA2d 519, 19 CR 379.

Notes used by savings and loan associations and some banks usually provide for a limited right of prepayment through use of a more complicated clause such as:

Privilege is reserved to make additional payments on the principal of this indebtedness at any time without penalty, except that,

for any payments made that exceed 20 percent of the original principal amount of this loan during any successive 12-month period beginning with the date of this promissory note, the maker agrees to pay, as consideration for the acceptance of such prepayment, six months' advance interest on that part of the aggregate amount of all prepayments in excess of 20 percent.

The clause refers to prepayment as a privilege given to the borrower, although in fact it also imposes a six months' interest penalty on the borrower for prepayment of over 20 percent of the original principal. Lenders call these "prepayment privilege" clauses; borrowers call them "prepayment penalty" clauses. Some institutions omit all reference to prepayment in the note, leaving for negotiation at a later time how much the borrower must pay in addition to the principal to pay off the loan.

A "lock-in" clause may also be part of the prepayment clause. It temporarily or permanently prohibits all prepayment. See *Trident Center v Connecticut Gen. Life Ins. Co.* (9th Cir 1988) 847 F2d 564. In the clause below, the borrower is prohibited from prepaying for the first three years of the loan:

Privilege is reserved to make additional payments on the principal of this indebtedness after three years from the date of this note.

The following additional limitation may be added:

Such interest will be paid whether prepayment is voluntary or involuntary, including any prepayment effected by the exercise of any acceleration clause provided in this note or the deed of trust securing it.

Involuntary prepayment is analyzed in §7.24. For discussion of prepayment charges when the obligation has been accelerated by the beneficiary, see §7.25.

§7.21   2. Validity

Because a creditor may refuse prepayment in the absence of a clause permitting it, it follows that the creditor may demand consideration from the borrower for accepting prepayment. See *French v Mortgage*

Guar. Co. (1940) 16 C2d 26, 104 P2d 655. It also follows that the creditor may bargain with the borrower in advance for the consideration it will receive for permitting the borrower to prepay. *Abbot v Stevens* (1955) 133 CA2d 242, 284 P2d 159; *Grall v San Piego Bldg. & Loan Ass'n* (1932) 127 CA 250, 15 P2d 797; *McCarty v Mellinkoff* (1931) 118 CA 11, 4 P2d 595. Thus, both the technique of stating a penalty in the original note and the device of bargaining over the penalty when the borrower seeks to prepay are valid. Only if the courts find the charge exorbitant are they likely to intervene on the borrower's behalf. *Lazzareschi Inv. Co. v San Francisco Fed. Sav. & Loan Ass'n* (1971) 22 CA3d 303, 99 CR 417; *Hellbaum v Lytton Sav. & Loan Ass'n* (1969) 274 CA2d 456, 79 CR 9. It appears that this is an area the judiciary believes to be best regulated by the legislature. See §7.24.

Contentions that such provisions are penalty or forfeiture clauses have been rejected on the ground that prepayment involves no breach by the borrower. *Meyers v Home Sav. & Loan Ass'n* (1974) 38 CA3d 544, 113 CR 358; *Lazzareschi Inv. Co. v San Francisco Fed. Sav. & Loan Ass'n, supra.* Borrowers' contentions that the provisions constitute invalid restraints on alienation have similarly failed. See *Sacramento Sav. & Loan Ass'n v Superior Court* (1982) 137 CA3d 142, 186 CR 823. Claims that prepayment clauses are invalid liquidated damages provisions have also been rejected. See *Pacific Trust Co. TTEE v Fidelity Fed. Sav. & Loan Ass'n* (1986) 184 CA3d 817, 229 CR 269 (prepayment charge upheld against junior lienor who sought to redeem property following senior acceleration).

The right to the prepayment charge is not waived when the lender inadvertently accepts payment without imposing the charge, as long as the lender then acts promptly to collect it. *Sanguansak v Myers* (1986) 178 CA3d 110, 223 CR 490.

§7.22   3. Legislative Regulation

Civil Code §2954.9 gives owner-occupiers of one-to-four-unit residential real property the right to prepay their loans entirely after five years; before then, prepayment charges are limited to six months' advance interest on the amount prepaid over 20 percent of the original principal amount. (Under CC §2954.9(a)(3), a noncommercial seller has the right to prohibit prepayment in the year of sale. See *Donahue v LeVesque* (1985) 169 CA3d 620, 215 CR 388.) Similar restrictions apply to loans arranged by loan brokers (Bus & P C §10242.6) and made under the Consumer Finance Lenders Law (Fin C §24473) or under the Cal-Vet Loan Program (Mil & V C §987). Prepayment charges are barred in installment land contracts (CC §2985) and after rate increases in variable interest mortgages (CC §1916.5(a)(5)).

Civil Code §2954.10 restricts imposition of prepayment penalties following acceleration under a due-on-sale clause. See §7.25. If the property consists of one-to-four residential units (not necessarily owner occupied), the charge is totally barred; for other property, the charge is valid only if express language is included in the note and signed separately by the borrower. There may be a prepayment penalty on a commercial loan if the required language is included in the note and signed. For a form provision for commercial loans, see 1 California Real Property Financing §3.39 (Cal CEB 1988). See also *Tan v California Fed. Sav. & Loan Ass'n* (1983) 140 CA3d 800, 189 CR 775, which the legislature overturned by enacting CC §2954.10.

Under the Garn-St. Germain Depository Institutions Act of 1982 (12 USC §1701j–3; see §7.12), Federal Home Loan Bank Board regulations prohibit prepayment penalties following acceleration under a due-on-sale clause on loans on owner-occupied residences. 12 CFR §591.5(b)(2). Prepayment restrictions also apply to Federal Housing Administration insured loans (24 CFR §207.253) and Veterans Administration guaranteed loans (38 CFR §36.4310). The federal Truth in Lending Act also requires disclosure of prepayment charges. 15 USC §1638(a)(11); 12 CFR §226.6(b).

§7.23   4. Prepayment Charges and Usury Laws

In the cases cited in §7.21, the courts held not only that a lender may validly charge for permitting prepayment but also that the existence of a prepayment penalty does not make the loan usurious. See *French v Mortgage Guar. Co.* (1940) 16 C2d 26, 104 P2d 655; *Abbot v Stevens* (1955) 133 CA2d 242, 284 P2d 159; *Grall v San Diego Bldg. & Loan Ass'n* (1932) 127 CA 250, 15 P2d 797. The courts also held that prepayment is voluntary and that a debtor cannot convert a lawful transaction into a usurious one by his or her own act. In any case, most commercial lending institutions are exempted from California's usury laws. Cal Const art XV, §1. Other categories of lenders are exempted by statute. For listings of exempt lenders, see 1 California Real Property Financing §§5.47–5.48 (Cal CEB 1988). A usury argument will therefore almost never protect a borrower from imposition of a prepayment penalty.

§7.24 5. Involuntary Prepayment

Prepayment of the loan can occur because of contingencies partially or entirely outside the parties' control. Justification for imposing a prepayment charge becomes less obvious as the reason for the prepayment moves farther away from a voluntary prepayment elected by the trustor.

When the loan is prepaid because of events outside the borrower's control, but within the lender's control, whether a prepayment charge will be permitted is problematic. Involuntary prepayment occurs when external events produce payments such as fire insurance or condemnation awards, and the deed of trust gives the beneficiary the option of permitting the trustor to retain the funds or of applying them to the loan balance. (Prepayment charges following acceleration for default, or under a due-on-sale clause, are covered in §7.25.) In such cases, the courts may hold either that the prepayment clause was not intended to be applied in this way (see *Tan v California Fed. Sav. & Loan Ass'n* (1983) 140 CA3d 800, 189 CR 775) or that the implied covenant of good faith prohibits the lender from simultaneously electing to have the funds applied to the loan and to impose a charge for prepayment (see *Schoolcraft v Ross* (1978) 81 CA3d 75, 146 CR 57; *Milstein v Security Pac. Nat'l Bank* (1972) 27 CA3d 482, 103 CR 16; see also *999 v C.I.T. Corp.* (9th Cir 1985) 776 F2d 866). For discussion of the lender's right to accelerate for the trustor's failure to maintain fire insurance on the property, see §7.26. (Code of Civil Procedure §1265.240 provides that the lender may not collect a prepayment penalty in a condemnation action, but the scope of the section is apparently limited to the issue of whether the condemning agency must pay the penalty and does not resolve the question of whether the beneficiary may claim the penalty independently from the condemnee-trustor.)

When neither party has discretion over how to apply proceeds arising from external events, so that the beneficiary's receipt of the prepayment is as involuntary as the trustor's prepayment, imposition of a prepayment charge is more likely to be held justifiable. See *Lazzareschi Inv. Co. v San Francisco Fed. Sav. & Loan Ass'n* (1971) 22 CA3d

303, 99 CR 417 (charge upheld when trustor was forced to sell property under judgment for marital dissolution and buyer elected to obtain new financing).

§7.25 6. Prepayment Charges if Obligation Accelerated

If the note contains an acceleration clause, the beneficiary may declare the entire principal balance due when the trustor misses a payment. See §§7.2–7.6. If the note or deed of trust has a due-on-sale clause, the loan may be accelerated if the trustor sells the property. See §§7.10–7.18. Imposition of a prepayment charge following exercise of a due-on-sale clause is barred by CC §2954.10 for residential property and otherwise allowed if the statutory formalities are met. See §7.22.

Early cases support the conclusion that a lender may both accelerate for default and charge a prepayment penalty when the penalty and the interest actually paid do not exceed the maximum allowable interest over the entire life of the loan. In *Sharp v Mortgage Sec. Corp.* (1932) 215 C 287, 9 P2d 819, the court held that, if the amount of interest is otherwise proper, it does not become excessive and usurious when the duration of the loan is shortened because the lender accelerates after the borrower defaults. The court also held that a debtor cannot make the creditor guilty of usury by a voluntary default. In *French v Mortgage Guar. Co.* (1940) 16 C2d 26, 104 P2d 655, the court held that, if it is not usurious to accelerate for default, neither is it usurious to charge a prepayment penalty. See *Trident Center v Connecticut Gen. Life Ins. Co.* (9th Cir 1988) 847 F2d 564. For discussion of bankruptcy courts' treatment of prepayment formulas that increase the interest rate on default, see §6.52.

II. AMOUNT IN DEFAULT

§7.26 A. Fire Insurance Proceeds

Clause A2 of the title company form deed of trust (see App B) provides:

To protect the security of this Deed of Trust, Trustor agrees:

2. To provide, maintain, and deliver to Beneficiary fire insurance satisfactory to and with loss payable to Beneficiary. The

amount collected under any fire or other insurance policy may be applied by Beneficiary upon any indebtedness secured hereby and in such order as Beneficiary may determine, or at option of Beneficiary the entire amount so collected or any part thereof may be released to Trustor. Such application or release shall not cure or waive any default or notice of default hereunder or invalidate any act done pursuant to such notice.

The standard acceleration clause in promissory notes (see App A) provides in general language that the beneficiary may accelerate the balance due if the trustor defaults on any of the obligations under the deed of trust. See 1 California Real Property Financing §3.10 (Cal CEB 1988). See also §§7.2–7.6. Clause B6 of the form deed of trust (see App B) contains a similar provision.

Financial Code §§1227.2 and 7461 and CC §2924.7 expressly permit beneficiaries to accelerate loans for the borrower's failure to keep insurance payments on the property current (as well as for failure to pay taxes, rents, and assessments). Under these sections, the lender is not required to show that the security has been impaired in order to accelerate; the sections thus negate the decision in *Freeman v Lind* (1986) 181 CA3d 791, 226 CR 515, in which the court had held that the beneficiary must show impairment of security. The better course for the lender, however, is to make the insurance payments in the meantime. If the property is damaged by fire before the foreclosure sale, the beneficiary faces the further risk that a judgment against the trustor may be limited to recovery of the premiums that should have been paid, or may be barred altogether by the antideficiency rules, if the failure to insure is treated as a form of waste (see §4.40). See *Cornelison v Kornbluth* (1975) 15 C3d 590, 125 CR 557; Leipziger, *The Mortgagee's Remedies for Waste,* 64 Calif L Rev 1086 (1976). It is safer for the beneficiary to pay the insurance premiums itself and add the amounts advanced to the principal debt. *Campbell v Realty Title Co.* (1942) 20 C2d 195, 124 P2d 810.

Civil Code §2955.5 prohibits the beneficiary from requiring a borrower to carry hazard insurance in an amount in excess of the replacement value of the improvements on the property.

Loan agreements frequently require the trustor to pay installments of the insurance and taxes to the beneficiary on a regular monthly basis. These funds are then held by the beneficiary in an impound account and used to pay the insurance and taxes directly. Title company forms seldom provide for tax or insurance impounds. See CC §§2954, 2954.8, and 2955 for statutory regulation of impound accounts.

§7.27 1. Beneficiary's Right to Proceeds

The second sentence of clause A2 of the form deed of trust (see §7.26, App B) gives the beneficiary the option of applying the insurance award toward the debt or permitting the trustor to take the funds. Under its terms, the beneficiary is not required to show impairment of its security in order to appropriate the entire award (*i.e.*, when the balance of the debt is $50,000 and the value of the security is $1 million, the lender could still demand that the entire $20,000 insurance award be applied to reduce the debt rather than to repair the property or be retained by the trustor). The literal language of the clause does not, however, control.

In *Schoolcraft v Ross* (1978) 81 CA3d 75, 146 CR 57, the court held that the trustor was entitled to use the insurance proceeds to rebuild the damaged improvements, despite inclusion of such a clause in the deed of trust, on the ground that the implied covenant of good faith and fair dealing requires that the beneficiary show that the security was impaired before applying the proceeds to reduce the debt. Subsequently, in *Kreshek v Sperling* (1984) 157 CA3d 279, 204 CR 30, the court permitted the trustor to keep the insurance award (without using the funds to rebuild) on a showing that the value of the security far exceeded the loan balance. See Moless, *Fire Insurance Covenants in Deeds of Trust: Death of Contract?*, 16 Lincoln L Rev 97 (1986).

The legislature enacted Fin C §§1227.2 and 7461 in 1987 (see §7.26), and CC §2924.7 in 1988, providing that a beneficiary is not required to show impairment of its security in order to apply the insurance proceeds to the debt. These sections were intended to overturn *Kreshek v Sperling, supra.* The legislature provided, however, that the sections do not overturn the decision in *Schoolcraft v Ross, supra,* "insofar as it provides that a lender may not prohibit the use of insurance proceeds for the restoration of the security property absent a showing that the lender's security interest in the property has been impaired." Stats 1987, ch 397, §5. Thus, a trustor proposing to use the funds for restoration should be able to do so, except when he or she is in default (see *Ford v Manufacturer's Hanover Mortgage Corp.* (9th Cir 1987) 831

F2d 1520). When the trustor is current on the loan, it is difficult to see how the beneficiary can demonstrate impairment of security when the property will be restored to its pre-fire condition. In the absence of a proposal to rebuild, the beneficiary has the superior claim to the proceeds without any impairment of its security. For discussion of recovery of insurance proceeds *after* a foreclosure sale, see §8.8.

Even if the security is impaired, the beneficiary's right to all or part of the insurance proceeds still depends on the language of the deed of trust. If the instrument merely compels the trustor to carry insurance, but does not provide that the proceeds will go to the beneficiary, the beneficiary may not be able to claim them. Compare *Alexander v Security-First Nat' l Bank* (1936) 7 C2d 718, 62 P2d 735, with *Lee v Murphy* (1967) 253 CA2d 205, 61 CR 174. In addition to language in the deed of trust entitling the beneficiary to the proceeds, the beneficiary should require that the trustor's insurance policy name the beneficiary as a loss payee. If a loss occurs after a foreclosure sale and the policy has not been rewritten to reflect the beneficiary's interest as the foreclosure purchaser (and did not previously name the beneficiary as loss payee), the proceeds are not payable to the beneficiary. *Reynolds v London & Lancashire Fire Ins. Co.* (1900) 128 C 16, 60 P 467.

The mortgagor's federal income tax treatment of an insurance award depends on how the funds are used. If they are used to repair the damage, there are no tax consequences and the insurance funds are not income. IRC §1033; Reg §1.1033(a)–2(c). If the funds are not used for repairs, but are instead pocketed by the mortgagor, there is gain or loss equal to the difference between the amount received and the mortgagor's basis in the property. Reg §1.1033(a)–2(c). The mortgagor must also report gain or loss if the mortgagee elects to have the funds applied to reduce the debt and the mortgagor does not thereafter acquire a replacement property. Reg §1.1033(a)–2(c). A mortgagor who uses the funds to purchase similar property within two or three years (depending on the nature of the property) may defer recognition of any gain under the involuntary conversion provisions of IRC §1033. Section 1033 does not apply to losses. Any loss resulting from an involuntary conversion will be recognized or not recognized under other Internal Revenue Code sections, *e.g.,* IRC §§1231, 165.

Receipt of insurance proceeds by the mortgagor and their ultimate use have no tax significance to a third party lender unless the mortgagor uses the proceeds to repay the loan. For a seller reporting under the installment method, application of the funds to reduce the debt will accelerate gain under IRC §453. See §7.5.

§7.28   2. Allocation of Proceeds Among Beneficiaries

If the proceeds of a fire insurance policy are to be paid to the beneficiary rather than to the trustor, and there are several encumbrances on the property, the proceeds are not allocated pro rata among the lienors. The entire recovery is awarded to the senior lienor, up to the amount of its lien (*Woody v Lytton Sav. & Loan Ass' n* (1964) 229 CA2d 641, 40 CR 560), as long as its security instrument so provides (*Alexander v Security-First Nat' l Bank* (1936) 7 C2d 718, 62 P2d 735).

§7.29   B. Attorneys' Fees

Clause A3 of the title company form deed of trust (see App B) provides:

To protect the security of this Deed of Trust, Trustor agrees:

3. To appear in and defend any action or proceeding purporting to affect the security hereof or the rights or powers of Beneficiary or Trustee; and to pay all costs and expenses, including cost of evidence of title and attorneys' fees in a reasonable sum, in any such action or proceeding in which Beneficiary or Trustee may appear.

Clause A5 of the form deed of trust requires that the trustor reimburse the beneficiary for any sum expended by the beneficiary under any of the deed of trust provisions. Because other clauses entitle the beneficiary to appear in any proceedings concerning senior liens (A6), bring judicial foreclosure (A6), appoint a receiver (B5), enforce payment of all obligations of the trustor (A6), and conduct a private foreclosure sale (B6), and in each instance permit the beneficiary to employ counsel, the beneficiary should be able to recover attorneys' fees from the trustor for most litigated and nonlitigated disputes between them arising from the deed of trust provisions. Under CC §1717, which makes attorneys' fees provisions reciprocal, the trustor should also be entitled to recover attorneys' fees when he or she is the prevailing party. *Nasser v Superior Court* (1984) 156 CA3d 52, 202 CR 552; *Valley Bible Center v Western Title Ins. Co.* (1983) 138 CA3d 931, 188 CR 335. For further discussion of the application of CC §1717, and recovery of attorneys' fees in general, see California Attorney's Fees Award Practice (Cal CEB 1982).

Because the beneficiary is concerned, in the instances enumerated, with its remedies under the deed of trust rather than the note, it is proper for the attorneys' fees clause to appear in the deed of trust instead of in the note (see *Hellier v Russell* (1902) 136 C 143, 68 P 581), although the note usually contains such a clause as well. See App A. If the beneficiary wants to be able to recover attorneys' fees, the deed of trust should contain attorneys' fees provisions, because there is no independent statutory right to such fees and they are not recoverable unless provided for by contract or statute (CCP §1021). Although CCP §730 appears to provide for attorneys' fees in any judicial foreclosure action, the section has been interpreted to mean that they may be awarded only when the mortgage so provides, and then in an amount set by the court, regardless of what the mortgage provides (see §7.32). *Hotaling v Montieth* (1900) 128 C 556, 61 P 95; see CCP §726. On the other hand, CC §2924c appears to require payment of attorneys' fees as a condition of reinstatement, whether or not the deed of trust calls for them. See §7.30. It is doubtful, however, that this section would permit a beneficiary to recover attorneys' fees when reinstatement is not the issue (*i.e.*, after expiration of the reinstatement period), although CCP §580c appears to allow them, by implication. But see *O'Connor v Richmond Sav. & Loan Ass'n* (1968) 262 CA2d 523, 68 CR 882.

§7.30   1. Reinstatement

If the beneficiary has recorded a notice of default and the trustor wishes to reinstate during the reinstatement period (see §2.17), CC §2924c requires payment not only of all arrearages but also of trustees' or attorneys' fees of $200 plus a decreasing percentage of the unpaid balance over $50,000. In *Sweatt v Foreclosure Co.* (1985) 166 CA3d 273, 212 CR 350, the court held that the unpaid balance, rather than the amount of the defaulted payment, is the appropriate measure of the trustees' fees. Because the statute refers to trustees' and attorneys' fees disjunctively, it does not appear that the beneficiary may claim both, even though both are incurred. Also, the fees should actually be incurred, which means that the beneficiary should have a bill from an attorney (or a trustee) for what it claims, and the attorney should not be house counsel. See *T. L. Reed Co. v Kruse* (1934) 220 C 181, 29 P2d 856. But see *Wiener v Van Winkle* (1969) 273 CA2d 774, 78 CR 761.

Civil Code §2924c refers to trustees' or attorneys' fees incurred in connection with recording the notice of default and instituting foreclosure proceedings. If the beneficiary has incurred additional attorneys' fees for other services related to the deed of trust that are recoverable under the deed of trust, it may also be entitled to recover them from the trustor as a condition of reinstatement, if the fees are included in the notice of default. *Buck v Barb* (1983) 147 CA3d 920, 195 CR 461; *Bisno v Sax* (1959) 175 CA2d 714, 346 P2d 814. See §3.51. In this instance, previously incurred attorneys' fees are like any collateral advances made by the beneficiary, which may be added to its claim. See §7.37. On reinstatement, see §2.17.

§7.31　　2. Foreclosure and Redemption

Civil Code §2924c does not govern attorneys' fees when there has been a foreclosure (as opposed to notice of default and reinstatement; see §7.30) and the issue is:

■ Whether the surplus from the sale may be applied to attorneys' fees;

■ Whether attorneys' fees may be included in any deficiency judgment against the trustor;

■ Whether a trustor redeeming before the sale must also pay attorneys' fees as part of the cost of redemption (see CC §§2903–2905); or

■ Whether a lender can include its attorneys' fees as part of its credit-bid.

If the beneficiary brings an action for judicial foreclosure and the deed of trust provides for attorneys' fees, CCP §726 provides that the trial court may award attorneys' fees in an amount "not exceeding the amount named in the mortgage." A somewhat similar provision, CCP §580c, governs attorneys' fees for private foreclosure sales, but §580c differs from CCP §726 in that §580c does not limit recovery to the amount stipulated in the deed of trust or require that attorneys' fees be stipulated at all in the deed of trust. The decision in *Hotaling v Montieth* (1900) 128 C 556, 61 P 95, however, limits attorneys' fees to situations in which the security instrument provides for them, and probably governs.

Not only should the beneficiary have an attorneys' fees clause in the note and deed of trust, but it should also have an attorneys' bill in its possession. A clause in the loan documents does not entitle it to attorneys' fees not actually incurred. See *T. L. Reed Co. v Kruse* (1934) 220 C 181, 29 P2d 856; *Patterson v Donner* (1874) 48 C 369. Although in *Wiener v Van Winkle* (1969) 273 CA2d 774, 78 CR 761, a creditor was awarded attorneys' fees despite the fact that the attorney was working on a contingent fee basis, both the attorneys' fees clause and the contingent fee agreement were specially worded.

Possessing a bona fide bill from an attorney is, however, no guaranty that the amount billed will be the amount recovered. The bill must be reasonable, which means that it will depend on the time spent by the attorney, the size of the debt, and the nature of the issues. *Shannon v Northern Counties Title Ins. Co.* (1969) 270 CA2d 686, 76 CR 7; *O'Connor v Richmond Sav. & Loan Ass'n* (1968) 262 CA2d 523, 68 CR 882. If the beneficiary foreclosed judicially and the attorney appeared in court to handle the proceedings, the trial judge already has sufficient evidence of the services and their value. *Hellier v Russell* (1902) 136 C 143, 68 P 581; see Anno, 18 ALR3d 733 (1968). If the services were for other aspects of the case, however, evidence concerning them should be offered. See *O'Connor v Richmond Sav. & Loan Ass'n, supra*; *Bisno v Sax* (1959) 175 CA2d 714, 346 P2d 814. For discussion of making the necessary evidentiary showing for an attorneys' fees award, see California Attorney's Fees Award Practice, chaps 6, 8 (Cal CEB 1982).

§7.32   3. Recovery of Attorneys' Fees

When some aspect of the deed of trust is being litigated, attorneys' fees can generally be sought, and the amount determined, as part of that action. On procedures for seeking attorneys' fees, see California Attorney's Fees Award Practice (Cal CEB 1982). When there is no judicial action, however, as in the case of a nonjudicial foreclosure, the beneficiary can seek attorneys' fees by filing an action for an accounting under CCP §1050. If the trustor claims that the balance due on the note is the amount required to redeem and to receive a release of the deed of trust, but the beneficiary claims attorneys' fees in addition, the trustor may add a cause of action for accounting to an action asserting the trustor's right to the property, such as an action to set aside the sale. See *Inskeep v Bear Creek Co.* (1942) 54 CA2d 723, 129 P2d 401. When a sale has been completed and the trustee does not know how to distribute the surplus, an action for accounting to determine attorneys' fees may be combined with an interpleader action filed by the trustee or a straight action for money filed by the trustor or other claimant. See *Johns v Moore* (1959) 168 CA2d 709, 336 P2d 579. The beneficiary has the same right as the trustor to seek an accounting, because the beneficiary may incur penalties for wrongful refusal to request reconveyance if the proper amount has been tendered to it. CC §2941; *R. G. Hamilton Corp. v Corum* (1933) 218 C 92, 21 P2d 413; *Hewlett v Evans* (1922) 56 CA 344, 205 P 492.

An action for accounting brought by the trustor presents the risk that the trustor may have to pay the beneficiary's attorneys' fees in that action, and the trustor may feel that it is not worth incurring attorneys' fees just to determine whether attorneys' fees have already been incurred. Under the wording of the deed of trust, any action in which the beneficiary is compelled to appear regarding its security entitles it to attorneys' fees, and the accounting action is plainly of that sort. *Hewlett v Evans, supra.* Despite such a clause, however, the court need not award fees to the beneficiary. See *Inskeep v Bear Creek Co., supra.* Furthermore, CC §1717 provides that either party may recover attorneys' fees when there is an attorneys' fees clause in the contract. Thus, a trustor who is victorious in an accounting action, in a claim to the surplus from a sale, or in opposition to a deficiency judgment is entitled to recover attorneys' fees from the beneficiary. See *Golden W. Credit Corp. v Maury* (1969) 270 CA2d Supp 913, 75 CR 757.

§7.33   4. Other Actions

Whenever a beneficiary is forced to appear in an action to defend its security, the deed of trust entitles it to attorneys' fees. See §7.32. This rule clearly applies when the security is threatened by paramount title or a senior lien. *Mitsuuchi v Security-First Nat'l Bank* (1951) 103 CA2d 214, 229 P2d 376. In *Shannon v Northern Counties Title Ins. Co.* (1969) 270 CA2d 686, 76 CR 7, a challenge to the beneficiary's security came from the trustor. The holder of a third deed of trust spent 16-1/2 days in trial resisting the trustor's suit for $50,000 damages for fraud and an injunction against foreclosure and was awarded $500 attorneys' fees because most of the trial concerned the fraud, rather than foreclosure, and the note was for only $1500. In *Wagner v Benson* (1980) 101 CA3d 27, 161 CR 516, however, the court awarded the lender attorneys' fees incurred in defending against fraud allegations because the defense was necessary to the lender's ability to collect on the note. See also *IMO Dev. Corp. v Dow Corning Corp.* (1982) 135 CA3d 451, 185 CR 341; *Johns v Moore* (1959) 168 CA2d 709, 336 P2d 579.

The trustee, as well as the beneficiary, may be entitled to attorneys' fees when there is a bona fide necessity for its appearance. See *Title Guar. & Trust Co. v Griset* (1922) 189 C 382, 208 P 673. When the dispute is solely between the beneficiary and the trustor, however, the trustee's appearance is only technically necessary, and the trustee is not entitled to attorneys' fees. *Field v Acres* (1937) 9 C2d 110, 69 P2d 422. See also *Mitau v Roddan* (1906) 149 C 1, 84 P 145. The holder of surplus funds arising from a foreclosure sale, who brings an interpleader action, may be awarded attorneys' fees. CCP §386.6.

A subsequent owner of the encumbered property who successfully enjoins the lender's attempt to accelerate the loan may be entitled to recover attorneys' fees under CC §1717 (see §7.29) even though he or she is a nonassuming grantee (and therefore technically not bound by the covenants in the deed of trust). *Saucedo v Mercury Sav. & Loan Ass'n* (1980) 111 CA3d 309, 168 CR 552 (overruling *Pas v Hill* (1978) 87 CA3d 521, 151 CR 98, on this issue). See also *Jones v Drain* (1983) 149 CA3d 484, 196 CR 827. Although such a nonassuming grantee would not be personally liable for attorneys' fees, he or she would have to pay them as a practical matter to avoid foreclosure and would therefore be entitled to recover them when successful under CC §1717.

§7.34 C. Taxes and Senior Liens

Clause A4 of the title company form deed of trust (see App B) obligates the trustor to keep taxes and senior liens current. Taxes are sometimes handled by imposing an impound account under which one twelfth of the taxes are paid to the beneficiary as part of each monthly payment. See CC §§2954, 2954.1, 2954.8, and 2955 for statutory regulation of impound accounts. In some cases, the beneficiary must pay interest on the impound account. CC §2954.8. Most title company form deeds of trust contain no provision for impound accounts. If a wraparound or all-inclusive deed of trust is used, the beneficiary will also collect from the trustor the amounts due on the senior lien. See §8.31.

§7.35 1. Taxes

Taxes resemble senior liens in that failure to pay them may invite foreclosure and sale of the property. The trustor's failure to pay taxes is a form of waste. See *Osuna v Albertson* (1982) 134 CA3d 71, 184 CR 338. On waste, see §§4.40–4.42. The foreclosure sale eliminates all junior liens. See §§2.28, 3.24. Even though taxes may not be due until after the deed of trust is executed, the tax sale will nevertheless pass title free from the deed of trust because liens for real property taxes have statutory priority over all other liens on real property. Rev & T C §2192.1. Compare *California Loan & Trust Co. v Weis* (1897) 118 C 489, 50 P 697, with *Guinn v McReynolds* (1918) 177 C 230, 170 P 421. Other charges included in the tax bill may not be entitled to the same priority. See *County of Butte v North Burbank Pub. Util. Dist.* (1981) 124 CA3d 342, 177 CR 282.

The beneficiary is entitled to demand that the trustor keep the taxes current. *Donkin v Killefer* (1939) 32 CA2d 729, 90 P2d 810. If the trustor does not pay the taxes, the beneficiary may either institute foreclosure proceedings directly or pay the taxes and foreclose if it is not reimbursed. Both the deed of trust and the Civil Code permit the beneficiary to choose the second alternative. Clause A6 of the title company form deed of trust (see §7.37, App B) permits the beneficiary to pay all debts necessary to protect its security and recover from the trustor. Civil Code §2876 permits the holder of a lien to satisfy prior liens, including tax liens, for its own protection and to recover back through its own lien. *Stafford v Russell* (1953) 117 CA2d 326, 255 P2d 814. On senior liens, see §7.36; on the beneficiary's right to act, see §7.37.

§7.36 2. Senior Liens

When the trustor defaults on a first deed of trust, the position of the holder of the second deed of trust is often unenviable. If the default is not cured, the senior lienor may foreclose, thus eliminating the junior lien. See §§2.28, 3.24. The junior lienor may attempt to foreclose simultaneously, whether or not the junior deed of trust is current, on the ground that a default by the trustor on the first deed of trust is also a default on the second. Even without foreclosing, the junior may seek to share in the proceeds of the foreclosure sale. See §§2.28, 3.48. The junior's participation in the sale is limited, however, to any surplus left after the senior has been paid in full, and distress sales rarely generate much of a surplus. Beyond that, the junior can hope only to sue on the debt as a sold-out junior, assuming that CCP §580b is no bar. See §§4.8, 4.32. Like anyone else, the junior may bid at the senior foreclosure sale, but the junior bid must be all cash. Unlike the foreclosing senior, the junior cannot credit-bid even the amount of the junior lien at the senior sale, unless this has been prearranged. *Nomellini Constr. Co. v Modesto Sav. & Loan Ass'n* (1969) 275 CA2d 114, 79 CR 717; see §§2.23, 3.59. A junior lienor who purchases at the senior sale is entitled to have any surplus applied to its own debt. *Pacific Loan Management Corp. v Superior Court* (1987) 196 CA3d 1485, 1491, 242 CR 547, 551.

To avoid these problems, a junior may prefer to avert a senior foreclosure by making the payments directly on the first deed of trust (see CC §2924c), tacking these payments onto the junior deed of trust, and then foreclosing on the junior deed of trust. The junior may then sell the property subject to the first deed of trust and apply the sale proceeds to the junior debt. See *United Sav. & Loan Ass'n v Hoffman* (1973) 30 CA3d 306, 106 CR 275. The junior may also effect a presale redemption from the senior deed of trust (see CC §§2903–2905), but this again compels the junior to produce cash for the full amount of that lien.

As with taxes (see §7.35), both the deed of trust and the Civil Code permit the junior lienor to keep senior liens from default, add the amounts paid to the balance on the junior debt, and be subrogated to the extent of the amounts paid. CC §§2876, 2903–2905; *Windt v Covert* (1907) 152 C 350, 93 P 67; *Churchill v Woodworth* (1906) 148 C 669, 84 P 155; *Johns v Moore* (1959) 168 CA2d 709, 336 P2d 579. Payments made by a junior are added to the junior lien, but they retain many characteristics of the senior lien. For instance, if the trustor is subject to personal liability on the junior deed of trust but not on the senior, a junior who pays off the senior lien and combines the amounts on foreclosure may obtain a deficiency judgment for only the junior portion of the debt. See *Windt v Covert, supra.* If the junior is able to obtain an assignment of the senior deed of trust, the junior may exercise the rights contained in the senior instrument (including the power of sale) without automatically losing the junior lien by merger. *Strike v Trans-West Discount Corp.* (1979) 92 CA3d 735, 155 CR 132. The junior's redemption of the senior lien, however, does not entitle the junior to compel an assignment of the senior lien. *Snider v Basinger* (1976) 61 CA3d 819, 132 CR 637. Junior wraparound deeds of trust usually contain special provisions concerning the servicing of the senior debt. See §8.31.

When a senior beneficiary either pays taxes or advances money to the trustor to pay them, lien creditors junior to the senior may claim that these are optional future advances not entitled to priority over their claims. See §8.34. The senior should, however, be able to claim that the payments (a) either were obligatory or were made to protect the security under CC §2876 and (b) were not future advances made under the future-advance clause. *Savings & Loan Soc'y v Burnett* (1895) 106 C 514, 39 P 922; *Turner v Lytton Sav. & Loan Ass'n* (1966) 242 CA2d 457, 51 CR 552; *Hesse v Railway Fed. Sav. & Loan Ass'n* (1941) 46 CA2d 111, 115 P2d 519. The senior's right to advance these funds need not, however, put the junior in jeopardy. The junior may declare a default under the junior deed of trust because of the trustor's failure to pay these necessary expenses, and may insist that the trustor either reimburse the senior or pay the junior an amount equivalent to what the senior advanced, as a condition for reinstating the junior deed of trust. *Manning v Queen* (1968) 263 CA2d 672, 69 CR 734.

Because clause A6 of the title company form deed of trust (see App B) permits the beneficiary or the trustee to pay any lien that in either party's judgment "*appear(s)* to be prior or superior" (emphasis added), the beneficiary need not obtain the trustor's consent to pay a prior lien directly when the trustor fails to pay. If a junior lienor pays off a senior lien, however, the junior's right to declare a default may turn on a subsequent determination of the validity of the discharged debt. In *Security-First Nat'l Bank v Lamb* (1931) 212 C 64, 297 P 550, the beneficiary paid off an assessment being challenged by the trustor in court and foreclosed when the trustor refused to reimburse it. The supreme court held that under the deed of trust the beneficiary could pay off any claim that, in the beneficiary's sole discretion, either was or appeared to be a lien. That decision may have rested in part, however, on the facts that the trustor could have paid the assessment under protest, there were heavy penalties for nonpayment, and the trustor ultimately lost the challenge to the assessment. On the other hand, in *Vilkin v Sommer* (1968) 260 CA2d 687, 67 CR 837, when the junior made payments on the senior deed of trust that benefited the junior rather than the trustor, the junior was not allowed to demand reimbursement. But see *United Sav. & Loan Ass'n v Hoffman, supra.*

§7.37 D. Beneficiary's Right To Act; Reimbursement

Clause A6 of the title company form deed of trust (see App B) provides in part:

6. Should Trustor fail to make any payment or to do any act as herein provided, then Beneficiary or Trustee, but without obligation so to do and without notice to or demand upon Trustor and without releasing Trustor from any obligation hereof, may make or do the same in such manner and to such extent as either may deem necessary to protect the security hereof . . . .

Thus, the beneficiary may pay the insurance premiums, taxes, or senior liens as necessary to protect its security. *Stafford v Russell* (1953) 117 CA2d 326, 255 P2d 814. Even without a specific clause in the deed of trust, the beneficiary has this right. CC §2876.

Clause A5 of the form deed of trust specifically obligates the trustor to pay on demand sums expended by the beneficiary or trustee under the provisions of the deed of trust, including advances authorized by clause A6. All such advances become part of the basic secured obligation, permitting foreclosure for nonpayment. CC §2876; *Windt v Covert* (1907) 152 C 350, 93 P 67.

Even without a provision in the deed of trust such as those in clauses A5 and A6, the beneficiary may still pay taxes and senior liens when necessary to protect its security and add these sums to its own lien. CC §2876; *Windt v Covert, supra.* Without a provision such as clause A5, the beneficiary will not be able to obtain a personal judgment for any deficiency represented by the unpaid taxes or senior liens if the trustor had no personal liability for those amounts. In *Windt v Covert, supra,* a junior mortgagee was denied a deficiency judgment for the amount of a senior lien that was paid to protect the junior lien. The mortgagor had taken the property subject to the senior lien but had not assumed the obligations of the senior lien. The junior lien was created by a deed absolute given as security. Thus, no special clause such as A5 existed in *Windt* by which the mortgagor promised to pay sums advanced by the mortgagee. The mortgagee could rely only on the lien rights granted by CC §2876. No court has ruled on whether a clause such as A5 creates a personal obligation on the trustor with respect to taxes and senior liens when an obligation does not otherwise exist. In any event, even if foreclosure is the beneficiary's only remedy, the proceeds of the foreclosure sale must first be applied to the sums paid for taxes and senior liens. *Windt v Covert, supra.* Thus, if the value of the security is sufficient to cover at least the amounts advanced by the beneficiary for taxes and senior liens, a deficiency judgment can still be obtained for the entire balance of the debt (assuming there is no purchase-money (see CCP §580b) or private-sale (see CCP §580d) bar). See §§4.14, 4.23.

Clause A5 also provides for interest at the legal rate on sums advanced by the beneficiary or trustee. Even without such a provision, advances for taxes or other prior liens made by the beneficiary to protect its own interest become a part of the indebtedness secured by the mortgage or deed of trust (CC §2876) and bear interest at the legal rate (*Beeler v American Trust Co.* (1946) 28 C2d 435, 170 P2d 439). The lender may wish to provide that, instead of such advances bearing interest at the legal rate, they be added to the indebtedness and bear interest at the same rate as the promissory note. See 1 California Real Property Financing §4.48 (Cal CEB 1988). A lender subject to the usury law may wish to provide that any such sums advanced by the lender bear interest at the maximum permissible rate regardless of the interest rate specified in the promissory note. For discussion of usury restrictions, see 1 Real Property Financing §§5.45–5.49.

§7.38   E. Condemnation and Damages Awards

Clause B1 of the title company form deed of trust (see App B) provides:

1. Any award of damages in connection with any condemnation for public use of or injury to said property or any part thereof is hereby assigned and shall be paid to Beneficiary who may apply or release such moneys received by him in the same man-

ner and with the same effect as above provided for disposition of proceeds of fire or other insurance.

§7.39   1. Condemnation Awards

When property is taken for a public use, the award must compensate the beneficiary as well as the trustor. CCP §1265.220. The beneficiary does not need an entitling clause in the deed of trust to be able to share in the award. It is well accepted in California that a public entity cannot take property subject to a deed of trust without compensating the beneficiary. See *Stratford Irr. Dist. v Empire Water Co.* (1943) 58 CA2d 616, 137 P2d 867. See also *Bellows v L. A. Dock & Terminal Co.* (1922) 56 CA 168, 204 P 858. Any award made by the condemning authority would be subject to the lien of the deed of trust under the doctrine of substitute security, which treats the award as replacing the reduced value of the real property security. *American Sav. & Loan Ass'n v Leeds* (1968) 68 C2d 611, 614 n2, 68 CR 453, 456 n2.

Without a clause in the deed of trust, the lender can claim no greater rights in the award than those necessary to protect its security interest from impairment. *Sacramento & San Joaquin Drainage Dist. v Truslow* (1954) 125 CA2d 478, 270 P2d 928. Thus, for example, if the secured debt is $100,000 and the property value exceeds $400,000, a taking of $50,000's worth of the property does not impair the security, and the owner may probably retain the entire award. Courts have held that a lender is similarly restrained, even with such a clause, by an implied covenant of good faith that requires it to exercise its discretionary control over the award to permit the trustor to retain all of it except that which is necessary to protect the lender's security from being impaired. *Milstein v Security Pac. Nat'l Bank* (1972) 27 CA3d 482, 103 CR 16. See also *Schoolcraft v Ross* (1978) 81 CA3d 75, 146 CR 57. This rule may be less strictly applied in federal court. See *Miller v Federal Land Bank* (9th Cir 1978) 587 F2d 415. Thus, clause B1 in the title company form deed of trust (see §7.38, App B) constitutes only a security assignment rather than an absolute assignment of the award, and the beneficiary is restrained from obtaining more than such entitlement allows. See *Duarte v Lake Gregory Land & Water Co.* (1974) 39 CA3d 101, 113 CR 893.

The *Milstein* rule has been codified in CCP §1265.225, which provides that, when there is a partial taking, the lienholder may share in the condemnation award only to the extent necessary to prevent an impairment of the security. The lending industry's response to *Milstein* has been to revise, in some instances, the deed of trust form to give the lender absolute discretion without regard to adequacy of the security. Whether such clauses eliminate the obligations of good faith that the courts find in these instruments is open to question. For discussion, see 1 California Real Property Financing §4.44 (Cal CEB 1988).

The point at which security is impaired is not governed by any generally accepted standard. In *Cornelison v Kornbluth* (1975) 15 C3d 590, 125 CR 557, the supreme court suggested application of a "debt-equivalency" test, *i.e.*, that impairment exists when the value of the security goes below the outstanding indebtedness. *Cornelison* involved waste rather than condemnation, however, and it has been suggested that the differing policies involved in the two situations should lead to different tests. *People ex rel Dep't of Transp. v Redwood Baseline, Ltd.* (1978) 84 CA3d 662, 149 CR 11; see §4.40. The *Redwood Baseline* case suggested numerous alternative ways of deciding when security had been impaired:

■ Original ratio (when the ratio of security to debt after the taking falls below that original ratio of security to debt);

■ Pretaking ratio (when the ratio after the taking falls below what it was immediately before the taking); and

■ Conservative lender (when the remaining value of the security falls below what a conservative lender would consider reasonable).

(The opinion also mentions two other possible standards, which the court found generally unacceptable in California: (1) giving the lender the entire award, as is done in many other jurisdictions; and (2) determining the market value of the security, which depends too much on external considerations.)

The decision in *Redwood Baseline* suggests that the test to be applied should depend on the trial court's evaluation of all the circumstances, including whether the original transaction was a sale or loan; the availability of a deficiency judgment; the repayment terms; the interest rate compared to prevailing rates; the original, pretaking, and posttaking ratios of security to debt; the size of the debtor's equity, absolutely and as compared to the loan; the debtor's payment record; the remaining life of the loan; the effect of the partial taking on the remainder of the property, taxes, and assessments; whether the loan is or has been in default or is likely to be in the future; and the marketability and value of the security. The court indicated that this was a partial list of factors.

Condemnation awards receive federal income tax treatment similar to that given to insurance awards under IRC §1033. See §7.27.

§7.40   2. Damages Awards

Despite ambiguous language, clause B1 of the title company form deed of trust (see §7.38, App B) also appears to include damages recovered from nonpublic tortfeasors by the trustor. See *United States Fin. v Sullivan* (1974) 37 CA3d 5, 112 CR 18. The clause does not, however, cover an award received by the trustor, as purchaser, from the vendor for fraud in conjunction with the sale. *American Sav. & Loan Ass'n v Leeds* (1968) 68 C2d 611, 68 CR 453. The beneficiary may, of course, have direct rights of action against such third persons, and nothing in the clause interferes with those rights. See §7.26.

III. OTHER ISSUES UNDER COVENANTS OF DEED OF TRUST

§7.41   A. Reconveyance

Clause B4 of the title company form deed of trust (see App B) provides:

4. Upon written request of Beneficiary stating that all sums secured hereby have been paid, and upon surrender of this Deed of Trust and said note to Trustee for cancellation and retention and upon payment of its fees, Trustee shall reconvey, without warranty, the property then held hereunder. The recitals in any reconveyance executed under this Deed of Trust of any matters or facts shall be conclusive proof of the truthfulness thereof. The grantee in such reconveyance may be described as "the person or persons legally entitled thereto."

Reconveyance is extensively regulated by statute. Civil Code §2941(b) requires that the beneficiary instruct the trustee to reconvey after satisfaction of the debt, and further requires that the trustee execute and record a full reconveyance within 21 days after receipt of the beneficiary's request and specified documents. Failure of either beneficiary or trustee to comply subjects the violator to liability for actual and penal damages. CC §2941(d); see *Pintor v Ong* (1989) 211 CA3d 837, 259 CR 577. Furthermore, CC §2941.5 makes willful violation of CC §2941 a misdemeanor. Amendments to CC §2941, effective July 1, 1989, provide a procedure for a title company to prepare and record a release of the obligation if a reconveyance has not been executed and recorded within 75 days of satisfaction. CC §2941(b)(3). See also CC §§2939, 2939.5, and 2940, concerning discharge of a mortgage, and CC §2941.7, which provides a procedure for obtaining a release of the lien of the deed of trust when a request for reconveyance cannot be satisfied. The trustee has the power to demand, before executing a reconveyance, that the beneficiary provide a lost instrument indemnity bond when the original papers cannot be produced. *Huckell v Matranga* (1979) 99 CA3d 471, 160 CR 177.

Civil Code §2941(b)(1)(C) requires that the note and deed of trust be returned to the trustor or the trustor's heirs, successors, or assignees, on written request, after reconveyance. Violation of CC §2941 is a misdemeanor. CC §2941.5. Clause B4 (see above) provides otherwise, however, and the practice of title companies and many institutional lenders, when acting as trustees, is to retain both the note and deed of trust even after the loan has been fully paid. Whether the clause can override the requirements of CC §2941 and justify retention of these documents is unknown.

The provision making recitals in the reconveyance instrument conclusive may have the effect of estopping the trustor, or any other party to the instrument, from denying their truthfulness. See §§6.39 and 7.42 for discussion of the effect of recitals in a trustee's deed given to a foreclosure purchaser. A forged deed of reconveyance is void and does not extinguish the lien or priority of the deed of trust, even against a subsequent bona fide purchaser or encumbrancer. *Wutzke v Bill Reid Painting Serv.* (1984) 151 CA3d 36, 198 CR 418.

§7.42   B. Default

Clause B6 of the title company form deed of trust (see App B) provides:

6. Upon default by Trustor in payment of any indebtedness secured hereby or in performance of any agreement hereunder,

all sums secured hereby shall immediately become due and payable at the option of the Beneficiary. In the event of default, Beneficiary may employ counsel to enforce payment of the obligations secured hereby, and shall execute or cause the Trustee to execute a written notice of such default and of his election to cause to be sold the herein described property to satisfy the obligations hereof, and shall cause such notice to be recorded in the office of the Recorder of each county wherein said real property or some part thereof is situated.

Prior to publication of the notice of sale, Beneficiary shall deliver to Trustee this Deed of Trust and the Note or other evidence of indebtedness which is secured hereby, together with a written request for the Trustee to proceed with a sale of the property described herein, pursuant to the provisions of law and this Deed of Trust.

Notice of sale having been given as then required by law, and not less than the time then required by law having elapsed after recordation of such notice of default, Trustee, without demand on Trustor, shall sell said property at the time and place fixed by it in said notice of sale, either as a whole or in separate parcels and in such order as it may determine, at public auction to the highest bidder for cash in lawful money of the United States, payable at time of sale. Trustee may postpone sale of all or any portion of said property by public announcement at such time and place of sale, and from time to time thereafter may postpone such sale by public announcement at the time and place fixed by the preceding postponement. Trustee shall deliver to the purchaser its deed conveying the property so sold, but without any covenant or warranty, express or implied. The recitals in such deed of any matters or facts shall be conclusive proof of the truthfulness thereof. Any person, including Trustor, Trustee, or Beneficiary, may purchase at such sale.

After deducting all costs, fees, and expenses of Trustee and of this Trust, including cost of evidence of title and reasonable counsel fees in connection with sale, Trustee shall apply the proceeds of sale to payment of all sums expended under the terms hereof, not then repaid, with accrued interest at 7 percent per annum; all other sums then secured hereby; and the remainder, if any, to the person or persons legally entitled thereto.

This clause covers, in general, the power-of-sale provisions. Power-of-sale procedures are regulated by statute (CC §§2924–2924h) and are discussed in chap 2.

Clause B6 first provides that the beneficiary may accelerate the installment obligations on the trustor's default. See §7.2. It then provides that the beneficiary or the trustee will record a notice of default. See §2.12. The second paragraph requires that the beneficiary deliver all documents to the trustee together with an appropriate demand that the trustee proceed under the power of sale. This provision is obviously for the benefit of the trustee, as well as the trustor, and helps prevent improper foreclosure sales. The third paragraph provides for the trustee to conduct a foreclosure sale of the property and issue a trustee's deed to the high bidder. See §§2.23, 2.26. Finally, the clause covers disposition of the sale proceeds. See §2.29.

Both CC §2924 and clause B6 contain provisions concerning the conclusiveness of the recitals in the trustee's deed. Under CC §2924, recitals concerning the giving of proper notice are made conclusive in favor of any bona fide purchaser. The provision in clause B6 is much broader; it attempts to make all recitals in the trustee's deed conclusive, without regard to whether the party attempting to take advantage of the recitals is a bona fide purchaser. Although the broader provision of clause B6 would not be binding against those (*e.g.,* junior lienholders) who did not join in the deed of trust, the trustor might be estopped by this clause from denying the truthfulness of the deed recitals even concerning matters not within the scope of CC §2924. See *Mersfelder v Spring* (1903) 139 C 593, 73 P 452. But see *Garfinkle v Superior Court* (1978) 21 C3d 268, 146 CR 208. See also §6.39 for discussion of the conclusiveness of trustee's deed recitals.

Although most standard title company deed of trust forms, including the one reprinted in App B, impose no notice requirements other than those prescribed by the Civil Code, the default provisions of some deeds of trust contain additional notice requirements. If such requirements appear in a deed of trust, they must be complied with in addition to the Civil Code notice requirements. Under CC §2924e, a junior lienor of residential real property, or a junior lienor whose lien does not exceed $300,000, may request notice of any delinquency of four months or more on the senior lien, even if no notice of default has been recorded.

The standard title company default clause, such as the one in this section, is not adequate for use with a wraparound or all-inclusive deed of trust. On wraparound instruments, see §§8.31–8.33. Wraparound instruments involve special foreclosure problems concerning whether the bid must include the amount of the senior debt and whether the sale under the wraparound deed of trust is subject to the senior loan or whether the senior loan will be paid out of the sale proceeds.

An attorney representing a wraparound lender should contact the title company or other entity to be named as trustee before the deed of trust is executed. The trustee may require that a wraparound deed of trust contain special provisions relating to the foreclosure sale. A typical provision follows:

Irrespective of any provision of this deed of trust [the all-inclusive deed of trust] to the contrary, any demand for sale delivered to the trustee for the foreclosure of this deed of trust shall be reduced by such unpaid balance, if any, of principal, interest, and charges existing on [the existing deed of trust]. Satisfactory evidence of such unpaid balance must be submitted to the trustee before sale.

C. Successors and Assigns

§7.43　1. Rights Under Deed of Trust

Clause B7 of the title company form deed of trust (see App B) provides:

7. This Deed of Trust applies to, inures to the benefit of, and binds all parties hereto, their heirs, legatees, devisees, administrators, executors, successors, and assigns. The term Beneficiary shall mean the holder and owner of the note secured hereby; or, if the note has been pledged, the pledgee thereof. In this Deed of Trust, whenever the context so requires, the masculine gender includes the feminine and/or neuter, and the singular number includes the plural.

Even without this clause, a successor in interest to the trustor takes subject to the deed of trust and must keep the secured note from default or lose the property by foreclosure. *Rodgers v Peckham* (1898) 120 C 238, 52 P 483. An assignee must be mentioned specifically only in order for a covenant for the addition of something new to real property, or for the benefit of some part of the property not then in existence, to run with the land. Civil Code §1464 codifies this rule, which is known as the "rule of *Spencer's* case."

The burdens imposed on the trustor by the deed of trust do not appear to impose any personal liability on nonassuming grantees (see *Cornelison v Kornbluth* (1975) 15 C3d 590, 125 CR 557), but they nevertheless remain as conditions of the deed of trust that continue to burden the land. Thus, foreclosure remains a deterrent to noncompliance with any of the terms of the deed of trust, not just a deterrent to nonpayment of the debt. See §4.41.

The benefits of the deed of trust run to the trustor's successors. Thus, successors may be able to enforce subordination or release provisions and can insist on a deed of reconveyance on full payment. *Sacramento Suburban Fruit Lands Co. v Whaley* (1920) 50 CA 125, 194 P 1054. The beneficiary cannot decline to accept full payment from a successor to the trustor, even though the successor did not make or assume the original note. See *Sacramento Suburban Fruit Lands Co. v Whaley, supra.*

Benefits and burdens also run to transferees of the note and deed of trust. The assignee of the note and deed of trust may enforce them against the debtor to the extent that the original creditor could have done so. See §1.17. Consequently, it may be more advantageous for a junior lienor to purchase the senior lienor's note than merely to pay it off. Compare *Strike v Trans-West Discount Corp.* (1979) 92 CA3d 735, 155 CR 132 (junior lienor who purchases senior deed of trust may conduct sale under power-of-sale clause), with *Snider v Basinger* (1976) 61 CA3d 819, 132 CR 637 (paying co-tenant cannot take advantage of power of sale if no assignment of deed of trust). For discussion of the *Strike* decision, see 2 CEB Real Prop L Rep 122 (Oct. 1979). An assignee of the note may have even greater rights than the original payee to the degree that the assignee qualifies as holder in due course. See Com C §§3104, 3302, 3305; §§1.18–1.19. Conversely, the transferee of the note and deed of trust is also bound by it and must therefore honor any provisions for subordination, release, or full reconveyance when the conditions have been met.

§7.44   2. Perfecting the Transfer

Assignments of a mortgage or deed of trust can be recorded and operate as constructive notice from the time of recordation. CC §2934.

Recording an assignment of a deed of trust does not, however, constitute notice to the debtor, and payments that the debtor makes to the original beneficiary who still holds the note are protected until the debtor receives actual notice of the assignment. CC §2935. Furthermore, recording an assignment of the mortgage does not protect a subsequent transferee against a prior transferee who actually holds the note, because considerations of commercial convenience have caused free transferability of the note to prevail over the recording statutes. See Com C §3304; §§1.18–1.19. Civil Code §2937 requires that the mortgagee or beneficiary of an instrument secured by single-family residential real property notify the borrower whenever it transfers the servicing of the indebtedness, and the borrower is not obligated to make payments to the new servicing agent until the notice is given.

If the transferor of the note and deed of trust files for bankruptcy, the transferee may be reduced to the status of a general creditor unless the transfer was perfected. Taking possession of the documents is the only sure way of perfecting a transfer; merely recording the assignment is insufficient. See Com C §9304(1); *In re Staff Mortgage & Inv. Corp.* (Greiner v Wilke) (9th Cir 1980) 625 F2d 281; *In re Bruce Farley Corp.* (Starr v Bruce Farley Corp.) (9th Cir 1980) 612 F2d 1197. But see *In re Golden Plan* (Bear v Coben) (9th Cir 1987) 829 F2d 705. Perfection may be necessary whether the transfer was made outright or was merely intended as security. *In re Executive Growth Invs.* (Rechnitzer v Boyd) (Bankr CD Cal 1984) 40 BR 417. See also *In re Woodson Co.* (Fireman's Fund Ins. Co. v Grover) (9th Cir 1987) 813 F2d 266 (investors in bankrupt had loaned money to it, as opposed to buying notes from it).

Outside of bankruptcy, the perfection requirement is occasionally ignored because of other equitable considerations. See *Domarad v Fisher & Burke, Inc.* (1969) 270 CA2d 543, 76 CR 529 (estoppel in favor of public; see §1.17).

Chapter 8: **Multiple Security, Parties, and Obligations**

8

Multiple Security, Parties, and Obligations

§8.1   I. INTRODUCTION

The model for discussion in the other chapters of this book is a single creditor, holding a single deed of trust, on a single parcel, securing a single note, and executed by a single debtor. This chapter discusses the special collection problems that are generated when any of these factors is multiplied.

A creditor who takes multiple security in the form of an additional deed of trust on other property, to afford further security for a single debt, does not automatically improve its position by doing so. Mishandling some of the security can jeopardize the creditor's ability to reach the rest of it or to recover on the debt itself. See §8.2. Multiple security does not require multiple-security instruments; the provisions of the standard deed of trust concerning insurance proceeds and rents and profits confer rights on the beneficiary to other assets. See §§8.3–8.8. When the additional security consists of the assets or personal liability of a third person, such as a guarantor, endorser, or subsequent owner of the property, the antideficiency rights of the third person may complicate collection still further. See §§8.9–8.27.

When the situation is reversed and one deed of trust secures multiple notes, different problems arise. The rules that apply when one creditor holds several notes are discussed in §§8.28–8.29. The problems encountered when different parties hold the notes are discussed in §8.30. Wraparound notes present a special type of multiple-note situation in which one or more notes are included within another note. See §§8.31–8.33. Future advance and dragnet clauses present yet another multiple-obligation situation, in which otherwise unrelated debts are brought under the security agreement, frequently with unintended consequences for the parties. See §§8.34–8.48. Finally, subordination agreements involve rearrangement of the respective priorities between persons holding different notes secured by the same real property. See §§8.49–8.52. Release and partial release clauses are also covered in connection with the discussion of subordination.

§8.2 II. MULTIPLE SECURITY

For purposes of the discussion in §§8.3–8.8, the term "multiple security" refers to the most commonly encountered situation, *i.e.,* more than one security instrument, referring to more than one asset but securing a single note. Possible variations include multiple assets within a single-security instrument or multiple-security instruments referring to a single asset. When multiple-security instruments each secure a separate note, no multiple-security problem is presented, although there may be multiple-note problems (see §§8.28–8.31).

A creditor whose note is secured by two deeds of trust rather than one is no better off with respect to application of the security-first aspect of the one-action rule (CCP §726; see §4.4), *i.e.,* the creditor is still prohibited from suing the debtor on the note without first foreclosing on the security. As with the singly-secured creditor, the multiply-secured creditor may elect judicial or nonjudicial foreclosure, although the multiplicity makes the election more complicated. See §§8.3–8.6. The creditor's choice is further complicated if the multiple security is "mixed," *i.e.,* consists of both real and personal property. See §8.7.

§8.3 A. Judicial Foreclosure

A creditor seeking judicial foreclosure must include all the real property security for the note in one action. Omitting any part of the security entitles the debtor either to insist on its inclusion (as an affirmative defense) or thereafter to treat the omitted property as free of the lien (as a sanction defense). *Walker v Community Bank* (1974) 10 C3d 729, 734, 111 CR 897, 900. In no event may the beneficiary file two separate foreclosure actions when multiple real property security covers a single obligation. *Stockton Sav. & Loan Soc'y v Harrold* (1900) 127 C 612, 60 P 165. Assertion of the affirmative defense forces the creditor to include the balance of the security in the foreclosure action, thus eliminating most of the problems created by the multiple security. The discussion that follows assumes that the debtor has not asserted the one-action rule as an affirmative defense.

The sanction defense operates not only to bar subsequent judicial foreclosure on the omitted security but also to prohibit a trustee's sale. Although no "action" is involved when the second sale is nonjudicial, a private sale is nonetheless outlawed if there has formerly been a judicial foreclosure. Thus, the effect of the sanction defense is to eliminate entirely the lien on all omitted security. *Walker v Community Bank, supra.*

Despite the sanction defense, the beneficiary probably may obtain a deficiency judgment following a judicial foreclosure even if some of the security was omitted from the action and sale. *United Cal. Bank v Tijerina* (1972) 25 CA3d 963, 102 CR 234; see *Walker v Community Bank* (1974) 10 C3d 729, 741 n6, 111 CR 897, 905 n6. Earlier decisions had leaned to the contrary on the ground that a deficiency judgment was proper only if *all* the security had been exhausted by the sale. *Hall v Arnott* (1889) 80 C 348, 22 P 200; *Bull v Coe* (1888) 77 C 54, 18 P 808. But see *Mascarel v Raffour* (1876) 51 C 242. In later decisions, however, the courts held that a trustor who permits the beneficiary to omit some of the security is subject to a deficiency judgment measured according to the property actually sold. *Walker v Community Bank, supra; United Cal. Bank v Tijerina, supra.* This situation is analogous to that in which a trustor who, having permitted the beneficiary to sue directly on the note (omitting all the security), suffers a personal judgment as a result. See *Salter v Ulrich* (1943) 22 C2d 263, 138 P2d 7. The omitted property is freed from the lien, but its omission does not preclude a deficiency judgment. *Walker v Community Bank, supra.* If part of the security is omitted because it has become worthless (*e.g.*, it was taken at a senior foreclosure), the beneficiary may ignore it entirely and seek a deficiency judgment following sale of the remaining security. *Investcal Realty Corp. v Edgar H. Mueller Constr. Co.* (1966) 247 CA2d 190, 55 CR 475; see *Dickey v Williams* (1966) 240 CA2d 270, 49 CR 529. See also §§4.4, 4.7.

If part of the security is omitted because the beneficiary previously released it from the lien (as opposed to simply omitting the security from the action), the trustor must be given credit for its value in the foreclosure action. *Woodward v Brown* (1897) 119 C 283, 51 P 2. This holding is somewhat inconsistent with the rule that a beneficiary may not unilaterally divest itself of its security before foreclosure (see §4.7), and is certainly more helpful to the beneficiary than a rule that the beneficiary is completely barred from a deficiency judgment because of the release.

§8.4   B. Nonjudicial Foreclosure (CCP §§726, 580d)

The principles discussed in §8.3 have not been applied with strict consistency to cases in which the first foreclosure sale is extrajudicial rather than judicial. The doctrine of *Walker v Community Bank* (1974) 10 C3d 729, 111 CR 897 (that security omitted from an initial judicial foreclosure cannot thereafter be sold, even under a power of sale; see §8.3), presupposes that the out-of-court sale is close enough to an "action" to come under the one-action rule. CCP §726. Consequently, when a trustee's sale comes first, one might expect the one-action rule to bar subsequent sales of any omitted security. The stated policy against multiplicity that underlies CCP §726 should apply to trustees' sales as well as to other judicial sales. Nevertheless, the courts take it for granted that a trustee's sale conducted first is not an action within the scope of CCP §726 and permit successive piecemeal extrajudicial foreclosure sales in multiple-security cases. *Hatch v Security-First Nat'l Bank* (1942) 19 C2d 254, 120 P2d 869.

Code of Civil Procedure §580d prohibits a deficiency judgment after a nonjudicial foreclosure sale (see §§4.14–4.16), but courts have held that this section does not prohibit the multiply-secured creditor from holding a second, separate foreclosure sale on security omitted from the first sale, because pursuit of additional security is not considered to be pursuit of a deficiency judgment. *Freedland v Greco* (1955) 45 C2d 462, 289 P2d 463. Thus, a bank holding one deed of trust on the debtor's city property and another deed of trust on country property (both securing the same note) may conduct an extrajudicial sale on the city property and, thereafter, a second sale on the country property (as long as part of the debt remains unsatisfied after the first sale). The second sale may be judicial or nonjudicial, because nothing in CCP §580d governs this choice. A deficiency judgment will not be permitted following the second sale, however, even if it is a judicial sale, because of the §580d sanction following the first sale. *Freedland v Greco, supra.* Thus, a first private sale permits further sales but destroys any chance of a deficiency judgment; there is no advantage in making the second sale judicial.

When there is only one deed of trust covering separate parcels, a trustee's sale should include all the real property security, because the courts will probably deny the creditor the right to conduct more than one extrajudicial sale (and incur more than one set of trustees' fees and costs) under the same deed of trust. See *Stockton Sav. & Loan Soc'y v Harrold* (1900) 127 C 612, 60 P 165.

§8.5   C. Fair-Value Limitations (CCP §580a)

In *Hatch v Security-First Nat' l Bank* (1942) 19 C2d 254, 120 P2d 869, the supreme court held that the fair-value provisions of CCP §580a do not apply to a creditor that disposes of its multiple security through piecemeal extrajudicial sales. The debtor's argument that there should be no second sale until the fair value of the property sold at the first sale has been established was rejected on the grounds (1) that the pursuit of additional security is not the same as pursuit of a deficiency judgment and (2) that the legislature did not intend to protect property that is only secondarily liable for the debt.

It is difficult, however, to find a significant difference between selling additional security and recovering a deficiency judgment, which is then satisfied by levy and sale of the debtor's other assets, much like a foreclosure sale of additional security. The statement that the other property is only "secondarily liable" seems irrelevant in light of the fact that it is owned by the same debtor who is primarily liable for the debt. It is not the property but its owner who suffers when property is sold for less than its fair value. Protection of additional security by fair-value standards would also justify the continued existence of CCP §580a, which would apply to such situations (see §§4.21, 4.33). In the absence of fair-value protection, a debtor who posts multiple security runs the risk that all of it may be sold to satisfy the obligation, even though the value of any one item of security might be more than sufficient to satisfy the debt.

Because CCP §580d already prohibits a personal judgment if the first sale is extrajudicial, there is no reason to apply a fair-value test following the final sale. A deficiency judgment, as such, would not be available in any event, regardless of whether the final sale was conducted after a judicial foreclosure or under a power of sale. See §8.4.

If the first foreclosure sale is judicial, the one-action rule prohibits the creditor from taking any further action to foreclose (see §8.3), but the creditor in effect waives the omitted security and receives a true deficiency judgment for the unsatisfied portion of the debt after sale of the included security. *Walker v Community Bank* (1974) 10 C3d 729, 111 CR 897. In such a situation, the fair-value provisions of CCP §726 apply to the security sold. The value of the omitted security is probably irrelevant to the fair-value determination. See *United Cal. Bank v Tijerina* (1972) 25 CA3d 963, 102 CR 234.

§8.6   D. Purchase-Money Restrictions (CCP §580b)

When the seller divides the unpaid purchase price into two distinct notes, one secured by a deed of trust on the real property sold and the other secured by a deed of trust on other real property of the buyer, only the first note secures purchase-money and comes under the provisions of CCP §580b. The second is a nonpurchase-money note and is thus exempt from §580b. *Roseleaf Corp. v Chierighino* (1963) 59 C2d 35, 27 CR 873; see §4.34. The two notes together must not exceed the basic debt. *Freedland v Greco* (1955) 45 C2d 462, 289 P2d 463. Thus, a money judgment is possible in such cases, either as a deficiency judgment under the other security exception to CCP §580b or as a direct judgment for payment of an unsecured note.

The result is quite different, however, when the purchase price is represented by a single note secured by several deeds of trust, some of which may be on property other than that purchased. The other security exception (see *Roseleaf Corp. v Chierighino, supra*) no longer applies because the single note cannot be divided into parts separately secured by purchase-money and nonpurchase-money security. See *Loretz v Cal-Coast Dev. Corp.* (1967) 249 CA2d 176, 57 CR 188. Each deed of trust secures the entire note, *i.e.*, all the proceeds of a foreclosure sale would be applied to the note, and none would be treated as surplus as long as there was a balance due on the note. Thus, there is no way for a creditor to obtain a money judgment in this situation. A unified judicial foreclosure of both deeds of trust would bar a deficiency judgment under CCP §580b, and a separate trustee's sale of the other security would bar a deficiency judgment under CCP §580d. (The same would be true of any attempt by the creditor to split the existing single note into secured and unsecured fractions by stipulating in the loan agreement to the limited value of the security. See *Loretz v Cal-Coast Dev. Corp., supra.*) To obtain a CCP §580b advantage from multiple security, the creditor must divide the price into separate notes and secure them separately (which will defeat any attempt to profit from underbidding at piecemeal trustees' sales because the situation no longer involves true multiple security; see §8.2).

§8.7   E. Combined Real and Personal Property Security

Personal property security is not subject to antideficiency rules. Com C §§9501, 9504; *KMAP, Inc. v Town & Country Broadcasters* (1975) 49 CA3d 544, 122 CR 420; *Bank of Cal. v Leone* (1974) 37 CA3d 444, 112 CR 394. A creditor who holds only personal property security may first sue on the note without disposing of the collateral, or may obtain a deficiency judgment after a sale of the collateral, even if the sale is extrajudicial. There is no right of redemption after sale of the collateral, and there is no fair-value limitation on any subsequent deficiency judgment. The creditor may also bring a separate action to obtain possession of the personal property before exercising one of the foregoing remedies regarding that security. When multiple personal property security is involved, these various procedures may be combined in almost any order. Com C §9501.

When combined real and personal property security is involved, the creditor is subject to Com C §9501(4). This section (enacted in its present form in 1985) gives the creditor the option of treating the personal property as real property and selling all the security at a "unified foreclosure" sale (judicial or nonjudicial), similar to that outlined in *Walker v Community Bank* (1974) 10 C3d 729, 111 CR 897 (which predates the current version of Com C §9501(4)). Alternatively, the creditor may conduct "separate foreclosure" sales of the real and personal property, subjecting the real property to the real property foreclosure rules and the personal property to the rules of Com C §9501. (Section 9501(4) also provides for a third "combination foreclosure" option, under which some of each class of security may be included in a unified foreclosure and some in separate foreclosures.)

When a unified foreclosure is undertaken, the personal property is treated as real property and is therefore subject to the debtor's right of reinstatement (CC §2924c; see §2.17), which is not otherwise the case under the Commercial Code. When a unified foreclosure is carried out by judicial sale, and the creditor then seeks a deficiency judgment, this recharacterization of the personal property security may lead to its being subjected to a fair-value requirement (see §8.5).

When separate foreclosure sales are conducted, and the real property is sold at a trustee's sale, a deficiency is barred even though one would otherwise be permitted under the Commercial Code after a sale of the personal property. Com C §9501(4)(c)(iv). If the real property is sold at a judicial sale, a deficiency judgment might be permitted because omission of the personal property security is tolerated in such a case and no rule of real or personal property security prohibits a deficiency. The real property security would be subject to a fair-value standard, but the personal property security would not, because this is not a unified foreclosure.

For analysis of these and other variations, see Hirsch, Arnold, Rabin, & Sigman, *The UCC Mixed Collateral Statute—Has Paradise Really Been Lost?*, 36 UCLA L Rev 1 (1988); Hetland & Hansen, *The "Mixed Collateral" Amendments to California's Commercial Code—Covert Repeal of California's Real Property Foreclosure and Antideficiency Provisions or Exercise in Futility?*, 75 Calif L Rev 185 (1987); and Bernhardt, *The Mixed Multiple Collateral Muddle,* 9 CEB Real Prop L Rep 101 (July 1986).

§8.8   F. Insurance and Rents as Multiple Security

If the deed of trust gives the beneficiary recourse to other assets, these also constitute multiple security. Fire insurance proceeds are security if the insurance was required by the deed of trust. *Redingler v Imperial Sav. & Loan Ass'n* (1975) 47 CA3d 48, 120 CR 575. On the beneficiary's right to insurance proceeds apart from a foreclosure, see §§7.26–7.28. Rents held by a receiver appointed under a rents-and-profits clause are also security. See §5.11. On the right to rents before foreclosure, see §§5.2–5.32. The discussion in this section is limited to the beneficiary's right to collect insurance proceeds or rents after foreclosure. The beneficiary's right to utilize the proceeds before foreclosure is a separate issue, subject to special good-faith constraints (see §7.27) and also possible application of the one-action rule (CCP §726).

If the beneficiary has foreclosed, it may later recover insurance proceeds paid on an earlier loss because these are treated as additional security, similar to a deed of trust on other property (see §8.2). *Redingler v Imperial Sav. & Loan Ass' n, supra.* The *Redingler* opinion did not clarify whether the sale was conducted after a judicial foreclosure or under a power of sale, but the characterization should have been the latter. A prior trustee's sale does not bar subsequent steps to collect on additional security. *Freedland v Greco* (1955) 45 C2d 462, 289 P2d 463; *Hatch v Security-First Nat' l Bank* (1942) 19 C2d 254, 120 P2d 869; see §8.4. If the first foreclosure were judicial, omission of the insurance policy from the action could be a ground for releasing it from the beneficiary's claim. *Walker v Community Bank* (1974) 10 C3d 729, 111 CR 897; see §8.3.

Rents usually become additional security for the beneficiary only after they have been collected by a receiver appointed under the rents-and-profits clause of the deed of trust. A turnover of the rents in accordance with a final judgment in the receivership action could be treated as exhausting the one-action standard of CCP §726, thus barring a subsequent trustee's sale (see §5.14). See *Walker v Community Bank, supra.* Consequently, the beneficiary should have the trustee's sale conducted before the receivership results in a final judgment.

The beneficiary must bid less than the amount of the debt to obtain insurance proceeds or rents after foreclosure. See *Cornelison v Kornbluth* (1975) 15 C3d 590, 125 CR 557; *Armsey v Channel Assoc.* (1986) 184 CA3d 833, 229 CR 509. A full credit-bid terminates the beneficiary's entitlement to any additional security, even if it later discovers that the property was damaged before foreclosure. *Universal Mortgage Co. v Prudential Ins. Co.* (9th Cir 1986) 799 F2d 458. A creditor wishing to receive the rents collected or any insurance proceeds available will usually underbid by an amount equal to the rents or proceeds. See chap 5. See also Johnson & Smith, *The Case Against the Full Value Bid,* 12 CEB Real Prop L Rep 141 (July 1989).

§8.9 III. MULTIPLE PARTIES

The sections that follow discuss the liability and defenses of persons other than the original trustor or borrower who may be liable for payment of the note or for a deficiency judgment following foreclosure.

These other potential parties include guarantors (see §§8.10–8.18), endorsers (see §8.19), and subsequent owners of the security (see §§8.20–8.27). Their potential liability, their indemnification rights, and the role of the antideficiency rules in resolving these issues are discussed in §§8.10–8.27.

There may be more than one borrower, *e.g.,* when the note and deed of trust are executed by spouses who own the property in some form of joint ownership. Such transactions do not present special multiplicity problems; collection procedures and the antideficiency rules apply no differently than if there were only one borrower. The same is true when there are two makers of the note, although only one of them is trustor under the deed of trust; the other maker is protected by CCP §726 just as if he or she were also a trustor. See *Pacific Valley Bank v Schwenke* (1987) 189 CA3d 134, 234 CR 298. When there are two trustors, but only one maker of the note, foreclosure procedures are unchanged; the maker alone is subject to personal liability, and the trustor may be entitled to indemnification from the maker for loss of the security on foreclosure, if their arrangement was an accommodation agreement. See *Caito v United Cal. Bank* (1978) 20 C3d 694, 144 CR 751.

§8.10   A. Guarantors

A beneficiary may have its note guaranteed by a third party while also having it secured by a deed of trust on the trustor's property. In that case, the creditor has potential claims against the property (under the deed of trust), against the trustor (on the note), and against the guarantor (on the guaranty agreement). The beneficiary may sue the guarantor directly on the guaranty before taking any other action, may sue the guarantor for a deficiency after foreclosing on the security, or may even sue on the guaranty after first suing the trustor on the note. This scenario, however, omits the impact of the antideficiency rules on the creditor's options, discussed in §§8.11–8.18. A guarantor who is forced to satisfy the beneficiary's claim has reimbursement rights against both the trustor and the security, but those rights are also subject to the antideficiency rules. In some cases, the antideficiency rules give the guarantor a defense against the beneficiary solely because the trustor has a potential antideficiency defense against the guarantor (see §8.18).

Guarantors are sometimes referred to as "additional security" (*Gott-schalk v Draper Cos*. (1972) 23 CA3d 828, 100 CR 434; *Heckes v Sapp* (1964) 229 CA2d 549,40 CR 485), but this characterization ignores the many statutory provisions that apply specifically to guarantors. Before 1939, California's many code sections covering sureties did not apply to guarantors, who therefore had no greater rights than those accorded to any other secondary security furnished by the trustor. Legislative abolition of the guarantor-surety distinction, however, and the inclusion of guarantors under protection for sureties (CC §2787) require significantly different treatment for guarantors than for other types of security. As discussed in §§8.11–8.18, the guarantor's purse is an asset of a different nature from the trustor's real property or even the trustor's purse. *Union Bank v Gradsky* (1968) 265 CA2d 40, 71 CR 64. For discussion of guarantors, see 1 California Real Property Financing, chap 7 (Cal CEB 1988).

For federal income tax purposes, a guarantor who is required to repay the debt and is unable to recover from the trustor may be able to deduct the payment as a bad debt under IRC §166. If the guaranty was made in the course of business, it is treated as a worthless business debt (Reg §1.166–9(a)); if the transaction was for profit, although not in the course of trade or business, it is a nonbusiness bad debt (Reg §1.166–9(b)). In either case, the guarantor must have received reasonable consideration for the guaranty. Reg §1.166–9(e). When the guarantor has subrogation rights against the debtor, the bad-debt deduction is not allowed until those rights become totally worthless. Reg §1.166–9(e).

§8.11   1. One-Action Rule

The one-action rule is said to be for the benefit only of the principal debtor and therefore to be inapplicable to parties who are secondarily liable, such as guarantors or sureties. *Murphy v Hellman Commercial Trust & Sav. Bank* (1919) 43 CA 579, 185 P 485. It has also been asserted that a guarantor is outside the one-action rule because the guaranty agreement is separate and distinct from the deed of trust (see, *e.g., Adams v Wallace* (1897) 119 C 67, 51 P 14), but the statutory assimilation of guarantors and sureties makes that proposition no longer tenable. CC §2787; see *American Guar. Corp. v Stoody* (1964) 230 CA2d 390, 41 CR 69. For discussion, see 1 California Real Property Financing §7.2 (Cal CEB 1988).

A different interpretation of CCP §726 might have been expected in light of CC §2809, which provides that a guarantor's obligations cannot be more burdensome than those of the principal, but the courts have ruled that §2809 does not prohibit the beneficiary from suing the guarantor without first foreclosing under the deed of trust, even though the beneficiary could not do so against the trustor (see §4.4). The courts have held that both guarantor and principal are similarly liable for the entire debt, and the fact that the trustor is liable only after a foreclosure sale does not mean that the trustor's burden is lighter than that of the guarantor, who is liable before and after such a sale. *Everts v Matteson* (1942) 21 C2d 437, 132 P2d 476; *Loeb v Christie* (1936) 6 C2d 416, 57 P2d 1303. Protection comparable to the one-action rule may be found in CC §2845, which entitles the guarantor to insist that the security be exhausted first when the creditor seeks relief against the guarantor. *United Cal. Bank v Maltzman* (1974) 44 CA3d 41, 118 CR 299; *Moffett v Miller* (1953) 119 CA2d 712, 260 P2d 215. This right may be waived, however, and most printed guaranty forms include a waiver. *Engelman v Bookasta* (1968) 264 CA2d 915, 71 CR 120; *American Guar. Corp. v Stoody, supra*. Civil Code §2845 is thus markedly different from CCP §726 in this respect. See §4.47.

When the guarantor has waived CC §2845 protection and the creditor proceeds against the guarantor first, the action is one to compel payment of the debt according to the guaranty and does not involve the real property security. Once the guarantor has paid, he or she becomes subrogated to the security and may employ it against the trustor to the same extent as could the original beneficiary. The guarantor is no different from other subsequent holders of the secured note and may take any action against the trustor that is not prohibited by the one-action or antideficiency rules. *Union Bank v Gradsky* (1968) 265 CA2d 40, 71 CR 64. (On rights of transferees of the mortgage paper, see §1.18.) A creditor who first forecloses judicially, however, must include the guarantor in that action or waive any rights against the guarantor. See §8.14.

It is unclear whether the trustor has a one-action defense against a beneficiary who has obtained an unsatisfied judgment against the guarantor and then sues the trustor. The beneficiary has had its one action, and its failure to include all its security in that one action (*i.e.*, its failure also to foreclose on the real property) may release the unincluded property (and persons) from further liability. See *Walker v Community Bank*

(1974) 10 C3d 729, 111 CR 897. On the other hand, the trustor has not been made a party to any previous action, and nothing in CCP §726 seems intended to insulate the trustor from being named in a lawsuit merely because there was a prior lawsuit between other parties over the same instrument. See §8.17 concerning a one-action rule defense by the trustor against the guarantor.

§8.12 2. Deficiency Judgment Following Foreclosure

The situation is more complicated when the lender seeks relief from the guarantor after it has foreclosed on the security. The issue then is the beneficiary's right to a deficiency judgment against the guarantor and depends on the nature of both the foreclosure action and the security. See §§8.13–8.16. For discussion of guarantors and antideficiency rules, see 1 California Real Property Financing §§7.3–7.6 (Cal CEB 1988).

§8.13 a. Deficiency Judgment Following Trustee's Sale

A lender who first disposes of nonpurchase-money security through its power of sale is thereafter barred from obtaining relief against the guarantor. *Union Bank v Gradsky* (1968) 265 CA2d 40, 71 CR 64. For discussion, see 1 California Real Property Financing §7.6 (Cal CEB 1988). The rationale is that the lender is estopped under CCP §580d. The beneficiary's action in conducting a trustee's sale of the encumbered property vests the trustor with immunity from a deficiency judgment. CCP §580d. The trustor's defense is good against both the beneficiary and the guarantor. If the beneficiary could still recover a deficiency judgment from the guarantor after such a sale, the guarantor would be denied the right of subrogation against the trustor solely because of the kind of sale the beneficiary chose to conduct. On the guarantor's right to recover from the trustor, see §8.17. Because the beneficiary could have averted this predicament either by foreclosing judicially or by suing the guarantor before the foreclosure, the beneficiary is the one who must suffer from its election of remedies. It is estopped because it has elected "to pursue a remedy which destroys both the security and the possibility of the surety's reimbursement from the principal debtor." *Union Bank v Gradsky* (1968) 265 CA2d 40, 46, 71

CR 64, 69. See also *Union Bank v Brummell* (1969) 269 CA2d 836, 75 CR 234. Such an estoppel operates only prospectively, *i.e.,* the estoppel does not force the beneficiary to return any security it had previously reached before it conducts a nonjudicial foreclosure sale. *Krueger v Bank of America* (1983) 145 CA3d 204, 193 CR 322.

In *Union Bank v Gradsky, supra,* the court allowed for the possibility of waiver (because all the antideficiency protections may be waived by a guarantor) but held that the conventional waiver language used in such instruments is not a waiver of this specific estoppel defense. See also *Indusco Management Corp. v Robertson* (1974) 40 CA3d 456, 114 CR 47. In *Mariners Sav. & Loan Ass'n v Neil* (1971) 22 CA3d 232, 99 CR 238, the court held that the defense had been waived. The court also indicated that the beneficiary may avoid the estoppel defense by tendering the note and deed of trust to the guarantor before selling the property on foreclosure. In *Krueger v Bank of America, supra,* however, the court held that a tender made by the beneficiary (and rejected by the guarantor) did not immunize the beneficiary from a *Gradsky* defense after the beneficiary then sold the collateral at a nonjudicial foreclosure sale.

The *Gradsky* rationale does not apply in purchase-money situations because the trustor's CCP §580b protection bars the guarantor from indemnification in any event. Thus, the lender's selection of a trustee's sale over judicial foreclosure causes no additional detriment to the guarantor. *Bauman v Castle* (1971) 15 CA3d 990, 93 CR 565. For the same reason, the *Gradsky* rule does not apply if the guarantor has already released its subrogation rights against the debtor. *Consolidated Capital Income Trust v Khaloghli* (1986) 183 CA3d 107, 227 CR 879.

§8.14 b. Deficiency Judgment Following Judicial Foreclosure

A nonpurchase-money lender who begins by first judicially foreclosing on the security should be able to recover a deficiency judgment against a guarantor who was included in the action. The one-action rule compels inclusion of the guarantor if the beneficiary seeks a deficiency judgment against the guarantor. *Titus v Woods* (1920) 45 CA 541, 188 P 68 (guarantor proper, but not necessary, party). As a precaution, the guarantor should be named regardless of the rights he or she may have waived, because the trustor has an independent right to demand a single foreclosure action against all the security, including the guarantor's. *Walker v Community Bank* (1974) 10 C3d 729, 111 CR 897; see *Union Bank v Gradsky* (1968) 265 CA2d 40, 71 CR 64; *Heckes v Sapp* (1964) 229 CA2d 549, 40 CR 485. When the guarantor and the trustor are named as defendants in the foreclosure action, there is obviously no estoppel defense available to the guarantor under the principles of *Union Bank v Gradsky, supra*; see §8.13.

It is probably also true that a creditor who underbids at its foreclosure sale becomes subject to a fair-value defense by the guarantor as well as by the trustor. On fair-value protection of the trustor, see §4.17. A deficiency judgment following the sale may be entered against the trustor, the guarantor, or both. The trustor clearly has fair-value protection, but it is unsettled whether the beneficiary can avoid complying with the fair-value rules by seeking a deficiency judgment only against the guarantor. There is no reason to believe, however, that such a scheme would work, because the logic of *Gradsky* would apply. See §8.13. Following the foreclosure sale, a deficiency judgment cannot be entered against the trustor except after a timely fair-value hearing. If the beneficiary could underbid and recover the entire difference from the guarantor, the guarantor would be left with an unrecoverable loss due solely to the beneficiary's action. Furthermore, failure to hold a fair-value hearing within three months after the sale would bar any recovery against the trustor, imposing the entire loss (not just the loss of the difference between the amount bid and the fair value) on the guarantor. This situation arises only because the beneficiary has credit-bid both less than it is owed and (possibly) less than the property is worth; thus, the consequences must fall on the beneficiary, who can credit-bid a larger amount, rather than on the guarantor, who must make a cash bid. The same result is probably mandated by CC §2809, which requires that the guarantor's burden be no more onerous than that placed on the principal. Although some early California cases appear to hold to the contrary, these results were reached before guarantors were given suretyship protection by CC §2787. See *Everts v Matteson* (1942) 21 C2d 437, 132 P2d 476.

A more difficult question is whether fair-value protections will be applied in favor of a guarantor who has waived both CCP §580d protection and the *Gradsky* estoppel defense and is being sued for a deficiency judgment following a private sale by the beneficiary. The applicable statute in this situation is CCP §580a, and the fact that the sale is nonredeemable is an argument in favor of giving the guarantor at least this much protection. Another argument is the policy of CC §2809 that the surety's obligation should be no more burdensome than the principal's. But see *Bank of Am. Nat'l Trust & Sav. Ass'n v Hunter* (1937) 8 C2d 592, 67 P2d 99. The guarantor's waiver of estoppel rights, however, constitutes an agreement that the beneficiary may completely destroy the guarantor's right to reimbursement by a trustee's sale, and thus the estoppel logic of *Gradsky* no longer fits. The entire problem would also be mooted by a specific waiver in the guaranty of fair-value protections.

c. Guarantor's Antideficiency Protection Against Purchase-Money Lender

§8.15 (1) CCP §580b as Guarantor Defense

The supreme court has not ruled on whether a guarantor is protected by CCP §580b, *i.e.*, whether a guarantor can be held liable for a deficiency judgment following a foreclosure sale of purchase-money security. Several courts of appeal have ruled that a guarantor is not protected, but their logic may not persuade the supreme court. Some courts have held that the legislature did not intend to protect guarantors. See *Katz v Haskell* (1961) 196 CA2d 144, 16 CR 453. Legislative extension of suretyship protection to guarantors (CC §2787; see §8.10), however, seems to indicate the opposite. Decisions denying protection to guarantors have also been based on the analogy between guarantors and endorsers (*Roberts v Graves* (1969) 269 CA2d 410, 75 CR 130), but this rationale overlooks some important distinctions between the two. See §8.19. It has also been claimed that the overvaluation and stabilization policies (see §§4.27–4.28) are satisfied by limiting CCP §580b protection to purchasers. See *Heckes v Sapp* (1964) 229 CA2d 549, 40 CR 485. In fact, however, a seller who demands the additional security of a guarantor over and above a security interest in the property is more, rather than less, likely to be overvaluing the property; imposing personal liability on a guarantor who receives neither the real property nor the loan proceeds is manifestly a destabilizing factor in a declining economy.

The lower courts have also ruled that the provisions of CC §§2809 and 2810 do not apply to guarantors of mortgage debts. *Heckes v Sapp, supra; Gottschalk v Draper Cos.* (1972) 23 CA3d 828, 100 CR 434.

Civil Code §§2809 and 2810 provide, respectively, that a surety's obligation should be no more burdensome than the principal's, and that a surety is not liable if the principal is not originally liable (unless the surety knowingly assumes that liability).

The decisions in *Heckes* and *Gottschalk* inform the purchase-money creditor that a deficiency judgment can be recovered if the security is inadequate as long as the judgment is against the guarantor rather than the debtor. By demanding a guarantor (or by tailoring the transaction so that the deeper pocket guarantees rather than incurs the debt), the creditor escapes application of CCP §580b. The essential principle behind §580b (that a seller must look only to the security, in accordance with the policy of *Brown v Jensen* (1953) 41 C2d 193, 259 P2d 425; see §4.34) is thus frustrated. A result more consistent with *Brown* would be that the guaranty of a purchase-money note is as worthless as its assumption by a subsequent purchaser of the property. See §§8.23–8.26 on assuming purchase-money obligations. When there is no personal obligation to assume, there is also no personal obligation to guarantee. Guarantor purchase-money protection should be an essential corollary to the rule of *Brown v Jensen, supra.* It is therefore possible that the California Supreme Court will grant §580b protection to guarantors.

§8.16   (2) Sold-Out Junior's Right To Recover From Guarantor

Because a nonpurchase-money sold-out junior is free to sue the trustor directly following the loss of the security (*Roseleaf Corp. v Chierighino* (1963) 59 C2d 35, 27 CR 873; see §4.34), the junior may also bring a similar action against the guarantor. *Lange v Aver* (1966) 241 CA2d 793, 50 CR 847 (action against endorsers). In *Heckes v Sapp* (1964) 229 CA2d 549, 40 CR 485, the court held that a sold-out purchase-money junior is similarly entitled to sue the guarantor, but this reasoning has not yet been validated by the supreme court. See §8.15.

§8.17   d. Guarantor's Relief Against Trustor

A trustor who is sued by the guarantor for reimbursement is as fully protected by the antideficiency rules as a trustor who is sued directly by the beneficiary for a deficiency judgment. *Heckes v Sapp* (1964) 229 CA2d 549, 40 CR 485.

A guarantor who was first sued by the beneficiary, and satisfied the debt without a foreclosure, is subrogated to the beneficiary's position and thus holds the security. CC §§2848–2849; *Sanders v Magill* (1937) 9 C2d 145, 70 P2d 159; *Union Bank v Gradsky* (1968) 265 CA2d 40, 71 CR 64. The guarantor may foreclose, either judicially or nonjudicially. *Union Bank v Gradsky, supra.* The trustor would have no CCP §726 defense in such a case because the former action was against the guarantor, not the trustor. If a nonjudicial sale is chosen, the guarantor is barred by CCP §580d from further recourse against the trustor. If the foreclosure is judicial, the guarantor's deficiency judgment will be limited by the fair-value provisions of CCP §726. If the guaranteed obligation was for purchase-money, the guarantor will be barred from any personal recovery by CCP §580b. The guarantor's right to reimbursement under CC §2847 is subordinated to the trustor's basic antideficiency protections. *Heckes v Sapp, supra.* If that were not so, a lender could bypass the antideficiency protections by having every debt guaranteed, and a commercial guarantor industry with recourse against borrowers would promptly appear.

§8.18   e. Alter Ego Theories

Because guarantors have less protection than trustors, it is not surprising that a lender may prefer to have its debt guaranteed as well as secured and, on occasion, to designate the borrower as a guarantor rather than a trustor. Such attempts often backfire, however, because if a court rules that the guarantor of a secured debt is the debtor in disguise, the guarantor-debtor is immediately vested with all the protections the law furnishes to trustors. *Engelman v Gordon* (1966) 242 CA2d 510, 51 CR 627. Thus, the guarantor will usually be accorded one-action protection (see *Valinda Builders v Bissner* (1964) 230 CA2d 106, 40 CR 735), CCP §580b protection in purchase-money cases (see *Roberts v Graves* (1969) 269 CA2d 410, 75 CR 130; *Valinda Builders v Bissner, supra; In re Wilton-Maxfield Management Co.* (Coast Fed. Sav. & Loan Ass'n v Crawford) (9th Cir 1941) 117 F2d 913)), and CCP §580d protection for private-sale foreclosures (see *Union Bank v Dorn* (1967) 254 CA2d 157, 61 CR 893).

A guarantor will most commonly be found to be the purchaser's alter ego when he or she is an individual behind a corporate trustor (*Valinda Builders v Bissner, supra;* see *Kincaid v Gomez* (1969) 274 CA2d

839, 79 CR 539) or a general partner of a partnership trustor (*Riddle v Lushing* (1962) 203 CA2d 831, 21 CR 902). Even in these situations, however, courts sometimes distinguish between trustor and guarantor. See *Roberts v Graves, supra; Engelman v Gordon, supra.* The surest way for the lender to invite trouble is to insist that the intended purchaser find someone else to take title so that the purchaser can become the guarantor instead. See *Union Bank v Brummell* (1969) 269 CA2d 836, 75 CR 234. See also *Mariners Sav. & Loan Ass'n v Neil* (1971) 22 CA3d 232, 99 CR 238. (Note that the alter ego theory is used in reverse in these cases: It is the defendants who claim that they are the alter egos of their own corporation, while the lender contends that they are not.)

Issues presented by intrafamilial guaranties have not been satisfactorily resolved. In *Mariners Sav. & Loan Ass'n v Neil, supra,* a husband who guaranteed a note signed by his wife and secured by a deed of trust on her separate property was denied alter ego protection despite his contention that the loan proceeds were used to satisfy "community debts." Enforcement of his guaranty made the community property liable for a deficiency, although the property would have been exempt if the husband had been the maker rather than the guarantor of the note (because of CCP §580d protection following the trustee's sale). Other peculiar results are possible under the *Mariners* logic. The community property is liable for the debts of either spouse (CC §5120.110), but the separate property of either spouse is usually not liable for the other spouse's debts (CC §5120.130). Assume that the husband owns a car as his separate property, the spouses own a boat as community property, and they now buy a house in which both will reside. Their purchase-money note falls under CCP §580b. If both sign it, the creditor cannot go beyond the house to reach either the boat or the car. If the wife alone signs the note, however, and the husband then guarantees it, he subjects his car and possibly the boat to the satisfaction of a deficiency judgment. Such results would be avoided if the courts were to treat spousal guaranties as alter ego transactions.

In *Everts v Matteson* (1942) 21 C2d 437, 132 P2d 476, the mortgaged property was sold to a purchaser who both guaranteed the mortgage and assumed it. Because an assuming grantee of mortgaged property is treated as the principal debtor (see §8.22), the guaranty was held invalid as an attempt to guarantee one's own debt. As a result, the purchaser was treated as a debtor protected by the antideficiency rules.

§8.19 B. Endorsers

Under the Commercial Code, a payee of a note who endorses it over to another becomes liable for its payment if the maker fails to pay. Com C §3414. The fact that the endorsed note is secured by real property does not change this basic rule of commercial paper. Endorsers are usually denied one-action and antideficiency protection on the ground that recourse against them is not an action for either foreclosure or a deficiency judgment. *Engelman v Gordon* (1966) 242 CA2d 510, 51 CR 627; *Stephenson v Lawn* (1957) 155 CA2d 669, 318 P2d 132; *Nuetzel v Mackie* (1927) 80 CA 768, 253 P 166. See also *Lange v Aver* (1966) 241 CA2d 793, 50 CR 847 (CCP §580a); *Katz v Haskell* (1961) 196 CA2d 144, 16 CR 453 (CCP §580b).

There is no compelling need to give an endorser the benefit of these protections because endorser liability merely amounts to refunding the price received for sale of the note (except when the note was sold at a discount). See *Brady v Reynolds* (1859) 13 C 31. An endorser is a former payee of the note who has since sold it. Calling on the endorser to satisfy a deficiency judgment requires the endorser to return the consideration received for the sale of the note. The loss occasioned by an insufficiency of the security thus falls on the transferor rather than the transferee of the security instrument because of the endorsement. (The loss can be shifted by a nonrecourse endorsement.) An endorser who is then unable to recover further against the trustor (because of the antideficiency rules) is in no worse a position than before he or she sold the note. When the endorser's position is worsened, as might occur if the holder first conducts a trustee's sale under a nonpurchase-money note, or if there is underbidding, then estoppel doctrine may apply. *Union Bank v Gradsky* (1968) 265 CA2d 40, 71 CR 64; see §8.13.

§8.20 C. Subsequent Owners of Property

A transfer of mortgaged property introduces additional parties into the picture. The new owner of the property, even when free from personal liability on the original obligation, nonetheless has an interest in how that obligation is treated because his or her interest in the property will be lost on foreclosure if the obligation is not paid. Moreover, because the appearance of a new owner does not by itself relieve the former owner of existing liability, a transfer is not merely a simple substitution of one obligor for another, but rather the addition of a second party having a concerned (financially if not legally) with paying the note. When the new owner undertakes personally to pay the original note (*i.e.,* "assumes" it), without a simultaneous release of the original debtor by the creditor, two parties become legally obligated to pay the note. The antideficiency rules qualify this rule substantially, however, as discussed in §§8.21–8.27.

§8.21   1. Transfers to Nonassuming Grantees

Real property may be transferred even though it is subject to a mortgage or deed of trust (although operation of a due-on-sale clause or similar security provision may alter this result), but the transfer does not eliminate the existence of the encumbrance on the property. Thus, the grantee takes title to the property subject to the mortgage, whether or not the deed so provides. The fact that the mortgage remains in existence means that the property may be sold on foreclosure of the mortgage if the debt is not paid, even though the property is no longer owned by the original debtor. Consequently, the new owner is a necessary party to a judicial foreclosure action (*Goodenow v Ewer* (1860) 16 C 461) and also has the right to reinstate the obligation (CC §2924c), or redeem the property from the default (CC §§2903–2905), before a foreclosure sale.

A grantee who did not assume the existing obligation when purchasing the property is not liable for a deficiency judgment after a foreclosure sale. *Treat v Craig* (1901) 135 C 91, 67 P 7. A deficiency judgment can be entered only against those liable on the basic obligation, *e.g.,* makers or guarantors of the note; a stranger to the note does not become liable merely by acquiring secured property. See *Braun v Crew* (1920) 183 C 728, 192 P 531; *Snidow v Hill* (1948) 87 CA2d 803, 197 P2d 801; *Wolfert v Guadagno* (1933) 130 CA 661, 20 P2d 360; Comment, *Assumption of Mortgage Debt by Grantee of Mortgaged Premises: Necessity for Express Promise,* 8 Calif L Rev 447 (1920).

The original owner of the property may or may not be an essential party to foreclosure proceedings. As maker of the note, he or she remains liable on it until released by the holder, and a transfer of the security to a third person is not the equivalent of a release by the holder (even if the holder has consented to the transfer under a due-on-sale clause; see §8.20). The one-action rule limits liability on the note, however, to a deficiency judgment following a judicial foreclosure sale of nonpurchase-money security; when the obligation is for purchase-money, the former owner is not personally liable on the note. The original owner may therefore be ignored when purchase-money security is involved, the foreclosure is nonjudicial, or the beneficiary does not intend to seek a deficiency judgment against the original owner. *San Diego Realty Co. v Hill* (1914) 168 C 637, 143 P 1021.

2. Transfers to Assuming Grantees

§8.22   a. Nonpurchase-Money Situations

A subsequent owner of real property can agree to become personally liable for the debt by assuming it when the property is transferred to him or her subject to a deed of trust. The beneficiary can enforce the assumption agreement whether it takes the form of a direct promise to it or of a promise made by the grantee to the grantor to assume the grantor's liability. See, *e.g., Bogart v George K. Porter Co.* (1924) 193 C 197, 223 P 959; *Birkhofer v Krumm* (1935) 4 CA2d 43, 40 P2d 553. Although the latter agreement appears to be a third party beneficiary contract (see CC §1559), the California theory under which it is enforced is premised on equitable subrogation principles: A creditor may reach any security given to the surety for performance of the obligation. CC §2854. As applied, this theory holds that on assuming the debt the grantee becomes the principal debtor, and the grantor becomes a surety; if the grantee does not pay, the beneficiary may enforce the promise of assumption made to the grantor. *Hopkins v Warner* (1895) 109 C 133, 41 P 868. The third party beneficiary explanation is rejected in California on the ground that it might entitle the beneficiary to sue the grantee without first foreclosing, in violation of the one-action rule. *Lewis v Hunt* (1933) 133 CA 520, 24 P2d 557. See also *Birkhofer v Krumm, supra.* However, the courts could have permitted the creditor to enforce an assumption agreement as a third party beneficiary, subject to the limitations of CCP §726, by permitting collection of a deficiency judgment from the assuming grantee, but only after foreclosure. In any case, the foundation of equitable subrogation is third party beneficiary doctrine, because that doctrine substitutes the grantee for the trustor as primary debtor. See Nelson & Whitman, Real Estate Finance Law §§5.12–5.13 (2d ed 1985).

The differences between the third party beneficiary and equitable subrogation rationales are more than theoretical; they lead to contrasting results in various situations. Under third party beneficiary theory, for example, the grantor cannot release the grantee from his or her promise without the beneficiary's consent, although equitable subrogation theory permits such a release. *Biddel v Brizzolara* (1883) 64 C 354, 30 P 609. Another difference between the two theories is that under California's equitable subrogation rule there is nothing to assume from a grantor who is not liable for a deficiency judgment. *Mottashed v Central & Pac. Improvement Corp.* (1935) 8 CA2d 256, 47 P2d 525; *Case v Egan* (1922) 57 CA 453, 207 P 388.

The grantee's assumption of the debt does not discharge the grantor-trustor from liability, although it does reduce the grantor to surety status. *Everts v Matteson* (1942) 21 C2d 437, 132 P2d 476; see *Layton v West* (1969) 271 CA2d 508, 76 CR 507; *Birkhofer v Krumm, supra.* Thus, the grantor is not protected from a deficiency judgment (see *Braun v Crew* (1920) 183 C 728, 192 P 531) but may seek reimbursement from the grantee for any judgment that he or she pays; each successive owner may look to subsequent owners who assume the debt. *White v Schader* (1921) 185 C 606, 198 P 19; *Robson v O'Toole* (1919) 45 CA 63, 187 P 110.

Under the statute of frauds (CC §1624(f)), an assumption agreement must be in writing to be enforceable, in contrast with early cases in which the courts held that an assumption could be implied from the fact that the grantee did not pay the grantor the full price (see *Banta v Rosasco* (1936) 12 CA2d 420, 55 P2d 601). An agreement that the buyer will take the property "subject to" the deed of trust is not an agreement to assume. *Wolfert v Guadagno* (1933) 130 CA 661, 20 P2d 360.

An assuming grantee is liable on the debt, but only for a deficiency. An assumption agreement does not make the grantee into a guarantor who may possibly be sued before foreclosure. *Security-First Nat'l Bank v Chapman* (1939) 31 CA2d 182, 87 P2d 724; see §8.10. See also *Shuey v Mulcrevy* (1917) 34 CA 218, 166 P 1019. Assuming grantees are thus protected by the one-action rule. *Lewis v Hunt, supra.* The fair-value provisions and CCP §580d also undoubtedly apply.

b. Purchase-Money Considerations

§8.23   (1) When Loan Was Originally for Nonpurchase-Money

If the deed of trust given by the grantor secures a nonpurchase-money loan, and the grantee assumes the debt under circumstances in which a similar new loan would be a nonpurchase-money loan (and thus outside the scope of CCP §580b), the grantee does not have §580b protection. *Brown v Jensen* (1953) 41 C2d 193, 259 P2d 425; *Stockton Sav. & Loan Bank v Massanet* (1941) 18 C2d 200, 114 P2d 592; *Paramount Sav. & Loan Ass'n v Barber* (1968) 263 CA2d 166, 69 CR 390. For example, if the grantor originally borrowed from a third party to improve a commercial structure, and later sold it to persons who assumed the loan and who did not use the structure as their personal residence, the loan is not a purchase-money loan and has no §580b protection.

There is also probably no CCP §580b protection for a subsequent purchaser who assumes an originally nonpurchase-money loan, even though a new loan to the assuming purchaser would come under §580b, *e.g.*, when money was initially borrowed for a vacation and secured by a deed of trust on a single-family dwelling, which was then sold to purchasers who assumed the loan and resided in the dwelling. There is dictum in several cases that the nature of a loan is determined at its inception and may not be changed thereafter (see *Stockton Sav. & Loan Bank v Massanet, supra*; *Jackson v Taylor* (1969) 272 CA2d 1, 76 CR 891). See also Riesenfeld, *California Legislation Curbing Deficiency Judgments,* 48 Calif L Rev 705, 715 (1960).

Giving CCP §580b protection to the assuming grantee of a nonpurchase-money loan would nullify the assumption agreement to the detriment of the seller. If the purchasers are protected by §580b, they are protected against both the seller and the lender. The seller is liable to the lender for any deficiency judgment, however, because he or she has not been released from liability on the note. If the seller is liable for a deficiency, and if §580b protects the assuming grantees, their promise to the seller to pay the debt is meaningless, although it may have been an important factor in setting the purchase price. Holding them to their promise to assume seems more equitable than giving them §580b protection despite their promise. *Union Bank v Gradsky* (1968) 265 CA2d 40, 71 CR 64. Although the buyers could have taken out a new loan (perhaps from the same third party) and obtained §580b protection, they did not do so. Furthermore, a new loan would undoubtedly have paid off the existing loan and thus released the seller. In three-party situations, the principals are free to tailor the transaction to suit their needs regarding the deficiency rules. *Kistler v Vasi* (1969) 71 C2d 261, 78 CR 170. The buyers may prefer to assume the existing loan to take advantage of a lower interest rate; the price they pay for this is deficiency exposure.

§8.24 (2) When Loan Was Originally for Purchase-Money

When the original borrower qualified for CCP §580b protection, the issue is whether that protection will be extended to new purchasers of the property. There are separate considerations for loans made by the vendor and loans made by third parties. See §§8.25–8.26.

§8.25 (a) Vendors

When the assumed loan was initially a purchase-money loan made by the original seller, one court has held that subsequent grantees who assume the loan have the same purchase-money protection as the original purchaser. *Jackson v Taylor* (1969) 272 CA2d 1, 76 CR 891. The court held that the seller remained a seller concerning the loan and did not become a third party lender in relation to the new purchasers. See also *Cornelison v Kornbluth* (1975) 15 C3d 590, 125 CR 557; *Weaver v Bay* (1963) 216 CA2d 559, 31 CR 211. This result is consistent with the general proposition that one cannot assume a loan from a party not personally liable on it, and also with the dictum that a purchase-money loan retains its nature. See §8.23. The assumption agreement's unenforceability does not harm the trustor, who is immune from a deficiency judgment under CCP §580b. Thus, when the loan assumed was originally made by the vendor, the assuming grantees are not liable for a deficiency judgment, despite their assumption agreement and regardless of whether the property is commercial or residential.

Sellers' efforts to use subsequent sales by their purchasers as a means of terminating CCP §580b protection have met with mixed results. In *Shepherd v Robinson* (1981) 128 CA3d 615, 180 CR 342, the seller, who originally held a purchase-money third deed of trust, agreed to a refinancing on resale of the property, contributed some of his own funds to the refinancing, took back a new and larger note (signed by both the original and new purchasers), and subordinated the note to a new senior loan. The court held that the net result of this activity was that he remained the seller with respect to the new purchasers, so that they had §580b protection. In *Goodyear v Mack* (1984) 159 CA3d 654, 205 CR 702, the court suggested that it would have reached the same result as the court in *Shepherd* except for the fact that the seller in that case exchanged the security for "other security" as part of a refinancing on resale, so that the new note and deed of trust did not retain their purchase-money status. See also *LaForgia v Kolsky* (1987) 196 CA3d 1103, 242 CR 282. In *Wright v Johnston* (1988) 206 CA3d 333, 253 CR 418, however, the court held that a seller who subordinated to a later refinancing, originated by a subsequent owner of the property, was thereby exempted from CCP §580b provisions and could recover on the note; the later subordination altered his original status as a seller. Under the rule of *Spangler v Memel* (1972) 7 C3d 603, 102 CR 807 (see §4.35), subsequent subordination should be irrelevant because it has no connection to overvaluation in that the price was determined much earlier. There is equally little connection, however, between assisting in refinancing and thus being considered a seller, as the decisions in *Shepherd v Robinson, supra,* and *Goodyear v Mack, supra,* imply. Sellers should be aware that it is difficult to predict the success of efforts to modify the CCP §580b status of their loans after they have been made. See §4.47 concerning attempts by the debtor to waive antideficiency protection.

§8.26   (b) Lenders

Purchase-money protection under CCP §580b probably continues when a third party purchase-money loan is assumed, *e.g.,* when the seller first obtained the loan to purchase the property as a personal residence, but the new buyers do not intend to reside there. Technically, there is nothing for the buyers to assume, because the seller has no personal liability. That a new loan made to the buyers would not be a purchase-money loan may be irrelevant if the parties are treated as free to create or eliminate purchase-money protection. See *Kistler v Vasi* (1969) 71 C2d 261, 78 CR 170, discussed in §4.30. If there is a due-on-sale clause in the deed of trust, the lender may compel the purchaser to take out a new nonpurchase-money loan rather than permitting assumption of the old loan. See §7.12.

§8.27   (c) Grantee as Guarantor

In *Everts v Matteson* (1942) 21 C2d 437, 132 P2d 476, the buyers were required to guarantee, as well as to assume, the seller's loan, which worked in their favor because it qualified them for protection (under CCP §580a) as principal debtors and canceled their guarantor status. In *Indusco Management Corp. v Robertson* (1974) 40 CA3d 456, 114 CR 47, a subsequent nonassuming purchaser guaranteed the seller's original nonpurchase-money note and was treated throughout the opinion as a guarantor rather than a grantee for CCP §580d purposes. Neither case involved purchase-money security, and the distinction between assuming and guaranteeing makes most sense in the nonpurchase-money area. If the note was initially for purchase-money, however, neither an assumption nor a guaranty of it by the purchaser will accomplish much (*i.e.,* the purchaser probably retains CCP §580b protection).

IV. MULTIPLE OBLIGATIONS
§8.28   A. Multiple Notes and Noteholders

The problems discussed in this section and in §§8.29–8.30 arise when one security instrument secures several notes, debts, or obligations. For a variety of reasons, a creditor may hold more than one note from the debtor. For example, the creditor may (1) have a single obligation split into separate notes or (2) make additional loans later, taking new and additional notes for the loans instead of consolidating each advance into a new, larger, single note.

The nature of the debt determines the nature of the note. For example, if a debt is secured, the note representing it is a secured note, regardless of what it says. *Schwerin v Shostak* (1963) 213 CA2d 37, 28 CR 332. Similarly, if the debt was originally a purchase-money debt, so is the note evidencing the debt, even if it is not the original note. *Jackson v Taylor* (1969) 272 CA2d 1, 76 CR 891; *Lucky Inv. v Adams* (1960) 183 CA2d 462, 7 CR 57.

If each note is secured by a separate deed of trust on a separate parcel, the notes may be treated entirely independently. *Roseleaf Corp. v Chierighino* (1963) 59 C2d 35, 27 CR 873. If each note is secured by a separate deed of trust, but the deeds of trust are all on the same piece of property, they may or may not constitute separate liens. If, for example, the deeds of trust have dragnet clauses, thereby securing all the notes, or if the notes all have cross-acceleration clauses or similar interlocking language, they may all merge into a single obligation. *Union Bank v Wendland* (1976) 54 CA3d 393, 126 CR 549. But see *Wong v Beneficial Sav. & Loan Ass'n* (1976) 56 CA3d 286, 128 CR 338. See §§8.34–8.48 on dragnet clauses. Even without such clauses, however, a court may link all the obligations together. *Union Bank v Wendland, supra* (concurring opinion of Elkington, J.).

If the liens are treated separately, a foreclosure sale under any one of them should eliminate any junior liens and leave the senior liens intact, as would occur if the liens were held by third parties. See §3.23. If the beneficiary becomes the purchaser at the foreclosure sale, however, its acquisition of both title and the remaining liens will effect a merger of the fee and lien interests. *Stockton Sav. & Loan Soc'y v Harrold* (1900) 127 C 612, 60 P 165.

If multiple notes are secured by the same deed of trust, the creditor is compelled by CCP §726 to foreclose on all of them together and, if the property lacks sufficient value to cover all the notes, the creditor's remedy is to seek a deficiency judgment (if one is permitted). *Walker v Community Bank* (1974) 10 C3d 729, 111 CR 897. Piecemeal sales may, however, be allowed. CCP §728; see *Furesz v Garcia* (1981) 120 CA3d 793, 174 CR 803. For discussion of the order of sale, see §3.55.

§8.29   1. Payment of Multiple Notes

A debtor who is obligated to a single creditor under several notes may indicate how the payments must be allocated. CC §1479. In the absence of any indication by the debtor, CC §1479 permits the creditor to make the allocation and also provides that, if neither party makes an allocation, the proceeds must be applied to interest then due, to principal then due, to the oldest matured obligation, to unsecured obligations, and to secured obligations, in that order. *Sunlight Elec. Supply Co. v Pacific Homes Corp.* (1964) 226 CA2d 110, 37 CR 802. Among secured obligations, if the liens securing several notes held by one creditor are separated by third party intervening liens, then the creditor's senior note will be treated as first paid (in the absence of express contrary language) to protect the intervening lien. *Pike v Tuttle* (1971) 18 CA3d 746, 96 CR 403.

§8.30 2. Separate Noteholders With Common Security

A debtor may execute several notes, in favor of different payees, and secure all of them by a single security instrument. See *Mercantile Trust Co. v Sunset Road Oil Co.* (1917) 176 C 461, 168 P 1037. If the notes are all in favor of one creditor, he or she may transfer them to different persons, all of whom will share the common security. *Wilson v McLaughlin* (1937) 20 CA2d 608, 67 P2d 710. Even if the creditor holds a single note, it may be divided among transferees through the sale of participation interests in it. *Jefferson Sav. & Loan Ass'n v Lifetime Sav. & Loan Ass'n* (9th Cir 1968) 396 F2d 21. In all these instances, there is a multiplicity of notes, all secured by a single or common security instrument, as well as a multiplicity of noteholders.

Fractionalized interests in a single note secured by a deed of trust, or multiple notes secured by deeds of trust of equal priority, may be securities within the meaning of Corp C §25019 and therefore be subject to all the applicable requirements of the Corporate Securities Law (Corp C §§25000–25706). *People v Schock* (1984) 152 CA3d 379, 199 CR 327. The *Schock* court relied on federal securities law precedents to support this decision, and it is likely that a similar conclusion would be reached under federal law. In *Leyva v Superior Court* (1985) 164 CA3d 462, 210 CR 545, the court held that fractionalized interests in a deed of trust are securities if, under the "risk capital" test, the investors are dependent on the promoter's success for a return on their investment. Title 10 Cal Code Regs §260.105.30(e)(1) seems to indicate that the securities laws would apply if interests were sold to more than ten people.

The rule that the security follows the debt (see §1.17) renders irrelevant the mechanical problem of how a single deed of trust is apportioned when it secures several notes or certificates parceled out to different persons. Each transferee is entitled to a portion of the security regardless of what actually happens to the deed of trust.

The question of which portion of the security goes to each transferee was settled by the California Supreme Court in *Phelan v Olney* (1856)

6 C 478, in which it held that each transferee is entitled to a prorata share of the security in the absence of a contrary agreement. This means, for example, that, if the total obligation is $100,000 but the property securing it is worth only $75,000, each note is then 75 percent secured. As various notes are paid off, the ratio of debt to security will improve unless part of the property is exonerated under a release clause. *Crane v Danning* (9th Cir 1968) 397 F2d 781; *Wilson v McLaughlin, supra.*

This California prorata rule must be distinguished from two protanto rules followed in some other jurisdictions. One such rule holds that the first transferee obtains priority over later transferees so that, if the security is inadequate, the first is paid in full and the second takes what is left over. Under the other protanto rule, the holder of the note that first falls due has priority and is therefore to be paid in full before the other holder receives anything. Such rules of priority are rarely what the parties intended or expected. See Nelson & Whitman, Real Estate Finance Law §5.35 (2d ed 1985).

Under California's prorata rule, no noteholder should receive a greater benefit from the security than any other noteholder. Assume that two notes of equal priority from a common debtor secured by a common deed of trust are held by different parties; one note was due yesterday, and the other is due next year. Clearly, the holder of the delinquent note may foreclose, even though the other note is in good standing, because the deed of trust always calls for foreclosure on nonpayment. *Mercantile Trust Co. v Sunset Road Oil Co., supra*; *Redman v Purrington* (1884) 65 C 271, 3 P 883. Whether the foreclosure is judicial or private, whether or not the other note is due, and whether or not the other noteholder has recorded a request for notice of default, the holder of the other note should be notified of the proceedings, brought into them, and permitted to share in the sale proceeds. The second holder may be joined as a Doe defendant if his or her identity is unknown. *Baumann v Bedford* (1941) 18 C2d 366, 115 P2d 437.

The holder of the nondelinquent note must be included in the foreclosure proceedings because any other approach necessarily treats the two holders as unequal. This becomes apparent from a consideration of the status of a second holder who is excluded from foreclosure proceedings held by the first. Does the second holder still have a lien on the property securing the note? An answer either way is unsatisfactory. If the omitted noteholder still has a lien (because the lien of that note was not foreclosed), then the security was sold subject to it, which is equivalent to giving the omitted lien the priority of a senior lien. If, on the other hand, the second holder no longer has a lien (because the entire deed of trust was foreclosed at the sale under the prohibition against piecemeal foreclosures (CCP §726)), the omitted noteholder has been reduced to the status of a junior lienholder wiped out by a senior sale. The second noteholder can be treated as an equal only by being brought into the first noteholder's foreclosure.

Inclusion of all noteholders in the foreclosure sale is easy to justify technically when cross-acceleration clauses permit each note to be declared in default if any other note is unpaid. In that case, the other noteholders may join the action merely by declaring defaults themselves. *Redman v Purrington, supra.* Their inclusion should also be proper when the property constituting the security is indivisible, because CCP §728 permits sale of the security for payment of the "entire debt and costs." The other noteholders should also be included even when the single deed of trust covers separate parcels (as in a blanket deed of trust) and when the notes evidence separate debts (as in a dragnet-clause situation, *i.e.*, two notes representing entirely unrelated obligations under one deed of trust), because there is no other way to effectuate the prorata rule.

Dictum in *Hohn v Riverside County Flood Control & Water Conserv. Dist.* (1964) 228 CA2d 605, 39 CR 647, states that when two notes are secured by one deed of trust, the nonforeclosing holder of one note is permitted to share only in the surplus from the foreclosure. The opinion in *Hohn* cited as authority the decision in *Grattan v Wiggins* (1863) 23 C 16, which depended on a special agreement between the two creditors entitling one to full payment at the expense of the other notes. In the absence of a special agreement, a prorata rule, rather than a protanto rule, should be applied. *Phelan v Olney, supra.*

§8.31   B. Wraparound Notes

When a wraparound ("all-inclusive," "overriding," or "hold-harmless") note and deed of trust are used, the face amount of the obligation includes some other, existing obligation, which the holder of the wraparound note will pay off while being paid by the maker of the wraparound note. For example, *C* gives *B* a promissory note for $50,000, which "wraps around" an existing $40,000 note held by *A, i.e., C* must pay *B* $50,000, but *B* will pay *A* $40,000. Thus, the $50,000 note wraps around the $40,000 note and in effect represents a new obligation to *C* of only $10,000. For discussion of the wraparound deed of trust and all-inclusive note, see California Real Property Sales Transactions §§5.26–5.37 (Cal CEB 1981). For discussion of wraparound notes in foreclosure proceedings, see *Armsey v Channel Assoc.* (1986) 184 CA3d 833, 229 CR 509, discussed in §8.33.

Wraparound notes and deeds of trust are often employed as substitutes for second deeds of trust. Using the same numbers as above, if *C* already owed *A* $40,000, secured by a first deed of trust, and wanted to borrow $10,000 more from *B, C* could give *B* a $10,000 note secured by a second deed of trust or, alternatively, could give *B* a $50,000 wraparound note secured by a second deed of trust. With a conventional second deed of trust, *C* makes separate payments to *A* and to *B*; with a wraparound note and deed, *C* makes payments only to *B,* who in turn makes payments to *A*.

The chief reason for using wraparound instruments is to profit from an existing lower interest rate on the loans that are wrapped around. See Real Property Sales §5.27. For example, if there is an existing first deed of trust of $40,000 at 8 percent interest, a wraparound second deed of trust of $50,000 at 10 percent interest generates far more interest income to the wraparound lender than would a conventional second deed of trust of $10,000, even at 12 percent interest, because the wraparound generates its new interest on the total loan and not just on the additional funds. To the debtor, the wraparound arrangement may permit smaller monthly payments than would two independent notes covering two unconsolidated debts. There may also be significant tax advantages to one or both parties. See Real Property Sales §§5.31–5.32.

The federal income tax principle that a seller recognizes income when any existing mortgages assumed (or taken subject to) exceed the seller's basis does not apply to an existing mortgage that remains on the property and is wrapped inside another mortgage. Thus, a seller who is prepared to take back a second mortgage subject to an existing first mortgage on the property may defer recognition of income from discharge of the first mortgage by having the second mortgage wrap around the first. *Professional Equities, Inc.* (1987) 89 TC 165. (Both mortgages are included in the buyer's basis in either event, as part of the property's acquisition cost.) For discussion, see Taxation of Real Property Transfers §§3.80, 3.82 (Cal CEB 1981).

§8.32 1. Uses of Wraparound Instruments

The major use of wraparound loans is to capitalize on the attractive lower interest rates of existing first deeds of trust. See California Real Property Sales Transactions §5.27 (Cal CEB 1981). If property is being sold subject to a low-interest first deed of trust, the seller may take back a wraparound second deed of trust at a higher rate covering the unpaid balance of the purchase price. Alternatively, an owner of property seeking to refinance may obtain a wraparound loan from a third party for the additional funds, instead of paying off the existing loan and taking out a new one or adding a conventional second deed of trust.

Wraparound financing may also be used to reduce or alter the payment schedules on existing loans, rather than as a source of new money. Thus, if an owner of property has an existing first deed of trust with a low interest rate, which calls for high monthly payments, a wraparound lender might agree to make those payments for the owner while accepting a smaller monthly payment from the owner each month. In effect, the wraparound lender is making a second loan to the owner each month of the difference between the two payments, and the wraparound second deed of trust is actually a future-advance mortgage. See §§8.34–8.48. Alternatively, the owner may not be able to meet the regularity of fixed-amount periodic first-loan payments, which could then be taken over by the wraparound lender in return for a more irregular payment schedule from the owner.

Finally, a wraparound arrangement can be used by other third parties (*e.g.,* guarantors) to ensure that obligations are paid regularly and perhaps also to gain some compensation. For example, the guarantor of a note requiring monthly payments of $100 could take a wraparound note from the principal calling for payments to the guarantor of $110 per month.

§8.33 2. Problems With Wraparound Instruments

There is little significant case law to guide practitioners in their use of wraparound instruments. A major worry raised by the use of wraparound financing is the possibility of usury. Although the total interest the borrower pays may fall below the legal limits, the effective interest received by the wraparound lender on the amount actually advanced may exceed that amount. If the seller takes back a wraparound note and deed of trust, the transaction should be exempt from usury limits under the time-price differential doctrine, which distinguishes a credit sale of property from a loan or forbearance, freeing the credit sale from the restrictions of Cal Const art XV, §1. *Boerner v Colwell Co.* (1978) 21 C3d 37, 145 CR 380; *Verbeck v Clymer* (1927) 202 C 557, 261 P 1017. For discussion, see Hyman, *Proposition 2 and the California Usury Law,* 3 CEB Real Prop L Rep 25 (Mar. 1980); Brown, *The Current Status of the Time-Price Differential Doctrine in California,* 2 CEB Real Prop L Rep 93 (Aug. 1979), and 3 CEB Real Prop L Rep 109 (Oct. 1979). If the wraparound financing is provided by a third party, usury limitations may possibly be avoided if the wraparound lender is personally liable on the senior indebtedness and agrees to pay it. See discussion and authorities cited in California Real Property Sales Transactions §5.29 (Cal CEB 1981).

Another concern is ensuring consistency between the provisions of the senior loan and wraparound loan concerning matters such as insurance, late charges, and impounds. Other important issues in the use of wraparound loans are whether the wraparound lender's obligation to pay the senior loan is absolute or conditional, the rights of the borrower to pay or prepay the wrapped-around loan, and the nature of the foreclosure proceeding when only the wraparound note is in default. For discussion of issues concerning wraparound financing, see Real Property Sales §§5.26–5.37. It is often useful to provide in the wraparound note for appointment of a collection agent to receive the wraparound payments and disburse the payments on the senior obligation.

Finally, care should be taken in foreclosing the wraparound instrument. See, *e.g., Armsey v Channel Assoc.* (1986) 184 CA3d 833, 229 CR 509, in which the foreclosing beneficiary under a wraparound deed of trust purchased the property by credit-bidding only the amount of its own lien and took title subject to the underlying liens. The beneficiary was thus able to claim the fire insurance proceeds against the trustor's contention that no indebtedness remained after the credit-bid. See §7.42 on foreclosure problems of wraparound loans.

§8.34　　C. Future-Advance and Dragnet Clauses

The standard title company form deed of trust (see App B) states that the real property is given as security

for the purpose of securing payment of the indebtedness evidenced by a promissory note, of even date herewith, executed by

Trustor in the sum of $_ _ _ _ _ _, any additional sums and interest thereon hereafter loaned by Beneficiary to the then record owner of said property, which loans are evidenced by a promissory note or notes, containing a recitation that this Deed of Trust secures the payment thereof . . . .

This provision assumes that the deed of trust and promissory note are executed contemporaneously. There is no legal requirement, however, that a security instrument come into existence simultaneously with creation of the underlying obligation. Whenever a debtor gives a deed of trust to secure an existing loan, there is a time lag between the date of the original note and the date on which the security is given. Consider the following two situations, neither of which is very different from giving a deed of trust to secure an existing loan:

■ A bank holds a $100,000 unsecured note from its debtor and is prepared to grant an additional loan of $150,000 if the debtor provides real property security worth $250,000.

■ A debtor requests a total loan of $250,000 and is prepared to furnish an equal amount of security, but currently needs only $100,000 and wants to delay receiving the rest and paying interest on it until a later time.

In each example it is possible to use two separate notes, for $100,000 and $150,000, respectively, secured by two separate deeds of trust on the same property. One of the deeds of trust, however, would have to be subordinate, which may not be permissible under banking policy or regulations. The lender could also use a single note for $250,000 in each case, but this would be cumbersome if the two loans had different interest rates, terms of payment, maturity dates, or other terms. Consequently, lenders prefer to use two notes and one deed of trust in each of these situations. In the first example, the deed of trust would recite that it secured an earlier note for $100,000 and a contemporaneous note for $150,000. In the second example, the deed of trust would refer to a current loan of $100,000 and a future loan or advance of $150,000. See CC §2884; *London & San Francisco Bank v Bandmann* (1898) 120 C 220, 52 P 583. For discussion of deeds of trust written to secure multiple notes, see §§8.28–8.30.

There would be no problem in either transaction if the deeds of trust were written as indicated, but commercial lenders do not care to tailor deeds of trust for each individual situation when a standard form can be drafted to fit many cases. In fact, lenders in the past attempted to extend the wording to cover every other conceivable obligation that either existed or might someday exist in favor of the lender. In one deed of trust, the clause read (see *Wong v Beneficial Sav. & Loan Ass'n* (1976) 56 CA3d 286, 292, 128 CR 338, 341):

FOR THE PURPOSE OF SECURING: (1) Payment of the sum of $28,000.00 with interest thereon according to the terms of a promissory note or notes of even date herewith, made by Trustor, payable to the order of the Beneficiary, and extensions or renewals thereof; (2) payment of such additional amounts as may be hereafter loaned by Beneficiary or its successor to the Trustor or any of them, or any successor in interest of the Trustor, with interest thereon, *and any other indebtedness or obligation of the Trustor, or any of them, and any present or future demands of any kind or nature which the Beneficiary or its successor may have against the Trustor, or any of them, whether created directly, or acquired by assignment, whether absolute or contingent, whether due or not, whether otherwise secured or not, or whether existing at the time of the execution of this instrument, or arising thereafter;* (3) performance of each agreement of Trustor herein contained; and (4) payment of all sums to be made by Trustor pursuant to the terms hereof.

This clause, with italics, appeared in a 1963 deed of trust. The comparable provision in the standard title company form deed of trust (see App B) now in common use is more modest because of cases and comments warning lenders of the dangers of overly broad language. The title company form in App B brings other obligations under the security of the deed of trust only if the notes involved so specify. A true dragnet clause (as appears in *Wong v Beneficial Sav. & Loan Ass'n, supra*) extends the deed of trust to cover every conceivable past, present, or future obligation between debtor and creditor, whether or not it is related to the present loan. This is why such clauses are called "dragnet"; they sweep into the deed of trust far more debts than the parties generally intended. *Wong v Beneficial Sav. & Loan Ass'n, supra.* These clauses are also often referred to as "anaconda" or "debt accrual" clauses. *Berger v Fuller* (Ark 1929) 21 SW2d 418; see *Capocasa v First Nat'l Bank* (Wis 1967) 154 NW2d 271, 275.

§8.35   1. Validity

Under CC §2891, the existence of a lien does not entitle the lienor to anything other than satisfaction of the original obligation secured by the lien. See *De Leonis v Walsh* (1903) 140 C 175, 73 P 813; *Mahoney v Bostwick* (1892) 96 C 53, 30 P 1020. This rule does not prohibit parties from agreeing that a lien will secure more than one obligation. *Ricketson v Richardson* (1861) 19 C 330; *Hocker v Reas* (1861) 18 C 650. The deed of trust could specify with precision all obligations or future advances that it secures and will secure, but the drawback of such precision for the creditor is that advances that are not described or that exceed the amount stated are unsecured. *Keese v Beardsley* (1923) 190 C 465, 213 P 500. But see *London & San Francisco Bank v Bandmann* (1898) 120 C 220, 52 P 583. Because the courts have long held that a future-advance clause is valid even though it does not state the upper limit of future advances (*Tapia v Demartini* (1888) 77 C 383, 19 P 641; *Oaks v Weingartner* (1951) 105 CA2d 598, 234 P2d 194), creditors naturally prefer to use future-advance clauses and avoid wording that might hinder them at a later time. Indeed, use of very broad terminology has been judicially approved as being the best way for parties to agree that everything loaned will be covered. *Sather Banking Co. v Arthur R. Briggs Co.* (1903) 138 C 724, 72 P 352.

Such clauses took a different form in the nineteenth century. Instead of stating that the mortgage secured more than one debt, the language recited that the mortgage secured a debt much larger than the amount actually loaned to the mortgagor; *e.g.,* if a bank loaned $10,000 to a mortgagor, the mortgage would say it secured a debt of $25,000. Because of dicta in *Tully v Harloe* (1868) 35 C 302 to the effect that this approach might result in a fraud on creditors, such language was dropped and replaced by clauses similar to that in *Wong v Beneficial Sav. & Loan Ass'n* (1976) 56 CA3d 286, 128 CR 338.

Between the debtor and the creditor, there is no need for a dragnet clause at all. A parol agreement that the deed of trust will cover an additional loan is valid. *Anglo-Californian Bank v Cerf* (1905) 147 C 384, 81 P 1077; *Banta v Wise* (1901) 135 C 277, 67 P 129. But see *American Sav. Bank v Kemp* (1913) 21 CA 571, 132 P 617. In fact, no agreement is necessary at all if the additional amount advanced is necessary to protect the security. CC §2876; *Churchill v Woodworth* (1906) 148 C 669, 84 P 155; see §§7.34–7.37. Because third parties may be able to attack such unwritten understandings, however, it is safer to refer to other loans in the original deed of trust. See *Langerman v Puritan Dining Room Co.* (1913) 21 CA 637, 132 P 617; §§8.43–8.48.

§8.36   2. Disputes Over Security

When a security instrument contains a dragnet clause, and more than one obligation exists between debtor and creditor, a variety of disputes may arise. If only the debtor and the creditor are involved, a disagreement may occur when the debtor tenders sufficient funds to pay off the original debt, but the creditor refuses to release the security unless other claims are also satisfied. The same dispute may occur in a different context if the creditor forecloses on its security because of the debtor's failure to satisfy the primary obligation, the foreclosing creditor seeks to have the surplus from the foreclosure sale applied toward satisfaction of its other claims, and the debtor contends that he or she is entitled to the surplus. The parties' contentions may be reversed if the creditor forecloses and receives funds sufficient to cover only the primary claim and then seeks independent legal redress for nonsatisfaction of its other claims, while the debtor contends that the other claims were secured by the deed of trust, making foreclosure the creditor's only remedy (under CCP §726; see §§4.3–4.10) or barring further recovery after a private foreclosure sale (CCP §580d; see §§4.14–4.16). See *Union Bank v Wendland* (1976) 54 CA3d 393, 126 CR 549.

More complicated disputes arise when a third party, either a junior creditor or a purchaser of the asset given as security, comes into the picture. Assume that *A* lends *B* $100,000 and takes back a deed of trust with a dragnet clause; *C* then lends *B* $150,000 and takes back a second deed of trust on the same property. *A* now lends an additional $200,000 to *B*; *B* pays no one; a foreclosure and sale produces $250,000. No one denies that the first $100,000 of the sale proceeds go to *A*, but to whom does the next $150,000 go? *A* contends that its second loan of $200,000 was a proper future advance secured by its dragnet clause and shares priority with its first loan; *C* asserts that *A*'s $200,000 loan is a third lien, subordinate to *C*'s second lien for $150,000. Answers to disputes such as these are not entirely certain. For discussion, see §§8.43–8.48.

§8.37   a. Preexisting Debts

The clause in the title company form deed of trust (see §8.34, App B) does not purport to cover preexisting debts. Thus, neither party can contend that the debtor's earlier, unsecured obligations to the creditor could have become secured by execution of the deed of trust. The broader clause also quoted in §8.34 (used in *Wong v Beneficial Sav. & Loan Ass'n* (1976) 56 CA3d 286, 128 CR 338) makes it appear that any earlier obligations are automatically secured by the words "any other indebtedness or obligation of the Trustor, or any of them."

The danger that all the debtor's existing obligations to the beneficiary automatically become secured whenever the debtor executes a deed of trust containing a dragnet clause was eliminated by the decision in *Gates v Crocker-Anglo Nat'l Bank* (1968) 257 CA2d 857, 65 CR 536. In *Gates*, a deed of trust executed by several co-tenants to secure a contemporaneous obligation was held not to secure the preexisting debt of one of them. Despite the fact that the language of the dragnet clause, like the wording of the clause in *Wong*, specifically covered obligations of any of the trustors, the court ruled that preexisting debts of only one trustor were not secured by the other trustors' interests in the property unless the others expressly consented or acquiesced. The basic logic of the decision (*i.e.*, that such clauses should not be read to include debts of which the trustor is unaware) extends beyond the co-tenancy situation and includes existing obligations either not specifically enumerated in the deed of trust or not explicitly called to the trustor's attention. Compare *Wong v Beneficial Sav. & Loan Ass'n, supra*, with *Lomanto v Bank of America* (1972) 22 CA3d 663, 99 CR 442.

Because it is easy to include specific existing obligations if the parties so intend, failure to do so constitutes a ground for a court to infer that no such intent existed or that, if it did, it was a secret intent harbored by the creditor and not shared with the debtor. See, *e.g., National Bank v Blankenship* (ED Ark 1959) 177 F Supp 667, aff'd sub nom *National Bank v General Mills, Inc.* (8th Cir 1960) 283 F2d 574; *First v Byrne* (Iowa 1947) 28 NW2d 509; *Farmers Nat'l Bank v De Fever* (Okla 1936) 61 P2d 245; *Sowder v Lawrence* (Kan 1929) 281 P 921; *Iser v Herbert Mark Bldg. Corp.* (NY Ct App 1930) 171 NE 757. Parol evidence is admissible to show what the security covers (*Shaver v Bear River & Auburn Water & Mining Co.* (1858) 10 C 396), but the burden is on the proponent to show that both parties intended that the preexisting loan be included. See *Anglo-Californian Bank v Cerf* (1905) 147 C 384, 81 P 1077; *Payne v Morey* (1904) 144 C 130, 77 P 831.

§8.38   b. Future Advances

Civil Code §2884 permits creation of a present lien to secure a future obligation. See also UCC §9–204. This rule can perhaps be reconciled with CC §2872 (making a lien accessory to an obligation) if the deed of trust provides that the lien secures the debtor's present promise to repay to the creditor all credit later extended. Nelson & Whitman, Real Estate Finance Law §12.7 (2d ed 1985). Thus, a deed of trust containing a future-advance clause is valid even if no debt exists at its inception (*Moss v Odell* (1901) 134 C 464, 66 P 581), or if the debt has been temporarily reduced to zero (*Frank H. Buck Co. v Buck* (1912) 162 C 300, 122 P 466). But see *Fickling v Jackman* (1928) 203 C 657, 265 P 810.

A future-advance clause is not necessarily separate from a dragnet clause. The dragnet clause in *Wong v Beneficial Sav. & Loan Ass'n* (1976) 56 CA3d 286, 128 CR 338, quoted in §8.34, contains a future-advance clause by its reference to "amounts as may be hereafter loaned." If all mention of existing obligations were omitted from that dragnet clause, it would then be only a future-advance clause. When the disputed second obligation is a future advance, creditors tend to refer to the clause as a future-advance clause because future-advance clauses have frequently been judicially upheld. Debtors prefer to refer to such clauses as dragnet clauses to capitalize on the negative implications of that word. Problems of the validity, construction, and scope of such clauses, and the priority created by them, however, have nothing to do with the label.

The clause contained in the title company form in App B and quoted in §8.34 confines future loans covered by the deed of trust to those in which the promissory note expressly recites that it is secured by the deed of trust. The clause in *Wong,* however, purports to secure future notes whether or not they refer to the existing deed of trust, and would sweep under the deed of trust such items as a trustor's subsequent checking account overdraft or a missed payment on an automobile loan, if either were handled by the same bank.

California courts have consistently preferred a construction of dragnet clauses that is faithful to the parties' actual expectations rather than to the literal wording of the clause. As early as 1889, the California Supreme Court held that even an expansive dragnet clause did not permit the creditor to buy up an obligation owed by the debtor to a third party and to include it under the creditor's mortgage. *Moran v Gar-*

demeyer (1889) 82 C 96, 23 P 6. The *Moran* case actually extends beyond its rule, because it involved a situation in which the debtor obtained a second loan from a secured creditor by endorsing over a note that the debtor was holding from a third party; it was this note that the supreme court held to be unsecured. The court of appeal announced the same rule 16 years later in *Provident Mut. Bldg. & Loan Ass' n v Shaffer* (1905) 2 CA 216, 83 P 274, again in a situation more favorable to the creditor than the rule made it appear. In *Provident,* the secured creditor advanced $300 above the original loan to pay a materialman for goods supplied to benefit the real property secured by the mortgage, but the creditor was not allowed to add the $300 to the mortgage.

Some dragnet clauses attempt to cover the situation confronted in these decisions by adding to the clause, "payable to or otherwise acquired by beneficiary," but it is doubtful whether this will help. The loans held unsecured in *Moran* and *Provident* fit literally into the future-advance clauses of those mortgages. Their exclusion from the security in those cases was based more on the perceived inequity of permitting a creditor to subject its debtor to such claims than on any inadequacies in the language of the clause.

Even when a secondary obligation was originally created solely between debtor and creditor, it does not necessarily come under the dragnet clause. In *Moran v Gardemeyer* (1889) 82 C 102, 23 P 8 (a companion case to the *Moran* decision cited above), a note recited that it was secured by a crop mortgage and did not refer to the existing real property mortgage under which the creditor wanted to secure this note. The supreme court held that, if the note had said nothing about security, it could have come under the real property mortgage, but because the note expressly referred to other security it was not secured by the real property mortgage. See §8.40.

§8.39 (1) Relationship Between Loans

The relationship between two loans may determine whether a court will find that the parties intended to secure both by the same deed of trust. For example, if the first loan is made to enable the borrower to erect improvements on the real property, and the purpose of the second loan is to finance more improvements on the same real property, a court is likely to find that the two loans are secured by one deed of trust. See *Union Bank v Wendland* (1976) 54 CA3d 393, 126 CR 549.

If there is little connection between the loans, a court may find that the parties did not intend (either when executing the security instrument or when making the second loan) that the second loan should fall under the security. *Moran v Gardemeyer* (1889) 82 C 96, 23 P 6. Thus, Alabama has refused to let creditors sweep unrelated negligence or rent claims under their mortgages. *Monroe County Bank v Qualls* (Ala 1929) 125 S 615; *Albertville Trading Co. v Critcher* (Ala 1927) 112 S 907. See also *McCollum v Braddock Trust Co.* (Pa 1938) 198 A 803. Under the rationale followed by the courts in these cases, the phrase "all other indebtedness" is construed to mean all other debts similar to the primary debt. See *Beavers v Le Sueur* (Ga 1939) 3 SE2d 667.

California courts have applied a similar test. Civil Code §3136 (former CCP §1188.1) gives preference to senior construction loans over mechanics' liens for optional as well as obligatory advances if the funds were used to pay for actual improvements to the property. See §8.46. This code section would be sufficiently narrow to be unimportant here were it not for the holding in *Turner v Lytton Sav. & Loan Ass'n* (1966) 242 CA2d 457, 51 CR 552, in which the court extended former CCP §1188.1 to a different dispute over priorities between a junior and a senior lienor. Considerations of notice and whether the advance was optional or obligatory, which are most important in a priority dispute (discussed in §§8.43–8.48), may not control in disputes between only the debtor and the creditor. It is not hard to argue by analogy, however, that if a junior lienor is to be further subordinated only to advances that actually relate to the property, the debtor's property should also be subject only to the liens of other advances that relate either to the property or to the original loan. See also *Fricker v Uddo & Toarmina Co.* (1957) 48 C2d 696, 312 P2d 1085; *Hoover v Agriform Chem. Co.* (1969) 268 CA2d 818, 74 CR 325.

Under this test, items such as overdrafts on a checking account or personal unsecured loans, which are different in nature from the original transaction, would not be included within the security unless (a) the parties had specifically described them, stating in the deed of trust that such items were to be secured; or (b) the parties subsequently executed notes or other instruments of indebtedness that specified that such debts are secured by the deed of trust. Once they are so described, the debtor cannot argue that they were not intended to come under the deed of trust. As long as the creditor relies instead on the very general wording of the dragnet clause, however, it leaves itself open to the charge that the debtor did not know what the clause meant. In light of the past success of debtors' arguments in cases such as *Moran v Gardemeyer, supra, Lomanto v Bank of America* (1972) 22 CA3d 663, 99 CR 442, and *Gates v Crocker-Anglo Nat'l Bank* (1968) 257 CA2d 857, 65 CR 536, creditors will not solve their problems by writing increasingly broad dragnet clauses, but rather by tending toward more specificity in describing subsequent obligations to be included.

§8.40   (2) Reliance on Security

The decision in *Moran v Gardemeyer* (1889) 82 C 102, 23 P 8 (a companion case to *Moran v Gardemeyer* (1889) 82 C 96, 23 P 6, discussed in §8.38), illustrates another kind of test to determine whether the debt comes within the scope of the dragnet clause. In *Moran,* the court held that the second loan was not secured by the real property mortgage because the promissory note recited that it was secured by a crop mortgage. The creditor thus could not claim to have relied on the real property security in making the loan. One rationale for this result is that the dragnet clause constitutes a continuing offer by the borrower to secure further loans under the security and, to determine whether the lender accepts the offer when a second loan is made, the lender's intent must be ascertained. The lender cannot be considered to have intended to accept the real property security when it takes different security instead. See *Bloom v First Vt. Bank & Trust Co.* (Vt 1975) 340 A2d 78; *Second Nat'l Bank v Boyle* (Ohio 1951) 99 NE2d 474.

Under this rationale, an automobile loan (with the vehicle as security) should not come under a deed of trust held by the same bank. Even a personal loan from the bank, although not separately secured, might be disqualified if examination of the bank's records and books shows that the bank was not relying on its deed of trust when it made the loan. Compare *Hollywood State Bank v Cook* (1950) 99 CA2d 338, 221 P2d 988, with *Langerman v Puritan Dining Room Co.* (1913) 21 CA 637, 132 P 617. On the other hand, one court has held that reliance is demonstrated when the second note is secured by a deed of trust on exactly the same property as that securing the first note. Both notes are thus covered by the first deed of trust, making the second deed of trust superfluous, even though that may not have been the parties' actual intention. *Union Bank v Wendland* (1976) 54 CA3d 393, 126 CR 549. This holding may make splitting a loan into two notes, secured by separate first and second deeds of trust on the same property, impossible whenever the first deed of trust contains a dragnet clause not expressly drafted to exclude the second note. In such a case, a recital in the second note that it is secured by the second, not the first, deed of trust may be insufficient to create two separate notes.

There is no way for a lender to use a dragnet clause so broad as to satisfy the reliance requirement in advance. The dragnet clause in the title company form in App B eliminates this problem by limiting coverage to future notes that actually recite that they are secured. Such a recitation also provides the best evidence of actual reliance.

§8.41   c. Contemporaneous Obligations

The same considerations for determining whether preexisting or subsequent notes between the parties come under the dragnet clause (see §§8.39–8.40) should also control when the "other" note is executed at the same time as the secured note. Assume that the debtor signs two notes and one deed of trust. One note recites that it is secured by the deed of trust and the other says nothing about the deed of trust. If the deed of trust recites that it secures the first note, and also contains a dragnet clause reciting that everything else is secured, does it cover the second note?

The logic of cases dealing with preexisting debts (see §8.38) dictates that the second note in this instance is unsecured because the parties' failure to secure it specifically by precise language in either the note or the deed of trust indicates a lack of intent to secure the second note. See *First v Byrne* (Iowa 1947) 28 NW2d 509; *Farmers Nat' l Bank v De Fever* (Okla 1936) 61 P2d 245; *Sowder v Lawrence* (Kan 1929) 281 P 921; *Iser v Herbert Mark Bldg. Corp.* (NY Ct App 1930) 171 NE 757. On the other hand, if the note is given for a purpose clearly related to that of the first note (see §8.39), and if the failure to secure the note expressly can be explained, the court may find contrary intent. This result occurred in *Wong v Beneficial Sav. & Loan Ass' n* (1976) 56 CA3d 286, 128 CR 338 (discussed in §8.34), in which a single real property development was divided into eight separate parcels, each serving as separate security under eight individual deeds of trust for eight separate promissory notes. The motive was to exceed the loan limits that would have been imposed on an undivided project. The court held that the dragnet clause served to tie the parcels together and to prevent the release of any one parcel without payment of the entire debt.

§8.42   d. Undesirable Effects of Dragnet Clause

The discussion in §§8.36–8.41 assumes that it is the creditor who asserts that another debt is secured, but this is not always the case. A bank with a dragnet clause in its deed of trust may decide to ignore the clause and contend that the other loan is unsecured, for any of the considerations that may motivate the bank to prefer unsecured over secured loans. The moment a loan becomes secured, hindrances as well as benefits attach to it. Personal collection actions are barred by CCP §726. *Roseleaf Corp. v Chierighino* (1963) 59 C2d 35, 27 CR 873. The lender's right to attach the security for the second loan may also be lost. CCP §487.020; *Western Bd. of Adjusters v Covina Publishing* (1970) 9 CA3d 659, 88 CR 293. If the deed of trust is foreclosed by trustee's sale, CCP §580d will bar any later personal action on the second note, making it entirely uncollectible. *Union Bank v Wendland* (1976) 54 CA3d 393, 126 CR 549; see §4.14.

§8.43   3. Disputes Over Priorities

A junior creditor can take advantage of the same arguments available to a debtor (see §§8.36–8.41) concerning whether an obligation is secured by a senior deed of trust. In fact, the junior can often go further than the debtor and argue that, even if a side obligation is secured between debtor and senior creditor, it nevertheless is lower in priority than the junior's lien. Such an argument plainly works in the following situation: *A* lends *B* $100,000 and takes back a deed of trust that also secures future advances; *C* then lends *B* $150,000, taking back a second deed of trust and giving *A* actual notice of this fact. Then, despite the notice, *A* voluntarily lends $200,000 more to *B* for a note secured by the original deed of trust. In this case, there is no doubt that *A*'s deed of trust secures $300,000 in loans to *B*, and that *A* may take this much out of sale proceeds after a foreclosure. But there also is no doubt that *A* cannot take out its second $200,000 until after *C* has been paid, because *C*'s lien for $150,000 is prior to *A*'s lien for $200,000, even though *C*'s lien is junior to *A*'s lien for $100,000. *Garcia v At-*

majian (1980) 113 CA3d 516, 169 CR 845; *Reidy v Collins* (1933) 134 CA 713, 26 P2d 712.

Two facts exist in this case that entitle *C* to leapfrog *A* for partial priority: (1) *A*'s second loan was optional (see §8.44), and (2) *A* had actual notice of *C*'s lien before it made the second loan (see §8.48). If either factor had been absent, *C* would not have achieved this priority.

§8.44   a. Optional Versus Obligatory Advances

If, in the example in §8.43, *A* had originally bound itself to make a second, later loan to *B* of the $200,000, *A* would have been protected even though it made the second loan after it knew about *C*. Obligatory advances do not lose priority even when made with notice of the second lien; to attain preferred status, however, the lender must make optional advances without notice of the intervening lien. *Lumber & Builders Supply Co. v Ritz* (1933) 134 CA 607, 25 P2d 1002. The deed of trust, which is the only recorded document relating to the original transaction between *A* and *B*, rarely states whether future advances are optional or obligatory, and there is no requirement that it do so. In fact, *A* may offer evidence of a parol commitment to lend more to *B* later on. Proof of this oral agreement is all that is needed to defeat a junior lienor who claims priority based on having given notice before the second advance was made. *Lumber & Builders Supply Co. v Ritz, supra* (criticized in Note, *Mortgages & Trust Deeds: Future Advances: Priority Over Intervening Liens,* 22 Calif L Rev 705 (1934)); *Machado v Bank of Italy* (1924) 67 CA 769, 228 P 369. But see *Langerman v Puritan Dining Room Co.* (1913) 21 CA 637, 132 P 617.

This rule requires that the junior creditor take numerous steps to protect itself: It must check the state of record title, discover the senior deed of trust, record its own deed of trust, and notify the senior. Having done all that, the junior still must obtain a beneficiary statement from the senior, indicating the state of the account on the senior encumbrance. Civil Code §2943 entitles the junior to obtain this information from the senior lender. Although CC §2943 does not specifically mention future advances, a senior lender would have difficulty claiming priority for later advances that it asserts are obligatory if they were not mentioned to the junior in response to a beneficiary statement requested under §2943. A person requesting a beneficiary statement is entitled to rely on its contents in accordance with its terms. CC

§2943(d)(1). The junior can also request an estoppel certificate from the beneficiary with respect to future advances.

There are legal as well as evidentiary problems concerning future advances. Advances may appear obligatory in form when in substance they are not, or a creditor may be under a real, though not contractual, compulsion to advance more funds to protect the security. See §§7.34–7.37.

§8.45 b. Revolving Line of Credit Problems

One of the most difficult priority problems faced by the real property practitioner is determining the priority of a revolving credit obligation. These obligations may arise from complex commercial lines of credit secured by real property or from a personal line of credit (offered by many lending institutions) that is secured by a single-family residence. The basics are the same for both of these types of lines of credit: Funds may be borrowed, repaid, and reborrowed over a specific time period, subject to specific conditions and secured by a lien on real property.

Although no recent cases have considered the priority of advances under revolving credit loans, the principles involved should be the same as those discussed in §§8.44 and 8.46. If the advances are obligatory and subject only to satisfaction of certain objective conditions, they should be entitled to priority relating back to the date on which the deed of trust or mortgage was recorded, regardless of whether the lender has actual notice of any subsequent junior encumbrances. Given the implication in many California contracts of covenants of good faith, fair dealing, and commercial reasonableness, even conditions that on their face are subjective or optional may be considered obligatory. See *Cohen v Ratinoff* (1983) 147 CA3d 321, 195 CR 84.

Title companies now offer endorsements for title insurance policies insuring revolving credit loans. One form of endorsement is reproduced on the following page:

TO 2140 D (8—84)

ENDORSEMENT

ISSUED BY

Ticor Title Insurance Company of California

Attached to and forming a part of Policy of Title Insurance No.

The Company hereby assures the Insured that, notwithstanding any terms or provisions in this policy to the contrary:

Advances made subsequent to the Date of Policy pursuant to the terms of
                                              which are secured by the insured mortgage, shall be included within the coverage of this policy not to exceed the face amount of said policy, provided that said vestee is the owner of the estate or interest covered by said policy at the date any such advances are made and subject to the limitations hereinafter set forth.

The Company further assures the Insured that such subsequent advances shall have the same priority over liens, encumbrances and other matters disclosed by the public records, as do advances secured by the insured mortgage as of Date of Policy, except for the following matters, if any, disclosed by the public records subsequent to policy date:

   a.   Federal tax liens.

   b.   Liens, encumbrances or other matters, the existence of which are actually known to the
        Insured prior to date of such advances.

   c.   Bankruptcies affecting the estate of the vestee prior to date of such advances.

The total liability of the Company under said policy and any endorsements therein shall not exceed, in the aggregate, the face amount of said policy and costs which the Company is obligated under the conditions and stipulations thereof to pay.

This endorsement is made a part of said policy and is subject to the schedules, conditions and stipulations therein, except as modified by the provisions hereof.

IN WITNESS WHEREOF, the Company has caused its corporate name and seal to be hereunto affixed by its duly authorized officers.

Dated:

                              TICOR TITLE INSURANCE COMPANY OF CALIFORNIA

                        By _____   President

                        Attest _____   Secretary

T.I. ENDORSEMENT 43

Principal Office: 6300 Wilshire Boulevard, P. O. Box 92792, Los Angeles, California 90009

§8.46   c. Construction Loan Problems

Construction loans frequently involve issues of obligatory versus optional advances. See California Mechanics' Liens and Other Remedies §§1.67–1.68, 6.10 (Cal CEB 1988). Often, the proceeds of a construction loan are transferred in a lump sum ("assigned") into a special account from which the funds are paid to the borrower or the contractor as progress payments for work completed. This permits the borrower to avoid paying interest on unused money and allows the lender to monitor construction to ensure that the job conforms to the plans. Typically the borrower makes interest-only payments on the funds actually disbursed until the entire loan proceeds have been disbursed, and then the borrower goes to a fully amortized loan repayment schedule. If the borrower defaults on repayment before the loan funds are fully disbursed, but after junior lienors have recorded their liens and notified the construction lender, the construction lender faces real risks if it takes over and uses the remaining funds to complete the project and also claims that its deed of trust gives it a first lien for the total amount of the loan on the completed project. *A-1 Door & Materials Co. v Fresno Guar. Sav. & Loan Ass'n* (1964) 61 C2d 728, 40 CR 85; *Miller v Mountain View Sav. & Loan Ass'n* (1965) 238 CA2d 644, 48 CR 278.

The construction lender may argue that there were no future advances because the entire loan was made when the money was put into the special account. Compare *Valley Lumber Co. v Wright* (1905) 2 CA 288, 84 P 58, with *Lanz v First Mortgage Corp.* (1932) 121 CA 587, 9 P2d 316. See also Nelson & Whitman, Real Estate Finance Law §§12.1, 12.7 (2d ed 1985). The junior lienor can argue, however, that the obligation was specious, because the construction loan agreement undoubtedly permitted the lender to withhold further disbursements once a default occurred, so that all payments made thereafter were optional rather than obligatory. Compare *Fickling v Jackman* (1928) 203 C 657, 265 P 810, with *Citizens' Sav. Bank v Mack* (1919) 180 C 246, 180 P 618. The senior may respond that, even if the later payments were optional, they were nevertheless necessary to protect the security. Because a half-finished project is a liability, and because the remaining payments actually improved the property, benefiting juniors as well, the lender should not be denied priority. See CC §3136; *Turner v Lytton Sav. & Loan Ass'n* (1966) 242 CA2d 457, 51 CR 552. See also CC §2876; *Savings & Loan Soc'y v Burnett* (1895) 106 C 514, 39 P 922; *Machado v Bank of Italy* (1924) 67 CA 769, 228 P 369.

Lenders often obtain protection, before making an advance that could be construed as being optional, by procuring an endorsement to their title policy from the CTLA 122 series, ensuring that the additional advance will have the same priority as the original loan. See Mechanics' Liens §§6.10, 8.6, 8.28–8.31.

§8.47   d. Wraparound Loan Problems

A wraparound or all-inclusive deed of trust provides that the holder of the wraparound note (*i.e.,* a note that "wraps around" a senior note; see §§8.31–8.33) will make the payments on the senior debt, usually out of the payments that the debtor is obligated to make to the wraparound lender. The wraparound noteholder's obligation to service the senior debt may be absolute, but it is usually made conditional on the debtor's not being in default to the wraparound lender. If the obligation is unconditional, the payments to the senior lender by the wraparound lender are probably obligatory advances with priority over inferior liens. See §8.44. In such a case, a lienholder junior to the wraparound loan might argue that payments made on the senior debt after the debtor is in default on the wraparound loan are optional advances and are not entitled to priority. Because they are payments made to protect the security, however, they should have priority. CC §2876. For discussion of payments on senior liens, see §7.36. The wraparound lender may also be subrogated to the security position of the senior lienholder. See *Caito v United Cal. Bank* (1978) 20 C3d 694, 144 CR 751. For discussion of whether making the wraparound lender's duty to pay the senior lien conditional may cost the wraparound lender lien priority in a dispute with other creditors of the debtor, see Healy, *A Legal View: Wrap-Around Mortgages,* 51 Title News 6 (1972); Cochrane, *Wrap-Around Mortgage Financing,* Legal Bull 185 (Sept. 1971).

§8.48   e. Actual Versus Constructive Notice

The holder of a second deed of trust usually has it recorded and often also records a request for notice of default on the first deed of trust under CC §2924b (see §2.15). Neither of these two steps deprives the holder of the first of priority for optional future advances made thereafter. Recording the second deed of trust gives constructive notice of its contents to all who come after, but it does not constitute notice to senior lienors already of record. *Savings & Loan Soc' y v Burnett* (1895)

106 C 514, 39 P 922; *Lanz v First Mortgage Corp.* (1932) 121 CA 587, 9 P2d 316. Similarly, recording a request for notice of default does not impart notice of an interest in the property. CC §2924b(f). A junior who seeks full protection must see that the senior has actual knowledge of the junior lien. See *Tapia v Demartini* (1888) 77 C 383, 19 P 641; *Atkinson v Foote* (1919) 44 CA 149, 186 P 831.

This requirement is based on sensible policy considerations. An experienced junior lender obtains a title search before any funds are advanced, thus ensuring discovery of the existence of the first deed of trust. The junior should also be held to the expectation that it will read the terms of the recorded deed of trust, including its dragnet clause. A prudent junior will then write the senior, asking whether any agreements exist with regard to obligatory future advances. Civil Code §2943 may provide a vehicle for obtaining this information, although it does not specifically mention future advances. See §8.44. In the same inquiry, the junior can inform the senior of the junior's status for protection against optional advances. The junior should also obtain an estoppel certificate or statement of condition from the senior setting forth the provisions regarding future advances. If mere recordation of the junior deed of trust were considered to be sufficient notice to the senior, the senior would be compelled to run a new title check before each advance or progress payment, a burden that would be cumbersome, unnecessary, and destructive of continuing lines of credit and open-account financing.

Although the constructive notice imparted by recordation is not adequate to protect the junior, the senior's actual knowledge of facts sufficient to create a duty of inquiry should protect the junior. For example, if the junior is a contractor, subcontractor, or material supplier, the senior may be charged with notice of the junior lien if it had actual knowledge that work had commenced or materials had been delivered to the property, even though there is no actual notice that a contractor or supplier has a claim. *W.P. Fuller & Co. v McClure* (1920) 48 CA 185, 191 P 1027.

§8.49 D. Subordination and Release Provisions

Clause B3 of the title company form deed of trust (see App B) contains provisions authorizing the beneficiary to release portions of the security ("reconvey all *or any part*") and to subordinate the lien of the security to another lien. Subordination is the beneficiary's agreement to accept a deed of trust with a lower priority than it would otherwise have. On subordination, see 1 California Real Property Financing §1.75 (Cal CEB 1988); California Real Property Sales Transactions §§5.39–5.54 (Cal CEB 1981). The general principles of priority of liens are:

■ First in time, first in right (CC §2897), subject to operation of the recording laws (CC §1214); and

■ Primacy for purchase-money liens over other liens (CC §2898), again subject to the recording laws.

Under these two principles, deeds of trust and other liens take initial priority according to their respective times of recordation, except that purchase-money deeds of trust prevail over preexisting judgment liens.

Release, or partial release, refers to the possibility of removing from the coverage of a blanket deed of trust one or more of the parcels of real property serving as security. For example, if a deed of trust covers ten acres, there is a partial release when one of the acres is withdrawn from the deed of trust and no longer constitutes part of the security. Without a release provision, the entire acreage continues to secure the entire debt. CC §2912; see §8.52. For discussion of release provisions, see 1 Real Property Financing §1.76; Real Property Sales §§5.55–5.67.

Subordination and release are matters of concern to developers assembling raw land for subdivision and construction. A purchaser who intends to have the seller take back a deed of trust for part of the purchase price must ascertain in advance that the seller will accept a deed of trust inferior to the deed of trust given to a bank to secure a construction loan. On subordination as an element of seller financing, see Real Property Sales §§5.38–5.54. If a purchaser intends to sell the property as individual lots over time, it is essential that the lender (seller or bank) agree in advance to release parcels from the blanket mortgage as they are sold. Thus, in the first situation, the purchaser's offer to buy will include the stipulation, "Subject to the seller's accepting a deed of trust which shall be subordinate . . . ." In the second situation, the purchaser's offer will recite, "Subject to inclusion in the deed of trust of a provision for release of various land from the deed of trust as follows . . . ." Without such clauses, neither subordination nor release can be forced on the beneficiary. See *Karlsen v American Sav. & Loan Ass'n* (1971) 15 CA3d 112, 92 CR 851.

The time for working out satisfactory subordination or release arrangements is when the seller and purchaser first enter into negotiations for sale of the real property. The California courts frequently refuse to grant specific performance against a seller who refuses to sell when the terms of subordination or release have not been drawn with sufficient specificity to minimize the seller's risk. See Real Property Sales §§5.42–5.43, 5.59; California Real Property Remedies Practice §§5.8–5.10 (Cal CEB 1982). To be enforceable, the subordination or release provision must be both specific and fair; a purchase and sale agreement that merely calls for execution of a subordination or release clause, without actually setting it forth, is unenforceable. *Handy v Gordon* (1967) 65 C2d 578, 55 CR 769 (subordination); *White Point Co. v Herrington* (1968) 268 CA2d 458, 73 CR 885 (release). In the case of subordination, courts first held that the details of all the provisions of the subordinating loan—including, but not limited to, use of the proceeds from the senior loan, its maximum amount, interest rate, maturity, points, prepayment, and acceleration provisions—must be set forth in the purchase and sale agreement. *Magna Dev. Co. v Reed* (1964) 228 CA2d 230, 39 CR 284. This strict rule has been eroded somewhat, however, by more recent decisions in which the courts have held sellers liable for damages for refusing to honor contracts containing release clauses that would have been too ambiguous to support specific performance. See *Larwin-Southern Cal., Inc. v JGB Inv. Co.* (1979) 101 CA3d 626, 162 CR 52; *Yackey v Pacifica Dev. Co.* (1979) 99 CA3d 776, 160 CR 430. A subordination clause was held to be for the buyer's benefit, so that the buyer could waive it and obtain specific performance against a reluctant seller, in *Reeder v Longo* (1982) 131 CA3d 291, 182 CR 287 (directly contradicting decision in *Magna Dev. Co. v Reed, supra*).

In the case of a partial release clause, it may be necessary to draft a complete release plan, including the release price per parcel and all restrictions on releases, such as maximum or minimum size and continuity, plus provisions for the relationship between regular installment loan payments and partial releases. *White Point Co. v Herrington, supra.* A release map of the property is helpful. Often, however, so much specificity is not possible early in the planning of the project. At the very least, the clause should specify maximum and minimum lot sizes for release. It must adequately protect the releasing party (the lender) with respect to adjacent parcels, access, utilities, and the like in order for the developer to obtain specific performance. *Eldridge v Burns* (1978) 76 CA3d 396, 142 CR 845.

The release clause should also require that a subdivision map be recorded before the first parcel is released. Otherwise, a foreclosure sale on only a part of the development might constitute an illegal lot split. Govt C §66499.30; see California Subdivision Map Act Practice §2.3 (Cal CEB 1987).

The subordination clause or subordination agreement must also comply with the requirements of CC §§2953.1–2953.4, unless either the subordinating loan or the loan to be subordinated exceeds $25,000 (CC §2953.5). These provisions generally require large-print disclosure of the subordination provisions.

§8.50   1. Implementing Subordination or Release Provision

In addition to incorporating complete terms for subordination or release into their purchase and sale agreement, the parties must include those terms in the deed of trust securing the loan. The parties may insert enforceable subordination or release provisions in the mortgage instrument even though their earlier contract omitted them; the former potential unenforceability of the contract (for lack of certainty) is immaterial if the parties eliminate the uncertainty with appropriate language in the deed of trust. Even if the subordination or release clause is still somewhat inadequate, the courts are less willing to undo a transaction entirely because of it than they would have been to permit either party to withdraw before the transaction closed. Thus, a court may be willing to countenance results that fall short of total rescission.

The final step in implementing a subordination or release clause is for the terms of subordination or release actually to be carried out. Subordination and release provisions differ with respect to this last step.

A subordination agreement is performed either by having the deed of trust recite that it is subordinated to some other instrument or, alternatively, by delaying its recordation until the other instrument has first been recorded, so that priorities are established by the time of recordation. CC §2897. On the distinctions between executory and executed subordination agreements, see California Real Property Sales Transactions §5.41 (Cal CEB 1981). A release agreement is first implemented by including the provisions for release of individual parcels in the blanket deed of trust, but final performance occurs only when individual parcels are actually released from the blanket lien. There are subsequent concerns in each case, but they are naturally of different sorts.

The primary concern of a subordinated lender is that all the proceeds from the senior loan be properly spent on the property itself, to increase the security value of the property correspondingly and thus to protect the subordinated security interest. For instance, if a seller conveys raw land worth $500,000 to a developer and agrees to accept back a note and deed of trust for $400,000, that deed of trust can safely be subordinated to a construction loan deed of trust for $1 million only if the finished product (land and buildings) has a value of no less than $1,400,000. Thus, it is probably necessary that all the construction funds actually be expended on the property in order to produce this value. A subordinated seller whose security is not thus protected may have remedies against either the purchaser-developer for failing to spend the funds properly (*Joanaco Projects, Inc. v Nixon & Tierney Constr. Co.* (1967) 248 CA2d 821, 57 CR 48), against the subordinating lender for failing to supervise the construction loan (*Gluskin v Atlantic Sav. & Loan Ass'n* (1973) 32 CA3d 307, 108 CR 318; *Middlebrook-Anderson Co. v Southwest Sav. & Loan Ass'n* (1971) 18 CA3d 1023, 96 CR 338; *Miller v Citizens Sav. & Loan Ass'n* (1967) 248 CA2d 655, 56 CR 844; but see *Gill v Mission Sav. & Loan Ass'n* (1965) 236 CA2d 753, 46 CR 456), or against the escrow agent or other third parties for failing to ensure that the vendor was properly protected (*Starr v Mooslin* (1971) 14 CA3d 988, 92 CR 583 (attorney); *Timmsen v Forest E. Olson, Inc.* (1970) 6 CA3d 860, 86 CR 359 (broker); *Ruth v Lytton Sav. & Loan Ass'n* (1968) 266 CA2d 831, 72 CR 521 (escrow); *Capell Assoc. v Central Valley Sec. Co.* (1968) 260 CA2d 773, 67 CR 463 (escrow); *Schoenberg v Romike Prop.* (1967) 251 CA2d 154, 59 CR 359 (broker)).

Conversely, when the subordinating loan is for acquisition rather than construction, so that the funds from it go to the seller, there is no need for special judicial protection of the subordinated lender. See *Ray Thomas v Fox* (1982) 128 CA3d 361, 180 CR 253. See also *Schneider v Ampliflo Corp.* (1983) 148 CA3d 637, 196 CR 172.

The primary concern of the parties under a blanket deed of trust with a release provision is that the provision be clear enough both to bind the parties when they seek the release of individual lots (see *Eldridge v Burns* (1978) 76 CA3d 396, 142 CR 845; *Lawrence v Shutt* (1969) 269 CA2d 749, 75 CR 533) and to protect them against the claims of either junior creditors or purchasers of other lots that releases have been improperly made. See §8.52. Even when the order of release is specified clearly, however, the buyer must be careful that the selection of release parcels does not appear to a court to be inequitable. See *Eldridge v Burns* (1982) 136 CA3d 907, 186 CR 784.

§8.51   2. Subordination Without Subordination Clause

Subordination can be accomplished without enabling language in the deed of trust if both trustor and beneficiary agree and if there are no third parties with valid grounds to object. The trustor and the beneficiary can agree at any time to subordinate the lien of their instrument to some other lien, and they need merely execute a separate subordination agreement to accomplish this purpose. *International Mortgage Bank v Eaton* (1918) 39 CA 39, 177 P 880. When the trustor is entirely unaffected, the beneficiary can probably subordinate its lien unilaterally, without the trustor's or rival lienor's consent. The trustor's consent is undoubtedly needed if the trustor would suffer, as might occur if the beneficiary subordinated its nonpurchase-money lien to a previously junior purchase-money lien, thus increasing the trustor's exposure to liability for a deficiency. The language of clause B3 of the standard form deed of trust (see App B) would not be read as constituting such consent. See *Lomanto v Bank of America* (1972) 22 CA3d 663, 99 CR 442.

The parties can also accomplish a form of "de facto" subordination by having the subordinated lender agree to delay recording its deed of trust until after the subordinating lender (usually a construction lender) has recorded its instrument. See California Real Property Sales Transactions §5.41 (Cal CEB 1981). Yet another form of informal subordination can occur through judicial application of the doctrine of equitable subrogation. See *Smith v State Sav. & Loan Ass'n* (1985) 175 CA3d 1092, 223 CR 298. Under this doctrine, a lender who refinances a senior lien, without actual knowledge of existing junior liens, is subrogated to the priority position of the senior lien, and junior liens remain in their subordinated position even though they are prior in time to the new, subrogated lien.

§8.52   3. Release Without Release Clause

When there is no release clause whatsoever, or when there is only a clause similar to clause B3 of the title company form deed of trust (see App B), the trustor has no right to demand partial releases of the property from the lien of the deed of trust as the debt is reduced. If a debt of $1 million is secured by a mortgage on 100 acres, the entire $1 million must be paid before a single acre can be freed from the mortgage; the trustor cannot demand that an acre be released from the mortgage for each $10,000 paid. CC §2912; see *Karlsen v American Sav. & Loan Ass'n* (1971) 15 CA3d 112, 92 CR 851; *Miller v Federal Land Bank* (9th Cir 1978) 587 F2d 415.

Even when there is no release clause, however, trustor and beneficiary may agree that some part of the property may be released from the blanket mortgage. Such a release should be enforceable between the parties but may be objectionable from the point of view of third parties. Under CC §§2899 and 3433, junior creditors and transferees have the right to marshal assets. A junior creditor who has a lien on only part of the property subject to the senior blanket mortgage may insist that the senior foreclose and first sell off that part of the property not also subject to the junior lien. This is known as the "two-fund rule" and may prohibit the senior beneficiary and the trustor from agreeing to release parcels that are not subject to the junior lien without first obtaining the junior's consent.

The junior needs this protection to ensure that lots subject only to the senior lien not be released for less than their share of the property's value. Otherwise, the remaining lots will bear a disproportionately large share of the balance and reduce the junior's prospects of being paid out of the surplus. Suppose, for example, that the senior holds a blanket mortgage on 100 lots securing a loan of $1 million, that each lot has a value of $15,000, and that a junior lienor holds a second mortgage on lots 1–10. Because the lots together are worth more than the senior lien, the junior can expect to receive a surplus of $5000 out of each lot when and if there is a senior foreclosure. If the senior releases lots 11–100 for only $800,000, however, the remaining ten lots would secure the balance of $200,000, or $20,000 per lot, thus depriving the junior of any chance for a surplus on foreclosure. See *Woodward v Brown* (1897) 119 C 283, 51 P 2. Business and Professions Code §11013.1 prohibits a subdivider from selling lots subject to a blanket mortgage unless it includes an enforceable release clause. See California Condominium and Planned Development Practice §3.31 (Cal CEB 1984).

Appendix A

Promissory Note

DO NOT DESTROY THIS NOTE: WHEN PAID, THIS NOTE AND DEED OF TRUST SECURING IT MUST BE SURRENDERED TO TRUSTEE FOR CANCELLATION BEFORE RECONVEYANCE WILL BE MADE

PROMISSORY NOTE SECURED BY DEED OF TRUST

$_ _ _ _ _ _   _ _ _ _ _ _ _ _, California

_ _[date]_ _

FOR VALUE RECEIVED, the undersigned, _ _[name(s) of maker(s)]_ _, _ _[jointly and severally]_ _ promise(s) to pay to _ _[names of payees]_ _, _ _[or order]_ _, at _ _[state address]_ _, or at such other place as the holder may from time to time designate by written notice to maker(s), the principal sum of $_ _ _ _ _ _, with interest from this date until paid at the annual rate of _ _ _ percent on the balance remaining from time to time unpaid. Principal and interest will be due and payable in lawful money of the United States of America without set-off, deduction, or counterclaim, in monthly installments of $_ _ _ _ _ _ _ _[or more]_ _. Payment will commence on the _ _ _ day of _ _[date]_ _, and be made on the _ _ _ day of each month thereafter until the principal and interest are fully paid, except that final payment of principal and interest, if not sooner paid, will be due and payable on the _ _ _ day of _ _[date]_ _.

[Add late-charges provision (see §7.8), if desired]

Each payment will be credited first to _ _[*late charges due under the terms of this note, then to*]_ _ interest then due, then to principal. If default occurs in the payment of any installment under this note when due, or in the performance of any of the agreements in the deed of trust securing this note, the entire principal sum and accrued interest will at once become due and payable, without notice, at the option of the holder of this note. Failure to exercise such option will not constitute a waiver of the right to exercise it in the event of any subsequent default.

Maker(s) agree(s) to pay the following costs, expenses, and attorneys' fees paid or incurred by the holder of this note, or adjudged by a Court: (1) reasonable costs of collection, costs, expenses, and attorneys' fees paid or incurred in connection with the collection or enforcement of this note, whether or not suit is filed; and (2) costs of suit and such sum as the Court may adjudge as attorneys' fees in an action to enforce payment of this note or any part of it.

This note is secured by a deed of trust executed this date.

[Add, if purchase-money note]

This note constitutes a portion of the unpaid balance of the purchase price of the real property purchased by maker(s) and securing this note.

[Add nonrecourse provision, if desired]

Maker(s) will have no personal liability for any deficiency on this note, and the only remedy available to the holder will be foreclosure pursuant to law as provided in the deed of trust securing this note.

> ___*[Signature(s) of maker(s)]*___
> _ _*[Typed name(s)]*_ _

Comment: This form note is included in this appendix as an illustration of promissory notes in common usage, rather than as a guide for a custom-drafted note. An attorney drafting a promissory note will usually prefer to draft it to fit the facts of the particular transaction. For form provisions to be used in custom-drafting a promissory note, see 1 California Real Property Financing, chap 3 (Cal CEB 1988).

The note should indicate the parties' capacities, *e.g.,* a California corporation, a general or limited partnership, a husband and wife. If there is more than one maker, the promise to pay should be joint and several so that the payee may sue each promisor for the full amount of the debt. If there is more than one payee, they should be designated "A *and* B" when payment must be made to both. If designated "A *or* B," payment to just one will reduce the debt pro tanto. Individual payees may wish to be designated as joint tenants to create survivorship rights in the note. See §§1.27–1.29 for discussion of parties.

If negotiability is desired, the note should be made payable to the named payees "or order." See discussion of negotiability in §§1.18–1.19.

Unlimited rights to prepay the note may be created either by adding the words "or more," as indicated in the form, or by providing that payments may be made "on or before" the due date. If neither of the phrases "or more" or "on or before" is used, there will be no right to prepay except as otherwise provided in the note or as provided by CC §2954.9 when the loan security consists of one-to-four-unit residential property. See §§7.19–7.25 for discussion of prepayment rights.

A provision accelerating the maturity of the note in the event of either monetary default or default of any of the collateral obligations under the deed of trust is essential for an orderly foreclosure. See §§2.17, 3.37, 7.2–7.6. The extent to which the obligation may be accelerated by other events (*e.g.,* sale, bankruptcy, dissolution, death) is subject to negotiation. See 1 Real Property Financing §§3.9–3.10. The form note contains no provision for acceleration of the loan on transfer of title (due-on-sale provision) or on any events other than default. See §§7.2–7.6 for discussion of acceleration provisions; §§7.10–7.18 for discussion of due-on-sale clauses.

Attorneys' fees may be awarded only if the note provides for them. CC §1021. Any attorneys' fees clause should provide not only for payment of attorneys' fees actually incurred but also for other costs of collection whether or not an action is filed. Under CC §1717, the courts must construe even a unilateral attorneys' fees clause "both ways" so that any prevailing party can recover its reasonable attorneys' fees from the other party. See the discussion of attorneys' fees provisions in §§7.29–7.33.

From the debtor's perspective, it is important that the note recite that it is secured by a deed of trust so that subsequent transferees cannot claim holder-in-due-course status and seek to bypass the one-action rule (CCP §726) by suing on the note without first foreclosing on the security. See §1.19.

If the note is for a purchase-money obligation, and the right to a deficiency judgment is barred by CCP §580b, that fact should be recited, and the optional nonrecourse clause should also be included in the note. Even though the absence of these clauses would not defeat any antideficiency protection rights the maker would otherwise have against the original holder (under CCP §580b), the presence of the nonrecourse clause could avoid any later dispute over the applicability of §580b to the note. This may be particularly important if the note is subordinate to another deed of trust. See *Spangler v Memel* (1972) 7 C3d 603, 102 CR 807, discussed in §4.34. It is unsettled whether the note must also recite that it (and the deed of trust) are purchase-money instruments to enable the maker to plead the antideficiency provisions of CCP §580b against a holder in due course of the note. As a precaution, any purchase-money note should recite this fact.

Use of a nonrecourse clause also lessens the maker's risk that the payee will improperly assign the note and later claim, when the debt is finally paid and the note is to be canceled and returned, that the note is "lost."

Even in nonpurchase-money situations, the parties may agree that the payee will be limited to foreclosure of the security. If so, the nonrecourse clause could be used without the purchase-money clause. Some lenders prefer to limit the nonrecourse provision by adding exceptions for fraud, misapplication of funds, waste, or breach of representations and warranties concerning the presence of toxics. For discussion, see 1 Real Property Financing §3.52.

See §§7.7–7.9 for discussion of the validity of late-charges provisions and a suggested clause. See also 1 Real Property Financing §§3.11–3.14.

To qualify as a holder in due course (see 1.19), a transferee of the note must obtain the proper endorsement. Com C §1201(20). In *Pribus v Bush* (1981) 118 CA3d 1003, 173 CR 747, the court held a separate but stapled paper ineffective as an endorsement because the information it contained could have been placed directly on the note. Consequently, the assignee did not take free of defenses as would a holder in due course. The holding has been effectively overturned by the legislature, which subsequently modified Com C §3202(2) to make it clear that an attached paper (an allonge) is effective as an endorsement even if there is sufficient space for the endorsement on the instrument.

Appendix B

Title Company Short-Form Deed of Trust

[*Front side of deed of trust*]

Recording Requested By)
)
)
)
After Recording Return To)
)
)
) (Space above this line for recorder's use)

___

DEED OF TRUST AND ASSIGNMENT OF RENTS

THIS DEED OF TRUST, made this _ _ _ day of _ _[*date*]_ _, be-tween ① _ _ _ _ _ _ _ _ _ _ _, herein called Trustor, whose address is _ _ _ _ _ _ _; ② _ _ _ _ _ _ _ _ _ _ _, a corporation, herein called Trustee; and ③ _ _ _ _ _ _ _ _ _ _ _, herein called Beneficiary, WIT-NESSETH: That Trustor irrevocably grants, transfers, and assigns to Trustee in trust, with power of sale, that real property in the County of _ _ _ _ _ _ _ _, California, described as:

④ [*Legal description*]

⑤ TOGETHER WITH the rents, issues, and profits thereof, SUB-JECT, HOWEVER, to the right, power, and authority given to and conferred upon Beneficiary by Paragraph 5 of Part B of the provisions incorporated herein by reference to collect and apply such rents, issues, and profits, for the purpose of securing payment of the indebtedness evidenced by a promissory note, of even date herewith, executed by Trustor in the sum of $_ _ _ _ _, ⑥ any additional sums and interest thereon hereafter loaned by Beneficiary to the then record owner of said property, which loans are evidenced by a promissory note or notes, containing a recitation that this Deed of Trust secures the payment thereof, any lawful charge made by Beneficiary for a statement regarding the obligations secured hereby requested by or for Trustor, and the performance of each agreement herein contained. ⑦ The provisions of Part A and the provisions of Part B of the Deed of Trust recorded in the office of the County Recorder of each of the following counties in California on _ _[date]_ _, in the Book and at the page designated after the name of each County, which provisions are identical in each Deed of Trust, shall be and they are hereby incorporated herein and are made an integral part hereof for all purposes as though set forth herein at length.

County	*Book*	*Page*
Alameda		

[List other counties]

⑧ In the event the herein described property, any part thereof, or any interest therein is sold, agreed to be sold, conveyed, or alienated by Trustor, or by the operation of Law or otherwise, all obligations secured by this instrument, irrespective of the maturity dates expressed therein, at the option of the holder thereof and without demand or notice shall immediately become due and payable.

⑨ Trustor requests that a copy of any Notice of Default and a copy of any Notice of Sale hereunder be mailed to him at his address given herein.

Comment: For discussion of use of title company long- and short-form deeds of trust, see §1.24. Although the provisions are identical, the parties to a transaction often prefer to use the long form because it can more easily be modified to accommodate the terms of the transaction.

The following points are keyed to the numbers in the text on the front side of the short-form deed of trust:

① When the trustors are the same as the obligors on the note, they should be named on the deed of trust in the same manner as they are named on the note. See the Comment to the form note in App A. For discussion, see §1.27.

② On deed of trust forms supplied by title companies, the title company's own name usually appears as trustee. A third party trustee is not essential; the beneficiary can be named as trustee with all attendant powers. *Bank of Am. Nat'l Trust & Sav. Ass'n v Century Land & Water Co.* (1937) 19 CA2d 194, 65 P2d 109; *California Trust Co. v Smead Inv. Co.* (1935) 6 CA2d 432, 44 P2d 624. If this is done, however, the trustee's duties may be imputed to the beneficiary. There is an additional danger that the instrument will be treated as a mortgage instead of a deed of trust. *First Fed. Trust Co. v Sanders* (1923) 192 C 194, 219 P 440; *Godfrey v Monroe* (1894) 101 C 224, 35 P 761. See §1.28 for discussion of trustees.

③ The beneficiary should be named in the same manner as on the note. See the Comment to the form note in App A. For discussion of the beneficiary, see §1.29.

④ The deed of trust must either contain a complete legal description of the property or incorporate by reference the description in a previously recorded document. See §§1.30–1.34 for discussion of the property given as security.

⑤ For discussion of rents-and-profits clauses, see chap 5.

⑥ For discussion of future-advance and dragnet clauses, see §§8.34–8.48.

⑦ Generally, only the front side of a title company short-form deed of trust is recorded. The provisions on the reverse side were previously recorded in a fictitious deed of trust to which this deed of trust refers. The actual recording data will vary, depending on which title company's form is used. See §1.24. The provisions printed on the reverse side of the short form will appear in this portion of the long form instead of the recording data.

Incorporation of the fictitious deed of trust is authorized by CC §2952; *Karrell v First Thrift* (1951) 104 CA2d 536, 232 P2d 1. Because almost all title company short-form printed deeds of trust actually contain, on their reverse side, all the provisions included in the fictitious master form, the only advantage of this procedure is that it permits the beneficiary to record only the front side of the deed of trust; the reference to the fictitious terms saves separate recordation of the reverse side. These reverse side provisions are, with minor exceptions, virtually identical in all title company printed forms. The form in this appendix divides the reverse side into collateral obligations designated "Part A" (¶¶1–6) and mutual agreements designated "Part B" (¶¶1–9). Other title company forms may not make this distinction but instead may simply number the provisions consecutively. In the long-form deed of trust, these collateral obligations and mutual agreements are contained in the body of the form before the signature line rather than reprinted on the reverse side of the form and incorporated by reference. The provisions are usually identical, regardless of whether the short-form or long-form deed of trust is used.

⑧ Most short-form deeds of trust do not contain a due-on-sale or due-on-encumbrance clause. If such a clause is required, see §7.10. For discussion of such clauses, see §§7.11–7.18.

⑨ Government Code §27321.5 requires that the deed of trust contain a request for notice of default and notice of sale to be recordable. See §2.14.

[Reverse side of deed of trust]

DO NOT RECORD

THE FOLLOWING IS A COPY OF THE PROVISIONS OF PART A AND THE PROVISIONS OF PART B WHICH ARE INCORPORATED BY REFERENCE IN THE DEED OF TRUST APPEARING ON THE REVERSE SIDE HEREOF.

A. To protect the security of this Deed of Trust, Trustor agrees:

1. To keep said property in good condition and repair; not to remove or demolish any building thereon; to complete or restore promptly and in good and workmanlike manner any building which may be constructed, damaged, or destroyed thereon and to pay when due all claims for labor performed and materials fur-

nished therefor; to comply with all laws affecting said property or requiring any alterations or improvements to be made thereon; not to commit or permit waste thereof; not to commit, suffer, or permit any act upon said property in violation of law; to cultivate, irrigate, fertilize, fumigate, prune, and do all other acts which from the character or use of said property may be reasonably necessary, the specific enumerations herein not excluding the general.

2. To provide, maintain, and deliver to Beneficiary fire insurance satisfactory to and with loss payable to Beneficiary. The amount collected under any fire or other insurance policy may be applied by Beneficiary upon any indebtedness secured hereby and in such order as Beneficiary may determine, or at option of Beneficiary the entire amount so collected or any part thereof may be released to Trustor. Such application or release shall not cure or waive any default or notice of default hereunder or invalidate any act done pursuant to such notice.

3. To appear in and defend any action or proceeding purporting to affect the security hereof or the rights or powers of Beneficiary or Trustee; and to pay all costs and expenses, including cost of evidence of title and attorneys' fees in a reasonable sum, in any such action or proceeding in which Beneficiary or Trustee may appear.

4. To pay at least ten days before delinquency all taxes and assessments affecting said property, including assessments on appurtenant water stock; when due, all encumbrances, charges, and liens, with interest, on said property or any part thereof, which appear to be prior or superior hereto; all costs, fees, and expenses of this Trust.

5. To pay immediately and without demand all sums expended by Beneficiary or Trustee pursuant to the provisions hereof, with interest from date of expenditure at the amount allowed by law in effect at the date hereof.

6. Should Trustor fail to make any payment or to do any act as herein provided, then Beneficiary or Trustee, but without obligation so to do and without notice to or demand upon Trustor and without releasing Trustor from any obligation hereof, may make or do the same in such manner and to such extent as either

may deem necessary to protect the security hereof, Beneficiary or Trustee being authorized to enter upon said property for such purposes; appear in and defend any action or proceeding purporting to affect the security hereof or the rights or powers of Beneficiary or Trustee; pay, purchase, contest, or compromise any encumbrance, charge, or lien which in the judgment of either appears to be prior or superior hereto; and, in exercising any such powers, or in enforcing this Deed of Trust by judicial foreclosure, pay necessary expenses, employ counsel, and pay his reasonable fees.

B. It is mutually agreed that:

1. Any award of damages in connection with any condemnation for public use of or injury to said property or any part thereof is hereby assigned and shall be paid to Beneficiary who may apply or release such moneys received by him in the same manner and with the same effect as above provided for disposition of proceeds of fire or other insurance.

2. By accepting payment of any sum secured hereby after its due date, Beneficiary does not waive his right either to require prompt payment when due of all other sums so secured or to declare default for failure so to pay.

3. At any time or from time to time, without liability therefor and without notice, upon written request of Beneficiary and presentation of this Deed of Trust and said note for endorsement, and without affecting the personal liability of any person for payment of the indebtedness secured hereby, Trustee may reconvey all or any part of said property; consent to the making of any map or plat thereof; join in granting any easement thereon; or join in any extension agreement or any agreement subordinating the lien or charge hereof.

4. Upon written request of Beneficiary stating that all sums secured hereby have been paid, upon surrender of this Deed of Trust and said note to Trustee for cancellation and retention, and upon payment of its fees, Trustee shall reconvey, without warranty, the property then held hereunder. The recitals in any reconveyance executed under this Deed of Trust of any matters or facts

shall be conclusive proof of the truthfulness thereof. The grantee in such reconveyance may be described as "the person or persons legally entitled thereto."

5. As additional security, Trustor hereby gives to and confers upon Beneficiary the right, power, and authority, during the continuance of these Trusts, to collect the rents, issues, and profits of said property, reserving unto Trustor the right, prior to any default by Trustor in payment of any indebtedness secured hereby or in performance of any agreement hereunder, to collect and retain such rents, issues, and profits as they become due and payable. Upon any such default, Beneficiary may at any time without notice, either in person, by agent, or by a receiver to be appointed by a court, and without regard to the adequacy of any security for the indebtedness hereby secured, enter upon and take possession of said property or any part thereof, in his own name sue for or otherwise collect such rents, issues, and profits, including those past due and unpaid, and apply the same, less costs and expenses of operation and collection, including reasonable attorneys' fees, upon any indebtedness secured hereby, and in such order as Beneficiary may determine. The entering upon and taking possession of said property, the collection of such rents, issues, and profits, and the application thereof as aforesaid, shall not cure or waive any default or notice of default hereunder or invalidate any act done pursuant to such notice.

6. Upon default by Trustor in payment of any indebtedness secured hereby or in performance of any agreement hereunder, all sums secured hereby shall immediately become due and payable at the option of the Beneficiary. In the event of default, Beneficiary may employ counsel to enforce payment of the obligations secured hereby, and shall execute or cause the Trustee to execute a written notice of such default and of his election to cause to be sold the herein described property to satisfy the obligations hereof, and shall cause such notice to be recorded in the office of the Recorder of each county wherein said real property or some part thereof is situated.

Prior to publication of the notice of sale, Beneficiary shall deliver to Trustee this Deed of Trust and the Note or other evidence of indebtedness which is secured hereby, together with a written request for the Trustee to proceed with a sale of the property described herein, pursuant to the provisions of law and this Deed of Trust.

Notice of sale having been given as then required by law, and not less than the time then required by law having elapsed after recordation of such notice of default, Trustee, without demand on Trustor, shall sell said property at the time and place fixed by it in said notice of sale, either as a whole or in separate parcels and in such order as it may determine, at public auction to the highest bidder for cash in lawful money of the United States, payable at time of sale. Trustee may postpone sale of all or any portion of said property by public announcement at such time and place of sale, and from time to time thereafter may postpone such sale by public announcement at the time and place fixed by the preceding postponement. Trustee shall deliver to the purchaser its deed conveying the property so sold, but without any covenant or warranty, express or implied. The recitals in such deed of any matters or facts shall be conclusive proof of the truthfulness thereof. Any person, including Trustor, Trustee, or Beneficiary, may purchase at such sale.

After deducting all costs, fees, and expenses of Trustee and of this Trust, including cost of evidence of title and reasonable counsel fees in connection with sale, Trustee shall apply the proceeds of sale to payment of all sums expended under the terms hereof, not then repaid, with accrued interest at 7 percent per annum; all other sums then secured hereby; and the remainder, if any, to the person or persons legally entitled thereto.

7. This Deed of Trust applies to, inures to the benefit of, and binds all parties hereto, their heirs, legatees, devisees, administrators, executors, successors, and assigns. The term Beneficiary shall mean the holder and owner of the note secured hereby; or, if the note has been pledged, the pledgee thereof. In this Deed of Trust, whenever the context so requires, the masculine gender includes the feminine and/or neuter, and the singular number includes the plural.

8. Trustee is not obligated to notify any party hereto of pending sale under any other Deed of Trust or of any action or proceed-

ing in which Trustor, Beneficiary, or Trustee shall be a party unless brought by Trustee.

9. Beneficiary may from time to time or at any time substitute a Trustee or Trustees to execute the trust hereby created, and when any such substitution has been filed for record in the office of the Recorder of the county in which the property herein described is situated, it shall be conclusive evidence of the appointment of such Trustee or Trustees, and such new Trustee or Trustees shall succeed to all of the powers and duties of the Trustee or Trustees named herein.

Comment: The provisions on the reverse side of the short-form deed of trust are discussed in the following chapters and sections:

A1	§§4.40–4.42	B1	§§7.38–7.40
A2	§§7.26–7.28	B2	§2.17
A3	§§7.29–7.33	B3	§§8.49–8.52
A4	§§7.34–7.36	B4	§7.41
A5	§7.37	B5	chap 5
A6	§7.37	B6	§7.42
		B7	§§7.43–7.44
		B9	§2.7

Table of Statutes, Regulations, Rules, and Rulings

CODE OF CIVIL PROCEDURE

Table of Cases

Dobbins v Economic Gas Co.
(1920) 182 C 616, 189 P 1073:
§§3.4, 3.45

Dockrey v Gray (1959) 172 CA2d
388, 341 P2d 746: §2.29

Domarad v Fisher & Burke, Inc.
(1969) 270 CA2d 543, 76 CR
529: §§1.17, 7.44

Donahue v LeVesque (1985) 169
CA3d 620, 215 CR 388: §§7.19,
7.22

Donkin v Killefer (1939) 32 CA2d
729, 90 P2d 810: §7.35

Dool v First Nat'l Bank (1929) 207
C 347, 278 P 233: §1.25

Dool v First Nat'l Bank (1930) 107
CA 585, 290 P 478: §1.9

Downey Sav. & Loan Ass'n v Metz
(In re Metz) (9th Cir 1987) 820
F2d 1495: §6.55

Downing v Le Du (1890) 82 C 471,
23 P 202: §§3.7–3.8, 3.52

Duarte v Lake Gregory Land &
Water Co. (1974) 39 CA3d
101, 113 CR 893: §§4.42,
7.39

Duff v Randall (1897) 116 C 226,
48 P 66: §3.7

Dugand v Magnus (1930) 107 CA
243, 290 P 309: §§2.27–2.28

Duley v Westinghouse Elec. Corp.
(1979) 97 CA3d 430, 158 CR
668: §1.12

Durrett v Washington Nat'l Ins. Co.
(5th Cir 1980) 621 F2d 201:
§6.56

Dyer Law & Collection Co. v Abbott
(1921) 52 CA 545, 199 P 340:
§4.6

E

Eagles, In re (California Thrift &
Loan Ass'n v Downey Sav. &
Loan Ass'n) (Bankr 9th Cir
1984) 36 BR 97: §§3.76, 6.50

Eastland Sav. & Loan Ass'n v
Thornhill & Bruce, Inc. (1968)
260 CA2d 259, 66 CR 901:
§§2.29, 5.21, 5.38

Easton v Ash (1941) 18 C2d 530,
116 P2d 433: §§4.40–4.41,
6.18

Ehring v Western Community
Moneycenter (In re Ehring)
(Bankr 9th Cir 1988) 91 BR 897:
§6.56

Ehring, In re (Ehring v Western
Community Moneycenter)
(Bankr 9th Cir 1988) 91 BR 897:
§6.56

Eigenhuis v Morris (1934) 136 CA
333, 28 P2d 928: §6.40

Ekmann v Plumas County Bank
(1932) 215 C 671, 12 P2d 433:
§§1.11, 6.18

Eldridge v Burns (1982) 136 CA3d
907, 186 CR 784: §8.50

Eldridge v Burns (1978) 76 CA3d
396, 142 CR 845: §§8.49–8.50

Eldridge v Wright (1880) 55 C 531:
§3.74

Ellis, U.S. v (9th Cir 1983) 714 F2d
953: §§3.51, 4.46

Engelbertson v Loan & Bldg. Ass'n
(1936) 6 C2d 477, 58 P2d 647:
§2.12

Engelman v Bookasta (1968) 264
CA2d 915, 71 CR 120: §8.11

Engelman v Gordon (1966) 242
CA2d 510, 51 CR 627:
§§8.18–8.19

Enos v Cook (1884) 65 C 175, 3 P
632: §1.32

Entz-White Lumber & Supply, Inc.,
In re (Great W. Bank & Trust v
Entz-White Lumber & Supply,
Inc.) (1988) 850 F2d 1338: §6.55

Equitable Mortgage Co. v Fishman
(In re Charles C. Stapp, Inc.)
(9th Cir 1981) 641 F2d 737:
§5.10

Hopkins v Warner (1895) 109 C
133, 41 P 868: §8.22
Hoppe v Hoppe (1894) 104 C 94,
37 P 894: §3.20
Hotaling v Montieth (1900) 128 C
556, 61 P 95: §§7.29, 7.31
Hotchkiss v Darling (1933) 130 CA
625, 20 P2d 343: §2.20
House v Lala (1963) 214 CA2d
238, 29 CR 450: §3.79
Houser v Superior Court (1932)
121 CA 31, 8 P2d 483: §6.27
Hubbard v University Bank
(1899) 125 C 684, 58 P 297:
§3.25
Huckell v Matranga (1979) 99
CA3d 471, 160 CR 177: §§1.12,
2.11, 7.41
Huene v Cribb (1908) 9 CA 141, 98
P 78: §2.5
Hulm, In re (First Fed. Sav. & Loan
Ass'n v Hulm) (8th Cir 1984)
738 F2d 323: §6.56
Humboldt Sav. Bank v McCleverty
(1911) 161 C 285, 119 P 82:
§2.23
Hunt v Dohrs (1870) 39 C 304:
§3.37
Hunt v Smyth (1972) 25 CA3d 807,
101 CR 4: §§2.17, 6.20,
6.38–6.39
Huntoon v Southern Trust &
Commerce Bank (1930) 107 CA
121, 290 P 86: §1.28
Huntsman, James Richard (1988)
91 TC 917: §1.15
Hurt v Pico Inv. Co. (1932) 127 CA
106, 15 P2d 203: §3.10
Hutchison v Barr (1920) 183 C 182,
190 P 799: §3.15

I

I. E. Assoc. v Safeco Title Ins. Co.
(1985) 39 C3d 281, 216 CR
438: §§2.6, 2.14

IMO Dev. Corp. v Dow Corning
Corp. (1982) 135 CA3d 451,
185 CR 341: §7.33
Idaho v Arnold (In re Arnold) (9th
Cir 1986) 806 F2d 937: §6.55
Imperial Coronado Partners, Ltd. v
Home Fed. Sav. & Loan Ass'n
(In re Imperial Coronado
Partners, Ltd.) (Bankr 9th Cir
1989) 96 BR 997: §6.52
Imperial Coronado Partners, Ltd.,
In re (Imperial Coronado
Partners, Ltd. v Home Fed. Sav.
& Loan Ass'n) (Bankr 9th Cir
1989) 96 BR 997: §6.52
In re _____ (*see* name of
relator)
Indusco Management Corp. v
Robertson (1974) 40 CA3d 456,
114 CR 47: §§1.9, 8.13, 8.27
Inskeep v Bear Creek Co. (1942)
54 CA2d 723, 129 P2d 401:
§7.32
International Mortgage Bank v
Eaton (1918) 39 CA 39, 177 P
880: §8.51
Investcal Realty Corp. v Edgar H.
Mueller Constr. Co. (1966) 247
CA2d 190, 55 CR 475: §§1.29,
2.23, 8.3
Isaacson, Estate of v Commis-
sioner (2d Cir 1988) 860 F2d 55:
§1.15
Iser v Herbert Mark Bldg. Corp.
(NY Ct App 1930) 171 NE 757:
§§8.37, 8.41
Italian Am. Bank v Canepa (1921)
52 CA 619, 199 P 55: §1.27

J

Jack v Wong Shee (1939) 33 CA2d
402, 92 P2d 449: §1.27
Jackson v Taylor (1969) 272 CA2d
1, 76 CR 891: §§8.23, 8.25,
8.28

M

Sather Banking Co. v Arthur R.
Briggs Co. (1903) 138 C 724, 72
P 352: §8.35

Saucedo v Mercury Sav. & Loan
Ass'n (1980) 111 CA3d 309, 168
CR 552: §7.33

Savings & Loan Soc'y v Burnett
(1895) 106 C 514, 39 P 922:
§§2.21, 7.36, 8.46, 8.48

Savings Bank v Asbury (1897) 117
C 96, 48 P 1081: §6.15

Savings Bank v Central Mkt. Co.
(1898) 122 C 28, 54 P 273:
§§4.8, 4.11

Sawyer v First City Fin. Corp.
(1981) 124 CA3d 390, 177 CR
398: §4.13

Scheerer v Cuddy (1890) 85 C
270, 24 P 713: §5.26

Schneider v Ampliflo Corp. (1983)
148 CA3d 637, 196 CR 172:
§8.50

Schock, People v (1984) 152 CA3d
379, 199 CR 327: §8.30

Schoenberg v Romike Prop. (1967)
251 CA2d 154, 59 CR 359:
§8.50

Schoenfeld v Norberg (1970) 11
CA3d 755, 90 CR 47: §1.31

Schoolcraft v Ross (1978) 81 CA3d
75, 146 CR 57: §§7.24, 7.27,
7.39

Schubert v Lowe (1924) 193 C
291, 223 P 550: §6.47

Schwerin v Shostak (1963) 213
CA2d 37, 28 CR 332: §8.28

Scott v Paisley (1926) 271 US 632:
§2.6

Scott v Security Title Ins. & Guar.
Co. (1937) 9 C2d 606, 72 P2d
143: §§2.3, 2.21

Seccombe v Roe (1913) 22
CA 139, 133 P 507: §§6.39–
6.40

Second Nat'l Bank v Boyle (Ohio
1951) 99 NE2d 474: §8.40

Security Pac. Fin. Corp. v Nelson
(In re Nelson) (9th Cir 1985) 761
F2d 1320: §1.27

Security Pac. Nat'l Bank v
Cassavant (1988) 205 CA3d
127, 252 CR 175: §4.24

Security Pac. Nat'l Bank v Wozab
(rev granted Aug. 24, 1989,
S010502; superseded opinion at
210 CA3d 1119 (advance
reports), 258 CR 850): §4.5

Security-First Nat'l Bank v
Chapman (1939) 31 CA2d 182,
87 P2d 724: §§4.6–4.7, 8.22

Security-First Nat'l Bank v Cryer
(1940) 39 CA2d 757, 104 P2d
66: §§2.24, 3.59

Security-First Nat'l Bank v De La
Cuesta (1936) 15 CA2d 302, 59
P2d 542: §2.20

Security-First Nat'l Bank v Lamb
(1931) 212 C 64, 297 P 550:
§7.36

Security-First Nat'l Bank v Marxen
(1938) 28 CA2d 446, 82 P2d
727: §5.26

Seidel v Larson (In re Seidel) (9th
Cir 1985) 752 F2d 1382: §6.55

Seidel, In re (Seidel v Larson) (9th
Cir 1985) 752 F2d 1382: §6.55

Seidell v Tuxedo Land Co. (1932)
216 C 165, 13 P2d 686: §1.17

Seidell v Tuxedo Land Co. (1934) 1
CA2d 406, 36 P2d 1102: §6.39

Sellman v Crosby (1937) 20 CA2d
562, 67 P2d 706: §2.17

Sepulveda v Apablasa (1938) 25
CA2d 381, 77 P2d 526: §1.30

Ser-Bye Corp. v C.P. & G. Mkts.
(1947) 78 CA2d 915, 179 P2d
342: §7.15

Sexton v Nelson (1964) 228 CA2d
248, 39 CR 407: §7.15

Shahen v Superior Court (1941) 46
CA2d 187, 115 P2d 516: §§6.27,
6.33

Vilkin

United Sav. & Loan Ass'n v
Hoffman (1973) 30 CA3d 306,
106 CR 275: §§2.23, 2.29, 5.23,
5.25, 7.36
United Sav. & Loan Ass'n v Reeder
Dev. Corp. (1976) 57 CA3d 282,
129 CR 113: §6.22
United Sav. Ass'n v Timbers of
Inwood Forest Assoc. (1988)
484 US 365: §§6.50, 6.52
U.S. v _____ (see name of
defendant)
U.S. Cold Storage v Great W. Sav.
& Loan Ass'n (1985) 165 CA3d
1214, 212 CR 232: §6.38
United States Fin. v Sullivan (1974)
37 CA3d 5, 112 CR 18:
§§4.41–4.42, 5.7, 7.40
U.S. Hertz, Inc. v Niobrara Farms
(1974) 41 CA3d 68, 116 CR 44:
§§1.28, 2.6–2.7, 2.14, 6.14, 6.36
Universal Farming Indus., In re
(Spacek v Thomen) (9th Cir
1989) 873 F2d 1334: §1.29
Universal Mortgage Co. v
Prudential Ins. Co. (9th Cir
1986) 799 F2d 458: §8.8

V

Valinda Builders v Bissner (1964)
230 CA2d 106, 40 CR 735:
§§4.48, 8.18
Valley Bible Center v Western Title
Ins. Co. (1983) 138 CA3d 931,
188 CR 335: §§6.34, 6.37, 7.29
Valley Lumber Co. v Wright (1905)
2 CA 288, 84 P 58: §8.46
Valley Title Co. v Parish Egg
Basket, Inc. (1973) 31 CA3d
776, 107 CR 717: §3.48
Valley Vista Land Co. v Nipomo
Water & Sewer Co. (1968) 266
CA2d 331, 72 CR 181: §1.9
Vance v Gilbert (1918) 178 C 574,
174 P 42: §3.33

Vance v Lincoln (1869) 38 C 586:
§6.10
Van Loben Sels v Bunnell (1901)
131 C 489, 63 P 773: §3.21
Van Loben Sels v Bunnell (1898)
120 C 680, 53 P 266: §1.13
Van Noy v Goldberg (1929) 98 CA
604, 277 P 538: §6.40
Van Valkenburgh v Oldham (1910)
12 CA 572, 108 P 42: §§3.7,
3.52
Van Vleck Realty v Gaunt (1967)
250 CA2d 81, 58 CR 246:
§§1.18, 4.38
Vasquez v Superior Court (1971) 4
C3d 800, 94 CR 796: §1.19
Vaughan v People's Mortgage Co.
(1933) 130 CA 632, 20 P2d 335:
§6.24
Vaughan v Roberts (1941) 45
CA2d 246, 113 P2d 884:
§§6.41, 6.44
Vella v Hudgins (1977) 20 C3d
251, 142 CR 414: §§6.39,
6.47
Venable v Harmon (1965) 233
CA2d 297, 43 CR 490: §§1.35,
4.36
Ventura-Louise Prop., In re (Great
W. Life Assur. Co. v Rothman)
(9th Cir 1974) 490 F2d 1141:
§§5.10–5.12, 5.24
Verbeck v Clymer (1927) 202
C 557, 261 P 1017:
§8.33
Verna v Dorman (In re Verna)
(Bankr CD Cal 1986) 58 BR
246: §6.56
Verna, In re (Verna v Dorman)
(Bankr CD Cal 1986) 58 BR
246: §6.56
Vierneisel v Rhode Island Ins. Co.
(1946) 77 CA2d 229, 175 P2d
63: §7.16
Vilkin v Sommer (1968) 260 CA2d
687, 67 CR 837: §7.36

W

Table of References

American Law Institute. Restatement (Second) of Conflict of Laws. 4 vols. St. Paul, Minn.: American Law Institute Publishers, 1971: §4.45

Bowman, Arthur G. Ogden's Revised California Real Property Law. Vol 2 (TI Corp-CEB 1975): §§1.27, 1.34, 3.27–3.28, 6.3

California Attorney's Fees Award Practice (Cal CEB 1982): §§3.43, 7.29, 7.31–7.32

California Civil Appellate Practice (2d ed Cal CEB 1985): §6.36

California Civil Procedure Before Trial. Vol 1 (Cal CEB 1977): §§3.10, 3.14–3.16, 3.26, 3.29–3.30, 3.52, 5.14, 5.17–5.18, 6.13, 6.29, 6.34, 6.36, 6.44

California Civil Procedure Before Trial. Vol 2 (Cal CEB 1978): §6.34

California Civil Procedure During Trial. Vol 2 (Cal CEB 1984): §§3.43, 3.52

California Civil Writ Practice (2d ed Cal CEB 1987): §6.36

California Condominium and Planned Development Practice (Cal CEB 1984): §8.52

California Debt Collection Practice. Vol 1 (Cal CEB 1987): §2.13

California Decedent Estate Practice. Vol 1 (Cal CEB 1986): §3.27

California Decedent Estate Practice. Vol 3 (Cal CEB 1987): §3.27

California Lis Pendens Practice (Cal CEB 1983): §§3.18, 3.45–3.46, 6.35

California Mechanics' Liens and Other Remedies (2d ed Cal CEB 1988): §8.46

California Real Property Financing. Vol 1 (Cal CEB 1988): §§1.4, 1.8–1.9, 1.14, 1.17–1.18, 1.20, 1.23–1.24, 2.5, 2.11, 2.22, 5.1, 7.8, 7.10, 7.12, 7.15, 7.22–7.23, 7.26, 7.37, 7.39, 8.10–8.13, 8.49, App A

California Real Property Financing. Vol 2 (Cal CEB 1989): §§1.4, 2.8, 4.1, 4.3, 4.5–4.6, 4.14, 4.17, 4.20, 4.23, 4.36, 4.40, 4.43, 4.45–4.46, 5.9, 5.14, 5.17, 6.11, 6.48–6.52, 6.55, 6.57

California Real Property Practice Forms Manual (Cal CEB 1988): §§1.5–1.6

California Real Property Remedies Practice (Cal CEB 1982): §§1.31, 1.35, 3.80, 4.36, 6.4, 6.12, 6.38, 6.45, 8.49

California Real Property Sales Transactions (Cal CEB 1981): §§1.4, 1.6, 1.8, 1.14, 1.20, 1.35, 2.27, 4.36, 7.5, 7.12, 7.19, 8.31–8.33, 8.49–8.51

California Residential Landlord-Tenant Practice (Cal CEB 1986): §§2.28, 3.16, 3.80, 5.38, 6.12

California Subdivision Map Act Practice (Cal CEB 1987): §8.49

California Title Insurance Practice (Cal CEB 1980): §§1.4, 1.6, 2.2, 2.14, 3.12

Cherkis, Laurence G., & Lawrence P. King. Collier Real Estate Transactions and the Bankruptcy Code. Looseleaf. New York: Matthew Bender, 1984: §6.48

Cowans, Daniel R. Cowans Bankruptcy Law and Practice. 3 vols. St. Paul, Minn.: West Publishing, 1987: §6.48

Debt Collection Practice in California. Vol 1 (Cal CEB 1987): §4.4

Debt Collection Practice in California. Vol 2 (Cal CEB 1987): §6.48

King, Lawrence P. Collier Bankruptcy Manual. 3 vols, looseleaf. Oakland: Matthew Bender, 3d ed, 1979: §6.48

————. Collier on Bankruptcy. 11 vols, looseleaf. New York: Matthew Bender, 15th ed, 1979: §6.48

Kratovil, Robert, & Raymond J. Werner. Modern Mortgage Law & Practice. Englewood Cliffs, N.J.: Prentice-Hall, 2d ed, 1981: §§5.10, 5.28

Miller, Harry D., & Marvin B. Starr. Current Law of California Real Estate. Vol 4. Looseleaf. San Francisco: Bancroft-Whitney, 2d ed, 1989: §3.72

Nelson, Grant S., & Dale A. Whitman. Real Estate Finance Law. St. Paul, Minn.: West Publishing, 2d ed, 1985: §§1.9, 1.11, 1.21, 3.1, 3.16, 4.1, 4.29, 5.26, 5.31–5.32, 5.38–5.39, 6.4, 6.15, 8.22, 8.30, 8.38, 8.46

Real Property Exchanges (Cal CEB 1982): §§1.6, 1.8

Secured Transactions in California Commercial Law Practice (Cal CEB 1986): §§1.2, 1.34, 6.57

Taxation of Real Property Transfers (Cal CEB 1981): §§1.8, 1.13, 1.15, 2.30–2.31, 7.5, 7.19, 8.31

Witkin, Bernard E. California Procedure. Vols 2, 4–5. San Francisco: Bancroft-Whitney, 3d ed, 1985: §6.26

Table of Forms

Index

Agency—*cont.*
Term "trustee" inclusive of agent of trustee, 6.25
Trustee under deed of trust as common agent, 1.28

Agreements
See also **Contracts**
Agreement in which guarantor is debtor, invalidity of, 4.48
Assumption agreement, enforcement of, 8.22
Environmental indemnity agreement, 4.39
Holding agreement disguised as mortgage, 4.37
Listing agreement. See **Listing Agreement**
Parol agreement that deed of trust will cover additional loan, 8.35
Postponement of trustee's sale, agreement for, 2.24
Purchase and sale agreement. See **Purchase and Sale Agreement**
Renewal of mortgage, agreement for, 6.18
Subordination agreement. See **Subordination**

Alter Ego Doctrine
Guarantor as purchaser's alter ego, 8.18

Amortization
Negative amortization, 1.14

Antideficiency Rules
See also **Deficiency Judgments; One-Action Rule**
Application to both deeds of trust and mortgages, 4.2
Assuming grantees, rules affecting. See **Assuming Grantees**
Delayed trustee's sale, application of antideficiency laws to, 6.37
Endorsers, denial of antideficiency protection to, 8.19
Environmental indemnity agreements, treatment of, 4.39
Fair-value provisions, enforcement of, 4.2, 4.33, 5.23
History of antideficiency legislation, 4.1
Installment land sale contracts, application to, 4.36
Mortgage substitutes, application to, 4.37
Mortgagor losing protection of antideficiency rules, 1.18
Purchase-money mortgages (CCP §580b). See **Deficiency Judgments**
Rents, treatment of, 5.22
Sold-out junior and antideficiency laws
Generally, 4.31
Fair-value rules, 4.33
Nonjudicial sales, 4.32
Purchase-money restrictions, nonstandard transactions, 4.35
Purchase-money restrictions, other security, 4.34
Trustor's protection from antideficiency rules, 8.17
U.S. Government bound by state antideficiency laws, 4.46
Unsecured and partly secured notes, treatment of, 4.38–4.39